then a great Prince [illegible] of wickedness, for his goodness endures for ever, & of his tender mercys there is no end to his children. God Almighty keep & preserve yee to his eternall kingdom, so wisheth

Thy Friend in godly love & sincerity

WPenn

my Father being [?] son sends thee his love & a small present wth it.

I have been wth H. Moor. who is better acquainted wth us then formerly, & will I hope rightly [?] us to ye world; however, our life is hid wth Xt. in god.

THE PAPERS OF WILLIAM PENN

Volume One · 1644–1679

THE PAPERS OF WILLIAM PENN

Volume One · 1644–1679

EDITORS

Mary Maples Dunn · Richard S. Dunn

ASSOCIATE EDITORS

Richard A. Ryerson · Scott M. Wilds

Assistant Editor · Jean R. Soderlund

UNIVERSITY OF PENNSYLVANIA PRESS 1981

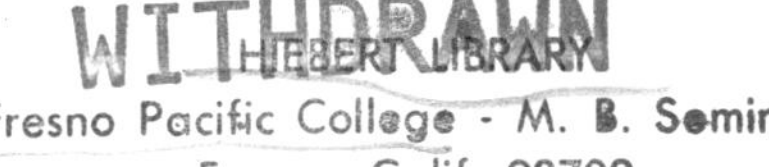

Printed in the United States of America

Library of Congress Cataloging in Publication Data
Penn, William, 1644-1718.
The papers of William Penn.
Contents: v. 1. 1644-1679.
1. Penn, William, 1644-1718. 2. Pennsylvania — History — Colonial period, ca. 1600-1775 — Sources. 3 Friends, Society of — History — 17th century — Sources. 4. Friends, Society of — History — 18th century — Sources. 5. Friends, Society of — Biography. 6. Pioneers — Pennsylvania — Correspondence. I. Dunn, Mary Maples. II. Dunn, Richard S. III. Title. F152.2. P3956 1981 974.8'02'0924 [B] 80-54052
ISBN 0-8122-7800-3 (v. 1)

Designed by Adrianne Onderdonk Dudden
Maps by Quentin Fiore

To
CAROLINE ROBBINS
and
to the
memory of
ALBERT COOK MYERS
HANNAH BENNER ROACH
and
FREDERICK B. TOLLES

•

Preparation and publication of this volume is made possible
through the support of

The American Philosophical Society
The Barra Foundation
Bryn Mawr College
Haverford College
The Historical Society of Pennsylvania
The McLean Contributionship
The National Endowment for the Humanities
The National Historical Publications and Records Commission
The Philadelphia Center for Early American Studies
Adolph G. Rosengarten, Jr.
The University of Pennsylvania

ACKNOWLEDGMENTS

The editors are deeply grateful to the following libraries and archives for granting permission to publish in this volume documents from their collections: the Bristol Record Office, Bristol, England; the British Library, London; the Bureau of Archives and History, New Jersey State Library, Trenton; the Chester County Historical Society, West Chester, Pennsylvania; the Church of All Hallows by the Tower, London; Dr. Williams's Library, London; the East Sussex County Record Office, Lewes, Sussex, England; the Historical Society of Pennsylvania, Philadelphia; Jordans Monthly Meeting, Bucks., England; the Library of the Religious Society of Friends, London; the Lilly Library, Indiana University, Bloomington, Indiana; the National Library of Ireland, Dublin; the National Maritime Museum, Greenwich, London; the New Jersey Historical Society, Newark; the Public Record Office, Dublin; the Public Record Office, London; the Quaker Collection, Haverford College, Haverford, Pennsylvania; and the Somerset Record Office, Taunton, Somerset, England.

Four institutions, Bryn Mawr College, Haverford College, the Historical Society of Pennsylvania, and the University of Pennsylvania — all participants in the Philadelphia Center for Early American Studies — are the sponsors of this edition. The editors are deeply appreciative of this cooperative institutional support. We are also very grateful to the National Endowment for the Humanities and the National Historical Publications and Records Commission, and to the American Philosophical Society, the Barra Foundation, the McLean Contributionship, and Adolph G. Rosengarten, Jr., for their generous grants.

A special word of thanks is due to James E. Mooney, Director of the Historical Society of Pennsylvania, to Peter J. Parker, Chief of Manuscripts, to John H. Platt, Jr., Librarian, and to the other members of the Society staff, for providing the editors with attractive working space and congenial company, free access to the Society's manuscript and book collections, and expert help whenever needed.

Edwin Wolf 2nd and his staff at the Library Company of Philadelphia have supplied almost daily service. The editors have likewise received indispensable assistance from J. William Frost and the staff of the Friends Historical Library at Swarthmore College; from Edwin B. Bronner and the staff of the Quaker Collection at Haverford College; and from the libraries of Bryn Mawr College and the University of Pennsylvania.

Further afield, we have been courteously received by Martha L. Simonetti at the Pennsylvania State Archives; by William C. Wright and Rebecca Colesar at the New Jersey Bureau of Archives and History; by the Council of Proprietors of West New Jersey; and by the Union Theological Seminary Library. Richard P. McCormick and Henry S. Haines were particularly helpful in our New Jersey researches. In London, we wish to thank Isabel Witte Kenrick of the Historical Manuscripts Commission, and the staffs of the Public Record Office, the British Library, the Library of the Religious Society of Friends, Dr. Williams's Library, and the National Maritime Museum; in Oxford, the Bodleian Library; in Bedford, the Bedfordshire Record Office; in Dublin, the special assistance of Louis Cullen and David Dickson, and the staffs of the National Library, the Registry of Deeds, the Public Record Office, and the Friends Historical Library; and in Cork, the Cork County Library.

The editors also wish to thank Marianne Wokeck, Elizabeth Kogen, Maurice Bric, Billy G. Smith, and Neil Fitzgerald, all Fellows of the Philadelphia Center for Early American Studies, for research assistance on documents in this volume. Sister Irma Corcoran's index to the microfilm edition of The Papers of William Penn has been very useful to us. Members of our Advisory Board have been extremely helpful whenever called upon. Carolyn Jones assisted with word processing, Patricia Wells did proofreading and the index, and Christie Lerch did the copy editing. Adrianne Onderdonk Dudden designed the book, and Quentin Fiore designed the maps. Walter Heppenstall and Barton L. Craig at the Winchell Company and Edward Johnson-Muller and his colleagues at the University of Pennsylvania Press have worked with us on an exceedingly tight schedule in order to produce this complex volume in a matter of months. Charles Cullen of *The Papers of Thomas Jefferson* has helped us with technical problems. Last, but by no means least, we wish to thank George F. Farr, Jr., of the National Endowment for the Humanities and Frank G. Burke of the National Historical Publications and Records Commission for their active interest in this project and their advice on how to proceed from seventeenth-century manuscripts to twentieth-century magnetic disks and from disks to a printed book.

CONTENTS

ILLUSTRATIONS AND MAPS

THE PAPERS OF WILLIAM PENN

Volume One · 1644–1679

INTRODUCTION

For most students of history, the mention of William Penn (1644-1718) evokes a bland and boring image of a man who did good work in his time but has little to say to us today. No one questions Penn's credentials: he played a central role in shaping and protecting the Society of Friends; he founded an immensely successful colony in America; he was a tireless champion of such worthy causes as religious toleration, civil liberties, decent race relations, ethnic pluralism, economic enterprise, and participatory government. Scholars have studied his career in detail, and have puzzled over the man's singular combination of attributes, for Penn was simultaneously a religious enthusiast, visionary idealist, persecuted martyr, polemical disputant, political lobbyist, patrician gentleman, and proprietary landlord. But few people aside from these scholars try to deal with Penn at first hand. Few read his books, or examine his private papers, or try to engage directly with his ideas, arguments, and values. In consequence, he is not generally considered very seriously. We are left with Benjamin West's painting of Penn's treaty at Shackamaxon, a stodgy stereotype—in Frederick B. Tolles' words—of the benign partriarch dressed "in the Quaker Oats costume of shadbelly coat and cocked hat" who is "eternally dispensing peace and yard goods to the Indians."[1]

The present edition seeks to penetrate beyond this stereotype, and to demonstrate to a modern audience that Penn's writings are interesting, timely, and valuable. He was a voluminous author, who wrote, or collaborated in writing, nearly 140 books, pamphlets, and broadsides. He also wrote and received many thousands of letters, and kept extensive business accounts and legal records. Over 2600 of these letters and papers survive. There has been only one previous edition of his writings. Shortly after Penn's death, Joseph Besse collected 57 of his printed tracts and 66 of his manuscript letters in two folio volumes. Besse's compilation was published in 1726, and has been reprinted several times since. Readers interested in Penn's religious and political tracts can find them in rare book libraries, or reprinted in Besse. But Penn's personal correspondence and business papers are still largely in manuscript. Those letters that have been published are scattered in dozens of books and journals, most of them printed long ago, with incomplete or inaccurate texts, and without annotation.

Our edition of *The Papers of William Penn* seeks to remedy this sad situation. We focus upon Penn's manuscripts: his correspondence, journals, religious and political papers, and business records. There will be four volumes of these documents, arranged chronologically. The opening volume presents the young Quaker activist, 1644-1679. The second volume will cover the founding of Pennsylvania, 1680-1684. The third volume will deal with Penn's tortuous career in England, 1684-1699. The fourth volume will document his second visit to Pennsylvania and the political and business problems of his final years, 1699-1718. In a companion fifth volume, Edwin Bronner and David Fraser will publish an annotated bibliography of Penn's imprints, identifying Penn's numerous anonymous tracts and correcting previous misattributions. A scholarly edition of Penn's chief religious tracts by Hugh Barbour is also in preparation, complementing our effort to make the writings of this creative Anglo-American figure more widely available.

WP — as he will be referred to henceforth — was not a tidy or well-organized person, yet he took considerable pains to collect and preserve his papers. In doing so, he followed the example of his father, Admiral Sir William Penn, who kept journals of his voyages and other documents from his naval career, catalogued these documents, and began the family archive. When the Admiral died, WP kept his father's papers (see doc. 54 in this volume) and added his own. WP was doubtless also influenced by the Quaker custom of spiritual record-keeping. He felt keenly that Quaker testimonies and Quaker sufferings should be written down and collected for posterity (see doc. 103), and accordingly he documented his own experiences. He wrote journals when traveling (see docs. 35, 70, and 119), and he retained drafts of unpublished tracts (see docs. 26, 55, 57, 65, and 66). As early as 1670 his steward Philip Ford was collecting WP's incoming correspondence (see doc. 45), and by 1672 Ford was keeping detailed accounts of WP's income and expenditures (see docs. 139-50). WP employed several clerks to write fair copies of his tracts, and to make letterbook copies of his outgoing correspondence. Thirty-nine of the documents in this volume come from a letterbook compiled by WP's clerks in the 1670s. In the 1680s, when WP became the proprietor of Pennsylvania, his scale of record-keeping expanded. He kept copies of the hundreds of deeds he issued, along with a large collection of other American papers. By 1699, when his clerks prepared an index to these Pennsylvania documents, their list filled a hundred-page volume.[2] In this same year his clerks itemized the contents of a box filled with bundles of Irish and English business papers (see doc. 137). When WP died in 1718, he left two large accumulations of papers, one with his widow Hannah Penn in England, and the other with his agent James Logan in Pennsylvania.

During the eighteenth and nineteenth centuries, the manuscripts that WP left in Pennsylvania were dispersed into several collections. James Logan preserved his extensive correspondence with WP, together with other early Pennsylvania records of high value; these papers were kept by the Logan family, and eventually were deposited in the Historical Society of Pennsylvania in Philadelphia. Another large block of WP papers was kept by the proprietary governors of Pennsylvania until shortly before the Revolution, and then by American agents of the Penn family. Some of these papers were acquired by the Commonwealth of Pennsylvania and are now held in the state archives in Harrisburg; others passed to the Cadwalader family in the nineteenth century, and from the Cadwaladers to the Historical Society of Pennsylvania in the twentieth century. Other WP manuscripts left in Pennsylvania were marketed by dealers, and acquired by autograph collectors.

Meanwhile, in England, the central collection of WP's manuscripts was carefully preserved for over a century and added to by WP's heirs. His son Thomas Penn (1702-1775) made active use of WP's records when he became proprietor of Pennsylvania. Thomas Penn arranged and filed the family papers in his possession, searched for additional WP documents that might strengthen his proprietary claims and revenues, and vastly added to the family archive with his own accumulation of correspondence. Thomas Penn's collection passed after the Revolution to the custody of WP's grandsons, first to John Penn (1760-1834) and then to Granville Penn (1761-1844). These manuscripts were stored in the Penns' imposing country mansion, Stoke Park, Buckinghamshire. When Richard Penn (1783-1863), a great-grandson of WP, proposed to write a biography of his Quaker ancestor, Granville Penn's librarian obligingly showed him "huge trunks and drawers" of WP's manuscripts—and Richard abandoned the project as too difficult.[3] In 1833 Granville Penn himself published a biography of WP's father, Admiral Sir William Penn, and drew upon correspondence between father and son which has since disappeared. By the 1850s the Penn family was in financial difficulties. WP's great-grandson, John Granville Penn (1803-1867), sold

Stoke Park, together with the choicest family paintings, books, and relics. He moved the bulk of the family papers to a London warehouse, the Pantechnicon, where they were piled in disorder in a storage room and neglected for many years.

In 1870 the Penn family papers, including WP's chief manuscripts, were severely vandalized and nearly destroyed. A man whose identity has never been proven gained access to the Pantechnicon storage room and proceeded to tear into bits the bundles and volumes of papers he found there. Wearying of this task, he paid a wastepaper dealer to haul the whole lot—priceless books, pamphlets, and maps, as well as manuscripts—to a paper mill for pulp. Most probably this destroyer was one Captain Granville, whose father had been an illegitimate child of Granville Penn. Captain Granville had expected to inherit his half-uncle John Granville Penn's estate in 1867, but was cut out of his will, so perhaps he acted out of vengeance. Or perhaps he was eliminating documentary evidence of his father's bastardy.[4] Fortunately, the wastepaper dealer did not junk the surviving Penn papers and books. Instead, he sold them to an antiquarian bookseller, who divided the collection with a manuscript dealer. When the two dealers marketed their wares in 1870-1871, the Historical Society of Pennsylvania paid £555 to acquire 862 items or lots of Penn manuscripts—principally the papers of WP and of Thomas Penn.[5] Other family manuscripts, not stored in the Pantechnicon in 1870, later came onto the market in auctions at Sotheby's and Christie's. While private purchasers acquired a good many of these manuscripts, the great bulk of WP's surviving papers are now held, through purchase or gift, by public repositories in America and England.

Considering the near disaster of 1870, WP's papers have survived the vicissitudes of three centuries remarkably well. There are about 2600 known documents (exclusive of duplicates) written or received by WP; it is difficult to arrive at a more precise figure because the several WP manuscript collections contain hundreds of duplicates, near duplicates, and variant texts. About 2350 of these documents are original manuscripts or copies made in WP's lifetime. The remaining 250 are modern transcripts or printed versions of lost originals. About 90 percent of the known WP manuscripts are now stored in eight libraries. The Historical Society of Pennsylvania — henceforth referred to as HSP — has, of course, the central collection; it owns about 1350 WP documents (exclusive of duplicates), including the manuscripts of greatest individual value and interest. The HSP collection is extremely variegated and illuminates every aspect of the man's career. The second largest holding is in the Public Record Office in London, some 300 documents which illustrate WP's dealings with the English government as a Quaker activist, as a political ally of James II, and as the proprietor of Pennsylvania. The Friends Library in London holds the third largest group, about 150 documents tracing WP's activities within the Society of Friends. The Pennsylvania State Archives in Harrisburg holds a smaller number of documents detailing WP's relations with his colonists. The Bedfordshire Record Office in England holds a group of WP property deeds that once belonged to Granville Penn. The British Library in London has a valuable holding of WP correspondence. The Chester County Historical Society in West Chester, Pennsylvania, holds a miscellaneous collection acquired by Albert Cook Myers when he was planning an edition of WP's papers (see below). The American Philosophical Society in Philadelphia also has an important collection of WP papers. Beyond these large holdings, another 250 scattered WP documents have been found in about 80 libraries and private collections in the United States, Britain, Ireland, and Holland. The Pennsylvania land conveyances issued by WP are not included in this tabulation of WP documents; hundreds of such deeds can be found in Harrisburg, in the HSP, and in private hands. Undoubtedly other, more personal, WP documents remain in private hands and have not been traced. But the 2600 known documents make WP one of the best-recorded public figures in seventeenth-century England or America.

The need for a scholarly edition of these papers has long been recognized. As long ago as 1910, Albert Cook Myers (1878-1960) began work on a comprehensive multivolume edition. Myers intended to publish WP's complete works: his books and pamphlets, together with his correspondence and associated documents, supported by full annotation. Working hard up to 1921, and more fitfully thereafter, Myers searched out 1312 WP documents and made a transcript of each text. He visited many archives, and conducted field trips to every place in England, Ireland, or America where WP was known to have lived or visited. Myers assembled his voluminous research notes, together with copies of WP's tracts and documents, in an imposing series of 196 leather-bound volumes, now deposited in the Chester County Historical Society. Unfortunately, Myers never came close to finishing his project. His research notes are a mine of useful information, but he kept digging for more data until the weight of undigested evidence paralyzed his whole effort. Myers' documentary transcripts are accurate, and he discovered some WP documents which have since disappeared, but his collection of papers is quite incomplete. He was much more interested in WP's outgoing correspondence than in his incoming correspondence, and he never transcribed hundreds of documents owned by the HSP.[6]

Around 1960 Frederick B. Tolles (1915-1975) of Swarthmore College hoped to revive Myers' project, or to bring out his own edition. Tolles was the leading Quaker historian of his generation and the ideal man for the job, but he was forced to abandon his plan because of illness. In 1968 a Committee on the Papers of William Penn was formed under the energetic leadership of Caroline Robbins of Bryn Mawr College. This committee undertook to assemble a master file at the HSP of all known WP documents. In part it retraced the work of Albert Cook Myers by searching American and English libraries for photocopies of every known letter to or from WP, for manuscript drafts of WP's religious and political papers, business accounts, and legal records. The committee did not, however, collect copies of WP's published tracts, nor did it collect copies of most WP conveyances, deeds, indentures, or other formal business documents. Between 1969 and 1975 the committee staff, headed for most of this time by Hannah Benner Roach (1907-1976), accessioned and filed photocopies of 3031 documents obtained from 86 libraries and private holdings in the United States and Britain. They made these photocopies much easier for readers to use by preparing literal typescripts of most of them, and providing translations for documents written in foreign languages. In 1975 the HSP issued a microfilm edition of The Papers of William Penn in fourteen reels.[7] This microfilm edition, once duplicates are eliminated, presents about 2500 documents—or nearly double the number collected by Myers. There are more than 1000 letters by WP and 800 letters to WP. Here is indispensable raw material for any scholar doing primary research on WP, on early Quakerism, or on early Pennsylvania. But of course the HSP microfilm edition provides no editorial apparatus: no identification of persons or places, no elucidation of obscure textual passages, no cross-references from one document to another, and no commentary upon the secondary literature.

Since 1978 the present editors have been working on a select letterpress edition of *The Papers of William Penn.* This edition is jointly sponsored by the HSP, the Philadelphia Center for Early American Studies, Bryn Mawr College, Haverford College, and the University of Pennsylvania. We have received very generous support from the National Endowment for the Humanities and from the National Historical Publications and Records Commission. And we have benefited enormously from the previous labors of Albert Cook Myers, Caroline Robbins, and Hannah Benner Roach. Our edition is based upon the master file assembled for the HSP microfilm edition of 1975. But unlike the comprehensive microfilm edition, we are publishing a selection of WP's most interesting and representative letters and papers.

In this select edition we will print about one-quarter of the documents from the microfilm edition, together with a small number of new WP documents added to the master file since 1975. Our selection process is necessarily subjective, but we have been guided by the following principles. In deciding which letters and papers to exclude, we omit documents which survive only as abstracts or brief extracts. We also omit routine correspondence of minimal content, and form letters. In deciding which documents to include, we look for letters and papers which are clearly the product of WP's own mind, or which received his close attention. We look for documents which add in some way to the reader's understanding of WP's beliefs and actions. We print correspondence with a cross-section of persons significant to WP, people of the "lower sort" as well as historically important figures. In choosing between two letters which have much the same character and content, we prefer the letter which introduces a new correspondent, or which contributes new information or fuller argument. In selecting representative examples from a sizable group of letters and papers (in the present volume, for example, WP's correspondence with his Anglican, Presbyterian, and Baptist adversaries during the 1670s), we look for interesting variations in presentation and content. And we bring attention to previously neglected categories of documentation, such as WP's business records.

Our four volumes are shaped to reflect the four phases of WP's career: the ardent young Quaker of 1667-1679, the energetic colonizer of 1680-1684, the embattled veteran of 1685-1699, and the elder statesman of 1699-1712. However, we have fewer documents to draw upon for WP's early years than for his last years. Only 12 percent of the documents at our disposal are dated 1644-1679, 19 percent are dated 1680-1684, 26 percent are dated 1685-1699, and 43 percent are dated 1699-1718. Since we do not wish to concentrate unduly upon WP's declining years, we shall print a higher percentage of the extant documents from the 1660s and 1670s than from the 1700s. Our purpose throughout is to illuminate all aspects of WP's career. Our four volumes will present abundant evidence of the man's defects, mistakes, and failures, but evidence also of his talent and boundless vitality as a religious controversialist, spiritual leader, civil libertarian, land speculator, politician, and, above all, as the designer, promoter, and defender of a dynamic new settlement in America.

Our opening volume spans the first thirty-five years of WP's life, from his birth in 1644 through his political campaign of 1678-1679. For the chronology of WP's actions during these years, see pp. 24-26. The documents in this first volume are arranged in eleven sections, designed to articulate the principal phases of WP's early career. Within each section, headnotes introduce groups of documents or individual documents, and supply a running commentary upon WP's activities. The many hundreds of persons and places mentioned in these documents are identified (whenever possible) in the footnotes; these identifications may easily be located in the index, where the page references to them are set in boldface type. The seven maps in this volume are likewise designed to aid the reader in locating most places mentioned in the text. WP's chief surviving business records for the 1660s and 1670s are printed or abstracted in an appendix.

The microfilm edition of WP's papers contains 311 documents for the years 1644-1679 (see the list on pp. 655-62, below). In preparing the present volume, we have selected 145 of these documents, and have also incorporated 12 additional documents that are not included in the microfilm edition. Only 76 of the documents in this volume — or about half — have previously been printed. Many of these are extracts or abstracts, and most appear without annotation in such old-fashioned books as Joseph Besse's *A Collection of the Works of William Penn* (1726), Granville Penn's *Memorials of the Professional Life and Times of Sir William Penn* (1833), Samuel M. Janney's *Life of William Penn* (1851), or in early issues of the *Pennsylvania Magazine of History and Biography* and the *Journal of the Friends' Historical Society*.

Since this is an edition of WP's manuscript letters and papers, as distinguished from his printed tracts, our documents, with one exception, were not published in WP's lifetime. The sole exception — WP's account of his journey to Holland and Germany in 1677 (doc. 119) — was printed in 1694. We have decided to include the Holland journal because it parallels and complements WP's earlier Irish journal (doc. 35) and his Kent-Sussex journal (doc. 70). Furthermore, the Holland journal is virtually the only source of information for this trip, a major episode in WP's career.

There are many gaps in the documentary record for the years 1644 to 1679. The first twenty years are nearly a blank. WP's earliest known letter (doc. 5) dates from 1665. No letters survive between WP and his brother Richard, though we know that they corresponded (see doc. 35). No letters between WP and his sister Margaret dated before 1683 survive, though we know that they corresponded earlier. Only one extract of a letter from WP's mother has been found (see *Micro.* 1:270), and none from WP to her. Only one letter (doc. 41) survives from his wife Gulielma, an early letter written before their marriage, though we know that Gulielma wrote other letters during their courtship (see doc. 35), and we may surmise that she continued to do so after their marriage whenever they were apart. During the 1660s and 1670s WP was an exceedingly active correspondent, but distressingly few of his letters from these decades still exist. When WP kept his Irish journal (doc. 35) in 1669-1670, he recorded sending 70 letters, citing the date and addressee of each letter. Only one of these letters (doc. 36) survives. It is evident from WP's Irish journal that he generally wrote letters in batches, and he likewise received packets of letters from English correspondents. In the Irish journal he mentions 25 incoming letters, citing the author and date of receipt for each. One of these letters (doc. 40) survives. Later in the 1670s, WP's correspondence apparently expanded. During a twenty-six-month span in 1672-1674, Philip Ford's accounts (docs. 139-44) show that Ford paid for the posting or receipt of WP's letters on 476 occasions. About half the time Ford paid for multiple letters, so it is reasonable to surmise that WP wrote or received nearly 1000 letters during this period. The master file has only 35 letters to or from WP dating from these months. Most of WP's early business records have likewise disappeared. As doc. 137 shows, WP possessed 14 bundles of letters, leases, conveyances, mortgages, rentrolls, and other papers from the 1660s and 1670s detailing his property transactions in Ireland, England, and New Jersey. We have found few, if any, of these papers. All in all, the 300 surviving WP documents for the years 1644 to 1679 probably constitute no more than 5 percent of the letters and papers that he wrote and received during these years.

Many of WP's early papers appear to have been shredded by Captain Granville at the Pantechnicon in 1870. Twenty letters to WP from his father have not been seen since they were printed in 1833, though if Captain Granville tore these letters up he was not systematic, for another eight letters between father and son, stored at the Pantechnicon in 1870, escaped destruction. WP's letterbook of 1667-1675, the source for more than a quarter of the documents in this volume, was damaged in 1870. This letterbook was ripped into three sections, and the last section — consisting of some ninety pages, to judge by one of the three indexes we have to this book—was probably demolished. The other two fragments were salvaged, but the forty-two-page opening section lost the upper inner corner of every page. In the auctions of 1870-1871, the two surviving sections of the letterbook were sold separately. Fortunately, the HSP acquired both sections, so the volume has been reconstituted as far as possible. Fortunately, also, the documents in the lost third fragment were mainly duplicates of letters from the Holland journal of 1677.[8]

This much-abused letterbook of 1667-1675 is a volume of very special importance for students of WP's early career. WP called it "A Book off Letters and some [other] Papers, given forth at severall times [as] required off the lord {& other wise in zeal & a good understanding of the tru[th]}, wether to Friends, Ruli[ng] People, or any perticuler persons, by me William Penn, from the 7th month in the year 1667."[9] In its present form, the letterbook is a quarto volume of 180 pages, containing copies of 82 letters, unpublished tracts, and other miscellaneous papers. Most of the letters are addressed to WP's anti-Quaker adversaries (see, for example, docs. 18, 31, 33, 71, 74, 76, and 89). Several of the draft tracts copied into this book (see, for example, docs. 55, 57, 65, and 66) are more readable than the pamphlets WP was publishing during this period. The letterbook was compiled, probably over several years, by three clerks, who are identifiable by their handwriting. Scattered through the volume are WP's own notations and corrections.[10] Many of the documents are undated. The copyists did not proceed in chronological order, though they began the volume with letters dated 1671 and worked forward in a general way, reaching 1675 by p. 180, and apparently concentrating on 1676-1678 in the lost final section. The clerk who entered most of the documents from p. 98 onward was Mark Swanner, a German refugee who was on WP's payroll in 1677, to judge by the Ford accounts (see doc. 146), but not in the early 1670s. Swanner made at least two copies of WP's Holland journal, and he drafted a number of Pennsylvania documents in the 1680s.

In the manuscript vault of the HSP, stored on the same shelf with the letterbook of 1667-1675, are two other slim volumes of particular value and interest: WP's Irish journal of 1669-1670 and his journal of travels in Holland and Germany in 1677. The Irish journal is a diminutive pocketbook, kept by WP himself, and filled with daily entries; it is described more fully in the headnote to doc. 35. If WP used a similar pocketbook to record his journey to Holland and Germany in 1677, it has disappeared. The manuscript Holland journal owned by the HSP is a copy by Mark Swanner; it is described more fully in the headnote to doc. 119.

WP always wrote in a great hurry. His letters and papers convey the urgency of his affairs and the passion of his convictions. He was a writer of many moods, often at his most forceful when deeply angry (see doc. 33 and 74), or, at the opposite extreme, when rapturously exalted (see doc. 55). He was never a graceful stylist, but he could turn a pungent phrase, as when he called the vice chancellor of Oxford University a "Poor Mushrom" (doc. 53), or when he declaimed against the "Idle Fancyes, nauseating gestures, ridiculous Sounds, &, vile Conceits" of the schismatic Quaker John Perrot (doc. 71).

The reader of this volume will find many other documents besides the letterbook and the travel journals of exceptionally high value and interest. The 16 letters between WP and Admiral Penn which we have chosen disclose a fascinating relationship between father and son. With so much of WP's family correspondence missing, the five intimate letters of July-August 1670 from WP's friends (docs. 41-45) are particularly welcome; ironically, these letters escaped the debacle of 1870 because they had been intercepted by government spies in 1670 and were filed among the State Papers in the Public Record Office. WP's correspondence with his fellow Quakers—particularly with George and Margaret Fox and Robert Barclay—tells much about the inner history of the Society of Friends in the 1670s. Docs. 112-18 illuminate WP's first effort at American colonization, in New Jersey. Docs. 125-27 and 130-34 divulge something—though less than one would like—of WP's political efforts in 1678-1679. For readers who want the other side of the story, a number of WP's correspondents vigorously challenge his Quaker beliefs and actions: for example, the Irish lords Orrery, Broghill, and O'Brien (docs. 19, 39-40); the Anglican Henry More (doc. 90); the Presbyterian Richard Baxter (docs. 95, 98); and the schismatic Quaker William Rogers (doc. 124). Last, but not least, WP's business records, particularly Philip Ford's accounts (docs. 139-50), detail WP's spending habits and demonstrate that he faced sizable financial problems in the late 1670s.

For readers willing to be patient with WP's seventeenth-century prose and ready to grapple with his ardent religiosity and his combative personality, the documents in this volume display a bold and resourceful young rebel against religious conformity, against political oppression, and against social convention. During the 1660s and 1670s WP fought and suffered for his beliefs. He was jailed four times, and endlessly insulted in print and in person. Yet WP stood up to his father and achieved reconciliation with him on his own terms. He disputed eagerly with religious opponents of every possible shade. He lobbied tirelessly with government officials; he petitioned Parliament; he appealed directly to the king. He exhibited boundless energy, whether in preaching for hours at a Quaker meeting, or traveling long days by horseback through England, Ireland, Holland, and Germany, or sitting at his desk pouring out letters and tracts. All of this effort was deeply rewarding to WP, for within the Society of Friends and within his own Quaker family he experienced great joy, love, and peace. In short, he was a young man far removed from Benjamin West's Quaker Oats stereotype: a man of many attributes, who was neither bland nor boring.

1. Frederick B. Tolles, *Quakers and the Atlantic Culture* (New York, 1960), p. 116.
2. Nicholas B. Wainwright, "The Penn Collection," *PMHB* 87:393.
3. Wainwright, "The Penn Collection," p. 405.

4. For further discussion of this bizarre episode, see Wainwright, "The Penn Collection," pp. 406-15.

5. Hampton L. Carson, *A History of the Historical Society of Pennsylvania* (Philadelphia, 1940), 2 vols., 1:383-89.

6. "A Report of a Survey of the Albert Cook Myers Collection of William Penn Material in the Chester County Historical Society," by Mary Maples [Dunn], Joseph E. Illick, and Frederick B. Tolles, unpublished but circulated Oct. 1959.

7. This is a film of Roach's file, exclusive of duplicates. See Caroline Robbins, "The Papers of William Penn," *PMHB* 93:3-12; *Guide to the Microfilm of the Papers of William Penn* (Philadelphia, 1975).

8. The letterbook, as we now have it, ends in the middle of a document on p. 180. The book was possibly assembled in two stages, for one of WP's clerks compiled a pair of indexes (to recipients and to first lines) which covers the documents through p. 180, whereas another clerk compiled a third index to documents from pp. 1-267. This third index gives the first lines of 15 documents in the lost third section. Eleven of these documents were letters duplicated in the Holland journal of 1677; two were copies of WP's address to James II in 1687 and the king's reply [see *Micro.* 5:766]; another two documents have not been identified.

9. This title is in WP's hand, at the top of the opening page. When the HSP rebound the book, the dates 1667-1675 were stamped on the spine because the last dated document toward the close of the book in its present form is dated Oct. 1675. Actually, the earliest dated document (doc. 4) is from 1664, and several of the undated documents (such as doc. 126) were written around 1678.

10. This letterbook may be the only one kept by WP during the 1660s and 1670s. It seems to have been the sole source of early WP letters and papers available to Joseph Besse when he compiled his edition of *The Works of William Penn* in the 1720s. Besse printed about 30 documents from pp. 1-180 of the letterbook, and another 13 documents from the lost final section. See *Works,* 1:2-186. All of the letters printed by Besse from the missing section are included in doc. 119.

EDITORIAL METHOD

No method of textual reproduction has yet been devised that solves the double problem of the historical editor: how to be completely faithful to a text composed long ago and to make this text fully intelligible to a present-day reader. The problem enlarges as the editor moves backward in time. Seventeenth-century habits of word choice, spelling, capitalization, and punctuation were far different from current standards. And seventeenth-century Quaker texts present a special editorial challenge. Early Quaker epistles are filled with Biblical quotations and echoes. Often they are composed in a private style, deeply meaningful to the Friends who received and read them, but difficult for outsiders to penetrate. The chief Quaker, George Fox, used a semiliterate style all his own. Early Friends, when writing to each other, customarily referred to fellow Quakers by initials only: as "my love to dr G.F. M.F. G.W. I.P. G.S. & J.B." Here the modern editor faces a grim choice. He can either make a faithfully literal but unintelligible transcript (with or without footnotes to identify the six persons and explain why the last-named was more probably John Burnyeat than John Bolton); or he can introduce a forest of square brackets ("my love to dr G[eorge] F[ox] M[argaret] F[ox] G[eorge Whitehead] I[saac] P[enington] G[ulielma] S[pringett] & J[ohn] B[urnyeat]"); or he can produce a readable but unfaithfully free translation ("my love to dear George Fox, Margaret Fox, George Whitehead, Isaac Penington, Gulielma Springett, and John Burnyeat").

Other textual difficulties encountered by the editors of *The Papers of William Penn* are common to most historical editing projects. Some of our documents are nearly indecipherable. WP's orthography is generally legible, but since he wrote in a hurry his words often jumbled onto the page faster than he could sort them into sentences or arguments. His letters have many slips of the pen, and erratic spelling, punctuation, and capitalization. WP's working drafts of documents are studded with deletions, corrections, and insertions. His clerks could not always read his hand, so their copies of WP's documents are marred by errors and blanks. Documents from WP's vandalized letterbook of 1667-1675 have lacunae where the pages are torn. And lost WP documents that survive only in nineteenth-century transcripts have been so altered by previous editors that the original wording and format cannot be restored.

A generation ago, most historical editors aimed for a happy compromise between literal and modernized textual reproduction. Current practice tends toward a more strictly literal method, particularly when printing documents from the seventeenth century or earlier, where modernization robs a text of much of its original character. In this edition, we aim to print a completely faithful transcript of each original text, including blemishes and errors. When the original text has been lost, we aim to print a completely faithful transcript of the best surviving copy. In this way we try to preserve the form and style of WP's seventeenth-century papers, and to introduce no further changes into his modernized papers. In general, our editorial interpolations [enclosed in square brackets] within the text are minimal. On the other hand, we provide considerable annotation. In the footnotes we clarify textual passages and identify persons and places. In the headnotes and footnotes we comment on the chief substantive issues raised in the documents. In this way we try to make each text fully intelligible to the reader. Some editors prefer to let the texts speak for themselves, but we believe that many of WP's documents are difficult to understand or appreciate without considerable editorial assistance.

Our editorial rules may be summarized as follows:

1. Each document selected for publication in *The Papers of William Penn* is printed in full. The only exception to this rule occurs in the appendix, where several property deeds are abstracted (docs. 151-52).

2. Each document is numbered, for convenient cross-reference, and is supplied with a short title.

3. The format of each document (including the salutation and complimentary closure in letters) is rendered as in the original or copy, with the following two exceptions. Endorsements are treated as dockets, and entered into the provenance note (see below). If a document is undated, an initial date line is supplied [within square brackets]. If a document is dated at the close but not at the opening, an initial date line is supplied [within square brackets], and the closing date line is retained.

4. The dating of documents poses a further editorial problem. Englishmen in WP's lifetime employed the Julian, or Old Style, calendar, which was ten days behind the Gregorian, or New Style, calendar used by most continental Europeans — and adopted by Englishmen and Americans in 1752. Seventeenth-century Englishmen started the new year officially on 25 March, but since 1 January also had currency as New Year's Day, some writers double-dated for the period 1 January to 24 March. In addition, the Quakers employed their own nomenclature. They numbered the months, March being the first month and February the twelfth. They also numbered the days of the week, Sunday being the first day and Saturday the seventh.

In this edition, when a document is dated in Quaker form, a "heathen" translation of the month is supplied [within square brackets]. When a document written between 1 January and 24 March is dated according to the previous year, a "modern" translation of the year is supplied [within square brackets]. Otherwise, the Old Style calendar is retained. For example, WP's birthday, 14 October, is not changed to 24 October, the Gregorian or New Style date of his birth.

5. The text of each document is rendered as follows:

a. Spelling is retained as written. Misspelled words are not marked with an editorial [sic]. If the sense of a word is obscured through misspelling, its meaning is clarified in a footnote.

b. Capitalization is retained as written. In seventeenth-century manuscripts, the capitalization of such letters as "c," "k," "p," "s," and "w" is often a matter of judgment, and we cannot claim that our readings are definitive. Whenever it is clear to us that the initial letter in a sentence has not been capitalized, it is left lower case.

c. Punctuation and paragraphing are retained as written. When a sentence is not closed with a period, we have inserted an extra space.

d. Words or phrases inserted into the text are placed {within braces}.

e. Words or phrases deleted from the text are ~~crossed through~~.

f. Slips of the pen are retained as written, and are not marked by [sic].

g. Contractions, abbreviations, superscript letters, and ampersands are retained as written. When a contraction is marked by a tilde, it is expanded.

h. The thorn is rendered as "th," and superscript contractions attached to the thorn are brought down to the line and expanded: as "the," "them," or "that." Our justification for this procedure is that we no longer have a thorn, and modern readers mistake it for "y." Likewise, since modern readers do not recognize that "u" and "v" were used interchangeably in the seventeenth century, we have rendered "u" as "v," or "v" as "u," whenever appropriate.

i. The £ sign in superscript is rendered as "l."

j. The tailed "p" is expanded into "per," "pro," or "pre," as indicated by the rest of the word.

k. The long "s" is presented as a short "s." The double "ff" is presented as a capital "F."

l. Words underlined in manuscript are *italicized.*

m. Blanks in the manuscript, missing words, and illegible words are rendered as [blank] or [missing word] or [illegible word] or [illegible deletion]. If a missing word can be supplied, it is inserted [within square brackets]. If the supplied word is conjectural, it is followed by a question mark.

6. Immediately following each document, a provenance note supplies the following information:

a. A symbol indicating the nature of the document: such as ALS or Draft. See the list of Abbreviations and Short Titles, pp. 20-23, for the explanation of these symbols.

b. A reference to the source of the document: such as the manuscript collection where the original is located, or the book where the best surviving transcript is located. See the list of Abbreviations and Short Titles, pp. 20-23, for the symbols used to identify the chief depositories and printed sources.

c. A reference to the HSP microfilm edition of The Papers of William Penn (1975), indicating on which reel and frame the document in question can be found. For example, *Micro.* 1:270 means that the document begins on the 270th frame of the first microfilm reel. See the Calendar of Microfilmed WP Documents, 1644-1679, on pp. 655-62. Documents not included in the microfilm edition are listed on pp.663-64.

d. The docket and address, if any. Comments on the physical condition of the document are added here, whenever appropriate.

7. Special procedures have been employed in rendering the texts of the Irish journal (doc. 35) and the Holland journal (doc. 119). See the headnotes to these documents.

TECHNICAL PROCEDURES

In preparing the text and editorial apparatus for the printer, we have used a Wang Word Processor, System 5. The word processor captures text on magnetic disks, displays it on a screen, and prints copy at high speed. Each document selected for the volume was keyed into the word processor from the typescript prepared for the microfilm edition by Hannah Benner Roach and her staff. Print-outs produced from the magnetic disk were then compared twice with the original manuscript (or best surviving transcript), and corrections were entered into the word processor. At a later stage, footnote numbers, editorial interpolations, provenance notes, headnotes, document titles, and footnotes were added to each document. After revisions were made in the editorial apparatus and each document was copyedited, our text was in finished form, but our print-outs from the word processor looked like typescripts. In order to convert our text into set type, we inserted codes on the disks designed to command a computer-driven typesetter to produce different sizes and styles of type for headings, text, and notes, to lead and space the lines of type, and to position the text on each page. From our encoded disks, the Winchell Company of Philadelphia then processed the text through its Penta computer and produced galley proofs in Baskerville type on its Linotron 202 typesetter. These galleys were reviewed by the editorial staff (chiefly for errors introduced at the encoding stage), corrections were made, and page proofs produced.

Using word processing equipment in historical editing has several advantages. Text or editorial matter is quickly and easily inserted, deleted, moved, or corrected; no new errors are introduced in surrounding text when corrections are made. Perhaps the largest savings of staff time come at the typesetting stage. Because the typesetting unit composes directly from our magnetic disk, no new textual errors are introduced at that stage. This is particularly useful in reproducing seventeenth-century text, where unusual spellings and phrasings would make a compositor's task difficult and the final proofreading of hand-set galleys extremely tedious and time-consuming.

ABBREVIATIONS AND SHORT TITLES

ACM
: Albert Cook Myers Collection of William Penn Materials, Chester County Historical Society, West Chester, Pennsylvania.

AD
: Autograph document, not signed.

ADf
: Autograph draft.

ADfS
: Autograph draft, signed.

ADS
: Autograph document (deed, will, diary, etc.), signed.

AL
: Autograph letter, not signed.

ALS
: Autograph letter, signed.

Alumni Cantabrigienses
: John Venn and J. A. Venn, *Alumni Cantabrigienses, Part 1: From the Earliest Times to 1751* (Cambridge, 1922-1927); 4 vols.

Alumni Oxonienses
: Joseph Foster, *Alumni Oxonienses: The Members of the University of Oxford, 1500-1714, Vol. 1: Early Series* (Oxford, 1891).

Baronetage
: G. E. C. [George Edward Cokayne], *Complete Baronetage* (Exeter, England, 1900-1909); 5 vols. plus appendix.

Beck and Ball
: William Beck and T. Frederick Ball, *The London Friends' Meetings* (London, 1869).

Besse
: Joseph Besse, *A Collection of the Sufferings of the People called Quakers* (London, 1753).

BL
: British Library, London.

Braithwaite, *Beginnings*
: William C. Braithwaite, *The Beginnings of Quakerism* (London, 1912).

Braithwaite, *Second Period*
William C. Braithwaite, *The Second Period of Quakerism*, 2d ed., ed. Henry J. Cadbury (Cambridge, 1961).

Burke's *Ireland*
Sir Bernard Burke, *Burke's Landed Gentry of Ireland*, 4th ed., ed. L. G. Pine (London, 1958).

Burke's *Peerage*
Sir Bernard Burke, *Burke's Peerage, Baronetage, and Knightage*, 96th ed. (London, 1938); 2 vols.

CCHS
Chester County Historical Society, West Chester, Pennsylvania.

Copy
Contemporary copy.

Cross, *Christian Church*
F. L. Cross and E. A. Livingstone, eds., *The Oxford Dictionary of the Christian Church*, 2d ed. (Oxford, 1974).

CSPD
Mary Anne Everett Green, et al., eds., *Calendar of State Papers, Domestic Series, 1603-1704* (London, 1857-1972); 85 vols.

CSPI
C. W. Russell, J. P. Prendergast, and R. P. Mahaffy, eds., *Calendar of the State Papers Relating to Ireland, 1603-1670* (London, 1870-1910); 13 vols.

Cunningham
Peter Cunningham, *A Handbook for London, Past and Present* (London, 1849); 2 vols.

D
Document in the hand of a clerk, not signed by the author.

DAB
Allen Johnson and Dumas Malone, eds., *Dictionary of American Biography* (New York, 1928-1938); 20 vols. plus index and supplements.

Df
Draft in the hand of a clerk, not signed by the author.

DNB
Leslie Stephen and Sidney Lee, eds., *Dictionary of National Biography* (New York and London, 1885-1900); 63 vols. plus supplements.

DQB
Dictionary of Quaker Biography, Quaker Collection, Haverford College, Haverford, Pennsylvania; multivolume series in typescript.

DS
Document in hand of a clerk, signed by the author.

Endy
Melvin B. Endy, Jr., *William Penn and Early Quakerism* (Princeton, 1973).

FLL
Library of the Religious Society of Friends, London.

Fox
Norman Penney, ed., *The Journal of George Fox* (Cambridge, 1911); 2 vols.

Fox, *Short Journal*

Norman Penney, ed., *The Short Journal and Itinerary Journals of George Fox* (Cambridge, 1925).

Fuller and Holme

Abraham Fuller and Thomas Holme, *A Compendious View of Some Extraordinary Sufferings of the People call'd Quakers* (Dublin, 1732).

Grubb

William Penn, *My Irish Journal, 1669-1670,* ed. Isabel Grubb (London, 1952).

GSP

Genealogical Society of Pennsylvania Collections, housed at HSP.

HSP

Historical Society of Pennsylvania, Philadelphia.

Janney

Samuel M. Janney, *The Life of William Penn* (Philadelphia, 1852).

Jenkins

Howard M. Jenkins, *The Family of William Penn, Founder of Pennsylvania, Ancestry and Descendants* (Philadelphia, 1899).

JFHS

The Journal of the Friends' Historical Society (London).

LBC

Letterbook copy (as from William Penn's Letterbook).

Lewis

Samuel Lewis, *A Topographical Dictionary of Ireland* (London, 1837); 2 vols.

London Monuments

Royal Commission on Historical Monuments (England), *An Inventory of the Historical Monuments in London, Vol. IV. The City* (London, 1929).

LS

Letter in hand of a clerk, signed by the author.

MBE

Minute book entry (as from Privy Council Minute Book).

Memorials

Granville Penn, *Memorials of the Professional Life and Times of Sir William Penn, Knt.* (London, 1833); 2 vols.

Micro.

The Papers of William Penn, Microfilm Edition, Historical Society of Pennsylvania (1975); 14 reels plus guide. References are to reel and frame.

MS, MSS

Manuscript, manuscripts.

Muirhead's *England*

Findlay Muirhead, ed., *England,* in The Blue Guides series (London, 1920).

Muirhead's *London*

Findlay Muirhead, ed., *London and Its Environs,* in The Blue Guides series (London, 1919).

New Bible Dictionary
J. D. Douglas, ed., *The New Bible Dictionary* (Grand Rapids, Mich., 1962).

Nobility and Gentry
An Alphabetical Account of the Nobility and Gentrey, Which are (or lately were) related unto the several Counties of England and Wales (1673; reprint ed., London, 1892).

OED
The Oxford English Dictionary (Oxford, 1933); 12 vols. and supplement.

Oxford Classical Dictionary
N. G. L. Hammond and H. H. Scullard, *The Oxford Classical Dictionary,* 2d ed. (Oxford, 1970).

PDS
Printed document (such as WP's conveyances of land), signed.

Peare
Catherine Owens Peare, *William Penn* (Philadelphia, 1956).

Peerage
G. E. C. [George Edward Cokayne], ed., *The Complete Peerage,* 2d ed., ed. Vicary Gibbs, et al. (London, 1910-1959); 13 vols.

Pender
Seamus Pender, ed., *A Census of Ireland, circa 1659* (Dublin, 1939).

Pepys
Robert Latham and William Matthews, eds., *The Diary of Samuel Pepys* (Berkeley, 1970-); 9 vols., index forthcoming.

PMHB
Pennsylvania Magazine of History and Biography.

PRO
Public Record Office, London.

PRO, Dublin
Public Record Office, Dublin.

Sandwich, *Journal*
R. C. Anderson, ed., *The Journal of Edward Mountagu, First Earl of Sandwich,* vol. 64 of Publications of the Navy Records Society (London, 1929).

Transcript
Modern (eighteenth–twentieth century) copy.

VCH
W. Page, H. A. Doubleday, et al., eds., *Victoria History of the Counties of England* (London, 1900-); multivolume series in progress.

Wing
Donald Wing, ed., *Short-Title Catalogue of Books Printed in England, Scotland, Ireland, Wales, and British America and of English Books Printed in Other Countries, 1641-1700* (New York, 1951); 3 vols.

Works
[Joseph Besse, ed.], *A Collection of the Works of William Penn* (London, 1726); 2 vols.

A WILLIAM PENN CHRONOLOGY, *1664–1679*

1644	*14 October.* Born in London.
c. 1653	Begins studies at Chigwell Grammar School, Essex.
1656-1660	Penn family at Macroom Castle, county Cork, Ireland.
1657	First hears a Quaker preacher, Thomas Loe.
1660	*October.* Enters Christ Church College, Oxford.
1662	Expelled from Christ Church College for religious nonconformity.
	Goes to France.
1663	Begins studying theology at Moses Amyraut's Protestant Academy at Saumur, France.
1664	*August.* Returns to London.
1665	*February.* Enters Lincoln's Inn to study law.
	April. With the English fleet preparing for war; at Whitehall Palace.
1666	*February.* Goes to Ireland on business for his father.
1667	*Late summer-early autumn.* Becomes a Quaker; is arrested at Cork.
	November. Returns to England.
1668	Argues with his father over religion.
	Visits the Duke of Buckingham to get Quakers out of prison.
	October. Death of Thomas Loe.
	October-November. Controversy with Thomas Danson and Thomas Vincent; writes *The Sandy Foundation Shaken.*
	December. Imprisoned in the Tower of London for blasphemy.
1669	*February.* Controversy with Lodowick Muggleton begins.
	Writes *No Cross, No Crown,* and *Innocency with Her Open Face* while in the Tower.
	July. Released from the Tower.
	September. Leaves London for Ireland on business and missionary work.
	October. Arrives in county Cork, Ireland.
1670	Writes *A Seasonable Caveat Against Popery,* and *The Great Case of Liberty of Conscience.*

August. Returns to London; is arrested for preaching.
September. The Penn-Mead trial.

1671 *January-February.* Publishes *Truth Rescued from Imposture.*
February-July. Imprisoned at Newgate for preaching.
August-October. First journey to Holland and Germany.
October-November. Journey through Suffolk.

1672 Controversy with John Faldo begins; publishes *Quakerism a New Nickname for Old Christianity.*
Controversy with John Morse begins; publishes *Plain-Dealing with a Traducing Anabaptist.*
Publishes *The New Witnesses Proved Old Hereticks,* attacking Lodowick Muggleton.
4 April. Marries Gulielma Springett and moves to Rickmansworth in Hertford.
September-October. Missionary journey through Kent, Sussex, and Surrey.

1673 Controversy with William Mucklow; publishes *The Spirit of Alexander the Coppersmith Justly Rebuked.*
Controversy with Thomas Hicks; publishes *Reason Against Railing.*
Friendship with Robert Barclay begins.

1674 First appearance at court since 1668; first meeting with the Duke of York since 1665. Lobbies against the persecution of Quakers; works to get George Fox out of Worcester prison.

1675 Writes *A Treatise of Oaths* and *England's Present Interest Discover'd.*
January. Son Springett Penn (1675-1696), WP's first surviving child, is born.
January-February. Arbitrates a dispute between two Quakers over New Jersey lands and becomes a trustee of West New Jersey.
October. Controversy with Richard Baxter.
October. Begins work with the new Quaker Meeting for Sufferings.

1676 *April.* Meeting at Draw-well, Yorkshire, concerning the Wilkinson-Story schism in the Society of Friends.
Summer. Aids Barclay's efforts to secure the release of imprisoned Scottish Quakers.
July-September. Arranges for the division of New Jersey into East and West parts, and for the settlement of West New Jersey.
Fall. Moves to Warminghurst in Sussex.

1677 *March.* Issues the West New Jersey Concessions.
July-October. Journey to Holland and Germany.

1678 *February.* Debates William Rogers concerning the Wilkinson-Story controversy.

March. Daughter Laetitia Penn (1678-1746) born.

Becomes involved in Whig politics in an effort to secure religious toleration.

1679 Publishes *England's Great Interest in the Choice of This New Parliament,* and *One Project for the Good of England.*

March-July. Tries to secure the election of Algernon Sidney to Parliament.

THE EARLY YEARS

1644–1665

The first six documents below are all that survive of what WP wrote, and most of what was written about him, before his twenty-first birthday; fortunately, each highlights a central element in his youthful experience.

WP's baptism in a parish church in the shadow of the Tower of London (doc. 1) locates him at the center of English politics and society. His parents' position in that society, however, was quite modest in 1644. His father was a young commander in the Parliamentary navy, his mother a refugee from the recent rebellion in Ireland. Doc. 2, WP's first surviving composition, shows a dramatic elevation in status. This Latin tribute to a fallen prince identifies its sixteen-year-old author as a gentleman commoner at Oxford's most prestigious college, Christ Church. By 1660 WP's father was a knight and an admiral, and the son was well placed to move easily into the upper ranks of English society.

The year 1664 shows a more mature, interesting, and troubled WP. Since adolescence he had developed an inner life of religious piety, and in the winter of 1661-1662 he was expelled from Christ Church college for publicly criticizing the ceremonies of the Church of England. Doc. 3 suggests that his father's effort to save him for the world by sending him to France had met with some success, but WP had soon tired of the stylish life of Paris and turned to the solid Huguenot theology of Saumur. And although he returned to London as a polished man of the world in dress, conversation, and possibly even amorous behavior, he was also still searching for a life of sober, quiet Christianity. WP's first surviving English composition, "Ah Tyrant Lust" (doc. 4), makes this point forcefully.

In 1665, WP began the study of law at Lincoln's Inn, attended court, and joined the English fleet that was preparing to fight the Dutch (see doc. 5). In April (doc. 6), he was dealing with the king and his chief courtiers and officials, pressing his father's claim to contested Irish lands and relaying messages from the navy to the king. He was also forming firm friendships, especially with the Duke of York, that would survive his later conversion to Quakerism. Thus these early documents disclose an interplay between the social advantages, varied educational experiences, and political contacts that WP was acquiring and the profound inner life that he was cultivating, producing a most unusual Quaker, and a quite remarkable Englishman.

1
BAPTISM

[23 October 1644]

23 william Sonn of william pen[1] & margaret his wife[2] of the Tower Liberty[3]

D. Parish Register. Church of All Hallows by the Tower, London. (*Micro.* 1:003).

1. William Penn (1621-1670) was the son of Giles Penn, a Bristol draper, merchant, and mariner, and Joan Gilbert. Penn became a captain in the Parliamentary navy in the year of WP's birth and rose rapidly in naval service to become one of the commonwealth's most important admirals. *DNB*.

2. Margaret Jasper Vanderschuren Penn (1610?-1682) was the daughter of John Jasper, a Rotterdam merchant. She first married Nicholas Vanderschuren (d.1641 or 1642), a Dutch merchant, in 1631 or earlier, and lived in Kilrush, County Clare, Ireland, until the Irish uprising of 1641. She then took refuge in London, where she married William Penn on 6 June 1643. Jenkins, pp. 16-21, 46; Peare, p. 11; ACM, vols. 49, 49A, 49B, 50.

3. Extending east and northeast from the Tower of London. The Penns lived on Great Tower Hill Road just north of the tower moat in 1655, and perhaps also in the 1640s, in a house whose courtyard abutted the old city wall. The medieval church of All Hallows is located in the Great Tower Ward, a few hundred yards west of the Tower. John Stow, *A Survay of London* (London, 1598, 1603; 1890), pp. 152-59; Cunningham, 2:840-41; A. E. Daniel, *London City Churches* (New York, 1896), pp. 15-27; Peare, p. 9; Jenkins, p. 31; *London Monuments*, 4:176; P. Gibson to WP, Mar. 1712, *Memorials*, 2:615.

2
VERSES ON THE DEATH OF HENRY, DUKE OF GLOUCESTER

[November 1660]

Publica te Dux Magne,[1] dabant Jejunia genti,
  Sed facta est nato Principe[2] festa dies.
Te moriente, licet celebraret laeta triumphos
  Anglia; solennes solvitur in lachrymas.
Solus ad arbitrium moderaris pectora; solus
  Tu dolor accedis, deliciaeque tuis.

Gul. Penn. eq. Aur. fil. natu Max. ex
AEd. *Christi,* superioris ordinis
Commensalis.[3]

The Nation's need, Great Duke, gave thee to us.
And now, when England celebrates with joy
The birthday of a Prince, she yet must weep
That thou art dead; thou who dost sway all hearts;
Thou who wast once our joy, but now our sorrow.

W.H.A.[4]

Printed copy. *Epicedia Academiae Oxoniensis, in Obitum Celsissimi Principis Henrici Ducis Glocestrensis* (Oxford, 1660). (*Micro.* 1:004).

1. WP's earliest surviving composition, written as he turned sixteen, mourns the death of Henry Stuart, Duke of Gloucester (1639-1660), Charles II's popular and widely admired youngest brother. Henry died of smallpox in London on 13 Sept. 1660. This verse appeared in a collection of sixty-seven poems memorializing Henry, written by a broad range of Oxford professors, young scholars, and cathedral clerics. The greatest concentration of authors were from Christ Church, WP's college, and the volume may have been planned and executed there, perhaps by the energetic Dr. John Fell (1625-1686), who contributed a poem. Fell is designated as "Eccles. Christi Subdecanus," which suggests a publication date of Nov. for the volume, since WP entered Christ Church on 26 Oct., and Fell became dean of the college on 30 Nov. *Epicedia,* [p.18]; *DNB.*

2. Henry's brother James, Duke of York (1633-1701) celebrated his twenty-seventh birthday on 15 Oct. 1660; this is probably the birthday to which WP refers. It is interesting that young WP, whose career was to be so closely intertwined with James', paid him this early formal tribute. *DNB.*

3. "Will. Penn, eldest son of a knight of the Court, of Christ Church, gentleman commoner."

4. This translation is by William H. Appleton, and appears in ACM, vol. 1.

3

UNKNOWN AUTHOR TO SIR WILLIAM PENN

Aprill 24 1664

Dr[?] Sr I have lately heard ~~that~~ a very good Caracter of yr Son for it ~~seeme he~~ {happen} that {he who} was my servant {abrode} ~~find~~ (wayting now on Mr Osburne) finds him at Saumurs.[1] where he is in particular ~~reputation~~ note of outdoing most of his Country men. and I am heartily rejoiced at it, for france is a very fertile soyle and will {aboundantly} improve the ~~Ste~~ Seeds accoording to their nature that come into it; and indeed the whole Suceesse of a traveler is in a kind of Crisis, of what Inclinations he carryes with him, and what Conversations he lightes in{to at} first. That tryall it Seemes is over ~~and now~~ {with Mr. Penne whom} you may {now} venter ~~him~~ {for ought I heare} amgts the Goths and vandalls. I know he had the advantages thorough ~~yr bounty and~~ Indulgence ~~you~~ {to} keepe pace with the best sort of Companye amonght whom the best things are Cravued; ~~and~~ {yett} I know not a greater Errour of the ~~Wisest~~ {wise} men of that Country than that they place a value on Expence. wch is quite opposite to the Italian maxime of gran Speza, poco Cevrello[2]. however {the humour of} each Country must have {allowance} ~~its mode~~, and he that either improoves his knowledge or his reputation as[3] the extraordinary expence of a few pistoles[4] will returne home noe great looser.

AL. Dreer Collection, HSP. (*Micro.* 1:012). Docketed: To Sr Wm Penne.

1. This town on the Loire River, near Nantes, was the site of L'Academie Protestante de Saumur, founded in 1591, a flourishing center of Huguenot culture until the revocation of the Edict of Nantes in 1685. WP enrolled in the academy in 1663 to study with the French theologian Moise Amyraut (1596-1664). For details see Endy, pp. 98-100; Peare, pp. 40-42. WP probably remained at Saumur, rooming in Amyraut's house, until the master's death early in 1664. When WP's Irish friend Lord Broghill boarded with his brother at Amyraut's house in 1662, they paid £168 per month (Orrery MSS 16/7074, National Library, Dublin).
2. Possibly "Cervello," or "Cerviello." This phrase, spelled "gran spesa, poco cervello" in modern Italian, means "big expense, little brains." Translation by Nancy Dersofi, Department of Italian, Bryn Mawr College.
3. "At."
4. A gold coin, worth about 16s. 6d in 1664. *OED*.

4
AH TYRANT LUST

[1664][1]

Ah Tyrant Lust could I thy ~~Hunger~~[2] {Power} stay,
And rout thy Force, [illegible deletion] {that wou'd} my Soul betray
~~un~~To the ~~devils watch~~[3] {Infernal Find}, & thus resigne
my ~~It's~~ Peace, my Joy, yea all I can call mine,
I'd as soon offer up a Sacrifice
To him whose Laws thou'st made me to despise:
I Say to his just wrath, for how, alas, could I
Shew him my Love & not pluck out mine eye![4]
All dallelahs[5] be gone, I you conjure,
No more your witchcrafts can my Soul endure;
And all Polluted ones, & blacker with Sin,
Then Leopards Spotts, or th' Ethiopians Skin;
Your In, makes their Outsides abasht to see[6]
What's fair without, within should blackest be.
And let me silently converse with those[7]
That in a faithful God their Trust repose:

That covenante & that commune with him,
whose motto's holiness, & knowes no Sin.
So will my wearied Soul find ~~peace &~~ {Sollid} rest,
not from without, but in an armed breast,
That's proof, where ~~th'Devils~~ Fiery darts nere
can prevail
wh~~en~~ile Heavens power is the Souls Coate of male.
And feed midst Xts Dr[8] sheep on mountains high,
above the world & all its vanity.[9]
There will she leap, there will she Dance, & Sing
Sweet ~~Her~~ Hallelujahs unto Christ her King;
where Raptures ne~~v~~'er grow barr'n nor Fountains dry
But overflow with joy eternally.

1664.

LBC. WP's Letterbook, 1667-1675, HSP. (*Micro.* 1:009). The text, evidently copied in the 1670s from the original that has been lost, is in a clerk's hand, as are the corrections in ll. 2 and 4. The date at the end is either in the clerk's hand or in the hand which makes all of the other corrections, and which may be WP's.

1. In the year in which he wrote this poem, WP manifested signs of a deep uncertainty over the proper course for his life. Upon WP's return from the continent, Samuel Pepys noticed only "the vanity of [his] French garbe and affected manner of speech and gait" (30 Aug. 1664); moreover, Pepys thought that WP was far too persistent in paying social calls on Pepys's young wife. And in 1665, WP would enter Lincoln's Inn to study law (Feb.), visit the royal court, and argue with Pepys over the meaning of a line in a French song (Sept.). Pepys, 5, 14 Sept. 1664; 22 Mar., 13 Sept. 1665. This poem affords a brief glimpse of WP's continuing inner struggle with the temptations of the world; whether it refers to a passion for a particular woman, however, is not known.

2. Possibly "Anger."

3. Possibly "witch."

4. The exclamation point is written over a question mark.

5. Delilah, mistress and betrayer of Samson. Judg. 16:4-20.

6. "In" and "Outsides" were capitalized after being written in lower case.

7. Christians who have escaped the anguish of the world, the sort of people WP found among the Quakers in 1667.

8. "Christ's Dear."

9. This whole line is written above a deleted, mostly illegible, line.

5
TO SIR WILLIAM PENN

From Harwich,[1] 23d April, 1665

Honoured Father,

We could not arrive here sooner than this day, about twelve of the clock, by reason of the continued cross winds and (as I thought) foul weather. I pray God, after all the foul weather and dangers you are exposed to, and shall be, that you come home as secure. And, I bless God, my heart does not in any way fail; but firmly believes, that if God has called you out to battle, he will cover your head in that smoky day. And, as I never knew what a father was till I had wisdom enough to prize him, so can I safely say, that now, of all times, your concerns are most dear to me. It's hard, meantime, to lose both a father and a friend. &c.

W.P.

Original lost. Printed, *Memorials*, 2:317. (*Micro.* 1:014).

1. An Essex port on the North Sea. WP had come to Harwich from the English fleet, which was assembling at Gunfleet Bar, a few miles offshore, in preparation for the first major battle of the Second Dutch War. In the three months prior to this letter, WP had spent most of his time in London, where he entered Lincoln's Inn to study law on 7 Feb., and where he probably pressed his father's claim to his Irish lands in March. Pepys encountered him on 22 Mar. while visiting the Duke of York. Admiral Penn, meanwhile, was with the fleet in the Thames estuary. WP probably joined his father at sea in late March or early April; he was now returning to London as a messenger. Sandwich, *Journal*, pp. 194, 198; Pepys, 17 Feb., 4, 22, 25, 28 Mar., 25 Apr. 1665.

6
TO SIR WILLIAM PENN

Navy office[1] 6th May 1665

Hond: Father

Being not able to give you any Considerable account off anything more then my Journy,[2] and straingly being disapointed off dispatching a packet the other day, you may well wonder my undissign'd silence: but meeting with this opertunity, I shall both acquaint you with what I then thought fitt your takeing notice, and begg your pardon others negligence not my own, Impede its Conveyance At my arrivall at Harwich ~~where I~~ (which was about 1 off the clock on the sabbath day, and where I stayd till three,) I took post for London and was at London the next morning by all most daylight: I hasted to whitehall[3] where not finding the King[4] upp, I presented my selfe to My Lord off Arlington,[5] and Coll Ashbournham[6]—at his Magesties Knocking, he was Inform'd that there was an express from the duke,[7] at which earnestly sciping[8] out of his bed, came only in his gown and slipers. who when he saw me, said Oh ist you, how does Sr Will:[9] he askt how you did at three severall times: he was glad to heare your Message about the Ka:[10] after Interrogating off me above halfe an hour ~~Bid~~ bid me goe now about your business, and mine too: as for the Dutchess,[11] she was pleasd to ask severall questions and so dismist me: I delivr'd all the letters given me: as for the Irish business[12] all is, as, it was, only Mrs. wallis[13] presen'd an other petition, I beleve uneffectuall enough. however to besure, Mr Southwell[14] has promest to Informe me whether its success is worth a counter one:—I am In some hopes as to the young Gentleman[15] you so much desire; for sinc he saw her, which never was but about three dayes sinc he is very much taken with her, and Protested seriously, that he approv'd the Judgment off Sr Peter Hammond who thought her a pritty woman and vow'd he was not acquainted, nor had he sene A finer: — the famely is very Kind, and familier, they Come hether often: Sr J have Gott your sale made, I hope to please you, but I wish rather it may profitt you: Reports here speake off A fight betwixt the Prince and DeRuler:[16] By some belev'd, by some not: My Lord Cheif Justice hide,[17] Cozen Germain[18] to the Chan^{lr}[19] diyd suddenly about four dayes since signing A writt off error: The great Lady hard by, and her Husband, are very spightfull, and unkind: Sr J. M.[20] much more the Contrary: My Mother was to see my Lady Lawson,[21] and she was here: this is all at present I can Informe you off. I pray God be with you, and be your armour in the day off Controversie: In the deepes they that feare him shall escape, and Learn rightiousness: It was good Councill given to Israell, that when their hosts went out to Battle, they should forbear every evel thing: May that Powr be your salvation for his names sake, and so will he wish and pray that is with all tru veneration

Hond Father
Your obedient Sonn & ser:
Wm Penn

The Great Lady: told My Lod Du: at the other end of the town, that you would have made a difference betwixt her and her husband.

ALS. Penn-Forbes Collection, HSP. (*Micro.* 1:015). Addressed: For Sr Will Penn Knt: | thes. Docketed: 6th May. 1665.

1. On the east side of Seething Lane, a few hundred yards northwest of the Tower of London. Admiral Penn and his family had residential quarters here from 1660 until shortly before his death in 1670. The Navy Office was destroyed by fire in 1673. *London Monuments,* 4: endpaper map; Pepys, 1:xxix-xxx; P. Gibson to WP, Mar. 1712, *Memorials,* 2:615.

2. From the English fleet to Harwich. WP refers to his brief letter of 23 Apr. 1665 (doc. 5).

3. This palace on the bank of the Thames River at Westminster was the chief royal residence from 1529 until its destruction by fire in 1698. Cunningham, 2:911-18.

4. Charles II (1630-1685; effective reign, 1660-1685).

5. Henry Bennet (1618-1685) was created first Earl of Arlington in 1663, and at the time of this letter was principal Secretary of State. *DNB.*

6. John Ashburnham (1603-1671) was Groom of the Bedchamber to Charles II. *DNB.*

7. The Duke of York, the King's brother, was Lord High Admiral, and in command of the English fleet from which WP had just come. *DNB.*

8. Possibly "leiping" or "leeping."

9. Admiral Penn.

10. Possibly a code symbol.

11. Anne Hyde, the Duchess of York (1637-1671), daughter of the Earl of Clarendon, who married James in 1660. She became the mother of two queens of England, Mary and Anne. *DNB.*

12. WP here refers to Admiral Penn's ultimately successful efforts to get Charles II to confirm his title to his Shanagarry lands in County Cork. This matter was resolved in 1667. See doc. 11 below.

13. Audrey, the wife of Colonel Peter Wallis, the rival claimant to Admiral Penn's Shanagarry lands.

14. Probably Robert Southwell (1635-1702), who was a clerk of the Privy Council from 1664 to 1679, and became deputy vice-admiral of the Province of Munster in Ireland in 1665. Southwell was knighted shortly after WP wrote this letter, succeeded his father as vice-admiral of Munster in 1677, and was principal Secretary of State for Ireland from 1690 to 1702. Alternatively, WP could be referring to Southwell's father Robert (1607-1677), but the elder Southwell spent most of his life at the fortified port of Kinsale, where he was a prominent figure and major landowner under both Cromwell and Charles II. Both Southwells had known Admiral Penn and WP well for many years and could aid them in their Irish affairs. *DNB*.

15. WP probably refers to a suitor to his sister Margaret, perhaps to Anthony Lowther, whom she married in Feb. 1667.

16. The rumor was false. Prince Rupert (1619-1682), Charles II's first cousin, was operating an English squadron in the North Sea, while the Dutch admiral Michal De Ruyter (1607-1676) was at this time far south in the Atlantic. For the confused state of English opinion on the disposition of Dutch naval forces, see Pepys, 13 Apr., 16, 20 June, 15 July, 31 Aug., 5, 6 Sept., 12, 18, 24, 29 Oct., 22, 24 Dec. 1664, 15 Jan., 4, 23, 27 Feb., 4 Mar., 8 June, 4, 14 July 1665; Sandwich, *Journal*, pp. 193, 197, 199, 200, 202, 204, 207 (19, 20, 23, 25, 30 Apr., 5 May 1665).

17. Sir Robert Hyde (1595-1665), Chief Justice of the King's Bench, died on the bench on 1 May 1665. *DNB*.

18. First cousin. *OED*.

19. The Lord Chancellor, Edward Hyde, first Earl of Clarendon (1609-1674), was the dominant figure at the early Restoration court. Clarendon opposed the Second Dutch War (1665-1667), but failed to keep English merchants and the Duke of York from dragging England into the conflict through their attacks on Dutch trading posts and colonies in Africa and North America. In 1667 he fell from power, and spent the remainder of his life in exile, writing his celebrated history. *DNB*.

20. Probably Sir John Mennes (1598?-1671), an admiral and a colleague of Admiral Penn's on the Navy Board, where he served as comptroller. Pepys confirms WP's remark that Mennes was of a most agreeable disposition. *DNB;* Pepys, 2 Jan. 1666.

21. Isabella Lawson, the wife of Admiral Sir John Lawson (d. 1665), a long-time naval colleague of Admiral Penn's. A few weeks after this letter was written, Lawson received a wound at the battle of Lowestoft on 3 June 1665 that caused his death, of gangrene, on 29 June. His career closely paralleled that of Admiral Penn, although he had been more radical both in religion (an Anabaptist) and in politics (a republican). Thus in May 1665, Lady Lawson and Lady Penn found themselves in quite similar situations. *DNB*.

IN IRELAND

1666–1667

The following documents concern WP's visit to Ireland in 1666-1667. Early in 1666 the elder Penn sent WP, just turned twenty-one years old, to Ireland to oversee the family's estate. With the Restoration, Irish land titles were in chaos, and Royalists competed with Cromwellian soldiers and native Irish for recognition of their claims. The Act of Settlement of 1660 outlined rules for settling conflicting claims and established a Court of Claims in Dublin to enforce the act, to issue letters patent, and to give good title to lands. Admiral Penn's lands at Macroom, where the family had lived in the 1650s, were returned to their former owner, and the admiral was given other lands near Kinsale and Cork as compensation.

Young WP's Irish mission had two purposes: to secure good title to the new lands from the Court of Claims, and to make leases with the tenants there. Admiral Penn may also have hoped that WP's stay at the worldly viceregal court in Dublin would temper his interest in religion. Doc. 7 introduces WP to Sir George Lane, secretary to the Lord Lieutenant of Ireland. Docs. 8, 11, 12, 13, and 14 concern WP's settling of claims and making of leases. Docs. 9 and 10 treat Lord Lieutenant Ormonde's offer of a captaincy of troops at Kinsale to WP, an offer ultimately rejected by WP's father.

7
SIR WILLIAM PENN TO SIR GEORGE LANE

[8 February 1666]

Hon^rd^ S^r^—

I cannot leave his Maj^ties^ service in England to attend my owne affaires in Ireland as things now stand. I have therefore sent the bearer my Son in my stead. And humbly desire the Continuation of your favour to him as it hath unfaylingly been hither to to mee. I have instructed him how great my obligation [is to you?][2] (which I hope shortly to solve in part) & desire that hee should become bound with mee ever to remaine

Honor[d] S[r]
yo[r] most obliged & very
humble ser[t]
W Penn

London 8: febr 65

ALS. National Library, Dublin. Printed, *Memorials*, 2:429. (*Micro.* 1:021). Addressed: These | For Sr George Lane | Dublin. Docketed: S[r] Will Penn | Dat. 8 Febr | Rec 16 Mar | 1665 | By his Son.

1. Sir George Lane (1620-1683), of an English family landed in Ireland since the time of Queen Elizabeth, was Secretary of War, Clerk of Star Chamber, Keeper of Records, and member of the Privy Council for Ireland. As secretary to the Duke of Ormonde while Ormonde was Lord Lieutenant of Ireland, and as one of the principal Secretaries of State for Ireland in 1666, Lane was an important contact for young WP. Loyal to Charles II during the Commonwealth, in 1676 he was created Viscount Lanesborough of Longford. *CSPI, 1663-1665*, pp. 624-25; *1666-1669*, pp. 72, 74, 78; *Baronetage*, 3:159; *Peerage*, 7:422-23.

2. This phrase has been partially erased or obliterated.

8

FROM SIR WILLIAM PENN

[5 May 1666]

Son William,

The bearer is Major Rowse,[1] one of my tenants in Eniskelly;[2] I desire you afford him all the Irish favour in your power, and that you continue him my tenant at as easy terms for him as conveniently you may. If any of the king's ships are at Kinsale,[3] or Cork,[4] &c., and he hath occasion for convoy, write to the commander to afford it him. I am

Your affectionate father,
W. P.

Navy Office, May 5th, (66.)

Original lost. Printed, *Memorials*, 2:571. (*Micro.* 1:022).

1. John Rowse or Rous (d. 1671), sometimes called "major" or "captain" by the Penns, received from Cromwell grants of leases of Garrymore, 157 acres in the parish of Ichtermurrough, County Cork, in 1659. These lands, originally the property of Maurice Fitzgerald, were in the barony of Imokilly, and were given to Sir William Penn as partial compensation for Macroom and other lands Penn lost to the Earl of Clancarty. Rowse's original lease of 1659 specified an annual rent of £40 for the first ten years and £48 for the remainder of the twenty-one-year term. In 1669 he leased Garrymore from WP for an annual rent of £38. Calendar to Cromwell Rolls, 1655-1659, PRO, Dublin, transcript in ACM, vol. 145; will of John Rous, 1671, PRO, Dublin, abstract in ACM, vol. 145; Grubb, pp. 57, 84, 95.

2. Imokilly, the barony in County Cork where about two-thirds of Sir William Penn's Irish lands lay, is intended.

3. Kinsale, a seaport near the mouth of the Bandon River about fourteen miles south of Cork City, was important as an English garrison and naval and shipping center. In 1666 it was an English town; native Irish were forced, at least officially, to

live outside its walls. In 1659 Kinsale and its liberties contained 2197 persons. Pender, pp. 119, 210-11; Lewis, 2:230-34.

4. Cork, the capital of County Cork, is on the river Lee, about twelve miles inland from the sea. As entrepôt for much of southeastern Ireland, its provisioning of beef and butter to the West Indies and to the British Navy and its export of tallow and hides to England were of primary importance in WP's day. In 1659 Cork City, its suburbs and liberties, contained about 4826 persons, 1607 English and 3219 native Irish, with English predominating in the city proper and Irish in the suburbs and liberties. Pender, pp. 191-95; Lewis, 1:408-20.

9

TO SIR WILLIAM PENN

[4 July 1666]

Honourable Sir,

When I was at Carrickfergus[1] with my Lord of Arran, Sir George Lane, in my Lord Dunagle's[2] house, called me aside, and told me, the character my Lord Arran[3] had pleased to give his father, obliged him to write you a letter on my behalf; which was, to surrender your government and fort.[4] My lord lieutenant[5] himself, before a very great company, was pleased to call me to him, and asked, Whether you had not done it, and why?[6] I answered, that you once intended it, and that his lordship had promised to favour your request. To assure you of my lord's design, I saw the letter under his own hand, but am to seek whether Sir George Lane sent it or no, which I am to ask of yourself; my lord lieutenant telling me several times, he wondered you never answered his letter. I excused it, by the remoteness of your present residence from London. If there be any under-dealing, 'tis the secretary's fault, not my lord's. However, sir, I humbly conceive it may be necessary you take notice of my lord's kindness in a letter by the very first, since he has asked whether you had writ me any thing in reference to it. I beseech your answer to this, as also, if you please, an acknowledgment to my lord lieutenant's and Lord of Arran's great and daily kindness. I wish, sir, you may have respite from your troubles, and some refreshment from your continual toils, (we supposing the fleet to be near out).

I am, sir,
Your most obedient son,
Dublin, 4th July, 1666. W.P.

Original lost. Printed, *Memorials,* 2:430-31. (*Micro.* 1:026).

1. Carrickfergus, a seaport on Belfast Lough, County Antrim, was long an English stronghold. In May 1666 the English garrison, short on provisions and unpaid for nine months, mutinied and seized the castle and town, but loyal troops under Arran and Ormonde recaptured the town and restored English rule. Young WP was part of Arran's contingent. Lewis, 1:269-74; *CSPI, 1666-1669,* pp. 110-24; Peare, pp. 52-54.

2. Sir Arthur Chichester (1606-1675), created Earl of Donegall in 1647, became governor of Carrickfergus in 1661. *Peerage,* 4:389-90.

3. Richard Butler (1639-1686), fifth son of James, first Duke of Ormonde, was created Earl of Arran. At the time of this letter he was a privy councilor for Ireland. *Peerage*, 1:225.

4. WP means the castle and fort at Kinsale, of which Admiral Penn held the captaincy and government.

5. James Butler (1610-1688), first duke of Ormonde, was loyal to the English crown throughout his life. As commander of the English army in Ireland, he defeated the Roman Catholics at Kilrush in 1642 and at Old Ross in 1643. Created Lord Lieutenant, he concluded peace with the Irish in 1646, but was compelled later that year to turn control over to parliamentary forces. He went into exile with Charles, and at the Restoration the king made him Lord Steward of the Household and Privy Councilor for Ireland, and restored him to all his Irish lands and titles. In 1661 he was created Duke of Ormonde in the Irish peerage, and served again as Lord Lieutenant, 1662-1669 and 1677-1685. *Peerage*, 10:149-54.

6. Ormonde wrote to the Admiral from Carrickfergus, 29 May 1666: "Remembering that formerly you made a motion for the giving up your Company of foote heere to your sonne, and observing his forwardnesse on the occasion of repressing the late Mutiny among the Souldiers in this Garrison, I have thought fitt to lett you know that I am wishing to place the Command of that Company in him, and desire you to send a resignation to that purpose." Penn-Forbes Papers, HSP. Sir William, as vice-admiral of the fleet, was preoccupied with the Anglo-Dutch naval war, but he did not want WP to take over his Irish posts. See doc. 10, and Pepys, 4 June, 1, 21 July, 1 Aug. 1666.

10
FROM SIR WILLIAM PENN

July 17th, 1666.

Son William,

I have received two or three letters from you since I wrote any to you. Besides my former advice, I can say nothing but advise to sobriety, and all those things that will speak you a Christian and a gentleman, which prudence may make to have the best consistency. As to the tender made by his grace my lord lieutenant,[1] concerning the fort of Kinsale, I wish your youthful desires mayn't outrun your discretion. His grace may, for a time, dispense with my absence; yours he will not, for so he told me.[2] God bless, direct, and protect you.

Your very affectionate father,
W. P.

Original lost. Printed, *Memorials*, 2:432. (*Micro.* 1:027).

1. The Duke of Ormonde. See doc. 9. Admiral Penn advised Ormonde on 7 Aug. 1666 that he would not give up control of Kinsale. The Admiral planned to settle in Ireland after the Second Dutch War ended. *Memorials*, 2:432-33. Ormonde apparently did not receive Admiral Penn's refusal well. After reading the Admiral's letter, Ormonde "said Nothing, but that he designed it for My Sake to whom he was willing to be Kind." WP thought Ormonde's displeasure would "ware off." WP to Sir WP, 18 Dec. 1666 (not filmed), [John Penn], *The General Address (in Two Parts) of the Outinian Lecturer to His Auditors* (London, 1822), p. 17.

2. Perhaps the Admiral was afraid that if Kinsale were to be transferred to WP, the family would lose the post and its attendant advantages in Ireland.

11
FROM SIR WILLIAM PENN

[2 February 1667]

Son William,

I have yours of the 26th ultimo[1], and am glad you are well returned to Dublin. I wish you (may) find that agreement with W.[2] prove according to your relation, and so I shall be satisfied; my frame of mind being, for *"peace with all men, so far as in me lieth."*[3] The Earl of Ossory[4] left London this day, bound for Dublin; he hath received commands from his majesty and his royal highness to favour your business all he can: and such was his goodness, that he offered me no less, without asking. So that if you foresee any difficulty, it is advisable you stop until his arrival, and then fail not to apply yourself unto him, whom, I have cause to judge a very generous, worthy, noble person. I have no news for you. The Lord keep you unblameable, and return you with comfort to me,

Your very affectionate father,
February 2d, (66.) W. Penn.

Original lost. Printed, *Memorials,* 2:379. (*Micro.* 1.032.)

1. Unfortunately, WP's letter of 26 Jan. 1667 to his father is lost.

2. Probably Colonel Peter Wallis (d. 1679), who claimed Admiral Penn's Shanagarry lands. Of an English family resident in County Cork since at least 1595, Wallis served as a major and colonel of troops loyal to Oliver Cromwell and was rewarded with grants of leases of Shanagarry and Ruskemore in the barony of Imokilly, Cork, in 1658 and 1659. In 1660 he was high sheriff for Cork; Charles II pardoned him in 1661. Under the Act of Settlement he applied for the Shanagarry lands in exchange for forfeited lands on the Great Island near Ross in County Wexford. In 1660, before the Act of Settlement, Sir William Penn had been granted Shanagarry and other lands in Cork in compensation for his surrender of Macroom and other lands to the Earl of Clancarty, as ordered by Charles. Several supplementary orders from the King and Privy Council, and the Act of Settlement itself, confirmed Penn's title to the Cork lands, and Wallis turned tenant, probably in 1661. But Wallis continued to pursue his claim with the commissioners for executing the act, and resolving the case was one of WP's primary missions in Ireland. WP appeared to have settled the matter before he left Ireland in 1667, and Wallis leased the Shanagarry lands in 1668. Wallis willed the leases of the "castle house and castle plowland of Shanagary" to his wife Audrey in 1679. *CSPI, 1647-1660,* p. 700; *1660-1662,* p. 318; Burke's *Ireland,* p. 737; copies of Cromwellian leases, abstracts of wills, and other documents from the PRO in Dublin in ACM, vol. 47; *Memorials,* 2:617-19.

3. Rom. 12:18: "If it be possible, as much as lieth in you, live peaceably with all men."

4. Thomas Butler (1634-1680), Earl of Ossory, eldest son of James, first Duke of Ormonde, a royalist and associate of Arlington. In his father's absence from Ireland he sometimes acted as Ormonde's deputy. *DNB.*

12
FROM SIR WILLIAM PENN

[6 April 1667]

Sonne William
I have yors that says wee must stand to the Ld Lt [1] & Councells valluation but doe hope better, however Gods will must be don, lett mee give yo this [two letters deleted] caution that yo make noe more hast then good speede but nowe yo must not mistake mee for my meening is that noe advantage be lost by hudling[2] on anything I know alsoe theres danger in delays. & now if ever. but if I must speeke plainer tis this I have reson to beleve yo have kindnesse for a person on this syde the watter.[3] I wish that may not make yor tyme there tedius, but agayne I saye, if it benot posable to get more I wish at this tyme we had every thing that might give us good title to what wee have
The powes[4] goe to sea in one ship the younger clarke to the Capt the other {to} learne his trade but soe as the Capt wd be Kind to him the ship is the dover[5] God be thanked we are in helth ~~I~~ My selfe the worst God blesse yo I am

yor very afft father
Apll 6 (67) W Penn

ALS. Penn-Forbes Papers, HSP. (*Micro.* 1.033). Addressed: For William Penn Esqr | These att | ~~Dublin~~ in | Ireland. Docketed: Sr W Penn | Aprl 67. In another hand, "Dublin" has been deleted from the address and an illegible word substituted.

1. The Duke of Ormonde.
2. Hurrying, or pushing hurriedly without order or ceremony. *OED*.
3. The lady has not been identified.
4. Possibly Littleton Powys (1648?-1732) and his brother Thomas Powys (1649-1719), sons of a Shropshire gentleman, who were the right age for cadet naval service in 1667. Both later became judges at the court of King's Bench. *DNB*.
5. The *Dover,* a 46-gun ship of the White Squadron, carried 170 men under Capt. Jeffrey Pearce. On 2 Mar. 1667 it was ready to take on provisions, and it returned to Plymouth on 19 Apr. with a prize of Spanish wool and salt. Sandwich, *Journal,* p. 272; *CSPD, 1666-1667,* p. 545; *CSPD, 1667,* p. 39. For Capt. Pearce's career, see John Charnock, *Biographia Navalis* (London, 1794), 1:116-17.

13
FROM SIR WILLIAM PENN

Apll 9o (67)

Sonne William
I have yors wch tells me you are taking out letters Pattens for my estate there & that you intende to waite upon our Noble freind Sr Edward Dearing[1] to Kinsale & soe for England,[2] I acknowledg my

obligations greete to Sr Edward & should be well pleased you or I were capeable of demonstrateing our gratitude by some waie more reall then in ~~another~~ a matter soe formoll as those things are [illegible deletion] {soe that} I woud not have you neglect any reall surcomstance that may prove to our reall advantage to performe such shaddows, And I doubt not but you will be possest of the letters Pattens & have all other formallities past before you thinke of coming home though I thinke I shalbe the gladest person to see you not withstanding any Expectations you {might} have from flattering women. And certainly it wil nither be honorable or honest to leve the worke you have in hand untill ~~until~~ it be througly perfect & then com on Gods name the sooner the better. Mrs Norton formerly Sr John Lawsons daughter, was I thinke maried yesterday to Sr John Chitchley[3] I am sure if it be not past tis concluded upon by all persons concerned & wil be spedily performed but I thinke it was don as I sayd Yesterday; pray consider these things prudently with the understanding of a man & let mee spedely heire from you that the letters Pattens be past & that you have possession by the sherif & all other things don, for I long to know it; & Expect further directions for making of New leases but lerne our interest througly & give good words to all, & for certaine they shall have Just dealing at last, but som consideration must be had to the Vast Expences I have allwaies bin att about those lands besyds its not prudent upon many accompts to make long leases at present ~~with~~ when that businesse is don & you intend on I wish Mr Amery[4] might com with you. pray let it be soe contrived. I thanke God I am better then at the writing of my last, soe that we are now all inhelth. God blesse you amen I remayne

yor very afft father
W Penn

ALS. Penn-Forbes Collection, HSP. (*Micro.* 1:035). Docketed: My Father Sr Wm Penn | Apll 67 | B.

1. Sir Edward Dering (1625-1684), was one of the seven commissioners appointed to execute the Act of Settlement for allocating Irish lands. As a member of this court of claims, and, after 1667, as a privy councilor for Ireland, he became known for his favoritism toward English Protestants, and developed close relations with Ormonde and Arlington. At the termination of the court of claims in 1669, he became a commissioner of the privy seal, and of the treasury, in England. Maurice F. Bond, ed., *The Diaries and Papers of Sir Edward Dering* (London, 1976), pp. 1-29; *Baronetage,* 2:6-7.

2. The court of claims for executing the Act of Settlement and the related Act of Explanation adjourned on 25 May 1667 to reconvene on 15 Oct. Admiral Penn's lands were certified by the court of claims on 29 Mar. and enrolled on 22 Apr., so WP had little excuse to remain in Ireland after that date. *CSPI, 1666-1669,* p. 369. Court of Claims, 4:129-35, as cited in ACM, vol. 144; Record Commissioners, *15th Annual Report* (Dublin, 1825), p. 95.

3. Isabella Lawson, daughter of Sir John Lawson, had married in 1665 Daniel Norton (d. 1666) of Southwick, Hampshire. Her new husband, Sir John Chicheley (d. 1691) entered the navy after the Restoration, serving as captain of several ships. He was knighted in 1665, appointed a commissioner of the navy in 1675, and became one of the lord commissioners of the admiralty in 1681. Pepys, 6 July 1665; *DNB.*

4. Thomas Amory (d. 1667), an Irish merchant of English birth, became victualler of his majesty's ships in Ireland in 1660, and settled at Galy, Listowel, County Kerry. He sat for Ardfert in the Irish parliament from 1661 to 1666. In 1666 he wrote to Ormonde's secretary suggesting that fire ships be put at Kinsale as a precaution against a rumored French invasion and naming Captain William Crispin, WP's cousin, as his agent. Gertrude E. Meredith, *The Descendants of Hugh Amory, 1605-1805* (London, 1901), pp. 23-24.

14
FROM SIR WILLIAM PENN

[21 May 1667]

Sonne William

I have yo^{rs} from Imokilly wch calls for noe greete answer. I wish yor business there were setld Leases for one Year given & the rents Recived I should alsoe be glad that letters Pattens were dispatchd but in that You would doe well to consid^{r} & advice With yor freinds what privilledges & Royalltys would be convenient & advantagos & indever the obtayning of them which things being don I know not what should keepe yo^{u} there for after this I hope yo^{u} will neede noe more instructions from mee concerning aught in that Kingdom at present. Publick news yo^{u} must Expect from others, for what concerns our owne there. I hope yor sister is with childe[1] Mr Lowther[2] who hath bin a very kind husband went yesterday towardst Yorkeshire on fryday Last Capt Holdcroft buried his Only Childe wch hath put him & his wife in a sad estate[3] I wish yo^{u} would condole with him in a few lines I account him a very good as well as a wise man besides he is very kind to us all. he hath declard Mr Lowther his Haire at Walthamstowe wch I thinke is 200^{l} per ano & I beleve he will alsoe have his paternall estate [two letters deleted] in Glostershire wch is about 400^{l} per ano more[4] We are God be praysed in health I had Lately a very witty & freindly letter from Sr Robt Southwell who desired to be kindly remembred to yo^{u}. My service to all that famely if this finds yo^{u} nere them And if ~~this~~ yo^{u} see W Pen[5] pray desire him from mee to have a very great care of the Kings stores comited to his {charge soe} that in his office hee may be found wise & honest & desire Capt Crispine[6] to affoard him his utmost assistance God blese yo^{u} in soule & body I remayne

yor very aff^{t} father

Navy Office May 21st (67) W Penn

I have all waise bin a greete debtor to My L^{d} of Orraries[7] kindnesse Y^{r} relation of his to y^{o} seems to poynt at some thing y^{o} had noe minde to be plainer in but I judge it not amisse y^{o} had when I remember some Stories that have com on this syde the watter.

W.P.

ALS. HSP. (*Micro.* 1:042). Addressed: For William Penn Esq[re] | at S[r] William Pettys[8] house in | Dubline | Ireland. Docketed: S[r] W[m] Penn to his Sonn | May 21. 1667.

1. The Admiral was clearly impatient for a grandchild. WP's sister had been married for three months, and at this date may have indeed been pregnant—but only newly so, since her first child was born eight-and-a-half months later.

2. Anthony Lowther (c. 1640-1693) of Marske, Cleveland, Yorks., married Margaret Penn (1647-1718) on 14 or 15 Feb. 1667. Lowther, son of Robert Lowther, a well-to-do citizen and draper of London, and Elizabeth Holcroft, was member of parliament in 1679 for Appleby. The Lowthers had nine children; the first, Margaret, was born 8 Feb. 1668 and was baptized 21 Feb. 1668 at St. Olave, Hart Street, London. ACM, vol. 49B.

3. William Holcroft, son of Sir William and Gertrude Holcroft, was buried at Walthamstow on 17 May 1667. He had matriculated at St. Edmund Hall, Oxford, on 28 July 1665 at the age of 16. Parish register of St. Mary's, Walthamstow, extract in ACM, vol. 49B; *Alumni Oxoniensis*, 2:728.

4. Captain Sir William Holcroft (c. 1618-1689) was Anthony Lowther's uncle. Lowther did inherit Holcroft's copyhold estate in Walthamstow, though the paternal estate in Broad Blunsdon, Wilts., went to another nephew. John Paul Rylands, *Notes on the Families of Holcroft* (Leigh, Lancashire, 1877), as cited in ACM, vol. 49B.

5. Ensign William Penn (d. 1676), son of Admiral Penn's uncle, George Penn, was an officer in the army of Charles II, and, since the Restoration, clerk of cheque at Kinsale. His will, made and probated in 1676, named wife Joan, sons James and William, and daughters Amey and Margaret. *CSPD, 1671,* p. 97; *1660-1662,* p. 580; O. F. G. Hogg, *Further Light on the Ancestry of William Penn,* (London, 1964); abstract of will in ACM, vol. 49.

6. William Crispin (1627-c. 1682), deputy victualler at Kinsale, and husband of WP's first cousin, Rebecca Bradshaw. His father had been master of the *Fellowship,* Admiral Penn's 28-gun ship, during the Civil War. The younger Crispin served in the Admiral's squadron in the 1653 campaign against the Dutch, and in Penn's West Indian expedition of 1655. Having shifted allegiance from Cromwell to Charles II, Crispin obtained various offices at Kinsale, including that of deputy victualler. After Ensign William Penn's death in 1676, he became clerk of cheque and muster master at Kinsale. Crispin died en route to Pennsylvania in the winter of 1681-1682, to which WP had commissioned him chief justice, surveyor general, assistant to the governor, and primary commissioner for settling the province. WP later confirmed his purchase of 5000 acres in Pennsylvania to his children as a free gift. See M. Jackson Crispin, "Captain William Crispin," *PMHB* 53: 97-131.

7. Roger Boyle (1621-1679), first Earl of Orrery, son of Richard Boyle, first Earl of Cork. He bore the title Baron Broghill from 1627 to 1660. During the civil wars, fighting first for Charles I and then for Cromwell, he played a leading role in the suppression of the Irish Catholic rebellion. When Richard Cromwell's government seemed hopeless, he returned home to Ireland, secured control of Munster, and was instrumental in gaining Ireland for Charles II. A member of the Convention Parliament, he was created Earl of Orrery in 1660. As one of the lords justice for Ireland, he helped draw up the Act of Settlement for Ireland, and the mention of Admiral Penn's debt to Orrery probably refers to the earl's help in securing Penn's Irish estates. Orrery was Lord President of Munster until 1668, when he resigned over a dispute with Ormonde. He was imprisoned shortly thereafter for defrauding the King's subjects, but this parliamentary action was stopped by Charles. *DNB.*

8. Sir William Petty (1623-1687) had been employed to make a detailed survey of Ireland. Petty's maps, known as the Down Survey, were the most exact and most detailed then known. Though he was close to the Cromwells, he acquiesced in the Restoration, and Charles knighted him as a founder of the Royal Society in 1662. Under the Act of Settlement, the Down Survey was declared the only authentic record for reference in resolving disputed claims. Through his friendship with Petty, WP presumably had excellent access to these maps. *DNB.*

15
FROM LORD SHANNON

The following document illustrates the polished Restoration social world in which WP circulated on the eve of his religious conversion. Lord Shannon, the brother of the Earl of Orrery (see doc. 14), was a member of the Boyle family — the wealthiest and most talented family in Ireland. Although he was nearly the age of WP's father, he seems to have been a close comrade. Shannon's elegant letter, with its references to WP's female companion and to his book lending, also hints that WP was enjoying himself as an Irish magnate.

Balinre[1]
20th August 1667.

My excuse for not waiting on you, dear Sir, though it does not run the same ground with that you are pleased to give yours; yet it bowls at the very same mark, a restraint, for you say you had given me the honor of a visit if you had not been arrested with a feverish cold; and I answer you, that I had given myself the honor of waiting on you if I had not been clapped up in a pair of gouty stocks. And sure mine is the more strange, for I left you in a young lady's company; and to Keep in that inconstant, intemperate torrid zone, to meet with heat and colds, and feverish distempers is usual; but to clap a Justice of Peace in the stocks in his own house is something extraordinary, and a good excuse to you, though a bad one for me. And truly if I may speak to you as a soul-doctor, instead of a young Monsieur, and make you my confessor, considering the errand I designed at Cork, my lameness was but like a rub to an overthrown bowl,[2] which proves a help by hindering it. And my lameness has also done me this farther favor, to give me not only an excuse, but a resolution never to drink passing two wine-glasses a day, so that I shall drink no more like Captain Shannon, but like St Timothy; a little for the stomach sake, and not much for the company's. Here are all the virtues I can hope for, by my distemper, which has almost left me; (I hope the virtues will not). The book you sent, though Sir John Suckling[3] says all translations are but like hangings turned the wrong side outward; the same figures of them are to be seen, but the lustre is not; yet truly it is extraordinary good; and nothing but the happiness of your company to fetch it, would make me desire to part with it. The obliging, complimental part of your letter, I am very proud of, because I fancy I know you, and therefore believe you too real to write them as most do, more to shew their wit, than to express their meaning, and so indeed they are generally taken, for fine words, not real intentions. And though the sense of my own disability renders me unworthy of so great a happiness, as your friendship; yet I shall not doubt the punctual payment of it, when I have an engagement for it under your hand; which I do very thankfully and pleasingly embrace; (as we do wives, till death us do part,) and do assure you it has made me so faithfully and totally yours, that ever hereafter to offer you my service, would be but an injurious compliment; since I should but entitle you to that by gift, which is your own by right: upon which score you may, dear Mr Penn, ever command

Your affectionate faithful
humble servant
Shannon[4]

I hope to see you in two or three days at Cork.

Original lost. Copy, FLL. (*Micro.* 1:050).

1. Ballinrea or Shannon Park, the seat of Viscount Shannon, about seven miles from Cork City. The castle, built in the reign of King John and occupied by the earls of Desmond for nearly 200 years, passed to Richard Boyle, first Earl of Cork, and from him to his son Francis, created Viscount Shannon. Lewis, 1:278-79; Pender, p. 204; *Peerage,* 11:655.

2. In the game of bowls, an impediment by which a bowl is diverted from its course. *OED.* Shannon's gout fortunately diverted him from doing or saying something ill-advised in Cork.

3. Sir John Suckling (1609-1642), royalist poet and playwright. The passage about translations does not appear in the standard Suckling canon. See L. A. Beaurline, ed., *The Works of Sir John Suckling* (Oxford, 1971), 2 vols. Shannon may refer to a passage from James Howell (1594?-1666), *Familiar Letters,* Bk. I, sec. 6, let. 27, or to a similar passage from Cervantes. See Eugene E. Brussell, ed., *Dictionary of Quotable Definitions* (Englewood Cliffs, N. J., 1970), p. 578.

4. Francis Boyle (1623-1699), created Viscount Shannon in 1660, was the fourth surviving son of Richard Boyle, first Earl of Cork. With his brothers he distinguished himself at the battle of Liscarroll, helping to suppress the Irish rebellion of 1642. In 1660 he carried a letter from his brother Roger, Lord Broghill, to Charles II in Brussels, inviting him to come to Ireland. He later served as a privy councilor for Ireland and as captain of a troop of horse. His wife Elizabeth was one of Charles II's mistresses. *Peerage,* 11:655-56; 6:706.

Though the exact time of WP's conversion to Quakerism is uncertain, it apparently took place in Cork in the late summer or early autumn of 1667. According to the Harvey MS (*JFHS* 32:22-26), an early-eighteenth-century memoir, WP was convinced after hearing Thomas Loe, a public Friend who was traveling in Ireland, speak in Cork. WP had heard Loe many years before in Macroom, when he was a boy, and he was now profoundly affected by Loe's message. Though WP described himself at this stage as not yet "throuly a Friend," he attended Quaker meetings in Cork. Admiral Penn's urgency in ordering WP home (docs. 16 and 17) may indicate that he had heard of his son's conversion. On 3 November 1667 WP was arrested with eighteen others at a Quaker meeting in Cork. Doc. 18 is his appeal for freedom to the Earl of Orrery; doc. 19 is Orrery's reply. Released from jail, WP returned to his father's house in England by way of Bristol, where he visited an old associate of Sir William's, the Quaker George Bishop. In a letter hand-carried by WP to the admiral (doc. 20), Bishop appealed to Sir William to understand his son's religious experience.

16
FROM SIR WILLIAM PENN

[12 October 1667]

Sonne William

I have writt severall letters to yo^{u} since I received any fro. yo^{u} By this I agayne charge yo^{u} & strictly command that yo^{u} com to mee with all posable speede in expectation of yor complyance I remayne

yor aff^{t} father

Navy Office October 12° (67) W Penn

ALS. Granville Penn Book, HSP. (*Micro.* 1:050). Addressed: For William Penn | Esqr | These | with speede. Docketed: Sr Wm Pen to his son | Octob^{r} 12 1667.

17
FROM SIR WILLIAM PENN

[22 October 1667]

Sonne William

I hope this will find yo^{u} in health. The cause of its writing is to charg^{e} yo^{u} to repaire to mee with all posable speede presently after the reciept of it & not to make any stay there (Bristoll)[1] or any place upon the roade untill it please God y^{o} see mee (unles for necesary rest & refreshm^{t}.)

yor very aff^{t} father

October 22° (67) W Penn

ALS. Granville Penn Book, HSP. (*Micro.* 1:055). Addressed: For William Penn Esqre | These att Bristoll. Docketed: Sr Wm Pen to his son | Octob 22^{d} 1667.

1. Apparently at one time WP planned to return to England shortly after 18 Oct. Lord Shannon to WP, 14 Oct. 1667, *Micro.* 1:052. Bristol, with its large Quaker population, was a tempting place for WP to tarry. He reached Bristol sometime in November and was there as late as 30 Nov.

18
TO THE EARL OF ORRERY

[c. 4 November 1667]

The occasion may seem as strange as my cause is Just but your lordship will no lesse expresse your Charity in the on than your Justice in the other.

Religion wch is at once my crime & my Innocency makes me a prisoner to a maiors malice,[1] but my own freeman, for being in The assembly of the people called Quakers, there came severall Constables, backt wth soldiers, rudely & arbitraryly requiring every mans appearance before the maior, & amongst many others violently haled me wth them Upon my coming before him he charged me for being present att a Riotous & Tumultuary assembly, & unless I will give bond give bond for my good behaviour, (who chalenged the world to accuse me Justly wth the contrary) he would commit me, I asked for his authoryty, for I humbly conceive wthout an Act of Parliamt or an act of State it might be Justly termed too great officiousness, his answer was, a Proclamation in the year 1660,[2] & new Instructions,[3] to revive that dead & ~~dormant~~ antiquated order. I leave your Lordship to be Judge if that Proclamation relates to This concernmt, That only was designed to suppress fifth Monarchy[4] killing spirits, & Since the Kings Lord Lieut[5] and your self, being fully persuaded the Intention of these called Quakers by Their meetings was really the service of God Have therefore manifested A Repeal by a long continuance of freedome, & I hope your Lordship will not now begin an [blank] severitie by indulging soe much malice in one [per?]son, whose actions savour Ill wth His neerest neighbours, but that there may be a speedy releasmt to all, for attending Their Honest callings, wth The enjoymt of their families, & not to be longer separated from both.

And Tho To dissent from a nationall sistem imposed by Authoritie renders men hereticks yett I dare belive your Lordships better read [in?] Reason and Theologie Then to subscribe a maxim soe vulgar & untrue for Imagining most Visible Constitutions or Religious Govermt suited to the nature & genious of a civill Empire, It cannot be ranked in the [blank] of herisie but to Scare a multitude from Such inquiries as may create divisions fatall to a Civill ~~policie~~ policie, & Therefore att worst deserves only the name of Disturbers.

But I presume my Lord the acquaintance you have had wth other Countryes[6] must needs have furnished you wth This Infallible Observation that diversitie of faith, and worships contribute not to the Disturbance of any place where morall uniformity is barely requisitt to preserve the peace, it is not long since you were a very good soliciter for that liberty I now crave,[7] & conclude no way so effectuall to improve or advantage this Country as to dispence wth freedome in things relating to Conscience. And I suppose were It riotous or Tumultuary, as by some vainly imagind. Your Lordships inclinations as well as duty would entertain A Very remote Opinion.

My humble supplication therefore to you is that, soe malicious & Injurious a practice to innocent English men may not receive any countenance or Incouragem^t^ from your Lordship for as it is Contrary to the practice else where & a bad argum^t^ to Invite English hither, soe wth submission, will it not resemble that Clemencie and English spirit that hath hitherto made you Honorable.

If in this case I may have used too great a liberty, it is my subject; nor shall I doubt your pardon: since by your authority I Expect a greater, wch never will be used unworthy an honest man.

And y^r^ Ldps faithfull
&c:
WP

LBC. WP's Letterbook, 1667-1675, HSP. (*Micro.* 1:057). Docketed: This a letter by me Sent to the Earl of Orrery Ld Pres^dt^ of Munster, from Cork Prison 1667 before throuly a Frd. The docket is in WP's hand; the letter is in a clerk's hand.

1. Christopher Rye, mayor of Cork in 1667-1668, was well known for his persecution of Quakers. According to reports sent to the National Meeting Record of Sufferings in Dublin, Mayor Rye made 28 arrests of Cork Quakers in 1667 and 71 arrests in 1668. Several persons were imprisoned half a dozen times. WP was arrested by Rye, probably on 3 Nov. 1667, with 18 others, listed as follows: "John Tailor, James Knowles, Stephen Harris, Phillip Dymond, William Penn, Francis Rogers, Henry Bennett, James Dennis, George Webber, William Hawkins, George Gamble, William Steele, James Toghill, John Gossage, Christopher Pennock, Richard Pike, John Moore, Thomas Robins, Thomas Mitchell for being mett together to worship god, were committed to prison, by Christopher Rye Mayor." National Meeting Record of Sufferings, 1655-1693, pp. 46, 49-50, Friends Historical Library, Dublin; C. B. Gibson, *History of the County and City of Cork* (London, 1861), 2:391.

2. On 10 Jan. 1661 a proclamation was issued prohibiting meetings of Quakers and Anabaptists and instructing that the Oath of Allegiance be tendered to those attending such meetings. Braithwaite, *Second Period,* p. 9.

3. The First Conventicle Act of 1664 (22 Car. II, cap. 1), apparently the "new instruction" to which WP refers, outlawed attending any conventicle or religious meeting other than those following the prescribed Anglican liturgy. It expired in 1669.

4. The Fifth Monarchy men, a fanatical sect that originated about 1649, pressed for the establishment of the "fifth monarchy" mentioned in Dan. 2:44, the reign of Christ and his saints which would supersede the four monarchies of the ancient world. In Jan. 1661 a group of them tried to overthrow the royal government, taking to the London streets with cries of "King Jesus, and the heads upon the gates." They were quickly suppressed, and their leader Thomas Venner was executed. Braithwaite, *Beginnings,* pp. 18-19; Braithwaite, *Second Period,* p. 9; *DNB.*

5. The Duke of Ormonde.

6. Orrery had been educated in France and Italy under a tutor, a Mr. Markham, who was possibly a relative of the Penns. *DNB.*

7. WP's reference is uncertain, though Orrery apparently understood what he meant. See Orrery's reply, doc. 19, below.

19
FROM THE EARL OF ORRERY

Charleville.[1] the 5th 9th [November 16]67.

Sir,

This morning betimes I received a letter from Mr Mayor of Corke,[2] which gave me an account of his proceedings the last Sunday, with several People called Quakers, who were met against the Laws & Proclamations at Corke. I could not but approve what he did, since he is a sworn Magistrate to execute the Laws & Proclamations of the King. But in hopes that Mildness may operate on such offenders, I did then advise him to reprove & admonish them not to hold meetings against the law, under the eye of the Magistrate, & in the King's Garrisons, & so to release them.

As soon as I had sent the Mayor this letter, I received one from Yourself alone, & another subscribed by You together with several others;[3] I confess I was surprised & sorry to see You thus associated; & apprehending what I should say unto You (seeing You now joined with the Quakers) would be of little validity with You, I sent this day by the Post to Your Father a Copy of Mayor's letter to me with my opinion on it to him. I cannot tell what the Meeting was for, but I am sure the words which the Mayor lays to Your charge after Your being brought before him, as well as Your being (as he says You were) their spokesman, was very unseeming, & such as I hope you will not be guilty of again. I cannot comprehend what You mean by my being not long since so good a Solicitor for that Liberty which you say you Crave;[4] but tho' I should understand it as possibly you mean it; Yet even that itself does evidence the liberty which it seems You would have cannot be allowed by me, unless it be first allowed by his Majesty's authority. And till which, You ought not to expect that I shall violate my Oath which is to govern His Majesty's subjects in this Province according to the law which is the only rule by which actions lawful & unlawful are to be judged; & tis' the law which I shall make my rule, & I advise you to do the like; but if your Conscience be against the Law, I would not say when I must transgress it, for if you do so after this fair warning You cannot expect that I will hinder the Magistrates from doing their duty. In hope you will follow this friendly advice, I subscribe Myself,

Sir,
Your affte Friend & Servant
Orrery

Copy in the hand of Granville John Penn. FLL. (*Micro.* 1:060). Addressed: For Mr Wm Penn | at Corke.

1. Charleville, Orrery's seat in Cork county, was built in 1661 and named after Charles II. As Lord President of Munster, Orrery kept his court here. The house was burned in 1690 by soldiers loyal to James II. G. Hansbrow, *Improved Topographical and Historical Hibernian Gazeteer* (Dublin, 1835), p. 166.

2. Christopher Rye.

3. WP's letter is doc. 18 above; we have not found the second letter, in which WP joined, but it was presumably written by some or all of the 19 Quakers arrested by Rye on 3 Nov.

4. See doc. 18, above.

20
GEORGE BISHOP TO SIR WILLIAM PENN

[30 November 1667]

My Antient freind[1]

Haveing this Opportunity by the hand of thy Son; whoe is now upon his Journy towards thee, I could not let it slipp; but by it give thee to Understand my Love, & Antient respect wch, as it hath been heretofore, soe it is still continued, although I have not heard from thee, since being at Bristoll, when thou camest from Ireland, in Order to the bringing in of this day, thou wast wth mee.[2] Soe, my friend, I am glad of the Opportunity to present thee, & thy wife, wth my Love, & doe rejoyce to see the Mercy to yor family; & that the Loveing kind-ness of the Lord hath Visited this thy Son, to give him the true sence, & Conviction of that, wch all along since his Childhood, hee hath sought to Understand; To whom I hope you will bee tender, & rather receive him into yor Armes, & Love, then by any kind of Esstraingedness, put sadness on him, or Temptation as to that, wch is his Conscience to God; wch is out of the Power of Man; & wch Man hath nothing to doe with, & is to bee cherished. And rather Account it (as indeed it is) yor Mercy, that hee is come to know that wch gives to Escape the Pollutions of the World, & to wch the blessing of God is, then to bee taken upp wth any kind of displeasure or troble for the same. Soe I leave the matter, & him wth you, desireing that the Goodness of the Lord may Encompass yor habitation, & whe~~n~~r{in} you have done amiss to let you see it, & forgive you; & when ther is any desire, or Breathing after the Lord in You, to quicken, & Encrease it; & to give you the Light of the Knowledge of himselfe in the face of Jesus Christ; wch is above all the World, & the Powers, & Pleasures & Vanities thereof wch Perish, & pass away, & reel, & totter, & are filled wth Anxieties, & Vexations, & encompassed with Temptations, in wch the Enemy is, whoe hunteth after the Precious life, & seeks to undoe a Man for Ever. For, what will it profit a Man to gayne the World, and loose his Soul & what shall a Man give in Exchaing for his Soul? Soe these things are to bee preferred, & at length a Man must goe to his Long home, & come before his Judge;

whoe is noe respector of Persons; nither doe Riches, or Greatness take with him; & Eternity attends a Mans Condition for Ever. Soe, my Freinds, yor Welfare I desire in the Lord, & how Ever you may think of mee, or my Principle, unto wch yor Son is turned; Yet I am in Peace wth the Lord, & doe lie downe in his bosome, whoe is my Safeguard, & Everlasting Reward; In whom I Salute you both, & yor Children, being, as you have Ever knowne mee.

Yo^r affectionate, & wellwishing
Bristoll. 30th 9th m^o 1667. Friend Geo: Bishope

ALS. WYN/15/3, National Maritime Museum, Greenwich. (Not filmed). Addressed: For Gen^ll William Pen | at London | these. Docketed: [in WP's hand] George Bishop | 30-9mo-67 | to my father | at my first | convincem^t. [in another hand] Mr George Bishop to s^r Wm Penn.

1. George Bishop (d. 1668) was one of the few persons who could conceivably have persuaded Admiral Penn to accept WP's religious conversion. The two men had shared parliamentary military service in the 1640s and 1650s before Bishop turned Quaker in 1654. It is not easy to trace Bishop's career, since several men of the same name were active in radical causes, but our man was probably born in Bristol, became an army captain, and took the Leveller side in the famous Putney debates of 1647. He was an intelligence agent for the republican Council of State in 1649-1653. Admiral Penn wrote to Bishop in October 1652 to announce a naval victory over the Dutch, and addressed him as "Honoured Countryman" and "my worthy friend." After Bishop converted from political to religious radicalism, he became a Bristol brewer and served as "ringleader or archbishop" of the local Quakers, according to a hostile witness. He was certainly a central figure in the Bristol Men's Meeting, and wrote a number of tracts. When WP visited him in 1667, Bishop had just published the second edition of his *New England Judged,* in which he denounced the Massachusetts Puritans for persecuting the Quakers. One year after this letter, Bishop's funeral was attended by an extraordinarily large crowd. G. E. Aylmer, *The State's Servants* (London, 1973), pp. 272-74; *Memorials,* 1:446-50; *CSPD, 1668-1669,* p. 59; Russell Mortimer, ed., *Minute Book of the Men's Meeting of the Society of Friends in Bristol, 1667-1686* (Bristol Record Society, 1971), pp. 3-4, 194.

2. Admiral Penn had come from Ireland to England about March 1660, when it was clear that a major political change was in the wind, with the Long Parliament finally dissolved and elections under way for a new parliament. The borough of Weymouth offered Penn a seat in this Convention Parliament (which invited Charles II to resume the throne) on 2 Apr. 1660. Evidently Penn passed through Bristol on his way to London and there saw Bishop, who remained stoutly opposed to the royalist new day. After the Restoration, Bishop continued to agitate against government policy; he was threatened with deportation to Barbados in 1665. *Memorials,* 2:209-10, 218, 221; Braithwaite, *Second Period,* pp. 9-10, 29, 54, 651.

THE YOUNG QUAKER CONTROVERSIALIST

1668–1669

The next three documents illuminate WP's personal life during a crucial period. His conversion very quickly propelled him into a public life as a controversialist, religious leader, writer, and lobbyist; from 1668 he was regularly in the public eye. But we know little about his inner experience of becoming a Quaker, about his new friendships, even about his courtship. In docs. 22-23 we see how deeply WP was affected by the death of his spiritual guide Thomas Loe. In doc. 21 we learn something directly of the young convinced, in rebellion against his father, upsetting family expectations.

Other evidence that his father was angry and disappointed comes from a later date. See in particular 13 September 1677, doc. 119, below. According to the Harvey MS, the father told his son he had educated him for a position at court, and wept at WP's stubborn fervor (*JFHS* 32:24). WP, doc. 119, the Harvey MS, and *Works,* 1:4 all assert that the father turned the son out of his house. The same sources record a reconciliation; the Admiral visited WP in the Tower ("Account of my life since Convincement," n.d. [c. 1689?], *Micro.* 6:208), and petitioned the privy council for his release (Sir William Penn to King Charles, 31 Mar. 1669, *Micro.* 1:137). One wonders what role doc. 21 played in either quarrel or reconciliation. On the one hand, it clearly states WP's rejection of the world of his father and his discomfort with the easy morals and fierce political competition of the Restoration world, with perhaps a continuation of the distrust of himself which is sensed in the poem "Ah Tyrant Lust" (doc. 4). On the other hand, it is an equally clear statement of his spiritual state and his new sobriety, and offers brief notice of several Quaker testimonies, for example about the Light, perfectability, and against swearing. The Admiral must have been angry when he first read it; but perhaps WP's relation also helped him realize that he had to give up hope for a worldly career for his firstborn.

21
THE TWO KINGDOMS OF DARKNESS AND LIGHT

[1668]

A Relation, & Description of the Nature & Fruits of the Two Kingdoms of Darknesse & Light, as they were collected out of the holy Truths declar'd in Scripture, as the Requirings of the Lord to be presented to my Father, who at that time was in high Wrath against me, because of my separation from the World, & Testimony against it, that the Deeds thereof were Evil.

Dear Father,
Fearing that Words may create Wrath, & that Reasons or Citations, though most true in themselves may loose much of their native force, & usual success, when by a Child alledged unto his Parent, it seems good unto the Lord (who first put it into my Heart) that I should only offer unto thee, a few Words out of his own written will, as discovering the most inward qualifications, as well as external Garb & Appearance of those two Spirits, that act or lead the Sonns & Daughters of Men, either to serve the God of this World, or the God of Heaven.

The Spirit & Practice of this World,	*contrary to*	*The Spirit & Doctrine of Christ.*
1. PERSECUTION		LOVE
Genes. 5.[1] v. 14. And the Officers of the Children of Israel, which Pharo's Taskmasters had set over them, were beaten, & demanded, Wherefore have ye not fulfilled yr taske in making brick, both yesterday, & today, as heretofore. v. 15 Then the Officers of the Children of Israel came & cryed unto Pharao, saying v. 16. There is no straw given us, & they say to us make Brick.		Matth. 13 28. And he said unto them, an Enemy hath done this (that is, sowne teares, or false Doctrin) the Servants said unto him, Wilt thou, that we gather them up? [29] But he Said Nay, least while ye gather up the teares, ye root up also the wheat wth them. Luk. 6. 27. But I say unto you, Love your Enemies. 29. And unto him, that smiteth thee on the one Cheek, offer also the other.
Psalm 17. v. 11 They now have com		Romans. 12. 19. Dearly beloved, aveng not

passed us in our stepps
v. 12. Like as a Lyon that is greedy of his prey.

Isaiah 3.
v. 15 What mean ye, that ye beat my People to peeces, & grind the faces of the poore.
chap. 29
v. 21 That make a man an offender for a Word, & lay a snare for him, that reproves in that gate, & turn aside the just for a thing of nought

Jeremiah 20.
v. 1. Now Pashur the Son of Immer the High Priest heard that Jeremiah prophesied,
v. 2. Then Pashur smote Jeremiah the Prophet, & put him in the stoks.

Matthew 27.
v. 30. And they spitt upon him, & took the read & smote him on the head.
v. 35 And they Crucified him.

Acts. 5.
v. 40. And when they had called for the Apostles, & beaten them, they lett them go.
Chap. 7.
v. 59. And they stoned Stephen calling on God.

your selves, but rather give place unto wrath, for it is written, Vengeance is mine, I will repay it, saith the Lord.

2. MOCKING

Psalm. 35.
16. With Hypocritical Mockers in Feasts they gnashed upon me.

Psalm. 69.
10. When I wept & chastned my Soul, that was to my reproach.

SILENCE.

1. Peter. 2.
23. Who, when he was reviled, reviled not again.
Chap. 3.
9. Not rendring railing for railing.

12. They that sat in the Gate spoke against me & I [was] the Song of Drunkards.

Jerem. 20.
10. For I heard the Defaming of many, Report say they, & we will report.

Matt. 27.
31 And after that they had moked him, they took the Robe off from him.

Luk. 23.
11. And Herod wth his Men of Warr set him at nought & moked him.

Hebrews 11.
36. And others had tryal of cruel Mokings

Jude 17.
But Beloved, remember the Words of the Apostles of our Lord Jesus Christ.
18. How that they told you, there should be Mockers in the last time, who should walk after their own Ungodly Lusts.

3. PROPHANESS, SWEARING, UNCLEANNESS, DRUNKENNESS BLOOD, WANTONNESS & PLEASURE	in Opposition to	HOLINESS, REVERENCE, CHASTITY TEMPERANCE FORBEARANCE, MODESTY & MODERATION

Jerem. 23.
11. For both, Prophet & Priest are Prophane, yea in my House have I found their Wickedness.
12 They committ Adultery & walk in Lyes, they strengthen the Hands of the Evildoers;

1. Cor. 6.
20. For ye are bought with a price, therefore glorifie God in yr body & in your Spirit, wch are God's[2]

Matth. 5.

that none returnes from his Wickedness.[3]
10. For the Land is full of Adulterers, & because of Swearing the Land mourneth.[5] For from the Prophets of Jerusalem is profaness gone forth into all the Land.

34. But I say unto you; Swear not at all

James 5.
14. But above all things swear not.[4]

1. Cor. 6.
18. Flee Fornication;
[19] Know ye not, that your Body is the Temple of the Holy Ghost.

Rom. [1]3.
13. Let us walk honestly as in the day, not in rioting & drunkeness, not in Chambring & Wantonness.

Hosea 4.
2. By swearing & Lying, & killing & stealing, & committing Adultery they break out, & Blood toucheth Blood
3. Therefore shall the Land mourne. Whoredom, & Wine, & new Wine take away the Heart
Chap. 5.
2. And the Revolters are profound to make slaughter, though I have been a Rebucker of them.

Isaiah 1.
15. Your hands are full of Blood

Esekiel. 22
9. In thee are men that carry tales to shed blood

Isaiah 5.
11. Wo unto them that rise up early, that they may follow strong drink, that continue till wine inflame them.

1. Thessal. 5.
7. Therefore let not us sleep as do others, but let us watch, & be sober.
8. Let us, who are of the Day, be sober.

Ephes. 5.
1. Be ye therefore Followers of God as dear Children.
2. And walk in love as Christ hath loved us,
3. But Fornication & all Uncleanness, or Covetousness let it not be once named amongst you, as becometh Saints.
4. Neither filthiness, nor foolish talking, nor jesting, which are not convenient, but rather giving thancks.
5. For this ye know, that such have no inheritance in the Kingdom of God.
8. For ye were sometimes Darkness, but now are the Light.
9. For the Fruits of the Spirit is in all goodness & righteous-

12. And the Harp & Viol. tabret & the Pipe, But they regard not the Work of the Lord

Chap. 3.

18. In that Day I will take away the bravery & their tinkling ornaments about their feet, their Caules & their round tires,
19. their Chaines, & the Bracelets & the Mufflers
20 the Bonnets, the ornaments of the Leggs, the Headbands, the Tabelets & the Earrings,
21. the Rings & Nose Jewels, the Chairgable suits of apparel, the Mantels, the Wimples, & the Crisping pinns.

Amos 6.

3 Ye that put farr away the Evil Day, & cause the Seat of Violence to come near,
4 That lye upon Beds of Ivory, & stretch themselves upon their Couches, & eat the Lambs out of the Flock, & the Calves out of the midst off the staule:
5. That chant to the sound of the Viol, & invent Instruments of musick, like David.
6. That drinck wine in Bowels, & anoint themselves wth the chief oyntment, but they are not grieved for the affliction of Joseph.

Zephaniah 1:

8. And it shall come to pass in the Day of the Lord's Sacrifice, that I will punish the Princes & the Kings Children, & all such w[ch] are clothed wth strang apparel.

ness & Truth.

10. Proving what is acceptable unto the Lord.
11. And have no Fellowship wth the unfruitful works of Darkness, but rather reprove them.

Titus 3.

3. For we our Selves also were Disobedient, foolish, Deceived, serving divers Lusts & Pleasures, living in malice, & envy, hatefull, & hating one an other.
4. But after the Love of God appeared,
[5] not by Works of Righteousness w[ch] we have done, but according to his mercies he saved us by the washing of Regeneration, & renewing of the holy Ghost.—

Romans 12

2 And be not (therefore) conform'd to this World, but be ye transform'd by the renewing of your Mind, that ye may prove what is the good & acceptable Will of God

1. Tim. 2.

9 And let your Women adorn themselves in modest Apparel, wth shame fac'dness & Sobriety, not wth broidered hair, or Gold, or pearls, or costly Array.
10. But (which becometh Women, professing Godliness) with good Works,

1. Petr.

3.4. & a meek & quiet spirit, which in the Sight of God, is of Great Price.
5. For in this manner the holy Women of old adorned themselves.

1. Petr. 1.
14. (And so walk as obedient Children, not fashioning your selves according to your former Lusts.
15. Because it is written, Be ye holy, for I am holy.[6]

Galat. 5.
19. Now the Works of the Flesh are manifest, Adul[tery] Fornication, uncleanness, Lasciviousness.
20. Idolatry, Witchcraft, Hatred, Variance, Emulations, Wrath, Strife, Seditions, Heresies.
21. Envyings, Murders, Drunkenness, revillings, & such like of which I tell you, that they wch do such things, shall not inherit the Kingdom of God.

1. Petr. 4.
3. (And let) the time past of your Life suffice to have wrought the Will of the Gentiles, when we walked in Lasciviousness, Lusts, Excess of Wine, revilings,[7] Banketings[8] & the like.
4. Wherein they thinck it strange, that you run not wth them to the same excess of Riot, speaking evil of you.
5. Who shall give an account unto him, that is ready to judge.

There might be more Instances of the genious Temper & Complexion of the Worldly Spirit, but it would be too large & prolix. In short, The Contrary to these recited qualities are the proper Fruits of the Lords Spirit.

2. Petr. 1.
4. Whereby are given unto us exceeding great promises, that by these ye might be partaker of the Divine Nature, having escaped the Corruption that is in the World through Lust.
5. And besides this add unto your Faith Vertue, & to Vertue Knowledge, to Knowledge Temperance,
6. to Temperance Patience, to Patience Godliness
7. to Godliness, Brotherly Loving-kindness, & to Kindness Charity.
8. For if these things be in you, & abound, they make you, that you shall neither be barren, nor unfruitful in the Knowledge of our Lord Jesus Christ.
9. But he that lacketh these things, is Blind, & hath forgot-

ten that he was purged from his old Sins.

10. Wherefore the rather, Brethren, give diligence to make your calling & Election sure, for if you do these things, ye shall never fall.

11. For so an entrance shall be ministred unto you abundantly into the Everlasting Kingdom of our Lord & Saviour Jesus Christ.

Revel. 2.

10. (And) fear none of those things, wch you shall suffer.

2. Timoth. 3.

12. For he that lives godly in Christ Jesus must suffer Persecution

Luke 9.

23. And he that will be my Disciple must take up his dayly Cross, & follow me

Mark 8.34

Matth. 16.24.[9]

Hebrews. 6.

5. (But) it is impossible for those who have once tasted

6. of the powr of God, & the glories to come,

7. if they fall away, to renew them again unto Repentance.[10]

IN A WORD

Philip. 3.

15. Whereunto we have attained, let us walk by the same.[11]

1. Peter 4.
17 For the time is come, that Judgment must begin at the House of God, where then shall the ungodly & Sinner appear.[12]

Galat. 5.
16. If ye walk in the Spirit, ye shall not fulfill the Lusts of the Flesh.

By these few Scriptures, (by such as beleeve them) may be clearly discerned the Fruits of the Spirit of this World, & the Spirit of the Lord Jesus Christ in its Appearances, Operations & Requirings, by which most pure & holy Spirit have I been made daily desirous of dying to all the Sin, Pomp, & vain Fashions of this World that I might be found in a Continual beholding of the Lord's Glory, which stains, & brings down the Pride of all Flesh untill there be a perfect changing into his Image & Likeness from Glory to Glory; Even so come LORD JESUS.

LBC. WP's Letterbook, 1667-1675, HSP. (*Micro.* 1:068). Relations between WP and his father appear to have been at their worst after he returned from Ireland in Dec. 1667 and before he was confined to the Tower in Dec. 1668. Hence, it is most probable that this "relation" was composed sometime in 1668. WP took some liberties with his text, omitting phrases which were not necessary to his argument, presumably in order to make his points with economy. The missing phrases have not been supplied here. There are occasional errors in transcribing Biblical references, and sometimes WP moved on to a new verse without taking note of it. In such cases, missing or incorrect references are corrected either in square brackets or in footnotes. WP may have used a Bible with notes by John Canne (d. 1667?), pastor of a congregation of English independents in Amsterdam, and editor of a reference Bible with notes which first appeared in 1647, published in English in Amsterdam. This was the first English Bible with full marginal references. Another edition appeared in 1662, and a third in 1664. See *DNB;* A. S. Herbert, ed., *Historical Catalogue of Printed Editions of the English Bible, 1525-1961* (London and New York, 1968), p. 195. WP may well have acquired a reference Bible for his studies in Saumur. Years later he acquired another edition of the Canne Bible (London, 1698), which is now owned by the HSP and housed in the Library Company of Philadelphia.

1. Exod. 5, not Gen. 5.
2. This could be read as "2," but "20" is correct.
3. Verse 14, not 12.
4. Verse 12, not 14.
5. Verse 10 ends here. WP moves on without note to verse 15.
6. Verse 16, not 15.
7. Should be read "revellings." The same is true in Gal. 5:21, below.
8. Should be read "banquetings."
9. Mark 8:34 and Matt. 16:24 recount the same speech by Jesus as Luke 9:23.
10. These are from Heb. 6:4, 5, 6, not 5, 6, 7.
11. Verse 16, not 15.
12. The last phrase is from verse 18.

22
TO GULIELMA SPRINGETT

[7 October 1668]

To D^{r} G S.[1]

This salutes thee in that wch is unfeigned; Time will not permit a long Epistle; Therefore in short know, that after a tedious Sicknesse, but many signal manifestations of Gods Glorious power & overcoming love (as time will bring to light, & publick View) Dear Tho. Loe[2] yesterday about the 9th hour in the morning, left the Body, & is ascended far above all Visible & Created things to the full possession of the pure Eternal Rest & sabboth of the holy God;[3] Having unspeakeably finisht his Testimony, & fought, like a Valiant Souldier, the good Fight: Whose Works follow him, & have Eternis'd his Memorial amongst the Faithful. Whom my soul loved, whilst alive; & bemoanes, now dead: & yet have pure fellowship with that which lives for ever. This day we lay the ~~vessel~~ {Body} in the Ground, as having done its Makers work, & well. And being it's thus; let us all presse after the Inheritance he hath obtained, through travels, tryalls, perils, temptations, afflictions, Cruel mockings; & what not: so shall it be well with us.

Fare well.
W. P.

LBC. WP's Letterbook, 1667-1675, HSP. (*Micro.* 1:100).

1. Gulielma Maria Springett (1644-1694), first wife of WP, and the posthumous daughter of Sir William Springett by Mary Proude Springett Penington (see doc. 23, n. 2). She inherited considerable estates in Kent, Sussex, and Ireland from her father and was said to be worth £10,000. She became a Quaker at fifteen. She was well educated—her tutor was Thomas Ellwood (1639-1713), a Friend, and an acquaintance of Milton—and apparently conducted her own business with her tenants. She was said to have skill at "physic." According to Ellwood she was "in all respects a very desirable Woman (whether regard was had to her outward Person, which wanted nothing to render her completely Comely: or to the Endowments of her mind, which were every way Extraordinary and highly Obliging, or to her outward Fortune, which was fair . . . . " She was much sought after for marriage; one suitor was John Vaughn, third Earl of Carbery (1640-1713), a patron of the poet John Dryden, and said by Pepys to be "one of the lewdest fellows of the age." She resisted such suitors, however, and lived with her mother until her marriage to WP, at the relatively late age of twenty-eight, in 1672. It is thought that they met in 1667, and it is not known why the courtship was protracted. She gave birth to seven children (including one set of twins) of whom three survived her. Her health was not strong. On her deathbed she said, "I never did, to my knowledge, a *wicked* thing in all my Life." A general account of her life is available in L. V. Hodgkin, *Gulielma: Wife of William Penn* (London, 1947); see also S. Graveson, ed., *The History of the Life of Thomas Ellwood* (London, 1906), pp. 181-82, 215-20, 223; ACM, vol. 54; the Harvey MS (a narrative written in 1729, based on WP's report to Thomas Harvey about 1700), *JFHS* 32:25.

2. Thomas Loe (d. 1668) lived near Oxford, and was convinced by John Camm in 1654. He became a minister in 1657, and travelled frequently in Ireland. He has been called "the Apostle of Ireland"; it was there, in 1667, that he convinced WP. According to the Harvey MS, WP had heard Loe speak in Admiral Penn's house in Cork when he was a child. WP was twelve or thirteen when Loe began his ministry. DQB; *JFHS* 32:22-26.

3. Ten days later WP wrote a longer account of Loe's death to Gulielma Springett's stepfather, Isaac Penington. See doc. 23, below.

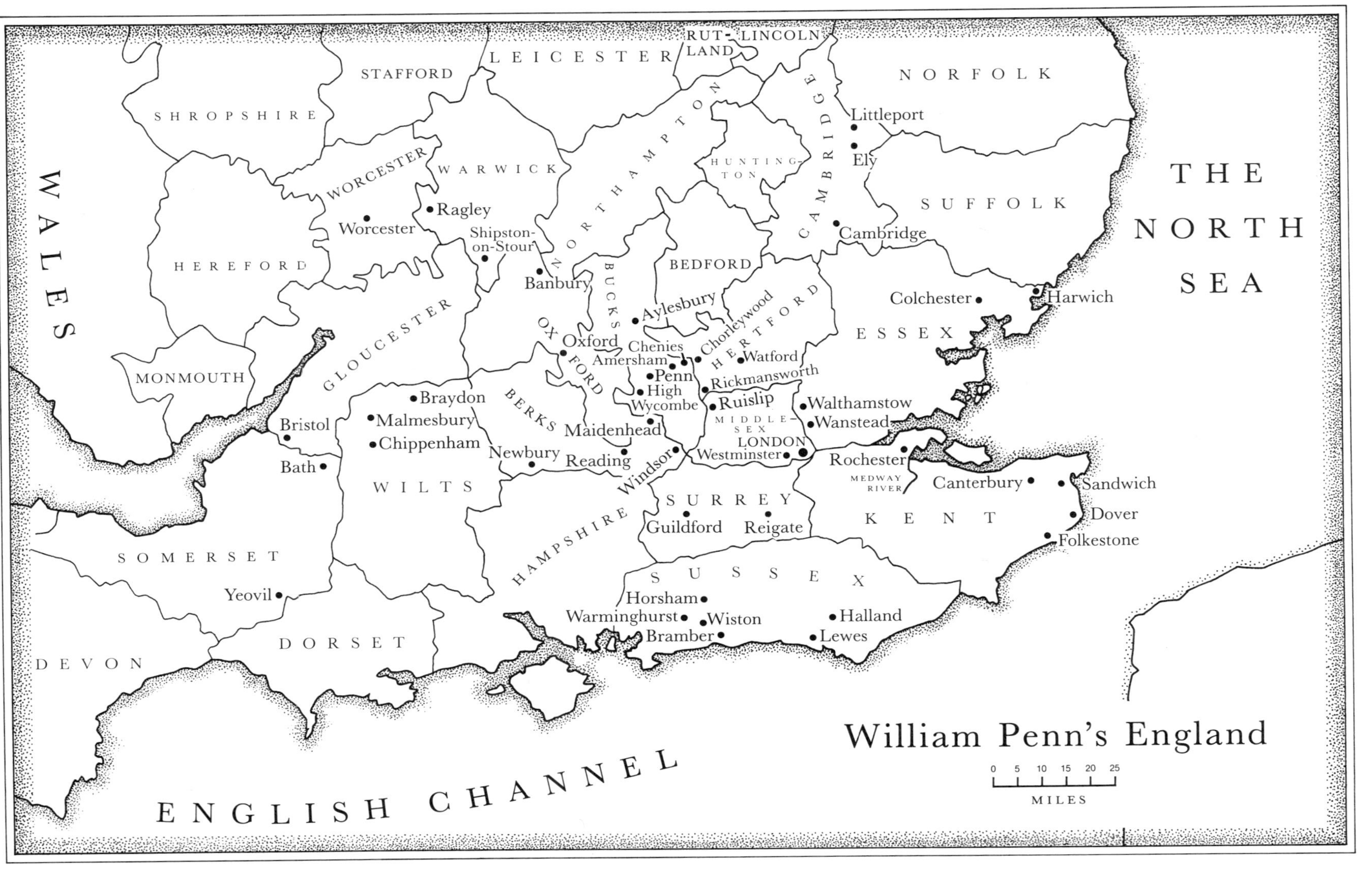
William Penn's England
0 5 10 15 20 25
MILES
THE NORTH SEA
ENGLISH CHANNEL
WALES
STAFFORD
LEICESTER
RUT-LAND
LINCOLN
NORFOLK
SHROPSHIRE
WORCESTER
WARWICK
NORTHAMPTON
HUNTINGTON
CAMBRIDGE
SUFFOLK
HEREFORD
MONMOUTH
GLOUCESTER
BUCKS
BEDFORD
HERTFORD
ESSEX
OXFORD
BERKS
MIDDLESEX
WILTS
SURREY
KENT
SOMERSET
HAMPSHIRE
SUSSEX
DORSET
DEVON
MEDWAY RIVER
Littleport
Ely
Cambridge
Colchester
Harwich
Ragley
Worcester
Shipston-on-Stour
Banbury
Aylesbury
Chorleywood
Chenies
Amersham
Watford
Penn
High Wycombe
Rickmansworth
Ruislip
Oxford
Walthamstow
Wanstead
Braydon
Malmesbury
Chippenham
Bristol
Bath
Maidenhead
LONDON
Westminster
Rochester
Newbury
Reading
Windsor
Canterbury
Sandwich
Dover
Folkestone
Guildford
Reigate
Yeovil
Horsham
Warminghurst
Wiston
Bramber
Halland
Lewes

23
TO ISAAC PENINGTON

[17 October 1668]

I: P.[1]

I very dearly salute thee in a measure of that pure everlasting light of God, wch is the life of them that believe. I understand by thy dear wife[2] of thy desire to be informed concerning the sickness & death of dear Tho: Loe; wch was thus. G.W.[3] Tho: L. & my selfe being the 6th day was a week, after thou leftest us at Wickham,[4] at the Dk of Buckinghams,[5] in relation to friends liberty, he was taken suddenly ill, wch necessitated him to leave us & hasten to the house of one Ann Cullen (a friend) who lived near, where after 3. hours, we found him by excessive reaching[6] very feavorish. My business called me to the city, so that I left them, that evening he was brought by coach to Ann Greenhill's, where he remained about a week at times very ill, & by reason off the continuall noise her house was exposed to, & consequently injurious to his repose, we removed him to Ed: Man's,[7] where we {had} all hopes of his speedy recovery; inasmuch as the retiremt of the chamber in wch he lay occasioned great rest; but having an infirm inside & an extraordinary feavor, the strength of his constitution could not long support it, for about {ten} ~~10~~ days together he daily decreased, & some day's before he left us we expected his departure, but he was not given up by some. About 4 days before he dyed, I fell sick my selfe, but hearing at wt point it was wth dear Tho: I could not long keep my bed, but got up, & though in a sweat, yet I hastened to him, whom I found in a sweet readiness to be gone. Friends stood much affected round his bed. Wn I came in & had set my selfe upon the bed side, severall heavenly expressions fell from his mouth, & so shook was he by the power of the Lord, & over come by the ravishing glory of his presence, that it was wonderfull to all friends; whose testimony concerning his departure was, that they judged it impossible for any to have layn so long, wth more patience, resignation & lamb-like innocency, then he did, yet truly bold & couragious; his expressions, as I writ them down were these, Glory, glory, for thy powers known—Good is the Lord—then taking me by the hand, he spake thus, Dear heart, bear thy cross, stand faithfull for God, & bear thy testimony in thy Day & generation, & God will give thee an eternall crown of glory that none shall ever take from thee: there is not another way, this is the way the holy men of old walked in, & it shall prosper. God has brought immortality to light, & immortall life is felt, glory, Glory to thee for thou art worthy—My heart is full, wt shall I say—his love overcomes me, my cup runs over, my cup runs over, glory, glory to his name forever—he is come, he has appeared & will appear: friends, keep your testimony.

Live wth God & he will live wth you — be not troubled, the love of God overcomes my heart — Many more were his expressions then I can here insert; but this effected more then all outward potions: for it so enlivened his sp^ts & raised him, that I think he soon after got up, & walked about, saying to us many times w^n I have been going, the Lord has shined upon my tabernacle & raised it: but it was the will of the lord, that after all his Labours, perills & travells, he should lay down the body amongst his ancient friends: for after some little time, so greatly did his distemper encrease, & his life sink, that we all gave him up, death appearing in almost every part, he lay some short while speechless; his sp^t being centred, life & death struggles strongly, at last he went away wth great stillness (being the 5^t instant) having finished his testimony & left many demonstrations of his service, & much fruits of his diligent labo^rs; having fought like a valiant Souldier the good fight & overcome, whose works follow him, & have eternised his memoriall amongst the faithfull, whom my soul loved, whilst living, & bemoans now dead; & yet have pure fellowship wth that wch lives forever — the day following we laid the vessell in the ground as having done its masters work & will. So, dear I:[8] it is good that we all press after the pure & unchangeable mark; that in our generation we may all honour Gods name & truth, that the unborn generations may call us blessed. So wth my dear love to thy self, wife & family, I remain, in true love,

Thy sincere friend
London. 17. of 8. Mon: 1668 Wm Penn

Copy. Penington MSS, FLL. (*Micro.* 1:102).

1. Isaac Penington (1616-1679), eldest son of Sir Isaac Penington, Puritan and Lord Mayor of London, 1642-1643. He and his wife (see below) had been Seekers, and became Quakers in 1658. Penington, who was imprisoned six times, lost considerable property because of his refusal to take oaths. He was a voluminous writer of mystical religious literature. DQB; Fox, 1:445; Maria Webb, *The Penns & Peningtons of The Seventeenth Century* (London, 1867), chaps. 1-3, 7.

2. Mary Proude Springett Penington (c. 1625-1682), daughter and heiress of Sir John Proude of Kent, married in 1642 Sir William Springett (c. 1620-1644), by whom she had two children, John and Gulielma Maria, who married WP. In 1654 she married Isaac Penington. She had full courage of her convictions and wrote a lively account of her life. See Norman Penney, ed., *Experiences in the Life of Mary Penington* (Philadelphia, [1911]); see also DQB.

3. George Whitehead (c. 1636-1723), was a Quaker whose career in many ways paralleled that of WP, although he was convinced much earlier (c. 1650), and bridged the pre- and post-Restoration generations. Like WP, he was particularly vigorous in pursuit of a national policy of toleration and sought royal support for it. Both came to similar positions on what constituted Quaker orthodoxy. *DNB;* Braithwaite, *Second Period,* pp. 82-85, 177-78, 667; Endy, pp. 77, 168, 183, 293.

4. Probably High Wycombe, Bucks., which is about five miles from Cliveden, the Duke of Buckingham's country residence in 1668. The Peningtons were probably living in Amersham at the time (Webb, *Penns & Peningtons,* p. 214), which was six miles from High Wycombe.

5. George Villiers, second Duke of Buckingham (1628-1687), a politician, wit,

and notorious rake. His personal life was disorderly and his politics inconsistent, but he regularly advocated religious toleration, which accounts for Friends' interest in him. In 1668 and 1675 he urged relief for Protestant dissenters; in 1678-1679 he was a Whig; in 1685 he wrote a tract in support of toleration, *A Short Discourse upon the Reasonableness of Men's having a Religion, or Worship of God* (London, 1685). WP was friendly with Buckingham at least from 1668, and Buckingham, as he wrote in 1678, was "heartily Mr Pens friend" (Granville Penn Book, Penn MS, HSP). WP wrote two tracts in favor of Buckingham's tract, *A Defence of the Duke of Buckingham's Book* (London, 1685), and *Annimadversions on the Apology of the Clamorous Squire* (London, 1685), and hoped to bring Buckingham into James II's government (*Micro.* 5:723). After Buckingham's death, WP had his letters to the duke destroyed, and said, a trifle defensively, "my only business with him, ever was, to make his *superior quality & sense, usefull to this poor Kingdom* that he might not dye under the guilt of misspending *the greatest talents that were among the nobility* of any Country." (*Micro.* 6:438a). On Buckingham, see *DNB;* Winifred, Lady Burghclere, *George Villiers, Second Duke of Buckingham, 1628-1687* (New York, 1903), pp. 128, 198, 306, 309; and John Harold Wilson, *A Rake and his Times: George Villiers 2nd Duke of Buckingham* (New York, 1954).

6. Retching or vomiting. *OED.*

7. Edward Mann, hosier, a prominent London Friend. His country house was at Ford Green, near Winchmore Hill, north Middlesex, about thirty miles east of High Wycombe.

8. Isaac.

In the first decade of his convincement as a Quaker, WP frequently engaged in controversy or debate with critics of the sect. These debates were sometimes conducted entirely in print, but just as frequently they were vocal and public, with the ground rules set in advance. The following three documents (24-26) illustrate WP's first such contest, in 1668. The end result was eight months in prison.

According to WP, who published his version of the debate and the points in dispute in *The Sandy Foundation Shaken* (London, 1668), it all began when two women, mother and daughter, attended a Friends' meeting out of curiosity, and stayed to be convinced. They were the parishioners of a nonconformist Presbyterian clergyman, Thomas Vincent, and Vincent was furious. By WP's account, Vincent said he would just as soon they went to a bawdy house as to a Quaker meeting, because of the Quakers' "erroneous and damnable doctrines." WP and one of his colleagues, George Whitehead, asked for an opportunity to respond to these insults, and the debate took place in Vincent's house. Several Presbyterian clergymen, including Thomas Danson and William Maddocks, attended with Vincent, who dominated the encounter. Vincent's tactics, as WP told the story, included breaking the debate by prayer, and ending it, before the Quakers had their full say, by putting the candles out. The audience, WP said, behaved with "levity and rudeness . . . Laughing, Hissing, Shoving, Striking." WP and Whitehead did not believe that they had had a fair hearing, and asked for a second meeting. Vincent refused a public session, but agreed to see them privately. WP and Whitehead, thinking themselves publicly insulted, wanted a chance for public refutation, and refused Vincent's offer.

What had started as an informal debate escalated into a battle of the books, after WP published *The Sandy Foundation Shaken*. It first prompted Vincent's version of the affair in *The Foundation of God standeth sure* (London, 1668), to which William Maddocks contributed a chapter. This differed from WP's account in emphasis and detail: for example, Vincent defended his right to close the meeting, by saying that WP and Whitehead rambled and failed to come to the point; and whereas WP had complained that Vincent would not argue from the Scripture, Vincent ridiculed what he saw as the Quakers' inability to pursue an argument according to formal rules of logic. Vincent said that there had been another meeting prior to the one reported by WP, and that he was just ready to agree to a third when he heard that WP was preparing a book against him.

Thomas Danson was next to enter the lists with *A Synopsis of Quakerism: or a Collection of the Fundamental Errours of the Quakers* (London, 1668), and George Whitehead followed with *The Divinity of Christ* (London, 1669) in answer to Vincent and Danson. Doc. 26 is a manuscript version of WP's response to Danson. It is clearly unfinished, and was never published.

Although a number of the Quakers' "erroneous and damnable" doctrines were criticized by Vincent and Danson, chief amongst them were their interpretation of the Trinity and of the divinity of Christ. In *The Sandy Foundation Shaken,* WP denied the existence of three separate persons in the Trinity; this argument was substantially repeated in doc. 26. Unfortunately for WP, this was generally interpreted as a denial of the divinity of Christ. He was arrested and held prisoner in the Tower of London until he published an "apology," *Innocency with Her open Face* ([London], 1669), in which he passionately asserted his belief in the divinity of Christ. WP did not reconcile this belief with his denial of "personality" in the Trinity, and he did not recant on the latter subject. A letter from WP to another Presbyterian, John Collinges, written five years later, in January 1674 (doc. 76), below, is yet another explanation of his views on the Trinity and his belief in the divinity of Christ. His ideas were virtually unchanged.

24
TO THOMAS VINCENT AND THOMAS DANSON

[31 October 1668]

T.V.[1] T.D.[2]

Judging ourselves injur'd as well by being refus'd a Competent time, to justifye our so much condemned Principles, as by those unchristian & untrue Characters past upon us of [blank] granted upon our Desires a second meeting, we do hereby request, [blank] be some Day the next Week about the tenth hour in the morning at y[r] own meeting, where & when we shall not fail with a few sober Friends to meet you, as well to clear ourselves, & Principles;[3] as to demenstrate the unreasonable Tenents of our Adversary's. Your Answer is expected by

Your Friends
G W.
31-8th Mo. 1668. W P.

LBC. WP's Letterbook, 1667-1675, HSP. (*Micro.* 1:106). Docketed: To Tho: vincent & T. Danson. There are two blanks in the original. The first is nearly a line long; the second about ten characters long.

1. Thomas Vincent (1634-1678) was noted for his bravery during the fire and plague. He apparently had not been much involved in controversy before his confrontation with the Quakers. His house, the scene of these meetings, was in Spitalfield, a district in the east of London, so called from St. Mary Spital, a church outside of Bishopgate. In 1669 Vincent was preaching in Hand Alley, Bishopgate Street, "in a special room new built with galleries." *DNB;* A. G. Matthews, ed., *Calamy Revised* (Oxford, 1934), pp. 13, 156, 503.

2. Thomas Danson (d. 1694) was a more ardent controversialist than Vincent. He entered the lists against the Quakers with a tract, *The Quakers Folly Made Manifest to all Men* (London, 1659). Whitehead attacked that work in *The Voice of Wisdom uttered forth* ([London], 1659), and Danson responded with *The Quakers Wisdom descendeth not from above* (London, 1659). Anthony Wood said that Danson was well educated, and knew Latin, Greek, Hebrew, Chaldean, Syriac, and Arabic. *Athenae Oxonienses* (London, 1721), p. 1016.

3. This meeting did not take place.

25
TO THOMAS DANSON

[November 1668?]

Tho. Danson.

My Importunity, if such, was for the Truths sake, thy meeting for my Importunities. What Intention is by the Usual front of our persecution I am to learn. But if that bouldnes be the true Interpretation, know that we are & shall be bold & valiant for our God on Earth. But whilst thou wouldst appear forward to give a meeting, thou hast so stufft thy Letter with Conditions Very hardly to be embrac'd; that unless thou wilt admit Some alteration, our meeting will be to little Purposs.[1] As for the Place, I will leave it to thy Choyce, & any time also betwixt this, & the Seventh Day Evening. The Auditory I would not consist of less then 50. of each: but as many more as thou wilt. My manner of Argument shall not be rambling;[2] but Scriptural; whose mode I take to be the best. And for my Positions or Hypotheses are four; & I conceive Stated in Terms very intelligible, because Scriptural, which with few words & much moderation I shall be ready to maintain, viz. 1st. That Christ the Light of the World hath given unto every man such a measure of Light, that by believing, & following of it man may be saved, & delivered from Death & Darckness, & led into the Position of Life.[3] 2ly. That a State from Freedom of Sin is attainable in this Life.[4] 3ly. That Sanctification is Antecedent to Justification.[5] 4ly. That the Father, Son, & Spirit, are not one Eternal Substance, subsisting in three Distinct & Separate Persons. The First I have not materially altered. The 2d. is in terminis thy own. The 3d. mine. And the 4th. is now by me denyed in the very terms, it was by thee Asserted at the Publique Disputation in Spittle-Yard. To all which I shall Expect thy Speedy & Positive Answer. Which, if Affirmative; I shall not fail, without Passion or Prejudice, as one that Really Covets nothing more, then the right Information of such Persons, whose understandings have been so vail{e}d by Ignorance, as to Embrace {humain} Tradition for {divine} Truth. If on the Negative; the world shall Otherwise know the Equity both of our Principles & our Practice. Fare well.

Thy loving Friend,
because a Lover of
Enemies, W P.

LBC. WP's Letterbook, 1667-1675, HSP. (*Micro.* 1:065). Insertions in the next-to-last sentence are in WP's hand.

1. In fact, it did not take place.
2. Vincent had accused Penn of rambling in his account of the Presbyterians' debate with the Quakers, *The Foundation of God standeth sure,* p. 21.
3. The Quaker doctrine of the Divine Light was untenable for Presbyterians like Danson and Vincent. Among other things, it allowed Quakers to bypass the authority of the clergy as interpreters of the word of God. It is possible that the secretary made an error in this sentence and that WP intended "possession" rather than "position."
4. Presbyterian Calvinists believed that, since Adam's fall, mankind had been corrupt and not perfectable on earth.
5. Strict Calvinists believed that "justification," or the decision by God that one will be free of the penalty of sin, was unconditional, and could precede faith (conversion), repentance for sins, and the achievement of a sanctified life. For a good discussion of WP's ideas on these and related theological points, see Endy, and Hugh Barbour, *The Quakers in Puritan England* (New Haven, 1964).

26
REPLY TO THOMAS DANSON

T. Ds Answears noe Answers.
or
A short Reply to T. D. Answears to
W Ps Argument.[1]

[1668 or 1669]

1) To W.Ps Arg. that saieth if therebe 3 distinct persons, then 3. destinct substances, he Ans. I deny the Consequence, because Per-

son is not predicated of Father. son. & ho: Ghost A like as it is of ~~men~~; the Creature, [illegible] In god is noles [no less] 3 subsisting in one ~~nature~~ Individuall nature; in man a subsisting of 3 in 3 ~~devided not~~ severall natures of the same kind this he backs withe wt [?] ~~Reply~~. In {Wottans}[2] ~~his~~ definition of A person as may be seen Pg 2, preceeded which he makes choice off above others, he acknowledges A Person to be ~~An~~ A severall or singular thing that subsists by it selfe in A nature Indued with understanding. in the same page he tells us it signefys someone Indued with understanding distinct from an other; and in the following page that it is a word us'd in th scripture to express the distinction off Fa. son. & spirit in the godhead [illegible deletion] & one from an other. ~~Now we say iff it be true that A person supposes one that hath~~ Rep. iff A person signefys some thing that subsists by it selfe then A substance, for all things Are either substances or accidents[3] whose propertys are the 1 to subsist by themlves the last to be inherent In the first, so that iff 3 distinct things that subsist by them selves then 3 distinct substances, & Conseq: 3 distinct gods. next he says A person is some one thing Indued wth understanding, if soe, then 3 distinct understandings; which being Infinite Conseq. 3 distinct gods. again if the word Person serves to distinguish fa: son & sp: {one from an other} ~~then since he doth Confess the father is an Infinite Intelligent substance~~, and yet that each of 3[?] persons are Intelligent substances, what is but to say that there be 3 substances, for if the father be an Intelligent substance yet not the son, the son An Intelli. sub. and not the spit the spi. An intelligent substance but neither Fa: nor ~~&~~ son. are not these consequently 3 distinct Intelligent substances, & so 3 gods. ~~I know not wt he means by 3 in one nature~~ the last part of his Answear is A paradox; for how Can ~~mans na~~ the nature of man kinde be 3, or 3 men be said to subsist In 3 severall natures. there is but one nature In all, and therefore [illegible deletion] when it is In 3 We Call them men. & iff the devine nature be In 3 distinct so as that one is not the other, it must follow that there would be 3 distinct gods.[4]

2 to W Ps 2 Arg. Either the devine persons are finite or Infinite if infinite then 3 distinct Infinites. and so 3 gods. he Answears thus we may deny the disjunction; finitenesse and Infinitenesse are not personall, but essentiall propertys[5] for In the notion of the nature [those?] propertys are contained before you consider that nature as In A person; R. A notion Indeed but An Antiscripturall one, I appeale to the unlearned fo whom he says his Book is Intended if they learned this In the simplicity of the scriptures; how Can A person be seperate from his essence; and if A person be an Intelligent devine substance is it not Infinite; was not the person of which T.D. says X to be the Express Image Infinite; and since he sayth the Image is distinct from that of which it is an image, & Conseq. the spi. from the son; what Can any man of sense Conclude but that here be 3 distinct infinites.

but he urgeth that though all the propertys in the devine nature agree to each person yet will it not follow that there be 3 infinites; because there are not 3 devine natures; but how weak this is will easely appeare; for since no person is without his own nature, and that what belongs to his nature belongs to him It follow that in persons finite or Infinite, they must be according to their natures; now if the person of the Fa. so. & sp. are not distinctly Infinite then not distinctly god. but if each be god the[n] each Infinite, and since one is not an other but 3 distinct Persons it follows they will [be] 3 gods. besides; how incongruous is it to say their Cannot be 3 infinites ~~nesses~~ but their will be 3 natures; for it were to say that be cause there be 3 finites ~~nesses~~ there fore thre natures; or becaus 3 men therefore 3 humain natures; ~~but since it is manifest~~ or because 3 {rationall or} reasonable creatures therefore three rationalitys, or kinds of reasons. but since Pe. James & Jo.[6] are said to be men from A participation off the [blurred] rationall nature, so will it unavoiudably follow that 3 distinct persons from their respective participation off the devine nature will be properly gods. his 2 & 3 Ars fall to the ground, for his distinction betwixt an individuall, & severall natures hath bee all ready refuted. since that is not Individuall which may be affirm'd off 3 or is Common to 3.

3 To W: Ps 3 Arg. If each person be god, & that G. subsists In 3 Pers then In each Per. are 3 Pers as god, & so from 3 they will Increase to 9. he Ans. thus, if he understands the tearms god as we doe, of god essentially no such Conseqs. will follow no more then this Instance. if Peter James, & Jo. if each per. be man & that man subsists in those 3 pers then each of those 3. persons are 3 pers, or men, and so from 3 they will Increase to 9. to which I Rep. that neither did will. P. understand god as he would have him that is without wt was Compleat to his being namely his subsistance as well as essence, but as A Person from wch the godhead is inseperable and the devine nature from which the person is Inseperable, neither is the instance of any force. for 1 that W. P. understood by the word person for god distinct from the other too is evident since his last arg. was to show that the consequence off 3 distinct pers in one sub. made 3 gods, Wherefore he now comes to show, how that if each distinct person be god according to his Arg. and yet that In god subsists 3 persons according to yr opinion then in each person or god would be 3. &c: next the Instance is Invallid; and that because he supposes W.P. to have understood God without his subsistance; and so he would bring in man without his person; by which I shall observe wt T.D makes of god: just soe much of the devine nature or god when Considered from the 3 persons, as I should make the nature of man Considered distinct from {all men;} which would (as he learnes it else where) be But A notion indeed. ~~but~~ for man doth not signefy nature in that sense, but when that rationall nature {subsists} in P.J. & J. they are said to be 3 men as if the whole

nature subsisted In ~~one man~~ Paul, he and it might be only styld man; so if the devine nature subsist but one way or in one, then Is It called god, but it Can never subsist In 3 distinct persons, who shall each of them have the propertys thereof, as men have of the rationall nature but they must be acknowledg'd for 3 gods. therefore It ought to run thus, if each of those before mention'd persons, P.J. Jo. be a {compleat} man, and {yet} that A man subsist In 3 persons, then, P. being a man subsist In 3 persons or men James, & Jo. the same; which is most notoriously absurd. as for his 2 Arg. To the same Arg. in wch he thinks that W.P: hath catch'd at somw^{t} in their writers he did not well understand, wch he would represent of their judgements, that nature and Person in the godhead, or god are one thing.[7] I rep. that ~~no wonder if he means~~ no wonder W.P. found somthing he did not understand, that is how it Could Consist ~~and hang~~ with the scriptures, or hang together; which is discover'd {to be} so contradictory: and as for his straing distinction about nature & per. I would fain Know that if the devine nature be An eternall sub. how it can so be with^{out} subsisting, and how its so subsisting Can be distinguish'd from itselfe; againe when T.D or any for him will tell us how the same numericall substance can subsist In 3 distinct manners or persons at the same time, so as that each person hath the whole nature, and yet no multiplicati[on] of the same nature; or how that ~~Infinite~~ {unety of the} substance, can have other wise then A unety in subsisting, or since {there is} no substance but {w^{t}} subsists from {& by} itselfe, how itself being but one can by itselfe subsist in 3 distinct ways. again how it can being Infinite subsist so and not be 3 Infinites omnipotents, &c: I say when T.D hath resolv'd us these things or any els it will be time to ~~Consider~~ credit his unscripturall distinction. he further offers to prove it from the ~~propertys~~ {attributes}. off begetting & being begotten, off Mercy & justice, that one is not an other & yet proper to the same nature. & as one Includs not the other so neither does the notion of the Fa, the son. &c. to which I resp. that he is very much mistaken In his argueing, for what is it more than to say, that mercy in Peter does not includ justice In Peter, therefore Peter and Jo. are not to [two] men: for as I have before prov'd, of whom the humain nature may be affirmed, {they are men} as for instance P. hath humain nature Ja. hath hu. na^{t} Jo: hath hum. nat. therefore ~~P. J. J. are 1~~ P is A man. Ja is a man. Jo. is a man; so of the Godhead may be affirm'd that is god, now iff the godhead be affirmed off 3 distinct Persons, that the 1 has the godhead the second the God^{h} the 3 the godhead, w^{t} is it but to say the 1st god distinct from the second as Pe. from Ja. the second distinctly god from the 3 as Jam. from Jo. and conseq. 3 gods. wherefore ~~to argue~~ It's granted that the Fa. does not Includ the son or the son the spirit upon that hypothesis or arg. becausit it appeares they are rather 3 distinct substances; but iff therebe One only substance, and that but one In subsisting, & yet Fa. so. & sp. that on[e] sub. It will then follow, that they doe includ one the other, how diversly so ever denominated to us. but here I must A little minde the Reader Concerning T.Ds tearmes. as P. 13 where he distinguishes betwixt nature Person, and godhead or god, now I query what is god but his nature, what is ~~this~~ devine nature but god what is that he understands by person but the devine nature and god. and that by god he supposes nature look P 11. 12, where he opposes W.P. {2&} 3 Argu [space] before he made them but 2. now 3. Thus doth he mangle and splitt that holy & eternall unety. and I appeale to all sober people iff it is not gross Impudence In T.D to make it one of the 200 Grand errors mentioned In the title page that they deny the scriptures to be A rule; who Instead of being guided by their plain expressions, hath employ'd the tearmes of old heathenish phelosphy, who in the first P. of his epistle, he acknowledges to have been given over to the most fond, & beastley errours about the natur of god. And for his guide in this concerne, he hath accepted Aquinas,[8] the great {ador'd} saint Thomas off Rome, and one off the most renown'd doctors off the Romish church, which may ~~show~~ Informe well-meaning Protestants to what refuge our adversarys run.

4 To W.Ps 4th Arg. he only tells us its Answear'd In the 2d; to witt, the Persons are either finite, or infinite & so 3 gods; but since his Ans to the 2d prov'd no answear, ~~it~~ {W.Ps Arg.} remains still to be disprov'd. for whats proper to mans nature is proper to Peter as A man; and what is in the devine nature is not seperable from the subsisting of it, or Person. therefore infinite; and iff 3 such Pers then consq. 3 infinites.

5. To W.Ps 5th Arg. if those 3 distinct Pers are one wth the godhead, then are they each one with An other (wch he sayth is the sum) he Answrs thus, that Rule quae conveniunt in uno tertio conveniunt Inter se[9] which perhaps (W P) does not understand, that these things which are one with some 3d thing are so Among them selves is to be understood that they are one among themselves only in respect of that wherein they agree, not simply as in this plain Instance, david was A man & Soloman was A man; they two Agree In A 3d thing (viz) humain nature will it therefore follow that they are one person. nothing less, So the Fa. & so: are not one per. but one god, or one in that de:[10] nature in wch 3d they two meet. To wch I rep. It matters not whether W.P. understood that rule, si[nce?] his own words, & T.D Confesse he understood the meaning of it; but if T.D. would have us hereby to observe ~~his pedantry, we~~ he did its true his pedantry both here and in allmost every page by broaken Latin sentences and Philosophicall axioms ~~give us~~ he to much affords us the occasion. ~~but~~ yet If T.D. understood his own Arg. & this rule better he would not have misunderstood W.P. for who sees not, that since they Acknowledge the person or subsisting of the substance to be inseperable from the substance, that the 3 {distinct} persons will at last resolve into one; for

iff the 3 per^{s} are really one with the substance, (as necessary to Compleat it) the[y] are really one amongst them selves being In the on[e] substance, otherwise they will {be} really distinct and really the same amongst themselves; and the one sub. wth wch they really are the same will be more times that which it is for there Can be no multiplication of persons in the same Individuall nature; otherwise if the whole nature be in each distinct per. then is the nature multeply'd 3 times as in 3 distinct men; but since by T.D. the 3 Persons are one with {not only wth the} same but the same individuall nature they must be {really the} same amongst themselves, ~~or els~~ as for Instance iff Pe. Ja. Jo. had but a one soul & body they might be 3 names but they could never be 3 ~~men~~ Persons; And for his Instance In da. & sol. it quite subverts his whole matter. ~~for iff he will be~~ An here I would desire constancy In him to his own words. for iff da. & So. {be a man & A man} ~~are two men~~ because off the reaso. nature [illegible deletion] affirm'd of & communicated to them {and so two distinct men,} then will it follow that the Fa. ~~& son being~~ is god & the son is god because of the devine nature if Communicated {to} & affirm'd of them: and ~~since~~ so two gods; nor can this be avoiaded; but to answear the reason of his Instance; its very sophisticall; for in da. & sol. are to distinct rationall {souls or} beings of the same nature {wherefore 2 men}, but in ~~go~~ the Fa. & the son one being or soule but 2 ways of subsisting[11]

ADf. ACM MS, CCHS. (*Micro.* 1:114). This is the very rough draft of a tract which was never published.

1. T.D.'s answers were in Thomas Danson, *Synopsis of Quakerism: or, A Collection of the Fundamental Errours of the Quakers* (London, 1668). WP wrote in direct response to points raised by Danson, and therefore used Danson's terms and examples.

2. Anthony Wotton (1561?-1626) was a divine with puritan tendencies, a well-known and popular preacher, lecturer at All Hallows, Barking, from 1598 to 1626, and author of a number of books. *Sermons upon a part of the first Chapter of the Gospel of St. John, preached in the Parish Church of All Hallows Barking, in London* (London, 1609) is apparently the tract referred to here.

3. In theological discourse, 'substance' is the permanent reality (in Christian doctrine on the Trinity, the underlying being of which all three are one), as contrasting with changing and visible 'accidents,' or attributes not essential to that permanent reality.

4. WP does not take up Danson's essential distinction, that "the Word Person is not praedicated of Father, Son, and Holy Ghost, and of Creature *univoce;* that is, the same Word does not signifie wholly the same thing in God, and the Creature: But in God, Three Persons notes a subsisting of three in one Individual Nature; in Man, a subsisting of (three) Peter, James, and John; suppose for instance, Three divided, or several Natures of the same kind." Earlier in the tract, he wrote "and what the Scripture hath revealed to us, concerning that distinction in the God-Head, cannot be apprehended by us, under any other Notion." Danson, *Synopsis,* pp. 10, 3-4. On this point see also Hugh Barbour, "William Penn, Model of Protestant Liberalism," *Church History* 48:169.

5. Danson, *Synopsis,* p. 11: "Yet will it not follow, that there are *three* Infinites, but only one; because there are not *three* Divine Natures, but only one; of which one Nature, Infiniteness is a property."

6. P. J. & J. or Peter, James, and John. A comparison of the Trinity to three men being one man (or three apostles being one apostle) is developed in this section, and the apostles' names are almost always abbreviated. Hugh Barbour believes WP adopted this argument from the Socinian John Biddle (1615-1662), *Apostolical & True Opinion*

Concerning the Holy Trinity (1653). See "William Penn, Model of Protestant Liberalism," p. 169.

7. Danson, *Synopsis*, pp. 13-14: "I rather think he hath catched at somewhat in our writers, which he did not well understand, which he would represent as our Judgments, (and thence deduce his absurd Consequence) (*viz*) that Nature and Person in the God-Head, or God, are one thing. For the Nature of God is so simple, that it admits of no parts or Accidents. The *three* Persons are not *three* parts, either essential or Integral of the God-Head; . . . so nor can we say, that the Notion of the Father, as one Person in the God-Head, includes the Son; nor the Notion of the Son, as one Person in the God-Head, includes the Father; though each of those Persons are the Divine Essence, or God . . . which we may thus Illustrate, and indeed confirm, by comparing the Acts of those absolute Attributes, and the properties of those relative Attributes. As punishing, is not an Act of Mercy; nor sparing, an Act of Justice; nor does the one Act include the other: So, nor does the Attributes of Mercy and Justice include each other. So as begetting is not being begotten, nor being begotten is not begetting; so nor does the Notion of the Father include the Son, nor of the Son, include the Father."

8. St. Thomas Aquinas (1225-1274), greatest figure of scholasticism, and author of *Summa Theologica*.

9. Danson, *Synopsis*, pp. 14-15: "If those *three* distinct Persons are one with the God-Head, then are they each one with another: That's the sum, though he multiplies the words. *Answ.* That Argument is grounded (though he does not express, nor perhaps understand it) upon that rule, *Qua conveniunt in uno tertio, conveniunt inter se.* Those things which are one with some third thing, are one among themselves, only in respect of that wherein they agree, not simply. As in this plain instance, *David* was a Man, and *Solomon* was a Man, they two agree in a third thing, *viz.* in the humane nature; Will it therefore follow, that they are one Person? Nothing less. So though the Father be God, and the Son God, it will not follow that they are one Person; for in personality, or manner of subsistence, they differ; but only it will follow, that they are one God, or one in that Divine nature, in which third these two meet." Both Danson and WP provide a translation of the Latin immediately after the phrase.

10. Divine.

11. WP's text ends at the bottom of a page, but is obviously unfinished. He had only responded to points raised in the first sixteen pages of Danson's tract, and did not deal with the remaining thirty pages of Danson's *Synopsis*. Either WP never completed his answer, or a part of the manuscript has been lost.

The following eight documents (27-33) illustrate WP's first extended term in prison. As a result of his objections to the doctrine of three persons in one God, which was understood by the government to be a denial of the divinity of Christ, WP was sent to the Tower in December 1668 (doc. 27). He was committed to close confinement, which meant that he had only a few approved visitors (doc. 30), and no exercise or fresh air. Conditions were undoubtedly unsanitary and unhealthy. Knowing that he was responsible for the imprisonment of his printer must have made the sentence harder. He occupied his time with writing. He wrote letters of explanation to Quaker comrades (docs. 28, 29), and a statement of defiance to an anti-Quaker adversary (doc. 31). He composed the first version of what was to become his greatest tract, *No Cross, No Crown.* Doc. 33, a letter to Lord Arlington, in which he passionately claimed his innocence and laid down the first elements of his case for liberty of conscience, is also a splendid early essay of great interest. Finally, he wrote the tract *Innocency with Her open Face,* which satisfied the government on the question of the divinity of Christ but did not proclaim the Trinity. WP emerged from the Tower (doc. 34) without having made a real retraction of the views expressed in *The Sandy Foundation Shaken,* and without having changed his mind about the Quakers.

27
ORDER OF THE PRIVY COUNCIL

[16 December 1668]

The Right Hono^ble^ the Lord Arlington his Ma^ts^ Principall Secretary of State,[1] having this day represented to his Ma^ty^ in Councill[2] That William Penn, author of the Blasphemous Booke lately Printed Intituled. The Sandy foundation Shaken &c^t^ had rendred himselfe[3] unto his Lord^sp^ & that thereupon in Order to his Ma^ts^ service he caused him to be Committed to the Tower of London[4] and likwise, that he had caused John Derby[5] who Printed the said Booke to be sent priso^r^ to the Gate House[6] which his Ma^ty^ well approving of did Order that the said Lord Arlington be, and he is hereby authorised and desired to give Directions for the Continuing the said Will. Penn, and John Darby Close prisoners in the respective Places aforesaid untill farther Order.[7]

MBE. PC 2/61/143, PRO. (Not filmed). Marginal notation: Wm Penn & Darby to | be kept Close Prisoners.

1. The extensive powers of the two principal secretaries of state included the authority to examine suspected persons, commit them to custody, and, under the Licensing Act of 1662 (14 Car. II. cap. 33), to license books. David Ogg, *England in the Reign of Charles II* (Oxford, 1955), 1:196.

2. The Privy Council, which in 1668 had forty-two members and a great deal of undefined power. According to Ogg, 1:190, it was "a nebula from which the separate ministerial departments were afterwards evolved, a great clearing-house of government."

3. WP did give himself up (see doc. 33, below), but there is no direct evidence to support the frequently repeated story that he did so because he had heard of the arrest of his printer. See, for example, Mabel Richmond Brailsford, *The Making of William Penn* (London, 1930), p. 253, and Peare, p. 82. It has also been suggested that he was arrested for failing to get a license for the book; see Brailsford, p. 252, and William I. Hull, *William Penn: A Topical Biography* (London, 1937), p. 182. But no specific charge of that nature has survived. The documents refer only to blasphemy, which of course could not be licensed.

4. The ancient fortress of London was used as a state prison until the nineteenth century. Admiral Penn was a prisoner there in 1655.

5. John Darby was a printer in London, Bartholomew Close. He was not licensed or bonded as required by the Licensing Act and was constantly in trouble for printing unauthorized satires, lampoons, and the like. He published Andrew Marvell's *Rehearsal Transposed* and in 1684 was convicted of printing a libel called *Lord Russell's Speech.* See Henry R. Plomer, *A Dictionary of the Booksellers and Printers who were at work in England, Scotland and Ireland from 1641 to 1667* (London, 1907), p. 61; and Plomer, *A Dictionary . . . from 1668 to 1725* (Oxford, 1968), p. 97. On the petition of Darby's wife, he was released from "close" imprisonment, but not from prison, in Jan. 1669; and, on his own petition, "to prevent the utter ruine of his Family," he was discharged in May 1669. See

PC 2/61/189, 289-90, PRO. WP probably kept up his connection with the Darbys. On 14 Feb. 1673 he paid Joan Darby £1. 10. 0.; see doc. 142. It is worth noting that Thomas Vincent's printer, Thomas Johnson, and his bookseller, William Burden, were also arrested but were held for only nine days. PC 2/61/159, PRO.

6. The Gate House was a prison in Westminster near the west end of the Abbey. It was torn down in the eighteenth century. Cunningham, 1:327-28.

7. The fullest treatment of this imprisonment is by John Bruce, "Observations upon William Penn's Imprisonment in the Tower of London, A. D. 1668," *Archaeologia* (London, 1853), 35:70-90.

28
TO LONDON FRIENDS

G.W. A.S. J.B. S.N. G.R: &tc.[1]

[December 1668]

Dr Friends & Brethren

In the everlasting Love of God, which hath called me out of my Fathers House, & from amongst my kindred & Acquaintance,[2] Yea, from the Glorys, Treasures and Pleasures of that Egypt & Sodom,[3] wherein Jesus lay crucified, I {very} dearly salute you all, with which my heart is replenisht, & my Cup at this time overflows[4] in true Love to the Holy Brethren, & praises overall to him, that hath thus visited me; For he has turned my Wilderness into a standing Water, & my dry ground into Water springs, & there makes my hungry Soul to dwell, that it may prepare a place for Habitation. And though I have been carried on the pinacle,[5] & not only all the allurements & Temptations, that have been us'd to beset me, have with fresh bate presented themselves together, But also more then I ever expected or thought their could have been, In a Word, what ever could take the proud, the Ambitious, the fearfull, the Worldly loving, & lastly the Wise part, have with no small Violence rush upon me. But to the Honour, Glory & renown of our God & Father, his everlasting Power hath preserved, yet the Vertue & authority of the Principle of Truth hath been tryed, & known herein over the Power & Spirit of the raging Adversary: So that I can Say, where or who should I go to for there only are the Words of eternal Life. And therefore Dr Friends, the reports (that ~~there~~ may have begotten Jealousies in some) of my turning from Jesus,[6] the Light, Truth, Way, & eternal Life, ~~its~~ {as} manifested amongst Dear Friends att this Day, is but some of the Smoak of the bottomless pitt, which the same glorious Light shall scatter, & utterly dispell. For by the fresh Sense, I have at this time of the presence of the Allmighty, & the measure of his Life that is wth me, it is layd on me to declare, that the God, who made all things, & in dayes past in divers manners hath appeared, and by divers Names, hath now manifested himself, below wch Apostacy in some degree or other raignes over all professions: And though in times past, & whilst in the World I heard his Voyce but knew him not that spoak (having allwayes had my heart & Eye towards what I thought was the best way, for which reason I could never joyn (though a Child) with any of their Carnal Professions, for which Testimony I have been in some sense a Sufferer at times from the 13th but Constantly from the 17th yeare of my age) I say, though Something I have had allwayes about me, that hath told me, whatever I did, yet now have I known him indeed (whatever others say of him) to be Jesus Christ the Son of the Living God; another then which there is not by whom Light & Salvation can be obtained.[7] And as for the occasion of my present Tryalls Dr Friends, it's like I may be censured by some in the World, however I have my [illegible deletion] {Record} with God; And it is not for nought, that the Inhabitants of that foundation have made so many Lyes, & whatever the World may report or insinuate, to shake the Love of Friends towards me; I know the Humble that only must be exalted, & that accurst Spirit of being some body, the publick principle I had, when a Stranger to Truth, did abhorr & detest: More is in my Heart than I can express; but let it suffice, that my Life, my Joy, & my Peace are in the pure Unity & that Love of the Father, wch doth abase & keep low, & gives only to seek the prosperity, renown & Exaltation of Christ Jesus the Light, Life & Truth over all Interests & Professions, that he alone may raigne in the Kingdoms of Men, whose right it is, & is worthy forever.

Towr 68. W P.

LBC. WP's Letterbook, 1667-1675, HSP. (*Micro.* 1:094). In the table of contents to the Letterbook, this document is called: ~~steadfast~~ {Love abides} in Tryal.

1. It is apparent that WP intended this letter to reassure a group of leading Friends. They probably were George Whitehead, Amor Stoddard, John Burnyeat, Samuel Newton, and Gerard Roberts. Whitehead has been identified in doc. 23. Stoddard (d. 1670), was an early Friend and companion to George Fox who settled in London sometime after 1656. See DQB; Fox, 1:431. Albert Cook Myers transcribed the third set of initials "I.P.," which, if correct, would suggest Isaac Penington. However, "J.B." seems the better reading to the editors, which suggests John Burnyeat (1631-1690). He was convinced by Fox in 1653, and travelled widely in the ministry. He spent a good deal of time with WP in Ireland in Nov. 1669. His works and autobiography were published in *The Truth Exalted* (London, 1691). See also DQB; Fox, 2:418; doc. 35, 17-26 Nov. 1669. Samuel Newton, a Friend active between 1665 and 1678, later joined WP in a petition to King and Privy Council, c. 1673. See *Micro.* 1:212; Fox, 2:422. Gerard Roberts (c. 1621-1703), was a wine cooper whose London house was a gathering place for Friends. See Fox, 1:434.

2. That is, his Quakerism, which initially alienated his father, and was unacceptable to his father's circle.

3. Rev. 11:8.

4. Ps. 23.5.

5. The allusion is to the temptation of Christ, Matt. 4:5 or Luke 4:9.

6. It is not clear whether WP thought that the possibility that he denied the divinity of Christ would alarm Friends, or whether there was some rumor that he was changing his mind about Quakerism.

7. This is a standard conversion pattern, and WP described it several times. See in particular doc. 74, below. On Quaker conversion patterns in general, see Howard H. Brinton, *Quaker Journals: Varieties of Religious Experience Among Friends* (Wallingford, Pa., 1972), pp. 4-5; and Louella M. Wright, *The Literary Life of the Early Friends, 1650-1725* (New York, 1932), pp. 155-97.

29
TO GULIELMA SPRINGETT

[December] 1668.

Dr G. S.
I thought it convenient to send thee a Copy of what my Masters Reply was to me,[1] when I brought him Word, how that the Bishop of London[2] would have him recant in Comen garden,[3] at an appointed time, before the Face of all the City, or else be a Prisoner during his Life.

Saith he, all is well, I wish they had told me so before, Since the expecting of a release put a stop to some Business; Thou mayst tell my Father, whom, I know, will ask thee, these Words, that my Prison shall be my grave before I will budge a jot, for I ow my Conscience to no mortall man, I have no need to fear, God will make amends for all, they are mistaken in me, I vallour not their Threats nor res[olu?]tions, for they shall Know, I can weary out their Malice & Peevishness, & in me shall they all behold a resolution above fear, Conscience, above Cruelty, & a baffle put on all their Designes by the Spirit of Patience, the Companion of all the tribulated Flock of the blessed Jesus, who is the Author & Finisher of the Faith that overcomes the World, yea Death & Hell too, Neither great nor good things we are ever arrived without Loss & Hardships: He that would reap & not Labour, must faint with the wind, & perish in disappointments; But a hair of my Head shall not fall, though they think to pull my Locks, without the providence of my Father that is over all.[4] The Day is at hand that it ~~just~~ shall be found just wth God to recompenes Tribulation upon them that trouble the innocent; And to them rest eternal that's glorious indeed. It's like they will be severer with me then formerly, & so I may want those opportunities of conveying Notes to thee, wherefore I caution thee, to be watchfull over thyself that thy Mind become not darkned, nor thy Light extinguisht, for thou knowst the Night to be farr spent, & dawnings thou hast seen; Waite for the Day Starr to arise, & follow it, & be a Child of the Son, that he may be thy Everlasting Light & Glory, farewell

Thy Loving Master
Towr Prison, 10^m 68 W.P.

LBC. WP's Letterbook, 1667-1675, HSP. (*Micro.* 1:108). The place and date at the end of the letter are in WP's hand.

1. The writer is probably Francis Cooke, WP's servant, who was given permission to see WP on 24 Dec. 1668, *Micro.* 1:112. WP must have told him to write to Gulielma Springett and Admiral Penn and given or dictated to him the body of the letter to be sent. The closing of the letter has given rise to some confusion about the addressee,

and in fact the letter seems to contain messages to G.S., the elder Penn, and the servant. The servant was not faithful. In *The Invalidity of John Faldo's Vindication On his Book, Called, Quakerism No Christianity* ([London], 1673), p. 415, WP said that his servant at the time of his imprisonment in the Tower (which must refer to Cooke) approached a friend of WP's, and pretending to be acting for the master, borrowed £40. WP said he never saw a penny of it, but repaid it because he did not want the friend to suffer because of his "Knavish Servant." The friend was Thomas Firmin (1632-1697), a wealthy Londoner, philanthropist, and Unitarian, who was initially attracted to WP because of his views on the Trinity, but later broke with him because he believed WP changed his mind in *Innocency with her Open Face*. See *DNB;* Vincent Buranelli, "William Penn and the Socinians," *PMHB*, 83:374.

2. Humphrey Henchman (1592-1675) had helped Charles II escape from England after the battle of Worcester in 1651; he was appointed bishop of Salisbury in 1660, and London in 1663. He was not hard on nonconformists, but WP later (1689?) wrote "that wch engaged the then Bp of London to be warm in my prosecution, was the credit some Presb. ministers had wth him, & the mistake they Improved agst me of my denying the Divinity of Xt & the Doctrine of the Trinity." See *Micro.* 6:208.

3. Probably Covent Garden, a fashionable residential area in this period. Sir Simonds D'Ewes writes of "the Coven or Common Garden in London"; James Orchard Halliwell, ed., *The Autobiography and Correspondence of Sir Simonds D'Ewes, Bart.* (London, 1845), 2:80.

4. George Fox wrote on 25 May 1677 that WP's hair "shed away" during this imprisonment. See doc. 110, below.

30
LORD ARLINGTON TO THE LIEUTENANT OF THE TOWER

[4 January 1669]

Itt is his Maties Pleasure, That you permitt & suffer Dr Edward Stillingfleete[1] to have accesse from time to time to William Penne now Pris[onr] undr yr Custody, wth in that his Maties Tower of London & to conferre with him, in ordr to the convincing him if it may be, of his blasphemous & Hereticall Opinions for wch &c. Jan: 4th 68/9.
To Lt of the Tower.[2]

Arlington

MBE. SP 44/30, PRO. (*Micro.* 1:132). Docketed: Dr Stillingfleet to see Penne.

1. Edward Stillingfleet (1635-1699) was a learned and distinguished Anglican spokesman. Appointed royal chaplain in 1668, he nevertheless was on good terms with nonconformists. He apparently convinced WP that he should write the "apology" *Innocency with her Open Face*. In WP's "Account of my life since Convincement," n.d. [1689?], *Micro.* 6:208, he wrote of Stillingfleet, "I am glad I have the opertunity to own, so publickly, the great pain he took, & humanity he shewd: and that to his moderation, learning and kindness I will ever hold my self obliged." It is interesting that during this year, George Whitehead, in *The Divinity of Christ, and Unity of the Three that bear Record in Heaven* (London, 1669) made a special point of citing Stillingfleet on justification and atonement, to strengthen the Quaker case. After the Glorious Revolution, Stillingfleet became bishop of Worcester. *DNB*.

2. Sir John Robinson (1625-1680) was Lord Mayor of London (1662-1663); MP for London (1660) and for Rye (1661-1679); Lt. of the Tower (1660-1679). The Lieutenant of the Tower was in charge of the prison; it was a position of status. Robinson played a formidable adversarial role in WP's life from 1669 to 1671. He worked actively for the Restoration in 1659 and 1660. He was also a vigorous churchman; his father had been a half-brother of Archbishop Laud. Pepys (17 Mar. 1663) said he was "a talking, bragging Bufflehead"; see also *DNB;* Burke's *Peerage;* Mary

Coate, ed., *The Letter-Book of John Viscount Mordaunt, 1658-1660*, Camden Society Publications, 3d ser., 69:163, 167, 177; *The Parliamentary History of England* (London, 1808), 5:37.

31
TO LODOWICK MUGGLETON

[11 February 1669]

Lodowick Muggleton,[1]

Having had a deep & Certain Sense of thy Insulting Spirit over the Death of that Valiant Champion, & painfull Servt of the most high God J C.[2] as if it was the Effect of thy silly Curse,[3] who for these 12 years hath in these Nations & Isles abroad, in all Straits, difficulties, & hard sufferings been an incessant Labourer for the Lord; & so impaired his Natural Health, that within these 12 months, or little more, I have known him 5 times sick, & 3. even unto Death (2 whereof, before he had ever seen thy face) I say, being sensible of thy Vaunts;[4] & it being now layd upon me—Therefore once more am I come in the Name & Authority of that Dreadful Majestie, which fills Heaven & Earth, to speak on this wise:[5]

Boast not, thou Enemy of God, thou Son of Perdition, and Confederate with the unclean Croaking Spirits reserved under the Chaines of Eternal Darckness; For in the Everlasting Glorious Light, thou despisest, art thou seen Arraigned, Try'd, condemn'd & Sentenced for a lying Spirit, & false Prophet, having Counterfeited the Commission & [blank] of that God whom the Heavens cannot Contain, hast bewitched a few poor silly souls. But their blood, o Muggleton, lyes at thy Door; & the Wrath of the Almighty is kindled agt thee: and his Eternal Power in his Servants the Qua: on whom thou hast passed thy Envious Cours's, shall suddenly grind thee to powder. And as formerly, so again on the behalf of the God of the Qua: whom I worship, I boldly Challenge thee, with thy [blank] God, & all the Host of Luciferian Spirits, with all your Commissions, Curses & sentences, to touch or hurt me; Practice your Skill & Power; behold, I stand in a holy Defiance of all your Enmity & Strength. And this know, That thou Mugg. with thy God art chained by the Spirit of the Lord, & on you I trample in his Everlasting Dominion, & to the bottomles Pit are you sentenc'd, from whence you came; where the Endles wormes shall gnaw, & tortur your Imaginary Souls to Eternity.[6]

Written, signed, & sealed by Commission Received
about the 5 hour of the 11th of the 12th Mo. 1668.
from the Glorious Majtie of the most high God who
fills Heaven & Earth; that lives in his servant

W Penn. Junior
(wp)
the seal

LBC. WP's Letterbook, 1667-1675, HSP. (*Micro.* 1:134).

1. Lodowick Muggleton (1609-1698), heresiarch, the founder with John Reeve (1608-1658) of a sect known as Muggletonians. They believed they were the two witnesses of Rev. 11 who would seal the elect and the damned before the second coming of Christ. Muggleton believed he had a commission from God to curse or bless anyone to eternity. He wrote a number of tracts against the Quakers, including *The Neck of the Quakers Broken* (Amsterdam, 1663 [more probably London, 1668]); *A Looking Glass for George Fox the Quaker, and other Quakers* ([London], 1667). In *The Acts of the Witnesses of the Spirit* (London, 1699, reprinted 1764), Muggleton recorded his answer to WP's letter, dated 16 Mar. 1669.

2. Josiah Coale (1632?-1669), convinced in 1654. A good deal of Coale's ministry was in America, which he visited first in 1657; banished from Virginia, he went by foot to New England where he was imprisoned several times. He was one of WP's close Quaker friends; William Sewel, *The History of the Rise, Increase, and Progress of the Christian People called Quakers* (London, 1725), p. 450. In 1668 he went with WP, Loe, and Whitehead to see the Duke of Buckingham and Sir Henry Berwick, Secretary of State, to secure relief for suffering Friends. See "Account of my life since convincement," n.d. [1689?], *Micro.* 6:208.

3. Muggleton cursed Coale on 17 Oct. 1668 (*Acts of the Witnesses*, pp. 116-20), and Coale died 15 Jan. 1669. Sewel, *History of the Rise and Progress*, p. 464, said he died of consumption. According to Fox, Coale worried on his deathbed that "when he was gone, *Muggleton* and his Company would boast against him." He urged the Quakers to publish his repudiation of Muggleton. This was done in Josiah Coale, *The Books And Divers Epistles Of the Faithful Servant of the Lord Josiah Cole* ([London], 1671), pp. 343-44.

4. Boasts or brags, *OED*. Coale said that he had heard that Muggleton "hath vaunted" about his death (*The Books and Divers Epistles*, p. 343). In Muggleton's answer to this letter, he cursed WP. See *Acts of the Witnesses*, p. 129.

5. In the paragraph that follows, WP's language and Coale's are very similar; the "chain," "false prophets," and "Bottomless-Pit" appear in Coale, *The Books and Divers Epistles*, p. 343. Presumably WP saw the manuscript, since he contributed to the volume. However, the imagery is all drawn from the Book of Revelation, and was appropriate for a response to Muggleton, who based his authority on Rev. 11. Moreover, Revelation was extremely important to the eschatology of dissenters (including Quakers) during the Restoration. For WP's own eschatology, see Endy, pp. 121-26, 138-46.

6. The challenge issued here started a controversy which lasted at least until 1673. WP attacked Muggleton in a pamphlet, *The New Witnesses Proved Old Hereticks* ([London], 1672), in which he described several visits to Muggleton, pp. 38-42. The writing is vivid and angry. WP must have been pleased with it, because he ordered two dozen copies sent to Ireland (see doc. 143, 26 Apr. 1673, below). Muggleton responded with *The Answer to William Penn Quaker, His Book, Entituled, The New Witnesses proved old Hereticks* (London, 1673).

32
TO LORD ARLINGTON

[19 June 1669]

To the Lord Arlington

S^r^, I know not any to whom the Inclosed may be so properly directed To As thy selfe. For as thou art Supreme Secretary of State, The Person to whom I did surrender my selfe, By whose order I was Committed, And who was pleas'd to take my examination here about a Note that was by some suspected to have fallen from me at Goreing[1] house; So thy great civility, & Candid promesses thou weret pleas'd to give me of thy Assistance are strong Incouragements not only to present thee with this true relation of my Case (back'd with some observations fetch'd from former Ages) which by the mouth of any of thy Attendants may quickly be understood) but also to expect An answear Altogether sutable.[2]

I make no Apology for my letter, as being troblesome &c: nor yet appeare so very sollicitous in the matter (the usuall style of suppleants) not for want of due respect to thee, or regard to my selfe, but because I think that the honner which will redound to thee, exceeds farr the advantage that Can succeed to me. since truly Great & Generous Minds gladly embrace every occasion to assist the helplesse, & then seem most foreward to Aid them, when nothing's to be gott besides the hazard of expressing It.

And I am well assur'd, that the kindnesse & justice It shall please thee to employ In my Concerne, Can never miss that Noble End with God & vertuous Men, as well as further obleidge me to respect & serve thee upon all occasions, with safety to my Concience.

Towr of London the WPenn
19th off the month Clld jun.
1669

ALS. SP 29/261, PRO. (*Micro.* 1:142). This is a covering letter for doc. 33. In the printed version in *Works,* 1:151-54, the first paragraph was attached to the main document, and the second and third paragraphs were dropped altogether.

1. Goring House, town house of Charles Goring, the Earl of Norwich, rented by Arlington in 1666 and sometimes known as Arlington House. Buckingham Palace now stands on the site. Cunningham, 1: 345. The "Note" was, apparently, incriminating.

2. Some of WP's biographers contend that Arlington imprisoned the son in order to attack the father. There is no evidence of that, and WP's statement here, and the terms of his argument for his own release, show no suspicion of hostility from Arlington, but rather the reverse. It is not clear how the story started. In the following document, WP mentioned rumors that his imprisonment was for political causes. For further discussion, see William I. Hull, *William Penn: A Topical Biography,* pp. 182-83; Brailsford, *The Making of William Penn,* pp. 254-57.

33
TO LORD ARLINGTON

[19 June 1669]

Were I Person as Criminal as my Adversarys have been pleas'd to represent me, It might well become me to beare my present sufferings without the least resentment of Injustice done; & to esteeme a vindication of my Cause as an aggrevation of my guilt; but since It's so notorious that Common fame (a most incompetent accuser) hath maliciously belyed me, & that from invincible testemonys I stand not guilty of what my Adversarys would have so peremptorely fastned on me (Always Confessing the eternall diety of Christ & unety of the

Father word & spirit) what better Interpretation Can be given of their great zeale, then meer peevishnesse, & high pretention to learning then foul Ignorance.
Strainge! that men esteem'd Christian should appeare so Indefatigable In writeing, preaching, & discourseing down the reputation off an Innocent man, by the most foul aspersions, black characters, & Exasperateing Imputations, that Spirits the most Incendiary Could Collect & Invent. In a word, to banish me the world, forbid me heaven, & furiously denounce me sequester'd of all, with the reserve of hell only, & there it selfe they have Intitl'd me to the last & most dismall station. But what's more admirable, these Persons have all this while mistook the very question; begging that which never shall be granted, & takeing that for granted which ever will remain a question; & In reality have been accuseing their own shaddows, makeing me suffer the punishments due to their Conceits, who least of all sinceerly am Concern'd In their heat. Such champions are they for religion, they seem to vow Its prosperety In the entire ruine of charety & moderation. Others there be I know who

> – Crimina rasis
> Librant in Antithesis–

Can insinuate their displeasure under more plausible expressions.

> –doctas possuisse figuras
> Laudantur–[1]

& Consequently with more seurety to themselves, though with lesse to me, may obtain their ends: But to indulge those poore pretences, & give reception to those hackny phraises & threadbeare Criminations, of *seditious fellow, erronious, factious & troblesome to the state under a meere Counter fitt of great illuminations &c* methinks need not a jury of twelve to Convict them of very gross Indiscretion: I am very confident those small Informers have little place with thee.
Who would be thought men of witt, & perhaps are so withall, but those that have It.
Three things I boldly Can affirme, & which should be reason enough for my enlargement with any but such as would Imprisone me for the use of it; Namely, that I not only never did deny, but always expressly own'd & maintain'd the eternall diety of Jesus X[t], & substantiall unety off Father, Word & Spirit. Next, that I am alltogether as Innocent of the first occasion of these disputes as he that In defense of his own life, strikes the Assassinat. It is prohibited to draw in garrisons, but 'tis not punishable In case of an attaque; should many be stifl'd upon the peoples Concours to see An Ambassader pass the streets, 'twere meerly Casuall, not necessary to his Appeareing there.–And lastly for my good behaviour, I freely engage & obleidge my selfe to such a Conversation, as suits wth justice, temperance, Industry & peace,

this I have been, am, & through the mercys of god allmighty dissigne to be:[2] however, my Adversarys will not have It so, who have bstow'd their amunition to less purpose then on woolsacks[3]: They are alas! gott to their old chimeras of fancying armies In the air, where they have been so hotly skermishing that hard It is to perswade them they only dreame, & Count realitys of fictions– My residence Is on a more sollid body. But as I am willing to beleive, had my Innocency been well observd my Confinement should not have given [illegible deletion] so great An approbation of their Imposters; so on the other hand since they are unquestionably manifested to be such, & that the more moderate of their Authors have given their retractions in publique Conversation, Expressing their great troble to have so greedely entertain'd & promoted such foul aspersions to the Incenseing the Civil magistrate against me (the Cause I say being thus removed) Its time the undeserved effect should cease. Otherwise, my liberty will seem to have been sacrefyc'd to the Inordinate passions of the most Inveterate part of A faction, or strongly to Confirme those In their Conjectures & reports, who Confidently tell It up & down, that my restraint is not Continued on any religious ground, but for some papers deeply Concerneing the safety of the King: both which are most unworthy the equety, greatnesse and honner of Authorety.
But Alas! why should these impudent forgerys, & malicious aggravations longer prevaile against a man that has broak no law, dispis'd no goverment, dethron'd no diety, subverted no faith, obedience, nor good life; but in words & actions hath Incessantly endeavour'd the effectuall promotion of all? What If I differ from some religious apprehentions publiquely Impos'd am I therfore Incompatible with the well-being of humain Societys? Shall It not be remembred with what successe Kingdoms & commonwealths have liv'd by the discreet ballanceing of Partys?[4] & if the Politicks of the more judicious & accute in those affairs are of any worth, They are not at a stand, but roundly tell us, It is their sense ~~not~~ that nothing's more Congeneous or naturall to the preservation of Monarchicall goverments.
Lett It not be forgotten, how under the Jewish Police,[5] the utmost requir'd to Intitle Straingers to freedom In Concientious matters, was their acknowledgement of the 7 *Noachical* Precepts[6] (never deny'd by me) nor was It better with them In latter times, then whilest the ballance was kept with evennesse among them, & that the *Par. Esseans, Saduces*[7] &c: had the free exercise of their distinct worships. This was no news amongst the Heathens neither; who knows not every tribe & almost every famely In Rome had Its particular *Sacra.*[8] Nay the fond dotages of the *Egiptian Isis* & *Serapis*[9] obtain'd Temples & devine honners among that wise people. Nor Can I omitt the great Candor of (that otherwise inhumain) *Tiberius*[10] to the Christians, who If *Eusebius Pamphilis*[11] be to be credited, not only made It death for any to persecute them, but had a rare good opinion of *Pilats* relation of

christ[12], & of the christian faith, though both were so distructive of his religion & the whole worlds. Nay, Since the Christian times Itselfe, who is not Ignorant of Ecclesiastical Story, and does not know the great variety of opinions & differing modes of worship that raign'd In *Egipt, Constantinople, Antioch* & *Alexandria?*[13] Indeed, where not? Nor doe we read It ever enterd Into the hearts of any for many generations to Molest them. And doubtlesse had not secular powr & Emperiall dignety been the Helen[14] both *Arrians* & *Anti-Arrians*[15] Courted, & fought for, they might have liv'd with greater securety & peace in their respective sentiments, & not have trobl'd the whole world, nor perplexd' themselves for so many ages by Civil Anemositys, that turn'd the Empire Into a meer wildernesse of Inexpressible Calamitys & divastations. And they who seriously reflect upon the Carriage of both those partys, may find reason enough to dread the very apprehention of A faction; & palpably discover the natural but fatall Consequences that Inevitably attend the exalting of any single party to the detriment of all the rest: This Maxime, *Socrates Scholasticus*[16] reports not to have been unseen, nor wholy left unpractised by the great wisdom of the Emperor Jovianus,[17] (first suggested by his beloved friend, & philosopher *Themistius*)[18] whos time, though short, had a most different successe from all that went before or follow'd after him: I omitt to mention the many testemonys, latter & present times, in these more Westerne Parts of the world not unknown to thee are able to afford, being [~~both~~] fresh & In vew. All wch strongly confirms the present matter.

For my own part I know none undeserving the Common benefitt of humain Societys,[19] but such whose principles are distructive of justice & fidelity, Industry & obedience in all matters relative of them (wherefore the Romans exil'd their *Mathematecos*)[20] of which neither my selfe nor any Q^kr^ living, can with any shew of reason be Impeached. But to Conceit that men must Forme their faith In God, & things proper to an other world by the prescriptions of mortall men, or else that they can have noe right to eat, drink, walk, trade, conferr, or enjoy their libertys or lives {in this}, to me seems both rediculous & dangerous: since 'tis most Certain the ~~undd~~ understanding Can never be Convinc'd by other Arguments then what are adequate to her own nature; which force is so remote from, that as it abundantly expresseth passion or Ignorance In those who are wont to use It; so experementally do we find, that its not only Insuccessfull by confirming those who really have reason on their side, but greatly obdurates the unreasonable; who are then most apt to loose sight of their own weaknesse, when they have so much reason to gaize upon their Persecuters: being well assur'd that whoever is In the right, he certainly is allways In the wrong, who by club-law & Corporall extremetys thinks to Illuminate, & Convince the understanding: They may Indeed make Hypocrates, not Converts; But If I am at any time Convinc'd, Ile pay the honner of It to truth alone, & not by Betray her dues, by a base & timorous hypocresy to any externall violence, or Compulsion under heaven.

Nor Indeed, are such Inquierys materiall, or those religious Waiters truly usefull, as well as that It is unlawfull to make so dilligent A search for Concience, and that In case they find her without the mark of publique allowance or that she does refuse to pay the Toll or Custom thats impos'd, Immediately to take her for A for fitt: No man is wont to Come & ask at any shop of w^t Religion the Master is, In order to A Bargen, but rather what's the price of this or that Commodety: Nor need men beat their brains, or Rack their Witts, how to Anotomize An Attom, or Cleave An hair in subtile disputations, that they may understand, whether *Whoordom, Perjury,* lying, cousening,[21] *Intemperance, injustice* &c: are unlawfull, or distructive off good order: So Certain 'tis that the well-being of all Politicall Societys, Is wholy Independent of the Airy Speculations & nice distinctions Employ'd by some about the mysterious points of divinity: which *Varro*[22] excellently confirms, who after his enumeration of the many sects among Philosophers to about 288, tells us, that notwithstanding their minute differences, they universally concluded, vertue to be the only means to present & future happinesse; Nor doe we once read that their *transmigrations,* their *entelechia,*[23] with their diversly assign'd Causes off beings &c: were ever fatall In the Subversion of states or Kingdoms. And were there as many opinions as might require A Geography as large, as that off lands, yet why the former should be more distructive off the whole mass or species off Mankind, then if the latter off the sollid body off the uneverse I know not; & think It a task too great for any man to performe. I doe not find the Earth to muteny Against the various Influences off Celestiall Bodys, nor doe the Mountains Impeach the vallys of disorder, and schisme. The English Barly Enacts no law against the Spanish grape; nor doe the mynes of Tinn In *Cornewell,* declame Against the golden ores of *India.* In short It's not the property of Religion (says Tertullian)[24] to persecute & compell Religion; which should be embrac'd freely for her selfe, not by force. She scornes to use those weapens to her defense, her Adversarys have employ'd to her depression: It being her priviledge alone to conquor naked of force or Artifice. And truly he that has not the election of his Religion In my opinion has None; for If that be Caesars,[25] nothing's Gods. But faith Is the Gift of god, & so it is no less that men beleive aright, {then} that they beleive at all[26] It's therefore (I conceive) unspeakably the King's Interest to Cleere all Prisons off Concientious Persons, & perpetuate that freedom, which here off late he has been pleas'd to Indulge; It is a rule among Politiciens, to omitt the execution of ~~those~~ laws, when the benefitt of their suspension exceeds that of their execution; which was not ill observ'd by [him] who being ask'd the reason of the like proceedings, Answear'd—

Resdurae & regni novitas me talia cogunt.[27]

For lett men say or conceit what they please, publique ruins have ever been the Immediate Consequences of such Infringements; & publique tranquility on the Contrary;[28] for uneformety of mind is not less impossible, then an exact resemblance of visage: And men must be new model'd In both respects, before they can be chaing'd to gratefy such desires.

However, my Case is singular, being wholy guiltlesse of what was charg'd against me, (namely, the denyall of the eternall diety of Christ, & the holy Spirit) And if the observation Cornelius *Tacitus* makes upon the Case of *Petronius Turpilianus*[29] be of any notice, who, thoug he did deserve the punishment inflicted, yet because 'twas done without due examination & Conviction, he suffer'd wrongfully; Then for a greater reason must my Confinement be injurious, who have been here shutt upp, above these 6 months, under A Strickt & close Imprisonment, from many common, & necessary affairs of life, without the least formall Cause or reason why, exhibited against me; Contrary I Conceive to the naturall priviledge of an Englishman, I am sure to the noble Tolleration of the christian Religion.

My hopes are, I shall not longer continue A Prisoner, meerly to perswade the world I am not Innocent, of what, In very truth I am not guilty; Nor yet that matters off lighter moment be sawght to prolong my restraint, because there is no law for an Inoffensive man to be depriv'd of so eminent A right as liberty. This were too neerly to resemble the tragicall Case of the Innocent daughter of the guilty *Sejanus*,[30] who, because the Roman laws allow'd not virgins to be strangl'd was first deflowr'd that she might be. My thoughts are otherwise off most off my superiors.

But above all, me-thinks that very name, Christian, Imports somthing of so holy, meek & Condescending a disposition, that such severetys can find no tollerable plea from those persons who have Intitl'd themselves unto It. For my own share, & the dispised Quakers (whos self denying life & doctrine I professe) As it is our principle, to live ourselves, & encourage others, In the persuit of just, sober & Industrious Courses (the truest grounds of Civil Societys & only ways to their prosperity) so In whatever we may differ or dissent from the publique establishment: It shall never find us remiss herein.

To Conclude, since my Adversarys have overshot the mark, that the accusation Is fictitious, & many of the more moderate have retracted their first opinions off me; after so strickt & silent an Imprisonment,[31] my resolutions to demean my selfe with all respect to Authorety, my concience only excepted; I think its time, & I desire I may be order'd

a release to follow my ordinary occasions; but if it should be scrupl'd or deny'd upon the least dissatisfaction unremov'd, I intreat the faver of an accesse to the King, before whom I {am} ready to give my true & just Answears to all such Interrogatorys as may concerne my present case. Or if It will not be allow'd I desire it would please thee to give me A hearing, to all those objections wch may be thought to Carry any weight; that If I must remain A Prisoner it may be Known for what: & In the mean while, that It would please thee to allow me that liberty of the *Towr* which is so Customary for Prisoners to enjoy after the first or second month of their restraint: & which both the season of the yeare, & my personall, emergent occasions do require.
A saying of the greatest man of his time, and one that liv'd not too long agoe to be remember'd. *Cornelius Tacitus* (not a strainger to thee) I [chuse] to close my discours, who upon his reflection on former severetys, by way of Comparison, extols the great clemency of *Nerva* & *Trajans* times,[32] [In] which the liberty of expression was not prohibited

> Rara temporum felicitate, ubi sentire quae velis, & quae [sentias] dicere licet.—[33]

W Penn

ALS. SP 29/261, PRO. (*Micro. 1:138*). There is also a copy certified by WP but very heavily edited in WP's Letterbook, 1667-1675, HSP. The Letterbook copy was the basis for the version in *Works*, 1:151-54, and is on the whole more polished and diplomatic than WP's original. There are many changes of spelling, punctuation, capitalization, and text. The more important changes are noted below. Dates of these three versions do not agree. The LBC is dated 5 May 1669; the printed version in *Works* is "1st of the 5th month,"; the original is not dated, but the covering letter is dated 19 June 1669. The covering letter also carries the address and docket. See doc. 33. The salutation in LBC and *Works* is in more Quakerly style: "To Hen: Bennet call'd Lord Arlington."

1. From Persius (A.D. 34-62), the first satire, ll. 85-87. "He balances the charges in smooth antithesis, and is praised for having fashioned learned rhetorical figures." Myra L. Uhlfelder, Department of Latin, Bryn Mawr College, supplied translations for Latin quotations.

2. Five sentences of text, from "Who would be thought men of wit" to this point, are omitted in LBC and *Works*. According to WP, "the first occasion of these disputes" was, of course, Thomas Vincent's insulting remarks about the Quakers.

3. A large package or bale of wool, sometimes used as a target. *OED*

4. This is an early expression of the idea of "balance," which was a persistent theme in WP's politics. See Mary Maples Dunn, *William Penn: Politics and Conscience* (Princeton, 1967), pp. 143-44, 155-57.

5. "Policy." In later versions it was changed to "Constitution."

6. The duties that could be required of Gentiles living among Jews, according to Biblical commands which preceded Mosaic law. The original seven precepts were: 1) obedience to authority 2) reverence for the divine name 3) abstinence from idolatry 4) from incest 5) from murder 6) from robbery 7) from eating flesh of living animals. The list grew, but these remained the most important, and only those pre-Mosaic laws which coincided with the laws enunciated at Sinai were included (e.g., circumcision was not required of Gentiles). See James Hastings, ed., *Encyclopedia of Religion and Ethics* (New

York, 1917). WP's word, "Noachical", is a variant of the more usual "Noachian". The *OED* gives this document as the only occurrence cited for "Noachical".

7. Pharisees, Essenes, and Sadducees. The Pharisees, c. 145 B.C. – 70 A.D., a Jewish religious party with a large following among common people, accepted oral tradition and exerted influence through the development of education and synogogue worship. The Essenes, second century B.C. to the second century A.D., were a Jewish ascetic sect whose life was highly organized and communistic. The Sadducees, a Jewish politico-religious sect, were opposed to the Pharisees, and represented the priestly aristocracy; they rejected oral tradition and accepted the written law only. In later versions of this document, the Essenes were replaced by the Scribes, originally Jewish scholars who knew the art of writing, later official teachers of Jewish law as based upon the old Testament and accumulated tradition. See Cross, *Christian Church.* The idea of balance amongst the three ancient sects originates in Flavius Josephus, *The Works of Josephus* (London, 1676), book 18, chap. 2, p. 477, and was cited by other proponents of liberty of conscience. See, for example, James Harrington, *A Discourse upon this Saying: the Spirit of the Nation is not yet to be trusted with Liberty* (London, 1659), where the same points were made.

8. The private religious rites of a *gens*, a family, etc., which the Romans observed carefully.

9. Isis and Serapis were Egyptian deities whose worship was organized into public cults in the Hellenistic Age. Isis became a leading goddess of the Mediterranean world; the cult had elaborate mysteries, ritual, and a professional priesthood. *Oxford Classical Dictionary.*

10. Tiberius Julius, Roman Emperor (42 B.C.–37 A.D.). *Oxford Classical Dictionary.*

11. Eusebius (c. 260-c. 340), Bishop of Caesarea, "Father of Church History." His *Ecclesiastical History* is the principal source for the history of Christianity from the Apostolic Age until his own day. Cross, *Christian Church.*

12. According to Eusebius, Pontius Pilate committed suicide. Cross, *Christian Church.*

13. The three ancient cities of Constantinople (now Istanbul), Antioch (in Syria), and Alexandria (in Egypt) were all seats of bishops in the early church (together with Rome), and all engaged in a struggle for supremacy.

14. Helen of Troy, fought over by the Greeks and Trojans.

15. Arianism was the heresy which denied the divinity of Christ, named for its author, Arius (d. 336). The Emperor Constantine called a council at Nicaea to counteract the heresy, and the Nicene Creed was promulgated in 325, under the leadership of Athanasius (293?-373), Arius' chief opponent. The issue disturbed the empire until the Council of Constantinople in 381; after that date, it continued to exist only among the Teutonic tribes. At its height, three parties could be identified, and Arianism was an issue in imperial politics. See Cross, *Christian Church.*

16. Socrates Scholasticus (c. 380-450), Greek church historian, native of Constantinople. His history was designed as a continuation of the work of Eusebius.

17. Flavius Jovian (c. 332-364), Roman Emperor, orthodox and earnest Catholic, supported Athanasius and the Nicene Creed.

18. Themistius (c. 317-388), Greek philosopher and rhetorician, though not a Christian, was favored by every emperor from Constantius II to Theodosius I because of his exposition of the ideology of monarchy. *Oxford Classical Dictionary.*

19. "Political Societies," in later versions.

20. Soothsayers or astrologers. Tacitus describes their iniquities in *Histories,* 1.18, and their banishment in *Histories,* 2.62.

21. Cozening, or cheating. *OED.*

22. Marcus Terentius Varro (116-27 B.C.), Roman writer and scholar, whose works were a mine of information.

23. Transmigration, or metempsychosis, is the doctrine that souls migrate from one body into another until completely purified; entelechy is the idea that there is a vital force in human beings urging them toward self-fulfillment. See Cross, *Christian Church.*

24. Quintus Septimius Florens Tertullian (c. 160-225), an African church father who wrote on a wide range of subjects, including religious toleration and persecution.

25. Matt. 22:21.

26. Nine sentences of text, from "Nor need men beat their brains" to this point, are omitted in LBC and *Works.*

27. "Res dura et regni novitas me talia cogunt," or "Harsh necessity and the newness of my kingdom." Virgil, *Aeneid,* Bk. 1:563.

28. Two sentences of text, from "It is a rule" to this point, are omitted in LBC and *Works.*

29. Cornelius Tacitus (b. A.D. 56), the great historian of imperial Rome, wrote that Petronius Turpilianus (d. c. 68), governor of Britain in 63, was executed by the Emperor Galba because he had accepted office from Nero. *Histories,* 1.6.

30. Sejanus, (d. A.D. 31), was a Roman prefect, commander of the guard, and consul under Tiberius, over whom he had great influence until charged with conspiracy, for which he was executed. *Oxford Classical Dictionary.* According to Tacitus, *Annals* 5.9, his family was also executed, and since it was unprecedented for a virgin to suffer capital punishment, his daughter was violated by the executioner before she was put to death.

31. In LBC and *Works,* there is an addition here: "without any legal course or just procedure, contrary to the Priviledges of every English man, as well as the meekness, forbearance & Compassion inseparable from true Christianity." WP continues with a request for intervention with the king and assurances of his loyalty, more characteristic of his thinking a few years hence.

32. Nerva was emperor of Rome, A.D. 96-98, and was succeeded by Trajan, A.D. 98-117. Both were enlightened and humane rulers.

33. Tacitus, *Histories,* 1:1, "in the rare happiness of the times when you may feel what you wish and say what you feel."

34
RELEASE FROM THE TOWER

[28 July 1669]

His Ma^ty being pleased this day to declare in Councill, That he is satisfyed as well by the Report of Dr Stillingfleete who was appointed to conferre with William Pen concerning some Hereticall & Blasphemous Opinions he had vented, as by what the said William Pen hath since published in Print, That he is sensible of the Impiety & Blasphemy of his said Hereticall Opinions, and that he doth recant and retract the same.[1] Did Order, That the said William Penn be, and he is hereby released from his Imprisonm^t in the Tower of London, Whereof Sir John Robinson Lieutenant of the Tower of London, & his Deputy there are to take notice, & to cause him to bee forthwith set at Liberty & delivered to his Father Sir William Pen.[2]

MBE. PC 2/61/372, PRO. (Not filmed). Marginal notation: Mr Pens Release from the Tower.

1. WP, *Innocency with her Open Face* ([London], 1669). WP did not really recant. He said he had been misunderstood about the divinity of Christ, and asserted his belief in it. According to Endy, pp. 281-87, WP's faith was strongly Christocentric.

2. William Sewel reported that some people thought WP's father had been involved in his imprisonment, "perhaps to prevent a worse treatment." *The History of the Rise, Increase, and Progress of the Christian People called Quakers* (London, 1725), p. 463. For discussion of WP's relations with his father, see the headnote to doc. 21. Braithwaite, *Second Period,* p. 64, citing a newsletter, said it was believed that WP was to be delivered to his father to be transported; and the Admiral did indeed send him out of the country, but to Ireland, to attend to the family estates there.

THE IRISH JOURNAL

1669–1670

35
MY IRISH JOURNAL

WP returned to Ireland in the fall of 1669, shortly after his release from the Tower. He had several purposes: to make new leases with his father's tenants in Cork, to settle his father's accounts in Kinsale, and to visit Friends along the way. WP had already secured his father's claims under the Act of Settlement (see headnote to doc. 7 and docs. 12 and 13); now he had to make the land profitable to the Penns by setting new rents, collecting arrears, and arbitrating disputes with his father's tenants. Admiral Penn had resigned the governorship of the fort at Kinsale, and WP had to work out arrangements with his father's successors at the fort, his cousins Captain Richard Rooth and Ensign William Penn (see doc. 45). For WP, however, the journey was primarily a spiritual one. There were many Friends in Cork, in Dublin, and elsewhere in Ireland, and WP spent most of his time in their company.

Doc. 35 is WP's journal of his Irish trip, beginning with his departure from London on 15 September 1669, and closing in Dublin on 1 July 1670. It is, next to the journal of his trip to Holland and Germany in 1677 (doc. 119), the most extensive travel diary he recorded. WP reports on his September visit to Bristol at the time of George Fox's marriage there, his arrival in Cork in October, his trip to Dublin in November, and his daily movements in county Cork from December 1669 to May 1670. He visited his father's lands in Imokilly, just southeast of Cork city, and in Ibaune and Barryroe, near Ross Carbery, and engaged in strenuous negotiations with his father's tenants. He was almost continuously on the move, and covered many hundreds of miles on horseback during his months in Ireland. Wherever he went he visited other Quakers (sometimes in prison), spoke in meetings, and offered what influence he could to ease their struggle with the local authorities. At the end of May he went back to Dublin to argue with the Lord Lieutenant and Privy Council for the release of imprisoned Friends. As the son of an important Englishman, WP was treated civilly by almost all of the officials whom he met, but he had only limited success in freeing his fellow Quakers. Notwithstanding his tendency to argue religion at table, he was entertained on his journey in households of every stripe, Protestant and Catholic, rich and poor, military and Quaker. The great majority of the people he dealt with, Quaker and non-Quaker, were colonists of English origin. WP showed very little interest in the oppressed native population—far less interest than he would show in the Indians of Pennsylvania a dozen years later.

The text of the Irish journal, written in a small pocket book, is extremely difficult to interpret. In Quaker style, WP identifies most persons by initials only. In English style, he misspells Irish surnames and place names. WP seems to have brought the journal up to date about once a week; he jotted entries hurriedly, and occasionally misnumbered dates and mixed up pages. The journal has been printed three times before: in a limited edition without annotation in 1910; in *PMHB* 50:46-84, again without annotation; and in a modernized form by Isabel Grubb (London, 1952). Of these versions, Grubb's is by far the best. Her volume is highly readable and well annotated. However, she takes great liberties with the text. Grubb expands abbreviations and alters Penn's wording at will; in effect she provides a free translation rather than a transcription.

In preparing this edition, we have retained WP's text exactly as he wrote it, but have expanded the hundreds of names initialed by WP, whenever they can be identified, within square brackets. In establishing the text we have collated the original manuscript with the previous editions and with a transcript made by Albert Cook Myers, and believe that we have deciphered a number of passages which baffled our predecessors. We have also made heavy use of research which Myers did in the Irish Public Record Office before it burned in 1922. Myers compiled biographical notes on nearly every person WP mentions in the Irish journal, supported by abstracts of documents destroyed in the fire, such as wills, tax records, and other official documents, as well as by information drawn from manuscript Irish Quaker records.

In annotating the Irish journal, we have drawn repeatedly upon the following sources, which are not specifically cited in the footnotes: ACM; Book of Survey and Distribution, County Cork, PRO, Dublin; Burke's *Ireland*; W. Maziere Brady, *Clerical and Parochial Records of Cork, Cloyne, and Ross* (Dublin, 1863); P. Beryl Eustace and Olive C.

Goodbody, *Quaker Records, Dublin, Abstracts of Wills* (Dublin, 1957); Fuller and Holme; C. B. Gibson, *History of the County and City of Cork* (London, 1861); Grubb; G. Hansbrow, *An Improved Topographical and Historical Hibernian Gazetteer* (Dublin, 1835); Lewis; Pender.

My Irish journall

Parted from London on the 15th of the 7th mo: [September] 1669:

7bre [September] 15th

I came to watford, to Ann Mericks,[1] A[mor]: S[toddard]: & J: G.[2] accompaning me

16

I came to I. P.[3] A[mor]. S[toddard]. & J[ohn]. G[iggour] being wth me; we had a meeting there; A[mor]. S[toddard]. left us & went for watford.

17

J[ohn]. G[iggour].. went for london, I remain'd there:

~~18~~

I left Amersham & took leave for my journy, but at maiden-head[4] mising of my sert [5] I return'd to I[saac]. P[enington's].

~~19~~ 18

I went with G[ulielma]. S[pringett]. to Pen-street,[6] return'd at night.

19

G[ulielma]. S[pringett]. S. H.[7] &c: went a foot to meeting at Russles,[8] & I with them. writt to Ailesberry for P. F.[9]

20

P[hilip]. F[ord] came early; I[saac]. P[enington]. Jo. P.[10] M[ary]. P[enington]. J[ohn]. G[iggour]. my selfe & P[hilip]. F[ord]. went for Reading: G[ulielma]. S[pringett]. & T. E.[11] accompany'd us beyoind Maiden-head. T[homas]. E[llwood]. & P[hilip]. F[ord]. exchaing'd horses; one at 05-10.00. the other at 09-00.00.—we arriv'd at Reading, visited the Prisoners.[12]

21

Jo[hn]. P[enington]. P[hilip]. F[ord]. & my selfe parted from Reading. I[saac]. P[enington]. M[ary]. P[enington]. & J[ohn]. G[iggour]. return'd home. we din'd at Newberry,[13] & lay at Mals-berry.[14]

22

We parted. Jo[hn]. P[enington]. went to Brist[ol]. by bath,[15] & wee two by chipnam.[16] we mett that night at Bristoll, they two lay at the In, I at D. H.[17] wth G[eorge]. W[hitehead]. I visited G. F.[18] M. F.[19] W & I. Y.[20] T. B.[21] & L. F.[22] that night;

23

I went to F. R.[23] to lye, they to T[homas]. B[isse]. wee remain'd there till the 23 of the next month, I lay at severall friends houses, we were

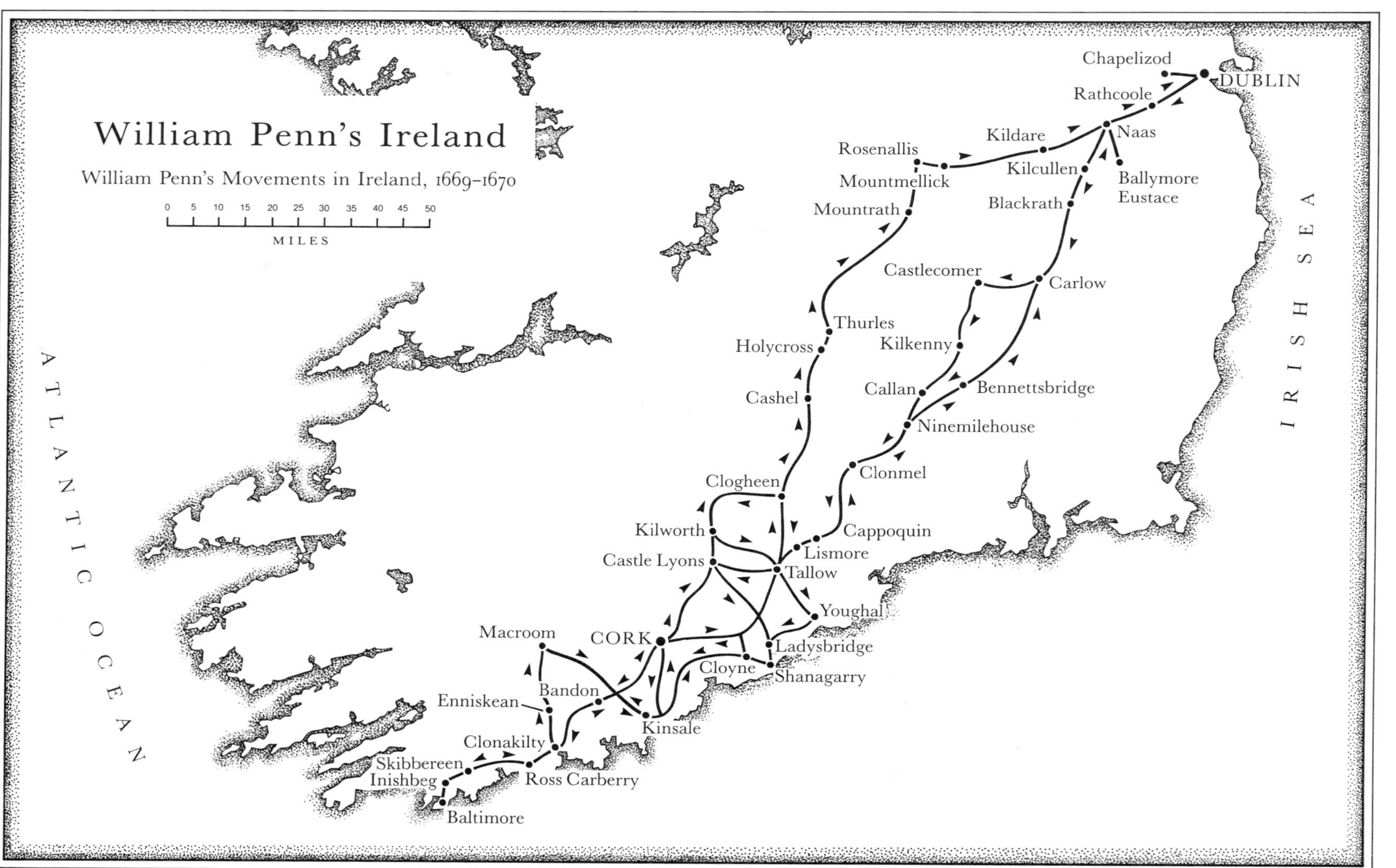
William Penn's Ireland
William Penn's Movements in Ireland, 1669–1670
0 5 10 15 20 25 30 35 40 45 50
MILES
IRISH SEA
ATLANTIC OCEAN
DUBLIN
Chapelizod
Rathcoole
Naas
Ballymore Eustace
Kildare
Kilcullen
Blackrath
Rosenallis
Mountmellick
Mountrath
Carlow
Castlecomer
Kilkenny
Bennettsbridge
Callan
Ninemilehouse
Clonmel
Thurles
Holycross
Cashel
Clogheen
Cappoquin
Lismore
Tallow
Kilworth
Castle Lyons
Youghal
Ladysbridge
Shanagarry
Cloyne
CORK
Macroom
Bandon
Enniskean
Kinsale
Clonakilty
Ross Carberry
Skibbereen
Inishbeg
Baltimore

very kindly entertaind; metings grew fresh. I was mov'd among others to testefy to G[eorge]. F[ox']s M.[24]

8b [October] 23.

we left bristoll, came to kingroad[25] accompany'd by T. S.[26] T. L.[27] C. H.[28] F[rancis Rogers]. & W. R:[29]

24

we sayl'd the wind being east N. east. gott beyoind Come 7 L.[30]

25

We arrived at the coave off Cork & lay there all night.

26

we Came to Cork. din'd at T. M.[31] visited the prisoners S. T.[32] being there, we lay at E. Pikes.[33]

27

W. M.[34] & my selfe went to the Mayors,[35] but to no purpose. I mett C. P.[36] F. S.[37] J. B.[38] we had a meeting in Prison at Night where we also had dined. I writt also to both Barronys to prepare them:[39] to R[obert]. S[outhwell]. for 30l payable to G. R.[40]

28.

Left Cork wth P. D.[41] W[illiam]. M[orris]. din'd at Killworth,[42] sup'd at clohane,[43] at A friends Inn. W. Laiford.[44]

29.

wee came to Jo: Fennills;[45] din'd at Cashall[46] at the Cow. past through holy Cross[47] (so call'd) from a superstitious conceit that a peece of xts cross was brought theither from Jerusalem {& by clas: town. where the English were murder'd by the Fitz: Pat:}[48] lay at Thurles, the Ancient manner hous off the D. of Ormonde[49]

30.

We came to J. Hutchinsons[50] a friend, who was gone before us towards Rosanalla.[51] past by Montroth, the Earles hous & town; where we saw the Iron-works.[52] lay at Rosannalla at W: Ed:[53]

31.

was the Generall meeting for Linster.[54] 2 friends spoak from Dub[lin]. W[illiam]. E[dmondson]. kept the meeting. & heavenly it was.

1. 9th mo [November]

we left w[illiam]. e[dmondson's]. stopt at Mt Melech.[55] Came to Kildare[56] & there lodg'd.

2.

we Came to the Naise,[57] their din'd, & Lay at Dub[lin]. at J. Gays.[58] I visitted M. Canon[59] & F. step.[60] that night.

3.

W[illiam]. M[orris]. P[hilip]. D[ymond]. & wee mett at my chamber. F[rances]. step[ney]. Came to see me. din'd & sup'd at home.[61]

4.

W[illiam]. E[dmondson]. came wth friends to the Citty. we were at meeting. W[illiam]. Ed[mondson]. G. G.[62] W[illiam]. P[enn]. spoak. P[hilip]. D[ymond]. W[illiam]. E[dmondson]. & G[eorge]. G[regson]. pray'd. din'd & sup'd at home.

5·

All friends mett at my Lodging to keep the Nationall meeting,[63] W[illiam]. E[dmondson]. W[illiam]. M[orris]. & G[eorge]. G[regson]. spoak. the sufferings off friends Came before us, Munster & Linster. but [not] Ulster were return'd. A Paper was sent to all the Provinciall mens-meetings to advise them to be more punctuall in the regestering of all sufferings; & to transmitt them in briefely to the nationall meeting. A paper by way of Addresse was carry'd by W[illiam]. M[orris]. & W[illiam]. P[enn]. to the Mayor who abus'd them, but did not releive the Prisoners of the Citty.[64]——sup'd at home, no diner.

6

wee mett at S[amuel]. Cla[ridge's]:[65] where wee drew up the Linst[er]. & Munst[er]. sufferings by way off Address to the Ld Lt.[66] din'd & sup'd at home.

7

wee mett at the little house, where W[illiam]. E[dmondson]. & one sharp[67] spoak. W[illiam]. E[dmondson]. & P[hilip]. D[ymond]. pray'd. J[ohn]. G[ay]. his wife & children were present. sup'd at home.

8

I Receivd A letter from J[ohn]. S[tepney]. about his daughters buriall,[68] haveing writt to him. Deane[69] came to me & W[illiam]. Ed[mondson]. about St[epney] at E. Gard.[70] din'd & sup'd at home.

9

Sr. G. Ascue[71] Came to see me all friends went wth M[ary]. Canning Jo[hn]. st[epney's]. daughter to our burying ground. they cary'd her with about 10 coaches. din'd & sup'd at home.

10

Coll. Packer[72] came to see me but T. Fouls said to meet Rob. & Lawrence[73] about a dispute, though deny'd by him. he affirm'd

1. that I was eternally damn'd if I did not own that christs death was to justify the vindictive justice of god.

2. that ~~christ~~ there were examples among the Martyrs that suffer'd more signally, & more with joy & peace, & more gloriously, & with greater triumph then christ did.

we went that afternoone, I An[n]. Gay. J[ohn]. P[enington]. P[hilip]. F[ord]. little D. ~~went~~ In a coach to chapple Izord to see C[ol. Richard]. Lawrence. he was in town. he makes Imagery.[74]

C[olonel]. law[rence]. & Ma. Jones[75] came to my Lodging, & Dr. Roules.[76] the last was quiet & affable. the other Passionate & Confounded, about the morall religion. & water baptisme. W[illiam]. M[orris]. present. din'd & sup'd at home.

11

Sr W[illiam]. Petty came to see me. stay'd 3 hours. he was very friendly.

E. Morcoe & her sister dyn'd at my Lodging. we went to the castle: receiv'd a slight account by C. Herle.[77] from thence to Col Shapcotes,[78] about C. Wallis.[79] he was kind. I {din'd,} sup'd at home.

12

I went to the Castle. C. H[erle]. very Civil but nothing done. visitted by fouls. Din'd & sup'd at home. Given 2 silver Candlestiks & suffers[80] to A[nn]. G[ay]. for their care & lodging.

13

Stay'd at home, writt {to Erl. of Dr.}[81] for England, to G[ulielma]. S[pringett]. I[saac]. & M[ary]. P[enington]. to E. J.[82] & E. B.[83] visitted by D[r. Daniel]. Rouls. he deny'd vindictive justice In the nature of good.
din'd & sup'd at home.
P[hilip]. D[ymond]. went for Eng[land].

14

we kept meeting at the old meeting hous. I declar'd about an hour. I pray'd afterwards. a great meeting. din'd & sup'd at home.

15

I went to the L[or]d. Dra. [Drogheda] about friends. he treated me wth all Civility. promessed his utmost Invited me to dine wth him at my pleasure. mett T. h. W[illiam]. M[orris]. G. W.[84] here at my Lodging. disputed wth fouls. din'd & sup'd at home

16

the Professors of all sorts declin'd a meeting. I din'd wth sr: w[illiam]. Petty. Sr. G[eorge]. Ascue came to see me; discoursed with Bird[85] about G[ulielma Springett's]. land.[86] Sup'd at home. visitted by J[ohn]. Stepney.

17

I went to the Earle of Draghedahs he treated me wth great civility. I meet the Earl of Arran & of Roscomon.[87] {R. H.} the Ld Jo.[88] C. T. L[or]d. D[rogheda]. G. T.[89] &c: I disputed wth wilson. was visitted by [Dr. Daniel] Rouls, F[rances]. Step[ney]. Jo[hn] st[e]p[ney] & ther kinsman. Capt.[90] J. Barniot[91] come to town & wth me. Din'd & sup'd at home.

18

I was wth Jo[hn]. Bur[nyeat]. in the morning. I din'd at home. discoursd wth C. Dis. & his sister M. F. we had a precious meeting at the Great hous. Jos. Step.[92] was with me at night. so was Jo[hn]. Bur[nyeat]. G[eorge]. Web[ber]. & an other friend. Sup'd at home also.

19

I was wth the Ld Kingston[93] who was very Civil & Kind. I went to Barry[94] & deliver'd him the Addresse in the morning, in the Afternoon I went to Councill, I mett the E[arl]. of D[rogheda]. there. the Address was not read, I mett also wth W. Fittz Geld[95] & Rob. F. G.[96] I din'd & sup'd at home.

20

visitted by j. Fouls. noe meeting can be had wth Prof[essors]. there came also W[illiam]. Bird & C. Sands[97] about G[ulielma]. S[pringett's]. businesse. the estate being neglected is gone, all but a 3d.—writt for England to my Fa[ther]. to A. P.[98] F[rancis]. R[ogers]. G[ulielma]. S[pringett]. din'd & sup'd at home. a letter resceiv'd from the chancellors chaplin, about T. S. j. visitted by Ingenious Bonnell[99] an account resceiv'd off the Revenu of this kingdom £219500.–

21

the Famely went wth me to meeting at Dublin, where I have been since the 2d Instant. J[ohn]. Burniot spoak, a good meeting it was in the powr of the allmighty. many people came amongst the rest severall off the Rude & Boisterous Gallants to gaiz on me, which they did for allmost an hour. meeting being done, we went out where I spoak to them very sharply, and so we parted. I sup'd at home.

22

I was at the Councill about friends, It satt not because of the Ld Lt Illnesse.[100] I mett there Sr G[eorge]. Lane, Sr A. Forbise,[101] Sr T. Jones.[102] Dr. Yarner[103] &c. they spoake merely to me, but I urg'd a relese of poore friends upon them 3 of them being Privy Councellors.[104] I went to the Castle saw C[apt]. Heade from thence to Sr G[eorge]. Askue so ~~home,~~ {to C[ol. Robert]. Shapcote} where I Gott the Articles of agreement betwixt C[ol. Peter]. Wallis & I.

I feed him wth 6 Cobbs.[105] I staled[106] the purchass of the Corke Inhabitants. from thence to Jo[hn]: Bur[nyeat's]. & so home where I din'd & sup'd.–

23.

I was visitted this morning by Lt. Coll. Young. I visitted Sr. J. Temple[107] & Sr G[eorge]. Lane. neither at home. T. Gooking[108] was to see me. Din'd at home.—Boneele din'd wth me. sup'd at home. J[ohn]. Bur[nyeat]. lay here that night.

24

Tho[mas]. Gook[in] C. Phair[109] & Dr [Daniel] Roules din'd here. T. Fouls come to see me. Dr. Hall[110] was to visit me also. I was at C[ol. Robert]. Shap[cote's]. he was not within. I went wth A[nn]. G[ay]. to J[ohn]. Bur[nyeat's]. W[illiam]. Bird come to see me at night din'd & sup'd at home.

25

I was at C[ol. Robert]. Shap[cote's] early but did little. from thence I went to J[ohn]. Burniots from thence to C[ol. Robert]. P[hair's] Lodging, where I meet sr st Jo: Brod.[111] where we discours'd of P[hair's]. matters. I Caus'd my hair to be cutt off & putt Into a wigg, because of Baldness since my Imprisonment.[112] I was at meeting, & a very heavenly one It was. I was with Coll. [Robert] Shap[cott]. where I ended my business about C[ol. Peter]. Wallis, & the Inhabitants of Corke. from thence to supper at home & so to J[ohn].

B[urnyeat's]. Lodging wth A[nn]. G[ay]. to take our leave of him. dind & sup'd at home.

~~27~~ 26

Jo[hn]: B[urnyeat]. went towards the mole[113] from this Citty of Dublin. C[ol. Robert]. P[hair]. Came to se me. so did Hawkings T. fouls, Disnee & Sr J.[George] Ascue: &—Bonneele. din'd & sup'd at home; nothing was done at Councill

27

Sr Aims Meridith.[114] C[ol. Robert]. Phair. Lt. Cll Walker din'd wth me at my Lodging. I writt to G[ulielma]. S[pringett]. to G[eorge]. F[ox]. to G[eorge]. W[hitehead]. to T[homas]. Fir[min]. to G[eorge]. web[ber]. to my Fa[ther]. to Fr[ancis]. R[ogers]. & to I[sabel]. Y[eamans]: din'd & sup'd at home.

28

I was at meeting, it was large. I declar'd 1h – & ½ – pr[ayed]: twice. the meeting was fresh & quiet. sup'd at home. friends came to my chamber at night where we had a precious meeting.–

29

Frinds were releas'd In this Citty wth great love & Civility from the Judges.[115] Nothing was done, nor is likely to be done at Councill. because of the Army & Revenues. Dr [Daniel] Roules & Jo. Scott[116] were to seen me, R. T.[117] E[lizabeth]. G[ardiner]. W. main & his wife[118] were here. several friends books were by me dispers'd G[eorge]. W[hitehead]. G[eorge]. F[ox]. E. B.[119] A R.[120] W[illiam]. P[enn]. primers.[121] &c:–my accounts ended wth Jo[hn]. Gay.–

30

we came from ~~Racole~~ Dublin to Racole;[122] J[ohn]. G[ay]. his wife, the children, S[amuel]. C[laridge]. A[nthony]. S[harp]. & another friend. I left orders wth J[ohn]. G[ay]. about all matters.—miles .6

1 of the 10th mo: [December] 1669

we left Racole.—they went with us 2 miles & so retur'd we bated[123] at blakwroth, & lay at Carloe.[124] where I sent for C. Chaffin.[125] gave him books to dispers.—

miles 26

2

we parted early from Carloe & pas'd through Castle Dirmont,[126] & bated at Killkenny[127] from thence we Came to Bat-Fouks[128] his hous where we lay.

miles .21.

3

we parted thence, & pass'd through Callin,[129] & bated at 9 mile hous call'd Grange Mac.Cleere.[130] and lay at Clonmell being .14 mile. sup'd wth Mead[131] wth home I had much dispute about originall sin.–

4

we chaing'd J[ohn]. P[enington's]. horse wth [John] Mead, & had one peece & 2 Cobbs to boote. we parted from Clonmell, famous for olivers seige,[132] its present strength, & great fruitfulnesse of soyle. we pass'd through the 4 mile water & came to Copper Fain[133] where in passing over the Blackwater, a river of great note, rapidity, & depth; the horses were so unruly, especially J[ohn]. P[enington's]. that we were all Endanger'd of drowning. J. P. was struck overboard & by mighty mercy, I & the Boatman caught & sav'd him. P[hilip] Fords hors slew over, & swome back portmantoe[134] or all to tother side, [three words cancelled] & whilest I & the ferry man were saveing J[ohn]. P[enington]. my horse & his had well neigh flung us both upon him & they upon us, which the god of mercys for his name sake prevented. we return'd, J[ohn]. P[enington]. Lost his hat; gott him to an Inn, putt him to bed, ply'd him wth hott cloths, strong waters, & what could be gott to preserve him; after 2 hours stay to drye & recruit him we past the Ferry & Came by lismore[135] the E^le^ off. Corks great seat, & so to Talloe, a road well Improv'd, & much English[136] where we lay at the signe of the George. miles 17.

5

we left Talloe & came to Capt bents.[137] we pas'd by a great company of Irish gather'd to the mass upon A hill. we din'd at C. B. went to se the vaile of shangary.[138] stop'd at Capt Boles farm he holds of my Fa[ther].[139] well Improv'd. from thence to C[apt. Richard]. B[ent's]. were we sup'd & lay.—

6

I left Capt [Richard] Bents & went to see C[ol. Robert]. Phairs wife;[140] & thence wth C[aptain]. Bent, his wife, & daughter went to Cork. where I went to see the prisoners that night.

7

we went to meeting, I spoak in the powr of the Ld God a fwe words to Backsliders. thence to diner at T[homas]. Mitchels. & so to Prison. & so home at E[lizabeth]. P[ike's].

8

I stay'd to write letters I Could not agree wth Capt Boles. I went to Prison. where I spoak a fwe words In the pure life. from thence home.

9

I left Cork. J[ohn]. Boles in company to Kinsale, C. Rooth[141] Came to visit me at the green dragon, & c[ousin Ensign William]. Penn.

10

I went to R[obert]. Southwel who was Civil. I received advice from him. from thence we went to the fort, where we dined, I gave the soldiers 2 cobs or plate peeces. — from thence I came to Cozen Crispins.

11

I left C[ousin William]. Crisp[in's]. & came to Immokilly, he Came wth us to the first Ferry 7 miles. I call'd at F[rancis]. Smiths, meett {Jo. Spat [?] &} P[riest Christopher]. vowel;[142] came to Capt Bents were was Ens. Cro:[143]

12

I sent P[hilip]. F[ord]. to Cork for Jo[hn]. Gos[sage]. with ~~a~~ letters to sherif feild & sheirif haray,[144] also to Jo[hn]. Gos[sage]: & S[amuel]. Thornton. I went to see C[ol. Robert]. Phairs wife. spoak some words there. sup'd at Capt Bents had much dispute wth Ens. Cro[ker]. disafected.

13.

I stay'd at home all day.[145] C. osb.[146] serj. Rouls.[147] Capt Freak.[148] P[riest Christopher]. vowel. Fran[cis]. Smyth. & old Francklan d[149] Come to see me the 2 first about land. but had noe positive answear till the 16 following, becaus P. Maskal[150] was not theer who opposes serj. Roul's now in possession of Ballelowrace & balleroe. Rid out Into the feilds In the evening. lay at Capt [Richard] Bents.

14

I went to see Ballelowrace & balleroe & Barris quarter, litt at serj [Samuel] Rouls, saw lissally, & Ballinwillin & Ballinvohir.[151] lay at C[apt. Richard]. Bents. J[ohn]. G[ossage]. & P[hilip]. F[ord]. came from Cork.

15

we went to admeasure Geiragh & Knocknegaple[152] Fr[ancis]. Smyth being there. & J[ohn]. Boles, it mounts to acres more then by the Civil Sirvay Cl. [Peter] Wallis came to me to see me. lay at C[apt. Richard]. Bents.

16.

F[rancis]. S[mith]. Serj. [Samuel] R[olles]. & Pr[iest John]: Mascall Come about the lands of Ballelowrace & Balleroe. It was determind for Rouls. much dispute at table Against the Priest; people satisfy'd. still at C[apt.]. Bents. J[ohn]. G[ossage]. & P[hilip Ford]. survay'd Fr[ancis]. S[mith's]. Land again.

17

we went to serj. [Samuel] Rouls to admesure his. we lay there that night.

18.

We made an End of [Samuel] Rouls his lands. Ballevallin & Lissally. C[apt. Richard]. B[ent].s & Came home that night.

19

F[rancis]. S[mith]. Came for a lease. we agreed at 42l per Ano. Serj. [Samuel] Rouls we also agreed with at 4.6 per Acre. with other Considerable Improvements on that halfe plowland. din'd & sup'd at home as I have done all that while. Received a Packet from Cork. one from G[ulielma]. S[pringett]. A[lexander]. P[arker]. R[ichard]. Pen[n]. T. Cook.[153] J[ohn]. & A[nn]. Gay

20.

we went to C[ol. Robert]. Phairs. we sup'd there; lay at C[ol.]. Phairs.

21

we went to C[apt.]. Boles his hous, admeasur'd his lands in part. din'd there. I returnd. & Jo[hn]: hull wth me. Jo[hn]. P[enington]. J[ohn]. Gos[sage]. & P[hilip]. F[ord]. stayd that night.—I writt for Eng[land]. to F[rancis]. R[ogers]. I[sabel]. Y[eamans]., G[ulielma]. S[pringett]. A[lexander]. P[arker]. G[eorge]. W[hitehead]. P. E. S. M. &c:

22

we went to Capt Boles finish'd his land, & so to Ahaddagh, to Ct Wakehams.[154] & lay there. J[ohn]. H[ull]. went to Ballicrenan.[155] mett wth Majr woodly.[156]

23

we went about admeasureing C[apt. John]. W[akeham's]. land; Fr[ancis]. Smith. & Sr. P. Smith[157] came to us; Articles were sign'd seal'd & deliver'd for 42l per Ano the first yeare, & 40l per Ano afterward. during 3 lives. S[amuel]. Thornton came in the while. return'd with him to C[apt. Thomas]. Boles, so to C[ol. Robert]. Phair who was come home. & thence to C[apt]. Bents hous where we lay. & had some service

24

he went to Cork. I to C[apt. John]. Walkhams, finish'd the admeasurementt there

25

was Pye Day.[158] none Could be gott to worke. J[ohn Penington]. J[ohn]. G[ossage]. P[hilip Ford]. & I. went to Cork. by C[ol. Robert]. Phairs. where we first dined. we lay at T[homas]. Cooks. visitted frinds In prison, first: S[amuel]. T[hornton]. lay wth me.

26

we went to a meeting at G. Bennetts[159] 4 miles out of Cork. we overtook J. Stubbs[160] & many Mallow[161] friends: we had a large, & blessed meeting; we returned to Corke. lay at T[homas]. C[ook's]. S[amuel]. T[hornton]. J[ohn]. S[tubbs]. & I lay together. we had a meeting at our lodgeing, the widdow Plasteed,[162] & T[homas]. Mitchell were there.

27

S[amuel]. T[hornton]. went for Mallow, J[ohn]. S[tubbs]. stay'd In Cork, & I came Into Immokilly to my Fathers hous. Shangary or old Garden.[163] haveing call'd At C[ol. Robert]. Phairs. we were Civilly treated: [one word deleted]

28

we went to se C[ol. Peter]. Wallis trenches In the great Bog where he has made a duble ditch 2 miles quicksetted & many great ditches a cross, by which It may become profitable land. Jo[hn]. P[enington]. fell Into a trench stepping over. J[ohn]: hul[l] Came to us. din'd supd at. sh[anagarry].

289

Major Farmer[164] & J[ohn]. Bolese came to me. I had advise from F[armer?]. din'd & sup'd at sh[anagarry]. I have perus'd Part of the Jesu. Book.[165]

~~29~~ 30.

I went to meet J[ohn]. S[tubbs]. but found him not. he Came late In the evening. wth C[hristopher]. Pennick. lay with me.

31

he went wth C[hristoper]. Pen[nock]. to Youghall,[166] where he had a meeting. I Carry'd him part of the way, and then return'd. mett at shangary Cll. [Roger] osborn. Rich. Hull.[167] F[rancis]. Smyth. Serj [Samuel] Roules & Jo[hn]. Bouls also G. Fitz-Gerald.[168] I did little businesse, they din'd here. we had some Controversy together about matter of liberty. serj. Rouls is to Conclude wth me about the businesse. G. F Gerald. would have a farme—none Can beset him. they left us, I went with them, so did J[ohn]. Hull C.ll. [Peter] wallis & J. Boles allmost to Ballicrenan. then returnd.–

1 of the 11th mo. [January 1670]

Cll. [Peter] Wallis J[ohn]. Boles & I. went to Inchy, found the hous out of Repair. thence to C^t^ [John] Walkhams & so wth J[ohn]. G[ossage]. & P[hilip]. F[ord]. home to shangary.–

2

we stay'd at shangary. all but J[ohn]. G[ossage]. & P[hilip]. F[ord]. went to gailes.[169] was about the Ans. to the Jesuits.

3

I was very busy about the Answear all day allmost. J[ohn]. Hull transcrib'd it.

4

J[ohn]. B[oles]. came to me, C[ol. Peter]. W[allis]. he J[ohn]. P[enington]. & I went to Cp^t^ [Michael] Gales rid Into the sea. J[ohn]. G[ossage]. & P[hilip]. F[ord] went to admeasure T[homas]. Francklands farme. & Return'd to Shangary that night. M[aj. Andrew]. W[oodley]. came to Dinner. J[ohn]. hull went to Corke & carry'd the first sheet to the press. J[ohn]. B[oles]. went home, & wodly to Gales.

5

I went an hour before day to Capt [Richard] Bents for advice. he come back [two letters deleted] two miles. I overtook Cp^t^ [John] Walkam & J[ohn]. B[oles]. I Concluded wth Capt. Walk for 90^l^ per An. for Fenore, Cur[roghticloghy]. Ball[ycarrowny]. Acre[doan]. Cond[on's acres]. Ball. & Seskens.

Major woodly & I have not quit agread. he went to Roleses & C. walk[ham]. home.

6

[one word deleted] Major [Andrew] woodly & I Could not Agree. I din'd & sup'd at shangary.

7

I writt much off my answear to the Jesuits: & J[ohn]. P[enington]. transcrib'd It.

8

I writt for england to G[eorge]. W[hitehead]. I[sabel]. Y[eamans]. F[rancis]. R[ogers]. & My Fa[ther]. I bought frize for M. Lowr[170] F. w. P. E. P. P. S[usanna]. M[itchell?]. I sent Another sheet to the presse. [Michael] Gale came we agreed at 82 per An^{o}

9

C^{t} [Michael] Gale Came again, we agreed still at the same price. I writt some of my answear.

10

Capt [John] Wakeham & J[ohn]. B[oles] came, the lease agreed upon & drawn. at 84 per An^{o} Serj. [Samuel] Rouls was also here, & agreed at 4^{s}-4^{d} per Acre.

11

C[ol. Robert]. Phair Came to see me. we went to [Michael] Gales. I had a letter from R[obert]. So[uthwell] [Capt. Richard] Rooth, M. Love.[171] about the souldiers pay. orders given about It. P[hilip]. F[ord] Returnd wth J[ohn]. Bu^{r}[nyeat] & S^{ll} [Thornton]–.

12

J[ohn]. Bur[nyeat]. J[ohn]. P[enington]. Sam^{ll} [Thornton] & I went to tallo. lost our way by 6 miles. we baited there. took a guide to cloheen. we were lost on the mountain,[172] fain to groape our way, at last gott Over, by many wonderful precipisces, & came to cloheen by an other guid from the foot of the mountain. being In all about 29 Irish miles. neer 50 English.

13

next morning we went to Jo[hn]: fennils. found S. Ecclis[173] there. had a meeting. J[ohn]. B[oles]. & S[olomon]. E[ccles] spoak. it was a most precious meeting, many friends were there. J. B.[174] G. Baker.[175] J[ohn]. Bouls &c. J. Hutchenson.[176] &c:

14

J[ohn]. B[urnyeat]. & S^{ll} [Thornton] went for Carloe, S[olomon]. E[ccles]; & J[ohn]. Fen[ne]^{ll} to Waterford & we returned by tallo wher we bated to shangary.

15

Ct. Gale Came hether. we Concluded at 90^{l} per An^{o}.

16

J[ohn]. P[enington]. & P[hilip]. F[ord]. & I went to C[apt.]. [Michael] Gales, putt out the gray gelden to grass. he gave me a stone Coult.[177] Came home to shangary again.

17

C[apt. John]. Walkham, Capt [Michael] Gale, Capt [John] Boles, Major [Andrew] woodly & Priest [Christopher] vowell Came to see me. finish'd with Capt Boles. at 62^{l} per An^{o}— I {had} much dispute at table wth vowell Farmer Landy[178] was there. I went wth P[riest]. V[owell]. to the strand.[179] much discourse with him. ~~P. F. went to Cork.~~

18

he Came again, & C[apt. Richard]. hulls wife & the lady Tents t'other two daughters.[180] Coll. [Robert] Phair & Suph & their wives, [Michael] Gale & Jo: Phair[181] came also to see mee. Phillip [Ford] went to Cork.

19

I writt more of my Answear. I went to C[ol. Robert]. Phairs. wth Capt. [Michael] Gale lay there meet Phillip [Ford] as We went, he returnd with us to C[ol]. Phairs. ~~went to Cap. Bents to preadvise them about Woodlys reference.~~

20

went to Cap. [Richard] Bents also, to advise about M[aj. Andrew]. Woodlys reference.[182] ~~to Phairs man 1s~~

20

Coll. [Robert] Phair & I &c: went to Gar[ret]. F[ts] Geralds of Lisguinland to vew Cloumain.[183] we din'd there, had a dispute wth the Priests [Christopher] Vowell & webb.[184] one Chaplen to the Ld Pres. the other at youghall. we return'd & parted upon the hill by the windmill. to the poor 1[s].

21

I went & Coll [Peter] Wallis to Coll. [Robert] Phairs, about the reference the land was returnd 4[s] 3[d] per Acre.[185] I paying quitrent.— I abated 6[d] per Acre, and that was 3[s] 9[d] per Acre. we so agreed on all sides. he before C[ol. Robert]. Phair {[Richard] Bent} [Jasper] Farmer, [Peter] Wallis &c: gave up Inchy the house not to touch & arrears of rent to pay. so we return'd home to C[ol]. Phairs ser[t] 1[s].

22

I mett Ger[ret]. F[ts] Ger[ld] about the windmill, we concluded on 44[l] per An[o] & what It shall be adjudg'd more worth by [Jasper] Farmer, & Gale. I paying quitrent.—

23

we stay'd within. I writt part of my letter to my Fa[ther]. we waited upon the Lord. went a walking.

24.

I made an end of my Fathers & writt one to my sister about Fran Cook. I receiv'd A letter from Cap[t] Smiths[186] wife at Ballicrenan, I answeard it;

25

I went to Capt [Thomas] Bols from thence to Coll. [Robert] Phairs & so to Capt [Richard] Bents. From thence to Cap[t] [John] Rous, agreed wth him. Phillip [Ford] went to Cork. I call'd At Coll fitz.Gerald. was not at home, mett him returning to Cap[t] [John] Boles. sup'd there, Came late to shangary.

26

Coll. [Roger] osborne, Capt [Richard] smiths wife, & hulls wife came to me at shangary about Capt Smiths farme, they earnestly sollicited for an abatement of the 4^{s}-6^{d}-per Acre, but I could not be moved from my Commission, & judgment. It was agreed that It should be so taken & Coll. osborne the securety. they return'd. much was added to my answear.

27

G[eorge]. Webber, S[usanna]. M[itchell]. & J. C.[187] came wth Phillip [Ford] from Corke. stay'd one night.

28

they return'd by Capt [Thomas] Boles, & C[apt. Richard]. Bents. there S[usanna]. M[itchell]. pray'd, we Carry'd them on their way to Carrigtohill.[188] & there Parted. they went for Corke. J[ohn]. P[enington]. & P[hilip]. F[ord]. & my selfe for Capt. [Richard] bents. & so to shangary. J. Bayly brought me a letter from J[ohn]. Gay.

29

I went to Coll. [Roger] osbornes Coll. [Peter] wallis & Jo: Baly accompaning me. the Coll. Lady [Mabel] Tent. M. Smyth. R[ichard]. & E[lizabeth]. hull &c: were very Civill, I agreed with smyth. obsborne is securety, the price is 4^{s}. 6^{d}. we return'd to shangary.

30

we stay'd at shangary, I proceeded In my businesse, in order to depart the next day. I writt a letter (very smart) to F[rancis]. S[mith].

31

we departed, Came to Capt [Richard] Bents. lay there that night. [four words deleted]

12th mo. [February] 1st.

M[aj. Jasper]. Farmer & M[aj. Andrew]. woodly Came to C[apt. Richard]. Bents I spoak to them. from thence we Went to Corke. J[ohn]. Boles being with us. we mett with Coll. [Robert] Phair. his wife. & severall of his Famely.—

2.

From Cork we went to Kinsale. I was at the Fort. was visitted by [Thomas] Gooking, & others. G[eorge]. Webber, & G. Gamball came to me about the burying place, bought of Jo: Galway.[189]

3

Severall din'd with us at Kinsale at the green-dragon. I went to see R[obert]. Southwell who receiv'd me civilly. we return'd to Cork.

4

I went from Cork, to w. Laifords, G[eorge]. G[amble]. P[hilip]. F[ord]. & J[ohn]. P[enington]. being wth ~~him~~

5

from cloheen, we came to Jo[hn]: Fennells, & there mett wth Sol[omon]: Eccles. & L. Cook.[190] we went thence to Cashell. to G[eorge]. Bakers.

6.

we had a meeting there being 1st day. Sol[omon Eccles]. spoak. then I. then lucretia [Cook]. Soll. & I. prayd. M: Martin & her sister were there. & many off the towns people. we return'd to Jo[hn]: Fennells.

7

we returnd thence to w[illiam]. L[awford's]. & thence to Killworth; had a meeting there. S[olomon]. E[ccles]. & I. spoak.

8

we went to Tallow, call'd at Capt Campains[191] a friend by the way. had a meeting at Talloe, where we were disturb'd by a busy Connestable. we refused to goe unlesse he produc'd his Commission, I spoak much to him, at last the man was smitt, & departed, Sol[omon Eccles]. pray'd & spoak, so did I. I had much discourse with. Rob: Cook.[192]

9

R[obert]. C[ook]. P. C.[193] S[olomon]. E[ccles]. W. H[194] his daughter, J[ohn]. P[enington]. G[eorge]. G[amble]. & my selfe Came to youghall; I visitted & Invited Ed[ward]: Landy to meeting, he did not deny me, yet Came not[195] we had a blessed meeting. both of us. spoak. sup'd at the Inn.

10

we left youghall, & w[illiam]. H[awkins]. his daughter, R[obert]. C[ook]. & P[eter]. C[ook]. & the rest of us Came to M[aj. Jasper]. Farmers, & thence to shangary, where we lay being Civilly treated.

11

we left J[ohn]. P[enington]. at shangary ill of a stopage In his throat at shangary & S[olomon]. E[ccles]. G[eorge]. G[amble]. & my selfe came to Coll. [Robert] Phairs, & so to Capt [Richard] Bents where we din'd: & I left my chesnut nag, takeing his daughters mare, & Came that night to Cork & lay at G[eorge]. G[amble's]. where Friends Came to see us. S[usanna]. M[itchell]. G[eorge]. W[ebber]. H. Fag.[196] J[oan]. C[ook]. R. B.[197] &c:–

12

We Continu'd at G[eorge]. Gamballs that day. I shav'd my head dind there, did somthing about my book. sup'd At G[eorge]. Webbers, with G[eorge]. G[amble]. his wife S[usanna]. M[itchell]. S[olomon]. E[ccles]. &c:–return'd to G[eorge] G[amble's]. lay there.

13.

we went to G[eorge]. Bennets 5 miles off to meeting had A precious one. S[olomon]. E[ccles]. S[usanna]. M[itchell]. & my selfe spoak returnd & sup'd At G[eorge]. G[amble's]. had a meeting at R[ichard]. Brocklesby [word deleted] S[olomon]. E[ccles]. S[usanna]. M[itchell]. & I spoak. it was A large convinceing meeting. lay At E. Erberys.[198]

14.

we din'd at eli[zabeth]. Erb[ury's]. & Came to Joan Cooks, sup'd there. G[eorge]. W[ebber]. spoak. S[usanna]. M[itchell]. pray'd. S[olomon]. E[ccles]. spoak.

15.

I writt for Eng[land]. to G[ulielma]. Sp[ringett]. & A[lexander]. P[arker]. din'd at S[usanna]. Mitt[chell's]. & lay there. sevell friends Came to town.

16

we had a great meeting being the 6 weeks meeting for Cork. S[olomon Eccles]. & S[usanna]. M[itchell]. spoak. & some others things, were well orderd as to truths affairs. we lay at G[eorge]. Gambels.

17

Coll. [Robert] Phair & I ended Priggs,[199] & [Michael] Gales businesse. S[olomon]. E[ccles]. J[ohn]. Hull. W[illiam]. Mor[ris]. J[ohn]. P[enington]. P[hilip]. F[ord]. & my selfe went to Kinsale,[200] ~~& thence to~~ bought some of w. Mask. Basketts.

18

we went to Bando[n] only will[iam]. Morrice. will Mask went with us to Bandon we had A meeting there. S[olomon]. E[ccles]. spoak. I also spoak. we were at the end disturb'd. for the Provost & Priest wth 3 Conestables Came to us. ~~We~~ I satisfy'd the Provest, nonplus'd the ~~Maj~~ [erased] Preist. writt him a challenge, & gott the victory.[201]

19.

we Came to Jo: Allens.[202] lay there.

20.

we had a large meeting there. S[olomon]. E[ccles]. & my selfe spoak. we lay there that night.

21

we came to Will[iam]: Morices that is S[olomon]. E[ccles]. G[eorge]. W[ebber]. J[ohn]. P[enington]. P[hilip]. F[ord]. & I; Jo[hn]: Allen Came with us. & return'd. we lay there.

22

we went to skippreen[203] will[iam] Morice Paul Morice[204] &c: with us. S[olomon]. E[ccles]. spoak: we return'd that night. that is W[illiam]. M[orris]. P[aul]. M[orris]. J[ohn]. P[enington]. P[hilip]. F[ord]. & I. but S[olomon]. E[ccles]. & G[eorge]. W[ebber]. went with J[ohn]. hull to his Island.[205]

23

Capt. Moore,[206] Abell Guilioms.[207] P. Maddox.[208] A. Clark.[209] W. Harris.[210] W. Berry.[211] Ed. Nuce.[212] & old [Thomas] Franckland. also. Philpott,[213] Arundall {Crowly,}[214] heart[215] German,[216] oheay.[217] & others. I Bargan'd wth A[bel]. G[uilliams]. C[apt]. M[oore]. & the rest parted civily. haveing appointed them their respective days. to ballance accounts, & to article for the time to come. severall din'd at W[illiam]. Morrices wth me. W[illiam]. M[orris]. J[ohn]. P[enington]. & P[hilip]. F[ord]. & I went that afternoone to J[ohn]. hulls Island to S[olomon]. E[ccles]. & G[eorge]. Webber. lay there. a pleasant & retir'd place. given me a Greek Psalter.

24

we all of us went to Ballamore,[218] had a meeting at J. Fens, S[olomon]. E[ccles]. & I spoak; he & G[eorge]. W[ebber]. stay'd but the rest return'd we to W[illiam]. Morrices, J[ohn]. hull to his Island.

25

~~I could not Agree with P. Mad. nor Ed. Nuce.~~ G[eorge]. Web[ber]. & Sol[omon]: Eccles Came to Wm Morris. I went to see the lands.

26

G[eorge]. Web[ber]. went to Cork. S[olomon]. E[ccles]. & [I?] went with him. saw J[ohn]. Stubs his farme. we returnd. I Could not agree with P[aul]. M[orris]. nor Ed[mund]. Nuce.

27.

Severall came to meeting from severall parts. Capt moors children,[219] & many others. S[olomon]. E[ccles] & I spoak. It was a precious meeting as I was ever In S[olomon]. E[ccles]. went to Jo[hn]: Allens

28

P[aul]. Mor[ris]. J[ohn]. P[enington]. J[ohn]. hull & I went to Bandon we went to meeting. I was call'd out by the Provests man; I had 3 hous discours wth the Provests very neere, & Brayly[220] wth many of the dirtyst people of the town. my staying prevented the breaking up of the meeting I endurd much In spirit, In reproaches, slanders, & the wickedness of the multitude: yet, in the end they were trampl'd upon In the dominion of the truth. we lay At S. Massys.[221]

~~29~~ 1st of the 1st mo: [March]

we return'd to Capt. [Emanuel] Moores at Ross, by M[ajor John]. Allens. we dyn'd At his hous, & sup'd there. Tho[mas]: – Gooking Came wth me from Ross to to Capt. [William] Morrices:[222]

2

I finish'd with Jo: Woods,[223] & Tho[mas]: Gookin went to Ross. I settled some of the proprietors; Warner[224] was with me, but nothing Concluded. D. Crowly, & D[avid]. Germin sign'd their Articles.–

3

Adam clark Came to me, I writt a letter to the Earle of Barrimore[225] by him. his businesse is unconcluded about Carrigroe. Walter Harris Came In the afternoone, he engag'd to discharge arrears, but agreed not for the future, only left It In suspence. J[ohn]. hull Came & lay with me.

4

I went to Ross, & J[ohn]. H[ull]. J[ohn]. P[enington]. P[hilip]. F[ord]. W[illiam]. M[orris]. & P[aul]. M[orris]. to Capt [Emanuel] Mores. there Breakfasted, & thence to Lt Ed. Clarks[226] thence to clanikilty.[227] Mett wth [Philip] Maddox. Concluded not.—from thence to Bandon, many Accompaning me good part of the way. from thence to Cork. I had the Preists letter & shall Answear It.

5

we, & many friends to the Number of 23 from Cork, to Youghall, others Came from other parts In order to the Next days meeting, S[olomon]. E[ccles]. & I lay at Rob: Sandarns.[228]

6

we had an exceeding great meeting & the people sober, & severall reach'd, all peaceable, & the Mayor himselfe said had he not been mayor he would have Come. we sup'd at the two Ends[229] being de-vided. & too many for one. S[olomon]. E[ccles]. S[usanna]. M[itchell]. J[oan]. C[ook]. G[eorge]. W[ebber]. P[hilip]. F[ord]. & I went to Ed[ward]. Landys, we much reach'd his love & hopes were begotten of him & so returnd, he accompaning of us a great part of our way.

7

~~W~~ I visitted M. Newlons father. a fine old man, & Civill, he lives highly, as to the outward. also J. Gerald, meett Governour osborne. Capt hull. Ens. Russell. & owen Silver[230] ended the Controversy wth him. but [Maj. Andrew] woodliff flinches. — we left youghall I brought friends to Carrigtohill, by the way at Corabby I chaing'd my dun[231] Nag for a flea bit mare. return'd to Coll. [Robert] Phairs sup'd there & then to Capt [Richard] Bents to bed.

9

writt for England, to fa[ther]. G[ulielma Springett]. P[hilip]. F[ord] went to Cork. I went to Coll. [Robert] Phairs stay'd till evening, then return'd to Capt [Richard] Bents Capt Bent was Come home. he has almost done his businesse with Barrimore–

10

we stay'd at Capt [Richard] bents. went over to Coll. [Robert] Phairs wth C[apt]. Bent. & din'd there. return'd to Capt Bents. I writt a sheet or two against Priest more[232] & purpose; effectv

11

Phi[lip]. Ford Came from Cork. the judge was Come to Cork. friends Imprison'd, great sevirity express'd.[233]

12

C[apt. Richard]. Bents man went to Cork, to Excuse his masters not Coming to town to the E[arl]. off Barrimore.

13

Phi[lip Ford]. went to Cork again for Capt [Richard] Rooth. Came not that day but [Capt. Richard] Bents man Came. he brought me a Packet. one letter ~~for~~ from my Fa[ther]. one from Gul[ielma Spring-ett]. one from T[homas]. Firm[in]. one from my sister.–
writ to the Judge.

14

Phil[ip Ford]. Came with my Cousen [Richard] Rooth from Cork. Friends barberously dealt with. Mayor & judge Agreed. many appear for them. my Cos. Rooth, & C[apt. Richard]. Bent agreed as far as could be. I have bought his stone-hors, for 15^{l}. that is, my Black hor of J[ohn]. Fen[nell]. & 9 pounds ster.

15

we Came all to Cork. C[ousin Richard]. R[ooth]. C[apt. Richard]. B[ent]. my selfe &c: I litt at Tho: Cooks. writt letters. went to the Prison, & saw D[ea]r. Friends. many Friends were at the sizes.[234]

16

I went to the Judge Could not speak to him in the morning. I went to G[eorge]. Webbers, saw [Lord] shannon, went wth him, Sr. St. Jo[hn]: Broderick. & Red: Bar.[235] to the Judge. discoars'd with him, effected but little. but cleer'd truth, & Came over the Judge.

17

W[illiam]. Mor[ris]. carry'd my letter to the judge, he seem'd Civil, but dealt wickedly. he affronted Jona. Demsey on our account. & in the County hall finish'd the matter against Friends ~~In the~~ that he should have done In the Citty hall. many appear'd for us. But nothing done for us. we waited to speak with the judge, prepar'd [the Earl of] Barrimore Ld Shannon, & Capt. [Emanuel] More; & writt the [judge?] A letter, deliver'd by the Ld Shannon but nothing done; only the tooles are not to be taken away, & Room to be given for lodging. the Judge went out of town, & left the Prisons full, & friends were fin'd 195 pounds. besides fees. one friend was beaten In the [word deleted] Court, but 'twas not regarded by judge nor Jury. a wickeder mayor nor judge has not been in the Citty of Cork since truth Came. we went to Prison inform'd friends, & went to our lodgeings.

18

I left friends In Prison P[hilip]. F[ord]. J[ohn]. P[enington]. & I went to Imokilly, by the lord shannons Capt [Richard] Ro[oth] & Jo[hn]: Gay accompanying us. the Ld. S[hannon]. made us wellcom from thence over both Passages[236] to C[apt. Richard]. Bents.

19.

I went to Col. [Robert] Phairs return'd at evening. I sett about a book against persecution Call'd the Great Case of L. of C. Debated & Defended.[237]

20

I writt much that day of the said discours I lay'd at Cap[t. Richard] Bents all the while.

21

I went, Phil[ip Ford]. with me to G[arrett]. F^{z} gerald & sing'd articles with him, cleer'd arrears with Capt R[ichard]. Smith. went to the lady [Mabel] Tents ended wth Coll. [Roger] osborne for himselfe, & Capt [Richard] Smith. we din'd there. return'd by shangary, Coll. [Peter] wal[lis]. brought us beyoind C[apt. Thomas]. bouls. we Call'd there. we found at Capt [Richard] Bents major [Andrew] Woodlife, at last Concluded with him, & pass'd articles betwixt us.

22

I proceed with my discours much. Coll. [Robert] Phair & Capt [Michael] Gayle Came to me. the business in suspense with Gale stil. & Coll. Phair also.

23

I proceeded & allmost finish'd my discours against persecution. P[hilip] F[ord]. went to [John] Rous, nothing don with him. still at C[apt. Richard]. Bents.

24

I proceeded still with my Book. Coll. [Robert] Phair ended with me. we left. Capt [Richard] Bents & Came to Cork. I went to visit Friends whose Tooles are taken from them. lay at Tho[mas]: Cooks.–

25

I spoak wth J. Gould did nothing. sent one sheet of the G[reat]. C[ase of Liberty of Conscience]. to dub[lin]. Jo[hn]: Gay. gave order for my little wig to be made into two cap borders. went tc prison. thence to G[eorge]. G[amble's]. his child just then Expird.[238] went to Bandon. saw S[arah]. Mas[sey]. & Th. Davis,[239] & Lay at Dash.[240]–

26

we went to Will[iam]. Mor[ris]. Call'd at Cohanakilty. twas very stormy. sent for Capt [Emanuel] More. he Came partly agreed with him. lay at W[illiam]. Mor[ris's].

27

we had A very good metting W[illiam]. Mor[ris]. spoak 3. myselfe 2. & once Call'd upon the lord god of life. Capt mors wife & [Edmund] Nuces son & daugh. were there. parted wth G. Bal.

28

W[illiam]. Mor[ris]. went towards Maryborrough upon Truths account.[241] A[bel]. Guil[liams]. came. but refus'd his arrears & so parted. his Distress[242] was sent for by F. & L. o.Hea. P[hilip]. Maddux was here. he was himself still & so he parted. no streis without arrears. A. Guil. came again. the businesse of[f] still. the Cattle violently rescued.[243]

David Ger[man]. had his lease.

~~29~~

J. Southwel sign'd articles for Carhow at 26^{l} per An^{o}.[244]

29

we went to D[avid]. Germ[an's]. din'd there. W[alter]. Harris & his Bro: J. Martin[245] came theither. we agreed not. all of us went to cheahbegg,[246] to vew the Irish mans farm. thence to Tho[mas]: Gookins. who was not within, & so to L^{t} Ed[ward]. Clarks. & agreed wth him at 40^{l} per An^{o}. a great Bargain in consideration of old friendship, & service Done my Fa[ther]. & his own great charge.[247] thence to A[dam]. Clarks. to whom I gave a letter to be sent to the E[arl]. of Barrimore. & so home by Ross to Will[iam]. Morris. where we lay–

30

we stay'd at home I writt much of my G[reat]. C[ase]. of L[iberty]. of C[onscience]. [Edmund] nuce Came. nothing done.

31

we went to T[homas]. Gookins. spoak wth P[hilip]. Mad[dox]. he was rude & surly, we passed thence to the slaveens, Geiragh, & Kile,[248] & so home again.

2d Mo. [April] 1st.–

Em Nuce Came to me but the leases were not Come. I writt more of my book. we stay'd at home. J[ohn]. H[ull]. came. W[alter]. Har[ris]. & J[ohn]. Mar[tin]. ended with me.

2

Ed[mund]. Nuce, & D. Crowly Came, the first had his lease, the last could not. It was not Come. we stayd at home, I did proceed in my book.–

3.

we had a good Meeting at W[illiam]. Morrices. Capt [Emanuel] Moors wife [Martha] was there. & J[ohn]. Hull.

~~3~~ 4

I went to capt [Emanuel] Moors. all of us went wth A[bel]. Gul[liams]. to Aghamilly.[249] he had distress. we return'd to Capt Moors & there lay.

5 ~~4~~

we all went to Ed[mund]. Nuces. thence Capt [Emanuel] Moore & I went to P[hilip]. Mad[dox's]. he was not at home. we return'd to Ed. Nuces. there din'd, & so came to Capt Moors. I gott my quit rent of the man of Geiragh,[250] but did not agree with him about the saile of his lease.

~~5~~ 6

P[hilip]. Mad[dox]. Came, I offer'd him his farme at 24l per Ano if J[ohn]. S[outhwell]. would give way. he would not & said he was resolv'd in his mind. Lt C. Mead Came, & din'd at Capt [Emanuel] Moors. Martha Moore her Daughter, little Manne[251] P[hilip Ford]. Jo[hn Penington]. & I walk'd to W[illiam]. Morrices but return'd at Night.–

~~6~~ 7

Capt [Emanuel] Moore, J[ohn]. Hul[l]. P[hilip Ford]. Jo[hn Penington]. & I went to Bandon. visitted Friends. E[arl of]. Barrimore was not their. lay at Lt [Richard] Dashwoods.

~~7~~ 8

we went to Cork. saw friends In prison, took fresh horses, & so for Castle Lyons.[252] A[dam]. C[lark]. & T. Hungerford[253] wth us. from Castle lyons we went to shangary in all .38 Irish miles.

8 9

we went to the lady [Mabel] Tents. Agreed wth the E[arl]. of Barrymore for 20^{l}, to have Carrigroe the 9 Gneevs[254] free, only quitrent Excepted. Coll. [Roger] osb[orne]. & his lady not being at home, Came into the yard as we were going out to take hors. we rid to Franck Smiths he was not within, we din'd there. so over the Ferrys to Cork. took our horses, & so for Bandon that Night. being 12 Irish miles after 6. lay at [Richard] Dashwoods.

~~9~~ 10

G[eorge]. Gambal Came to me. we broak fast & Mounted for Ross, overtook a Berring,[255] Barberous like the heathen. Came to Ross. J[ohn]. Hull was there. we lay there.–

~~10~~ 11

we Continu'd there. the sur^{v} G^{ll} of the harbers Came, went to Baltemore. J[ohn]. H[ull]. accompany'd him. the young Gookings Came.[256] W[illiam]. Berry Came, we concluded on 22^{l} 10^{s} for to release his farme but to have it one year.

~~11~~ 12

W. Freak Came. w[illiam]: Berry Came, for 6^{l} he surrender'd his years lease, that is he promessd to doe It. I was to meet him the day following at Clanakilty to resolve. W. Freke took Kilman at 22^{l} per An^{o} for Capt Freke.[257] A[dam]. Clark took Derreduff[258] at 24 per An: & 22 fine.

~~12~~ 13

we left Rosse, went [to] T[homas]. Gookins, sent for Berry he Came not, we went to him at Clanakilty, he bogl'd I fell out with him, & so return'd to Rosse to settle that businesse. I overtook Bohone the Irish tennant Brought him to Rosse. sen J. & L. Hart to distraine the Cattle on Berrys Farme.

~~13~~ 14

the dstress Came early the mony paid & Engag'd for to be paid. Berry Comes, was as before. I offered him what I at first did, & he demanded, he refus'd It before Capt [Emanuel] Moore, he Bid him be gon.

~~14~~ 15

Phil[ip Ford]. went to Cork mett berry, he submitted & leaft himselfe at my mercy. I meet him at Banduff[259] paid him 6^{l} & 20^{s} over & above, & finish'd our difference he acknowledgd his fault & so W[illiam]. M[orris]. & J[ohn]. H[ull]. & I Came to Ross. W[illiam]. Mor[ris]. Returnd we stay'd.—

16

we went up to m^{t} salem.[260] lay there.

17

P[hilip]. F[ord]. returnd from Cork we had a very good meeting. severall straingers Came. Mar[tha]. Moore stay'd & supp'd at W[illiam].

M[orris's]. we return'd to Ross. lay there. received letters from my Fa[ther].

18

C[apt. Emanuel]. More. & we went to Imscone. spoak to Ruddock,[261] did nothing & so to Macroom[262] by E. Pouels Island. stay'd there that Night ~~saw the Castle~~ lay at Chris Goulde.

19

Stay'd there that day, by reason of raine. saw the Castle & gardens. was at the widdow goulds bespoak 7 & 3 gallons of usquebough.[263]

20

we Came to kinsale. left Capt [Emanuel] more at Ballengloss to returne home-wards. we were wett saw. T[homas]. G[ookin]. C[ousin Richard]. R[ooth]. C[ousin William]. P[enn]. &c:

21

I went to see old R[obert]. Southwell, stay'd 2 hours with him, he & his wife were Civil to me, found no Papers but Ruddocks. din'd at my lodging. came to Cork. saw friends lay at the Slow.–

22

went to the Prison again, & so Into Immokilly.

23

Capt [Thomas] Boles & his son [John] Came, & sign'd their lease.

24

I follow'd my Book of L[iberty]. of C[onscience]. J[ohn]. B[oles]. Came heither.

25

I went to Ladys Bridge[264]. Coll. [Roger] osb[orne]. & M[aj. Andrew]. woodlif Came & took their leases 2 to osb. 1. for himselfe & 1. for [Francis] Smith. & woodly one for himselfe; went to [John] Rous gave order that he & [John] walkham should Come on the 27th Instant.

26

~~I went in wth my book. Coll P. & Gratricks came hether. I went to Ballicrenan, saw Coll. F: Gerald. G. F. Gerald. Sr. F. Hanly. &c:~~ P[hilip]. F[ord]. went to Cork. J[ohn]. B[oles]. Came. Joshua Mantle & his wife, I follow'd my Book.

27

I went to Ballecrenan J[ohn] Boles wth me. Call'd at Coll. F[itz]. Geralds & G[arrett]. F[itz]. Geralds, at ladys Bridge & saw sr F. Hanly. I Could doe little wth [Roger] osb[orne]. about C[apt. Richard]. Bents businesse.

28

v. Gratricks,[265] Coll. [Robert] P[haire]. &c: din'd here. Capt [John] Rous, & Let: Walkam[266] I ended wth Rous. at 33l per Ano dismist Joshua Mantle. Phillip [Ford] Came from Cork. & ald. Langer[267] lay here.

29

I went to meet Coll. [Roger] osb[orne]. at Curabby. Concluded on nothing, he said It was In agitation since the last 6th mo: call'd August. J[ohn]. Bo[les]. was with me. I went thence to Capt [Thomas] Boles his Barne & so to Coll. [Robert] Phairs where I dined.–

30

Will[iam] Freak Came hither. P[hilip Ford]. went to Cork. James Gold & tho[mas] Franck[land]. Came for a surcease of the Arrest. stay'd that night.

3d Mo:–[May] 1

they went to Cork. ~~I proceeded to my businesse.~~ [Michael] Gale struck up. & Concluded.

2

P[hilip Ford]. Came home, went with me to Inch & Walter Croker took possession. returned by Cloyn. there din'd & so home.

3

the Irish Inhabitants Came, they had their houses & gardens as before. two were maid serjeants to keep the Grass &c: Croning & Peirce. J[ohn]. Walk[ham]. Came. Tho[mas]. Franck[land]. & his son. I bought his sons hors. gave one ginny of earnest for 11. Sr. F. Hanly. & G[arrett]. F[itz]. Gerald Came the last had his lease. they sup'd & so returned.

4

Capt [John] Walkham went with me & P[hilip]. F[ord]. to Talloe, mett Coll: [Roger] osb[orne]. but not the Earle of Barri[more]. from thence we went to sr Boyl Maynards.[268] so to Walt[er]: Crokers. there the Lord Broghill mett us, went wth him to Castle Lyons. lay there.

5

I was at the Castle, I spoak wth the lord shannon, & Lord Barrimore. & his lady. did my businesse as well as I could & so return'd to Capt. [Richard] Bents. Capt. [John] walkham went to Aghaddagh. I writt away to castle Lyons to the Ld. B[arrymore]. & the Ld shann[on]: ~~receiv'd I~~

6 ~~7~~

receiv'd letters from the lord shannon & Ld. Barr[ymore]: stay'd at Capt. [Richard] Bents—w[alter]. croker went away.

~~7~~

~~w. croker went away~~ I made the stepps into the private walk. P[hilip Ford]. & I had som words.

7 ~~8~~

P[hilip Ford]. went to Cork. [Thomas] Franckland Came not. I injoy the lord that night.

~~9~~ 8

I injoy'd the lord that day. J[ohn]. P[enington]. & I waited in my chamber together I went to Capt [Thomas] Boles. had w: R. H. G. & J. O.

+ 9

P[hilip]. F[ord]. came from Cork. we went to [John] Rous, ended with him. had his security of 30 Beast. & 2 leases for the payment of 43l 10s—returnd to Cap. [Richard] Bents meet Tho[mas]: Mitchells & J. Haman.[269]

10

we Came to Cork, I writt to B[arrymore?]. to the Ld. shan[non]. to my Dr. B. 2[270] to the C. of Clan.[271] to E[lizabeth]. B[ailey]. to T. L. To T[homas]. E[llwood]. &c: P[hilip]. F[ord]. went Post to Dub[lin]. I saw Capt [Emanuel] Moore.–

11

we had a precious meting, P[hilip]. D[ymond]. S[usanna]. M[itchell]. G[eorge]. W[ebber]. W[illiam]. H[awkins]. J[ohn]. H[ull or Haman]. & my selfe spoak. I Prayd.

12

we went to Prison, stay'd mostly wth friends, J[ames]. Gold. & J[ohn]. B[oles] ~~spoke~~ were. here. I lay at Prison.

13

I stay'd the morning at T[homas]. Cooks about businesse went to Prison at night, spoak a fwe words. lay at home. I was with the Mayor about my books, he abus'd me with names, as, Cokscome, Jackanapes, fellow, foole &c.[272]

14

I writt by Capt. [Emanuel] more to the Provost & Burgesses of Bandon In answear to the Priest. I went to see friends. lay at Prison all night. disputed wth the collector.

15

we had A good meeting we were disturb'd. J[ohn]. H[ull]. & 3 more were stop'd they mist me, though they saw me, & Came for me. I Came home, I spoak twice.

16

went to Friends, sent a letter to charlevil. disputed wth Alder. Coult & Dunscum.[273] return'd to my lodgeing at tho[mas]: Cooks.

17

I was at Prison al day. We drew up A Paper of Friends sufferings to be sent for Dublin. I receiv'd an expresse from C[ousin William]. C[rispin].

18

we went to Kinsale. lay at the Fort; [illegible deletion]

19

wth old R[obert]. S[outhwell].—disputed wth him. ended wth C[ousin Ensign William]. Penn. din'd wth my C[ousin Richard]. Rooth, disputed much at table. return'd to Cork. Phillip [Ford] Came from Dublin nothing done. lay at T[homas]. C[ook's].

20.

I receiv'd A Packet from the Ld. Bryan from Charlevill, the Mayor upon a letter to him return'd the Books.[274] we went to meting. lay at T[homas]. Cooks.

21

we went Into the county at C[aptain Richard]. B[ent's]. fix'd T[homas]. Fr[anckland's]. leases & sign'd Jo[hn]: Boleses. writt to the tennants.

22

Jo: ~~P.~~ Boles Came to se us; we stay'd there.
~~they saw me, & Came for me. I spoak twice. I came to my lodging. disputed~~

~~16~~

~~I went to Prison, stay'd with friends till night. disputed much with~~[275]

23.

Capt. [Michael] Gaile has his lease finish'd. Cl. [Robert] Ph[aire]. came & his wife to see us.

24

Jo[hn]: Rous Came about his bond we ended the scruple. we came to Cork. saw friends, lay at T[homas]. Cooks, disputed wth a Popish Coll.–

25

I was at prison for the most part that day.

26

the Tennants came to town. sign'd G. Bale. leases. D[esmond]. Crow[ley]. lease, Lt. [Edward] Clarke, J[ohn]. South[well]. 2 of Adam Clarke. & Capt [John] Freke.

27

I writt to W[illiam]. Mor[ris]. I gave teig. oHeay a note for 4^{l} per An^{o} & young T. oHeay, fourty shillings. I receiv'd A statute staple[276] from Jeans Gold. for to secure a rent charge of 20 per An^{o}
sign'd Walt[er]. Harrises lease & James Martins: did much other business. went to Prison, & so to my lodgeing. & about 12 at night took Post for Dublin. gott to Talloe.

28

gott to clonmell. rid that night to Bennetts Bridge.[277]

29

gott to Carloe, & thence to Kilkullin,[278] & so to Dublin by Break of day following. being the

30.

Tho: Fearon[279] & R[obert]. Tur[ner]. Came to see me. — ~~nothing done~~ An order obtain'd, but to be on bayle not Excepted.[280]

31

I writt to the Ld. Lt.[281] & s^{r} Ellis Leighton the secretary[282] to have admission to the Ld. Lt. It was promess'd next day. visitted friends; I also writt to the chanceller.[283]

1. 4th mo.–[June]

I was with the chanceller, discours'd wth him. much promiss'd I was with the Ld. Lt. Mett the Earle of Arran there, I had kind admission. he promess'd me faire, we were Call'd Into the Councill, the Ld. Arr came for me, haveing first carry'd in our Papers. — an Order of reference was granted to severall to enquire about Friends sufferings.

2

I was with the Ld. Arran. we went to the meeting had A good one.

3

we went again to councill, I was with with the Ld. Arran at the Red house, his Coach brought me home. An order was granted for the release of Marys Borrough friends.–

4

the Ld. Arran, Ld. shannon, Ld. Kingston, Maj. Fairfax,[284] Buckly,[285] Lesson,[286] Sheifeild[287] &c. din'd with me.[288]
I writt for England to o. b. F.[289]

5

we had a large but hard meeting being the 1st day. Severall great ones, the Countess of Mt Allexander[290] & of Clancarthy, the lady harvy, &c: & gods powr was over them all. & they reach'd. had an other at my lodging Tho[mas]. Feoron & I spoak

6.

I was with the chanceller, also with the Ld. off Arran, & the Ld. Lt. in his closet alone. he promessed to release our friends & did so by order of Councill In the afternoone; my Fa[ther's]. businesse is also done.–

7

I was with the Ld. Shannon. & Sr St Jo[hn]: Bro[derick]: they eat with me

8.

I was at Councill, we obtained An answear, but [Matthew] Barry was base to us. the Ld: shannon went to take the Air, sup'd wth me.

9

I was at the meeting spoak there. we returned. I was wth the Ld shannon

10

I was with the Ld: Lt: [deleted illegible interlineation] shannon also at Councill. we were nothing better.

11

Tho: Feoran & I was together; I writt to my o. d. F. 2.[291]

12

we went to meeting the Ld. shan[non]: was with me at sup.

13

I was with the chanceller & the L[or]d. Ar[ran]: gave him Jo[hn]: hulls letter. We had an order for J[ohn]. H[ull]. at Coun[cil]. we waited there the L[or]d. shan[non]: was with me at sup.

14

the Jesuit would not meet me according to Promesse. the Ld. shannon & I was together.

15

~~we were~~ I was at the ~~chancellers, gave~~ ld. shannons. I went to the Councill I was Call'd In. heard, we obtain'd an order for the release of the remaining nine. also for J[ohn]. hull. — I gave the chanceller my letter. din'd at the {lady clanC[arty's].} the Ld. shannon sup'd with me.

16

I was at the Ld shan[non]. saw the Ear^{l} off ClanC[arty].[292] Ld. shan[non]. [Sir St. John] Bro[derick]. & his wife din'd with me. Phillip went to Cork with the orders;

17

I was wth the Ld. shan[non]. disputed there. din'd at home. he Came & [Sir St. John] Bro[derick]. after diner. was wth Coll. [Robert] shap[cote]. & Gov. stephens.[293] sup'd at home. visitted by Tho[mas]. Fearon. & Ab. Fuller.[294]

18

I was wth the Ld. shannon. also wth Coll. [Robert] shapcote & G[overnor Sir John]. stephens nothing yet done about the letters. din'd & sup'd at home.

19

we went to meeting, Tho[mas]: Fearon spoak 2. I. 2. two other friends once, apeece. return'd sup'd, & mett again at the old meeting house C. Bukly run the meeting.

20

I was wth the Ld. shan[non]. also wth old j^{d} Bouls din'd & sup'd at home. I was wth the Ld. Ranelaigh.[295]

21

I was at the meeting of Men-friends. we order'd severall businesses.

22

the Ld. shan[non]. & Mazereen[296] was with me.

23

I was sent for to the Lady Mt Allex[ander]. I disputed with the Papists, manifested their great folly. went home so to T[homas]. F[earon's]. to supper & so to the Ld. shan[non].

24

I was at home. I saw T[homas]. F[earon]. heard from P[hilip Ford]. from Cork receiv'd my B[ook]. off L[iberty of]. C[onscience].

25

I went in Coach to Ballymorriceushie[297] wth T[homas]. F[earon]. ~~he~~ Phi[lip Ford] & J[ohn]. P[enington]. came to town.

26

we had a good meeting there being the first returned at night. sup'd at home. receiv'd [a] L[etter]. from my o. b. F.[298] S[usanna]. M[itchell?]. & E[lizabeth]. B[ailey]

27

was at the Councill, gave two addresses one for C[ork]. & one for M[aryborrough]. one to the Ld. R[aneleigh]. & one to the Ld A[rran]. an order to fetch up F[riends]: by A pursuvant.[299]

28

we were at A meeting W[illiam]. E[dmondson]. judge. M. & T[homas]. F[earon]. but it disgusted F[rien]ds

29

I was wth the Ld. ~~sha~~ Lt he was kind. wth the Ld Ar[ran]. gave him a horse. with the chan[cellor]: the Ld. shan[non]. &c: dined wth the L[ady]. Mt. Alexander.

30

we went to meeting, Meet S[olomon]. E[ccles]. & W. S.[300] T[homas]. F[earon]. S[olomon]. E[ccles]. & W[illiam]. S[teele]. spoak. sup'd at my lodging.

31 [1 July]

I was wth Mazereen. dined wth M. Forster.[301] S[olomon]. E[ccles]. was at Councill obtain'd an order.[302]

AD. Penn Papers, HSP. (*Micro.* 1:144).

1. Ann Merrick (d. 1703) of Watford, Herts., a widow, had petitioned against tithes in 1659. She was one of two Friends who cared for Quakers imprisoned in Bridewell. Index to Female Petitioners Against Tithes, GSP.

2. Probably John Giggour or Jiggour (d. 1693), a Quaker, and Gulielma Springett's servant. Bucks. Quaker Register, GSP. John Gay could be intended, however. See n. 58.

3. Isaac Penington, then living in Berrie House, Amersham, Bucks. Maria Webb, *The Penns and Peningtons*, p. 214.

4. About 12 miles from Amersham, on the Thames in Berks.

5. John Giggour?

6. A hamlet in the parish of Penn, Bucks., 3 miles west of Amersham. *VCH, Buckinghamshire*, 3:235-36.

7. Probably either Sarah or Samuel Hersent, Quakers and domestic servants, first of Gulielma Springett and then of the Penns. Mortimer, *Minute Book of the Men's Meeting . . . Bristol*, p. 195. Both Sarah and Samuel appear frequently in the Ford Accounts, docs. 139-50.

8. William Russell's farm at Jordans in Chalfont St. Giles, Bucks., was frequently used for early Friends meetings. The meetinghouse at Jordans where WP and his family are buried is on this site.

9. Philip Ford (c. 1631-1702) of Aylesbury, Bucks., had been imprisoned with Isaac Penington in 1665 for refusing to take the oath. He seems to have been a shopkeeper, perhaps a clothier, in London about 1656, but his business did not prosper, and WP employed him in 1669 as his steward for £40 per year. After his return from Ireland he opened a shop at the sign of the Hood and Scarf in Mary le Bow Lane, London. His business accounts with WP in 1672-1674 and 1677-1680 are printed as docs. 139-50. He continued to serve as WP's business manager in the 1680s. By this point, by Ford's reckoning, WP owed him several thousand pounds. During the 1690s, Ford entered into a series of financial disputes with other Friends, but refused to submit to the arbitration of the meeting. About the same time, he began pressing WP for

payment of debts, which led to his claim to own all of Pennsylvania. After his death, his wife Bridget sued WP and eventually won her case against him.

10. John Penington (1655-1710), son of Isaac Penington and half-brother of Gulielma Springett. After accompanying WP to Ireland in 1669-1670, he attended Christopher Taylor's Quaker boarding school. He later corresponded in Latin with William Sewel, the Quaker historian of Amsterdam, published tracts attacking William Rogers and George Keith, and staged a public debate in 1696 with Keith. *DNB*.

11. Thomas Ellwood (1639-1713), Quaker and friend of John Milton, was Latin tutor to the younger Penington children in Amersham. On 28 Oct. 1669 he married Mary Ellis, a woman sixteen years his senior. Several times arrested, he devoted much of his life to combating internal division within Quakerism and to defending Friends against other dissenters, taking an active role in debating Jeremy Ives, Thomas Hicks, and George Keith. *DNB*.

12. At least three Quakers were then imprisoned in Reading, and would continue in jail until Charles II's pardon in 1672. Besse, 1:26-28.

13. Newbury, Berks., is about 17 miles west of Reading.

14. Malmesbury, Wilts., about 40 miles west of Newbury.

15. The largest town in Somerset, about 23 miles southwest of Malmesbury.

16. Chippenham, Wilts., about 9 miles south of Malmesbury. This is the more direct route to Bristol.

17. Dennis Hollister (d. 1676), a grocer in High Street, Bristol, was a member of parliament for Somerset in 1653 and was converted to Quakerism in 1654. His granddaughter was Hannah Callowhill, WP's second wife. Fox, 2:284; Mortimer, *Minute Book of the Men's Meeting . . . Bristol*, p. 204.

18. George Fox (1624-1691), founder of the Society of Friends, began preaching in 1648, was frequently imprisoned thereafter, and made numerous missionary trips throughout the British Isles, the West Indies, and British North America. As succeeding references in this volume show, WP worked closely with Fox from 1669 on.

19. Margaret Askew Fell Fox (1614-1702), the "nursing mother" of the Quakers. She met George Fox in 1652, and her home, Swarthmoor Hall, soon became a center of Quaker activity. Her first husband Thomas Fell (1599-1658) never became a Quaker. They had seven daughters and one son. The daughters were Quakers; the son was not. For her marriage to Fox, see n. 24. *DNB;* Isabel Ross, *Margaret Fell: Mother of Quakerism* (London, 1949).

20. William Yeamans (1639-1674), a Bristol merchant and Friend, married Isabel, daughter of Thomas and Margaret Fell, in 1664. After her first husband's death, Isabel Yeamans (c. 1637-1704) became an active missionary, traveling with WP to Holland in 1677. She later married Abraham Morrice (d. 1704). Ross, *Margaret Fell*, p. 178; Mortimer, *Minute Book of the Men's Meeting . . . Bristol*, p. 222.

21. Thomas Bisse, a Bristol merchant and Quaker, had married Anne Hersent (d. 1666), Gulielma Springett's maid. Mortimer, *Minute Book of the Men's Meeting . . . Bristol*, p. 195.

22. Leonard Fell (1624-1699), a public Friend, was not related to Thomas and Margaret Fell, but was a retainer in their household. He was convinced in 1652 and traveled frequently with George Fox or Margaret Fell. Fox, 1:409; Ross, *Margaret Fell*, p. 75.

23. Francis Rogers (d. 1694), a Bristol merchant and Friend with interests in co. Cork. His first wife was Elizabeth Erbury, daughter of a very early Friend of the same name in Cork. Mortimer, *Minute Book of the Men's Meeting . . . Bristol*, p. 213.

24. The marriage of George Fox and Margaret Fell was published in the Bristol Men's Meeting on 18 Oct., again at a joint men's and women's meeting on 21 Oct., and at a public meeting on 22 Oct. The marriage took place on 27 Oct. WP spoke at the meetings of 18 and 22 Oct. His testimony is recorded in Port. 10.53, FLL (not filmed).

25. King Road, or Kingsroad, is an anchorage on the Bristol Channel.

26. Either Thomas Salthouse (1630-1691), a Quaker preacher who signed the Fox/Fell marriage certificate, or Thomas Speed (d. 1703), a Bristol Quaker and merchant whose first wife was William Yeamans' widowed mother. *DNB;* Mortimer, *Minute Book of the Men's Meeting . . . Bristol*, pp. 214, 216.

27. Thomas Lower (1633-1720), an early convert to Quakerism, married Mary Fell, Margaret's daughter, in 1668. Lower was imprisoned frequently, and spent most of the years 1673-1686 in jail. *DNB*.

28. Charles Harford (1631-1709), an active Bristol Friend, was a soapmaker and later a merchant. He was a frequent sufferer and served on several disciplinary committees. Mortimer, *Minute Book of the Men's Meeting . . . Bristol,* p. 202.

29. William Rogers (d. 1711), brother of Francis Rogers, a freeman and merchant of Bristol, was a frequent sufferer. In the Wilkinson-Story controversy of 1675-1679, he strongly opposed Fox and WP. See doc. 102, n. 22; and doc. 124. Mortimer, *Minute Book of the Men's Meeting . . . Bristol,* pp. 21, 214.

30. Seven leagues beyond Combe on the Cornish coast.

31. Thomas Mitchell (d. 1691), a merchant, and his wife Susanna (d. 1672), were early Cork Friends. Thomas Mitchell had been arrested with WP at Cork in Nov. 1667. He died in London.

32. Samuel Thornton (d. 1685), a Friend of Hampsthwaite, Yorks., was frequently imprisoned. When he visited Ireland in 1669, he was arrested again; at a Friends' meeting held in his prison cell, eighty Quakers were locked in and denied food and drink for twenty-four hours, except for what they could get through a grate. Yorks. Quaker Register, GSP; C. G. Crump, ed., *The History of the Life of Thomas Ellwood* (New York, 1900), p. 15.

33. Elizabeth Pike (c. 1635-1688), widow of Richard Pike (c. 1627-1668), was convinced in Ireland in 1655. Her husband, a shopkeeper in Cork, died in prison in Cork in 1668; Elizabeth then married Andrew Vivers in Cork in 1670.

34. William Morris (c. 1620-1680), a former Baptist and a captain in the army, was convinced and turned out of his military office in 1656. He lived near Ross Carbery, and had been imprisoned for appearing in court with his hat on.

35. Matthew Deane, a violent persecutor of Friends.

36. Christopher Pennock (d. 1701), a Cork Friend, is mentioned in Besse as early as 1660. He immigrated to Pennsylvania, where he died. Besse, 2:467, 475, 478.

37. Francis Smith, one of WP's tenants, was a justice of the peace for Cork in 1671.

38. John Boles (d. 1702) of Kilbrie, later of Inch, co. Cork, was the son of Captain Thomas Boles, one of Sir William's largest renters.

39. WP was alerting his father's tenants in the baronies of Imokilly, between Youghal Bay and Cork Harbor, and Ibaune and Barryroe, southwest of Clonakilty.

40. Possibly Gerard Roberts.

41. Philip Dymond (1625-1679), a Cork merchant, was born in Devon and went to Ireland as a soldier under Cromwell. He was convinced in 1655 and suffered frequently thereafter. In 1667 he was imprisoned with WP (see doc. 18). By 1670 he was one of the wealthiest Quakers in Cork.

42. Kilworth, in northeastern Cork near the Tipperary border. WP was travelling from Cork to Dublin.

43. Clogheen, in southern Tipperary.

44. William Lawford or Laford (d. 1674) of Ballyboy, near Clogheen.

45. John Fennell (1626-1706), a Friend, was born in Wilts. and lived at Kilcommonbeg near Clogheen.

46. Cashel, Tipperary, was formerly the seat of the kings of Munster.

47. The abbey of Holy Cross, seven miles from Cashel on the Suir, contained a piece of the True Cross given by Pope Pascall II in 1110.

48. WP may mean Cassestown, in the parish of Thurles. Thurles was the site of a memorable routing of the English and their allies the Danes by the Irish under O'Brien of Thomond in the tenth century. "Fitz-Pats," in WP's usage, appears to be a synonym for "Irish."

49. Thurles, Tipperary, gives the secondary title of Viscount Thurles to the Butler family, earls and dukes of Ormonde.

50. James Hutchinson (d. 1689), a Friend, lived at Knockballymeager in northern Tipperary.

51. Rosenallis, in northern co. Leix.

52. Mountrath, Leix, where the Coote family, earls of Mountrath, manufactured iron until the local supply of firewood gave out.

53. William Edmondson (1627-1712), the first and most influential Quaker in Ireland. At the time of WP's visit, Edmondson was engaged in a long battle with the Anglican vicar at Rosenallis over payment of tithes. In 1671 he traveled to America with Fox. For other aspects of his long and important career, see *DNB*.

54. Leinster province, the easternmost in Ireland, contains twelve counties: Carlow, Dublin, Kildare, Kilkenny, Leix (Queen's), Longford, Louth, Meath, Offaly (King's), Westmeath, Wexford, and Wicklow. General Meetings of the Leinster Friends were held every six weeks.

55. Mountmellick, Leix, was an important center of Quakerism in Ireland and the scene of much persecution.

56. Kildare, co. Kildare, about 28 miles southwest of Dublin.

57. Naas, Kildare, about 15 miles southwest of Dublin.

58. John Gay (d. 1692) of Dublin, a former Cromwellian adventurer in Ireland, was a commissioner for settling lands in Ireland in 1654. In 1668 he was made chief marshall of the Four Courts in Ireland. In 1687 he was admonished for taking an oath, but he died a Quaker. His wife Ann (d. 1694), mentioned on 7 Nov., was also a Friend. They had four surviving children, three sons and one daughter.

59. Mary Canning, daughter of John and Frances Stepney and wife of George Canning, died four days later, on 6 Nov., at the age of twenty. According to the Dublin Quaker Register (ACM, vol. 142), "Many and Teadious were her Exersises & Tribulations for the Truth Sake, Both from her Father and From her husband, Whose Continued Cruelty Shortened her dayes." She was convinced four years before her death.

60. Frances Stepney (d. 1707), mother of Mary Canning, was a Friend, unlike her husband John.

61. That is, at John Gay's house in George's Lane.

62. George Gregson (d. 1690), a merchant, was born a Roman Catholic, but became one of the leading Friends in Ireland. He lived at Lisburn, Antrim, but travelled in Ireland and in England.

63. The Irish Quakers held a national meeting every six months. Fox attended the previous one in the summer of 1669.

64. See doc. 36.

65. Samuel Claridge (1631-post 1714) of Dublin, a merchant, came to Ireland with Cromwell's army in 1651. He was convinced about 1658, but was disowned in 1677 by the National Meeting for immorality. He later became an alderman of Dublin.

66. John Robartes (1606-1685), who fought in the Civil War with Sir William Springett and advocated toleration for dissenters in the 1660s, was Lord Lieutenant from Sept. 1669 to Apr. 1670. Hodgkin, *Gulielma*, p. 13.

67. Anthony Sharp (1642-1706), a merchant and clothier with legal training, was one of the most prominent Friends in Dublin, Master of the Weavers' Guild and later an alderman. He invested heavily in New Jersey lands, and both his son and nephew immigrated there. Albert Cook Myers, *Immigration of the Irish Quakers into Pennsylvania* (Swarthmore, Pa., 1902), pp. 383-85.

68. John Stepney, former sovereign of Kinsale and later a Commissioner of the Treasury for Ireland. See n. 59.

69. Possibly Joseph Deane (d. 1694), a shearman and a Dublin Friend.

70. Elizabeth Gardiner (c. 1606-1674) was a widow in 1669. One of the first convinced in Ireland, she used her house to entertain Quakers.

71. Sir George Ascue or Ascough, former colleague of WP's father, held several naval commands under Charles I and Cromwell, and received a pension of £300 a year in Ireland. At the Restoration he was appointed commissioner of the navy, and served as rear admiral in the Second Dutch War. He was captured by the Dutch and held until Oct. 1667; upon his release he retired to Ireland. Charnock, *Biographia Navalis*, 1:89-93.

72. Possibly Philip Packer or Parker, who was a captain in Munster in 1649.

73. T. Fouls is not identified; from WP's description, he held eccentric theological views and was eager to debate adversaries. Colonel Richard Lawrence (d. 1691), an upholsterer, operated a subsidized linen factory at Chapelizod, a village on the Liffey, a few miles west of Dublin.

74. Figured work on fabric. *OED*.

75. Possibly Margaret Jones (d. 1696), wife of William, early Dublin Friends, though her views expressed here do not seem Quakerly.

76. Daniel Rolls, a physician, lived in Dirty Butter Lane, Dublin.

77. ACM suggests that Captain Sir Richard Kyrle, soldier under Cromwell and assessor for claims under the Act of Settlement, is intended. Kyrle was later governor

of South Carolina. Caroline T. Moore and Agatha Simmons, *Abstracts of the Wills of the State of South Carolina, 1670-1740* (Columbia, S. C., 1960), p. 5.

78. Colonel Robert Shapcott, a lawyer, had been implicated in a plot to seize Dublin Castle in 1663. He was imprisoned, but received a royal pardon in 1664.

79. Apparently Captain Peter Wallis was again making claims on the Penn estate, hence WP's visit to assessor Kyrle and lawyer Shapcott. See doc. 11.

80. Snuffers.

81. Henry Moore (d. 1676), Earl of Drogheda, was privy councilor for Ireland. *Peerage,* 4:463.

82. Probably Elizabeth Jephson. See docs. 42 and 43.

83. Elizabeth Bowman. See doc. 42.

84. George Webber (d. 1674), Cork Friend, was convinced in 1655 and suffered frequently.

85. Probably William Bird of Dublin (d. 1681). See doc. 137.

86. Sir William Springett, Gulielma's father, inherited from his uncle Sir Edward Partridge half of Partridge's £600 adventure in Irish land. In 1653 and 1654 the rights in this land were confirmed to Gulielma as her father's sole heir, and with several others from Sussex and Kent she drew land in the southwest quarter of the barony of Deece, co. Meath. The group stated that they wanted to hold their land, worth in all £2300, in one lot, and chose Theobald Randell, citizen and grocer of London, to act for them. See 20 Nov. *CSPI, 1642-1659,* pp. 73, 74, 343; *CSPI, 1647-1660,* pp. 399, 560.

87. Wentworth Dillon (c. 1633-1685), Earl of Roscommon, was restored to his family's estates by Charles II. He was a favorite of the Duke of York, who made him captain of a band of gentleman pensioners. Though he spent most of his life in England, in 1669 he was in Ireland securing his estates.

88. Probably Richard, Lord Jones of Nevan (1641-1712). A former pupil of John Milton, in 1669 Jones was Chancellor of the Exchequer for Ireland. In 1670, on the death of his father, he became Viscount Ranelagh; in 1677 he was created Earl of Ranelagh. WP encounters him again, on 20 June 1670. *Peerage,*10:731-33.

89. Probably Colonel Gilbert Talbot, a Catholic and royalist, who was Orrery and Roscommon's brother-in-law and Lord Jones' uncle by marriage. Edward MacLysaght, *Calendar of the Orrery Papers* (Dublin, 1941), p. 182; Peerage, 3:420; *CSPI, 1669-1670,* pp. 313, 480.

90. Probably Lancelot Stepney, captain of a militia company at Kinsale.

91. John Burnyeat.

92. Joseph Stepney (d. 1693) was a merchant in Dublin.

93. John King (d. 1676), Baron Kingston, a former Cromwellian who helped restore the monarchy, was a privy councilor for Ireland and one of the commissioners of the Court of Claims. In 1669 he was joint governor of Connaught with Lord Berkeley. *Peerage,* 7:297.

94. Matthew Barry (d. 1695) in 1669 was deputy clerk of the Irish Privy Council. He had been secretary to the commissioners of the Court of Claims. *CSPI, 1666-1669,* pp. 468, 737.

95. Probably the William Fitzgerald who was Clerk of the Crown Peace, Prothonotary and Assize for Cork and Waterford. *CSPI, 1666-1669,* p. 633.

96. Robert Fitzgerald, son of the sixteenth earl of Kildare, was controller of the musters and cheques of the army and a privy councilor.

97. Robert Sandys (d. 1684) was colonel of a company of foot at Kinsale. MacLysaght, *Orrery Papers,* p. 100; *CSPI,1669-1670,* p. 388.

98. Alexander Parker (1628-1689), well-traveled Quaker missionary. *DNB;* Fox, 1:427. In 1672 WP traveled with Parker in Kent and Sussex; see doc. 70.

99. Probably Toby Bonnell, brother of Samuel Bonnell (d. 1662), who was appointed accountant-general in Ireland at the Restoration. Samuel Bonnell's patent as accountant-general passed to his pietistic son James (1653-1699) at his death, but in 1669 James Bonnell was pursuing his education in England. Toby Bonnell, James' uncle, seems to have acted as his deputy. *DNB;* C. Litton Falkiner, "Some Letters of Toby and James Bonnell," *English Historical Review,* 19:122-25.

100. John Robartes.

101. Sir Arthur Forbes (1623-1696), a Presbyterian and a royalist during the Commonwealth, was made a commissioner of the Court of Claims at the Restoration,

and in 1670 a privy councilor for Ireland. James II created him Earl of Granard. *DNB.*

102. Sir Theophilus Jones (d. 1685), originally a Cromwellian, was appointed scoutmaster general for life and privy councilor in 1661. As a member of the Restoration parliament, he had moved a grant of £30,000 to Ormonde on his becoming lord lieutenant. *DNB.*

103. Dr. Abraham Yarner (d. 1677), later knighted, was muster master general of the forces in Ireland, and fellow of the College of Physicians in Dublin.

104. Lane and Jones were privy councilors; Forbes would not become one until 1670.

105. A "cobb" was the Irish name for a Spanish piece of eight. *OED.*

106. Agreed to payment by installments. *OED.* The context is unclear, but see 25 Nov.

107. Probably Sir John Temple the younger (1632-1704), soliciter general of Ireland and one of the commissioners for executing the Act of Settlement, but possibly his father Sir John Temple (1600-1677), who was master of the rolls in Ireland. *DNB.*

108. Thomas Gookin, merchant and burgess of Kinsale and later sovereign of Clonakilty. *DNB.*

109. Colonel Robert Phaire (c. 1619-1682), of Cromwell's army in Ireland, and a regicide, was arrested in Cork in 1660, transported to London, and imprisoned in the Tower until 1662. In 1666 he was implicated in a plot to seize Dublin Castle, but was not prosecuted. In the 1650s he had attended Quaker meetings, but about 1660 became a Muggletonian. See W. H. Weply, "Colonel Robert Phaire, 'Regicide,' " *Journal of the Cork Historical and Archaeological Society,* 2d ser., 29:76-80; 30:20-26.

110. Dr. Jeremie Hall (d. 1689), formerly of Boothtown, Yorks., treated Orrery and other officials. MacLysaght, *Orrery Papers.*

111. Sir St. John Broderick (1627-1711) moved to Ireland during the Commonwealth and was knighted and made provost marshal of Munster at the Restoration. Under the Act of Settlement, he obtained large tracts of land in Cork near those of Admiral Penn.

112. See doc. 110 and 25 Mar. 1670.

113. A pier or breakwater. *OED.*

114. Sir Amos Meredith, of Marston, Devon, was a commissioner of appeals under the Act of Settlement. He died 5 Dec. 1669.

115. Mathias Foster, John Savage, William Steele, William Cleaton, John Windor, Dennis Rochford, Joseph Sleigh, and William Maine had been imprisoned for five weeks, "in which time they were indicted at the King's Bench, for being at an unlawful Assembly; but not being found by the Grand Jury, they were discharged by the Court."

116. Perhaps the Quaker John Scott, who died in Dublin in 1696.

117. Robert Turner (1635-1700), one of the earliest Friends in Ireland. In 1677 he became interested in colonization, and with other Friends acquired one whole share in West Jersey. In 1681, with WP and others, he purchased East Jersey from Sir George Carteret's estate, purchased 5000 acres in Pennsylvania, and subscribed £500 worth of stock in the Free Society of Traders. In 1683 he moved to Pennsyvlania, where he held several high public offices. Myers, *Immigration of the Irish Quakers,* pp. 257-62.

118. William Maine (c. 1637-1673), a native of Middlesex, went to Ireland in 1657. His wife was Elizabeth Mason, who married John Burnyeat after his death.

119. Edward Burrough (1634-1662), one of Fox's first converts, wrote more than twenty tracts. *DNB.*

120. Ambrose Rigge (c. 1635-1705) wrote numerous epistles and tracts. His *Good Old Way and Truth* was published in London in 1669. *DNB.*

121. John Perrot's *A Primer for Children* (1660, reprinted 1664) or William Smith's *A New Primer* (1663, reprinted 1668) may be intended.

122. The village of Rathcoole, co. Dublin, is about 10 miles southwest of Dublin. WP was returning to Cork to make leases with his tenants. His reckonings of distance on this trip appear to be in Irish miles, which are longer than English.

123. "Baited," or fed their horses. *OED.*

124. Blackrath, co. Kildare, is about twenty miles from Rathcoole, and Carlow, co. Carlow, is another sixteen miles beyond Blackrath.

125. John Chaffin (1607-1671) of Carlow was a Friend; because he had been a member of the Parliamentary army, he was sent as a prisoner to Ireland in 1662 and confined in Dublin Castle under Ormonde.

126. Castledermot is north of Carlow, not between Carlow and Kilkenny. Perhaps WP means Castlecomer, on one of the two routes from Carlow to Kilkenny.

127. Kilkenny, co. Kilkenny, closely identified with the Ormonde family.

128. Bartholemew Fowke (d. 1682) owned land in Tipperary and in Kilkenny. Foulkstown, co. Kilkenny, is about two miles south of Kilkenny.

129. Callan, co. Kilkenny.

130. Ninemilehouse is in Tipperary on the Kilkenny line.

131. John Mead was a merchant in Clonmel.

132. In 1650 the royalist garrison at Clonmel resisted Cromwell's army for two months, but eventually was forced to withdraw and the inhabitants surrendered.

133. Cappoquin, co. Waterford, on the Blackwater River.

134. A portmanteau is a leather case for carrying clothes and other goods on horseback. *OED.*

135. Sir Richard Boyle bought Lismore castle and manor from Sir Walter Raleigh.

136. In 1659 Tallow, co. Waterford, contained 44 English and 61 Irish, a greater proportion of English than in the surrounding countryside.

137. Captain Richard Bent (d. 1680) of Carrigacotta, now Castle Mary, just west of Cloyne in co. Cork, was an officer under Cromwell and received leases of land in 1659. He rented Lisally in Imokilly from Admiral Penn. His wife Mary, mentioned on 6 Dec., died in 1678; their daughters married Walter Croker and Andrew Ruddock.

138. The vale of Shanagarry, where the Penns had much of their Irish land, borders on Ballycotton Bay near the village of Shanagarry.

139. Captain Thomas Boles (c. 1608-1683) of Kilbrie, between Cloyne and Castlemartyr, helped to secure Cork for the Commonwealth in 1649. He leased Kilbrie, Sheanless, Carrigtohir, Teadbegg, Ballyvillin, and Ballinvohir (426 Irish acres) from Admiral Penn.

140. Robert Phaire in 1669 lived at Cahermone Castle, just east of Midleton. His wife Elizabeth (d. 1698), a Muggletonian, was the daughter of Sir Thomas Herbert, Charles I's faithful attendant in his last hours.

141. Captain Richard Rooth, called "cousin" by the Penns, had commanded the *Hound* during the Commonwealth and at the Restoration was made commander of the 100-gun *Dartmouth,* off the Irish coast. On 31 July 1669 he became governor of the fort at Kinsale, after Admiral Penn had relinquished this position because of his failing health. Later Rooth returned to active naval service. He was knighted in 1675. *CSPI, 1666-1669,* p. 764; Charnock, *Biographia Navalis,* 1:28-29.

142. Rev. Christopher Vowell (1640-1709) held several cures in Imokilly, and was chaplain at Charleville. Orrery considered him a lazy, drunken braggart. MacLysaght, *Orrery Papers,* pp. viii-ix.

143. Ensign Walter Croker, Richard Bent's son-in-law, lived at Lisnabrim, about two miles west of Tallow.

144. William Field and Richard Harvey were sheriffs of Cork in 1669. Probably WP was petitioning for relief for imprisoned Friends.

145. That is, at Captain Richard Bent's, now Castle Mary.

146. Colonel Roger Osborne (c. 1623-1680) held lands in Cork and in Tipperary.

147. Sargeant Samuel Rolle or Rolls (d. 1713) of Ballyfin, co. Cork, an Anglican, owned large tracts of land in Cork and leased Barries quarter, Ballinwillin, and Ballelowrace and Ballyroe, 172 acres in all, from Admiral Penn. In 1684 he purchased 5,000 acres in Pennsylvania.

148. Captain John Freke (d. 1688), a royalist, received several grants in Cork after the Restoration and rented Sleiveene, which later passed to Admiral Penn, from the crown.

149. Thomas Franckland (d. 1684), had leased Kilderrig (Coolederické) from the crown in 1659, but under the Act of Settlement the land was given to Admiral Penn, and apparently Franckland turned tenant. His son, mentioned on 3 May, was also named Thomas.

150. (Priest) John Mascall (d. 1701) held a number of parishes in the diocese of Cloyne, including Aghada and Inch.

151. Lisally was leased to Richard Bent; Ballinvillin and Ballinvohir to Thomas Boles. All three are within two miles southwest of Cloyne.

152. Francis Smith leased Knocknegeiragh and Knocknegappule from Admiral Penn. See also doc. 44.

153. Thomas Cook (d. 1706), a merchant and Quaker of Cork.

154. Captain John Wakeham or Walkham (d. 1715) of Aghada, an Anglican, had served under Robert Phaire in the Commonwealth army. He leased Curroghticloghy, Condon's acres, Ballycarrowny, Seskins, and Acredoan (295 acres total) in the parish of Aghada, and Fenore and Knocknagihy in Corkebeg parish (279 acres) from Admiral Penn. One other tract that he leased from Admiral Penn has not been identified. See 5 Jan. 1670.

155. Ballycrenane is on Ballycotton Bay, about three miles northeast of Shanagarry.

156. Major Andrew Woodley rented Inch and Doonepower (presently Powerhead) in Inch parish and Ballynatra in Corkebeg parish from Admiral Penn. He had to dispute Peter Wallis in order to get Inch. See 20 Jan. 1670.

157. Percy Smith of Ightermurragh (d. 1714), second son of Sir Percy Smith, grandson of the first earl of Cork, and brother of Mabel Tynte.

158. Christmas Day, when mince pies were served. *OED.*

159. George Bennett (c. 1628-1673), a Quaker, died in Kilgrohanemore parish, west of Cork city.

160. John Stubbs (c. 1618-1674), Quaker minister of northern England, was traveling in Ireland in 1669. Fox, 2:148; 1:418.

161. Mallow, co. Cork, about thirty miles north of Cork city.

162. Jacquet Playsted (d. 1684), widow of Thomas Playsted (d. 1662), a Cork merchant.

163. Captain Peter Wallis leased Shanagarry, 266 acres in Killeagh parish near Ballycotton Bay, from Admiral Penn. With nearby land which Wallis also rented from the Penns, Wallis' total acreage came to 1226, making him their largest tenant. Today one wall of the old manor house where Wallis lived and WP visited still stands. See doc. 11.

164. Major Jasper Farmer (c. 1623-1685) had been active in the army during the Commonwealth. In 1666 he was a member of the common council of Youghal. He purchased 5,000 acres in Pennsylvania and died on a voyage from Pennsylvania to Ireland.

165. Probably [Christopher Davenport], *An Explanation of the Roman Catholicks Belief* (1656), reprinted in 1670. *A Seasonable Caveat Against Popery* (1670) was WP's reply.

166. Youghal, about 25 miles east of Cork, on the seacoast.

167. Richard Hull (d. 1693) of Leamcon, co. Cork, a justice of common pleas knighted in 1678, married Elizabeth, daughter of Sir Henry Tynte.

168. Garrett Fitzgerald (d. 1689) was restored to his family's estate at Lisquinlan, co. Cork, in 1662. He also owned land near Corkebeg.

169. Captain Michael Gayle had served in Robert Phaire's regiment during the Commonwealth, and was implicated in the 1663 plot against Dublin Castle. He seems to have been a Muggletonian. Gayle rented Ballyronahane, Ballybraher, Coolenodigg, Carrigkilter, and Rathcully, 392 acres in the parishes of Cloyne, Killeagh, and Ballintemple, Imokilly, from Admiral Penn.

170. Probably Margaret Lowther, WP's sister. Frieze is coarse woolen cloth, especially that of Irish manufacture. *OED.*

171. Major John Love of Kinsale. See doc. 45.

172. The Knockmealdown Mountains are between Tallow and Clogheen.

173. Solomon Eccles (c. 1618-1683), Quaker minister, traveled widely in Ireland, the West Indies, and America. In Sept. 1669 he had run through Galway city naked with fire and brimstone on his head, denouncing Papists.

174. "J. B." is rubbed out in the original.

175. George Baker (1628-1703), a Quaker of Cashel, Tipperary, was born in Herts. and moved to Ireland in 1650.

176. Probably James Hutchinson.

177. A "stoned" animal, in contrast to a gelded one, has not been castrated. *OED.*

178. Probably not the Edward Laundy, Youghal merchant, mentioned on 9 Feb.

179. The seashore.

180. Lady Mabel Tynte, widow of Sir Henry Tynte and wife of Col. Roger Osborne; she continued to use her first husband's surname and title after her marriage

to Osborne. She had six daughters. One of them, Elizabeth Tynte, married Sir Richard Hull.

181. Probably John Phaire (d. 1677), Col. Robert Phaire's son.

182. Woodley disputed Peter Wallis' claim to the lease of Inch, and Wallis gave up the claim. See 21 Jan.

183. Sir William Penn held 236 acres at Clonmain, in Ightermurragh parish, a few miles from Shanagarry.

184. The Rev. John Webb (b. c. 1644) was chancellor of Cloyne and rector of Youghal and other parishes in the diocese of Cork and Ross.

185. This was a typical price for Admiral Penn's land in Imokilly. Michael Gayle, for example, rented 392 acres for £82 per year, or just over 4 s. per acre. Irish land sold for about £2 per acre, so WP received a ten percent return on his property. Marquis of Lansdowne, *The Petty Papers* (London, 1927), 2:109.

186. Captain Richard Smith rented Ballyhonick and Ballyline, 200 acres total, in Imokilly.

187. Joan Cook (c. 1640-1693), wife of Thomas Cook of Cork.

188. Carrigtohill is a village between Midleton and Cork.

189. George Gamble (d. 1694) of Cork, was convinced in 1655. His father-in-law, Robert Phaire, influenced him to become a Muggletonian, at least for a time. In 1668 he was arrested with WP at a Quaker meeting. In the same year, he purchased a small plot of ground in the south liberties of Cork from John Gallway for a burial place. Part was to be used for members of his family, and apparently the rest for the Quakers, but Gamble's flirtation with Muggleton seems to have put its status in question.

190. Lucretia Cook was the wife of Edward Cook of Bandon, cornet of Cromwell's troop of horse. Both she and her husband were Quakers, and both were frequently imprisoned and fined.

191. Captain Thomas Campion (d. 1699) was a Quaker who lived at Leitrim, near Kilworth.

192. Robert Cook (c. 1646-c. 1726) of Tallow, later a merchant, was a vegetarian who flirted with Quakerism and insisted on wearing only linen clothes. He was Thomas Cook of Cork's nephew. *DNB*.

193. Peter Cook, a clothier and Quaker of Tallow, was the brother of Thomas Cook of Cork and uncle of "linen" Robert Cook.

194. William Hawkins (c. 1619-1706), a Quaker of Cork.

195. Edward Landy (d. 1686) was a Youghal merchant who had joined the Quakers in the 1650s. Grubb suggests that Landy's elevation to freeman of Youghal in June 1669 and bailiff in Sept. caused the tension between him and WP.

196. Henry Fagiter (d. 1686) of Cork, later separated from the Quakers.

197. Richard Brocklesby (d. 1696), a clothier in Cork, was convinced in the 1650s.

198. Elizabeth Erbury (c. 1627-1687), the first convinced in Cork, was a widow and the mother-in-law of Francis Rogers. Her home was a center for visiting Friends and for Quaker meetings.

199. Probably William Prigg of Skibbereen, a Quaker.

200. WP was going to Ibaune and Barryroe in west Cork to make leases with his tenants there.

201. The provost of Bandon, on the Bandon river about fifteen miles inland from Kinsale, was John Poole. Peter Hewitt was vicar.

202. Major John Allen (d. 1692), a Quaker, lived near Bandon.

203. Skibbereen, west Cork, is about thirty miles southwest of Bandon on Baltimore Bay.

204. Paul Morris (d. 1673), brother of William Morris, lived at Ballylongner, near Ross Carbery. In 1669 he served as a guide to George Fox when Fox visited Friends in Ireland.

205. John Hull lived on Inishbeg, an island in Baltimore Bay about four miles southwest of Skibbereen.

206. Captain Emanuel Moore (1620-1692) of Ross Carbery, whom Orrery described as "a good soldier" and one of the "chief men" of west Cork, had been cornet of horse in the Irish wars of 1641. In the 1660s he was a justice of the peace and lieutenant of a troop of horse. Later he became a burgess of Clonakilty and sheriff of Cork. In 1681 he was created a baronet. He appears to have leased land from Admiral

Penn in west Cork. Though Moore was not a Quaker, his wife and children attended Friends meetings, and WP was on good terms with the whole family, as later journal entries show.

207. Abel Guilliams (d. 1695) was a tenant of Admiral Penn's in west Cork. See 28 Mar., 4 Apr.

208. Philip Maddox (d. 1673) of East Gully, Ballymooden, Cork, rented lands, probably part of Carhow in Kilgariff parish about two miles northwest of Clonakilty, from Admiral Penn.

209. Adam Clark in 1659 had occupied Carrigroe and Killeleine (319 acres) in Rathbarry parish, near Castle Freke. This land was given to Admiral Penn under the Act of Settlement, and WP rented it to the Earl of Barrymore. Clark took Derryduff, 386 acres in Ross Carbery parish, instead. See 3 Mar., 8, 9 Apr.

210. Walter Harris (d. 1685) probably rented Courleigh, 75 acres near Carrigroe, from Admiral Penn. He had lived on this property in 1659.

211. Berry was one of WP's tenants in Ibaune and Barryroe. See 11-15 Apr. for WP's efforts to settle with him.

212. Edmund Nuce (d. 1693) had rented Keile, Derryvoreene, Maugh, Creaboy, and Farrane McShonig (230 acres total) in the parishes of Ardfield and Kilkerranmore from the crown in 1661. These lands passed to Admiral Penn under the Act of Settlement, and it seems likely that Nuce then rented them from the Penns.

213. Perhaps the John Philpot who was a tenant of Orrery in 1671. MacLysaght, *Orrery Papers,* p. 83.

214. Probably Desmond Crowly (d. 1683), a husbandman of Bandon.

215. Not identified, but see 13 Apr.

216. David German or Jermyn, a lieutenant in the Cork troop of foot, rented Creaghbeg (or Greah Begg), 129 acres in Kilkerranmore parish, Ibaune and Barryroe, from the Penns.

217. Perhaps Teague O'Hea. See 27 May. About 2,000 acres held by Admiral Penn in Ibaune and Barryroe had belonged before the Irish Rebellion to Daniel, John, Teague, Thomas, or William O'Hea.

218. Grubb suggests that Baltimore, a small fishing village southwest of Skibbereen, is intended.

219. Captain Emanuel Moore and his wife Martha had five surviving children, two sons and three daughters. Probably the meeting was in Ross Carbery, where the Moores lived.

220. Perhaps "brawling."

221. Sarah Massey (c. 1618-1698), widow of Daniel Massey (d. 1665), both early Friends. She lived at Bandon.

222. Morris lived at Castle Salem, now Banduff, about one mile northwest of Ross Carbery.

223. John Wood had held Ardquoky (65 acres) in Lislee parish in 1659. The property was given to Admiral Penn under the Act of Settlement, and probably Wood then rented it from the Penns.

224. Probably the Randall Warner, gent., who lived in Lislee in 1659. Perhaps he rented Bally McRedmond, the Admiral's other parcel of land in Lislee.

225. Richard Barry (1630-1694), Earl of Barrymore, a grandson of Richard Boyle, first earl of Cork. Barrymore and Adam Clark both wanted to lease Carrigroe, 219 acres in Rathbarry parish, near Ross Carbery. See 8 and 9 Apr.

226. Lieutenant Edward Clarke (d. 1685) had held Garranegoline, Kilkerranmore, and Gortnekerry (161 acres total) in Kilkerranmore parish under crown rental in 1659, and he became the Penns' tenant when these lands were given to the Admiral.

227. Clonakilty is about six miles northeast from Ross Carbery on Clonakilty Bay.

228. Robert Sandham (1620-1675) of Youghal, a Baptist in his youth, went to Ireland in Cromwell's army. In 1655 he was convinced, and the first Quaker meetings in Youghal were held in his house.

229. Perhaps WP means the two ends of town, or the two inns. The mayor of Youghal was John Farthing.

230. Owen Silver, baliff and alderman in Youghal, was a tenant of the Admiral in Imokilly. See also doc. 45.

231. Grayish brown. *OED.*

232. John Moore was archdeacon of Cloyne and held several parishes near Shanagarry.

233. See headnote to doc. 39.

234. Assizes. The persecuting judge who held this court has not been identified. The mayor of Cork who collaborated with him was Matthew Deane.

235. Redmond Barry (d. 1690) of Rathcormack, sixteen miles northeast of Cork, was a member of parliament for Fethard, Tipperary, in 1666.

236. Ferries from Cork to the Great Island and from there to Imokilly.

237. *The Great Case of Liberty of Conscience Once More Debated and Defended* (1670).

238. Daniel Gamble's death on 25 Mar. 1670 is recorded in the Cork Quaker Register.

239. Thomas Davis of Bandon, a Quaker and a clothier, bought land in West Jersey in 1678.

240. Lieutenant Richard Dashwood (c. 1624-1672) of Bandon had served in Robert Phaire's regiment during the Commonwealth.

241. Friends from Mountmellick were then imprisoned in Maryborrough, now Portlaoise, co. Leix.

242. A distraint or distress is a legal instrument authorizing the seizure of chattel property to satisfy an unpaid debt, commonly for rent due. *OED*.

243. A stress is a distraint or the goods seized in a distraint. *OED*. Apparently WP seized Abel Guilliams' cattle until he paid his overdue rent.

244. Probably John Southwell's lease was for either North or South Carhow in Kilkerranmore parish. The rent he contracted for is too small to be for both tracts, and Maddox may have retained part.

245. Walter Harris made John Martin one of the overseers of his estate in his will in 1685.

246. Creaghbeg, leased to David German. See n. 216. German probably sublet to an Irish tenant.

247. Edward Clarke's past relationship to Admiral Penn has not been determined.

248. Penn tracts in Kilkerranmore parish, Ibaune and Barryroe. Edmund Nuce seems to have rented some of this land.

249. Aghamilly, another Penn tract in Kilkerranmore parish, contained 192 acres.

250. Not to be confused with Geiragh in Imokilly.

251. Probably Emanuel Moore, Jr., born in 1667.

252. Castle Lyons, near Fermoy, north Cork, was the seat of the Earl of Barrymore.

253. Thomas Hungerford of Rathbarry had two sons who attended Trinity College, Dublin.

254. A "gneeve" is an Irish measure of land, one-twelfth of a ploughland. *OED*.

255. A burying.

256. Probably children of Thomas Gookins or of his brothers, who lived in Lislee parish.

257. William Freke (d. 1685). His relationship to Captain John Freke is uncertain, though he appears to have acted as his agent. The property seems to be Killeene, 100 acres in Rathbarry parish. At over 4 s. per acre, it was one of the more expensive of the Penns' rental properties in west Cork. See n. 185 and 258.

258. Derryduff, 386 acres in Kilkerranmore parish, Ibaune and Barryroe. Rented for £24 per year, at about 1 s. 4 d. per acre, it was perhaps Admiral Penn's cheapest land, though the rental of nearby Carrigroe, 219 acres for £20 or about 2 s. per acre, came close. Ibaune and Barryroe was not as fertile as Imokilly, and most rents there were lower. See n. 185 and 257.

259. Banduff was the old name for Castle Salem.

260. Grubb suggests that WP means Castle Salem.

261. Probably Captain Andrew Ruddock, who went to Ireland in Cromwell's army.

262. Apparently the Penns still had some interest in Macroom, the estate west of Cork where WP had grown up in the 1650s and which had been returned to the Earl of Clancarty under the Act of Settlement. See doc. 45.

263. Whiskey. *OED*.

264. About two miles north of Shanagarry.

265. Valentine Greatrakes (1629-1683) had served under Robert Phaire during the Commonwealth, and through his influence became a county magistrate and clerk of the peace for Cork. After the Restoration he became a celebrated healer, curing scrofula and ague by laying on hands. In 1666 he effected a number of cures in England, but failed in a demonstration before Charles II, and returned to Ireland. His procedure, which resembled a religious ceremony, attracted the support of the scientist Robert Boyle and the philosopher Henry More. More used Greatrakes to support his own theories of disease. *DNB;* Keith Thomas, *Religion and the Decline of Magic* (New York, 1971), pp. 202-4, 208-9.

266. Lieutenant Richard Wakeham (d. 1710), John Wakeham's brother.

267. John Langer had been an alderman in Youghal in 1663.

268. Sir Boyle Maynard (d. 1690) of Curryglass, Mogeely parish, about a mile north of Castlemartyr, owned lands in Tipperary and Waterford and sat in the Irish parliament for Youghal in 1661. His wife was a daughter of Sir Henry Tynte.

269. John Haman (d. 1692) of Cork, a Quaker, rented Clonmain in Imokilly from Admiral Penn.

270. Perhaps a reference to Gulielma Springett; cf. 4, 11, 24 June. See Hull, *William Penn, A Topical Biography*, pp. 102-3.

271. This lady cannot be specifically identified. There were three countesses of Clancarty in 1670, the widows of the first two earls of Clancarty, and the wife of the third earl. *Peerage*, 3:214-16.

272. See doc. 39.

273. Noblett Dunscombe had been sheriff of Cork in 1659 and mayor in 1665.

274. See docs. 39 and 40.

275. This cancelled passage throws light on WP's mode of composition. He wrote the journal entries for 10-16 May all at the same time, to judge by the ink and handwriting. In jotting down these entries, he inadvertently skipped two pages in completing 15 May and starting 16 May. On discovering this, he crossed out these entries, went back two pages, and rewrote 15-16 May in slightly variant language.

276. A bond of record. *OED*.

277. Bennet's Bridge, Kilkenny, about fifty-seven miles from Dublin.

278. Kilcullen, Kildare, about twenty-one miles from Dublin on the Liffey.

279. Thomas Fearon was an English Quaker minister from Cockermouth in Cumberland.

280. The council's order to the mayor of Cork for release on bail of the imprisoned Quakers excluded those held on writs of excommunication. WP wrote to the Archbishop of Dublin on 31 May, which suggests that some Quakers were held on such writs, which were under ecclesiastical jurisdiction. See doc. 127.

281. John, Lord Berkeley of Stratton (d. 1678), a royalist and favorite of the Duke of York, was made Lord Lieutenant in 1670. He was a proprietor of both Carolina and New Jersey, and in 1674 sold West Jersey to Edward Byllinge and John Fenwick. *DNB;* John E. Pomfret, *The Province of West New Jersey* (Princeton, 1956), pp. 56-58, 65-67.

282. Sir Ellis Leighton (d. 1685), secretary to the Lord Lieutenant, had been secretary to the Duke of York in exile.

283. Michael Boyle (c. 1609-1702) was Chancellor of Ireland and also Archbishop of Dublin.

284. Major Thomas Fairfax was commander of the King's company in the Dublin regiment of guards.

285. Henry Bulkeley, younger son of Viscount Bulkeley of Cashel, was an ensign in the Irish Guards.

286. Colonel Hugh Leeson went to Ireland as an officer of Charles I. He later became a member of parliament and mayor of Dublin.

287. Edmund Sheffield was cornet of Ormonde's own troop of horse.

288. Sheffield and Leeson had served with WP under the Earl of Arran in the suppression of the mutiny at Carrickfergus in 1666. *CSPI, 1666-1669*, p. 122.

289. Perhaps a reference to Gulielma Springett. See n. 269.

290. Katherine (d. 1675), widow of Hugh Montgomery, Earl of Mount Alexander, commander of the royalist army in Ulster in 1649, and sister of Richard, Lord Ranelagh. She was an Anglican, but her will directed that she be buried "neither vainly nor contemptuously."

291. See n. 279 and 286.

292. Callaghan MacCarty (d. 1676), Earl of Clancarty, formerly a monk in France, conformed to the Anglican church on his accession to the earldom, but died "out of communion with the Church of England." *Peerage*, 3:216.

293. Sir John Stephens (d. 1673) was governor of Dublin Castle. He had served under Ormonde in the Irish wars, shared Charles II's exile, and was employed by Ormonde on many important missions.

294. Abraham Fuller (1622-1694) of Moate, co. Westmeath, a Dutch-born Quaker convinced in 1659, wrote with Thomas Holme *A Brief Relation . . . of the Sufferings of the True Christians, the people of God (in Scorn called Quakers) in Ireland* (1672).

295. Richard Jones, identified on 17 Nov. 1669 as Lord Jones, had succeeded to his father's title as Lord Ranelagh.

296. John Skeffington (d. 1695), Viscount Massereene, was a Privy Councilor and a large landholder in northern Ireland, with a nonconformist background. *Peerage*, 8:544-45.

297. Ballymore Eustace, a village on the Liffey about twenty miles southwest of Dublin.

298. See n. 269 and 286.

299. A pursuivant is a state messenger with the power to execute warrants. *OED*.

300. William Steele of Dublin was a Quaker.

301. Probably Mathias Foster, a Quaker who had been released from prison in Dublin on 29 Nov. See n. 115. Note that WP met William Steele, who had been released with Foster, the previous day.

302. WP probably closed his journal at this point, several weeks before leaving Ireland, because he ran out of paper. The closing page of the notebook, containing WP's final two entries, also has (upside down) a business memorandum of 1662 in the hand of Admiral Penn. Several further pages are torn out, suggesting that the notebook had been earlier used by the elder Penn before his son took it over and started his journal from the other end.

IN IRELAND

1669–1670

WP's stay in Ireland from October 1669 through July 1670 is the best documented phase of his early career. In addition to the Irish Journal (doc. 35), with its invaluable record of his daily movements, the ten documents grouped below provide much supplementary information on WP's personal life and on his religious, political, and business activities. Docs. 36, 39, and 40 show WP as a lobbyist with the political authorities in Ireland, pressing for relief from Quaker arrests and Quaker harassments. Docs. 37 and 38 show his relationship with his father, rapidly failing in health, who is settling his affairs with WP as his heir. Docs. 41-45, intercepted by a government spy, introduce us to WP's inner circle of Quaker correspondents in England and Ireland.

36
TO MAYOR LEWIS DESMYNIERES [?]

To Sr J. Cor. of Suffolk[1]
To the May^{r} of Dublin in the Paper[2]

[5 November 1669?]

Friend,
It is the Duty of a Magistrate to hear & redress the Oppressed, not to revile them.
I came this Morning in Love to thy Person, & due Respect to thy place, in the behalfe of some imprisoned Friends, & with an Address (I think) unblameable: But instead of an Entertainement, becoming so innocent an Application, I, and They were most abusively called Rogues, Raskalls, inhuman Rogues, Whelps, deserving to be lasht out of the Town, & sent to Barbadoes; and our Paper ~~addrest~~ {refused} with Scorn, & {wth} the greatest Detestation flung to the ground.
What thinkest thou of this Usage? Was it the Good, the Temperate and Mercyfull Spirit in thee, or the Contrary? In what Chapter & Verses in Scripture or the Laws of the Land may the like Passages be found? but are they not expresly contrary to both?

Let me tell thee, that if we were as Contentious, as thou hast shown thyself Injurious, this Treatment would find a resurrection to thy great Disprofit.
But as becomes the Patient & Afflicted Followers of Jesus Christ, who by the Priests & Rulers of his time, with all his servants, became matter of Reproach & great Tribulation, we heartily forgive thee, & desire that God Allmighty would overrule thy Passions, & overcome thee with his Spirit of Moderation, that in all things thou mayst better become thy place, & answer the Just & mercyfull Ends of Laws & Government; I am, what once I was, (when better known to thee, & much more, in reality)[3]

Thy True Friend,
WP.

LBC. WP's Letterbook, 1667-1675, HSP. (*Micro.* 1:181).

1. The heading "To Sr J. Cor. of Suffolk" is in WP's hand, while "To the Mayr of Dublin in the Paper" is in the transcribing clerk's hand. If WP's attribution is correct, the letter is addressed to Sir John Cordell (1646-1690) of Melford Hall, Suffolk, and is dated later than 1680 (when Cordell inherited his baronetcy) and most probably in 1684, when Cordell as a justice was persecuting Friends. *Baronetage,* 3:52; Besse, 1:685. But none of the eighty-one other documents in this letterbook can be dated later than 1676, and Cordell was most actively pursuing Quakers in July 1684, when WP was in America. Possibly WP used this letter as a model for a protest to Cordell, but there is no other evidence of his going to Suffolk on behalf of persecuted Friends.

2. Cadbury attributes the letter to 5 Nov. 1669, when WP and William Morris carried a "paper by way of Address" to the Mayor of Dublin. See Henry J. Cadbury, "More Penn Correspondence, Ireland, 1669-1670," *PMHB* (1949) 73: 9-10; and doc. 35, 5 Nov. 1669, above. Lewis Desmynieres (d. 1689), mayor of Dublin in 1669, was a native of Amersfoort in Utrecht. He became a merchant and brewer in Dublin, and was made a free denizen of Ireland in 1655. *CSPI, 1647-1670,* pp. 572-73; *1669-1670,* pp. 241-42, 570; Pender, pp. 369, 620, 639; Arthur Vicars, ed., *Index to the Prerogative Wills of Ireland, 1536-1810* (Dublin, 1897), p. 131; John Lodge, *The Peerage of Ireland* (London, 1754), 2:170.

3. No past relationship between WP and either Desmynieres or Cordell is known, though the Desmynieres were living in Dublin on WP's earlier visits to Ireland.

37
WILL OF SIR WILLIAM PENN

Though not yet forty-nine, Admiral Penn was already gravely ill and in permanent retirement when he made the will below. He had resigned his office on the Navy Board in April 1669 and retired to his country house in Wanstead, Essex, where he lived out his last year in steadily deteriorating health. For a description of his illness at this time, see doc. 43. He died on 16 September 1670.

[20 January 1670]

IN THE NAME OF GOD AMEN I Sr William Penn of London Kt beeing of perfect minde and memory doe make this my last Will and

Testament this twentyeth day of January in the yeare of our Lord God one thousand six hundred sixty and nyne and in the one and twentyeth yeare of the Reigne of our Sovereigne Lord Charles the Second by the grace of God of England Scotland France and Ireland King Defender of the Faith &c in manner followeing And first I doe hereby revoake adnull and make voyd all {&} every former and other last Will and Testament Devise and Devises Bequest and Bequests by me heretofore at any time made or published My Soule I humbly recommend unto the mercifull hands of my ever Blessed Lord and Saviour Jesus Christ beseecheing him that through his meritts I may bee made pertaker of life eternall My Body I committ to the Grave to bee buryed in the Parish Church of Redclyffe[1] within the Citty of Bristoll as neere unto the Body of my Deare Mother[2] deceased (whose Body {lyes} there interred) as the same conveniently may bee And my Will is that there shall bee erected in the sayd Church as neere unto the place where my Body shall bee buryed as the same cann bee contrived an handsome and decent Tombe to remayne as a Monument as well for my sayd Mother as for myselfe the Charges thereof to bee defrayd by my executor hereafter named out of my personall estate And as for and concerneing my personall estate I doe hereby devyse the same as followeth And first I doe will and devyse unto my Deare Wife Dame Margarett Penn to bee payd unto her immediately after my decease the Summe of three hundred Pounds sterl together with all my Jewells other then what I shall hereinafter perticulerly devyse And I doe allsoe give and bequeath unto my sayd Deare Wife {The use and Occupation ~~of~~ dureing her Lyfe of} one full moyety of all my plate and howsehold stuffe and likewise all such Coaches and Coach-horses or Coach Mares and all such Cowes as I shall happen to have at the time of my Decease ITEM I doe Will and Bequeath unto my younger Sonne Richard Penn[3] the Summe of fower[4] thousand Pounds sterl together with my faverett diamond ring and all my Swords gunns and pistolls the said fowr thousand Pounds soe bequeathed unto my sayd Sonne Richard to bee payd and payable unto him so soone as he shall arrive at the age of one and twenty yeares and not sooner And my Will is that in the meane time and untill he shall arrive at the sayd age of one and twenty yeares my executor heareafter named shall pay unto my sayd Sonne Richard out of my personall estate the yearely Summe of one hundred and twenty Pounds which I hereby Devyse unto him for his support and mayntenance untill he shall attayne the age of one and twenty yeares and no longer ITEM I doe Will and Devyse unto my Deare Granddaughter Margarett Lowther[5] the Summe of one hundred Pounds sterl unto my two Nephews James Bradshawe[6] and William Markham[7] to each of them tenne Pounds sterl unto my two Nephews John Bradshawe[8] and George Markham[9] to each of them five Pounds sterl unto my Couzin William Penn[10] Sonne of George Penn[11] late of the Forrest of Brayden[12] in the County of Wilts gent deceased the

Summme of tenne Pounds sterl unto my Couzin Elianor Keene[13] the yearely Summe of six Pounds sterl to be payd unto her yearely dureing her life by my executor out of my[14] personall estate by quarterly Payments at the fower most usuall quarterly Feats[15] or quarterly dayes of Payment in the yeare ITEM I Will and Bequeath unto my late Servant William Badham forty shil to buy him a Ring unto my Servant John Wrenn[16] five Pounds sterl unto the Poore of the Parish of Redclyffe aforesayd in the Citty of Bristoll aforesayd twenty pounds sterl And unto the Poore of the Parish of S[t] Thomas[17] in the same Citty of Bristoll twenty Pounds sterl I doe allsoe Will and Devyse unto my eldest Sonne William Penn my Gold Chayne and Meddall with the rest and residue of all and singuler my plate howsehold stuffe goods chattells and personall estate not hereinbefore devysed {as also the s[d] goods & premises devised to be used by my s[d] Deare wife dureing her Life from & after the decease of my s[d] wife} And I doe hereby constitute declare nominate and appoynt my sayd Sonne William Sole executor of this my last Will and Testament And doe hereby appoynt him at my Funerall to give mourneing unto my sayd Deare Wife my sayd Sonne Richard my Daughter Margarett Lowther and my Sonne in Lawe Anthony Lowther the Husband of my sayd Daughter And unto D[r] Whistler and his Wife[18] and unto such of my Servants as my sayd Deare Wife shall for that purpose nominate the sayd Mourneing to bee payd for out of my personall estate hereby devysed unto my sayd executor And though I cannott apprehend that any differences cann fall out or happen betweene my sayd deare Wife and my sayd Sonne William after my decease in Relation to anything by me devised or lymmitted by this my Will or in Relation to any other matter or thing whatsoever yett in Case any such differences should aryse I doe hereby request and desire and as farr as in me lyeth require conjure and direct my said Deare Wife and my sayd Sonne William by all the Obligations of duty affection and respect which they have and ought to have to me and my memory That all such differences of what nature or kinde soever they shall bee by the Joynt consents and submission of my sayd Deare Wife and my sayd Sonne William bee at all times and from time to time referred to the Arbitration and Final Judgement and Determination of my Worthy Friend S[r] William Coventry of the Parish of S[t] Martins in the Feilds in the County of Middlesex[19] whome I doe hereby intreat to take upon him selfe[20] the Determination of all and every such Difference and Differences as shall from time to time or at any time after my Decease bee referred unto him Awards or Determinations by my sayd Deare Wife and my sayd Sonne William Penn for the totall prevention of all suites in Lawe or Equity which upon any occasion or misunderstanding might otherwise happen betweene them IN WITNESSE whereof I have unto this my last Will and Testament sett my hand and seale the day and yeare first above wrytten And doe publish and declare this to bee my last Will and Testament in the presence of those whose Names are subscribed as Wittnesses hereunto.

Signed Sealed Declared & Published[21] after theis words vizt [the use & occupation dureing her lyfe of][22] betweene the seaventh & Eighth lynes And theis words vizt [as also the sd Goods & premises devised to be used by my sd Deare wyfe dureing her lyfe from & after the decease of my sd wyfe] betweene the seaventeenth & Eighteenth lynes were interlyned in the presence of

R. Langhorne[23] John Radford[24]
Will: Markham

W Penn

DS. Penn Collection, Tempsford Hall Papers, HSP. (*Micro.* 1:216). Docketed: 20 Jan 1669 Sr Will Penns Original Will | Received the Will & Codicill | [from Chas Tucker] | [this 6th day of the month] | called Aprill | Wm Penn.

1. St. Mary Redcliffe, "the fairest, the goodliest, and the most famous parish church in England," in Queen Elizabeth's phrase. Admiral Penn's burial monument is mounted in the wall at the west end of the nave. Muirhead's *England*, p. 136.

2. Joan Gilbert Penn (c. 1580-1664) married Giles Penn (c. 1573-1645?) in 1600. Her family came from Somerset. ACM, vol. 49A

3. Richard Penn (c. 1655-1673) died at Rickmansworth on 4 Apr. 1673, before reaching his majority. See doc. 143, 7-25 Apr. 1673; Jenkins, pp. 46-47; ACM, vols. 49B, 50.

4. The "fower" here, and again in the passage "fower thousand Pounds" immediately following, has been written over an erased word, suggesting that the Admiral changed his mind about what sum to leave Richard.

5. Margaret Lowther (1668-1714) was the eldest child of Anthony Lowther and WP's sister, Margaret Penn Lowther. ACM, vol. 49B; Pepys, 8 Feb. 1668.

6. James Bradshaw (1646-1692?) was the son of Ralph Bradshaw and Rachel Penn Bradshaw (b. 1607), Admiral Penn's sister. In 1685, WP sent him to Pennsylvania as clerk of the colony council. ACM, vol. 49A; *Micro.* 5:219.

7. William Markham (c. 1635-1704) was probably the son of one of Admiral Penn's sisters; little is known about his family. WP sent him to Pennsylvania in 1681 and employed him as councilor, commissioner, and, from 1694 to 1699, as governor of the colony. ACM, vol. 49.

8. John Bradshaw (b. 1651) was James's younger brother. ACM, vol. 49B.

9. George Markham was apparently William's younger brother, as indicated by his smaller bequest.

10. See doc. 14 above.

11. George Penn (c. 1571-1632) was the Admiral's uncle. Jenkins, pp. 7-9; J. Henry Lea, *Genealogical Gleanings Contributory to a History of the Family of Penn* (Boston, 1900), app. 2, xlv.

12. The site of the Penn family's ancestral home, on the Gloucestershire-Wiltshire border. It was from here that the Admiral's father emigrated to Bristol by 1593. Jenkins, pp. 7, 8-9; ACM, vol. 49A.

13. Eleanor Keene (b. 1611) was the daughter of Admiral Penn's uncle George, and sister of William Penn of Kinsale. In 1635 she married Edward Keene (c. 1608-?). Lea, *Genealogical Gleanings*, app. 2, xliii.

14. Written over an erased word.

15. "Feasts."

16. Probably the John Wren who cleared ships' victuallers in their accounts in 1668 and 1669. *CSPD, 1667-1668*, p. 349; *1668-1669*, pp. 10, 202. After Admiral Penn's death, he seems to have become purser of two ships, the *Montagu* and later the *Swallow*. *CSPD, 1672*, p. 10.

17. The Admiral was baptized in the church of this parish, just north of St. Mary Redcliffe, in 1621.

18. Dr. Daniel Whistler (d. 1684), a Fellow of the Royal Society and a friend of Admiral Penn's from 1664 or earlier, had married Elizabeth Holcroft, Anthony Lowther's mother, after her first husband's death. See doc. 14 above; and ACM, vol. 49B, under "Holcroft."

19. The whole phrase "Sr William Coventry of Middlesex" is written in over an erased passage, and the spacing suggests that Admiral Penn originally intended to have two arbitrators before settling on Coventry alone. Sir William Coventry (c. 1628-1686) became secretary to the Duke of York in 1660, and a colleague of Admiral Penn's on the Navy Board in 1662. He was an important figure in the government from 1665 to 1667, but, along with Penn, he became a target of Parliamentary criticism after the Dutch attack on the Chatham Docks in June 1667. He was stripped of his offices and briefly imprisoned in the Tower. Upon his release in Mar. 1668, he retired from public life. Coventry was, like Penn, a moderate in politics, a bit of a "trimmer," and a man who had lost his political power when Penn made his will in 1670. *DNB;* Anchitell Grey, *Debates in the House of Commons* (London, 1763), 1:134, 137, 138.

20. The words "him selfe," and the word "him," later in the sentence, are written over erased words, again showing the Admiral's original intention of have two arbitrators.

21. From this point on, the text has been written in a different ink.

22. The brackets between this point and the close of the document are in the original text.

23. Richard Langhorne (d. 1679) was a lawyer, a member of the Inner Temple, and a Roman Catholic. He was later employed by WP as counsel, and was also the Jesuits' attorney in England. The first person accused by Titus Oates of involvement in the "Popish Plot" in 1678, he was imprisoned 7 Oct. 1678, tried 14 June 1679, and publicly executed at Tyburn 14 July 1679. *DNB;* Joseph Gillow, *A Literary and Biographical History, or Bibliographical Dictionary of the English Catholics* (London, n.d.), 4:127-31; John Kenyon, *The Popish Plot* (London, 1972), p. 74.

24. Unidentified. Widow Constance Radford, who paid rent to WP on 12 July 1672, 3 May 1673, and 11 Nov. 1673, was possibly John's wife. See docs. 140, 143.

38
FROM SIR WILLIAM PENN

Apll 29o (70)

Sonne William This coms inclosed in my letter to Mr Southwell[1] with whom I would have you ajust yr accot betwene us for my Cozn Will Pen as clarke of the cheqr [2] for two years & give him a faire aquitance {if}[3] he can with in one month send the ballance of it to mee as I have desired him its well other wise you must rect & send it wth what else you can spedely Mr Southwell is my good ould freind & I would have you according vallue & respect him I wish you had well don al yr busines there & that you were here, for I find my selfe to decline, But I would have the grand things so substantially effected as that wee may have no mor futer disputes or neglects in paymt of rent which at hand is dangerus but much mor so remote. I have writ you that Capt Rooth I intend to imploy after yor depart so that it would be nesesary you fully informe him the true estate of al things I have answerd every perticuller of all yor letters but have received no answer of myne nor so much as one line from you this 5 weeks as I take it, though I know others that have very Lately which I canot easily dejest for I am sure I have deserved yor duty if I nevr havet it shalnot be my falte. since my last by the helpe of John wren I have found that yo[r] Mother whilst I was at sea received seventy nine pounds 8[s] (the other 12[s] was it seems give to One of the Treas[rs] clarkes) this you must alow him upon cleering his accompt, pray Keepe out of harmes waie & the God of mercy direct & preserve you

I am yo[r] very afft father
W Penn

ALS. Penn-Forbes Collection, HSP. (*Micro.* 1:225). Addressed: For William Penn Esq[r] | These in the county of Corke. Docketed: S[r] W[m] Penn | April 29. 1670.

1. Robert Southwell (1607-1677) was sovereign of Kinsale in Apr. 1670, and since Sir WP was planning, because of ill health, to resign the governorship of the fort at Kinsale to his kinsman Richard Rooth, he naturally would have had accounts to settle with Southwell. Richard Caulfield, *Council Book of the Corporation of Kinsale* (Guildford, Surrey, 1879), pp. 421, 111, 114; *DNB*.

2. Apparently Admiral Penn meant to keep Ensign William Penn as clerk of cheque at Kinsale even after Rooth became governor of the fort. Cf. *CSPD, 1671*, p. 97.

3. Written over an illegible deleted word.

In the spring of 1670, Matthew Deane, the mayor of Cork, intensified his persecution of Friends, breaking up meetings, imprisoning male Quakers, confiscating their tools, and not allowing them to work in prison. In early May, Deane confiscated copies of one of WP's books, probably the just published *Great Case of Liberty of Conscience.* On 13 May, Penn met with Deane to try to recover the books but had no success, and, by WP's account in the Irish Journal, was abused with foul language. Three days later, John Hull and other Quakers were arrested in Cork, and on 18 May WP wrote to Roger Boyle, Lord Broghill, Orrery's son, for relief. Broghill was WP's contemporary, and the two had visited as recently as 4 May.

Though WP's letter to Broghill does not survive, the reply does. Broghill got his brother-in-law, Lord O'Brien, son of the Vice President of Munster, to intercede for Hull and WP. Deane returned Penn's books, but Hull and the others were not released — that required action by the Lord Lieutenant and Council, and though an order for the return of the imprisoned Friends' tools was issued on 30 March, Hull was not set free until 15 June. Doc. 39 is Broghill's reply to WP's lost letter of 16 May, and Doc. 40 is O'Brien's letter. Though both condemn Deane's abuse of a person of WP's standing, neither Broghill nor O'Brien approves of Quakerism, and O'Brien openly rejects WP's plea for religious toleration. (See Fuller and Holme, p. 72, where Hull's imprisonment is dated 1669, and the order in council, 30 Mar. 1670, PRO Dublin, trans. in ACM, vol. 48.)

39
FROM LORD BROGHILL

Charlevill the 18 of May 1~~6~~670

Sr

Soe soone as I receivd yr letter I shewed itt to my Brother oBryen[1] who hath promissed mee to doe some thing for you; Had I as much power as formerly I have had, itt should bee Imployed to serve you; & in the Capasity I now am in, Ile doe you what Kindenesse I can; I much wonder that the Maior of Corke should give any Gentleman bee hee of what Religion or sect soe ever such ill Language, as you send mee word he gave you, for ~~severall sorts of Religion~~ severall sorts of Religion, is but variety of opinions, wch certainely cannot make any man degenerate from beeing a Gentleman who was borne soe, & although the Maior of Corke & you differ about Religion, yet he ought to shew you that Civility as yr birth requiers; I shall come verry speedely to Corke & then, Ille gitt him to deliver you yr books, I hope to see you write ere Long as much in the defence of the Protestant religion, as you have, for the profession of the Quaquers, wch I am sure will bee a greate satisfaction to all yr freinds & in particular to Sr

Yr assured freind & servant
Broghill:[2]

ALS. Granville Penn Book, HSP. (*Micro.* 1:319a). Addressed: For my Esteemed freind | William Penn Esqr att | Corke. Docketed: Lord Broughall | 18th-May-1670.

1. William O'Brien (c. 1642-1692), later Earl of Inchiquin, was the son of Murrough O'Brien (c. 1614-1674), Earl of Inchiquin; he married Margaret Boyle, Broghill's sister, daughter of Roger, first earl of Orrery. In 1671 he was made privy councilor for Ireland; he died as governor of Jamaica. *Peerage,* 7:51-53.

2. Roger Boyle (1646-1682), second earl of Orrery, was styled Lord Broghill before his father's death in 1679. In 1669, he had acted in his father's absence as vice president of Munster, hence the reference to his current lessened power. *DNB; Peerage* 10:178.

40
FROM LORD O'BRIEN

Charleville 18th May 16[70]

Sir,

My brother Broghill shewed me yesterday a letter of yours wherein you complain of the Mayor of Corkes severity. Whatever be your opinion, I shall never incourage him to be uncivil to a person of your quality, wherefore I have writ the enclosed to him,[1] & wish it may work the effect that you desire. If it does not the cause of it must be attributed to the advantage the Law gives him over you, more than to my want of inclination to serve you, for you must give me leave to tell you that I cannot agree to the State of the Case as you represent it, but do see so much reason that the Law should be dessigned against you, that I am confident it was so. I confess prudence ought to be of great authority in a Magistrate; but I cannot allow that the extreme execution of justice is inconsistent with it when the forbearance of it may be more prejudicial to the greater concerns than would be the execution of it to those of a particular corporation. I fear all this trouble you undergo is because you dont believe not what you cant but what you wont believe, & as it is certainly possible for you to believe our faith, for it is reasonable, we must punish them that cant because they may & will not have it. Excuse this liberty I take & believe that in your particular you shall always find me ready to embrace the occasion of serving you, for I am really,

Your affte friend & Servant
O Bryan.

Your books, upon the enclosed will be restored, & I suppose John Hull[2] set at liberty.

Transcript. FLL. (*Micro.* 1:039). Addressed: For William Penn Esqre | Corke.

1. O'Brien's letter to Mayor Deane has not survived.

2. John Hull (c. 1612-1692) of county Cork, a merchant, accompanied George Fox on his trip to Barbados in 1671, serving as Fox's secretary. In 1672, he went to England with Elizabeth Miers, whom he married that year in London. With Fox he wrote *To the Ministers, Teachers, and Priests . . . in Barbadoes* (1672). In 1673, the Hulls were back in county Cork, but in 1689 they were "forced out of Ireland," and thereafter were supported by the London meeting until their deaths. Fox, 2:428; ACM, vol. 144.

The next five documents were written in July and August of 1670 and intercepted en route by an agent of Joseph Williamson, secretary to Lord Arlington. WP never received them, and they are today filed among the State Papers in the PRO. Several of these letters illustrate the severity of Quaker persecution in 1670: docs. 41 and 42 detail the impact of imprisonment upon Quaker families, and doc. 45 shows how closely government spies kept track of Friends' activities. These letters also reveal everyday, personal aspects of WP's environment which are seldom described in the more formal correspondence surviving from this period. Doc. 41, from WP's future wife, and doc. 42, in the artless syntax and spelling of Elizabeth Bowman, introduce two vigorous young women from his circle. Doc. 43 reports on WP's ailing and troubled parents, and docs. 44 and 45 discuss Irish business problems not mentioned in WP's Irish Journal. These letters have been annotated and printed in Henry J. Cadbury, "Intercepted Correspondence of William Penn," *PMHB* 70:349-72; and Cadbury, "More Penn Correspondence, Ireland, 1669-1670," *PMHB* 73:9-15. Our edition depends heavily upon Cadbury's work.

41
FROM GULIELMA SPRINGETT AND MARY PENINGTON

Pen[1] 16—5mo [July] 1670

W P

With the Salutation of that love wch is everlasting & wch is livingly felt at this time in my hart to {thee} & al that truly love the Lord & have given up there all to follow him in this day of trial [illegible deletion] I Salute thee wth the rest of thy company & friends there, yours of the 27 of 4th mo we received wch was very welcome to my Mother[2] but your selves would have been much more acceptable especially She being laitly deprived of the companie of my Deare father[3] who went to vissit friends at Reading & the Goaler sent for Armorer[4] who after a great deale of discourse & reviling language tendered him the oath & committed him to the Goal he hath since been had to the Sessions & tendered it again so that in short time {it is like} to come to a praemunire[5] unless God put a stop to theer wicked intentions we could rather if we might chuse that he had been in almost any other place but in al things we have learned to be content & desire to be given up wholly to his will wthout whom this nor any other trial could come on us & we know he orders al things for the good of those that put there trust in him. Friends heare abouts are generally well & meetings yet quiet wch we can not but looke upon as a great thing. expecially [illegible deletion] {when} we consider the grevious sufferings that friends meet wth all in other places wch are to teidous to mention in perticular, deare G F[6] was heare att two of our meettings & they were very large we were laitly att London & friends were very well, we Speake wi th Will Baily[7] who came the night before to Lond: from Barbadoes[8] he saw I P[9] there he was very well & the place agreed very well wth him we expect him home very shortly if nothing prevent Jo: Stubs was also heare and desired his deare love to thee T Es[10] deare love is to thee P F[11] & J P[12] wth mine dearly to them &c

Who am thy friend
in the lasting friendship
Guli: Springett

Elizabeth Walmslys[13]
deare love is to thee &c
as also S Hs[14]

Deare W P

Thy letter in wch thou kindly joyndest us I received wth a deep sence of thy love, as also thy prospering in the truth my deare Husband[15] & I am now seperated as G S hath informed thee but I entend to send it him I am very wel satisfied that the stay of my boy[16] is upon the account of thy Servis as for thy care Counsel & love I belive he hath not wanted it it is a great joy to me to heare of thy faithfulness & unweariedness in the worke of the Lord I being now deprived of my Husbands companie I am more honing[17] after my poore boy then I have been since ~~I~~ {he} went endeed this of my husbands inprisonment is hard very hard to me. but when I retire out of al affection & wait to see what the Lord will doe wth him there I am still as if the thing were nott

Thy intire friend
M P

my deare love is to P F & my poor child he hath increased his intrest in my love by his subjection to thee.

ALS. SP 63/328, PRO. (*Micro.* 1:230). Addressed: To | Captain John Gay att | his hous | In | Dublin | For Will: Pen | these.

1. The village of Penn, Bucks., three miles east of High Wycombe. Gulielma Springett and the Peningtons lived here briefly in 1670, while a house they had bought in nearby Amersham was being renovated. This area of Bucks. was a center of Quaker activity from at least 1658, when the Peningtons began holding meetings at Chalfont St. Peter, seven miles from Penn village. By 1671, Quakers were meeting at Jordans, five miles away, where they established a graveyard in which WP and Gulielma Springett Penn were later buried. Cadbury, "Intercepted Correspondence of William Penn," *PMHB* 70:356; Grubb, pp. 18, 61-62; *VCH, Buckinghamshire,* 3:143, 185, 193, 250.

2. Mary Springett Penington.

3. Isaac Penington.

4. Sir William Armorer (c. 1600-?) was an energetic persecutor of Quakers, with a particular fondness for imprisoning Friends who were visiting other Quakers already in prison. WP gives a vivid description of Armorer in *The Great Case of Liberty of Conscience* (London, 1670), in *Works,* 1:463-64. Also see *Persecution Appearing with its own Open Face, in William Armorer* (London, 1667), author unknown. Cadbury, *PMHB* 70:357.

5. A writ whereby a sheriff or constable was directed to summon a person accused of asserting or maintaining papal jurisdiction in England, and thus denying the ecclesiastical supremacy of England's sovereign. This writ, commonly used against Roman Catholic recusants, was also employed against Quakers (*OED*). Penington remained in Reading gaol under the praemunire until 1672, when he received a pardon following Charles II's Declaration of Indulgence.

6. George Fox. After meeting with Friends in the Penn village area, he visited imprisoned Quakers at Reading, and escaped without detection. Cadbury, *PMHB* 70:357; Fox, 2:163.

7. William Bayly (?-1675) was a Quaker sea captain from Poole who was convinced in 1655 and thereafter was often in prison for his belief. He died at sea on a return voyage from Barbados. Fox, 1:435.

8. Quaker preachers first visited Barbados in 1655; the island eventually had five meeting houses, and was the chief center of Quakerism in the West Indies. Fox, 2:412; Richard S. Dunn, *Sugar and Slaves* (Chapel Hill, 1972), pp. 103-6.

9. Isaac Penington (c. 1656-1670), the second son of Isaac and Mary Penington, went to Barbados with John Grove, a London Quaker sea captain, and drowned on

the return voyage. Cadbury, *PMHB* 70:358; S. Graveson, ed., *The History of the Life of Thomas Ellwood* (London, 1906), p. 175.

10. Thomas Ellwood.

11. Philip Ford.

12. John Penington, Gulielma's half-brother.

13. Elizabeth Walmsly, of Chalfont St. Giles, Bucks. was an active Friend, and, with her husband Thomas, a close friend of the Peningtons. Cadbury, *PMHB* 70:358.

14. Sarah Hersent.

15. Isaac Penington.

16. John Penington.

17. "Yearning."

42
FROM ELIZABETH BOWMAN

[16 July 1670]

deare frend

thine I[1] reseved[2] & Acorden to thy desire i have delvred the inclosed I have resaved 3 & she ass maney I delevred the last jost noue for she haeth bene here[3] to mete Margret Rouse[4] Abought her Mouthers Besenes that is in order to geat her relesed & E. J & her Mouther onderstanden Margrett Foxes Condeshon & that she being weth child & so nere ass she is [deleted] her time beingen out All Most thay are veary Endorstret[5] to prokure her Leberty which i hope thay well doue[6] Eliz: J is veary well ass to her hel heleth but for Aney thinge Eles thare is not much to bee sade ass to her Groeth in trueth for she is muche taken upe wethe her Mouthers Compney & such Like I Cane truly scay I am trobled for her scake for she is of a prety swete desposeshon & the wetnes of God is Awake in her thoeth not Minded by her I Could weshe weth all my hart that she wose[7] from that vane noteye[8] Compney & pray when the Ritest to her a Gane porswade her to Lefe this Contrey & to Goe for the Irlande for I doue belefe itt would bee beter for her soles goode & in short Everewaye doue not take Aney notest whot I have reten to her here haeth bene a frendly that is of thy Aqunta[nce?] that lefes att doblen money times att my house his name is John Gaye & I have Assested hee in whot hee desired of mee frends here are Generly veary well Evrey waye & wonderfully Cared one[9] in the pouer of the Lorde & kepes Metens in Armonenose[10] maner & a Gret body not wethe standene the Crulety of the Enemy whoase strenth & pouer never wose att soe gret a hede ass itt tese & Licke to bee I never saye itt soe bade neather Ever wose itt Ever so sense trueth aprede in this nashon thay torne hole fameles out of thar houses & imployments & grete thretnens is daly[11] My dere frend sense My last to the I have oltred my Condeshon bot I ded not prosed weth out the Conse[nt] & Advise of the Most of the Mens & wemes meten & hade a grete Maney of good oulde frens Compney thar[12] wose all so Eli: Jeps & her Mouther weth som over that that thay brot weth tham whou weare vearey much plesed weth thar [illegible deletion] beingen thare for Charles harese[13] wose thare & Cared one the meten & thar that Rased in som of tham I dou bee Leefe well never bee for goten by tham I fere I ame to tedyese

I hope that this Lines well Com
scafe to thy hande this weth
the rembrens of My dere Love to
the is all att present from thy
true frend

Lon: the 16th the 5 Mo: 70
Eliz: Bowman

ALS. SP 63/327, PRO. (*Micro.* 1:235). It is addressed, in a different hand: For William Penne | at John Gayes | house in Georg's | Lane | in Dublin | these dd | Ireland.

1. Elizabeth Baily (1639-1675) of St. Martin's in the Field, married Mathias Bowman, a London haberdasher, 28 June 1670. She died in childbirth. Cadbury, "Intercepted Correspondence of William Penn," *PMHB* 70:354.

2. Assuming that Elizabeth Baily Bowman is the "E.B." in WP's Irish Journal, he wrote to her on 13 Nov. 1669 and 10 May 1670 and received a letter from her on 26 June. See doc. 35, above.

3. It is impossible to tell what the enclosures were or for whom intended. WP did frequently send tracts to his friends and acquaintances. The confusion of feminine pronouns here is difficult to decipher. Perhaps the "she" who received enclosures is the E. J., or Eliz. J., or Eliz. Jepe referred to in several places in the letter. An Elizabeth Jephson signed Elizabeth Bowman's marriage certificate. Cadbury, *PMHB* 70:354.

4. Margaret Fell Rous (1633-1706), one of the daughters of Margaret Fell Fox and her first husband, Thomas Fell. She married John Rous of Barbados in 1662. She and her husband worked hard to get her mother out of prison in 1670. Margaret Rous was pregnant when this meeting took place; a son, Nathaniel, was born 9 Sept. 1670. Cadbury, *PMHB* 70:354; DQB.

5. "Interested"?

6. Margaret Fell Fox was imprisoned in Lancaster in Apr. 1670 under a praemunire, probably at the instigation of her son George Fell (c. 1638-1670), who quarreled with his mother over property and probably resented her marriage to George Fox. She received a complete discharge in Apr. 1671, six months after the death of her son. See Isabel Ross, *Margaret Fell: Mother of Quakerism* (London, 1949), pp. 226-29, and Norman Penney, "George Fell and the Story of Swarthmoor Hall," *JFHS* 29:51-61; 30:28-39. Cadbury believed this letter might confirm a charge by Francis Bugg (1640-1724), a Quaker until 1680 and then a fierce writer of anti-Quaker tracts, who wrote years later that Margaret Fox had imagined herself pregnant while in Lancaster jail. If true, other Quakers were remarkably silent about the affair. It is conceivable that the reference to being with child is to Margaret Rous. See *DNB*, and Francis Bugg, *A Finishing Stroke* (London, 1707), p. 241, as quoted in Cadbury, *PMHB* 70:355.

7. "Was."

8. "Naughty"?

9. "Carried on"?

10. "Harmonious."

11. Persecution was intense under the Second Conventicle Act, particularly in London. See Braithwaite, *Second Period*, pp. 75-81; Gerald R. Cragg, *Puritanism in the Period of the Great Persecution 1660-1688* (Cambridge, 1957), pp. 16-18.

12. Elizabeth Baily's meeting had apparently questioned whether her intended husband Mathias Bowman was a Friend. See [William Mucklow], *Tyranny and Hypocrisy Detected* (London, 1673), pp. 21-22.

13. Perhaps Charles Harris of High Wycombe, Bucks., a Friend in good standing in 1670, who later was a Story-Wilkinson supporter, and by the 1680s had separated from the Friends. See Cadbury, *PMHB* 70:352; Fox, *Short Journal*, p. 325.

43
FROM JOHN GAY

[23 July 1670]

Deare S^{r} I should in the first place excuse my selfe for not writeing to y^{u} all this tyme I have been in England but I shall decline that well knowing yor aptnes to put the best interpretation upon my neglects (as it deserve indeed to be called) I hope you have had noe want of me at Dublin since my absence, especially, haveing been there [deletion] yor selfe I have wasted most of my tyme at penshurst,[1] but intend now if God will to sett forward out of this towne towards home next third day being two or three days longer then I intended to stay here and is in respect to H S[2] at whose house I have layne in the Muse since I came last from pensh and very neere yor little freind[3] whoe I have severall tymes visited but as often missed being much abroad and more in finery then ever I suppose. she wonders at y^{u} and her fathers writeing and thinkes yor mad, and says that none can deale to any purpose or doe any good in medling betweene man and wife, but sayth she shall doe best her selfe wth him, and by writeing kindly to him hath made him kind wch she likes best at a distance and sayth he hath sent her 40^{l} wth great kind expressions excusing that it is noe more & that she knows how hard it is to get money in Ireland and hath ~~sent~~ sent his brother to her to pay her the rest {for him} if she need it before he can remitt. she sayth she thinks it {as} impossible for y^{u} to alter her by all yor writeing as it is for her to alter you by hers & much discourse of that kinde. Upon the last fift day I went to watford in Essex[4] to see yor father & mother where I came about the tenth hower & enquired for Sr Wm Pen who I was told was within, I told the servant I was there to waite on him & to present his sons duty him that was in Ireland, word was brought me from him forth wth that he was not well and had that day taken phisick and could not see me but that if I pleased to come some other tyme he would be glad to see me, soe I lighted and went in and enquired for yor mother and desired to know if I might not see her (who it seemed was abed as she told me after) where upon some person went to her and brought me word she would come presently wch after some tyme she did, and was very civell and gave me preserves and other fruite and drinkes. and much discourse we had & full of tears she was concerning y^{u} that y^{u} should continue of that Judgm^{t} still that was soe contrary to them and that y^{u} were growne lesse loveing to her since then before for she had not had one letter from y^{u} ~~there~~ since you went hence and wondered what the reason was except her husband might meet wth them and keepe them from her. I gave her all the assurance I could that you were as much ~~if not~~ or rather more affectionate & dutyfull to her as ever. and that I knew full well it was contrary to yor principles to be other wise and that y^u had lately writt a little letter or Booke in Ireland wch plainly spoke to that very perticuler.[5] and that I had brought 6 of them over wth me but had none left to give her wch I was sorry [deletion] for then she fell upon that strange rude way that was taken up amongst such as y^u of not putting of the [hat] and what a strange thing was it to speake to a King wth the hat on and that religion should be placed in such a thing. I told her that they placed noe manner of religion in it, and she might plainly see if she had ever read yor booke about hat worship &c.[6] I alsoe said what I thought right in yor commendations to her and that y^u had greate favor and respect wth the L L^t[7] and many greate {men} visited y^u and that the Lo. L^t had been very civell to y^u & others of them called quakers she sayd yor father had intended to make y^u a greate man but y^u would not hearken to him, I told her that y^u had (I questioned not) chosen the better parte, and would be rather {I hoped} greate in heaven much discourse we had of this kinde & not fitt all to be told y^u she told me yor sister was brought a bed a fortnight since of a Girle,[8] and that yor brother[9] was well but a little wilde & had been greetely enterteyned where he is in Italy. And now to come to yor father whoe she sayd with her wondered y^u did not come over and asked me when y^u would come over and that yor father would faine have y^u there to understand his estate and how he settles & leaves things for he is very ill of a dropsy scurvey & Jandies and hath a very greate belly & full of water & the fisick was to get out the water if possible but the doct^rs had given over and had sayd (between her & I she sayd) that the fall of the leafe would put him hard to it, and that if not then the first parte of the winter would carry him away[10] he seldome walks in the garden and not at all abroad but once a week to the place by blackwall[11] where the India shiping affaires is (I cannot give the name) being concerned there for a widdow of a clarke there lately dead. [deletion] his goeing to the bath[12] was lately consulted of by 4 doctors (she sd) 3 were against it & but one for it. they sayd that he would faint away either in the Journy or in the water or in sweating & therefore that was layd aside. I told her that by what I had perceived it was yor fathers minde {rather} to have you stay in Ireland then come hither and that certainly upon the least intimation that it was yor fathers pleasure y^u would come speedyly over, it being for his service y^u went & stayd there rather then yo^re owne inclination, the family being in disorder as she sayd two servant mades being sick of agues, and she under trouble I went away betweene 11 and 12. thence to Hackney[13] crosse a water out of Essex into Midlesex I thinke to Alderm Forths who marryed S^r H vanes daughter[14] being near travell where the lady vane was, wch I had notice of at fairlane[15] and there made my visit and came just as they were sitting downe to dynner and stayed there till almost sunn sett being very hott in wch tyme Sr Walter & Charles S^r H bretheren came in who I had opportunity of seeing.[16] I have given yu a tedious relation but not much more I suppose then expedient, if wee meet before yu come hither I may farther trouble yu wth ~~the~~ something of the like kinde. I have not this night wrote to my wife If you are yet at dublin pray excuse me to her being more ernest now of being my own messenger to her then of writeing. Isack penington hath been cruelly used by an evell minded Justice in or nere reading (wch it may be yu have heard) for onely goeing to visit freinds in prison at reading.[17] apprehended him & put the Oath of alleag[iance] to him & for refuseing. Comitted him there where he is. Greate courage and boldnes is given to freinds espetially of the ministry here, wch I have seene and heard wch makes the enemy much the more to rage and make spoyle as they have and cheifly in the country to the ruining of familys wch the Lord doth behold and in due tyme will recompence. I shall ~~all~~ ad noe [more] now but remaine dear freind

Yors to serve yu as far
as in my power
Jo: Gay:

London 23th of
the moneth called
July 70

ALS. SP 63/328/164-65, PRO. Addressed: To William Penn Esqe at John | Gays house in Georges lane | these | Dublin.

1. Penshurst Place, the manor house of Robert Sidney, Earl of Leicester. Gay was probably visiting Leicester's son Henry Sidney, for whom he served at various times as estate agent in Ireland. Philip Sidney, *The Sidneys of Penshurst* (London, 1910), pp. 267-78; ACM, vol. 143.

2. Henry Sidney (1641-1704), later Lord Romney, in 1670 was captain in the Holland regiment. His London house seems to have been in the Mews, at Charing Cross, near the royal stables. Cunningham, p. 551. WP had probably known Henry Sidney since the early 1660s, when both young men were studying with Protestant scholars; this is also when WP is believed to have met Algernon Sidney, Henry's older brother.

3. Possibly Elizabeth Jephson. See doc. 42, n. 3.

4. Probably an error for Wanstead, an Essex village adjoining Walthamstow, six miles east of London, where the elder Penns were living in retirement. In later documents this house of the Penns is referred to as being in Walthamstow.

5. *A Letter of Love to the Young Convinced* (1670).

6. *No Cross, No Crown* (1669).

7. John, Lord Berkeley of Stratton. See doc. 35, 31 May, 1 June, and 6 June 1670.

8. Elizabeth, daughter of Anthony and Margaret (Penn) Lowther, was baptized 31 July 1670 and buried 4 Aug. 1675 at Marske, Yorks. ACM, vol. 49B.

9. Richard Penn.

10. Sir William Penn died 16 Sept. 1670.

11. On the north bank of the Thames, about three miles east of the Tower and five miles from Wanstead.

12. A bathing spa, such as Tunbridge Wells in Kent or Bath in Somerset.

13. Hackney, Middlesex, about three miles toward London from Wanstead, was a favorite suburban residence for London merchants. Samuel Lewis, *A Topographical Dictionary of England* (London, 1838).

14. Albinia (b. 1644), daughter of Sir Henry Vane the younger (1612-1662), a

leading republican of the Commonwealth period, married Alderman John Forth of London in 1668. Cadbury, *PMHB* 70:363.

15. Fairlawne was a Vane family estate in Kent. Cadbury, *PMHB* 70:363.

16. Sir Walter Vane (1619-1674), a royalist (unlike his brother Henry) was knighted by Charles II. In 1668, he was appointed colonel of the Holland regiment. Charles Vane (c. 1621-1672) had been an agent of parliament at Lisbon in 1650. *DNB;* Cadbury, *PMHB* 70:363.

17. Isaac Penington was pardoned and released from Reading jail in 1672 following the Declaration of Indulgence. Besse 1:31. For his arrest, see doc. 41.

44
JONATHAN KEALY TO PHILIP FORD

The following document, from an unidentified Irishman to WP's agent Philip Ford, sheds additional light on WP's Irish business. Jonathan Kealy was employed to make maps of Sir William Penn's estates in Imokilly, Ibaune, and Barryroe. Sir William Petty had surveyed Catholic lands in Ireland in the 1650s, and his maps, known as the Civil Survey, or Down Survey, were the basis for distributing land under the Act of Settlement. When Kealy wrote to Ford, he had completed his work, but was lacking data on one tract of land which he asked Ford to search for in Cork; he also asked to be paid.

Dublin August the 5th 1670

When I reced thyne, I left my harvest and building and hasten'd hither to the end yo^{u} should not be disappointed, and now haveing almost finished, I intend on tewsday morning to begin my Journey towards Gowran,[1] and carry the mapps wth me; I would send them ere now but the surrounds[2] of Knocknegeiragh and Knocknegappule[3] hindred me for I [one word deleted] can finde them neither in Office nor privat hands. for they were reputed protestant intrest and were left unSurveyed; and haveing all the rest of the land described soe perfect [illegible word deleted] I am loath to insert them by Estimat; although I have them in the Barony mapp, I cannot bring them to the scale of the great mapp wthout committing an Error Therefore I must desire yo^{u} to enquire for the Booke of Survey of the protestant intrest of that County wch Mr Taylor and I made ~~made~~ up there in the yeare 16~~6~~59 out of wch yo^{u} may send me the Trace and number of Acres by the Post, and then yor maps wilbe as perfect as yor heart cann wish, I am sure that booke is in Corke therefore yo^{u} cannot miss it,

The Frames Box, Fees and other Materialls of those Maps cost me 4^{l}-17^{s}-00^{d}, and the Comon Rate given me by the office for makeing each Barony Map is 3^{l} soe that I have made up the three Baronyes:[4]

together wth the greate map wch I hope yo^u will compute together, and returne me to Kilkenny soe much money as will answer my paines, I assure yo^u I wish I had given 5^l that I had not undertaken them, because my loss of time about them is very greate. I chall continue at Gowran 10 dayes and shall goe thence to waterford soe that before I send the maps I expect they Letter and money wch is all at present from

Yo^r Lov^g Freind
Jo^n Kealy[4]

Excuse this scribling
for I have not time
to read it over

ALS. SP 63/328/193, PRO. Addressed: For Mr Phillip Ford | at Mr Thomas Cooke's | house in Corke | These.

1. A townland, parish, and barony in county Kilkenny. The town was incorporated by James I in 1608, and its castle was surrendered to Cromwell in 1650. Lewis, 1:667-68.

2. A surround is a perimeter map. Edmond Fitzmaurice, *The Life of Sir William Petty, 1623-1687* (London, 1895), p. 325.

3. Knocknegeiragh and Knocknegappule, 120 acres in Ballincona parish, Imokilly, was formerly owned by William Cotter, who, this letter implies, must have been a Protestant. Book of Survey and Distribution, county Cork, PRO Dublin; Grubb, p. 80.

4. Apparently Imokilly, Ibaune and Barryroe are intended, though Ibaune and Barryroe is one barony, not two.

45
FROM PHILIP FORD

Corke the 9th 6mo [August] 1670

Deare Friend

My last to thee was Post the 3 Day after thou wentst from hence[1] the 5th day following I went to King sayle & had the stoned horse to Capt Rooth who has taken him but would not Cum to a price but his keeping shall Cost thee nothing he saith, he purposeth to Ride him to Charlevell this weeke to give the Earle of Orery a Visit & as he likes him may Cum to a [price?] at his Returne which I shall indevour, as to the Remainder of the [men's] pay of thy fathers[2] he saith its not pd thee, thou knowest & w[hat] was more he gave the Acc^o: he did not proffer to pay it neither d[id] I see it Convenient to Aske for it at that time, I sent a lett^r to Capt Cr[ispin?] to Meet me at King sayle fort who Accordingly did, I Acquain[ted] him with w^t Orders thou left with me Concerning him & W[: P:] & likewise Capt Rooth I lett see thy fathers lett^r [3] According as thou bidst me, And likewise sent for the Ensigne W: P:,[4] to Cum to the Castle but he would not be seene nor none of his family but word brought back by Capt Rooths serv^t that he was gone over the watter to the towne, which was not soe. Capt Rooth seemd to wonder Very much at it that he Came not:

but Doutless Capt Rooth knew why he Came not but whilst we were in Expectation of his Cuming I propounded wt thou orderst me to Capt Crispin who was willing to Conclud that business betwixt the Ensigne & himself he having half the proffitt from the Day of the Ensignes entering Upon it he allowing him halfe of wt he has Receivd & giveing him halfe the bills that are Un pd & then Upon the paymt of the 72l:8s: he would give a Dis[charge] as to that[5] but would not Includ the Improvmts at MackRoone so that I [see?] no likely hood of ending that business Except their be an Allow[ance] granted him in one way or other, he having a bill of the Ensigne to g[ive] him half proffitt looks Upon him self as safe anough as to that so the Ensi[gne] not Cuming as the business was so it is then I told Capt Crispin that I had Order to Call on him for the 30l lett he sd he would Allow it in the money pd to the Ensigne as so much of his pte, or if he be sued then he must Cume Upon Old {R:} Southwell for his 40l stopt: & pay it out of that, as to Major Love he was not in a Condision to Make any Acco keepeing his bedd & every day Expecting his Death:,[6] Capt Rooth saith that he see wt Acco he gave thee which he Luked Upon as pretty equall, the same Day I was their John Hadock[7] had a Meeting at Rich Nunns in Kingsayle & Margaret[8] is to have one there next 6th Day as for Powell[9] he hath not brought in his Accos as he said to thee he would nor as I understand ever Intends but wt is owing he purposeth to keep towards his Improvts & for Tige Reerdon thou must send a writing under thy Mothers hand that its Due, & for Lumbard I Expect to here from thee wt to doe, Last ist Day was a meeting at Yaughall, George Harris, Margeret & S: Mitchell, severall there is that be Convinsed amongst whome is Major Farmers Daughter that is Marrd in that towne to a mcht:[10] he was at the Meeting with her After the Meeting was over M: & S: Mitchell went to the Babtist Meeting where they had good servis & severall of the Babtists Confesd to the truth, next first Day John Hadock is to have a Meeting there at Yaughall he is now in the west, I went to O. Silver for the 13l but he saith he hath not the Money neither would say when he would pay it but I thinke to send to him before next terme if he will not pay it I have Receivd no money since thou wentst I purpose to be with the Tennts in Imokelly this weeke as to the Mapp, if I Receive it shall pay him[11] his Mo[ney]: I sent thee the lettr [of] his as to the spannish worke being ten pieces & the Italian Introducktion [I] sent them from King sayle if there was more of them thou must send me word for I doe not Remember that ever thou tolst me the perticulers I have sent them to Bristoll to Francis Rodgers with another box of books 120 of Liberty Con:[12] 12:six [quires] of popery[13] which may be 300 books 59 lettr Lov[14] & the Odd sh[ee]ts to perfect them thou hadst away, likewise 2 pr shoes & all the lettrs since thou wentst, severall Friends have there Deare Love to thee, Friends in this Citty are Genrly well the Mayor Continues taking

Friends names but proceeds no further[15] My Deare Loe is to Friends in that City London & thereabouts as thou hast freedom to Acquaint them that know m[e] So desiring to here of thy well fare I Remain thy Friend in faithfullness to serve thee

Philip Ford

before the sealing hereof thyne per inclosure G: H: Came to hand wherein I Understand thy safe Arrivall at Bristoll which I & severall more here was glad of as to thy horses thou wouldst have sent I suppose thou Intends only thy gray geldi & Jo P:[16] for the Mare is sold to John Fennell & the stoned horse is with Capt: Rooth so that them two J P: & thyne I purpose to send to Mine=head[17] & so have them safely Convaid to Bristoll this Day I spoke to a mr of a ship that will Carry them but it w[ill] be next weeke before he sets sayle & I question whether I shall get them [sent?] or noe before here is not any ship for Bristoll but the Arthur & Mary & she Cannot Carry them,

P F:

ALS. SP 63/328/13-14, PRO. (*Micro.* 1:253). Addressed: To | Edward Man at the signe | of the Goulden Lyon nere | Bishops=gate | London | For Will: Penn.

Endorsed with the following summary: P. F. in his letter from Corke the 9th 6mo 1670. Directed to Edward Man at the Signe of the Golden Lyon near Bishops-gate, London for Will. Penn. Gives an account of a Meeting he was at Richard Nunns in Kinsale, & that Marget was to have one there the next 6th day. That the last 1st day was a meeting at Youghall where severall are convinced. & the Next 1st day anothr to be held their by Jo. Haddock. He speakes of a Spanish, 10 pieces & an Italian Introduction, wch he sent from Kinsale to Bristol to Francis Rodgers wth anothr box of books 120 of Liberty of Con. 12. 6 quires of Popery wch may be 300. books 59. letters Lov & the Odde Sheetes to perfect there wch he had away.

Further endorsed in the hand of Joseph Williamson:[18] Information. Seditious books out of Ireland W Penne. Oct. 1670.

1. Though the Irish Journal ends on 1 July 1670, WP apparently spent most of July in Dublin, returning to Cork en route to London about 1 Aug. See docs. 41, 42, 43; Richard Bent to WP, 1 Aug. 1670, *Micro.* 1:246.

2. Ford seems to mean the accounts remaining to be settled after the Admiral's relinquishment of the governorship of the fort at Kinsale.

3. Doc. 38.

4. Ensign William Penn.

5. Crispin as deputy victualler, Ensign Penn as clerk of cheque, and Rooth as new governor, would have had complex financial dealings with each other. All were related through the Penn family. The exact nature of their arrangements is uncertain.

6. Major John Love was deputy governor of Kinsale Fort. His will was dated 28 May and probated 5 Oct. 1670. ACM, vol. 144.

7. John Haydock (1640-1719) of Coppull, Lanc., a Friends minister, visited Ireland in 1669, 1671, 1676, and 1710. On 14 Sept. 1670, with ten others, he was committed to the county jail for attending a meeting in Wexford. Cadbury, *PMHB* 70:369.

8. Perhaps Margaret Sutton, a public Friend who visited Ireland in 1669. *JFHS* 10:158.

9. Perhaps E. Powell, whose island was near Macroom. See doc. 35, 18 Apr. 1670.

10. Elizabeth, daughter of Jasper Farmer, married another Friend, James Dowlan, in Youghall. Grubb, p. 82.

11. John Kealy. See doc. 44.

12. *The Great Case of Liberty of Conscience* (1670).

13. *A Seasonable Caveat Against Popery* (1670).

14. *A Letter of Love to the Young Convinced* (1670).

15. Whereas the Cork Quakers reported at least thirty-seven arrests in 1669 by Mayor Matthew Deane, in 1670 they reported no arrests and only four seizures of Quaker property. National Meeting Record of Sufferings, 1655-1693, pp. 57-58, 64, Friends Historical Library, Dublin.

16. John Penington.

17. Minehead, Somerset, a small port on the Bristol Channel.

18. Joseph Williamson (1633-1701) was secretary to Lord Arlington and chief of his spy network. *DNB*.

IN NEWGATE

1670–1671

In August 1670 and again in February 1671, WP was arrested and sent to Newgate prison in London. On the first occasion, he was brought to trial with his fellow Quaker William Mead, at the court of quarter sessions. The following six documents, 46-51, illustrate several key points in the Penn-Mead trial, which became a major event in the development of English liberties. The trial was important in WP's development as a defender of the Society of Friends, and as a proponent of religious freedom for all Englishmen.

When a London constable arrested WP and William Mead at an assembly of Quakers in Gracechurch Street in August 1670, Sir Samuel Starling, Lord Mayor of London, chose not to fine WP for nonconformist preaching but to try Mead and WP for conspiring to incite a riot (doc. 46). Starling was trying to intimidate London's Friends, who had been stoutly resisting all attempts to disperse their Gracechurch Street meetings. Doc. 47 suggests that he may also have had a personal animus against the Penns.

Docs. 48 and 49 comment upon the Penn-Mead trial of 1-5 September, which is fully recounted in *The People's Ancient and Just Liberties Asserted, in the Tryal of William Penn, and William Mead, with An Appendix, by way of Defense for the Prisoners* (London, 1670), in *Works*, 1:7-35, which was probably written jointly by WP and other Quaker leaders; in S.S. [Samuel Starling?], *An Answer to the Seditious and Scandalous Pamphlet, Entitled, The Tryal of W. Penn and W. Mead, at the Sessions held at the Old Baily, London, the 1, 3, 4, 5, of Sept. 1670* (London, 1671); and in WP's *Truth Rescued from Imposture, or A Brief Reply to a Mere Rhapsody of Lies, Folly and Slander; But a Pretended Answer, to the Tryal of W. Penn, and W. Mead, &c.* (London, 1671), in *Works*, 1:486-521, which was a reply to S.S.'s *Answer.* In the trial, Mead and WP successfully defended themselves and were acquitted by the jury, but were fined by the bench for contempt of court. In doc. 48, WP summarizes his argument that the trial was unjust and replete with errors. In his letter of 5 September to his father (doc. 49), he gives further details about the trial and the behavior of the court.

The actions of three men elevated this trial above a routine judicial persecution of religious dissent. Had Mayor Starling fined WP for preaching contrary to the Conventicle Act of 1670, or tendered him the *praemunire* loyalty oath, to which no good Quaker could swear, no jury would have been impaneled and WP would have become just another sufferer for his faith. Had WP ignored the specific charges in the indictment and argued broadly for freedom of speech and religion, he probably would have been convicted. Instead, he demonstrated to the jury that he had been preaching to an unarmed, peaceable crowd, and convinced them that he was not inciting a riot. Finally, had juror Edward Bushell accepted the court's fine for trespassing upon the bench's power to interpret law and for refusing to bring in a directed verdict, the trial would not have generated an important legal precedent. Bushell's successful suit against the London bench in the Court of Common Pleas strengthened the right of juries to decide matters of law as well as of fact, and granted them greater independence from overbearing magistrates.

Mead and WP, however, were able to leave prison only after paying stiff fines for contempt of court in refusing to take off their hats. WP wished to appeal this fine (docs. 49-51), but he changed his mind and allowed the fine to be paid so that he could see his dying father. For further accounts of the Penn-Mead trial, see Braithwaite, *Second Period,* pp. 68-73; Janney, pp. 56-74; Peare, pp. 109-25; and Mary Maples Dunn, *William Penn, Politics and Conscience,* pp. 12-18.

46
SIR SAMUEL STARLING TO THE KEEPER OF NEWGATE

London. [14 August 1670]

Receive into yo[r] Custody the Body of W[m] Penn herewith sent you, who was taken in the Street called Gracious Street[1] preaching seditiously, & causing a great Tumult of people in the sayd Street to be there gathered together Riotuosly & Routuously,[2] and him safely keep, untill he shall be legally discharged. Dated this 14[o] day of August 1670. and this shall be your Warrant.

To the keeper of Newgate.[4] Samuel Starling, Maior.[3]

LBC. WP's Letterbook, 1667-1675, HSP. (*Micro.* 1:261).

1. Gracechurch Street was a major thoroughfare in the east-central part of the City of London. After the Great Fire of 1666, London Quakers built residences and a meetinghouse at White-Hart Yard, formerly the site of the White-Hart Inn, a courtyard screened off from the street by houses at the corner of Gracechurch and Lombard

Streets. The Quakers to whom WP was preaching had gathered in the street itself after a detachment of soldiers had shut them out of their meetinghouse. *London Monuments,* 4: endpaper map; Beck and Ball, pp. 145-47; Braithwaite, *Second Period,* pp. 68-69.

2. In a "routous" or disorderly manner. *OED.*

3. Sir Samuel Starling (1625?-1674), Lord Mayor of London, was a merchant and (so his enemies charged) a persecutor of royalist sympathizers in the 1650s. At the Restoration he was named to the bench that tried and sentenced several regicides to death. He was elected Lord Mayor in 1669. Starling lived on the west side of Seething Lane, across from the Navy Office, and he probably knew Sir William Penn, and perhaps WP, personally. S.S. [Samuel Starling?], *An Answer To the Seditious and Scandalous Pamphlet,* pp. 4-9; WP, *Truth Rescued from Imposture,* in *Works,* 1:492-93; Pepys, 8 Sept. 1666; Daniel, *London City Churches,* p. 18.

4. The chief prison of the City of London, located near the twelfth-century gate of that name in City Wall. Muirhead's *London,* p. 324.

47
TO SIR WILLIAM PENN

15th of 7[6]th mo.[1] [August] 1670.
Second day morning.

My Dear Father,

This comes by the hand of one who can best allay the trouble it brings. As true as ever Paul said, that such as live godly in Christ Jesus shall suffer persecution,[2] so for no other reason am I at present a sufferer. Yesterday I was taken by a band of soldiers, with one Capt. Mead,[3] a linen draper, and in the evening carried before the mayor;[3] he proceeded against us[4] according to the ancient law; he told me I should have my hat pulled off, for all I was Admiral Penn's son. I told him that I desired to be in common with others, and sought no refuge from the common usage. He answered, it had been no matter, if thou hadst been[5] commander twenty years ago. I discoursed with him about the hat; he avoided it, and because I did not readily answer him my name, William, when he asked me in order to a mittimus,[6] he bid his clerk write one for *Bridewell,*[7] and there would he see me whipped himself, for all I was Penn's son, that starved the seamen.[8] Indeed these words grieved me, as well as that it manifested his great weakness and malice to the whole company, that were about one hundred people. I told him I could very well bear his severe expressions to me concerning myself, but was sorry to hear him speak those abuses of my father, that was not present, at which the assembly seemed to murmur. In short, he committed that person[9] with me as rioters; and at present we are at the sign of the Black Dog, in Newgate market.[10]

And now, dear father, be not displeased nor grieved. What if this be designed of the Lord for an exercise of our patience? I am sure it hath wonderfully laid bare the nakedness of the mayor. Several Independents were taken from Sir J. Dethick's, and Baptists elsewhere.[11] It is the effect of a present commotion in the spirits of some, which the Lord God will rebuke; and I doubt not but I may be at liberty in a day or two, to see thee. I am very well, and have no trouble upon my spirit[12] besides my absence from thee, especially at this juncture; but otherwise I can say I was never better; and what they have to charge me with is harmless. Well, eternity, which is at the door, (for he that shall come, will come, and will not tarry.) *that* shall make amends for all. The Lord God everlasting consolate and support thee, by his holy power and presence,[13] to his eternal rest and glory. Amen.

Thy faithful and obedient son,
My duty to my mother. William Penn

Original lost. Printed, *The Friend* 6(1833):170; Janney, pp. 57-58. (*Micro.* 1:262). Docketed: For my dear father, Sir William Penn.

1. In *The Friend,* (see provenance note) this letter is incorrectly dated 7th mo.; Janney's version is correctly dated 6th mo.
2. 2 Tim. 3:12.
3. William Mead (1628-1713) was a London merchant tailor and, like WP, a person of considerable property and social standing. He seems to have joined the Quakers shortly before this arrest. Mead quickly became active in Quaker affairs, working closely with Fox, Whitehead, WP, and other leading Friends in petitioning the government to cease persecution. Fox, 2:420; Braithwaite, *Second Period,* pp. 69-70, 207.
4. "Me," in Janney's text.
5. Janney inserts "a" here.
6. A warrant ordering the reception of a prisoner. Doc. 46 is a mittimus. *OED.*
7. A workhouse for the idle poor, rioters, and prostitutes, located between Fleet Street and the Thames. Muirhead's *London,* p. 340; Cunningham, 1:118-21.
8. Mayor Starling was referring to charges brought against Admiral Penn in 1668 by the Commissioners of Accounts that he sold between one and two thousand pounds worth of captured Dutch merchandise and kept the proceeds. This charge led to Penn's impeachment and suspension from the House of Commons in Apr.-May 1668. In the Commons debates over the charges against him, one M.P. argued that "the poor soldiers and sailors want pay, and the officers grow fat," while another charged that Penn was particularly culpable because "the wants of the soldiers and seamen [were] so well known to him." After the Penn-Mead trial, Starling and WP carried on their dispute over the Admiral's character in print. *Journals of the House of Commons,* 9:82, 85, 88, 92, 93; Grey, *Debates in Commons,* 1:133-41; *Memorials,* 2:460-86; Pepys, Mar.-Apr. 1668; Charnock, *Biographia Navalis,* 1:122; S.S. [Samuel Starling?], *An Answer To the Seditious and Scandalous Pamphlet,* pp. 6-7; Penn, *Truth Rescued from Imposture,* in *Works,* 1:497-99.
9. William Mead.
10. Just east of Newgate Prison. The sign of the Black Dog marked a private inn that housed persons awaiting trial who were of too high a social status to be put into the foul and dangerous prison itself. The Quakers believed, however, that they were put there in 1670 because the master of the inn and one inmate had recently died of spotted fever, which the authorities hoped they would contract. Cunningham, 2:586-87; *London Monuments,* 4: endpaper map; Peare, p. 110; Besse, 1:428.
11. Several congregations of Anabaptists, Presbyterians, and other dissenters, as well as Quakers, were being broken up and arrested all through the summer of 1670, both in London and in the countryside. *CSPD, 1670,* pp. 310, 343, 369, 384.
12. "Spirits," in Janney's text.
13. Janney has "Preserve."

48
EXCEPTIONS AGAINST THE PROCEDURE OF THE COURT

[5? September 1670][1]

The Exceptions of William Penn Junior, agt the Procedure of the Court[2] (in Relation to him) at the Old Baily[3] this Sessions; begun the 31st of the month called August, 1670.

1. That no Assembly of Persons, designing only to worship God without any disturbance or Tumult offered on their part in contempt of the Fundamental Laws of this Land, be it in the street itself, when the Soldiers by force of Arms, commanded of the Lieutenancy thereunto, Keep them out of their lawfull hired house,[4] can be Criminal according to the usual Statutes, & common Law of this Realm in force agt Riots, Routs, or unlawful Assemblies.

2d That yr proceedings agt me to the Loss of my Liberty & Propriety for Assembling after our accustomed manner to worship God, being voyd of any Intention or just discovery of the same to prejudice the Governmt or people of England, & to overrule me as a Rioter, or a Router; For so doing is contrary to the fundamental Laws of England, which I claim as my birth-right, & Inheritance, & as the Immutable Fundation of the English Constitution in point of Govermt.

3d That an Imprisonment or Amercement[5] upon the people of England for any Act of Religious worship, or that is the necessary Adjunct of the same, is destructive of the Great Charter,[6] that considers us not, as of this or that perswasion in matters of Religion, in order to the obtaining of our antient Rights & Priviledges: but as English men: Witnesse the Constancy thereof through all Revolutions of Religious opinions.

4th I Except agt the Indictmt as Defective & False in 6 eminent Particulars;[7] & more especially, since the law pretended to be broken, & those necessary parts thereof, which makes a Riot, are not rehearsed.

5th That unlesse the witnesses swear, The Meeting was, with swords & staves, & to the terrour of the Kings people, according to the words & Intent of the Statute; Their Evidence is invalid, & not according to the Law.

6th The Jury is not obliged to make or give their Verdict according to that Evidence itself, unless they in conscience & Law are satisfied of the Truth thereof, being wholely Judges of the Matter.

7th I cannot but except agt yr Illegal Proceedings in not suffering me to plead for myself, or to be fully heard either by way of Question, or Answer: nor yet to make, nor offer those material, & necessary Demands, & Objections; which is my undoubted Right. As (1st) That you of the Bench should be my Council;[8] & not with harsh menaces, & scornful Repartees to prevent or silence my legal & sober Offers. Nor yet (2d) When I asked Oyr[9] of the Law (you pretend I have broken) that you should deny it me, as a motion agt the honour of the Court; though the known Common rights of every Englishman. Neither (3d) should you hale me by violence from the Barr[10] into the Bayl dock[11] & then to give the Jury Charge in my Absence: which is notoriously agt the Law. Nor, when I called upon you to signifie as much; immediately to send me into the stinking Hole,[12] & then to say your pleasure of me to the Jury. And when they agreed not upon their Verdict; to minace & abuse them with severe Reflections. Nay, when the Verdict was agreed upon; you utterly refused it, and swore certain persons, to keep them lockd up all night, in order to obtain your ends; although I asked a Record of the ~~Bench~~ Verdict, & that the Sentence of the Bench ought to wait upon, & be pursuant to the Verdict of the Jury.

These Exceptions above written I make, as good in Law, if you deny me the Benefit of them, as being agt Law: & my Right, as an Englishman, I require you to give it me under your Hands & Seals. as you in the Like case ought to do.

LBC. WP's Letterbook, 1667-1675, HSP. (*Micro.* 1:263).

1. This text is the longer of two drafts of "exceptions" in WP's Letterbook, both written in a clerk's hand. The other draft, which may have been composed jointly by Mead and WP, and which refers throughout to "us," closely resembles this document in the first six numbered paragraphs, but has no par. 7. At its close, however, another hand, probably WP's, adds that if the court denies their exceptions, they intend to "joyn issue for tryall of their validity" (WP's Letterbook, 1667-1675, HSP., f. 57, not filmed), making it clear that this document was intended as the first step in opening a suit in the Court of Common Pleas against Starling's court. Because this draft of exceptions recounts the entire trial, it must have been composed no earlier than 5 Sept.

2. The quarter sessions of the City of London.

3. The London law court on Old Bailey Street. The building in which WP was tried was destroyed in the Gordon Riots of 1780. Cunningham, 2:603-5; Stow, *Survay of London*, p. 145.

4. The Quaker meetinghouse in White-Hart Yard, Gracechurch Street.

5. A fine levied arbitrarily, at the discretion of a justice. *OED*.

6. In the full account of the trial in *The People's Ancient and Just Liberties Asserted*, WP appealed repeatedly to the rights and privileges in the Great Charter of 1225 and its earlier version, Magna Carta (*Works*, 1:12, 13, 16, 18), and he and his friends appended a learned commentary upon the Charter and its legal legacy from the fourteenth century to their own day (*Works*, 1:23-35).

7. It is unclear just what "6 eminent Particulars" WP refers to here. Most of the points which follow in this document relate to the trial itself, while *The People's Ancient and Just Liberties Asserted* gives ten numbered objections to the indictment (*Works*, 1:19-21).

8. WP here appeals to the tradition that the court advise the accused of their legal rights. An anti-Quaker account of the trial shows that when WP directly asked the justices to perform this duty, the court's response was vague and perhaps deliberately evasive. S. S. [Samuel Starling?], *An Answer To the Seditious and Scandalous Pamphlet*, pp. 12-13.

9. The reading of a document or statute in court upon request. *OED*.

10. The railing before the judges' bench, where accused persons usually sat or stood during trial. *OED*.

11. A cagelike structure in the courtroom; prisoners were usually placed here on the day of trial and brought forward to the bar as the bench was ready to hear each case. Cunningham, 2:603.

12. Probably a cell in Newgate Prison.

49
TO SIR WILLIAM PENN

Ld. [London] 5. 7br [September] 1670

Dear Father.

Because I cannot ~~write~~ come, I write. These are to lett thee know that this morning about 7 we were remanded to the Sessions. The Jury after two nights & two days being locked up, came down & offerr'd their former verdict, but that being refused as not so positive, they explained themselves in answering not Guilty. Upon which the Bench[1] were amazed, & the whole Court so satisfyed that they made a Kinde of Hymne — but tht the Mayor Recorder Robinson &c:[2] might add to their Malice, they fined us to the number of about 12 of us, for not pulling off our hatts & keep[3] us prisoners for the mony An injurious trifle wch will blow over, or we shall bring it to the Common Pleas[4] because it was against Law & not by a Jury sessed.[5] How Great a dissatisfaction three of their actions have begott may ~~be seen~~ very reasonably be conjectured from the bare Mention of them (1) That the Jury was about 6 times rejected in their verdict & besides vaine fruitless illegall menaces, were kept two days & two nights without bed, tobacco provisions &c (2) that a Sessions should be held on the first day[6] (the designe we know) (3) that the Jury, only[7] judges by law should be fined 40 Marks[8] each. & to be prisoners till they have paid it and that without any Jury to pass upon [t]hem. However their verdict is accepted for us. because they did not dare deny it. This is the Substance. The Circumstances I shall personally relate if the Lord will. I am more concerned at thy distemper & the pains that attend it[9] than at my own mear[10] Imprisonment which workes for the best

I am Dear Father.
Thy obt Sonne.
Wm Penn.

Transcript. Coxe Collection, HSP. (Not filmed). A slightly variant copy of this document is printed in *The Friend* 7 (1833):59, and in Janney, pp. 72-73.

1. The justices on the bench were Lord Mayor Samuel Starling, presiding; John Howell, recorder; Thomas Bludworth, Richard Ford, William Peak, John Robinson, and Joseph Sheldon, aldermen; and Richard Brown, James Edwards, and John Smith, sheriffs. (*Works*, 1:9).

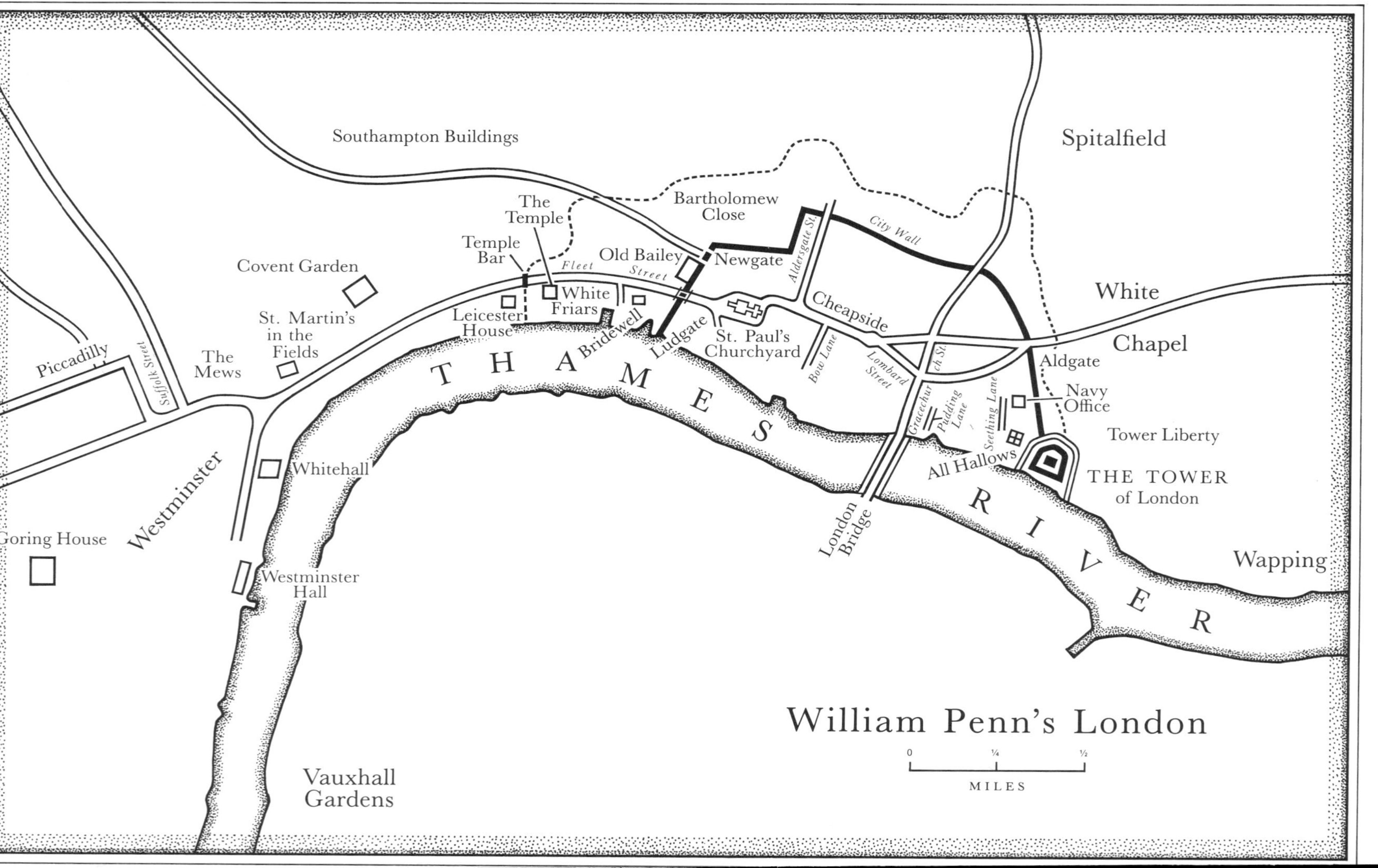
William Penn's London
0
¼
½
MILES
Southampton Buildings
Spitalfield
Bartholomew Close
The Temple
Temple Bar
Old Bailey
Newgate
Aldersgate St.
City Wall
Covent Garden
Fleet
Street
White Friars
Leicester House
Bridewell
Ludgate
St. Paul's Churchyard
Cheapside
Bow Lane
Lombard Street
White
Chapel
Aldgate
Navy Office
Tower Liberty
Gracechur
ch St.
Pudding Lane
Seething Lane
All Hallows
THE TOWER
of London
London Bridge
Wapping
St. Martin's in the Fields
The Mews
Piccadilly
Suffolk Street
Westminster
Whitehall
Westminster Hall
Goring House
Vauxhall Gardens
THAMES
RIVER

2. Mayor Starling, Recorder Howell, John Robinson, etc. Recorder Howell functioned as the court's prosecutor, and the account of the trial in *Works*, 1:7-18, shows that Howell, Starling, alderman Bludworth, and Robinson were the most active members of the court in prosecuting Mead and WP, and in hectoring the jury.

3. Janney and *The Friend* read "kept."

4. The Court of Common Pleas, one of the three superior courts of common law in England. WP and William Mead proposed to sue Starling and his colleagues if the justices did not withdraw the fines against them. They did not file this suit, but jurors Edward Bushell, John Baily, John Hammond, and Charles Milson did file suit in the Court of Common Pleas against Starling and his colleagues for fining them, and in 1671, Chief Justice Vaughn read his celebrated opinion in their favor (Bushell's Case), thereby sharply curtailing the power of justices to direct juries to bring in particular verdicts. William Cobbett, *Cobbett's Complete Collection of State Trials* (London, 1810), 6:999-1026.

5. Assessed.

6. Both *The Friend* and Janney omit "the" before "first day." WP was objecting to holding trial proceedings on Sunday, 4 Sept.

7. *The Friend* and Janney insert "the" before "only."

8. The equivalent of £ 26.13.4, a substantial sum in the seventeenth century. *OED*.

9. Admiral Penn had been seriously ill for several months, and died eleven days after WP wrote this letter.

10. Janney and *The Friend* read "mere."

50
TO SIR WILLIAM PENN

6 7br [September] 1670

D Father,

I desire thee not to be troubled at My present Confinement.[1] I could scarce suffer upon[2] a better account. nor by a worse hand: & the will of God be done It is more grievous & uneasy to me that thou shdst be so heavily exercized (God Ally knows) than any living worldly concernment. I am clear by the Jury, & they in my place.[3] They are resolved to lye[4] till they gett out by law; & they every six hours demand their freedom by advice of Councile. They[5] have so overshott themselves that the Generality of people much detest them. I intreat thee not to purchass my liberty They will repent them of their proceedings. I am now a prisoner notoriously against law. I desire the Lord God, In fervent prayers[6] to strengthen & support thee & anchor thy mind in the thoughts of the Immutable blessed state which is over all visible perishing concerns. I am Dear Father.

Thy obed Sonne Wm P.

Transcript. Coxe Collection, HSP. (Not filmed). Addressed: To My dr Father Sr Wm Penn. | Wanstead. Docketed: Letter of Wm Penn from New Gate. A slightly variant copy of this document is printed in *The Friend* 7 (1833):59, and in Janney, p. 73.

1. WP was still in Newgate because he would not pay his fine of forty marks for wearing his hat in court on 3 Sept. 1670. *Works*, 1:10.

2. *The Friend* and Janney read "on."

3. When the jurors acquitted WP and William Mead of conspiring to speak to a riotous assembly, they were fined and imprisoned for their verdict by the enraged

bench. Eight of the jurors paid their fine and were released, but four, led by Edward Bushell, sued Starling's court in the Court of Common Pleas, were released on bail, and finally won their case. See doc. 49, n. 4, above.

4. *The Friend* and Janney read "lay."

5. Mayor Starling and his colleagues on the bench.

6. *The Friend* and Janney read "prayer."

51
TO SIR WILLIAM PENN

Newgate, 7th Sept. 1670.

Dear Father,

To say I am truly grieved to hear of thy present illness, are words that might be spared, because I am confident they are better believed. If God in his holy will did see it meet that I should be freed, I could heartily embrace it; yet considering I cannot be free, but upon such terms as strengthening their arbitrary and base proceedings, I shall rather choose to suffer any hardship. I am persuaded some clearer way will suddenly be found out to obtain my liberty, which is no way so desirable to me, as on the account of being with thee.[1] I am not without hopes that the Lord will sanctify the endeavours of thy physician unto a cure, and then much of my worldly solicitude will be at an end. My present restraint is so far from being humour, that I would rather perish, than release myself by so indirect a course as to satiate their revengeful, avaricious appetites. The advantage of such a freedom would fall very short of the trouble of accepting it. Solace thy mind in the thoughts of better things, dear father. Let not this wicked world disturb thy mind, and whatever shall come to pass, I hope, in all conditions to approve myself, thy obedient son,

William Penn

Original lost. Printed, *The Friend* 7 (1833):179. (*Micro.* 1:269). Addressed: For Sir William Penn at Wanstead.

1. Within a few days after writing this letter, WP was released. Apparently WP decided to accept his father's offer to pay his fine so that he could see him before he died.

52
TO SAMUEL PEPYS

[4 November 1670]

I am so Farr from Flattering my selfe with the least hope of successe because I make the Insueing request that I have no greater reason to beleive the Contrary; It is my unhappynesse to be misrepresented by some, & wonderfully misunderstood by more; but no more off this.

My Poore Father was pleas'd to give me a sight of an Ingenious & Kind letter he receiv'd from thee[1] some time before he left it, & us; which assureing him how much thou wer't devoted on all occasions to serve his friends (because In doeing so thou servest thyn own) & because I am very unwilling to place but the vallue of a meer Complement upon It, I beseech thee to take the Condition of Lt Keen[2] Into Consideration. his friend Is gone, unlesse he finds him outliving himself In thee; his abilitys I know not; none a better judge then thy selfe; but of his gratitude I dare avouch, & for full performance off all due observance I freely offer my selfe for his security. but what need I trouble thee or my selfe with arguements of this Kind, when the* hand that presents it is all sufficient; nor doe I expect any thing here Can be obleidgeing but from the vertue It borrows off her; & least I should spoyle all, I am resolv'd I will conclude, In beseeching thee to gratefy her, since he Cant dare pretend to It, who, whate[ve]r thou beleivest, is

Thy very Affect
Reall Friend
Wm Penn

Ld: 4th 9bre 70
* my Cos.'n The. Turner.[3]

ALS. Granville Penn Book, HSP. (*Micro.* 1:274). Addressed: For My Worthy | Friend Samll Pepys | Esqr:

1. Samuel Pepys (1633-1703), the diarist, was appointed secretary to the Navy Board at the Restoration. Pepys quickly became a close acquaintance of his Navy Board colleague, Sir William Penn, and of every member of the Penn family except for WP, whom he saw only occasionally; and although he soon came to dislike all of the Penns, he was careful to maintain cordial relations with the family until the Admiral's death. Thus it was natural that WP should ask Pepys for a favor. Pepys's *Diary* (1660-1669) offers a few vivid portraits of the young WP, and is, despite its bias, the richest extant source for the personality of Admiral Penn. *DNB;* Pepys, 5, 9 July 1662, 1 July 1666, 21 Feb. 1667, 20 Apr. 1668 (on the Admiral and his family); 25 Jan., 1 Feb., 16 Mar., 28 Apr. 1662, 30 Aug., 5, 14 Sept. 1664, 25 Apr. 1665, 5, 13 Sept., 5, 29 Dec. 1667 (on WP).

2. Probably the son of Eleanor Keene, Admiral Penn's first cousin. A "Capt. Keene" received £12 from WP, 6 Mar. 1673; see doc. 143, below. This may be Captain John Keene of the English navy; see *CSPD, 1672*, pp. 263, 264, 311, 325, 390, 412, and *CSPD, 1673*, p. 63.

3. This line is in another hand, apparently Pepys's. Theophila Turner (1652-1686) was the daughter of Pepys's cousin Jane Pepys Turner. Pepys saw "The.," his usual abbreviation, very frequently. Pepys, 1 January 1660 n.; John Gough Nichols, ed., *The Topographer and Genealogist* (London, 1846-1858), 1:26, 3:505-7.

53
TO PETER MEWS

[November 1670][1]

Shall the multiplied Oppressions which thou[2] continuest to heap upon Innocent English~~men~~ {People} for their peceable Religious Meetings pass unregarded & unavenged by the eternal God, Dost thou think to escape his fierce wrath, & dreadfull vengeance for thy Ungodly & Illegal persecution of his poor Children; I tell the No, better were it for thee, that thou hadst never been born. Poor Mushrom, wilt thou war against the Lord, & lift up thyself in Battle against the Allmighty; Canst thou frustrate his Holy purposes, & bring his Determinations to nought, He hath decreed to exalte himself by us & to propagate his Gospel to the Ends of the Earth; Therefore dread to obstruct this mighty Work; & repent of thy proud, peevish, & bitter actings, if by any means thou mayst be forgiven of the Lord, & find Mercy with the God of our Salvation: Otherwise his righteous Judgments[3] shall lay hold on thee, & thou shalt be made to know, that He, the great Jehova rules amongst those of the Children of men whom thou robbest & persecutest; Yea the Laws of of the Land will rise up in Judgment, in due time, against thee to the disgracing & punishing of thee & the rest of thy Tyrannical Oppressing Brethren, who make your own Wills Laws to undoe persons & whole Families by; Is this according to the Gospel & Precepts & Practice of that Patient Suffering Lamb of God [Christ Jesus and his] poore Disciples, (incarnat Divels do no worse.

O the piercing Lips of the needy & the Oppressed dayly, because [of these things] verily they have entered the Eares of the great God of Sabbath, & becaus[e thereof] do his destroying Judgments impend this Voluptuous, Wanton, Evil Worl[d afflicting] the Innocent; And if thou goest on, & returnest not their own, whilst thou su[fferest] the Vain, prodigal, Lascivious to go unpunish'd, there thou shalt be overwhelm'd [with] the rest of that persecuting Cain-like race, in the Valley of ~~from~~ Armageddam,[4] w[here] God the Righteous Judge will plead with all flesh.

This reproof & Caution, take from one who is above the fear of Man, whose breath is in his nostrils, & must one day come to Judgment, because he only fears the Living God, that made the Heavens & the Earth, the Sea & Fountains of Water.

oxford 9th mo: 1670. (a true Coppy) W P.

LBC. WP's Letterbook, 1667-1675, HSP. (*Micro.* 1:271). Docketed: To P.M. Vice-Chanceller of Oxford. The manuscript is damaged on the right margin; the missing text has been supplied from *Works,* 1:154-55.

1. WP was in London on 4 Nov., and again on 2 Dec.; see docs. 52, 54. He probably stopped at Oxford just before or after visiting Gulielma Springett and the Peningtons in Bucks. Peare, pp. 128-29.

2. Peter Mews (1619-1706) was a vigorous opponent of nonconformity. As vicar of St. Mary's, Reading, he had labored to suppress nonconformist meetings in 1663 and 1667. He was elected president of St. John's College in 1667 and served as vice-chancellor of Oxford University from 1669 to 1673. In 1670 he was energetically persecuting Quakers and other nonconformists by placing informers in their ranks. Mews later became Bishop of Bath and Wells, and then of Winchester. *DNB;* Janney, pp. 77-78.

3. The "s" in "Judgments" is either blotted or deleted.

4. Rev. 16:16, 19:11-21; and Judg., chaps. 4-5.

54
TO THE COMMISSIONERS OF THE NAVY

London. 10ber [December] the 2d [16]70

I just now receav'd a Letter from you, intimateing a Draught of the River Medway[1] (belonging to the Navy Office) to have reman'd, in my deceased Fathers hands, with your desires it might be return'd, to answer that frequent use, the Kings Service, obliges you to make of it. But as I would shew my selfe extreamlie forward, to answer the Commands of the Board; espetially when attended with soe plausible a reason as any the least publique benefit; and also most cheerefully evidence, my great desires to be Just, by restoreing what ever I have noe reall right to: Soe I hope you will interpret it my duty (and but reason done my Fathers memory) to examine his Interest in it (in case I have it amongst the many other of his Draughts) since I have yet superstition enough (as some are pleas'd to call it) to vallue every the smallest Relique, that may be deem'd a badge of his Trade, wch rendred him what he was, and Us, his Relations, what we are. Not, that I would be thought to question your verity[2] at all, when you are pleas'd to tell me, it belong'd to that Office, and was in his hands; But the integrity of such Clarks, whose neglect, or carelessnes, in loseing, or mislaying it, may put them upon such an answer as beleiving it; passing with your present demands. I shall thus farre express my willingness & dilligence to answer your expectations, as to examine his Catalogue of Draughts, where if I find this, and not his, I shall dispatch it to you,[3] and if once his, I shall not however stick, to supplie your present exegency, confideing in your Generositie, to returne it, in some competent time to

Your very
Affect Friend
Wm Penn

LS. SP 29/286, PRO. (*Micro.* 1:279). Addressed: This | For the Ld Brouncker,[4] Sr John Mennes, | Coll: Middleton,[5] Sr Jer: Smyth,[6] Sall Pepys | Esqrs, principle Officers & Commissionrs, of the | Navy. Docketed: 10br: 2. 70 | Mr Wm Penn about the draught | of the River Medway.

1. This river in northern Kent was the site of the disastrous Dutch raid of 13 June 1667, which led to a public examination of the Navy Board and the impeachment of Admiral Penn in 1668. If the Admiral took this draft or chart of the river home from the Navy Office, he may have done so in order to prepare his defense against the impeachment charges. Muirhead's *England,* p. 20; Pepys, 11-15 June 1667; Ogg, *Charles II,* 1:309-21.

2. "Verity" is written over "veracity."

3. In response to a second inquiry from the Navy commissioners, WP wrote on 31 Dec. 1670 that he had searched through his father's papers and had not found the chart. *Micro.* 1:283.

4. William Brouncker (1620?-1684), second Viscount Brouncker in the Irish peerage, was appointed to the Navy Board in Nov. 1664, and became assistant to Comptroller Mennes, in charge of treasury matters, in 1667. *DNB.*

5. Thomas Middleton (d. 1672) had been appointed to the Navy Board on Admiral Penn's recommendation in 1667; he was surveyor of the naval yards. Pepys, 4 Nov. 1664, 5 Oct., 10, 19 Dec. 1667.

6. Sir Jeremiah Smith (1615?-1675) had been an admiral in the Second Dutch War, and was appointed to succeed Admiral Penn on the Navy Board as Comptroller of Victualling on 17 June 1669. *DNB*.

55
GOD'S CONTROVERSY PROCLAIMED

In 1670-1671 WP published a number of religious tracts, including *The Great Case of Liberty of Conscience* and *A Seasonable Caveat against Popery*. He also composed, but did not publish, the following exhortation, which is distinct in character from most of his other early religious writings. Introducing himself as a witness to the Lord, innocent of all wickedness, WP proceeds to speak and write with the voice of God. He proclaims dreadful judgment against the profane and the persecutors, and also sternly rebukes those "Professors of Religion" (referring here mainly to non-Quaker dissenters) who obey priests instead of God. This document is perhaps the best example we have of WP's public style when speaking in Friends' meeting, inspired by the inner light. His language is Biblical, and almost Calvinistic in its reliance upon the harsh imagery of Isaiah and Ezekiel, although he also draws heavily upon Revelation. Exact quotations from scripture are cited in the footnotes.

Gods Controversy proclaim'd to the Nation
through one of his Servants & Wittnesses W.P.

[1670]

Through the good Report & through the bad report[1] am I travelling on to the Holy Land of Rest, & eternal Habitation of Glory, which my Father hath layd up in store for the Righteous; And though many are the Troubles, Tryalls & Temptations in the Way, being Despised, Defam'd, reviled, evilly intreated, & counted by the Men of this Generation as Turbulent, factious, seditious, an Enemy to Caesar, & made a gaising-stock[2] to the World & a Spectacle to God, to Angels & to Men, yet have I peace with the Lord, & by his own eternal Power am I made both able & willing to endure the Cross, & despise the shame for the Possession of the glorious Mansion of Immortality, & that Inheritance which is reserved for the faithfull eternall in the Heavens. And being thus Innocent of all wicked Contrivations,[3] & thus devoted through the Spirit of my God to the service of his Voice & righteous Truth, which is but my reasonable Service for him that not only made me, but has stretch'd forth the Arm of his Love to gather me out of the many unstable Wayes, & off from the Sandy Foundations, & barren Mountains, as well as the Pollutions, & grosser Enormities of this vile & Impious World, Bold I am in his Holy Fear & dread to proclaim his Controversy wth this Nation having given up my Life, & all visible enjoyments into his wise Disposal being no wayes solicitous of my success, nor what may prove my Lot from the hands of this Evil generation, for my Eye is fixed on the recompens of reward, And I fear not the Wrath of mortall men, whose breath is in his Nostrills,[4] having beheld the glorious Majesty of him that is invisible.

To all Sorts of People in generall.

Thus saith the Everlasting Lord God Allmighty; Let all Flesh tremble before me, for behold I am come to judge the Inhabitants of the Earth in Righteousness; Sin & Ungodliness shall not stand before me, I will be as consuming Fire unto the Chaff, & as Everlasting burning to the stubble; O my dreadfull Controversy is with the Disobedient & those who have broken my Law, Judgment will I therefore lay to the line, & Righteousness to the plummet:[5] I will weigh the Nations as in a Ballance, & sett as a Refiners fire, & Fullers Sope,[6] & the Rebellious will be burnt up with the unquencheable Fire of my Wrath & Indignation; for the time of making Inquisition for blood[7] is come, & the Books shall be opened[8] & the dead judged, for I have taken to my self my great power, & I will raigne; Kings shall bow before me, & Princes fall at my rising, & the Nations will I dash like a Potters Vessel, & they shall know, that I God the Lord of Hosts am come to reign amongst the Children of Men, whose is the Dominion, & the Glory, & Kingdom for ever & ever. Therefore Wo, Wo, Wo to the Murderer & the Oppressor, the Unclean Person & Drunkards, the Lyer & Swearer, the Prophan; & such as live in Vanity. Repent, repent, & come unto me the Lord God Allmighty, Dread & fear my Name, give Glory only unto me, & no more worship the Beast, who hath reigned over Kindreds, Tongues & People, blinding their Eyes, ~~defiling their valouer,~~ & betraying their souls, into all manner of Abominations. But mind my Appearance in you, grieve not my spirit, that would seal you unto the Day of the fullness of your Redemption; For this know, that the Lord of Hosts tells man his thoughts & the purposes & Intents of his Heart. Who are faithfull in all my Wayes, & righteous in all my Judgments, whose goings forth were from everlasting, & of whose power & Truth there shall be no end. For be not deceived, I the Lord will not be mocked, what thou hast sown that must thou reap, & my ~~son is in my hand,~~ & my reward is with me: But my soul loathes your unclean sacrifices, & your Oblations are Abominations unto me, you have wearied me with your much babling, & your offrings are a trouble unto my soul; Why take ye my Name into your Mouths, you who hate to be reformed, & yet cry, is not the Lord of our side, None can call me Father but by the Holy Ghost: Therefore put away the Evill of your doings & cease to do evill, wash your selves, cleanse your selves, & purge your selves by true sorrow & repentance never to be repented of, & fear, & keep my holy Commandements, stand in aw & sin not, & then shall it be well with you; For my dreadfull Controversie is with the hypocrite & him that say, he is a Jew & is not, a Christian & is not, who exalteth the things that perish, & debareth the hidden Mystery of my Divine Life & Truth, who know not the Circumcision that is in the Spirit & not in the Letter, but rest in meat & drincks & divers washings, (which cleanse not as concerning the Conscience,) & holy Dayes, & never come to know Christ the Substance of all in you, to make an end of Sin, to finish transgression, & bring in everlasting righteousness. Yea, & with the Loose & Prophan also is my terrible Controversie, even Esau's race,[9] Cain's race,[10] & Ishmael's race,[11] that dwell in the Envy, malice, persecution & bitter mockings, adultery, murder, Theft, & all manner of Iniquity; I will pour out my fury on such, & the full viols of the plagues of my heavy indignation, unless they speedily repent: And herein am I just & equall in all my wayes, because my Light is come, & my glory is risen, yea my spirit have I poured out on all, & my Grace hath every where appeared, teaching men that denying Ungodliness, & Wordly Lusts, they should live soberly, righteously, & Godlikely in this present evill World, and this shall be the Condemnation of the World ~~of~~ {that} this Light hath shined in their hearts, & this Grace hath appeared unto them, & my Messengers have gone forth to declare the Sum, giving them to know the things that belong to their eternal peace, but they have loved Darkness rather than Light, & turned from my heavenly grace into Wantonness, & persecuted my Prophets, because their deeds were evil; Therefore behold, I will make such as a barren field, & a desolate Land, & a Wilderness wherein dwell beasts of prey: Overturn, overturn, overturn[12] will I by my own outstretched arm, till I have brought these things to pass, till the Lofty be brought down, the proud debased, the Hypocrite cutt off, & them that take Counsell against me & mine anoynted, confounded; and the Horn of my Salvation[13] will I exalt, & my holy mountain upon the top of all mountains, & to it shall the gathering of the Nations be, & Holiness shall be writ upon them to the Lord, and a Name will I gett myself in the Earth, & Satan will I chain, & the Holy Citty will I establish, & every exalted mountain will I lay low, & every low Valley will I exalt, & I the Lord God of Hosts will make a throughwork in the Earth, for I have decreed to raise up my holy plant of renown[?], & to sett my Son upon mine holy hill of Sion, that he may rule the Nations as with a rod of Iron, & bow down the strong mind, & lay low every exalted spirit, that he alone may reign whose right it is, And that the Government of the Hearts of the Sons & Daughters of Men may be upon his shoulders, that he may whip out all buyers & sellers, that I may come into my Temple,[14] that the Sun, Moon & Stares may give Light no more, that weak & beggerly Elements may be done away, that the Lamb only may be their Light, & I the Lord God their Glory; so shall knowledge cover the Earth, as the Waters cover the Sea, & Righteousness & true Judgment shall run down their streets, like mighty rivers, that I may rejoyce in the habitable part of my Earth,[15] & that my delight may be with the Children of Men, that I may be their God, & they my People.

Hear & harken unto these things, o ye Inhabitants of this Isle, for I the Lord have thundred out of Sion, & my powerfull Word is gone forth from Jerusalem, tremble you that hear these things, & let your Lipps quiver at the Voyce[16] thereof, that you may all rest in the day of trouble; for a Day of Sorrow, & a Day of Anguish, a Day of howling, & a Day of gnashing of Teeth is coming upon the Nations: And the Time of Babylons, that Harlot, that false Church, that sayes, she is the Lambs Wife,[17] & is not, but full of Abominations, being judged, her Bratts will I dash against the stones, her glory will I stayn, her pride will I lay in the dust, & her Cruelty will I recompence upon her head, she shall be a stinck amongst the People, & her Name shall be an hissing amongst the Nations; & the beastly power will I destroy, & the fals hireling prophet will I smite, & the Dragon that old Serpent will I overcome, that have defiled the kingdoms of the Earth, & eaten my People as Bread.

To all Persecutors,
Thus saith the Dreadfull Majesty on high.

I have beheld from myn holy Habitation, & my righteous soul is vexed, my spirit is grieved, & it repents me, that I have done good for you, O ye Rebellious, o ye stiffneked Persecutors, how often have I visited you in Lovingkindness, have not my Prophets & Servants risen early & late with line upon line, & precept upon precepts[18] to declare unto you, what I required at your hands that ye might live, but ye have hardened your selves against me & my reproofs; Ye have gone greedily to do wickedly, ye have turned Judgment backwards, perverted Justice, & oppressed & robbed the poor, the Widdow, & the Orphant, & establisht sin by allow of your own prescribing, your hands are full of blood, & you make a prey of the Innocent, your Hearts are not right before me, but full of all manner of abominations, O my Righteous Soul is grieved to behold these things, ~~the~~ {your} earth is full of Violence & Uncleanness, O what Wantonness, what swear, what Covenant breaking, what Whoredom, what Drunkenness, w^t^ prophanness, & w^t^ Cruel Contrivances to bring sufferings upon them that fear my name; O for these things, for these things I the Lord mourn, & I am become a stranger amongst you, you have forgotten {me} the Lord, & turn'd my grace into Wantonness, Therefore is my Decree gone forth, & my Judgments are ready to be revealed, for the Innocent I will avenge, & the poor & the needy that have no helper on your Earth, & your Devices will I bring to nought, & your Councills to hinder the progress of myn own Everlasting Truth will I confound & dissappoint; For I the Lord God of Host, am rising out of myn holy Habitations, & in Vengeance will I plead with you the cause of mine oppressed Heritage as wth the Amalekites & Philistins of old,[19] & though I may suffer you to go on for a while, yet behold, I will bring you to Judgment at the revealation of my righteous Tribunal of Glory, and in the patience & holy boldness will I keep my Children, my sheep & my little Lambs, & by the Blood of the Lamb, & the Word of their Testimony, & by not loving their Lives unto the Death shall they Conquer your Cruelty, & surmount all your tortures, & pure as the Gold out of the furnace shall they come, through these many Tribulations, to give Glory to my Name. But your Cup shall be fill'd thereby, & drinck it you shall at my hand of my dreadfull Vengeance, for I will recompence tribulation to such as trouble them, And though you thinck you are full, & rich, & want nothing, saying, is not God on our side; yet will I distress your Families ~~& your Faces with smoke~~ by strange plagues, famins, Wars, Earthquakes & Fire, & your Faces will smoak to gather paleness,[20] & your hearts shall faint & your hands tremble, & your knees smite together; And I will change your sweet smells into a stinck, your girdle into a rent, & instead of wellsett hair there shall be baldness, & for a stomacher a girding of sackcloath, & burning instead of beerly.[21] Your men shall fall by the sword of my Spirit, & your mighty men in my holy Warr[22] of Righteousness, that no flesh may glory, & your fine places will I lay desolate for the beasts of the field, & the measure which you have meeted to others will I meet to you again, you shall be brought into everlasting contempt, you shall become a byword amongst the People, & your memorial shall rot amongst the Children of men. I the Lord God of Hosts who brought my People of old out of outward Egypt, & am now bringing my People out of spiritual Egypt, & that overwhelmed persecuting Pharao & his Host in the red sea of my wrath,[23] will as faithfully perform these things in the Eyes of the Nations, & yet a {very} little while, & a great Voyce shall be heard in this Land, saying It is done, it is finished, the Lord God of Hosts hath spoken it.

To the Professors of Religion of all
Sorts within these Isles; especially
such as are scornfully called
Phanaticks or Dissenters.

This saith the Lord of Heaven & Earth to you all.

The Everlasting Day has dawned, the glorious Light doth shine & my heavenly brightness is risen to give you the sound understanding of those weighty things that concerne your eternal peace, when time shall be no more. O come down, come down from every exalted Imagination, & be ye separated from that spirit, which having only the form of Godliness denyeth the inward feeling of the power of the same, & that ingrafted Word, which like a living hammer breaks in peeces the stony heart, & like a sharp sword cutts down every corrupt Tree, & like devouring Fire consumes the bryars & Thornes, that under all your crying Lord, Lord, abounds in you. O my Controversie in Lovingkindness & in Judgment is also with you; for you have not answered the Heavenly Visitation of my glorious Dayspring from on high;[24] but have despised my Appearance in yr fleshly Wisdom as too mean & contemptible for you to stoop unto, & also evilly intreated my holy Messengers & Servants that come in my the Lords Name, whom I sent forth from their Fathers House as Sheep amongst Wolfes, that you might be gathered into their fold & with them lye down in the possessions of the Heavenly Bread which nourisheth up unto eternal Life, & of that Water, & Wine which comes down from above, that whosoever drinketh thereof, shall never thirst more. And this is my wonderfull work in the Earth, For behold my Tabernacle is with men, & I the Everlasting glorious Light am come, to put & end to the Sun, Moon, & Stares for evermore, & my eternal Arm of power is made bear, to smite the Image that hath reigned wth his golden Head of many Professions (out of the true hidden Life & Substance of all) & to bruise the Serpents Head,[25] that I may take the Dominion & the Power & the reign over the Works of my Hands, & finishing Sin & Transgression, that hath separated betwixt me & my People, I might bring in everlasting Righteousness, that so the whole Earth might be filled with the knowledge of me & the Beauty of my Holiness. But you have sett this Appearance to nought, ye, you have put it in a manger, you have not followed that Daystare which lead the Wise Men of old to offer Gifts unto this righteous Seed, Your Priests have boren rule over you; & you have not asked Counsell of me, but from men, whose breath is in their Nostrils, teaching their Traditions for Doctrins; O they have caused my People to err, speaking peace, when there is no peace to the Workers of Iniquity. O! why will ye dye? Return, return, you that are going on in your own strength & Wisdom, thinking your selves full & rich, & wanting nothing. Behold I the Lord God of Hosts weigh you all as in a Ballance, & know the purposes & Intents of yr Hearts; And your Bable of Profession will I tumble down by the dreadfull stormes of Persecution that I will suffer to come upon your Earth to trye them that dwell thereon, & your stubble will I consume with the seareing Fire of the same, that you may come to see yourselves poor, & naked, & wanting every good thing, then will you seek me early, & ask which is the way to that Jerusalem & that holy Hill of Sion, where the outward meats & Drinks & divers washings & SabbathDayes have no place; But where Christ is in my holy one because the substance of those shaddowy things, whom I have given a Light to lighten the Gentiles, & for my Salvation unto the Ends of the Earth, whose Dominion I will cause to increase to the four Corners of the Winds, for unto him (the hidden Life, the Substance of all) shall the gathering of the Nations be, And I will exalt my Name in the sense of my own Divine Life, reigning in the Hearts of the Children of Men; & to day, if you will hear my Voyce & live, bow before me that telleth you the thoughts & purposes of your Hearts, for I am the Lord God of Hosts, & think that your imitation of my Servants the Prophets & my Apostles in shadows & carnal Observations shall suffice, My Soul hates them, & I am weary of your Deceit; Therefore wash ye & purge ye from all wrath, Enmity, Backbiting, & every evill way, & abide in my holy Child Jesus, who is now come forth in Spirit this second time, without Sin unto the Salvation of your Souls; For I the Lord that hold Covenant through all Generations now have made good my Promise of old, I have poured {forth} my Spirit on all flesh, that they may be convinced of Sin, Righteousness & of Judgment, & blessed are they, who waite for the Operation of the Baptisme of the same, they shall sitt att the Table I will spread, & eat of that Bread, & drink of that drink, which nourisheth to all everlasting. But the rebellious Pharisee will I cutt off, it shall wither as a fig tree without fruit,[26] & the fiery tryalls[27] shall scorch him off the earth. For I am risen, yea I am gone forth like a mighty man of Warr, conquering & to conquer, And a black & a cloudy Day[28] will I bring over the Nations, & great anguish & Distress upon the People, And I will plead with all Flesh, & they that rest in fleshly Ordinances, that I may {over} turn all, & scatter all that would not my own Life, Power & Spirit should reign, & nothing shall be able to stand in that Day out of the Living Sense of my own eternall indwelling power; that the People may see glory of the resting place of my Heritage, & be prepared for me to temple & tabernacle in, that my righteousness may last forever, & myne holy Dominion from generation to Generation. But they who trust in Horses & Chariots[29] & mighty men of Warr after the Flesh for their Deliverance, I the Lord God of Heaven & Earth will bring their designs to nought, & frustrate their vain expectations; for I the Lord will bring only Deliverance to the distressed in Spirit, & grind the Oppressor to powder, mine own arm shall do it, & no flesh shall glory before me.

Penn 1670.

LBC. WP's Letterbook, 1667-1675, HSP. (*Micro.* 1:193).

1. 2 Cor. 6:8. This phrase, and much of the imagery and argument of doc. 55, is repeated in the closing paragraphs of "Injustice Detected" (doc. 57), written in Newgate

in Feb. 1671. Doc. 55 may also have been written when WP was in prison in Feb. or Mar. 1671; an Old Style construction of the date 1670 in the LBC would support this interpretation. In any case, doc. 55 is certainly animated by WP's keen resentment of his persecution by government officials and Anglican clerics.

2. Heb. 10:33.

3. Contraventions or transgressions.

4. Isa. 2:22.

5. Isa. 28:17.

6. Mal. 3:2.

7. Ps. 9:12.

8. Dan. 7:10.

9. Bondsmen; see Gen. 25:23-34.

10. Murderers; see Gen. 4:8-12.

11. Outcasts; see Jer. 41.

12. Ezek. 22:27.

13. 2 Sam. 22:3.

14. Matt. 21:12.

15. Prov. 8:31.

16. Hab. 3:16.

17. Rev. 17:1-5; 21:9-10.

18. Isa. 28:10.

19. See Moses' defeat of the Amalekites in Exod. 17:8-16; and David's defeat of the Philistines in 1 Sam. 17:1-51.

20. Jer. 31:6.

21. Copyist's error for "beauty." See Isa. 3:24.

22. Isa. 3:25.

23. See Exod. 14:13-30.

24. Luke 1:78.

25. Gen. 3:15.

26. Mark 11:13.

27. 1 Pet. 4:12.

28. Ezek. 34:12.

29. Ezek. 26:7.

The next group of documents (56-62) concern WP's incarceration at Newgate prison from 5 February to about 5 August 1671. This was his second imprisonment in Newgate within a year, and his third imprisonment in London within three years. As in August 1670, WP was arrested by the London authorities for speaking at a Quaker meeting, this time at Spitalfield. But in other respects, his experience differed significantly from the previous summer. Sir John Robinson, Lieutenant of the Tower, denied WP any opportunity to publicize his cause through a jury trial by summarily sentencing him to six months in Newgate under the terms of the Five Mile Act (doc. 56). In Robinson's view, Quakers were besotted fools and knaves, and he deliberately made an example of WP in order to check their civil disobedience (*CSPD, 1671-1672*, p. 40). WP wrote, or helped to write, a narrative denouncing Robinson's "illegall" methods (doc. 57), but he did not publish it, perhaps not wishing to risk a longer term in Newgate. "For my freedom I am no wayes carefull," WP boasted in doc. 57, and his poem from Newgate to Gulielma Springett (doc. 58) further expresses his bouyancy. But WP was beginning to alter his strategy against persecutors by turning to Parliament for relief. See his draft of a Quaker petition to Parliament (doc. 59).

As in his earlier jail terms, WP kept busy writing. Doc. 60 throws light on one of his Newgate tracts, *A Serious Apology*, written in answer to the Presbyterian Thomas Jenner. Doc. 61 shows him quarreling with a Catholic critic, Richard Langhorne. Jail conditions were harsh (doc. 62), and when WP was released, he avoided further immediate confrontation with the London authorities by taking a trip to the continent. This was to be his last stay in prison for many years—until 1708, when under utterly different circumstances he was sentenced to the Fleet for debt.

56
SIR JOHN ROBINSON AND JOSIAH RICRAFT TO THE KEEPER OF NEWGATE PRISON

[5 February 1671]

Middlesex

To the Keeper of his Maties Goal of Newgate,
for the said County, or to his Deputy there.

Whereas William Penn Esqr stands duely Convicted before us, whose Names are Subscribed, two of his Maties Justices of Peace for the said County, upon the Oaths of four Credible Witnesses, for assuming & taking upon him to preach in a certain unlawful Assembly, Conventicle, or meeting holden upon this day, being the fifth Day of this Instant Month of February, under Colour or Pretence of Exercise of Religion contrary to the Laws & Statutes of this Kingdom, within the Parish of Stepney[1] in the County of Middlesex, which Parish is within 5. Miles & less, of the City of London. And thereupon we tendred unto him the said Wm Penn the Oath prescribed in, & by an Act of this Present Parliament, made in the 17. Year of his Ma^tis^ reign, Entituled, An Act for restraining Non-Conformists from Inhabiting in Corporations: which Oath he hath refused to take & subscribe.[2]
These are therefore in his Maties Name to will & require you forthwith upon Sight hereof to receive into y^r^ Custody the Body of the said Wm Penn (whom we send you herewith) & him there safely to Keep without Bayle or main-prize[3] for the space of six months—for which this shall be y^r^ Warrant. Given under our hands & Seals the fifth day February Anno Domini 1670.

Vera Copia
M P. Robt Warner.
Cler. Newgate

LBC. WP's Letterbook, 1667-1675, HSP. (*Micro.* 1:319). Sealed: J. Robinson | LTen. Toure. | Josiah Ricroft.[4]

1. This parish included Spitalfield, where WP was preaching to Quakers in Wheeler Street at the time of his arrest. Cunningham, 2:765-67, 779-80; Beck and Ball, pp. 162-64.

2. This statute (17 Car. II, c. 2), popularly known as the Five Mile Act, was passed in 1665. It authorized a justice to levy a fine of £40 upon anyone not a cleric of the Church of England and a subscriber to the oaths required by the Act of Uniformity of 1662 who preached in or within five miles of any incorporated borough. Moreover, any two justices could imprison, for six months without bail, any offender against the Five Mile Act who would not swear a loyalty oath. Thus WP was committed to Newgate for six months. Besse, 1:xx-xxii; Andrew Browning, ed., *English Historical Documents, 1660-1714* (London, 1953), pp. 382-84; Braithwaite, *Second Period*, p. 52.

3. With no permission to obtain release by finding sureties to post bond. *OED.*

4. Josiah Ricraft (c. 1625-?), a Stepney merchant, had been a Presbyterian and Parliamentary propagandist in his youth. At the Restoration he renounced his Presbyterianism; he served as a justice of the peace in Stepney throughout the 1670s. *DNB.*

57
INJUSTICE DETECTED

The following narrative of WP's arrest and arraignment presents a puzzle in authorship. Ostensibly it was written by an anonymous eyewitness, with a postscript by WP. However, there is reason to suppose that WP composed the entire narrative himself, under the "eye witness" alias, in order to publicize his judicial mistreatment, as he had previously publicized the Penn-Mead trial in *The Peoples Ancient and Just Liberties Asserted.* "Injustice Detected" was copied into WP's letterbook, which otherwise contains only pieces written by WP. It is extremely similar in format to *The Peoples Ancient and Just Liberties,* with WP winning all the points in his debate with Robinson as he had previously with Mayor Starling. WP's speeches are quoted in such circumstantial detail that he seems the likely author, particularly since pro-Quaker bystanders were excluded from the court. Whoever wrote this tract, it was not published in 1671, perhaps because WP realized that Robinson would gladly extend his jail term if he were offered fresh provocation. It was first printed after WP's death, in a shortened version, in *Works,* 1:36-40.

Injustice Detected or a brief Relation
of the
Illegall Committment
of
William Penn
by him call'd
Sr ~~John Robinson~~, Lt of the Tower,
from an Eye- & Ear-Wittness

[February 1671]

Blessed are ye, when men shall revile you & persecute you, & ~~that~~ say all Manner of Evill against you (falsely) for my sake, Rejoyce, & be exceeding glad, for great is your reward in Heaven; for so persecuted they the Prophets, which were before you, Matt. 5. vs. 11.12. Gather up the fragments, that nothing be lost: Joh. 6. 12.

As Sufferings have ever been the portion of True Christians, so was it both their Prudence & their practice to record them, that future Ages might not only be told, it was no new thing, to suffer for Religion; but also be inform'd, what strength & Heavenly resolution attended them in their afflictions, to the confounding of their Adversaries, & renowning of both their Patience & their Principles amongst their Neighbours, that through such good Examples many might be enduc'd to constancy, and Perseverance.

It is a shame, yet a great Truth, that in our protestant Age there is no small occasion given to write after the Coppy of our Brethren the Martyrs; because we find those, who would [be] thought their Successors to follow the Example of their inhumane Persecutors, amongst whom, the Person[1] we are to mention, in this short relation has not acquit the meanest place or rank of reputation, having been from the first, as hearty a persecutor, as if he had receiv'd a pension for the purpose.

But before we give the Narrative of William Penns Committment, (attended with many circumstances of Folly & revenge) we shall observe some of the common Maxims, of that sort of Men, whose aimes are rather at the promotion of a party then a publick good: which will be a necessary Introduction to the matter.

First, That those very Principles, which in themselves are just, & have been so defended by some, have by those very men been frequently deny'd & opposed (under the notion of Mistake) when their scen of interest has been chang'd, as is notorious in the practice of those Protestants, who exclaim'd against that persecution in the Papists, they have avow'd for Christian in themselves.

2d There are a sort of men, who therefore covet Authority that they might promote their own aimes, either in the Advancement of themselves, or ruine of other men, rather then the benefit of the general.

3d Those Men, (perhaps ignorant as well as breakers of Law) being conscious to themselves of their irregular & passionate proceedings, diligently labour to perswade their superiours in power, of their Right, to an unlimited prerogative, to the end, that it might prove a Sanctuary for them, to secure themselves from the Hew & Cry of Law, whose penalty they have justly incurr'd: But of all men those are the greatest Enemies to King, Country, & Law. To the King, as loading him wth the Ignominy of their Oppressions, by avouching them with his Authority: To the Country, by reason of their sinister & monopolising practises. To the Law, by stopping the free course of it in their Defence whom they have wrong'd.

4ly Another eminent practice of these evil spies is to whisper the Ears of the supream Magistrat with misrepresentations of such peaceble inhabitants, as it's their interest or designe to ruine; that by complaining first they may prevent them, whose griefs give the greatest occasion for it. By all which the Populace suffer, & their Estates & Liberties become a prey to the fury, interest & revenge of meer Mercenaries.

Char{r}on in his excellent discourse of Wisdom[2] amongst many other Infelicites, which attend princes: he gives us this following, as one of the most pernitious, viz.

The seventh Misery: worse perhaps then all the rest: & more dangerous to the *Wheal*-publik,[3] is, That they are not free in the choice of men, nor in the true Knowledge of things: They are not suffered truly to know the state of their affaires, & consequently not to call & employ such as they would, & as were most fitt & necessary; they are shutt up & beset with a certain kind of People, that are by the greatness of their Houses & Offices, or by prescription, so far in Authority, Power & managing of affairs before others, that it is not Lawfull, without putting all to hazard, to discontent, or in any sort to suspect them; Now these kind of People that cover & hold as it were hidden the Prince, do provide thatt all the Truth of things shall not appear unto him, & that better men, & more profitable to the state come not near him, lest they be known what they are. It is a pittiful thing not to see but by the Eyes, not to understand but by the Eares of another, as Princes do; And that wch perfecteth in all points this misery, is, that commonly, & as it were by destiny Princes & great Personages are possessed by three sorts of People The plagues of human kind Flatterers, Inventers of Imposts & Tributs, Informers, who under a fair & false pretext of Zeal & Amity towards the Prince, as the two first, or of Loyalty & reformation, as the latter, spoil & ruinate bot[h] Prince & State. Char. of Wisdo Pag. 183, sect. 14.[4]
These particulars considered, we may not be ignorant of the measure of the times, & ought the less to wonder at this ensuing Narrative.

It is not unknown to many that William Penn (when {in} health & at Liberty) is a diligent frequenter of their Assemblies (whom the World in Contempt call Quakers), and amongst others on the 5th instant he was att a Meeting in Wheelerstreet, beyond Spittle-Fields,[5] where he had not been halfe an hour, before a Serjeant came with a Squadron of Souldiers, who immediately plac'd themselves at the door, yet at first hindred not any to enter (& none were terrified from it by their appearance) after they had been there a quarter of an hour, William Penn stood up (the Assembly being full) & spoke to the People, exhorting them not to be dismay'd at the rattling of Weapons of Warr, nor therefore to relinquish their Meeting to worship the Lord, for as God alone had been their strength, & by his own Arm had to that day preserv'd them, notwithstanding their bitter tryalls from all Powers; so he would continue to protect them to the end, if they endured in patience the Wrath of Men; particularly disowning all plots, Conspiracys or visible Wayes of relief or Defence, much less offence by an arm of flesh, admonishing all to eye God, & by Faith & patience only to seek Victory over such as evilly intreated them.

After he had spoak near half an hour, the Serjeant came & pulld him down, & lead him through the throng of the Meeting into the street, where the Constable & his Watchmen joyn'd the souldiers, & leaving the Meeting brought him to the Towr. by order from the Lieut[t]. As he went, he had some Discourse, both with the Constable & a Corporal, who told him, that there was notice at the Tower, that he would be there that day, which he much wondred at, but the[y] gave him to understand some unfair Dealing in the matter; However, he very chearfully came with them, & being brought to the Tower, a Guard was clapt upon him; & an Express dispatcht to the L[t] then at Whitehall, to inform him of this wonderfull success upon a single man; who (to shew himself no wayes wanting in what might compleat him a victime to his fury) return'd the Messenger with ordres to take Horse at the Tower, & ride for L[t] Coll. Ricraft[6] (his usual partner in those employs) In the mean time W. Penn receiv'd much more Civility from the souldiers etc then from those that sett them att work, The poor men professing their sorrow to be no better employ'd but particularly one thought it hard measure, that Papists should have that universal indulgence, & such innocent Assemblies be disturbt.

After 3. houres time (being evening) the L[t] came home, to committ an act fit for Darkness, but his Company not being gather'd, & things unprepared, he delay'd sending for W.P. near two houres more, at last the Persons (lookt for) being come, & (having taken their Cups as well as Councill together) W.P. was sent for by L[t] Gerrard, accompanied with a Fyle of Musketeers from the Guard; When come, he took a very solemne View of the Company, which was lazy & warm, particularly there were present those they call S. J. Robinson, S. S. Starling, S. J. Shelden,[7] L. C. Ricraft, But as men afraid of their work, however well they wisht it. They thought it the best prudence to have as few wittnesses as they could, & therefore gave strict order, that upon no account any person should be admitted up, unconcerned in the business. By this time the Lt began, as Speaksman for the rest,

J. Rob. What is this Persons Name?
Note The mittimus was allready writ, & his Name put in.

Const. Mr Penn Sr.

J. R. Is your name Penn?

W. P. Dost thou not know me? Hast thou forgotten me?[8]

J. Rob. I don't know you, I don't desire to know such as you are.

W. P. If not, why dost thou send for me hither.

J. Rob. Is that your Name Sir?

W. P. yes, yes, my Name is Penn, thou knowst it is, I am not ashamed of my name.

J. R. Constable, where did you find him?

Const. At wheelers street at a Meeting.-

J. R. Speaking to the People, you mean he was speaking to an unlawfull Assembly?

Const. I don't know indeed Sir Jo. He was there, & he was speaking.

J. R. Give them their Oaths

W. P. Hold, don't swear the Men, ther's no need for it, I freely acknowledge I was at Wheelerstreet, & that I spoak to an Assembly of People there.

J. R. & several others; He confesses it.

W. P. I do so, I am not ashamed of my Testimony.

J. R. No matter, give them their Oaths.
Note, they were sworn, to answer such questions as should be askt, upon which they gave the evidence before given by the Constable.

J. R. Mr Penn, you know the Law better then I can tell you, & you know that these things are Contrary to the Law.

W. P. If thou believest me to be better known in the Law then thyself, hear me; for I know no Law I have transgressed. All Laws are to be considered strictly & literally, or more explanatorily & lenitively.[9]
In the first sense, the Execution of many Laws, may be extrema Injuria the greatest wrong. In the Latter Wisdom & Moderation, I would have thee make that part {thy} choyce.
Now whereas I am probably to be try'd by the Late Act against Conventicles,[10] I conceave, it doth not reach me.

J. R. No Sir, I shall not proceed upon that Law.

W. P. What Law then? I am sure that was intended for the present standard, in these occasions.

J. R. The Oxford Act of Six Moneths.[11]

W. P. That of all Laws can't concern me; for first I was never in Orders, neither Episcopally nor Classically, & one of them is intended by the preamble of the Act.[12]

J. R. No, no, Any that speak in unlawfull Assemblies, & you spoak in an unlawfull Assembly.

W. P. Two things are to be considered; First that the Words, such as speak in any unlawfull Assemblies alters the case much; for such is relative of the preamble, & cannot concern persons in any other qualification, then under some ordination, or mark of Priesthood; I am perswaded thou knowst I am no such person, I was never ordain'd, nor have I any particular Charge or stipend, that may intitle me to such a function: And therefore I am wholly unconcern'd in the Word Such.[13]

2dly An unlawfull Assembly is too generall a Word, the Act doth not define to us, what it means by an unlawfull Assembly.

J. R. But other Acts doe.

W. P. That is not to the purpose, for that may be an unlawfull Assembly in one Act, that may by Circumstances not be so adjudg'd in another: And it's hard that you will not stick to some one Act or Law, But to accomplish your ends, borrow a peece out of one Act, to supply the Defects of an other, & a different nature from it.

J. R. Will you swear? Will you take the Oath that the Act requires you?

W. P. This is not to the purpose.

J. R. Read him the Oath—the Oath.

I, W. P. do swear, that it is not Lawfull upon any pretence whatsoever, to take Armes agt the King, & that I do abhorr that Trayterous position, of taking Armes by his Authority against his Person, or agt those that are commissionated by him in pursuance of such Commissions, & that I will not at any time endeavour any alteration of Government either in Church or State.

J. R. Will you take it, or no?

W. P. What need I take an Oath not to do that, it is my faith not to do, so farr as concerns the King.

Lt Price then swear it.

W. P. The Oath in that respect is allready answer'd, to all intents & purposes; for if I can't fight agt any man (much less agt the King) what need I take an Oath not to do it; should I swear not to do, what is already agt my Conscience to do.

J. R. You won't take the Oath then?

W. P. What if I refuse the Oath? not because of the Matter contained in it (wch only can criminate in the sense of the Act)[14] but of scrupeling any Oath, shall I therefore be committed to prison? This is most unequal. 'Twas ~~not~~ {about} fighting, the Oath & Act were designed, & not taking of Oaths;

Therefore the denying to swear, when there is a Denyall to fight or plott, is no equitable ground for committment

Note, but the Man was a little dimm'd, & at that time reason proof.

J. R. Do you refuse to swear?

W. P. Yes, & {that} upon better grounds, then those for wch thou wouldst have me swear; If thou wilt please to hear me.

J. R. I am sorry to see, you should put me upon this severity, it is no pleasant work to me.

W. P. Those are but Words, it is manifest, that this is a prepenst malice,[15] thou hast several times layd[16] the Meetings for me, & this day particularly.

J. R. No I profess, I could not tell you would be there.

W. P. Thyne own Corporal told me, that you had Intelligence at the Tower, that I would be at Wheelerstreet today, allmost as soone as I knew it myself; It's disingenious and partiall; I never gave thee occasion for such unkindness.

J. R. I knew no such thing, but if I had, I confess, I should have sent for you.

W. P. That might have been spar'd, I doe heartily beleeve it.

J. R. I vow Mr Penn I am sorry for you, you are an Ingenious Gentleman, all the World must allow you, & do allow you that, & you have a plentifull Estate, why should you render your self unhappy by associating wth such a simple People.

W. P. I Confess, I have made it my choyce to relinquish the Company of those that are ingeniously wiked, to converse wth those that are more honestly simple.

J. R. I wish you wiser.

W. P. And I wish thee better.

J. R. You have been as bad as other Folks.

W. P. When, & where? I charge thee to tell the Company to my Face.

J. R. Abroad & at home too.

Sr Jo^s^ Shelden (as is supposed) No no, Sr John that's too much; or words to that purpose.

W. P. I make this bold Challenge to all men, Women & Children upon Earth justly to accuse me with ever haveing seen me drunk, heard me swear, utter a Curse, or speak one obscen word (much less that I ever made it my practice) I speak this to God's glory that has ever preserv'd me from the power of those pollutions, & that from a Child begot an hatred in me towards them. But there is nothing more common then when men are of a more severe Life then ordinary, for loose persons to comfort themselves wth the Conceit, that they were once as they are, and as if there were no collateral or oblique Line of the Compass or globe, men may be said to come from, to the Artick pole, but directly & immediately from the Antartick. Thy words shall be thy burden, & I trample thy slander as dirt under my feet.

J. R. Well, Mr Penn, I have no ill will towards you; Your Father was my Friend,[17] & I have a great deal of kindness for you.

W. P. But thou hast & ill way of expressing it.

You are grown too high to consider the Plea of those you call y^r Forefathers for Liberty of Conscience ag^t the Papists, Cranmer Latimer, Ridly, Bradford &c.[18]

'Twas then Plea good enough, my Conscience wont let me go to Mass, & my Conscience wills that I should have an English Testament.

But that single plea, for separation then reasonable, is now by you that pretend to succeed them, adjudg'd unreasonable & factious.

I say, since the only just cause of the first revolt from Rome was a Dissatisfaction in point of Conscience, you cannot reasonably persecute others, who have right to the same plea, & allow that {to} be warrantable.

J. R. But you do nothing but stirr up the People to Sedition; And there was one of your Friends, that told me you preacht sedition, & medled with the Government.

W. P. We have the Unhappiness to be misrepresented, & I am not the least concern'd therein; Bring me that man that will dare to justifie this accusation to my face; And if I am not able to make it appear, that it is both my practice & all my Friends, to instill principles of Peace & moderation (& only to warr ag^t spiritual wickedness, that all men may be brought to fear God, & work Righteousness) I shall contentedly undergo the severest punishment all your Laws can expose me to.

And as for the King, I make this offer, that if any Living can make appear, directly or indirectly, from the time I have been called a Quaker (since from thence you date me seditious) I have contriv'd or acted any thing injurious to his person or the English Government, I shall submit my Person to your utmost Cruelties, & esteem them all but a due recompens.

'Tis hard, that I being innocent, should be reputed guilty; but the Will of God be done; I accept of bad report as well as good.

J. R. Well I must send you to Newgate for six Moneths, & when they are expir'd, you will come out.

W. P. Is that all? Thou well knowst a longer Imprisonment has not daunted me, I accept it at the hand of the Lord, & am contented to suffer his Will. Alas you mistake your Interest, you'le miss your ayme; this is not the way to compass y^r ends.

J. R. You bring your self into trouble, you will be heading of Parties & drawing People after you.

W. P. Thou mistakest, there is no such way as this to render men remarkable; you are angry that I am considerable, & yet you take the very way to make me so, by making this bustle & sturr about one peaceeble Person.

J. R. I wish your adhering to these things do not Convert you to something at last.

W. P. I would have thee & all men to know, that I scorn that Religion, wch is not worth suffering for, & able to sustain those that are afflicted for it. Mine is, & whatever may be my Lott for my constant profession of it, I am no wayes carefull, but resign'd to answer the will of God by the Loss of Goods, Liberty, & Life itself. When you have all, you can have no more; & then perhaps you will be contented, & by that you will be better inform'd of our innocency. Thy Religion persecutes, & mine forgives; And I desire my God to forgive you all, that are concernd in my Committment, & I leave you all in perfect Charity, wishing your everlasting salvation.

J. R. Send a Corporal with a File of Musketeers along with him.

W. P. No, no, send thy Lacky, I know the Way to New Gate.

{[In another hand] Here Insert the Mittimus, Page 98 in this Book being the Proper place for it.}[19]

The Lt of the Tower & Lt Coll. Ricraft having sign'd the Mittimus, & orders being given for a File of souldiers to assist the Constable & his Watchmen in accompanying W. P. to New Gate (being about 8. at Night) they took him away, not more readily then he was willing to go; Several Officers & other spectators follow'd him down staires, expressing much Civility & concern for him; some pittying his hard measure, others asking Forgiveness, that their men were employ'd about so unhandsome a work, & several promising to visit him, who after they had conducted him to the Tower Gate, left him to the Constable & Souldiers to guard him to his prison, which was accordingly done, & where he remaines, to compleat the remainder of his illegal committement.

It is worthy of further notice, that the Man[20] being (doubtless) conscious to himself of base malice & unjust revenge, thought not himself secure, but by his foul reports of this affair to the King, as is familiarly discourst, & by a Person of Note told the Prisoner since his confinement, as if the Quakers had congratulated W. Penn's restraint, & in a solemn manner return'd their thancks to this Lieutent for his Committinges of him: In as much as he was a Person, that made it his Business, to stirr up to sedition, & betray them into sufferings by such Doctrine, as rather tended to alter the Civil Government, then to establish true Religion; or words to this Effect.

But as the Devil is the Father of Lyes, so (if these things have been said) he will pay ~~him~~, the Man his Wages. For though a more malignant, & aggravated Charge could not well have been brought agt him, yet it is not less true, that there is nothing more notoriously false.

And Unhappy is that People, whose Adversaries shall have Liberty to suggest the vilest falsities to their Superiours, & at the same time be deny'd the just Liberty of a free Defence. I shall undertake for W. P. that if the King or any else by his Command, shall give himself the leasure of a hearing, he shall vindicate his Innocency wth as much clearness as with boldness he has & doth assert it.

The illegality of the Action was sufficiently evidenc'd by the Discourse of the Prisoner, & further many discret Lawyers affirms it. Nay it has been an adjudg'd Case, that no man is properly intended by that Act, that has not been either Episcopally or Classically ordained, which the Prisoner never was.

'Tis lamentable, that men peaceable & of good Example should be disturbed, under pretence of being seditious, & that by such as have not learnt the very Alphabeth of Morality; But how should we expect better from one, that a week after, committed a grave Matrone of this Citty, (& aged 60. yeares) to Goale upon the same Act for a non-conforming Person.

All the harm we wish the King is this:

1st That he would consider, how happy he might reigne King in all external Civil & Moral Affaires (his only employ) without meddling wth Church matters, or maintaining of the Interest of a Church Partie, not the tenth part of his Kingdom.

2d. That he had men of more Vertue, Wisdom, & Moderation to administer Justice, then the Man concern'd in this illegal Committment.

So would Oppression cease, Government be easie, Trade improv'd, Mercenaries discourag'd, the Inhabitants pleased, the King Establisht, & the whole Kingdom advanc'd in Tryumph over all the sad letts[21] & deplorable mischiefs it miserably labours under.

Having diligently perusd the Insuing Narrative, these are to certifie those to whose Hands it may come, that I can find no other defect in the whole relation (so far as I am concern'd in it) then that it's not the halfe of what past at the time of my Committment; But as the remainder would have signified much to my further Vindication, so can I acquit the Author for an impartial relator.

And for my freedom I am no wayes carefull, & therefore can never creep to obtain it; although they tell me, I only want[22] it because I don't seek it; but since my Conscience is dearer to me, then my Liberty desirable, I rather chuse by bonds to keep that of my Conscience then be so unlike those worthy Ancients who refused Deliverance as by a base crouching to free my Body & engoale my Mind.

No, through good report & bad report, acceptance & suffering, cheerfully am I travelling on to the eternal rest;[23] And the reproaches of my Profession (be it known to all) I esteem my Crown. I own myself one of the heavenly Camp & Host of God, who has fill'd my Quiver with Arrows & a strong strong Bow hath he put into my hands, & my arm is fresh, & my heart is bold to arch ag^{t} spiritual Wickedness, & that in the High Places first; And whether I live or dye, I leave it to the Lord, but it's the alone thing I desire, that if I dye, it may be for him, & if I live, it may be to him.

I am a Souldier & Follower
of the Lamb, who must have
the Victory (though it be
through many Tribulations

London, Newgate,
12th month. 1670.

POSTSCRIPT

And though we remain in peace with the Lord God, yet for his Names sake can we give ourselves no rest. And therefore it is, we are now constrain'd to warn all Persecutors in the Name of the Dreadfull God of Hosts, as they will answer it at his righteous Tribunal, Leave off your Cruelty & Oppression, & strengthen not the Bonds of the Innocent, vex not the Fatherless, neither spoil Widdow, nor oppress the poor, But repent you of all your ungodly purposes ag^{t} the Righteous; set open the Prison doores, put away the dayly evill of your doings, your Whoredoms, your Blasphemies, your Prophanness, your Treachery, your Drunkenness, your Swearing, your Murders, your Robberys, persecutions (that have ascended up unto Heaven, & are drawing down plagues upon Earth) O wash your selves, cleanse your selves, & humble your selves for all these things (you whose Day is not yet gone over your heads) or verily a swift Destruction will overtake you & famin like an armed man; for a Consumption is determin'd, & the Lord will rid himselfe off his Enemies; he will lay low the Lofty, bring down the Proud, & stain all their Glory, distress shall persue them, & a Canker eat them up, their pleasant places shall be as Deserts, & their stately statues become nests for the Birds of prey; And when Desolation & Destruction comes, they shall seek peace, but there shall be none found, Mischief shall come upon mischief, & rumor upon rumor, then shall the King mourn, & the Prince be clothed with Desolation, & the hands of the People of the Land shall be troubled. The Lord God of Vengeance will do unto them after their ungodly Way, & according unto their deserts will he judge them, Yea an hiss will he make them to the Nations; & a perpetual Contempt to all Generations. This is the Word of the Lord God of Heaven & Earth (unto them all) who lives & reigns in his holy Dominion forever.

WP

LBC. WP's Letterbook, 1667-1675, HSP. (*Micro.* 1:320). Notation after the signature in another hand: See also & Insert the Mittemus p 98.

1. Sir John Robinson.

2. Pierre Charron (1541-1603), French philosopher and close friend of Montaigne, is best known for his work *De la sagesse* (Bordeaux, 1601), translated into English as *Of wisdome, three bookes* (London, 1612; 1651) by Sampson Lennard (d. 1633).

3. The public good. *OED.*

4. This entire paragraph is quoted, quite accurately, from Charron, *Of wisdome,* 2d. English ed. (1651), b. I, chap. 49, sec. 14, p. 183.

5. The Quakers had recently built a meetinghouse near the corner of Wheeler and Westbury (later Quaker) Streets, in Spitalfield. Beck and Ball, pp. 162-63.

6. See doc. 56.

7. For Sir Samuel Starling, see doc. 46. Sir Joseph Sheldon was alderman of Farringdon Without the Walls, sheriff of London in 1666-1667, and Lord Mayor in 1675-1676. Henry B. Wheatley, ed., *The Diary of Samuel Pepys* (London, 1920), 7:7n.

8. Robinson had, in fact, met WP at Sir William Batten's house on 29 Jan. 1665 (Pepys), as well as at the Tower in 1668-1669, and at the Old Bailey in Sept. 1670.

9. Leniently. *OED.*

10. The Second Conventicle Act, passed in Mar. 1670.

11. The Five Mile Act of 1665 was passed at a parliament held at Oxford. It was an act "of Six Moneths" because it empowered two or more justices to sentence any preacher who would not take a loyalty oath to six months in prison. Besse, 1:xx-xxii; Browning, *English Historical Documents,* 8:382-84; Braithwaite, *Second Period,* p. 52.

12. The preamble to the Five Mile Act was aimed against "persons in Holy Orders" —whether Catholics who had taken episcopal orders or Presbyterians who had taken classical orders — who preached without taking the oaths prescribed by the Act of Uniformity of 1662. The Quakers, as WP was quick to point out, did not have an ordained ministry. But the Five Mile Act more generally embraced "all such person and persons as shall take upon them to preach in any unlawful assembly, conventicle or meeting under colour or pretence of any exercise of religion, contrary to the laws and statutes of this kingdom," and it was on this basis that the court proceeded against WP. Besse, 1:xx, xxi; Browning, *English Historical Documents,* 8:383.

13. See n. 12 above.

14. WP here argues that only those who rejected the content of the oath could lawfully be incriminated under the Five Mile Act; nothing in the statute, however, made provision for those who, like WP, objected to taking oaths on principle.

15. Premeditated malice. *OED.*

16. Set a watchman or informant at. *OED.*

17. Pepys reports three small dinner parties attended by Robinson and the Admiral, one with young WP in attendance, and one at the Admiral's house. Pepys, 9 Mar. 1663; 29 Jan. 1665; 11 Jan. 1666.

18. Thomas Cranmer, Archbishop of Canterbury (1489-1556); Hugh Latimer, Bishop of Worcester (1485?-1555); Nicholas Ridley, Bishop of London (1500?-1555); and John Bradford (1510?-1555) were all Protestant martyrs in the reign of the Catholic Queen Mary.

19. The mittimus is doc. 56, entered onto p. 98 of WP's Letterbook. This marginal note may be by Joseph Besse, who used the Letterbook in preparing his edition of WP's *Works.* Besse printed the dialogue between WP and Robinson from doc. 57 in *Works,* 1:36-40, and then inserted the mittimus at this point, skipping the closing pages of doc. 57.

20. Robinson.

21. Hindrances. *OED.*

22. Lack. *OED.*

23. Note the parallel here with the opening sentence in doc. 55.

58
AN HOLY TRYUMPH

[1671]

Your Goals & Prisons we defie,
By bonds we'l keep our Libertie.
Nor shall your Racks, or Torments make
Us, e're our Meetings to forsake.[1]
Nor all your Cruelties afright
Our Hearts, that own & love the Light.
No, death can never make us bend,
Nor make our Conscience condescend.
For that Seed's risen, wch will bow,
And lay your lofty Mountains low,
Your Hills shall fly away before
The Majesty that we adore.
And Heaven will display it self
Before your Eyes to our Releif,
And you that persecute shall know
A deadly Arrow from his Bow.
And vengeance, for a Recompense
He'l render you, in our Defence,
And overturn for evermore
False Prophet, dragon & the Whore.[2]

WP.

LBC. WP's Letterbook, 1667-1675, HSP. (*Micro.* 1:293). Docketed, in WP's hand: Sent to Dr G. M. Springet (my Dr. wife since) | writt ~~then~~ in newgate 1671.

1. WP indulged in poetic license here. The Conventicle Act of 1670 punished Quaker meetings with a ruinous schedule of fines, not "Racks, or Torments." The Five Mile Act of 1665, under which WP was imprisoned, imposed fines and jail sentences of six months. See doc. 56, above.
2. WP understood the dragon to be the devil and the whore to be the Pope or the Roman Catholic Church. Rev. 12:3, 17; 17:1-2.

59
PETITION TO PARLIAMENT

At the time of WP's imprisonment, both houses of Parliament, and particularly the House of Commons, were rabidly anti-Catholic and anti-dissenter. Having passed the Conventicle Act in 1670, Parliament staged a strong debate on the growth of popery in February-March 1671, and the Commons passed a new bill against seditious conventicles on 5 April 1671 and sent it to the Lords. The following petition was an effort to block such legislation. It is one of a series of Quaker petitions from the 1670s, mostly undated, which WP helped to compose, addressed to Parliament or to the king. For two other petitions, see *Micro.* 1:208; 1:212. While doc. 59 illustrates WP's energetic efforts to influence the political establishment, it should be pointed out that these efforts had little effect. There is no evidence in the *Journals of the House of Commons* or the *Journals of the House of Lords* that this petition, or any other Quaker petition, was considered or even received by Parliament during the 1670s.

[April 1671]

For as much as it hath pleas'd you to make an Act intituled: An Act for [Sup]pressing Seditions the Dangerous Practices ~~of~~ {of seditious} Sectaries &c.[1] and that [un]der Pretence of Authority from it, many have taken the ungodly Liberty of Plundering, Pillaging, and breaking into Houses to the ruin & Detriment of whole Families, not regarding the Poor, the Widdow~~s~~, & the Fatherless, beyond all President or excuse, And that we are inform'd, it is your purpose, instead of relaxing your hand, to supply the Defects of that Act by such explanatory clause~~ls~~, as will inevitably expose us to the fury & Interest of our several Adversaries;[2] that under pretence of Answering the Intents of the said Act, will only gratifie their private humors, & doubtless extend it beyond its Original purpose to the utter Destruction of us, & our suffering Friends;

We therefore estem'd our selves oblig'd in Christian ~~Charity~~ {Duty} once more to remonstrate

1st That we own Civil Government ~~&~~ {or} Magistracy, as ~~what is necessary to~~ {God's ordinance for the} punish~~ing~~{mt of} Evil doers, & ~~cherish him~~ {the praise of them} that do~~th~~ well; & though we cannot comply with those Laws that prohibit us to worship God according to our Consciences {as beleeving to be his alone prerogative to preside in matters of faith & worship.} yet we both owe & are ready to yeild obedience to every Ordinance of man {or ordinance} relating to human affairs & that for Conscience sake.

2dly That we deney & renounce, as an horrible ~~Iniquity~~ {impiety} all plots & Conspiracies; or to promote our {Interest, or} Religion by the blood & Destruction of such as dissent from us, or yet those that persecute us.

3dly That in all revolutions we have demenur'd[3] our selves with much Peace & Patience, {(disowning all contrary-actings)} notwithstanding the ~~more was~~ {numerous} provocations of ~~Evill~~ {Cruel} & Ungodly Men, which is a Demonstration of our harmless behavior, that ought not to be of little moment with you.

4ly {That} As we have ever liv'd most peacebly under all the Various

Governments, that have been since our first appearance (*nothwistanding we have been as their Anvil to smite upon,*) so we do ~~t~~hereby signifie, that it is our fixt resolution to continue the same, that were we cannot actually obey, we patiently shall suffer, (~~leaving our innocent Cause with,~~[4] ~~not daring to love our very Lives unto the death for our blessed Testimonies sake.~~) {thereby manifesting to the whole world, that we love God above all, & our neighbour as ourselves.}

And if this ~~doth~~ {prevailes} not ~~penetrate~~ with you to suspend ~~the~~ {your} thoughts of reinforcing ~~the~~ {y^{r}} former Act, We do desire {that} we {or some of our Friends} may ~~be heard impartially~~ {receive a free hearing from you} (as several of us ~~were~~ {had}, upon the first ~~at~~ Act for Uniformity) having many great {& weighty} reasons to offer against {all} such severe proceedings,[5] to the end all wrong measures of us & {of} our Principles may be rectified, & {that} you ~~may be~~ {being} better inform'd of both ~~us & them for such moderation will be well pleasing both to God & good men.~~ may remove our heavy burthens & let the oppressed free.

From us, who are now prisoners at Newgate (~~for Conscienees sake~~ on the behalf of our selves & all our Suffering Friends in England. &c

Wm Penn.
Jasp. Bath.[6]
Jo. Bolton.[7]
Th. Green.[8]
Newgate 2^{d} mo: 1671 Patr. Livingstone.[9]

LBC. WP's Letterbook, 1667-1675, HSP. (*Micro.* 1:342). Docketed: To the High-Court of Parliament. This heavily corrected draft is in the hand of one clerk and was revised by another, probably reflecting changes in wording made by WP and his fellow petitioners. Besse generally incorporated the revisions into his printed text in *Works,* 1:41-42. Where text is missing because of a tear in the opening lines, it is supplied from *Works,* 1:41.

1. The Second Conventicle Act, passed in Mar. 1670.
2. In Mar. 1671 the House of Commons debated a new bill designed to prevent and suppress seditious conventicles. After the Commons passed the bill (*Journals of the House of Commons,* 9:230), it died in committee in the Lords when the king prorogued Parliament on 22 Apr. (*Journals of the House of Lords,* 12:478-79, 483, 515).
3. Demeanoured or behaved. *OED.*
4. "God" is inserted here in *Works,* 1:41.
5. Altered from "proceedure."
6. Jasper Batt (d. 1702) of Somerset was convinced in the 1650s, and quickly became a leading Quaker preacher in his home county, where he was fined or imprisoned on more than a dozen occasions between 1657 and 1686. No record of Batt's incarceration in London in Apr. 1671 has been found outside of this petition. Fox, 2:495; Besse, 1:484, 577-649 passim.
7. John Boulton (c.1599-1679?) was a London goldsmith, and a Quaker by 1656. He was arrested at the Gracechurch Street meeting three times in 1670. After the last occasion, he was fined forty marks for refusing to remove his hat in court and another twenty marks "for trespass and contempts," and was committed to prison until he paid

the whole. Boulton was apparently still under arrest in Apr. 1671. Fox, 1:435; Besse, 1:369, 379, 385, 408, 409, 426-28, 439.

8. Theophilus Green was arrested twice in 1670 for preaching at Quaker meetings near London. At the Jan. 1671 quarter sessions he refused to take the oath of allegiance and was given an indefinite sentence in the King's Bench prison in Southwark. Doc. 58 suggests that he had been transferred to Newgate prison by Apr. He was eventually released from the King's Bench prison, under the royal pardon of 13 Sept. 1672. Besse, 1:415, 429, 437, 453, 701-2.

9. Patrick Livingstone, a Scottish Quaker, had been arrested in Dec. 1670 at a Friends' meeting in Stepney, and brought before Sir John Robinson, who sentenced him to six months in Newgate under the Five Mile Act. Besse, 1:431.

60
FROM GEORGE FOX

[24 May 1671]

Dear W:

To whom is my love & to friend that a way. I understand that thy answer to Gener,[1] is not all come up, so that for want of the rest of the sheets, they are feyne to put other things in the press. And now here being severall friends newly come out of Ireland who informes of the great want of this book in answer to his, I desire thee speed it up, laying a side all other things till it be done.[2] Indeed this should have been sent up befor now, and therefore I say hasten it to E H[3] here, that so it may be speedily printed off that our sd friends that came over may carry some of them back againe with them, and the rather becaus we understand that Gener makes a trade of his books in sending & selling of them up & downe. And therefore such a dirty thing should never rest till ~~we~~ {they} have them out of our hands to the place to whom they belong, & therefor I say speed them up to E. H:

london
m. 3. d. 24.

G F

LS. Penn-Forbes Papers, HSP. (*Micro.* 1.348.) Addressed: For William Penn | att | Tilleringreen. Docketed: Geo: Fox | 3mo 24.

Tyler's Inn Green, or Tyler's Green, a hamlet in the parish of Penn, Bucks., is intended in the address. Apparently the letter was to be forwarded to WP in Newgate by Gulielma Springett, who was "of Tyler End Green in the parish of Penn in the County of Bucks" in their first declaration of marriage. See doc. 67, below.

1. Thomas Jenner (1605-1676), Puritan minister, was the author of *Quakerism Anatomiz'd and Confuted* (Dublin, 1670). He had a variegated career, having held pastorates as a young man in Weymouth, Mass., and Saco, Me., then returning to England, where he was minister at Coltis Hall, Norfolk, 1652-1658, and finally moving to Ireland. He was chaplain to a Commonwealth Irish brigade which fought the Royalist uprising in Cheshire in 1659. When he published his anti-Quaker tract, he was living in Carlow. Frederick Lewis Weis, *The Colonial Clergy and the Colonial Churches of New England* (Lancaster, Mass., 1936), pp. 116-17; *Works,* 2:73; *CSPI, 1642-1659 (Adventurers),* p. 352; *CSPI, 1647-1660,* p. 405; *DNB; Alumni Cantabrigienses,* 2:469.

2. WP's answer, written with George Whitehead, was *A Serious Apology for the Principles & Practices of the People call'd Quakers, Against the Malicious Aspertions, Erronious*

Doctrines, and Horrid Blasphemies of Thomas Jenner and Timothy Taylor, in their Book, entituled Quakerism Anotamiz'd and Confuted (1671). It is addressed "To the King's Lieutenant-General, and General-Governour and Council of Ireland," and WP's conclusion was written from Newgate, 28 June 1671. Whitehead had already completed his portion of the tract, which was dated Kingston-upon-Thames, 1 Apr. 1671.

3. Ellis Hookes (c.1630-1681), salaried "recording clerk" of the London Friends from 1653, collector of accounts of sufferings, and joint author with Fox of an historical *Arraignment of Popery*. In 1671 he informed Margaret Fell that he had "left off all imployment in printing of books, by reason of weaknes." Fox, 2:402; Norman Penney, "Our Recording Clerks," *JFHS* 1(1903): 12-22, quotation on p. 18.

61
TO RICHARD LANGHORNE

[1671]

My inogenous[1] Friend;[2]
I am persuaded I was colder when I read thy Letter, then thou wast, w[hen thou writ'st] it, if I may have so much Credit with thee, And you Catholicks are famous [for believing] (though it be, ye know not what) I do declare my end of animadverting[3] [upon that] palliated[4] Confession, was no other then of presenting to the World the Cath[olick true] Creed, & I shall avouch the Authorities.[5]

My Ignorance in that matter will be best shewn, by the Temper & better [Reasons] & quotations of some Romanists; but it was ill offered & a Token of more Indiscr[etion] then I thought thee Capable of, to shew so much heat & Displeasure in rebuking min[e] But above all to estim my Ignorance invincible, & yet to offer me a friend of thine to help to rectifie my mistaken Understanding is a Contradiction, that may need my Charity. However me thinks there can be no reason in the World, why thou shouldst express so much Unkindness in thy letter, since my Ignorance hath been so beneficial to the Romans Cause (but if mine ha'nt, there's one has.)

Scolding I utterly abhor, & have been ever bred a step above so great rudiness, but I perceive some men estim it spleen, to divulge theirs. I can only say, that the Romish, I meant, I did not intend to proclaim him to be my friend L & am sorry, his concerns should do it;[6] It was the gald horse that was ever most apt to wince.

I am so far from baulking an encounter with any of thy Friends that if thou please, I desire he may be either Priest or Jesuit, it is my choyce.[7] By which thou mayst understand, I am not conscious of my self either of fear or Ignorance, though thou or thy Friend shewes not less, that dares not conferr in a free Auditory. For my own part I have no reason to embrace so unreasonable a Proposition, till my Religion can furnish me with all the revenge that Roman Catholiks can. If he please to come each having one or two Hearers on his own side, I shall franckly accept his visit, & believe it, that everyone who comes from thee, shall find a very candid reception. By a Protestant

I mean, that man who denies the common Errors charg'd & justly too upon the Romish Church. Next I claime a share in that Notion negatively, not as confessing all that some Protestants (vulgarly so called) hold, but deny in common with them the Authority, Antiquity, & Orthodoxality of the Romish Church, & by this in short thou mayst receive an account of the two things.

If I did not proced upon some undeniable Principles, I suppose I may collect thus much that I proceeded upon some deniable Principles & it is a great Truth, for I went upon a Discovery of a Romish ones coutcht under the dubious phrases of a Mungrell Protestant;[8] 'Twas too uncharitable to expect all what might be sayd methodically from so short a Discourse, and when let from it by the Pamphlet answerd. I know not what old fashion stuff that is I am charged to have revived, but it is not unknown to thee, I am no Lover of that new fashion, & am as great a Lover of that deserted old one. I grant that Protestants they call themselves, having much quitted their former Way of arguing with those of the Romish Faith but [wou]ldst thou know the reason of it, not because that was less invincible for un[?][veiling] but because they would expose themselves too much to other Separatists that [might] imploy their Arguments against you, against them; But this doth no wayes [rend]er me culpable, but the more plain & ingenuous to abet the Protestant Religion [upo]n the first basis. And I stand amazed to think, that so ingenious a Person as thy self shall overplay the biggot for a Religion that never yet did there dare stand the test of being read in known, I mean in vulgar Languages.

I am so far from thinking this enough that I am but the more warmly resolved to prosecute my Designe of publishing my larger Tract, & the rather, that thou mayst read Principles, & I hope sure footing too. Indeed I am sorry, that after I have defended myself against that apprehension of inceassting[?][9] any ag^{t} You, thou shouldst express so much persecution in a Letter that I look upon it as an earnest of a Romish Smithfield bargain.[10]

Take this abrupt Answer, & believe, that I am by my Principle to write as well for Toleration for the Romanists, as for thy true Friend

Newgate (a true coppy) WP.

To R. Lang. 1671.

LBC. WP's Letterbook, 1667-1675, HSP. (*Micro.* 1:289). The upper and lower corners are torn. Words in brackets have been supplied from the printed version in *Works*, 1:42.

1. Ingenuous. There are several peculiar spellings in this letterbook copy. Perhaps WP's clerk could not read his handwriting.

2. Richard Langhorne. See doc. 37, n. 23. In *Works*, 1:42-43, the addressee of this letter is given as R. Lany, and the mis-identification has persisted. In the LBC, the name is abbreviated and the *g* is so open that it is easily misread as a *y*. However, in the second index to the LBC (also in a seventeenth-century hand) the full name, there spelled Langhorn, is given.

3. Langhorne's letter, unfortunately, does not survive. He was obviously unhappy about a pamphlet published by WP, *A Seasonable Caveat Against Popery Or, A Warning to Protestants* ([London], 1670), written in response to *An Explanation of the Roman Catholic Belief,* perhaps by Christopher Davenport (or a Sancta Clara Franciscus), originally published in 1659, reissued in 1670, and intended to de-emphasize doctrinal differences between Catholics and English Protestants. See also doc. 35, 29 Dec. 1669, above. In *A Seasonable Caveat,* WP "animadverted," or commented critically, on ten such points of Roman Catholic belief (e.g., transubstantiation, prayer in Latin, ecclesiastical hierarchy, civil disobedience) in order to re-emphasize differences. WP was certainly rather ambivalent about Catholics. On the one hand, he said he wanted toleration for them, too; on the other, he believed that their doctrine demanded a primary obedience to authorities of the church, and that if they were given any civil power, their doctrine would commit them to persecution of nonbelievers. Mary Maples Dunn, *William Penn: Politics and Conscience*, pp. 137-39, and Endy, pp. 326-30, provide discussions of the relationship between these attitudes and WP's politics and ideas on toleration. WP also thought that Catholics in 1670, in order to achieve toleration or power, were concealing or glossing over these points. For example, in *A Seasonable Caveat,* the Catholic's suggestion that the church did not command people to pray in languages not understood (Latin) is attacked as an evasion by WP, who pointed out that Catholic doctrine, ritual, etc., were in Latin; only some books for private devotion were appearing in vulgar languages. WP's anti-Catholicism was probably also fueled by what he called the "barbarous" practices of Irish Catholics (see doc. 35, 10 Apr. 1670). Furthermore, Quakers were often persecuted under laws against the recusants, as Catholics were called; WP was therefore anxious to establish his great distance from Rome. Irritation against Catholics was in general rising in this period, and was connected with fears that Catholicism was gaining in the royal court. See John Miller, *Popery and Politics in England 1660-1688* (Cambridge, 1973), pp. 108-34.

4. Concealed. *OED.*

5. In *A Seasonable Caveat,* WP cited, in addition to scripture, classical authors and Roman Catholic theologians.

6. WP's tract did not identify Langhorne as the author of *An Explanation of the Roman Catholic Belief.* He may not have realized until he received Langhorne's letter that Langhorne was a Catholic, even though they had business dealings together; it was not generally known. Joseph Gillow, *English Catholics* (London), 4:128.

7. WP's tract concludes with several queries for Catholics to answer, asking, among other things, if they could or would grant others the toleration they wanted for themselves. Perhaps Langhorne was inviting him to a debate on these queries.

8. WP presumably means the Catholic author who tried to make Catholicism acceptable to Englishmen. There is more than a suggestion in the rest of the paragraph that WP believed that "old fashioned" beliefs about the shortcomings and dangers of Catholicism were correct; but that there was a trend toward severity to separatists and leniency toward Roman Catholics.

9. This meaningless word is replaced by "incensing" in *Works,* 1:42. See also *Works,* 1:468.

10. A sharp bargain in which the buyer is taken in. *OED.* That is, if Catholics were to win toleration and power, they would become persecutors. The use of the metaphor (a common one) may have been suggested by the fact that the Marian martyrs had been burned at Smithfield.

62
TO THE SHERIFFS OF LONDON

[3 June 1671]

Friends,[1]

Though we are a People, the Plainness of whose Principles will not admit of vain Complements, yet are we by them required to express our gratitude; And we must confesse, that since your being in office we have received many Instances of your kindness, for which you never will be condemned of God, or Vertuous Men, as well as that we send you by the bearer our sensible acknowledgments.

This done, we think it fit, to let you know, that though we are in a distinct House,[2] yet not in a distinct Capacity with meer fellons, unless it be, that the[3] have a free Prison, & we have none; For the keeper is so far from showing us that common respect, or have enjoy'd that differenc'd us from Malefactors: that we are not less restrained, if not as much abused; for one of us desiring Liberty to fetch some Bear,[4] the Turnkey thrust him back, calling him Loggarhead, Puppy, Rogue, &c. & that to several others.

In short; We are not willing to be Bondsmen at our own Cost; not for the Value of our House rent (with other additional Expenses) but our Testimony agt the insulting menaces & Extortions, of some of the Goalers, who would cast us into the common stinking Goale, And therefore are resolved to undergo that severity; Which is all at present from those that have wrong'd no man, but fear God, & have Peace with him

Newgate ~~4~~ 3~~th~~d: 4 Mo: 1671 Your True friends &c.

LBC. WP's Letterbook, 1667-1675, HSP. (*Micro.* 1:346). Docketed: To the Sherrifs of London.

1. The sheriffs for London and Middlesex in 1670-1671 were Dannett Forth and Patience Ward. Ward (1629-1696), the more prominent of the two, was later knighted, and chosen Lord Mayor. He was an ardent opponent of the high church party, and was so openly sympathetic to dissenters that he was falsely labeled, in the reign of James II, as a Quaker. *DNB*.
2. The prison inn at the sign of the Black Dog.
3. "They."
4. "Beer."

SETTLING DOWN

1671–1674

After his release from Newgate, WP spent the closing months of 1671 in missionary travel. In August he and Thomas Rudyard set forth for the Netherlands, where they joined Benjamin Furly. Very little evidence survives of WP's movements or missionary work during this continental trip. We know that in September, offended by the worldliness of Amsterdam, WP wrote "A Trumpet Sounded" (*Micro.* 1:351), a stern letter of warning to the Dutch people. In October he visited the Quaker-like community of Labadists in Germany; WP's account of this unsuccessful encounter is in doc. 63. Returning to England in late October, he visited Friends in Essex and Suffolk. In November, while in Suffolk, he grappled with the Quaker problem of how to avoid imprisonment for refusing to swear loyalty oaths. Doc. 64 gives his views on this issue, an important one for WP since he himself had been sent to Newgate in February 1671 for refusing to take an oath. It was probably also at this time that he learned firsthand about recent Quaker sufferings at the hands of a brutal Cambridgeshire magistrate. This inspired him to write doc. 65, another tract against persecution, which, however, he left unfinished and unprinted.

63
TO JOHN DE LABADIE'S COMPANY

Herwerden.[1] 8^{m} [October 16]71.

My Friends,[2]
I came in the Love of God to Visit you in y^{r} retirem^{t} many miles out of my way,[3] hoping to have found such a reception from you, as might have answered that great ~~Brute~~ {Noise} of Spiritual Reformation you have made, which is ever attended wth love, meeknes, sincerity, & godly courage, But in lieu thereof you seem'd to me as men surprised with fear, & in great pain to receive us: as if you had been so far from embracing my loving visit with a sincere & open wellcome, that you were shy—of suffering us to approach y^{r} house, & more y^{r} company.

Which I presently perceived to be an high effect of yr Jealousy, & Suspition of us. And though you may be so far opinionated of yr own strength as that you no ways fear'd the utmost Essays of any differing from you to bring an alteration upon your people (as [illegible deletion] indeed I had something to have spoken by way of Dissatisfaction in yr manner of proceeding, being to me not only dissonant from the Scriptures, but very incongruous with the natural Influence of the holy spirit. Yet I am very well satisfied, that our being led from yr door into a wet garden, whilst yr Assembly was not so [illegible deletion] {dispers'd} but wee might have cleard our Consciences, showes, that you were either voyd of that common Civility & humanity, which the spirit of God admits of, & encourages to, especially the Reception of strangers) which yr Nation highly pretends to, or else that {you} were excessively apprehensive of the success of our Visit to yr people.[4] But indeed I was willing to remain a while passive in this matter, & to employ that opportunity I had to the best service I could, hoping, that there might have been some good understanding; as on yr parts was much pretended to (declaring great & kind Apprehensions of us). But when we were gone, & in our journey had taken a View of yr Discourses, & particularly that, which you call a Dedication etc.[5] I must confess, I was a little Startled. Not that there should be so great Difference between us; for that I could have told any, before ~~I~~ [blank] ~~then~~. But that, whilst you should speak so many good things of us to our Faces as that we were the people of God; holy & good men; the best practical Christians in the world; that knew & enjoyed more of the Power of Godlines, then all else: that {all} others were in Babilon [blank][6] high Panegyriks: that yet you should tell the World, that we speak irreverently of the will of God: that you cannot comprehend, how we could be entred into the living knowledge of God: that in somethings we should be one with the Jesuits, & Manichees[7] etc. shows so much manifest Contradiction, as is highly inconsistant not only with the unerring unity with the eternal Spirit you pretend to be guided by; but that common prudence, charity, & indeed Sense, which many wordly men have to much caution to be guilty of. In fine I have but too great reason to believe, that you have over shott your work, & instead of keeping in that meek, low, self denying & suffering Spirit of Jesus, you are but [blank] to set up [blank] for yourselves, being very ignorant of that Death to this World through the [blank] Cross of Christ & Resurrection within to a new & heavenly life, the very [blank] of the last great spiritual Dispensation, wherein the primitive purity should be restored, & an end for ever put to those self-confident & fleshly Religions, that are in the World, which you pretend to. You are deeply acted [?] by an Exalted Spirit, whose best Revelations are mostly Phantastical Imaginations. As that one Instance of your [blank] did but too Evidently shew; & your express Assertion of the latitude of the Spirits motions, even to Murder &

Adultery; & w[t] not. My Friends, I could not be clear in my Conscience before the Lord, whose peace is more dear to me, then the Censures of the most-pretendedly refined Separatists can be terrible. And I do exhort you to turn your minds that [blank] spirit, & divine Light of God, out of your own runnings & willings, in Stillnesse to be guided, whose way is pure, sound, [blank] & convincing of Gain-sayers, which never led to sin, but is a Convincer of the World of it, & a severe condemner of the world for it. That experiencing a Dayly Increase of Victory in y[r] selves over the Spiritual (as well as Carnal) Wickednesse in high places; through your Obedience to the Cross you may become right-born sons, & Daughters by the Spirit of the Lord. And then I am well perswaded, that you will see y[r] selves to have been very near that Liberty & joy, which ends in very Loosness & Ranterisme.[8]

And I have a great Deal of reason to urge again upon you t'abett that unsavory & ambitious Title of Father, it being in that very Case only deny'd, & severely reprehended by Christ Jesus.[9] And the Apostles calling some of the Churches Children, no ways implys their constant calling of him Father, or that he Customarely assum'd or accepted it. And I have more Cause to question, whether J. Labadee has begotten those, that are at present well opiniated of him, into that most-Christian spirit; then he hath reason [blank] to receive or require that Great & superlative Title. Though I pretend not to say, he hath not great Cause to affirm, he hath but too much begotten them into his own Belief.

In short, I would not be thought to Strike at those tender desires, that may be in any of y[r] Company after God, & his most-spiritual Way to Life: but highly encourage such in their Separation from the fleshly religions & Worships of the World, that are not Effectual to the Converting of the Soul to God. Yet, I must needs Caution you of being too much lead by a more-refined Formal Spirit: & which mysteriously works to stop the pure in erring motions of the Lords Spirit: & that will lead you to as much Formality, as the somuch decry'd Directery, & Formalised Articles of Reformed Faith.[10]

[line left blank by the copyist]

that are with you, that they turn their minds to the blessed light & grace of God in their hearts, by that to be guided; & to eye that, as their Leader, & Instructour; & not to give away their Understandings unto men, whose breath is in their nostrils,[11] that may & do err: for that is no better State, then the Common Parish-people are in. That so they may come to enjoy Bread in their own houses, & water in their own wells. For this is the Tenour of the Second Covenant:[12] And cursed is that, which seeds self promotion, or to pretend to rule or guide the minds of any in this day of the shining-forth of the blessed light of the everlasting light.

So, my Friends, I have herein dealt faithfully & plainly herein; as seeing in the Eternal light of God your present State, & what your are driving at: That I may be clear in my Conscience, & that you may be advised & cautioned.[13] I am

Yr very truely well-
wishing Friend

To Jo: Delabadees Company. W P

LBC. WP's Letterbook, 1667-1675, HSP. Docketed: To the *family* {*Society*}— of *John Del'abadde* | then at *Herwerden* in Germany, being refused by him | and 2 deputys to see them. The address and docket are in WP's hand. The copyist evidently had great difficulty in reading this letter, and left many words blank.

1. Herford, a city now in West Germany.

2. This letter is addressed to John de Labadie and his followers. De Labadie (1610-1674) was a famous French divine who became a Protestant in 1650. He held pastorates in Geneva, London, and Amsterdam. His religious ideas had some similarity to those of the Quakers: he believed that the Holy Spirit guides the regenerate to truth, and to the interpretation of the Bible; that the church possesses the gift of prophecy through all time; that children of the regenerate are born without sin. He gathered a separatist community together in Amsterdam in 1669, believing that the regenerate should live together. They were subject to considerable persecution, and in 1671 accepted an invitation from Princess Elizabeth of the Palatinate, Protestant Abbess of Herford, to settle on her estates. The people there were much opposed to the Labadists, and the group moved to Altona (then in Denmark), where de Labadie died in 1674. Several small communities were established in the Rhineland and one in New Jersey, but the sect apparently did not survive beyond 1728. William Hull, *William Penn and the Dutch Quaker Migration to Pennsylvania* (Swarthmore, 1935), pp. 2-19; Cross, *Christian Church*; F. Ernest Stoeffler, *The Rise of Evangelical Pietism* (Leiden, 1965), pp. 162-69.

3. We know very little about WP's route on this trip to Holland and Germany, except that he stopped at Rotterdam and Amsterdam in the Netherlands, Emden and Friedrichstadt on the German North Sea coast, and Herford in the interior principality of Ravensberg, part of the electorate of Brandenberg.

4. WP was particularly anxious to meet Anna Maria van Schurman (1607-1678), de Labadie's most famous convert. She was considered one of the best-educated women of her time, and was a friend of Princess Elizabeth. Joyce Irwin, "Anna Maria van Schurman: From Feminism to Pietism," *Church History* 46:48-62, and Hull, *William Penn and the Dutch Quaker Migration,* pp. 3-4, 8.

5. It is not clear which of de Labadie's works is intended here. In *L'Impudant Manteur on L'Imposteur de Marque Antoene La Marque En son Libelle Difamatoire fait contre Mr. Jean de Labadie* (Amsterdam, 1670), he defended himself against charges of Quakerism in terms similar to those cited here.

6. "And such"?

7. Manichaeism was a dualistic religion based on a supposed primeval conflict between light and darkness. It taught that the object of religion was to release the particles of light which Satan had stolen from the world of light and imprisoned in man's brain. Severe asceticism was required, but enemies accused the Manichaeans of evil practices. The sect spread rapidly in the third and fourth centuries, but by the seventeenth century had disappeared, although its bad reputation remained. The Quaker concept of the light may have made them subject to charges of Manichaeism. See, for example, WP's dichotomy between light and darkness in doc. 21.

8. The Ranters were a radical English religious group which came into prominence in 1649. They believed in a pantheistic mysticism, and a complete spiritual liberty which led them to reject organized religion, even the authority of Scripture, and belief in the existence of sin. They expected a revolution in the social order and appealed to the urban poor. Some Ranters challenged conventional family mores, and advocated free love. These beliefs led to charges of blasphemy and sexual promiscuity, and to tremendous hostility against them. They were often compared with Quakers, to the discomfort of Quaker leadership. See A. L. Morton, *The World of the Ranters* (London, 1970), pp. 70-114. Christopher Hill argues that "the whole early Quaker movement was far closer to the Ranters in spirit than its leaders like to recall," in *The World Turned Upside Down* (London, 1972), pp. 186-207.

9. E.g., 1 Thess. 5:5. WP found the title "father" unsavory because it was used by Roman Catholic priests.

10. Formalism, in this sense, was an insistence on outward observances with a corresponding neglect of the inner spirit. *The Directory of Church Government* (1644) was a book of discipline written in Latin in 1586 by Walter Travers (c. 1548-1635), a Puritan divine, and issued in English in 1644 by those interested in introducing the Presbyterian system in England. "Reformed" churches were Calvinist, as opposed to Lutheran. Cross, *Christian Church*.

11. Isa. 2:22, a favorite verse of WP's. The marginal comment in the Geneva Bible is "cast of your vain confidence of man, whose life is so fraile, that if his nose be stopped, he is dead, and consider that you have to do with God."

12. Or New Testament. See especially Heb. chaps. 8-9.

13. The Labadists' rejection of WP continued to rankle. On 24 Nov. 1672 he wrote them another letter in a similar vein, complaining once more of their incivility. He called upon them to reject the authority of de Labadie, and "Returne, Returne, Returne to the Heavenly Grace & Light in your own Hearts" (see *Micro.* 1:446). In 1677, on his second visit to Germany, he remarked that "though they had received some Divine touches there was a danger that they would run out with time & spend them like prodigals." He visited the Labadists again on that occasion, and had a more satisfactory meeting. See 13 Sept. 1677, doc. 119, below.

64
ON LITIGATION AGAINST OATHS

[15 November 1671]

My dearly Beloved Friends & Brethern;

My Love is to you all in that blessed unchangeable Truth, & Seed & Covenant [of Life, whe]rein is our pretious Fellowship, & which hath been our Rock & Foundation f[rom the Day] that the Lord God eternal appeared unto us, & convinced us of the same, y[ea, the im]movable, Solid, Certain & Living Foundation, on which our Building hath ev[er stood sure] save[1] & unshaken, from all the Storms & Tempests that from the filthy rage[ing Sea have] risen against us, & in & upon which alone we can & shall only be able to stand [in all our] Exercises, Tryals & Controversies from & with this Ungodly Generation.

Now, my Friends, I am press'd in Spirit to write to you, as one amongst you, & in [the] Living Union of the Body, jelous with you of the honor of the Lord, & the renown & Su[c]cess of his blessed everlasting Way of Truth, more dear to me, then all visible Glorys, Tryumphs, Reputations, or any momentary Injoyement whatsoever; And that which lyes upon me, is this:

I have understood by several good Friends that there are some Endeavours, Earnest & pressing, to Comment[2] a Suit with the King for the Delivery of our Dear Friends, that are Sufferers upon the Oathes, by a formal Course of Law; I confess I was not a little startled at it, yet boar the thing several Dayes in my Mind, being in my Selfe very unwilling to interrupt such a prosecution, partly on the account of the greater Wisdom, and Councill of Friends thereto advise, & partly of the good that might succed, at least might be aim'd at in the thing. But these considerations not being sufficient to silence those stirrings that were in my selfe, & much less to surmount the Objection of not clearing my selfe according to the Order of Truth as received from the beginning, I was constrained after some dayes time thus to easie my spirit, in meekness & endeared tender Love unto you & for the blessed Truth of God.

The Ground of the Procedure in this matter must be this, That the Oaths runing in the Name of K. James,[3] & he Dead, such as require men to take them, would have them swear To be faithful to one that is not in being, which say the Prosecutors of this matter, is absurd & impossible:

To this I answer & object

1. The King never dyes {in their law} & they will say, that none did swear {to} that which died, but that which doth not dye, the political part, & Civill Government, & only to obey that which dyed, as that Corresponded w~~hich~~th what does not dye, to wit, *their Laws & Power.*

2. Say they, if this were not the meaning of it, then during the Interregnum, betwixt the one King's Death & the others Coronation, that formaly makes him King, there could be no Treason, no Murder, no Theft, no sedition &c. which being unreasonable & absurd, it follows, that the Oaths intend the Government, & that is allwayes in being, say they.

3. But let us grant, that our plea is valid in Sense, Reason & Equity; & that their Chamber Lawyers for great fees will whisper so; will these men stand it out against the Displeasure of Authority in open Court.

4. If they do, then consider, whether the Judges will think fit or the K. & Councill admit of such a Sentence against those oaths, as brands them for the greatest Oppressors in the World; For, what are they else, if they have so many years (not to say Ages) imprisoned People, & confiscated their Goods, without any Law, as must be, if these oaths be legally invalid.

5. Consider what probability there is of a Success upon them, who have the Law, that must condemn them, in their own hands; & who, in cases wherein they have less colour of Law or Justice stick not to comit dayly outrages upon our Persons & Estates.

6. That we do not only plead our own Cause, but that of the very Papists & other killing Spirits, who use to have our Testimony unmixed (mark that) for in breaking these oaths we do not break the Bond & Bullwark of Swearing down, which is our Single unmixt Testimony, but we overlook [that we?][4] inform them, how to make an other Law, that will prevent us of the present Plea [not to speak?] two Words King James; And so we render our Bonds but the more legally strong [against us. In?] Common & Universal Cases, it it[5] well, that our Testimony appear so, yet wherein [our Testimoney?] distinguisht us from all the Families of the Earth (at least in our Earth) there [should our?] Testimony be distinguishing & unmixed, that we not

spend our Labour to get two [words] chang'd, & leave the bondage standing, yea reinforced; But above all, that in Cases, [whi]ch concerne Conscience, not Civil Properly alone, as swearing doth, we should imploy [me]rcenary Lawyers, who made & maintain those very oaths; & they them is hard, yea very [h]ard to think on.[6]

Thus much in few Words my {Dear} Friends, opened in weighteness to me, & I could not be clear, but in communicating them to you, that so all things may be done, worthy of the blessed unchaingable Truth, & our immovable Foundation, the Law of the Spirit of Life, which makes free from the Laws & Lawyers of Sin, & gives the Tongue of the Learned into every mouth, wherewith to plead his own righteous Cause, & so a good Conscience become an able & bold Advocate; And herein my Soul knows peace with the Lord over the Floode, & every thing that would disturb, hurt, or set at work in that which does not the will of God, or seeks the one thing necessary above Martha's many unnecessary things;[7] If it suceed, it may be well, if not, I am clear. So in the pure Love of God I desire this may be received, in which I most dearly salute you all, resting in the Living Sense & Fellowship thereof

My Dear Friends
Your endeared
Friend & Brother
(a true coppy)
WP

Suffolk the 15th 9th mo: 1671.[8]

Friends here away are well, & Friends tender, & Meetings large.

Post-Script.

Besides, it ought to be well considered, that this attempt endevors a Disobligation & an intire absolution of the People from all Allegiance; for if these Oaths (or Laws,) that insew or warrant them be void & not legally in being, then such as the Government suppose them selves secure of, by their taking those Oaths, are released from all such Obligations, & the Government is insecure of the Obedience & Obligation therein required & intended, which, how strangly it will savour, is left with you to weigh. For the ground of one not taking the Oaths is not these two Words K. J. but our not swearing, therefore we should not give that for a reason which is not since if we would swear, we would not boggle at those words, therefore not swearing is the only reason. And how can we imploy those Lawyers to plead against Oathes, who are maintained by them, & who maintain them, & for money could plead as heartily for them, & so the~~ir~~ ground of their Plea is not Conscience, but Covetousness, the Root of all Evill. Christ, that lead us not to swear, is an only Advocate for not swearing, & there Truth leaves it.

LBC. WP's Letterbook, 1667-1675, HSP. (*Micro.* 1:366). A fragment of the first page is torn off at the upper right, and a fragment of the second page is torn off at the upper left. The missing words from the first page are supplied from an incomplete second copy of the document, also in the letterbook. For the missing words from the second page, see n. 4.

1. "Safe," in the second letterbook copy.
2. "Commence," in the second letterbook copy.
3. James I (1603-1625).
4. The next five lines of manuscript text are very difficult to read because a corner of the letterbook page has been torn out. We have placed conjectural readings of the missing words, followed by question marks, in brackets, so as to convey the sense of WP's argument.
5. "Is."
6. WP's argument here might seem to depart from his recent policy of fighting England's political and legal establishment through the courts (see docs. 46-51, 57-58). In the Penn-Mead trial and in his debate with Sir John Robinson, however, WP spoke to the tolerant and humane principles that he believed were embedded in English law. He hoped to convince the government that enforced oath-taking violated these principles. From WP's point of view, his fellow Friends should be objecting to oath-taking in general rather than to the wording of a particular oath. WP was strongly opposed to oath-swearing; he argued the Quaker position at length in *A Treatise of Oaths* in 1675.
7. Luke 10:41-42.
8. On 24 Oct. 1671, WP arrived at Harwich on a packet boat from Holland, according to a government spy, and immediately "associated himself with the Quakers of this town" (*CSPD, 1671*, p. 541). In the following weeks he visited Friends in Suffolk and Cambridgeshire.

65
NARRATIVE OF THE SUFFERINGS OF QUAKERS IN THE ISLE OF ELY

[November? 1671]

The Arraignment & Judgment of that Cruel Spirit of
PERSECUTION,
with a brief Discovery, of the
CAUSE, EFFECTS & END of it,
being
A true NARRATIVE of some of the Lamentable Sufferings of the People Called Quakers in Little Port in the Isle of Ely,[1]
occasioned by the Illegal & inhuman practices of
Edward ~~Patrick~~,[2] called a Justice, & Thomas Richman
an Apparator,[3] Brethren & Parties in Oppression.

By a Servant of the Lord, a Sufferer for his Truth, that sympathiseth wth his Brethren, & therefore cannot let their Sufferings go unrecorded, nor their Persecutors pass either undected or unrebucked.

W.P.
Written in the Year 1671.

Sect i. Persecution must not be deny'd by any to be the Devils ofspring, who dare not esteem Cain's Murder his Brother Abel's just punishment, for only worshipping the God, that made them, in a way to him most acceptable;[4] But we have great reason to fear, that the Persecutors of this age are quite as guilty, & not have[5] so penitent, who not only committ the same Impieties, but also think, they therein doe God service as well as themselves; And which aggravates the whole, they act it wth an unwanted Zeal & boldness ag^t^ the express Letter of the Scripture the fundamental Laws of England, & Common Safety of every Corporation, as if it were not so much their purpose to convert as ruin all Dissenters, that out of their ruins they may raise what they call fortunes to themselves. And that we may not be misunderstood but better enabled to defend our Charge ag^t^ Persecutors, we shall explain our meaning by it.

Sect. 2. By Persecutors we intend a Coercive Civil Power compelling us upon Corporal Punishment, to conform to such Articles of Faith & practise in point of Worship, wch in pure Conscience we cannot own or imbrace, or restraining us from the Profession of that Faith & practise in Worship, wch in pure Conscience we dare not deny or discontinue.

Sect. 3. This hath been the Work & Contrivance of the Devil almost from the beginning for ever since he made any wicked, he has put them upon persecuting the good, whole kingdoms have rung of it, & what storie is without it? It is as old as superstition, & where the one reigns the other thrives God never had a Message to the World but it met with Sufferings from both. His extraordinary Ambassadours have been ston'd to Death though they have come on the Ambassy of Peace, & whilst they sought the Worlds salvation, the World as earnestly indeavoured their Destruction. Thus was Abel's sacrifice an Offence to Cain, & instead of following his Example, he sought his Blood; The same Spirit withstood & reproacht the righteous preachings of Noah to the old World, & imbondaged Israel in the New one.[6] The Prophets became a Sacrifice to their own Nation;[7] But that's no wonder when we call to mind the reproachfull & Blasphemous Murder & Crucifixion of Christ himself, since the time of whose Appearance in the World Persecution has lived wth Christianity, & to have been a good Christian has been the only next Way to be persecuted as if to have no right to the World, were to serve him that made it, & the ready way to be persecuted out of it to profes strictly the Life & Doctrine of him who alone hath right to it. Calamities indeed too great to have been supported had not he sustain'd his People, to whom no thing is impossible. Thus have the best Servants of the Lord not miss'd the Violence of Persecution, as well as that the meanest of them never usd it.

Sect 4. But as it is both ag^t^ Scripture, & severly reprov'd by it, so doth it strike at the very foundation of our English Laws & Goverment, for though they have lately vaild them from the Eyes of common People by new & sharp Acts ag^t^ Dissenters, yet we well know, that the Ancient Constitution[8] of the Lands doth not regard this or that profession of Religion (much less allow of a Forfeture of those Civil rights & Priviledges upon a bare Non-Conformity in those matters) but considers us as English Men, & as a Civil Body & Society of People, trading & commercing together in such things as are of a Civil, external Nature & importance; For as there is not a Law extant that legally can invalidate the great Charter of England, so is there not the least mention made therein of the necessitie of our Conforming to any kind of Religion, in order to enjoy the benefit thereby confirmd,

Sect. 5. Nor indeed dare we in gratitude suppose so great weakness, Nay Cruelty in our Ancestors; since he that denies himself or Child the free injoyement of those Priviledges his reason, & Country intitule him to upon a Nicety in Faith or Worship doth either shew his Ignorance in supposing such an Ignobleness in them that are Changeable as nothing can ever work an alteration upon them, or else afford this great instance of their self-incharity & indiscretion that not being able to assure themselves of on years Constancy to a present Conviction much less their Posterity contrive wayes too far fit for their Liberty & Estates upon every such Change of Judgment, however rational, so that either we ought to continue in the Belief & Practise of what we do however hetrodox, or if they though a Dissent, let it be never so Christian to loose their Liberties or Estates; O strange Ignorance, Madness, yet so besotted & much more is every Persecutor in England that consents or executes such a Law, however it is unpardonable in a Protestant to deny Men their Civil Freedom upon or under religious Dissent, since they esteem'd it so great a Work of AntiChrist in the Papist, unless they think that Christianity in themselves, wch they adjudg'd inhuman in the Papist, wch doth but aggravate his Injustice, but this shewes that either Persecution was excusable in the Romans, or else that the Protestants are most condemnable, & it's strange to us that any should fancy the Name alters the Nature; No, the same {Anti-}Christian Spirit that burnd Thorp[9] & Bradford[10] has its Resurrection in some of the present Protestants to ruin us. The difference being but barely nominal. Nor will it be any excuse for them to say, we are Hereticks, for the Papists thought them for matter ~~being~~ in Controversie being not so much about what was true in itself, as what they believed to be so, (what was not of Faith, being Sin) & that they ought not to suffer for disbelieving a Religion they would not believe upon Conviction, nor for believing a Religion they were Convinced of, of wch their [word missing] would have them disbelieve.

Sect. 6. In short: Till men are capable of imbracing any Religion or worship wth out the use of their Understanding, Judgment, & Will (wch will be never) they must necessarily employ them in that great choyce, & therefore it is a moral impossibility to believe or perform any Article or Act of Religion, conscientiously without their due Conviction & Determination, wch not depending upon the Skill or power of an other man, it is the Top of Tyranny to give prescriptions or require Obedience in those matters. And this Challenge we are bold to make to all Persecutors in this Nation. First, to defend Persecution by any Argument that has not or might not be used by the Papists agt them, & which their own Arguments are suficient to refute; & secondly, to produce us one Instance throughout the whole scriptures & primitive storie, wherein the true Religion ever persecuted the False, And we will produce 10000. Instances, wherein the false has ever persecuted the true, wch made Tertullian say that 'tis not the property of the true Religion to compell, & therefore plac'd it as a Mark of Infamy upon the Heathens, that theirs did not convince, but force Proselyts; much might be said, if there had not been so much said already, & we did not designe Brevity at this time:

Sect. 7. It remains however that we say something to the Cause, Effects, & End of Persecution or reward of Persecutors before we proceed to rehearse the matter of Fact, that our Charge may appear both rationall & Christian.

Sect 8. The Cause of Persecution may as easily be known by it as the Child, that is the exact picture of its Father: For the Devil was a Murtherer from the beginning & since all accounts either proceed from the good or evil Principle, & that compelling, beating, confiscating, Imprisoning, Bannishing & killing about matters of Faith & Worship (which evill works make up that wch we call Persecution) cannot proceed from the good Principle wch we call God, who is Gentleness, Mercy, Longsuffering & Compassion it self, it must necessarily follow, that it is the Devills Ofspring, & he its Parent, But though he be the General Author of it, yet the Occasions wherefore he doth imploy it, are very many; some times out of meer hatred, because of that reformation that might ensue the free exercise of the true Religion; like those of old that Christ {Matt. 5.}[11] said, should hate & spitefull use his servants; some times out of self-Politie or Interest, endeavouring to cloud the Peoples Understandings from a clear Discerning of what would most attend to their Freedom & Happiness (as well as Discovery of their Wickedness) thus did the Jews when they persecuted Christ, least the People should beleeve & follow him; some times out of very revenge, as Cain murdered Abel; sometimes out of Derision, as both Jews & Gentiles did to the Apostles, when they were counted as the ofscouring of all things[12] & gazeing stoks[13] unto the World, but above all {as} the Scribes & Pharisees[14] served our Lord Jesus, when they crowned him wth thornes, & gave him Vinegar to drink, wreiting over his Head, This is the King of the Jews; & lastly some persecute out of an ignorant Zeal, as Saul did the Churches,[15] thereby thinking, he did God service, though all that while he crucified his only Son, who was & is the

Lord of Life & Glory. Yet notwithstanding these various prompts & Inducements to Persecution, it is the same Devil still, who makes use of the divers pasions & inclinations of men, to maintain his murthering Principle in the World, that he might perpetuate Contention wth human Society.

Sect. 9. As to the Effects of Persecution, they are indeed too many to be numbred, yet will we hint at such particulars as may best suite the bulck of this Discourse & answer our design in it.

1. The first bad Effect it works, is Contention, & that amongst Brethren; Whole states have been overrun wth the seeds of strife that Persecution hath sown, the biggest Empires in the World have not been strong enough to relief themselves from the ensuing ruin to such debates, Wittness the grand Contests of the third & fourth Century betwixt the Homousians & Arrians,[16] wth the rest of the subdivided separatists of those times.

2. Secondly, ~~by~~ this strife continued works Hatred, wch is the accomplishment to all Cruelty, it eats out all tyes of Friendship, & breaks the strongest bonds of natural affection, in so much that neither the Dictates of Grace nor sweetest influences of Nature are frequently powerfull enough to repell the strong motions of Enmity & despitefull Hatred

3 Thirdly, Hatred setts man a lusting after {the} Destruction of what they hate, as in Estate, by unreasonable Fines, illegally called Forfeitures (wth the Trebble Dammages extorted in such occasions) to the utter ruin of the Poor, the Fatherless, & the Widdow.

4 Fourthly, it hatches & brings forth Warrs, as in England, Scotland, France, Holland, Swizerland & Germany; to say nothing of antient times, whose happiness or Infelicity hath stood upon a toleration, each being the natural Consequences of each.

5 Fifthly, it has occasioned a Decay of Men & Trade, & consequently an increase of Povertie to the making Bankrumpt the wealthiest Kingdoms, & most potent Common-Wealths; Nay, it has been the very reason of that Advance the Turk has made in Europe as well as that it stumbles the Jews from all Conversion to the Christian Faith. Something of this the late Author of the Intreast of England[17] has evidently demonstrated by Instances fetcht from abroad of the Prosperity of those states who chiefly ow it to a toleration in Religion.

6. Sixthly, another Effect is to deprive men of the use of their Understandings, & Judgments as if they were such Ciphers as only signifie something behinde their figures that impose upon them. 'Tis a strange peece of Confidence, that any should think the greatest part of the World was born to believe them & distrust themselves, And what is yet stranger that they should allow a liberty to understand, judge, determin, trade & commerce in & about matters of an external & momentary importance; wch most properly concerns the regiment of this World, & yet deny freedom of Conscience those

Men in matters of an eternal concernment that relate to an other World, & whom they can never answer for: Certainly God was not less prospitious to man in furnishing him wth a spiritual discerning then he was in giving him a Natural one. But this great Absurdity is another Effect of Persecution.

7. Seventhly, it makes Hypocrites; for most are not made their Proselyts by Faith but Force, the supplies of Civil power, answering to the Defects of their Religion. But let their New Conformists be weighd in equal Ballance, & they will be found lighter then they were by a whole good Conscience. And so detestable is an Hypocrite, that it were better to profess an Errour conscientiously than a Truth hypocritically.

8. Eightly, The last & worst Effect, that we shall mention here, is Persecutions – Murder, but the Saints Martyrdom; How many thousands soules lye now under the Altar, who prove their beheading for the Testimony of Jesus & a good Conscience to be the cursed effect of the Spirit of Persecution. What Countries in the World remain unsprinkled wth their blood, read but the stories of all Nations & wt Slaugther do they tell us, hath been made in every Age: Yea in their most partial relations do we find describ'd those rivers, wch emptying themselves into one, make up that vast ocean of innocent blood that has been crying, how long, how long Lord God, holy & True etc. from Righteous Abel's day to this, & as certain as it hath been shed, so in that red sea will God devour & overwhelm Pharaoh,[18] & all his persecuting Host forever, for they shall have blood to drink, which leads me to the End of Persecution, or the Reward of Persecutors.

Sect. 10. Their Reward is commonly shame, if not some greater Judgment here But everlasting Burnings in the World to come. Of the first we have many Instances. For Cain had no sooner turned Murderer, but he turned Vagabund, nor had the old World long persecuted all Rigtheousnes out of it, ere the dreadfull Deluge overtook it; Egypt was no longer without Judgments then it was without Persecution, & that Pharaoh wch thought to cut of Israel in their march to the holy Land, was wth his Hosts cut off in that Attempt.

Sect. 11. And though Sodoms Transgressions were more ripe for Judgment, yet that which aggravated both the Sin & punishment was their Persecuting of those Holy Angels whom they had no sooner evilly intreated then Blindness fell upon them, & flaming fire upon their Citty.[19] Vengeance followed Saul whilst he persecuted David;[20] And the Gallowes that was design'd for Mordecha, hangd Haman the Contriver.[21] So Daniel's Enemies were torn, where he was only tried, & the Prison he Chose to loose his Liberty in that he might preserve his Conscience free, they wth their Liberty lost their Lives too.[22] In short Judas had not hang'd himself had he not betray'd his Master;[23] & Jerusalem might have stood till to day had not she Crucified the Lord of Glory. It were almost endless to go through those many

Volumes that have been written of God's Judgments upon Persecutors, & indeed our own times have not wholly left us without very remarkable Instances of God's Displeasure upon Persecutors; many have been struk (by an immediate hand) wth mortall Distempers, and not a few wth languishing sickness, whose own Convictions have been the sharpest Testimonies that have been given of the Impiety of their Actions. Others have gone distracted, & several have been manifestly curst in their outward substance unto their utter Ruin & Consumtion.

Sect. i2 In short, Persecutors have been so farr from being true Christians, that they have ever regenerated from true Men, For if they had had that Generosity, & Valour that render Men truly worthy or Noble, they would have abhorr'd oppressing those, who neither deserv'd it, nor yet have Power to relief themselves, so that they are not only apostatized Christians, but apostatized men.

Amongst that Number of Men, who have set that brand of Infamie upon their own Heads the persons concern'd in this Relation, have not been the least notorious as a few of those many Passages, their Cruelty has given occasion to observe, will further manifest which thus farr differ them from most imploy'd in the same work, that more Ignorance, Folly, Baseness & Cruelty has not appear'd by such aggravated Circumstances, so much in any as this grand {In} Justice of Ely.

1. Upon the 5th of the 11th month commonly called January 1670. Edward Patridge, calld a Justice & Thomas Richman his Informer, came to a Meeting of the People called Quakers, who were peaceably assembled wth no other design then to worship the only true God, where having taken their Names he, the said E. Patridge in a Frothy & Prophane manner wth as little witt as religion much abused and reflected upon them, the least he should be wanting to shew himself an Enemy to all Sobriety, he first rudely hal'd them out of the Meeting, then beat one of them, caus'd their Horses to be brought into the Meeting, where they made a Turd, & sent for drink to make merry; after he had made this boisterous prank, fitter for a ruffan then for a Justice, he sent for the Smith, & had the Doores lockt up; this being done, he charg'd several Town's Men to accompanie him to their purchased burrying place, who wth his own hands helped to pull down the pailes[24] that inclos'd it, treading & breaking many of them in peeces. Thus did this furious Man as one not contented wth his Cruelty ag^{t} the Living commit this Indecency ag^{t} the Dead, whom he has exposed to the Beasts of the Field, who have layn quietly inclosed for about ten years past. But what peece of Inhumanity is to great from a blind Romish spirited Persecutor to act.

2. Upon the 22th of the same Moneth the People of that Place being again conscientiously met to the purpose aforesaid, & one Samuel Cater[25] speaking the Words of Truth & Soberness to the People, the said E. Partridge came again wth his Informer & struck him twice w^{th}

his staff, violently pulling him down, wch when he had done, the said Sam. Cater kneeled down to pray, but this Man of Injustice, that he might shew his dislike to praying as well as preaching cruelly & undecently took him by the Nose, hald him by it of from his knees, nor was he contented wth this, for he fin'd the said Meeting 60l for the House, & the Speaker, & the rest what suited his prerogative will & pleasure.

3. Upon the 26th of the same Month, being kept out of their Meeting (their Lawfull hired House) they met in the Street, where wth his wonted Violence he pulld & tore them from the place, striking 4. of them several blows, to wch Cruelty he added the Injustice of illegal Fines.

4. Upon the 29th of the same Moneth upon the like of their peaceable Meeting together to worship God, these Partners in Malice & Envy were not wanting in their diligence to come nor in their Violence, when there to abuse them; for after they had been boysterously pull'd out, E. Partridge like the Man that valiantly encountered the Tree[,] fell heavily upon them. Some he bruised by sore blowes, others he punch'd on their Sides & breasts, pulling of the Hatts of several Men & Women, & wth a Boyish incivility afterwards kickt them into the dirt; & that he might give further evidence how little he deserv'd to be a Justice, & how much to be questioned by such as really are so; he very confidently incourag'd Rob. Pickering & Ed. Dunth. to take out of their House their seats & forms, & carry them into their publick place of Worship, thereby making their Temple[26] a Sanctuary for their Plunders, & that he might lett us know, how much such practises suited the Injustice of his Nature, he doth not stick to call them honest men, as if their breaking of the Law, by answering his illegal Commands, had been a sufficient Testimony of their Loyalty; Certainly, such men can never truly honour the King, nor serve the Goverment. And that he might leave nothing undone, wch was in his power to do, he issued out several Warrants to seise, & sell their Goods persuant to the fines impos'd upon them.

5 Nor was he willing to leave them so, but seem'd as resolute in his Oppression as they did in their Meeting; for upon the 20th of the Mon[th] called April, 1671. he came again into their Meeting, so blowne wth rage & malice, that more became an inrag'd Party than an impartial Justice, for after he had taken their Names, he pulld off the Hatts of several Men & Women, & fell heavily upon them wth his staffe, beating young & old men & Women, having not the least regard to Age or Sects[27] whilst his staff lasted wch not being so strong as his Envy, he took {another out of a wardsmans[28] hand} & imployd that upon their Heads, & shoulders wth the same violence, till he had broken that also. His sticks thus failing him, he betook himself to his hands & feet, & that he might prevent us in aggravating his Tyranny & Oppression, imploy'd them upon a poor old Woman, first pulling

her down, & then stricking her when she was down, from her he proceeded to several old men above 60. yeares of Age, whom he also beate, & th~~en~~rew several women in the Dirt, causing several spectators to cry out, he would kill them, he would kill them, to wch he had no more Witt, Law, or Humanity, then to say, If I do, I can answer it.[29]

LBC. WP's Letterbook, 1667-1675. (*Micro.* 1:294).

1. A district in northern Cambridgeshire; Littleport is five miles north of the cathedral town of Ely.

2. Later in the narrative spelled "Patridge" and "Partridge." See also Besse, 1:95.

3. Attendant to an official. *OED.* Besse calls this person Rickman, 1:95.

4. Gen. 4:4-5.

5. Half.

6. WP, following 2 Pet. 2:5, uses "the old World" to signify the wicked antediluvian society to which Noah preached in vain. In the "New" world after the Flood, Israel was conquered by Assyria in the eighth century B.C., and then by Babylon in the seventh century. *New Bible Dictionary.*

7. The prophets of Israel, living in the period of foreign subjugation, were rejected and villified by their own people. See the lamentations of Isaiah, Jeremiah, and Ezekiel, in particular.

8. The system of fundamental principles by which England was governed. See J. G A. Pocock, *The Ancient Constitution and the Feudal Law* (Cambridge, 1957).

9. William Thorpe was burned at the stake in 1407 as a heretical follower of John Wycliffe. *DNB.*

10. John Bradford was a Protestant martyr in the Marian persecution, burned at the stake in 1555. *DNB.*

11. "Matt. 5." is written in the margin. See Matt. 5:10-12.

12. 1 Cor. 4:13.

13. Heb. 10:33.

14. See doc. 33, n. 7.

15. See Acts, 7:58; 9:1-18.

16. For the Arians, see doc. 33, n. 15. To counter the Arian heresy, the Homoousians held that the Father and the Son were "of the same substance" and that Christ was in no way subordinate to God. This doctrine was adopted by the Council of Nicaea in 325 and became the orthodox position of the church. See Cross, *Christian Church.*

17. Perhaps a reference to *The Interest of England in the Protestant Cause* (1659), by John Durie (1596-1680), a Scottish evangelist who traveled throughout Protestant Europe and attempted to form an evangelical union of all Protestant churches on the continent and in Britain. Wing, 1:265; *DNB.*

18. See Exod. 14:21-30.

19. See Gen. 18:16-19, 25; 19:10-11.

20. See 1 Sam., chaps. 17-31.

21. Esther, chaps. 2-8.

22. See Dan. 6:10-24.

23. See Matt. 27:3-5.

24. Stakes forming a paling or fence.

25. Samuel Cater was in frequent trouble with the authorities. In 1662 he had been imprisoned in Cambridge for ten weeks; in 1670 he was fined for preaching in Norfolk, and again in Essex. In 1686 he would be released from another jail term in Cambridge Castle. Besse, 1:91, 94-95, 99, 204.

26. The Anglican parish church.

27. "Sex."

28. A warden, employed to watch over prisoners. *OED.*

29. Patrick's (or Patridge's) violent behavior is also recounted in Besse, 1:95-96. The abrupt ending to WP's narrative suggests that he left his intended pamphlet unfinished.

WP and Gulielma Springett were married on 4 April 1672. They had been courting for about three years (see docs. 22, 29, 35, 41, 58). Their marriage, one of the central events in WP's life, is discussed in the next four documents.

Quaker marriage procedures had been worked out in the 1650s. Betrothal was to be a slow process which gave everyone time to think things through. A couple, after full self-examination, should consult fellow Friends, parents, Meeting; only when all were agreed and willing to "liberate" them for marriage could the marriage be announced. WP and Gulielma Springett made their first declaration at a monthly meeting on 7 February 1672 (doc. 67). Their case was investigated, after which they received approval at the next monthly meeting on 6 March 1672 (doc. 68). The marriage took place at a third meeting, before the witness of Friends — and also WP's non-Quaker mother and brother—who all joined in signing the certificate (doc. 69), which was then presented to the magistrate.

Doc. 66, an undated manuscript probably written shortly before WP's betrothal, gives his interpretation of Quaker marriage. Friends had developed a doctrine which linked conversion to the nature of marriage in a new way: the converted were in relation to each other as Adam and Eve had been before the Fall. Fox was explicit about this on a number of occasions, but no more so than at his own marriage to Margaret Fell, which he explained "as a testimony that all might come uppe Into the mariage as was in the beginninge: & as a testimony that all might come uppe out of the wildernesse to the mariage of the lamb."

This concept of marriage brought in its train a number of problems to be worked out. For example, a person's interest in marriage had to "arise purely & simply from within," and one had to know "in coolness of mind" the Lord's intentions. Only then could one approach the intended, and if the couple then became sure, they could approach parents and the Meeting. This, of course, raised questions about the customary exercise of parental authority and the role of material wealth and social class in the making of marriages.

The general understanding of the purposes of marriage was undergoing considerable modification in the course of the seventeenth century. Traditionally these purposes had been defined as procreation, refuge from sin, and (only last) mutual support or affection. Many English men and women were now valuing conjugal affection more highly. The Quakers saw true marriage between the converted as a transcendent unity, which, among other things, relieved women from the burden of submission, and even childbearing took a lower place in Penn's order of "society, Assistance and Increase."

This concept of marriage was extremely important to Friends; it guaranteed a united family base for membership, it integrated doctrine and social behavior, and it helped to distinguish Quakers from Familists and Ranters. A measure of its importance can be seen in the fact that although WP apparently wrote only this one epistle devoted exclusively to the subject, George Fox wrote sixty between 1653 and 1689.

At the time of WP's marriage, Fox was concerned that some Quakers were evading the proper marriage procedure and other organizational rules (see the headnote to doc. 72). Therefore he embarked on a vigorous program to establish monthly and quarterly meetings for men and women, a program just about completed in 1671. Women were to concern themselves particularly with the oversight of marriage-making in order to maintain a united family base of membership. The exercise of group authority and the participation by women in decision-making of such importance were not easily accepted, and led to the Wilkinson-Story conflict (see the headnote to doc. 91).

66
RIGHT MARRIAGE

RIGHT MARRIAGE,
as it stands in the
LIGHT and COUNCIL
of the
LORD GOD,

To be read in his Fear & Wisdom, att all their Mens Mee[tings] who are gathered into the Name, Truth, & Light of Jesus
Testified unto in Soundness of Judgment, at the requirings of the Spirit of God, by his Servant W.P.[1]

[c. 1671]

God that created the World, & all things that dwell therein by the Word of his invisible & allmighty Power, made the Male, & of his rib made he the Female; for society, Assistance, & Increase, that he overall might be honoured & glorified in them & by them; wherefore their Love, Care & Service to each other in all things, were to stand in the Sence of, & Unity with that immortal Word which proceeded from God, by which they were created; So that though there was, & is a natural Affection that is commendable in its place, & necessary in the natural relation, wherein they also stood, yet were not thereby they to be ordered, but both that Affection, & they in whom it was, were to be ordered & guided in the Counsel & Wisdom of that creating Word of Life, nigh in their Hearts, which gives to every man his own rib; So of twain makes one again; Now this is the honourable Marriage, & the Bed undefiled {in the most excellent Sense} where the Lust of the Eye rules not, & the earnest & forward affections lead not out of the Sence & Unity of that living Word of God, ~~For that is the defiled Bed & Dishonerable Marriage, where the Love & Affection that goe forth from either Male or Female, to each other, are not honoured with the unity, Blessings, & Holy Leadings of the Spirit, & Word of God in the Heart, & not preserved in the undefiled Life~~; So that this, the Lord God eternal requires at the hand of every Male & Female, that are convinced of his pure Light, & Way, & Truth & Word of Life in the Heart, when ever any thing ariseth in his or her mind to lead forth into any Love or Affection, that immediately to the Light it be brought, where the true discerning is given, & that the Mind there waite {in humility wth patience} to know what is the good Will & pleasure of the Lord in that matter, & then the Creature shall come to a right understanding, whether that word of Life, which ~~so~~ created them, Male & Female, have unity therewith; {And when this duty hath been perform'd to the lord god their Creator, then, is it Incumbant, & the light so teacheth to acquaint their ~~outward~~ Parents & relations; for though their Consent is not of that absolute force as either to make or unmake a true marriage & they ought to walk cercumspectly towards their Children in this matter; yet it is the duty off the partys concern'd to seek it with all due respect, & in wisdom & patience; for that is acceptable with the lord & required of him.} And as they who have thus waited to feel & know the Lords right Judgment & Leadings {& the mutuall consent of the Parents, ~~if possibly to be obtain'd~~} have built their natural Affections upon the ~~Heavenly~~ {Right} Foundation of Unity with the Lord, by his own Spirit, & therein one with another, as the first & chiefest matter above all visible considerations therein, & come to obtain the desires of their Hearts, & the Lords Peace & Blessing upon them ~~as the truly [torn]ibles Married, & as having a Bed undefiled~~, so those who bring not their [torn] & affection unto this tryed Stone [?], & true Ballance, that it might be tryed [&?] [w]eighed {& who overlook the father that begot & the mother that painfully brought forth,} but rather in the Contrivance & Forwardness of their own minds, [~~and~~] {natural} {[and dev]iseings of their natural and [illegible deletion] worldly} Desires, as thinking they have a Liberty therein, because it's an outward relation, to begin & carry on such a thing {of themselves}; I testifie by the Living Power of the Lord, that such are not of the Lords {leading &} Joyning, but their own, and are Strangers to the Heavenly Leadings & Providences of the Lord in these matters; for the Lord joynes Male & Female through that very Word by which he created them, which is that invisible Word of Life & Power, that proceeded forth from God in the beginning, when all things were made good. So {lett} all [blotted out] take heed unto the Word that made them, Male & Female {wch lives & speaks in them} that so you, who are convinced of the blessed way of Light & Life, may feel the holy Orderrings of the same, in the rise, Progress, & Finishing of your Loves & Affections {~~walking clear of all,~~} that so you may have this Testimony in your selves {& yr relations (if not ennemys to the truth)} & in the Meetings whereunto ye belong ~~the like with you~~; that not your own Contrivances, ~~nor any outward~~ {~~extraordinary~~} ~~Consideration,~~ neither only your natural affection {or outward considerations} have joyned you together, but the Lord by his own Orderings, Counsell & Wisdom, whose you are; And here is the true Love {as} at the first, & the honourable Marriage as at the beginning, where all Deceits, selfe seekings, Self Exaltings {Irreverence to god, disregard of Parents & slight of friends} are judged down, by the Spirit & Word of God, that lives for ever & ever.

And therefore a few things are strong upon me to caution all off (that profess the Truth) in this weighty matter:

First, that none directly or indirectly out of any Favour, Affection or other end whatever do speak to, or advise & incourage {(without a special motion from the lord)} Male or Female to seek, or desire after each other in reference to a Marriage State, (for such shall not goe without their Condemnation) but that every thing of that kind arise purely & simply from within, the parties themselves, first {on the bottom aforesaid,} which keeps in coolness of mind, & ~~that~~ in the Lords Feare, ~~they may be ordered therein~~, & then no good Counsell is excluded.

Secondly, as none ought to be exalted above their measure in reference to the Truth, (& such alwayes know a safe Condition) ~~so that none be lifted up~~ so that none ~~(for that answs not the end of it being given)~~ because of the Truth that is meek & lowly {& makes & keeps so} ~~so that none~~ be lifted up above that outward Station & Condition, wherein the Lord hath placed them, and wherein a great share of their external Happiness [~~so much~~] in that visible relation doth consist; namely, in a suitableness, (not {so much} of outward wealth, which takes Wings & flies {a way}) as of Education, manner of Life, Temper & Disposition, wherein is a visible Harmony, which Truth destroys not; But is of good Savour, both in them that believe, & in them that perish.

Thirdly, that where ever God hath inriched any with his Heavenly [trea]surie of Life, or other wayes a good Condition in the Truth, Oh, that [torn] ever be tempted & drawn forth to make use of that indeared Love tha[torn] towards them for the Truths sake, nor of that interest the Truth has gi[torn] in their Hearts, therewith to allure them to their persons, {or impose themselves upon them in Con[torn] [torn]pect them so much on the one account cannot [torn]} & so for the Lo[torn] to them on the account of an invisible Relation, to draw out the Minds [torn] to their Persons, thereby to engage {them in} ~~to~~ an outward & visible relation {wch perverts the affection, or extorts & imposes wch ~~god will that is a meer extorting, &~~ [torn] {unrighteous} in the sight of god] ~~for God eternally blast that subtil~~ {~~never bless~~ [illegible deletion] & shows more of subtility &} self seeking, ~~self exalting Spirit~~ than of the Love [&] wisdom that are from above, by wch the people of the lord are to be order[ed.][2]

Fourthly, as the Life of Truth is beyond all Words, & that Words are vain without it, so where there is not a living indeared Love, justified in the sight of God, let there not be the least indeavour to {compel &} draw each other into any verbal Promises & engagements, be it directly or indirectly, particularly or generally, absolutely or conditionally, for it is {~~calling~~ [illegible deletion] an evil} ~~a wicked~~ Temptation & snare {~~before an other~~}; Since first Such mistrust God, & dare not venture their desires with his care & providence. 2dly, they are disingenuous to the Party, either in doughting of their Love, or the Constancy of it, or ~~they~~ else would {force &} tie them by words, beyond the true bond {~~of affection~~} of Union {& love ~~wch is~~} And lastly, such are self seeking, in that no man or woman in the Truth should seek to tempt, insnare, or oblige any by words, in whom that indear'd absolute Marriage Love ~~was~~ {is} not, ~~wherein the Love might~~ {& in whom that love does not naturally arise to} engage them, ~~unless they had~~ {without such ensnareing ties & bonds. Such have} some further end or designe in their mind of {selfe love,} outward accommodation or ~~&~~ advantage to themselves, {~~that so do,~~} & not a mutual happiness of partys [illegible] But this worldly {~~spirit and his Bed, God hath cursed for ever. & sptt~~} god never blest. nor never will.

Fifthly, that every one who is convinced of the blessed Way of Truth, I mean those, who have but just turned their Faces {~~& are~~} Zionward, may first {of} all seek the Kingdom of God, & the Righteousness thereof, in Faith & full Assurance that all other things convenient for them, shall in due time be added to them, that {somthing of} the invisible Marriage of the Lamb they may know {who are in a Single condition} before they seek after a visible Marriage with ~~the Creatures~~ {any}, that so whenever they go about to change their outward Condition, they may secretly wait to feel the Invisible Word of God's Power, that in the beginning made them ~~twain~~ Male & Female, to joyn them together, & of twain, to make them one flesh {Yea wch is more} & one Spirit, ~~& so~~ too, & so God's works wil praise him, & the right honourable Marriage, & the Bed undefiled will be truly Known & injoyed.

Sixthly, I have this Testimony to bear to the {generall} Goodness, Mercy, & Providence of the Lord in {my} many Exercises {both} inward & outward ~~(& some, wherein I have been as one alone)~~ that as I have trusted in the Lord, & been freely resigned up in my spirit [torn], both out of Desires & Despairs, Doubts & Confidences, in stillness to stand, to [torn] his good pleasure concerning me, I have evermore beheld his Salvation, & his pros[per]ing hand to bring to pass those things, that I have not ~~dared~~ desired {tho desierable} much less to [ex]pect them ~~being as against all hope~~; thus good it is, early to trust, & seek the Lord; & [torn]h that all those who make Profession of Gods unchangable Truth, might in all things waite, to be ordered by the immortal Word ~~of Life~~, who created them in the beginning, to use all things in {subjection to} that Life, Wisdom, & Dominion that {man had} ~~were~~ in the beginning, so would our Righteousness go forth as ~~the~~ Brightness, & our Salvation as the Lamp that burnes.

~~Seventhly, &~~ Lastly, O that ~~everyone~~ {thos}, who, through Faith, Patience, & an intire Resignation to the Lord, hath experienced his Goodness & Faithfulness to them {in the cours of their life & especially} in this one weighty matter, may forever be preserved in the Heavenly Sense & Orderings of that Creating Word {~~that has sustained them~~} that made them Male & Female, & of two one Flesh, that so they may not give way to the inordinate ~~aboundings of~~ Affection, for {that dishonours the bed yea} ~~that is a defiled bed (as well as grosser Pollutions) & such thereby~~ {& in a sense} puts asunder, what God, by his living Word first joyned together; neither can {meer} Affection preserve out of vain Jealousies, inconvenient surmises, harsh Words, & unbecoming Distances, through the Disappointment & Crosses that are in the World; but they will come, & embitter that Relation, which should be held in all tenderness & Constancy of endeared Love as ~~an~~ {the greatest visible} help & Comfort {of this life}. Therefore, ~~that~~ {lett} every one love each other as Christ loveth his Church, remembring, how they were brought together, & so lett them continue~~ng~~ in the Sense of that Life & powerfull Word that was in the beginning, which governs & subjects (but never subdues) the affectionate part, that whenever anything presents, that would draw forth into ~~lewd or~~ {inordinate or} Unkind thoughts, or Behaviour, there may be an abiding in that {pure} Love, which {[blotted out] keeps, covers} & overcomes all; that thus living, & thus dying, ~~each may take his or her~~ {they may take their} last Farewell, with this Testimony in both Consciences, that they have not been wanting to each other, but faithfully have kept Covenant together {before the lord}, & so give each other up in the weighty Sense of ~~that~~ {his} eternal Word, which first brought {& joyn'd} them together; ~~in this the invisible Life of it to~~ to live, one in Spirit {therin} to all everlasting; For these things are well pleasing to the Lord, who is the blessed rewarder of them that {love him &} fear him to the end.

LBC. WP's Letterbook, 1667-1675, HSP. This document was entered in the letterbook by a secretary and heavily edited by WP. The top corners of all four pages of the MS are torn, adding to the difficulties of transcription. This document is not dated, but is placed with a group of letters dated 1671, which suggests that it was written in the same year, or shortly before his marriage in 1672. No printed version has been discovered.

1. WP also gave eloquent testimony at the meetings preceding Margaret Fell's marriage to George Fox (18, 22 Oct. 1669, Portfolio 10, FLL). The earliest epistles concerning marriage are George Fox, Portfolio 36-19a, FLL, and Margaret Fell, Portfolio 36-19b, FLL. For Fox on his own marriage, see Fox, 2:154. On Quaker marriage in the seventeenth century, see Richard T. Vann, *The Social Development of Quakerism, 1655-1755* (Cambridge, 1969), pp. 181-83, and Arnold Lloyd, *Quaker Social History* (London, 1950), pp. 2, 6-7, 48-65. On changing attitudes toward marriage, see Lawrence Stone, *The Family, Sex and Marriage in England, 1500-1800* (New York, 1977), and for a somewhat different point of view, Peter Laslett, *Family Life and Illicit Love in Earlier Generations* (Cambridge, 1977).

2. The condition of the manuscript makes this point particularly difficult to interpret. It would appear that WP cautions against using one's spiritual stature among Friends to attract a potential marriage partner.

67
DECLARATION OF INTENTION TO MARRY

[7 February 1672]

Att a Meeting at Tho: Ellwood's on the 7th of 12th mo: 71.

William Penn of Waltamstowe[1] in the County of Essex and Gulielma Maria Springett of Tiler End Green[2] in the parish of Penn in the County of Bucks, proposed their intention of taking each other in marriage wherupon it was referd to Thomas Zachary[3] and Thomas Ellwood to enquire into the clearnes of their proceedings, and give an account to the next Meeting.

MBE. Upperside Monthly Meeting Minutes, 1669-1690, Buckinghamshire Record Office, Aylesbury. (*Micro.* 1:373).

1. WP had inherited his father's house in Wanstead, adjoining Walthamstow. His mother continued to live there after the Admiral's death, paying her son £19.10.0 in rent per annum (see doc. 144, 25 Mar. 1674; doc. 147, 12 July 1678; doc. 150, 24 Feb. 1680).

2. See doc. 60.

3. Thomas Zachary (c. 1624-1686), a Friend and citizen of London who also lived at times in Rickmansworth, Herts. and Beaconsfield, Bucks., was arrested and imprisoned in 1670 on the evidence of an informer for attending meeting at Jordans. In 1671, 1673, and 1676 he served on visitation committees for Upperside Monthly Meeting, Bucks. With John Burnyeat and Cuthbert Hurst, he purchased 1250 acres in Pennsylvania in 1682, and though apparently he never emigrated, his son Daniel was married in Philadelphia Monthly Meeting in 1700. Digests of Quaker Registers, Bucks. and Middlesex, GSP; Besse, 1:79-80, 473, 478; Walter Lee Sheppard, Jr., ed., *Passengers and Ships Prior to 1684, Penn's Colony* (Baltimore, 1970), p. 199; William Wade Hinshaw, *Encyclopedia of American Quaker Genealogy*, (Ann Arbor, Mich., 1938), 2:440, 696.

68
APPROVAL OF INTENTION TO MARRY

At a Meeting at Tho: Ellwood's on 6t of 1st mo: [March 16]71/2

William Penn & Gulielma Maria Springett, who at the last Meeting proposed their intention of taking each other in Marriage, came now to receive the Answer of friends and had their consent & approbation therin.

MBE. Upperside Monthly Meeting Minutes, 1669-1690, Buckinghamshire Record Office, Aylesbury. (*Micro.* 1:375).

69
MARRIAGE CERTIFICATE

[4 April 1672]

Whereas William Penn of Walthamstow in the County of Essex, and Gulielma Maria Springett of Penn in the County of Bucks, having first obtained the goodwill and consent of their nearest friends & Relations, did in two publick Monthly Meetings of the people of God called Quakers, declare their intention to take each other in Marriage, & upon serious & due consideration, were fully approved of the said Meetings, as by several weighty testimonies did appear.

These are now to certifie al persons whom it doth or may concern, that upon the fourth day of the second month in the year one thousand six hundred seaventy two, the said William Penn and Gulielma Maria Springett did, in a godly sort & manner (according to the good old Order & practise of the Church of Christ) in a publick Assembly of the People of the Lord at King's, Charle-wood[1] in the County of Hertford, solemnly and expressly take each other in marriage, mutually promising to be loving, true & faithful to each other in that Relation, so long as it shal please the Lord to continue their natural lives. In testimony whereof, we then present, have hereunto subscribed our names, the day & year aforewritten.

Margret Penn.	Martin Mason.[3]
Rich: Penn.	Tho: Dell.[4]
Isaac Penington.	Edward Hoar.[5]
John Penington.	John Puddivat.[6]
Mary Penington.	John Gigger sen.[7]
Mary Penington junr.[2]	Abraham Axtell.[8]
Elizabeth Springett.	John Costard.[9]
Alexander Parker.	Giles Child.[10]
George Whitehead.	Stephen Pewsey.[11]

Sam: Newton.
Wm Welch.[12]
Ger. Roberts.
Tho: Zachary.
James Claypoole.[13]
Tho: Rudyard.[14]
Robt Hodgson.[15]
John Jenner.[16]
Charles Harris.
Edward Man.
Sam: Hersent.
Rich: Clipsham.[17]
Robt Jones.[18]
Tho: Ellwood.

John Harvey.[19]
Elizabeth Walmsly.
Rebecca Zachary.[20]
Mary Ellwood.[21]
Jane Bullocke.[22]
Mary Odingsells.[23]
Elizabeth Murford.[24]
Mary Newton.
Frances Cadwell.
Helena Claypoole.[25]
Sarah Mathew.[26]
Sarah Welch.[27]
Mary Welch.[28]
Martha Blake.[29]

MBE. Upperside Monthly Meeting Records, RG 6/1338, PRO. (*Micro.* 1:376).

1. King John's Farm, a fifteenth-century half-timbered building in Chorleywood, adjacent to Rickmansworth, where WP and Gulielma lived after their marriage. ACM, vol. 53.

2. Mary Penington, Jr. (c. 1657-1726), only daughter of Isaac and Mary Penington, married Daniel Wharley (d. 1721), a woolen draper of London, in 1686. She had earlier agreed to marry Samuel Boulton, a London goldsmith and Quaker minister, and when their wedding plans were broken off, Boulton blocked her marriage to Wharley until Friends of Upperside Monthly Meeting decided that Boulton had given up his claim. Beatrice Saxon Snell, ed., *The Minute Book of the Monthly Meeting of the Society of Friends for the Upperside of Buckinghamshire, 1669-1690* (High Wycombe, Bucks. 1937), pp. 166, 179-81; Fox, *Short Journal*, pp. 299, 310, 322.

3. Perhaps the M. Mason who appears in the Ford Accounts (see doc. 139). Martin Mason wrote a paper "To both Houses of Parliament," dated 2 Nov. 1660, in which he stated that the mayor of Bristol could not prevent Friends from meeting while "two of them were left together." Braithwaite, *Second Period*, p. 10.

4. Thomas Dell, yeoman, of Hedgerly, Bucks., and a prominent member of the Upperside Monthly Meeting, for which he served on many oversight committees during the 1670s and 1680s. He was imprisoned in 1660, 1665, 1666, and 1683. Snell, *Upperside Minute Book;* Besse, 1:12, 77, 78, 82; Digests of Quaker Registers, Bucks., GSP.

5. Edward Hoar (d. 1686), weaver, of Great Missenden, Bucks., and a weighty Friend of the Upperside Monthly Meeting. Snell, *Upperside Minute Book;* Digests of Quaker Registers, Bucks., GSP.

6. John Puddivat (d. 1709), tanner, of Northchurch, Herts., another active member of the Upperside (Bucks.) Monthly Meeting. Snell, *Upperside Minute Book;* Digests of Quaker Registers, Bucks., GSP.

7. Probably the father of Gulielma's servant John Giggour. The elder John Gigger, or Giggour, was unable to work and ran into debt in 1673-1674. WP contributed half of the £10 raised in 1673 to help him out. Snell, *Upperside Minute Book*, pp. 19, 21, 25, 29, 33.

8. Abraham Axtell (d. 1687), mercer, of Chesham, Bucks., and member of Upperside Monthly Meeting. His wife Alice died in 1664; he and Mary Belson, his second wife, announced their intentions to marry on 3 Apr. 1672, one day prior to WP's marriage to Gulielma Springett. Snell, *Upperside Minute Book*, p. 13; Digests of Quaker Registers, Bucks., GSP.

9. John Costard, mealman, of Amersham, Bucks., and active member of the Upperside Monthly Meeting. Snell, *Upperside Minute Book;* Digests of Quaker Registers, Bucks., GSP.

10. Giles Child, clothier, of Amersham, Bucks., and member of Upperside Monthly Meeting. He joined Charles Harris and other supporters of Wilkinson and

Story (see doc. 107), in supporting his son Timothy Child's refusal to take his intentions to marry Mary Sexton before the women's meeting. The case brought the Wilkinson-Story controversy to a head in Upperside, and ended in the division of the Bucks. Quarterly Meeting. Snell, *Upperside Minute Book,* pp. 33, 103, 106, 108; Digest of Quaker Registers, Bucks., GSP.

11. Stephen Pewsey (d. 1686) of Beaconsfield, Bucks., and member of Upperside Monthly Meeting. He sided with Timothy Child in his refusal to take his marriage before the women's meeting. Pewsey was one of twenty-three Friends imprisoned at Aylesbury in 1683 for attending a meeting near Wooburn. He was released from jail when his fine was paid by the Beaconsfield authorities because they did not want to support his family. Snell, *Upperside Minute Book,* pp. xviii, 125; Besse, 1:82; Digests of Quaker Registers, Bucks., GSP.

12. William Welch, a London merchant. He was an active Friend from 1668 to 1672, although he apparently supported the schism of John Perrot (see headnote to doc. 71) briefly in 1669. Welch was released from prison by Charles II's pardon in 1672, and signed, with WP and others, a petition to the king against Friends' being convicted as Popish recusants (*Micro.* 1:212). Fox, 1:453; Fox, *Short Journal,* p. 359; Besse, 1:437; William I. Hull, *Benjamin Furly and Quakerism in Rotterdam* (Lancaster, Pa., 1941), pp. 217-20.

13. James Claypoole (1634-1687), merchant, active member of the Six Weeks Meeting of Friends in London, and representative to the Meeting of Sufferings in 1676. His brother, John Claypoole, married Oliver Cromwell's daughter Elizabeth in 1646. James emigrated to Pennsylvania in 1683 and served there as a member of the Provincial Council. Marion Balderston, ed., *James Claypoole's Letter Book: London and Philadelphia, 1681-1684* (San Marino, Calif., 1967), pp. 3-24; Fox, 1:457; Fox, *Short Journal,* pp. 296, 361; Besse, 1:484.

14. Thomas Rudyard (d. 1692), of London, was a lawyer who often used his skill for Friends' benefit, as in 1674, when he attempted to obtain a habeas corpus for George Fox's release from Worcester jail (see headnote to doc. 81). In 1670, Rudyard was tried for attending a Quaker meeting before the same jury that heard the case of WP and William Mead. He accompanied WP on his trips to Holland and Germany in 1671 and 1677. Rudyard was a proprietor of both East and West Jersey and served briefly as deputy governor of East Jersey. Fox, 2:273, 420; Fox, *Short Journal,* pp. 358-59; John E. Pomfret, *The Province of West New Jersey,* pp. 88, 91.

15. Perhaps Robert Hodgson of Reading; he was twice imprisoned in the 1650s for attempting to visit Friends in jail, preaching in the street, and refusing to take an oath. R. Hodson appears in the Ford Accounts, 8 July 1672 (doc. 140). Besse, 1:12, 228-29.

16. John Jenner was a joiner who did work for WP (see docs. 139-43).

17. Richard Clipsham (d. 1700), tailor, of Chalfont St. Giles, Bucks., and an active member of the Upperside Monthly Meeting. WP paid Clipsham £5 quarterly in rent (docs. 139-44), perhaps for land or outbuildings at Rickmansworth. WP rented his residence, Basing House, at Rickmansworth from John Skidmore at £40 per annum. Snell, *Upperside Minute Book;* Digests of Quaker Registers, Bucks., GSP.

18. Robert Jones (d. 1698), maltster, of Cholesbury, Bucks., and weighty member of the Upperside Monthly Meeting. He was jailed for refusing an oath in 1660, and he served on many monthly meeting committees for discipline and relief of the poor during the 1670s and 1680s. Snell, *Upperside Minute Book;* Besse, 1:76; Digests of Quaker Registers, Bucks., GSP.

19. Perhaps John Harvey, Quaker grocer, of Linton in Cambridge, who had goods distrained for his absence from national worship in 1677. His son John married Elizabeth Woodhouse of Berkhamsted, Herts., a member of the Upperside (Bucks.) Monthly Meeting, in 1683. Besse, 1:97; Snell, *Upperside Minute Book,* p. 119.

20. Rebecca Zachary (c. 1638-1694), was Rebecca York, second wife of Thomas Zachary. They married in 1664 in London; their three children were born between 1665 and 1671. Digests of Quaker Registers, Bucks., and Middlesex, GSP.

21. Mary Ellwood (c. 1623-1708), was Mary Ellis, who married Thomas Ellwood in 1669. She was an active member of the Upperside (Bucks.) Women's Meeting. In 1685, she helped to write a broadside denouncing Susan Aldridge of Wooburn meeting for speaking against Friends. Fox, 2:486; Snell, *Upperside Minute Book,* pp. 64, 146.

22. Jane Bullocke (d. 1687), of Edmonton, Middlesex, was in 1677 the principal of the Friends' Shacklewell school for girls at Hackney in North London. Fox, *Short*

Journal, p. 305; Braithwaite, *Second Period*, p. 528; Digests of Quaker Registers, London and Middlesex, GSP.

23. Mary Odingsells, spinster of Chalfont St. Peter, Bucks., was an active member of the Upperside Women's Meeting. She married Peter Prince (d. 1694), citizen and tallow-chandler of London, in 1685. Snell, *Upperside Minute Book*, pp. 64, 145; Fox, *Short Journal*, p. 330; Digests of Quaker Registers, Bucks., GSP.

24. Elizabeth Murford (d. 1693), member of Upperside (Bucks.) Monthly Meeting. She married Richard Baker of London, woodmonger, in 1672. Snell, *Upperside Minute Book*, p. 14; Digests of Quaker Registers, Bucks., GSP.

25. Helena Claypoole (d. 1688), wife of James, was Helena Mercer. They were married by a Calvinist minister in 1658 in Bremen, where James was apprenticed to a merchant. They moved to London soon after their marriage and joined the Society of Friends prior to 1661. Balderston, *Claypoole's Letter Book*, pp. 3-21.

26. Perhaps Sarah Mathews (c. 1641-1697) of Shoe Lane, Bride's Parish in London, and member of Peel Monthly Meeting. Sarah Mathew appears frequently in the Ford Accounts. She loaned WP £100 in 1672 or earlier, and he paid £8 per annum interest to her for seven years, finally repaying the principal on 7 Apr. 1679 (see docs. 139-48). Digests of Quaker Registers, London and Middlesex, GSP.

27. Sarah Welch, wife of William Welch. She became a Quaker in 1657 while in Edinburgh, and her room was probably the first meeting place for Friends in Rotterdam in 1661. Fox, 1:297, 453; Hull, *Benjamin Furly*, pp. 217-20.

28. Mary Welch (c. 1646-1696), daughter of William and Sarah Welch and second wife of John Osgood (c. 1634-1694), a Quaker linen-draper of Cheapside, London. They married in 1674. Fox, *Short Journal*, p. 317.

29. Martha Blake, of Upperside Monthly Meeting. She and Nicholas Horton, both of Penn, Bucks., received permission to marry in 1676. Snell, *Upperside Minute Book*, p. 42.

70

ON TRUTH'S ACCOUNT: JOURNEY THROUGH KENT, SUSSEX, AND SURREY

After his marriage WP lived with Gulielma at Basing House in Rickmansworth, eighteen miles northwest of London. The opening months of his married life are best documented in the accounts (docs. 139-41) kept by his steward Philip Ford, who shipped large quantities of groceries and household goods from London. According to Ford's accounts, WP spent more than £2000 during the closing nine months of 1672, and his income was only half this figure. In consequence, in July 1672 the newlyweds sold for £1000 three tracts of land in Kent which Gulielma had inherited (doc. 151). In this same month WP traveled to Kent and Sussex to collect rent from his wife's tenants (doc. 140, 9-13 July 1672). His journey, however, was not exclusively devoted to business. The governor of Sheerness Castle complained to Secretary Williamson on 6 August that WP and several Quaker brethren were busy proselytizing in the forested Weald of Kent (*CSPD, 1672*, p. 450). Heartened by his meetings with Friends in this region, WP promptly made a second missionary journey.

Doc. 70 is WP's record of this missionary journey, a three-week circuit of Quaker meetings in Kent, Sussex, and Surrey, from 11 September to 4 October 1672. This travel journal, though far briefer than WP's Irish journal (doc. 35), gives a somewhat fuller picture of his vigorous public ministry. He traveled 300 miles, and held twenty-three meetings in eighteen towns and villages. At the time of his visit, the Quakers in Kent and Sussex were enjoying a momentary respite from persecution, thanks to the Declaration of Indulgence issued by Charles II in March 1672, which suspended all penal laws against dissenting Protestants and Catholics. On his journey WP encountered several of the nearly 500 Quakers who had just been released from jail by the king's pardon. Doc. 70 demonstrates how openly and vigorously Quakers were meeting and worshipping. But in 1673 Parliament forced the king to revoke his declaration and to accept a new religious loyalty oath, the Test Act, which returned the Quakers to their former persecuted status.

My Journey on Truths account; through Kent, Sussex, & the Skirt of Surrey,[1] began the 11th Septembris, 1672. & ended 4th Octobris, 1672.

7th Month. [September 1672]

It being in my Heart to devote myself to the service of my God, in a way of visit to his People in the Countries of Kent & Sussex (as

8

it had ~~been layi~~ {for some time} upon me) on the 8th day of the 7th month in the year 1672. I left my own House at Rickmantsworth & my dearest Wife at Watford,[2] both in Heartfordshire, in order to my said journey. My Company was my Bro: J. P.[3] & W. G.[4] at whose House in London I lodged that Night.

9 10

The 9th & 10th I stay'd in that Citty, employing myself in seeing of Friends, & dispatching some papers then in the press. The 4th morn-

11

ing & the 11. instant Dr A. P.[5] myself, & Bro. J. P. left London in order to the afore mentioned journey, it being as well the intention of A. P. to visit the Friends of God in that Country, as it had been mine for some time. That Night we came to Tinsbery,[6] were lodg'd att the Widdow Clemens, had a little Meeting, but not being clear in our selves as well as that the Friends were unsatisfied with so short a

12

stay, we had a Large, Living & Open meeting the next morning in Rochester, in which the Lords presence was manifest, unto the laying low many exalted Professors, who were then there; from thence we parted that Day, bated[7] at littenburn,[8] & came to Canterbury, where we were lodged at the House of Tho: Tenterden,[9] Shoemaker, an honest tender man, & whose wife is of a sober, grave, & exemplary

13.

deportment. The next day we had a Meeting in the same House, but few besides Friends, who were comforted in us; we remained there

14.

that Night & the next Day, at which time there came a young Ruffin, son to the Defunct Earl of Lindsey,[10] he was high, peremtory, knowing, but pragmatical he often run out into unhandsome expressions against us, & very wicked epithsits he gave the Light, but God's power was over him, & he fell mightily under, in so much, that he came creeping in at Night, confessing to what had been said to him at noon, acknowledging his mistake & unhandsomness, & promising to be at Meeting next Day, being the first Day.

15.

About the 12th hour we went to the Meeting, which was soon crowded with all sorts of People, base & Noble, rich & poor, young & old, learned & unlearned, Men, Women & Children; And great was our Travail for the Seed's sake, & our weights were many, but the glorious Power rise and stained the Glory of all Flesh before us, & the grass withered in our Presence, & all Hearts seemed bare & naked, & we felt an Answer in most Consciences, so that we came away in Triumph over all, & Truth was sett upon the Head of that great Citty. In the Evening we had a good Meeting at our Lodging, which consisted mostly of Friends.

16

The next Day we went to Sandwich, accompanied by the Friends of Canterbury, & L. H.[11] of Dover, it rained & was very Dirty but our Joy was more then all which we received after a very open sound Meeting, which we had the same Day, many Professors being present, & all down; We lay there that Night att the House of Tho: Louten, a Master of a Ship.

17.

The next Day we departed thence to Nonington,[12] where we had a Meeting mostly of Friends, it being their Monthly Meeting; from thence we came that Night to Deal, and were lodg'd at Tho: Holi-

18.

mans[13] a Glover; The next day we had a very Convincing, open, Powerfull, & exceeding tender Meeting to the bringing all under, & our Spirits joyed in the God of our Life, who was our plentifull rewarder that Day. One Valentine Brooks[14] a notable wise man is there convinced; We left Deal that Night & came to Dover accom-

19.

panied of L.H. at whose House we lodged. The next Day we had a strong & sound Meeting, & was of good report among those that came, & there were very many Professors & others. The next Day

20.

we left Dover, for Fa{u}lkstone, & that Day had a pretious, sweet & Heavenly Meeting, whether the Priest came, was quiet, & several Professors, some came from Dover; never at a Meeting before, as several did from Deal to Dover; we rested there that Night. The next

21.

Morning I left Dr A. P. to be there on the next Day, being first Day, & on the 3th Day at Swinfield[15] at a Monthly Meeting, where he had heavenly good Service. I passed away accompanied ~~wth~~ {by} Ed. Tideman,[16] T. Tambridge,[17] & Bro. John, for Lid,[18] the Town where honest S. Fisher[19] was first National Priest, & then a Baptist Teacher.

22

We got thither that Night, & the next Day had a very large publick Meeting, whether T. Everden came, & Luke Howard, who was assistant. The Lord God appeared in his Power to the renowning of his Truth, & comforting of his People, & confounding of Gaynsayers. That evening we had a sweet & heavenly Meeting at my Lodging,

23.

where we might have halfe a hundert people; The next Day T. T.[20] & E. T.[21] returned for Faulkstone, & L. H.[22] T. E.[23] & Bro: John came with me to Wey,[24] where at a great Notionists[25] House, & Lover of Friends, I had a Meeting, & Gods Dreadfull Power trampled all false Coverings under foot, & the plain simple Truth was sett over all, & in good Dominion, I came to my Inn, but the Love of the Professors was so great, that they constrained me to one of their houses, where they entertained me with exceeding openheartedness.

24.

The Day following the Alarm being given, many of the Town came to J. B[26] about two miles from thence, whether many Friends, & Abundance from Ashford[27] resorted, the very Passengers stopt, & came in, & I mighty large meeting I had, & the glorious Power was so strong, opening, piercing, & tendring that Truth became of good savour, & all seemed to confess & rejoyce. From thence that Night I went to Ashford, where contrary to my desire, though according to my fear, the Town came crowding in, in so violent a manner, that people were forc'd to go out for breath; the parler, Kitchen, Entry, Garden etc. were cram'd. The Lord was with us, & the Way to the Everlasting Kingdom was declared in the Demonstration of Power & Spirit, as many confessed that never were at Meetings before. The

25.

next Morning we had an other Meeting, & desired it might be of Friends only, but many prest in unavoidably, we clear'd our Consciences, so I took my leave, L. H. & T. E. staying behind me for home, & myself & Bro: J. P. accompanied with two Friends went to Tenterden,[28] where we met A. P. & had a Meeting fresh & tender. From thence we all came to Cranbrocke,[29] & were lodg'd at J. Asfords[30]

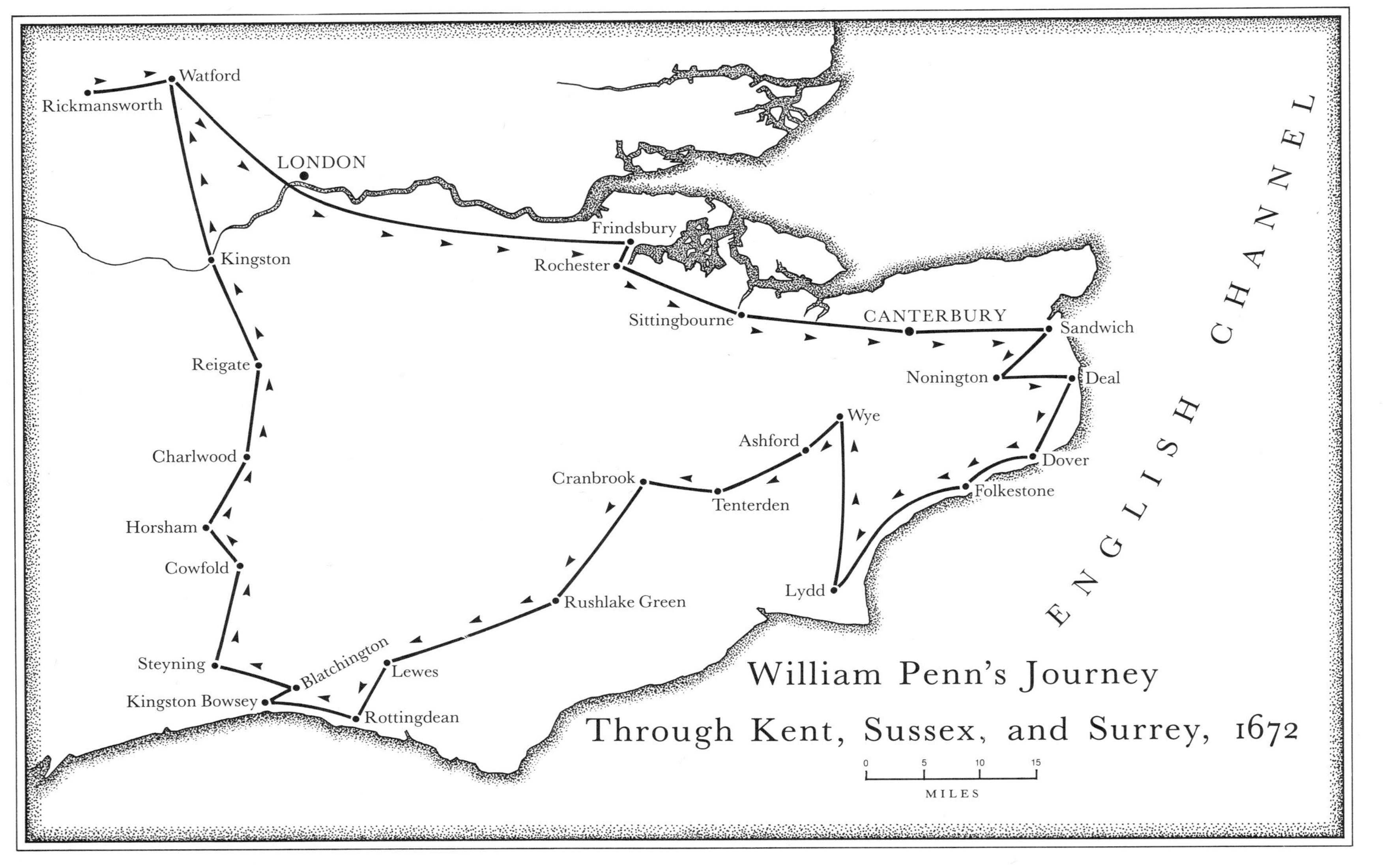

Rickmansworth
Watford
LONDON
Kingston
Frindsbury
Rochester
Sittingbourne
CANTERBURY
Sandwich
Nonington
Deal
Dover
Folkestone
Wye
Ashford
Tenterden
Cranbrook
Lydd
Rushlake Green
Reigate
Charlwood
Horsham
Cowfold
Steyning
Blatchington
Kingston Bowsey
Lewes
Rottingdean
ENGLISH CHANNEL
William Penn's Journey
Through Kent, Sussex, and Surrey, 1672
0
5
10
15
MILES

26.

that Night. Next Day we went to J. Colvils,[31] where we had a precious good Meeting, most Friends, & from thence came to J. Bennets,

27.

where we stay'd that Night, The Day following, accompanied by J. Asford we came to J. Elleses,[32] where we met with I. P.[33] & had a very living thorough Meeting, remain'd there that Night, and came

28.

next Day through much wett & dirt safe to Lewes, & are lodged att the Widdow Acres's.[34]

29.

This Day being the first of the Week we had in the same House a good Meeting, the Lords heavenly precious Power was with us, & a good sence there was, we came the same Night to Nicholas Beards[35] at Rottingdean,[36] where we lay, being by him accompanied thither.

30.

This Morning we left his House & came to Kingston bonsy,[37] much decay'd, some body in fault that has lived on rack rents, & not minded improvements; we came presently to Blechington, the Widdow & her 4 sons inhabiting there.[38] The Lord is with us.

Octobr. 1.

We went to Stening Town,[39] where we had a large & very sound & thorough Meeting, & the Lords presence & power was strong opening & refreshing among us, we lay at the same House, being the Widdow Blackfan[?][40] that Night.

2.

Next Day we passed to the House of Tho: Parsons,[41] where Amb. Rigg[42] met us, he spoak first, we had a precious time there with Friends, & things thus farr continued very well. We came that Night to Horsham to the House of A. R.[43] being about 5. Miles from T. P.s[44] House, & were kindly entertained. We came accompanied next

3.

Day by A. R. & his Wifes Mother[45] to Charlewood[46] in Surrey, where there was a very large & good Meeting, we went that Night to Rigate, & lay at the House of T. B.[47] being 8. miles.

4.

The following morning, we had a Meeting, & indeed the Lord seal'd up our Labours & Travills according to the Desire of my Soul & Spirit with his heavenly refreshments, & sweet living Power & Word of Life unto the reaching of all, & consolating our own Hearts abundantly: After Meeting thus clear of our work, it rise in the Liberty & sweet Love of the Lord in both our Hearts to go home to our Dear Wives & Families, wch we accomplisht that Day, so that Dr A. P. left me 5. miles on London Rode from Rigat & gott to Enfield[48] that Night being about 30. miles, & I went by Kingston[49] (where I stay'd one houre) cross the Country to my Dear Wife & got home before the 7th hour in the Evening being about 28. miles, & after the 12th hour of the Day.

And thus hath the Lord been with us in all our Travells for his Truth, & with his Blessings of Peace are we returned, which is a reward beyond all wordly Treasure.

Laus Deo in aeternum,
the End.

LBC. WP's Letterbook, 1667-1675, HSP. (*Micro.* 1:405). This journal was printed and annotated by Henry J. Cadbury, *PMHB*, 68:419-29. Our edition depends heavily upon Cadbury's work for the location and identification of most of the Friends whom WP met on his journey. We have moved WP's marginal dates to the center of the line to conform with the style of the Irish Journal (doc. 35).

1. The southern part of Surrey, along the Sussex border.

2. WP and Gulielma probably had a number of close acquaintances at Watford; Friends from Rickmansworth, Chorleywood, and Watford regularly met together (Snell, *Upperside Minute Book*, p. 30). WP had stayed with Ann Merrick at Watford in 1669.

3. WP's stepbrother-in-law John Penington, with whom he had traveled in Ireland in 1669-1670.

4. William Gibson (1629-1684), convinced about 1654, and an active Quaker preacher, writer, and sufferer in the 1660s and the 1670s, had just been released from prison under the Declaration of Indulgence pardon. *DNB;* Besse, 1:437.

5. Alexander Parker.

6. WP probably means Frindsbury, a small village just north of Rochester.

7. "Baited"; fed their horses. *OED*.

8. Probably Sittingbourne, about twelve miles east of Rochester.

9. This seems to be a mistake for Thomas Everden, a Canterbury Quaker shoemaker. See below.

10. The "young ruffian" was probably either James Bertie (1653-1699) or Henry Bertie (c. 1655-1734), sons by the second marriage of the late Montagu Bertie (c. 1606-1666), the second earl of Lindsey. Burke's *Peerage*.

11. Luke Howard (1621-1699), a shoemaker, was convinced in 1655 and became a leading Friend in Kent.

12. A village in eastern Kent, about seven miles southwest of Sandwich.

13. Thomas Holiman, a Deal Friend, had been arrested in 1660 for Quaker activity and imprisoned at Dover.

14. Cadbury thinks that this was Valentine Bowles, who had lived in Deal since at least 1659, and suffered for his faith in 1678, 1682, and 1684. Cadbury, *PMHB* 68:425n.

15. Swingfield, a village five miles north of Folkstone.

16. There were two Quaker Tiddemans, neither of them named Edward, in the area in this period: Henry Tiddeman of Timford, near Canterbury, and Henry Tiddeman of Preston, Kent.

17. Probably Thomas Tunbridge (d. 1688) of Folkstone, a Quaker minister and sufferer from 1660 to 1684.

18. Lydd, a small town fifteen miles south of Folkstone, in the Romney Marsh country.

19. Samuel Fisher (1605-1665), an Oxford graduate and a learned minister, who joined the Quakers about 1655. During the final decade of his life, he published many Quaker tracts and spent much time in jail. *DNB*.

20. Thomas Tunbridge.

21. Ed. Tideman.

22. Luke Howard.

23. Thomas Everden.

24. Presumably Wye, a village in eastern Kent, seventeen miles north of Lydd.

25. One who held extravagant religious opinions. The term, which was of recent coinage, appeared in other Quaker and anti-Quaker writings. *OED.*

26. Perhaps John Bennet, a Friend in southern Kent who suffered for his faith as early as 1656. In 1672 he was apparently living a few miles south of Cranbrook, near the border with Sussex. See below in the text, under 26 Sept.

27. A town in central Kent, four miles southwest of Wye.

28. A village in southern Kent, about twelve miles southwest of Ashford.

29. Cranbrook was a village in southern Kent, about eight miles west of Tenterden. In July 1672, WP and his wife had sold parcels of land in Cranbrook and in nearby Hawkehurst and Sandhurst that Gulielma had inherited. See doc. 151.

30. John Ashford of Cranbrook, a Quaker sufferer in Kent between 1660 and 1684.

31. John Colvil, or Colvill, of Cranbrook, a Quaker who had just been released from Maidstone jail when WP visited him. He suffered further persecution in 1682-1683.

32. Probably John Ellis (d. 1685), a yeoman of Rushlake Green, a Sussex village near Warbleton and about fifteen miles southwest of Cranbrook. Ellis regularly held Quaker meetings in his home.

33. Identification uncertain. This may be a mistake for A. P. (Alexander Parker), who had already separated from and rejoined WP once. It could also refer to Isaac Penington, John Penington's father; he had been released from prison in 1672.

34. Mary Akehurst (d. 1691), widow of Ralph Akehurst, of the Cliff, or Cliff Hill, near Lewes, about fifteen miles southwest of Ellis' home in Rushlake Green. She often held Quaker meetings in her house until 1675, when a meeting house at Lewes was completed.

35. Nicholas Beard (c. 1615-1702), a gentleman converted to Quakerism in 1655. Beard had just been released from prison as a result of Charles II's Declaration of Indulgence. He hosted meetings in his house until his death.

36. A village on the English Channel, about six miles southwest of Mary Akehurst's home near Lewes.

37. Kingston Bowsey, now called Kingston Buci, or Kingston by Sea, a village on the English Channel about eight miles west of Rottingdean.

38. Blatchington, two or three miles inland from the coast, was the site of Friends meetings from the 1660s. The widow was perhaps Joan Scrase (c. 1604-1675) of West Blatchington, who, with her sons Henry, Richard, John, and Walter, were all Quaker sufferers between 1660 and 1670.

39. Steyning, about eight miles northwest of West Blatchington.

40. Probably the widow of John Blackfan (d. 1672), Constable of Steyning when George Fox and Alexander Parker first preached there in 1655.

41. Either Thomas Parsons of Patchgate or Thomas Parsons, Jr., of Slafam or of Cowfold, is plausible. Thomas Parsons, Jr., of Cowfold held Quaker meetings in his house at this time. All of these villages are about five miles southeast of Horsham.

42. Ambrose Rigge had just been released, by a pardon resulting from Charles II's Declaration of Indulgence, from ten years in prison at Horsham.

43. Ambrose Rigge.

44. Thomas Parsons.

45. Elizabeth Luxford (d. 1689). It was at Thomas and Elizabeth Luxford's house in Hurstpierpont, Sussex, that Rigge had been arrested in 1662; he married Mary Luxford in 1664, while in prison.

46. A village about eight miles north of Horsham.

47. Perhaps Thomas Blatt, a tallow chandler and one of the first men to receive Quakers at Reigate; a John Blatt of Reigate held Quaker meetings in his home in the 1670s. This could also be a relative of John Bicknall, who held meetings in his home in the 1680s.

48. A town in the northeast corner of Middlesex, about ten miles north of London.

49. Kingston-upon-Thames, Surrey, about thirteen miles northwest of Reigate, where WP may have stopped at the house of John and Margaret (Fell) Rous. See Fox, 2:421.

71
TO WILLIAM MUCKLOW

WP spent most of his first two years of married life at Rickmansworth, with frequent visits to London. Gulielma bore him a daughter in January 1673, and twins — a boy and a girl — in January 1674; all three babies died within a few months of birth. Throughout this period, WP continued his energetic involvement in Quaker affairs. As a participant in the London Morning and Yearly Meetings, he helped to shape national policy. Between 1672 and 1674 he published twenty-two religious tracts, some of them very lengthy, all of them written in direct response to critics of the Society of Friends. During these years WP engaged in pamphlet wars with (among others) the Independent minister John Faldo, the Baptists Thomas Hicks, John Morse, and Jeremiah Ives, and the heresiarch Lodowick Muggleton.

The next ten documents (71-80) illustrate other aspects of WP's variegated work within the Society of Friends. As a member of the Upperside Monthly Meeting in Bucks., he served on visitation committees that were designed to monitor individual Friends' behavior and to preserve community discipline. Doc. 73 shows him examining a proposed marriage. In doc. 76 he defends his interpretation of the divinity of Christ in a letter to the Presbyterian John Collinges. Doc. 77 shows his friendship with Robert Barclay, the leading Scottish Quaker. WP also did what he could to stem the renewed persecution of Quakers after Parliament forced Charles II to rescind his Declaration of Indulgence in March 1673. Doc. 72 is a petition to the House of Commons, urging modification of the Test Act of 1673. Docs. 75, 78, and 79 are appeals to local justices for leniency in enforcing the penal laws of 1661-1670. Doc. 80 is a direct plea to the king, in the hope that Charles II still wished to pursue his toleration policy of 1672-1673.

There was a further problem, very bothersome to WP, which is illustrated in docs. 71 and 74: the emergence of a protest movement among some Friends, first against the ritual doffing of hats during prayer, then against the disciplinary practices and meeting structure advocated by George Fox. It had begun a decade earlier when the mystical John Perrot (d. 1665) opposed all ritual and form in Quaker worship and criticized Fox's organizing zeal as too authoritarian. Fox, for his part, believed that Perrot's mysticism was extravagant and that he was guided by delusions, not by the light within. In 1662 Perrot, discredited with the Quaker leadership, went to Barbados; he died in Jamaica in 1665. But Perrot left behind a circle of followers who shared his quest for the freedom and spontaneity of the early Quaker movement. In 1671 William Mucklow, Mary and John Pennyman, and Ann and Thomas Mudd openly rejected Fox's leadership and the majority position. WP tried to answer these people. Doc. 71 is his letter to Mucklow, defending the Quaker form of taking off the hat in prayer; WP's argument failed utterly, for Mucklow published *The Spirit of the Hat* in 1673, initiating a bitter pamphlet war with WP. Doc. 74, written at the height of this pamphlet war, is WP's passionate letter of denunciation to another schismatic, Mary Pennyman. The quarrel would continue, and widen and deepen, over the next decade.

Basingh[1] 11th 8th month [October] 1672

W. Mucklow[2]
There came a Letter last Night to my Hand, which was not more full of Queries then it filled me with surprise, but upon perusal of it, I found it to consist of many, I thinck 38. Questions, concluded by way of application or direction to me for a sober & sufficient Answer; And though I wondred, that a Man so unknown to me, who was scarcely born in the time of those unhappy Contests[3] which have left behind the brand of Schism & mark of deep Displeasure on thee against that Living Body, to which the Mercies of the Lord have incorporated me a member, an honor more desirable then to be the Companion of Kings, & for which my Soul bowes before the God of my Life, evermore desiring to be found in the footsteps of his despised Flock, Yet feeling the tender bowels of the Love of God, that would not W. M. should perish from of the Land of the Living by a wandering Self Separating or murmuring Spirit, I overlookt what ever might reason me out of the good Samaritans Charity,[4] & therefore with some of Gileads Balme[5] as I have received, shall I endeavour to heal that breach, which the Lord knows, has been to wide & too long made, if by any means there may at last be a coming under the Holy & due Chastisements of the Lord, & an exercising of the Mind in the Light that reproves for every unfruitfull thought; Which Will. I know has been thy State, & by which thy Mind has lost the sense of the blessed Wittness, so as to be thy Judge Rule & Guide into the pure, Living & Heavenly fellowship. Bear with me for the seeds sake whose Liberty from the prejudice or aggravating repining Spirit I earnestly seek & contend for, & not any other Conquest; For though Will. thou mayst fancy to thyself a pleasant Habitation, yet know it is desolate, & swept only to entertain a Spirit sevenfold worse than the first, & should it seem never so delightfull, yet in the eternal Light it is seen to be but that green Tree[6] under which thou delightfully play'st the Harlot every day. Be not moved at these Sayings, for I am not unacquainted with that state, which those Queries plainly tell me they come from. Oh the best Condition that is capable of

receiving in prejudice, is not unable of [three words missing] it, & very tall is that stature that can wade through those flows[7] & not stick therein by [two words missing] I shall attend thy Queries, & give them that Answer, which shall most simply arise in [two words missing] wherein I may be clear of thee, & at Peace in myselfe.

I find them to be unnecessarily multiplied, & the greatest part of them to be only [one word missing] or their Consequences aggravated into differing Expressions; wherefore I shall sum up the [one word missing] tendency of the whole into these three.

1. Whether under the Gospel Administration & in Gospel Worship there ought to be any [Cere]monies or forms practised.
2. Whether pulling of the Hat in time of Prayer be not a Ceremony or form.
3. Whether keeping it on be a sufficient ground for giving Judgment against such, as Sower[s] of Dissension, & out of the unity of the Body, & whether you are not the Men, that is, the Quakers (so called) or several of the Chief of them, that have so censur'd severall & consequently are not for Liberty of Conscience.

These I take to Comprehend the whole Letter, so far as concerning the Queries, except one or two particular trivels, that may be answer'd by themselves, or in my return to these four.[8]

The first Question admitts of a Distinction upon the Word Ceremony or Form; Ceremonies Typical, which shew fo^r^th a future Glory, or any mystical Dispensation, not yet revealed, neither proper to that, nor of that in which we are, & which was peculiar to the former Jewish State,[9] we utterly renounce as no wayes suitable to the Spiritual Worship of the Gospel; & whoever pleads their continuance or practice in the Christian Church is an Enemy to the Cross of Christ.

But again, though the Gospel Worship is of a more interior & Spiritual Nature, & the Life, Substance, & Vertue thereof consists in a weighty retirement of Mind from all Visible motions & performances, though never so true, yet that there is somewhat exteriour or bodily, that is relative & adjunctive to that Spiritual Worship is as rationall, & true in itself, as that the Body, which is the exteriour, case or forms of the Soul, is a relative, & bears a part in the Worship that is paid to God; So that then such a Form, or such a Ceremony (to use the Word indifferently & inoffensively) which is not Typical, Legall, or Superfluous, & which may not so properly be tearm'd the fruit as leaves of Religion, as being suitable to the state of the Body or that exteriour part of Man, which is but a Kind of Figur or Emblem of the Soul, we do say, is both Lawfull, Commendable, & Necessary. In short, as the Soul Worships, so does the Body, & though all exteriour Worship not arriving from the Interiour, as its root, Life & Vertue is hypocritical; yet where there is interiour, there will be many times an exteriour Discovery of the same by such an awfull, reverential demeanure as may suite the present sense, fear & Worship of the Mind, especially in publick Assemblies. Such Ceremonies are as relative to the Body, as the Body is to the Soul. For the Body being visible, it cannot be attended with an invisible respect, for that is the Minds; And it is high weakness to think that every visible gesture is a form or Ceremony, at [le]ast such an one as is to be exploded & condemned; for men may as well chide those [th]at of old worshipped God in Body, Soul & Spirit, & whose Bodies were Temples for the Holy Ghost, indeed that men worshipt God with their Bodies at all; But allow the Body to be visible or Exteriour, & allow it any share in the Worship of the Gospell, & it will inevitably follow, that a bodily reverence is not a superstitious or legall Ceremony, but what as properly suits the formal state of the Body, as interiour reverence doth the Spiritual state of the Soul. So that the Devil not being able to prevent the breaking in of the pure power of Godliness, would Serpentlike translate himself into the appearance of an Angel of Light, & seem to be for the Power more then any, yea, & so, as to exclude all form however, indispensibly necessary (who once persecuted the Power) that so he might spoile the Work of God by overdoing, & sow the teares of cursed Dissension (as a Spiritualist) among the Wheat, which in some semish, selfrighteous brittle, & Crazy Spirits have taken root; & that to the beguiling of some simple ones, but the Lord hath ranzomed, & yet will ranzom from the snare of that cruel Fowler,[10] such as have any integrity to him.

To conclude, such a Ceremony, or Forme, as is relative to the state of the Body, that is but as the formal part of Man, we do believe to be both Lawful, & that which the Spirit of the Lord has unity with, & has lead to, & doth countenance in, & that which under the pretence of greater Liberty or more clear illumination hath unlenkt itself, & gone out of the good & wholsome practice of the Body, O the Lord judgeth, & not we, by his own pure eternal Spirit & Power, as a delusive, Imaginary, unsubject, selfseparating & rending Spirit.

To the Second Query thus in the fear of the Lord. The pulling off the Hatt, little in itself, is of some weight to us; We deny it to be such a Ceremony or Form as is by thee struk at, & which I have already distinguisht about; And that it is not so, I may prove from thy own Queries. For thou grantest that the Spirit of the Lord may move to pull off the Hat in prayer; then say I no Anti-Gospel form, because if it were, as thou dost seem elsewhere to conclude, the Spirit of the Lord might move to perform an AntiGospel Ceremony, so that from thy own concession I infer, that the Lord's Spirit may move to do it, & consequently, it is so far from being an Anti-Gospel, as it may be a very Gospel form. Well then, this know, that as it is a mark of reverence among Men in the Fall, & therefore we deny it to their Persons, so in the deep reverence of our Souls & Spirits, & in the heavenly motion of pure Life do we pull off our Hats to Allmighty

God, to express that honor, homage, & reverent respect to the immortal King of Glory, which we cannot & dare not give to any mortal Man; And I affirm, that till bodies are excluded any share in Divine Worships, bodies ought to have, & will have exteriour as well as Souls interiour acts of Divine Reverence. And to be plain in God's Sight, they are but the Novices, the itching Eares, airy Notionists,[11] & stomaks, that cannot digest sound food, that boggle & startle, & are uneasy under that blessed Evangelical Order, that is now like the morning Sun, rising in its Glory & lustre among us the Lord's Heritage.

In short, that Spirit, which has betray'd in this matter, has exercised above the [three words missing] the Condition of the particular, the Obedience of the Cross, the Unity of the Body, the [one word missing] of the Lord, whose bond of peace would have been kept, if there had been but a [one word missing] Mind upon him out of the conceited, airy exalted Life. And had J. P.[12] esteem'd [his Bre]thren better then himself, as speaks the Scripture, there had not been that erring [two words missing] pure Power & deep Councill of the Lord; In so much, than when reproof came over [him] he grew froward, waspish, & selfseparating, the very badge of guilt & token of [his] Exaltation; for the true Spirit is meek. But his race is run,[13] though not the true o[ne] & the Lord has & will take vengeance for his Seed, his righteous Seeds sake. A[nd] I stand amazed to thinck how men that dare trust their own Understandings, & wou[ld] not suffer them to be brib'd to the aims & ends of such Sect-Masters, should believe, th[at] after the eternal God had broak forth in his Power, & raised Wittnesses to his day, & that great Work, which he is doing in the Earth, who knew both the Mysteries of Godliness & Iniquity, & by whom many were turned from Darkness to Light, that the Lord should in their Life time make use of J. P. to bring up a more excellent Dispensation, Viz. To keep on the Hat in time of Prayer, thereby judging Legality, Carnality, & Darkness to be the state of the first Messengers in whose testimony Life was known, & a Certain sound wittnessed, & the Mysteries of the Kingdom revealed; for my part, I should not so ill contrive my work by an Ambassador, who am a Mortal, as they make the Allwise God to have done in reference to this his great & marvellous Work in our Day. The Objection about the Hat in prophesie is not to purpose, for in that state men speak from the Allmighty God to mortall men, & in prayer they speak as mortall men to the immortal Glorious God. And though I may speak with my hat off, yet do I not that as an Act of reverence to the People, or as believing my self thereto oblig'd, but in my freedom & for meer Conveniency;[14] For that one & the same gesture may be in reference to distinct times & actions both necessary & indifferent, though not at the same moment of time, & in the same act or performance; As for the Scripture urg'd, if it must be an argument against Corporal

Homage & reverence, certainly, it is ill used & applyed, and tharfts[15] thy assertion that a man may be mov'd to pull off the Hat in prayer; for might I say, why not mov'd when thou prophesiest! And if mystically taken, why bodily moved at all, since one may be uncovered whilst covered. Indeed I take it so, yet that binds not from visible reverence, which attends publick bodily Worship, nor doth mistical interpretation hinder or tharft our reverent practice.

The third Query I answer thus. That the separating & singular practice of the Hat on in prayer to Allmighty God, is a very just ground for Friends to testifie against, and refuse Communion with such as persist therein, & that for these reasons.

First, because, that since they who keep on their Hats immediately before they did it, upon their first doing of it, confessing to the power of the Lord to be in the Body, and the presence, Councill & Wisdom of God {to} rest upon them, as they did; the Body dislikeing it, being grieved by it, & at last judging it, is to me an infallible mark that the practise was [an] intrusion, & not a motion from the eternal spirit, unless we should deny, that God has [giv]en greater Judgment to his Church, then the Individual members of it. For though the Moderate sort of the Church of Rome hold this to be a true position in itself, as it is, yet, herein the err, that Rome is not a true Church, which J. P. & his Followers denyed not the Body of Friends to be.[16]

Secondly; It made an absolute Division, & rent, & caused much Confusion, Heartburnings & Distances, & those who runn well, were thereby interrupted, & Men & Women were drawn off from their dayly Obedience, & the more weighty matters, appertaining to Life & Salvation, & were wholly allmost taken up with these debats & Contests, & since that of the Hat was the Cause thereof, Peace & Concord, & the prosperity of the Church not ensuing, which had it been of God, would have been known among Israel, & not have been judged as a strange Birth; I conclude, it was not of God, but of the conceited, singular, self-separating, self-Exalting Spirit, which is judged for ever.

Thirdly, If it had been right, it cost more then it was worth, & had J. P. been owned in that, his whymsies had been endless, at least whilst he had liv'd, and he that like Cor Dath & Abi.[17] against Moses, cryed out upon others as Task Masters & Oppressors, & Lords over God's Heritage, would have been thereby exalted as high as Lucifer, And therefore I am verily perswaded, that God put it in~~to~~ the~~ir~~ hearts of the Holy Elders to stop that Spirit, & stand against it forever, & I have a Testimony in my Heart, that it was not of God.

Fourthly, It was so slight a thing, as had it been right, it could add nothing to Life & Salvation, nor to the Edification of the Body, which is the End of every true motion: It would have carried neither interiour nor exteriour Homage, Service or benefit in the least, either to Persons in their own particular, nor the Church in generall.

Fifthly, That which to its Defenders seems strong for it, is that, which with me carries most against it, namely the Trivialness of the thing. For it was not a Time, a Day for the Devil to appear in any material or substantial opposition that in J. P. & others met with a rebuck, that utterly blasted the Serpents Designs. And therefore he thought to have found Friends asleep to these lesser matters; he would first endeavour to introduce his body by his head, which seems little, And if he could have once prevailed by J. P. agency in this one conceit, he would have drew in his whole Body, & Mass of Imaginations, till the blessed Truth had been overrun with his Ary Dreams, & the whole Body become a just Derision to all sober Men, which was mounting into good esteem with many, who either waited for the Kingdom, or wisht well to it & the subjects thereof. O endless had been the Idle Fancyes, nauseating gestures, ridiculous Sounds &, vile Conceits of that foolish man & his Adherents; I have seen that Spirit, & what it would have led to, in that which is eternal. O my Soul had loathed the very Name & Profession of Friends, had they been cover'd wth such Garments, as he would have cover'd them withall, whom finding in the Godly Aw, the sound Mind, the Powerfull practicall, experimental Minist[ry] [three words missing] profitable Imaginations of that Paratonian[18] Spirit, I closed with them, & my Sou[l] [two words missing] though {through} great Trouble & Distress, for which I can magnifie the Name of my God [two words missing] his Living Heritage. And my Soul rejoyces, that there were some that stood in [two words missing] were mighty with God & among men to the stoping that deluge, which my Soul sees [two words missing] Eye in a clear Day) would have come with great swiftness over the Church of God. [One word missing] So farr are Friends from resembling the Church of Rome as to her Degeneration, th[at it] was by such little things at first, when greater would not do, that the Devil that [one word missing] Serpent introduc'd his whole superstition & Idolatry, why that People has layn un[der] for many ages. Had the Romans kept to the Gospell as preach'd & settled in the first ag[e,] all had continued pure; & had J. P. kept to the pure power, & what it had establisht [as] fitt & necessary for Worship, Fellowship & Communion, the Church's peace had never been disturb'd, many Souls murdered, nor himself utterly rent off & lost from the Living Body, which my Soul has sometimes bitterly lamented. In short, it is not the Trivialness of the gesture, but that Spirit that thereby has taken Occasion, to begin a Separation, & to rend from the Body, as an other mark & badge then is that practice of the Body. And in the Vision, Power & Authority of the Lord God of Light & Life, I see it to be Curiosity, Imagination, singularity, airyness, & above the weighty seed, & judge it to be the birth of a stranger, & this judgment will stand for ever.

Sixthly, To me it seems to have been the sign & product of a

Judging Spirit, that judgeth the Body, & thinks worse of others then itself; Which shews that the Eye was out, & from watching over the particular Condition. This pufs up, & exalts self, gathers to self, which is a Sect-Master, & the same in ground, which loves to be called Master of men, & is exercised off from the daily Cross, the staggering, unstable ones by unprofitable things cast in their way; Yea it is the old Professing Notionall Spirit, that is above all form & Power to, & in the End proves nothing, but Dryness, Barrenness & meer Ranterisme.[19] For such as go into those things first grow weary of Obedience at home, & not being able to outdo the Brethren therein, then getts up for a Name by some singular Invention, & seeks to gather to that mark, that there may be a rending from that Body, & a setting up of self thereby. But God hath curs'd it, & it shall wither forever. And truly W. M. Friends have been tender in the General, & the Meetings, that in the Wisdom, Power, & tender Love of God were both erected & held three years since for these very matters, bow'd many, that they judged themselves, & therefore were not judged of us, who have through it found mercy, & can testifie, how sweet it is for Brethren to live together in Love, & to travell on wth the Flocks of the Churches Companions, where the shepheard is known, & his pleasant pastures wittnessed, & to which (who art a scattered sheep) I invite thee in the dear & tender Love of God as an unbyas'd Man in all respects, & can say that I am what I am in this Answer, only to the Lord God, & no mortal man, that thou wouldst come in, come home, & wander no longer among barren, dry, [illegible word] Imaginations, nor briary & thorny prejudices, that tear and scarch, & heal not; that so thou mayst partake of the Living refreshment, that is among us [on]ce more know the true fold, where the Flocks rest in unity & peace with the Lord God, their [lov]ing Shepeard, & one with an other. And well said of G. F.[20] whom thou slightly mentions, but we much value & respect as a Man of God, is no Liberty of Conscience; not as thou takest it, that other differing persuasions are to be persecuted. But that all Consciences out of Truth are in bondag'd by the God of the World, being his servants whom they obey, not having known the freedom that the Truth brings to. And Will. the Liberty of thy Conscience is not for us to own thee in thy separation, but for thee, by the Spirit of Judgment & the Spirit of Love to know a being made free from the Spirit of Singularity, & Self Separation, & Judging of the Body, as fallen, & its Elders as Tyrants & Oppressors; And if thou waitest low in the dread & fear of the Almighty, overlooking things that are behind, & shutting out all carnal reasonings, surmises, & prejudices that would hurt & hinder, & come to Meetings, & bear the Judgment, & esteem the stroak of the Righteous as Balme, & the reproof of a Friend as pretious oyntment; O Will. the Case would soon be chang'd & thou wouldst quickly feel some Love to arise, so tenderness begotten, & taking shame to self,

& a cleaving to the Body, yea, & some fervent resolutions to dwell wth us forever, & that, which has hurt thee, thou wouldst come to wound by the Spirit of Judgment that would go out of thy mouth against it.

And Will. though thou may'st sometimes feel a sense of the Lord's drawing nigh, yet let not that harden thee, but tender thee to the Body, & have a care, that thou runnest not away with those touches, & presently inferrs, I am justified, because thou waitest not to feel the Condemnation that would come; for to know the signification of the Lord's coming nigh to any is a very weighty thing. Therefore do not thou interpret God's visiting thee in reproof, or his long forbearance to thee a Justification of thee in thy separation from the Body, For I testifie for God, the Living God, that Spirit is not of him; And we are his People, his chosen, bought with a price, & redeemed through such tribulations as (to us) never were, since the World began, & he is our Lord, our God, our King, our Righteous Judge, & Holy Lawgiver, whose Lips preserves Knowledge, & from whose Mouth we daily receive his pure Law of Life to our Instruction, refreshment, & establishment forever.

Thus in general as to the Substance of the Queries, in soundness of Mind, yet in moderation & true Love; If thou requirest any further satisfaction, I shall at any convenient time discours things with thee, if thou are not herewith satisfied, which I greatly desire.

As to the Business that happened between J. B.[21] & thee, it was not my Concern; But this I think in the Fear of the Lord, that If J. B. had wrong'd thee, thou shouldst not have made so ill an use of it, as to have aggravated it against the Body, but either have been satisfied in clearing thy Conscience to him, or have born it. And truly, I think that spirit wch in thee put that needless & inoportun question, viz. Whether if I or my Wife were dead, would you give us a Burying amongst you, was too displeas'd & enrag'd at J. B.^s^ denyall of the other thing. For thy Child & Wife[22] I know what I have to say, when it is in my power, or I should be at that Meeting, when it should be proposed. But for thee Will. this I must say, tha[t] [three words missing] I would not lye among them dead, that I had no Fellowship with Living, & shouldst [three words missing] the same separating Spirit, in which thou standst at a distance from us, I must needs [two words missing]ness I could not accord, yet nothing, I hope, is so inhuman, as to refuse a burying plac[e] [two words missing] as dead, & so not to deny it thee; But as departed of us, or in the Fellowship & owned [two words missing] trouble of Spirit & some Lamentation over thee, I must tell thee, I could not agree. Now [two words missing] my plain & simple Answer in the fear of the Lord.

And Will. as for that Authority thou sayst, is taken by some, this, I say, if thou [are] griev'd after privat admonition, come forth & speak to the Church, & don't lye pinnt up [in pre]judice & black Saturnall Melancholy, & unfruitfull thoughtfullness, which misrepresent, & wrongs both thee & us. For my part, I have unity with the Elders, & all my Brethren & am glad there be men that in the holy plain, yet deep counselling power of the Lord stand over the Wise, Prudent, Self Contriving, headordering Spirit, that might arise to have the Government upon ~~his~~ {its} shoulders in any, & that keep to the holy power of God, & Judge by the Unity that has or has not, with whatever is proposed, & not as it is convenient or not convenient in mens Wisdom, which God will confound, & may those honest & good men live, & prosper, which is my Soul's desire; And when J. B. is gone to rest, he shall be then accounted by some of his very Enemies, what several feel him now to be, I mean, a good man, who loves the Power of the Lord, & acts with his whole Heart & understanding in Integrity & Zeal for God, little minding his own concerns. May the Church never have worse Servants nor less affected to the promotion of the pure unchangable Truth of the Lord God in their Day & Generation, according to his understanding.

Thus Will. have I at present clear'd my Conscience to thee in plainness & Honesty, not desiring to Justifie the guilty, nor condemne the righteous, the Lord knows; And O don't think it a disgrace for thee to embrace my loving, tender & wholsom Advice, which in God's Love I now send unto thee, but read, waite, & be low, patient, & in True aw before the Lord, & I shall not be without some hopes of thy restoration, among those that have flockt to come in att the Windows of our Tabernacle, & heavenly habitation. My Soul desires well for thee, O that thou mayst be saved, & be serviceable to the Lord in thy Generation, it is my hearts desire for thee, for I am

Thy truly wellwishing Friend.

LBC. WP's Letterbook, 1667-1675, HSP. (*Micro.* 1:414.) The salutation is in WP's hand; the text is in a clerk's hand. On each page of this MS the upper inside corner is torn; missing words are indicated in brackets.

1. Basing House, Rickmansworth.

2. William Mucklow (1631-1713) of Mortlake, Surrey, was among the Quakers jailed at Bridewell in 1662. A decade later he joined John Pennyman (see doc. 74) in protest against Fox's formalism; in Fox's words, they "became open opposers of truth" (Fox, 2:315). Mucklow's letter to WP has not survived; he seems to have raised most of the issues which he presented soon after in his anonymous tract, *The Spirit of the Hat, or the Government of the Quakers* (London, 1673). Here, Mucklow charged that the Quakers in their "Foxonian-Unity" were as authoritarian as the Catholics. He challenged rituals, like taking off the hat in prayer; disciplines, like scrutiny of proposed marriages; and the relationship between authority exerted by the meeting and liberty of conscience and the guidance of the light within. WP answered with *The Spirit of Alexander the Copper-Smith Justly Rebuked* ([London], 1673), comparing Mucklow's apostacy from Fox with Alexander's apostacy from Paul (Acts 19:33; 2 Tim. 4:14). Mucklow probably wrote the anonymous retort, *Tyranny and Hypocrisy Detected; or, A further Discovery of the Tyrannical Government, Popish-Principles, and vile Practices of the now-leading Quakers* (London, 1673). WP replied to this with *Judas and the Jews Combined against Christ and his Followers* ([London], 1673). Mucklow next wrote a pamphlet on *Liberty of Conscience asserted against Imposition* (London, 1673), which was answered by George Whitehead. After this flurry, Mucklow stopped publishing. Some years later, he renewed his fellowship with the Quakers. DQB; *DNB;* Fox, 2:273, 315, 448.

3. WP means that he was only a boy (and not yet a Quaker) when John Perrot had his quarrel with Fox. Perrot was an Irish Quaker who went on a famous mission to the Middle East in 1657 and returned by way of Italy, where he wanted to meet the Pope, and where he spent three torturous years in a Roman madhouse by order of the Inquisition. Back in London in 1661, he opposed any form in public worship and maintained that meetings should not be scheduled at all. He spent his last three years, 1662-1665, in America, and died unreconciled to the majority position. See Kenneth L. Carroll, *John Perrot, Early Quaker Schismatic* (London, 1971).

4. Luke 10:30-37.

5. Jer. 8:22.

6. Jer. 2:20.

7. Morass or quicksand. *OED.*

8. WP means "three."

9. The ritual observances of the Jews, which are detailed in Exod. 25-31, in Lev., and in Num. chaps. 1-10, 15-19, were rejected by all Quakers.

10. Ps. 91:3.

11. Holders of extravagant religious opinions. *OED.*

12. John Perrot.

13. Perrot had died seven years before.

14. WP is clearly having some difficulty here in maintaining a distinction between keeping the hat on before men and taking the hat off before God.

15. Thwarts?

16. Mucklow objected to WP's argument here in *Tyranny and Hypocrisy Detected,* and WP reaffirmed his position in *Judas and the Jews Combined against Christ.* See *Works,* 2:207-8.

17. Korah, Dathan, and Abiram. For their rebellion against Moses, see Num. 16:1-34.

18. Followers of Perrot.

19. Pantheistic mysticism. See doc. 63, n. 8.

20. George Fox.

21. John Boulton; see doc. 59, n. 7. Because Mucklow was disowned, Boulton had refused him the use of a Quaker burial ground. Mucklow complained about this again in *Tyranny and Hypocrisy Detected,* pp. 16-17.

22. Because Mucklow's wife was not a Friend, the Quakers had denied the validity of his marriage. Mucklow complained about this again in *Tyranny and Hypocrisy Detected,* p. 16.

72
PETITION TO THE HOUSE OF COMMONS

The following document shows WP trying to protect his fellow Quakers from renewed political persecution. In March 1672, Charles II, claiming the monarch's supreme power as head of the Church of England, had issued the Declaration of Indulgence, which suspended the execution of penal laws against dissenters, provided for the licensing of nonconforming ministers, and allowed Protestant dissenters to meet in public and Catholics in private. In September 1672 the king had pardoned 491 Quakers held in jails throughout England. When WP visited Friends in Kent and Sussex in September-October 1672 (doc. 70), their meetings were open and relatively unmolested. However, Parliament viewed the Declaration of Indulgence as an infringement upon its own right to make and repeal laws. In March

1673 the king was forced to suspend his declaration and to accept a new parliamentary statute, the Test Act, which required all officeholders to swear an oath of allegiance to the crown and to subscribe to a statement denying transubstantiation. The immediate effect was to remove the Duke of York and other Catholics from office, but the Test Act also alarmed Quakers, who denied transubstantiation but would not subscribe to oaths.

Doc. 72 asks that Parliament permit the Quakers to substitute a simple attestation for a loyalty oath. It is one of several undated petitions copied into WP's Letterbook. Besse supposed that the Quakers presented it in 1678, when Commons was debating a second Test Act, designed to exclude Catholics from membership in Parliament (*Works*, 1:117-18). But the Test Act of 1673 had more direct application to Quakers than the act of 1678, and the 1673 measure appears to be the "Bill against Popery" referred to in doc. 72. When WP addressed his *Treatise of Oaths* to Parliament in 1675, he stated that the Quakers had "again and again tender'd our solemn Yea or Nay" (*Works*, 1:612). Doc. 72 is one such effort. The petition was unrecorded and ignored by the House of Commons.

To the Commons of England
Assembled in Parliam[t]
The Request of the People
called Quakers.

[c. March 1673]

Besides those many & great sufferings we have sustained by the Execution of laws made ag[t] us, to the Ruin of many Industrious families, we have been many of us much damnifyed both in our Estates & Persons, sometimes even to Death itself by laws neither made against us, nor so much as designed ag[t] such a people as we are, & such principles, as we hold.

And understanding that you are pleased to Insert & Enact such a distinguishing Clause in the Bill against Popery, as that they, who will take the Oath, & subscribe a Declaration therein exprest, shall not suffer by such Lawes. And because for pure Conscience we cannot swear at all (in which we are not alone; for that many of the Philosophers, Jews, & many of the best Christians have had that same tendernesse) We intreat you to take our particular Case into yo[r] serious Consideration, & give us some relief: otherwise we are like to come under penalties, that belong not to us, because we cannot take this Oath: though the Ground of our refusal be not the matter, to which the penaltie is affixed; but the form of it. And that, which with all due Respect & Integrity we offer, is; *That our Word may be taken instead of an Oath.* And if we are found faulty; that we may undergo that penaltie, which shall be inflicted on the other case. That we, & our Families may not be exposed to the malice, self ends, or Revenge of any: which we shall certainly be, if you relief us not: Many of us having already suffered upon this single Account. And it is not to be thought by wise & Charitable men, that we have any ill Design in refusing to swear; since we allways refused in our own case: though to our great Detriment.

A Proviso for Friends Yea or Nay.

Provided always, & be it hereby further enacted & Ordained, That were any person or persons of the people commonly distinguished by the term Quakers, being by any Laws or statutes of this Realm required, to take any Oath, or Oaths, shall scruple the taking thereof; & yet shall be ready & willing to promiss, verifie, or attest by his or their solemn *Yea* or *Nay*, whatsoever is or shall be required by such Oath or Oaths: Then, & in such Case every such solemn avernm^{t}, promiss, or attestation shall from hence forth be received, admitted, & allowed of as fully, amply, & effectually to all Intents & purposes, as if Oath were made thereof according to Law. And if in Case any person or persons shall be found upon such solemn promiss, averment, or attestation to aver, promise, or attest any thing contrary to Truth, & be thereof lawfully convicted; that then every such person so thereof convicted shall suffer & incurr all such paines, penalties, & forfeitures, as by the laws & statutes of this Realm are to be incurred & inflicted by or upon any person or persons convicted, or guilty of willful perjury. And likewise, that no person or persons, who upon such scruple, as aforesaid, shall at any time hereafter refuse to take any oath or oaths; shall for or by reason of any such refusal incurr, suffer or undergoe any paine, penaltie or forfeiture whatsoever; any Law, statute or Custom whatsoever to the contrary in any wise not with-standing.

LBC. WP's Letterbook, 1667-1675, HSP. (*Micro.* 14:765). Docketed in WP's hand: about oaths.

73
A MARRIAGE DISCIPLINE

[4 June 1673]

Att a Meeting at Tho: Ellwood's on the 4th 4th mo: 73.

An Account being given by Edward Hoare that John Jennings & Mary Arnold (the first-Cousins) do not only continue & cherish that unlawfull affection to each other, wch friends have so often in tender love born testimony against,[1] but are also in danger of running into further Evil & inconvenience thereby; & their conditions being seriously & solemnly weighed & considered, there arose in some a desire once more in the love of God to visit them, & seek their restoration & preservation: whereupon it was agreed, that Edward Hoare do give notice unto them both, that some friends have a desire to see them at Tho: Zacharies upon the 7th day of this week between the 2d & 3d hours; & Isaac Penington, Wm. Penn Nich: Noy[2] & Tho: Zacharie declared their willingness & intention to be there.

MBE. Upperside Monthly Meeting Minutes, 1669-1690, Buckinghamshire Record Office, Aylesbury. (*Micro.* 1:530).

1. As early as 1671 first cousins John Jennings and Mary Arnold were reproached by Upperside Monthly Meeting, WP's home meeting, for "cherish[ing] an unlawful & unnatural affection towards each other" and for "inhabit[ing] together." Committees from the meeting visited them three times in 1671, culminating in a public declaration by the meeting in Jan. 1672 that "no such Persons, as thus go together in Marriage, are indeed of us and owned by us, what soever they may seem or pretend to be." In 1673, as doc. 72 shows, the Monthly Meeting tried again. The committee which WP served on found Jennings and Arnold "brought to a good degree of tenderness, giving some hopes of their recovery from the snare wherin they are entangled." But a month later another committee found them "stifly persisting in their unlawful affection." Four years later John Jennings came to the meeting to plead their case again, but found the meeting in "ful testimony agt. the thing," and left "somwhat broken & tendered." Snell, *Upperside Minute Book,* pp. iv, xii, 10-12, 23-24, 26-28, 56, 96, 98, 114-15. For the Quakers' objections to first-cousin and other "near kindred" marriages, see doc. 91, below, and Lloyd, *Quaker Social History,* pp. 57-59.

2. Nicholas Noy (d. 1708), a bodice-maker of Chipping Wycombe, Bucks., was frequently a visitor for Upperside Monthly Meeting. Snell, *Upperside Minute Book,* p. i; Digest of Quaker Registers, Bucks., GSP.

74
TO MARY PENNYMAN

Rickmansworth, the 22th of the 9Mo [November] 1673.

Mary Pennyman,[1]

I received a Letter ~~of~~ {from} thee, by the hands of T. Mudde[2] my Neighbour: what is of weight therein, I shall I hope, in Truth & Righteousness answer. First thou sayest that at the reading of what I printed against thee (to thy great Scandal) thou felt that Love which could forgive, as oft as I so writ.[3] I answer, there was no Enmity in my Heart against thee; neither did I take my aime directly at thee or at thy Actions: I had the publick Adversary in my Eye,[4] who could plead a Cause, he once {to my} ~~ac~~knowledg~~ed~~ scorned, only to abuse & scandalize me, my Wife & Friends.[5] What I said I will stand by in God's Day; but if thou canst forgive so well (which indeed is not hard, where no Offence is committed) learn thy Husband to do so, who hath been a reviler of our Friends behinde their back & a Promotor of the Book Tyranny & Hypocrisie detected[6] &c. by contributing to the Accusations therein mentioned, as himself confessed to W. P. Tell me, Mary, is it more refined Quakerism (I use the word innocently, our Enemies reproachfully) to strengthen the Spirit of the World against it, & pleasure those with Arrows ag^{t} us, that hate us as being Quakers at all? Answer me plainly; Is not the Devil in Professors & Prophane Joyed at it? And could thy Husband with all his pretended Innocency & Spirituality dip in the Dish with those Ishmaelites & Philistines?[7] Is it to convert People to the Truth, to strengthen them with Accusations ag^{t} the Professors of it, who have been old publick opposers of both, & who make no other use of such Informations then to pierce & wound the Principle through their sides that profess it, & in all things answer it not, as my Book often hints? Ah! Ham's Spirit[8] has entered him; My Soul with brokenness wisheth that he might not receive Ham's recompence, if it be not too late, & the Lord so please, & see what Defenders thou hast. Is it for thy Religious Credit to be propt up by such as are kind for their own Ends, & shew that Froth, Abuse & Envy, that their Book[9] plentifully discovers? It hath wounded your Cause abundantly with all Soberminded People. Do not therefore make me the Persecutor; Thou art not clear: & thy Husband hath manifested his Rage ag^{t} us by publick & clandestine Opposition & Insinuation: And in the Vision of the Infinite, Eternal, Allmighty God I testifie, that the Spirit in you which hath assaulted us, is one in {the} ground, though not in the Appearance with the Spirit of John Faldo,[10] Th. Hicks,[11] H. Hedworth,[12] & F. Chadwell;[13] for you both drive to the same End, & you equally strengthen the Spirit of this World against us, And it is Sport to that Generation, when either of you bring forth any thing ag^{t} the People, called Quakers. Thou sayest, it was not in thee, to desire any Mortall to plead thy Cause, & thou justifieth not the Doing of it. But Mary, some Mortals & no more have done it; here is, I fear, Equivocation to boot. Thou didst not desire it, but one good turn requires another, sayes the proverbe. Thy Husband help'd or closed with them for Matter of Accusation, thereby strengthening the Hands of the common Adversary to lay waste God's Heritage: For though he pretend to be the True Quaker, he helpt them that deny both the true Quaker & his Principle, & have writ ag^{t}, despised, & persecuted both. Oh! that God would be pleased to let him see this great Evill that he is fallen into. Now, could they do less then become your Advocates, such as they are. But why plead? Prophane not that Scripture in thy mind, as if the Earth helped the Woman; No, no; but the Dragon {doth} cast forth Waters: (The Multitude) {to} drown us {(if possible)} the True Church, coming now out of the Wilderness; but, Blessed be the Lord, {they} can not prevaile; nor shall any Weapon formed ag^{t} Sion.[14] Thou sayest, thou dost not justifie it, but dost thou condemn it! By no means; for then thy Husband will come under thy Censure, who thou sayest is innocent; which if he be, no body is guilty. Thou wishest I had had no Provocation. Oh Mary, glad would I be if this were spoken sincerely: Thou must either have been ignorant of thy Husbands Help to this Work, ~~& sorrow for it;~~ or else thou hast writ equivocatingly, or thou must have repented of his medling with; since no Man or Woman can wish a thing not to have been, which has been, & they accessory, without Repentance or Deceit; chuse thouwhhaps) upon thyself. We are {not} of thy mind, Thou art not so retired, as thou would have us believe. A Rich, Young, Neat, Sparkish Husband is a certain visible thing, & his Credit in the World an appendant, & I am of the mind, to speak plainly, that a great part of thy Delight is lodged in him. I will speak no more {least it be reputed} offensively {said}. I hope I have not in saying that. But thou sayst, He is an innocent Man, & bidst me have a care how I speak or affirm any thing of him; for I must give an account of it. So I must for what I affirm of thee or any else. Is there not a Singular Exaltation here. How canst thou admonish me not to be puffd up, that hast so puffd up the poor Man, that he is ever and anon ready to be cracked? Thou hast wrong'd him by these things; I testifie in the Truth of God that your Humility is feigned, & your Exaltation high; & thou hast entered that poor Man, & help'd to his being beguil'd, by swelling him beyond his place, as if he were some God on Earth, for which Seed of the Serpent J. P.[15] has a large ground. Mary, be not displeas'd that I am thus plain; I should play the Hypocrite with thee, if I writ not as I do: Thou canst gird thyself, & speak & write smooth & soft; I am anothers, & I write & speak as I feel it, & not in demure Images. The Evil {one hath that Way to make his Work go for God's, who will sometimes appear Mild to Bad as well as Good, & sooner Enraged ag^{t} the Good then Bad.} I call to mind thy Secret grudgings of old ag^{t} the Generality of Friends that laboured more especially, thy faire Carriage, & backbiting Characters; thereby shut up thy Spirit from that Fellowship, which would have been a Strength & preservation unto thee. Thy Husband may call to mind how he used to reflect in my tender Seasons as to Truth upon the most eminent Travellers amongst us, enough to overset so small a saile in so great a Sea of Exercise as I was in. I had writ to your Paper ag^{t} Quaker-Preachers,[16] & my self in particular 3 or 4 sheets of you both, & your Carriage within & without to Friends & others; Certainly a smart Rod, but I had Compassion I stayed my hand, if yet you would mend, little expecting the 2d part to the same Ungodly purpose, but as yet it lyes by me.

In thy Advice to me, that I should have a care of the knowledge that puffs up, I wish I may follow it to the end; Yet this I will say, That the knowledge of God from the Living Wittness from 13 years of Age hath been dear to me, from 16 I have been a great Sufferer for it at the University; By that Inward Work alone I withstood many. I never addicted my selfe to Shool-Learning to understand Religion by; but allwaies even to their Faces rejected, & disputed ag^{t} it. I never had any other Religion than what I felt, excepting a little Profession, that came wth Education. I had no Relations that inclined to so solitary & Spirituall a Way; I was as a Child alone; yet by the Heavenly Expressings of the Scriptures to my Understanding, & more immediate Inspirations was I confirmed & abundantly comforted. I was a secret Mourner by the Waters of Babylon, & underwent heavy stripes from my Relations, {(afterwards by them repented of)} & that frequently, only for my inward Perswasion sake, wch was too strong for all Opposition or Allurements in the End. And though I was, a while in the midst of this World's Glory both in this & other Countries; yet it was rather to know that I might the better condemn them with a Vanity of Vanity; All is Vanity & Vexation of Spirit, then to sit down & to be married with {them.} At last my Soul meeting with Truth, that is, the knowledge of that Inward tender Principle, that overinclined me to Righteousness, Mercy & Peace, to be the Truth in the inward parts that I was to have my regard to, I embrac'd it wth gladness of Heart, though it was as sharp to me as a well pointed Dart, because of Iniquity. So that Mary, the knowledge that puffs up, I have never been much exercised in. 'Tis not confuting Priests, maintaining Truths, sound Doctrine, that puffs up; No, I can live in Love wth my Brethren, & think them, as the Apostle saith, better then my self. But Mary, exalted Apprehensions of greater Light then others, larger Discoveries then others, More Self Denial then others, Watching for others Infirmities, & Judging Common Decency & Conveniency, as thou must know that thou hast done; This is the Pharisee; I am holyer then thou; here's is the conceited puffed up state, of which, oh that you both, & I & all may have a care of, especially of the feigned Humility; for underneath that seeming nothingness lurks the greatest Exaltation; & such by crying down all Hight, raise themselves up higher than ever {as if others were only fitt to be pittyed, yourselves justified & commended;} I say, have thou a care of this & thy Husband too: And do not thou greaten him, to obtain thy own Ends on him; for some think thou hast betrayed much {of} the Simplicity that was once in him, through thy fair Speeches, & unfit Applause. O remember your own Infirmities, & consider your ~~own~~ outgoings, & lay to Heart, that deep Reproach you have brought upon the Living God, his Way & People, & let Sorrow take hold of you, for these Provocations, if yet the Lord will forgive you. Truly, my Soul is deeply affected for you; & I could say, Oh that these things might never be laid to their Charge: But this I of a Truth know, that through deep Judgment upon that *Watching, Judging Spirit,* that hath rendred others worse, & your selves better then you are, you must come, or Remission, & lasting Peace you shall never witness. Much I could say, but at this time my Spirit is closed. Only had John Pennyman sought Peace & pursued it, he would never have busied himself so much in other Folks matters, Assumed the Office of an Inquisitor, Abused

Men behind their Backs, have blazed abroad some Miscarriages to confirm Professors Envious Inventions. In short, have declined Meeting G. F. since his Return,[17] notwithstanding his Loving Invitation, & least of all have upbraided & reviled him in his Letter to Joh. Osgood[18] about the Burial of his Child, since no man was more willing to answer what he seemed to desire, by giving his Judgment among others so freely & meekly in the Matter. I could rejoyce to be serviceable to you, though in the meanest Capacity of your Restauration, if yet it may be. But for that Spirit, which hath led you into that distance from us, God that lives forever, hath both clearly & frequently satisfied my Soule, in the Wrongness of it, & that it is for Eternal Judgment. Thus in plainness, Meekness, & a true Sorrowing Love for you, I conclude this Letter, who am thy true Friend

W P

LBC. WP's Letterbook, 1667-1675, HSP. (*Micro.* 1:536).

1. Mary Heron Boreman Pennyman (1630?-1701) was an early Quaker who was imprisoned in London in 1662 in the aftermath of the uprising of the Fifth Monarchy men. Her husband, Henry Boreman, died in Newgate, leaving her with three children and pregnant with a fourth. After keeping an oil shop in Leadenhall Street, London, she decided to go out of business in 1670, "in *pure Obedience* to the Leadings of HIS own SPIRIT of Life, made Manifest in My Mortal Body," and went to live in Tottenham with two other widows. One of those may have been Jane Ward Lead (or Leade) (1623-1704), a mystic who helped to found the Philadelphians (a sect whose members rejected form and ritual), and had also refused to work for a living. In 1671 Mary Boreman married John Pennyman. The Pennymans lived together until her death in 1701, in continuous quarrel with the Quakers, and frequently on the move through the English countryside. For biographical details, see Norman Penney, ed., "The Cambridge Edition of the Journal of George Fox," *JFHS* 23:23; Besse, 1:366, 389; Fox, 2:432; *DNB.* Numerous letters and short pieces by Mary Pennyman are included in her husband's publications. See especially *The Ark is begun to be Opened* (London, 1671); *A Short Account of the Life of Mr. John Pennyman* (London, 1703); and *John Pennyman's Instructions to his Children* (London, 1674).

2. Thomas Mudd of Rickmansworth. He and his wife, Ann Mudd, were close friends and followers of the Pennymans, frequently mentioned in Pennyman's *A Short Account.* The Quakers were accused of pulling Ann Mudd down when she wanted to speak in meeting ([Mucklow], *Tyranny and Hypocrisy Detected,* p. 15); WP said "she hath been so Unhappy as through her Excess of Affection to *J. Pennyman,* to be a Sharer with him in his perverse Out-Cryes against us" (*Judas and the Jews Combined against Christ,* p. 40). Ann Mudd gave her own interpretation in *A Cry, A Cry: A Sensible Cry for many months together hath been in my Heart for the Quakers Return out of that Egyptian Darkness they have long lain in* (London, 1678).

3. In *The Spirit of Alexander the Copper-Smith,* pp. 13-14, WP attacked the Pennymans for their "Prodigal Feast" at the Merchant Taylor's hall in London in celebration of their marriage, and he attacked Mary Pennyman for exchanging simple clothing for things like a "Silk Farendine Gown" (a mixture of silk and wool) and a satin bodice. Mary Pennyman may have used clothes to provoke Quakers; in 1677 she said she "was made [by the spirit] to wear Lace on my Head" and attend a Quaker meeting (Pennyman, *A Short Account,* p. 87). In *Judas and the Jews,* pp. 61-63, WP repeated his charges. He often referred to her as Mary Boreman, presumably because Friends did not recognize her marriage to Pennyman.

4. WP refers to John Pennyman (1628-1706), Mary Pennyman's husband, a highly successful London wool draper. In 1658 he was attending Quaker meetings, but by 1661 was meeting with followers of Perrot. The real breach came about 1670 when Quakers thought he had decided the Bible was not necessary to those inhabited by the

spirit and that he had burned the Bible (and his collection of Quaker tracts) in the Royal Exchange. They, in effect, disowned him, finding him "broken in his brain or distracted" ([Mucklow], *Tyranny and Hypocrisy Detected,* p. 7). Pennyman protested his innocence and spent the rest of his life both feuding with Quakers and trying to establish fellowship with them. In 1679 he published a series of extracts from WP's tract, *An Address to Protestants of All Persuasions.* In 1681, on sending WP some of his other publications, he wrote: "And I knowing Your Self of an Intelligent and Inquisitive Mind, after such Matters, was willing to send you one of Each [tract]; by which, in Seeing, you may See, and in Reading, may Understand, in some measure, what My Work, and Service, of late hath been." The letter is signed "Your Respectfull, and Truly loving Friend" (*A Short Account,* pp. 1, 7, 10, 21-22, 121).

5. The cause which Pennyman could plead, having once scorned it, was the Perrot cause. In *Judas and the Jews,* p. 23, WP said that Pennyman had once joined in a unity of spirit against Perrot, saying that the spirit which led Perrot to keep his hat on in prayer was "The spirit of witchcraft and of the Devil."

6. *Tyranny and Hypocrisy Detected* (1673) was written by William Mucklow. See doc. 71.

7. That is, betray the Quakers. WP recalls what Christ said of Judas, Matt. 26:23, "He that dippeth his hand with me in the dish, the same shall betray me." WP quoted this verse on the title page of *Judas and the Jews.*

8. Gen. 9:18-29. Seventeenth-century interpreters concluded that when Ham showed derision and contempt for his drunken father Noah, he was cursed and his posterity were doomed to slavery.

9. *Tyranny and Hypocrisy Detected.*

10. John Faldo (1633-1690), a nonconformist minister, said to have been a chaplain in Cromwell's army. He engaged for four years in an extended controversy with WP, a controversy which saw nearly a dozen titles into press. See doc. 83; *DNB;* Hull, *William Penn,* pp. 146-47.

11. Thomas Hicks, an Anabaptist, first attacked the Quakers in *A Dialogue between a Christian and a Quaker* (London, 1672) and then in *A Continuation of the Dialogue* (1673). WP counterattacked in *Reason Against Railing, and Truth against Fiction* (1673). This controversy, like that with Faldo, continued for two more years of polemical exchange.

12. Henry Hedworth was a Socinian or early unitarian about whom little is known. He also engaged in controversy with WP; he opened, anonymously, with *The Spirit of the Quakers* (London, 1672); WP answered with *The Spirit of Truth Vindicated* ([London], 1672); Hedworth's rejoinder was *Controversy Ended* (London, 1673); and WP concluded the contest with *A Winding-Sheet for Controversie Ended* ([London], 1672). See Hugh Barbour, "William Penn, Model of Protestant Liberalism," *Church History* 48:168-70, and Vincent Buranelli, "William Penn and the Socinians," *PMHB,* 83:369-81. The controversy with Hedworth also produced a short letter to a female apostate; see WP to Elizabeth Wadle, n.d. [c. 1672], *Micro.* 1:372.

13. Little is known about Frances Chadwell. According to Mucklow, Chadwell was ill-used in Quaker meeting, pushed, pinched, kicked, pulled down, thrown out (*Tyranny and Hypocrisy Detected,* p. 14). WP said Chadwell was a liar and drunk who "had as good as confest that he had been Hired by some Professors to Disturb us" (*Judas and the Jews,* pp. 38-39).

14. Rev. 12:1-6, 13-16; and see Isa. 54:17.

15. John Pennyman.

16. Probably John Pennyman, *For the Preachers and Leaders of People called Quakers* (1673). WP's answer unfortunately does not survive.

17. From the West Indies and America, which Fox visited in 1671-1672.

18. John Osgood (1634?-1694), linen-draper in Cheapside, a Friend who served on many committees for London Monthly Meeting and presented a petition to the king in 1679. According to Mucklow, *The Spirit of the Hat,* pp. 30-31, Osgood had refused to wear his hat in prayer, and when he wanted to marry Rebecka Travers in 1667, the meeting raised difficulties. In *Judas and the Jews,* pp. 83-84, Osgood proclaimed his orthodoxy. WP's reference to the burial of a child is not clear.

75
TO DANIEL FLEMING

In his continuing efforts to protect Quakers from political harassment (see doc. 72), WP here appeals directly to a local magistrate, Daniel Fleming, who had discretionary power in enforcing the persecuting laws. Fleming was a longtime enemy of Quakers, but he also seems to have disliked other dissenters, so WP tried to coax him into toleration by stressing "the implacable Hate and Persecution" of the Independents and Baptists toward Quakers. WP's further efforts to lobby for the Quakers are shown in docs. 78-80.

[1673]

The Obligation, Thy[1] Civility laid upon the Person that is now my Wife, when in the North, anno 1664.[2] is, with her being so, ~~made~~ {become} mine. Not to acknowledge, though I could never retaliate it, were a Rudeness I have not usually been guilty of; for however differing I am from other Men circa Sacra,[3] & that World, which respecting men, may be said to begin when this ends; I know no Religion that destroyes Courteisie, Civility & Kindness, which rightly understood, are great Indications of true Men, if not of good Christians. Certainly there is such a thing, as [illegible deletion] Civil uniformity, where a Religious one may be inobtainable, and methinks there can be nothing more irrational, then to sacrifice the Serenity of the one to an adventrous (if not impossible) procurement of the other. Let Men be Men before Christians, & not repute that the best Way of making them the last, which inevitably destroys the very Constitution of the first. Natural Affection, Quiet Living, Honest Commerce, & an Exemplary Life so strongly plead for Toleration of Opinion, that where Opinion aims not at the Destruction of Government, 'tis high pitty, & not a little Injustice to molest those that are so qualified. It is not my purpose to Dispute for Liberty of Conscience, but recommend it: Several Discourses are extant, which with me seem Irrefutable, I hope the Insuccessfulness of such severity as hath been acted, will be an Unanswerable Argument with them to leave it, with whom other Reasons would not prevaile: though I cannot think but a Person of those Parts, several have represented thee to have, would have been satisfied with less Cost of Controversy. For, indeed, there can be nothing more Irrational then to fancy that external Penaltys should work right Conviction or Information upon the Conscience in the Understanding of any: Sure I am it is beneath the True Religion to do so; as well as unbecoming one that hath been so served, to use that Ill Argument against others.

But the Scean is changed, & from the Severity of Magistrates, we are

fallen under the implacable Hate & Persecution of some Co-Dissenters. 'Tis for our Credit they quarrel us, especially, that they begin. Truth then best advocates her Innocency into Mens Consciences, when it is most questioned: she loses nothing by being tried; but the Woolfs-Skin the Wolf in Sheeps Cloathing is wont to cast upon Her; & I no waies doubt of that success in our Undertakings for her Defence. An Independent, & an Anabaptist, both Preachers, have lately bedirted us in three Discourses, they have publisht against us,[4] 'tis said with no smal Applause; but then it is to be understood, with our Enemies, or such as know us not: for them we have Charity, therefore have we writ; for truly, neither is the Truth hurt in herself; nor are we brought into the least Doubt of our Holy Faith by them: Our Unhappiness is, we are not understood; & Envy takes great Care, we should not. I have sent with this our Answers;[5] Be pleased to accept and peruse them; I hope, I need not say impartially, to a Man of so much Wisdom & Prudence. I leave the Consequence with Allmighty God, to whom we must all render our Account for the Deeds done in this Mortal Body, whether they be good or evill.
Excuse my Freedom, & accept of my Acknowledgment of former Favour, & be assured, it shall ever meet with a gratefull, returne from

Thy sincere Friend,
however unknown,
WP

Rickmersworth
73.—[6]

LBC. WP's Letterbook, 1667-1675, HSP. (*Micro.* 1:472). Docketed in WP's hand: Justice Fleming | a Justice of Coram[7] & Dep[t] Lieft. in westmerland.

1. Daniel Fleming (1633-1701) of Rydal, Westm., and Coniston, Lancs., was appointed sheriff of Cumberland at the Restoration and deputy lieutenant for Lancaster in 1674. Though he was a frequent persecutor of Friends and other nonconformists, he went along with the Declaration of Indulgence, calling it "great news," but hoping that dissenters would be content with it and not demand anything more. In 1681 he was knighted, and he later sat for Cockermouth in Parliament. *DNB; CSPD, 1671-1672*, p. 311; *CSPD, 1673-1675*, p. 246.

2. WP's reference here is mysterious. In 1664 Fleming was instrumental in imprisoning George Fox and Margaret Fell in Lancaster; why he was civil to the young Quaker Gulielma Springett is not clear, unless he was interested in her large inheritance. Nothing is known about Gulielma's visit to the north in 1664. *CSPD, 1664*, pp. 433, 444, 489, 523-24.

3. Concerning religion.

4. The Independent minister John Faldo and the Anabaptist preacher Thomas Hicks between them published four anti-Quaker discourses in 1672-1673: *Quakerism No Christianity* and *A Vindication of "Quakerism No Christianity"* by Faldo, and *A Dialogue between a Christian and a Quaker* and *A Continuation of the Dialogue* by Hicks.

5. Presumably copies of WP's replies to Faldo and Hicks. In answer to Faldo, he published *Quakerism a New Nick-Name for Old Christianity* (1672) and *The Invalidity of John Faldo's Vindication* (1673). In answer to Hicks, he published *Reason Against Railing and Truth Against Fiction* (1673).

6. Added in WP's hand.

7. WP means that Fleming was a member of the county quorum of justices.

76
TO JOHN COLLINGES

From my house in Rickmansworth,
the 22th of the 11th Month,
[January] 1673[/4]

John Collenges[1]

Although of all times the present may seem improper for English Men & Protestants to open a Gap, or whet up an Edge to Controversie;[2] yet since so publick an occasion hath been given by thee[3] (a Man, I hear, under the Character of a Doctor of Divinity) I hope, all sober People will have me excused, that I defend my self against such scandalous Attacques, so undeserved as well as unexpected on my part. I intend nothing bitter or prolix; What may yet be needfull (if any thing, after the honest & full Answer already made) is briefly this:

First, Thou introducest thy Reflection with a Design to shew what Ignorance puts man under the State of Damnation; & what knowledge is necessary to Eternal Life; Let us see if that be followed honestly & clearly, & not made a pretext for undue Censure & publick Reproach.

The Matter insisted upon relating chiefly to us on this occasion, was that we in common with Socinians, do not believe Christ to be the Eternal Son of God; & I am brought for Proof of the Charge. To this hath been already answer'd, that my Book, called, the Sandy Foundation Shaken toucht not upon this; but Trinity, & Separate Personality, &c.[4] But this will not serve thy turn, thou must both accuse us, & then wring & rack our Books to maintain it. I have two things to do; first to show I express nothing that divested Christ of his Divinity; next, declare my true Meaning & Faith in the matter. I am to suppose that when any Adversary goes about to prove his Charge ag[t] me out of my own Book, he takes that which is most to his purpose; Now let us see, what thou hast taken out of that Book so evidently demonstrating the Truth of thy Assertion. I find nothing more to thy purpose then this, that I deny a Trinity of Separate Persons in the Godhead; Ergo What? Ergo, William Penn denies Christ to be the only true God; Or, that Christ the Son of God is not from Everlasting to Everlasting God. Did ever Man yet hear of such Argumentation? Doth J. Collenges know Logick no better (but which is more condemnable in a Minister) hath he learnt Charity so ill? Are not Trinity & Personality one Thing, & Christ's being the Eternal God an other? Must I therefore necessarily deny his Divinity, because I justly reject the Popish Skool-Personality? This savours of such Weakness or Disingenuity as can never stand with the Credit of so great a Scribe to be guilty of. Hast thou never read of Paulus Samosatenus that denyed the Divinity of Christ,[5] & Macedonius that oppugned the Diety of the Holy Ghost?[6] And dost thou in good Earnest think they were one in Judgment with Sabellius, that only rejected the imaginary Personality of those times?[7] who at the same instant own'd & confessed to the Eternity & Godhead of Christ Jesus our Lord. It is manifest then, that though I may deny the Trinity of Separate Persons in one Godhead, yet do not consequentially deny the Deity of Jesus Christ.

And now I will tell thee my Faith in this Matter. I do heartily believe that Jesus Christ is the only true & Everlasting God, by whom all things were made that are made in the Heavens above, or the Earth beneath, or the Waters under the Earth. That he is as omnipotent, so omniscient & omnipresent, therefore God; This is confest by me, in two Books printed a little before the ~~*Sandy Foundation Shaken*~~, *Guide mistaken,* p. 28. & *Truth Exalted,* p. 14, 15. also at large in my *Innocency with her open Face.*[8] I think I have dealt very honestly with thee, I am sure to the Satisfaction of my own Conscience, & it is not my fault, if it be not to the better Information of thine. But as thou confessest, the Scripture hath no Word for Trinity, so thou undertakest to prove Personality from it, & calls it a Foundation: But certainly this retorts with great sharpness upon thee; for first, This being a Foundation, as thou sayest, it follows, that there is a Necessity of its being known & believed in order to salvation. But I do aver, first, that there is no Scripture for it; next, that Ten Thousands, yea Millions of People, calld Christians, neither do understand, nor (which is more) can understand any such thing, so mean are their Capacities, & so intricate & obscure is the thing itself. What Dangerous Inquiry, & Wanton Curiosity is that which cannot set down with this Scripture Definition, There be Three that bear record in Heaven, The Father, the Word, & the Spirit? It is more truly Religious, if not to deride, at least to reject Human Inventions & Pagan Philosophy, the chief Ingredients that make up the School Definitions,[9] & acquiesce in the naked Text of Holy Writ, unless the Comment were more clear & Unquestionable; Clear it is not, & for Unquestionable the Present Protestant Notion calls it Popery; as if it were an infallible Mark of sound Doctrine, to cry up the Fallibility of all Doctrine; A piece of new fashion'd Divinity, that is, not two removes from Atheism. Next, Thou sayest, There be three Individual, Intelligent, Incommunicable Substances; I never heard that asserted so plainly before: It is so far from proveing what is laid down, that it seems with me to overthrow it; for I can see no Difference between οὐσία & ὑπόσασις, Being & Substance: 'Tis true, the Schools say, the οὐσία, or being is communicable but the ὑπόσασις or Substance is incommunicable;[10] But the very arrant Nonsense of such cleaving of Atoms appears in this, That my Substance is as communicable as my Being, & this as incommunicable as that; for how can my being be communicated &

my Substance incommunicated. Never scorn Transubstantiation[11] while thou canst call this a Foundation, & a Doctrine indispensible to Salvation. The confusion both ancient & modern Doctors have been brought into by their human Inquisitions after this Mystery, sufficiently proves, how much better it is to let it alone, for they do but fool themselves in meddling, & more in determining about things they are at last forced to say they do not understand.

For Satisfaction, Thou knowest, or ought to do, that it is a Form belonging to the Civil Law, was never read in Scripture; I have this to say, That the Friend took me right, namely that I chiefly opposed the Impossibility of God's otherwise pardoning, &c.[12] And thou showest great unacquaintance[13] with some late Writers, & such too, as go for no smal Divines, viz. D. Owen,[14] R. Fergeson,[15] & T. Vincent (at least the two first) that make this the only Reason, why I oppose all Satisfaction, because no Divine ever asserted the Impossibility, &c. & J. Owen assures thee, if thou wilt believe him, that Zarnonitius, Casmannus, Salinacius, Para'us, Piscator Lubartus, Lucius, Camero, Voetius, Amaraldus, Placa'us, Rivetus, Wala'us, Thysius Altingus, Maresius, Essenius, Arnoldus, Turretinus, Baxter, &c. went upon that very hypothesis that is by me oppugn'd,[16] & by thyself denyed. J. Owen in his Epist. to his Doctrine of the Trinity & Pers. & Satisf. of Christ.[17] He that would not have me mistaken on purpose to render his Charge against me just, whether it be so, or no, may see in my Apology for the *S. F. S.*[18] that I otherwise meant then I am charactered. In short, I say, both as to this & the other point of Justification, that Jesus Christ was a Sacrifice for Sin, that he was set forth to be a propitiation for the Sins of the whole World, to declare God's Righteousness for the Remission of Sins that are past, &c. to all that repented & had faith in his Son. Therein the Love of God appeared, that he declared his good Will, thereby to be reconciled, Christ bearing away the Sins that are past,[19] as the Scap Goat did of old,[20] not excluding inward Work; for till that is begun, none can be benefitted, though it is not the Work, but God's free Love that remits & blots out, of which the Death of Christ, & his sacrificing of himself was a most certain Declaration & Confirmation. In short, that declared Remission to all who believe & obey for the sins that are past, which is the first part of Christ's Work (as it is a Kings to pardon a Traiter before he advanceth him) & hitherto the Acquittance imputes a Righteousness (in as much as Men on true Repentance are reputed as clean of Guilt, as if they had never sinned) & thus far justified; But the compleating of this by the Working out of Sin inherent, must be by the Power & Spirit of Christ in the Heart, destroying the old Man & his Deeds, & bringing in the new & Everlasting Righteousness: So that I writ against, is such[21] as extended Christ's Death & Obedience; not to the first, but this second part of Justification; not the pacifying Conscience as to past Sin, but to compleat Salvation without clensing & purging from all filthiness of Flesh & Spirit by the internal Operation of his holy Power & Spirit. Concerning these two Points I refer thee to two Books written not long since by me, called, Quakerism a new Nickname for old Christianity; & Reason agt Railing; in which these Points are fully discussed; As also The Divinity of Christ writ by G. W.[22] Our Unhappiness hath been that our Enemies have charged their oblique Consequences from our Principles back upon us for our very Principles; As thus: If we say that the Scriptures are not able to [resist at?] Temptation, they will infer, That we deny the Scriptures to be any Means, whereby to resist Temptation. And if we say, That good Works are necessary, they teach that we hold good Works Meritorious. Lay this aside, & read us with a serious, unprejudic'd Mind, & I doubt not thou mayst yet be better satisfied of us. But if thou are not & thinkst it fit to tell the World so, remember, Thou wilt draw the Controversy upon thy own head, which will be assuredly undertaken, & closely followed by such of us as hope to acquit themselves by God's holy Assistance, with success to the Cause they defend. So wishing thy better Information of the Truth of God, & greater Moderation, yea, Love towards them that profess it, even the poor, despised Quakers, the Spiritual Christians of this Age (for your outside ones make but up refined Babylon, the Mother of all Abominations,[23] wch now deluge Christendom so called) I remain Thy friend ~~to Good work.~~

LBC. WP's Letterbook, 1667-1675, HSP. (*Micro.* 1:596). This letter was printed in *Works,* 1:164, with a few substantive variations, noted below.

1. John Collinges, D.D. (1623-1690) was a Presbyterian divine, controversialist, and author. He was apparently involved much less in controversy after the Restoration. *DNB.* There is no published exchange between him and WP.

2. Parliament was in session from 7 Jan. 1674 to 24 Feb. 1674, and in strong pursuit of papists. Any increased persecution of Roman Catholics would have repercussions for Friends. WP may also have continued to hope for a special bill to ease Protestant dissenters. See headnote to doc. 80, below.

3. Perhaps Collinges had preached a sermon attacking WP's theology.

4. Socinians were unitarians. This letter makes clear that in 1674 WP had the same convictions and intellectual difficulties with the concept of the Trinity as he had when he published *The Sandy Foundation Shaken* (London, 1668). See also the headnote to doc. 24 and docs. 25 and 26, above.

5. Paul of Samosata (3rd cent.) was a heretical bishop of Antioch, deposed for his teaching on the person of Christ. He taught that Christ differed only in degree from the prophets. Cross, *Christian Church.*

6. Macedonius (d. c. 362), deposed Bishop of Constantinople. He was a "Semi-Arian," and was believed to have denied the full Godhead of the Holy Ghost. Cross, *Christian Church.*

7. Little is known of Sabellius, who was probably a third-century theologian of Roman origin. Sabellianism is an alternative name for "Monarchianism," an early form of unitarianism. Cross, *Christian Church.* Barbour, *Church History,* 48:170, says that in this letter WP admitted that Friends were Sabellians.

8. *The Guide Mistaken, and Temporizing rebuked* (London, 1668); *Truth Exalted* (London, 1668); *Innocency with Her open Face* ([London], 1669).

9. That is, those of the schoolmen, or scholastic philosophers and theologians collectively. *OED.*

10. WP provides his own translations. The second of the two Greek words is correctly written ὑπόστασις, not ὑπόσασις.

11. Roman Catholic belief in the conversion of the substance of the bread and wine of the Eucharist into the substance of the body and blood of Christ. Rejection of a belief in transubstantiation was a part of the oath imposed in the Test Act of 1673. Cross, *Christian Church.*

12. In Christian theology, satisfaction generally refers to the payment of a penalty due to God on account of sin. WP objected to the doctrine, primarily on the grounds that it would make it "altogether impossible for God to remit or forgive without a Plenary Satisfaction." *The Sandy Foundation Shaken,* p. 16.

13. In *Works,* this reads "acquaintance," not "unacquaintance."

14. John Owen, D.D. (1616-1683), was a noted theologian, a nonconformist and congregationalist. Despite his dissent, he was held in general esteem because of his learning, his temperate tone, and the respect he gave his opponents. His works were voluminous. WP admired him. *DNB;* Peter Toon, ed., *The Correspondence of John Owen (1616-1683),* (Cambridge, 1970).

15. Robert Ferguson (d. 1714), was a Calvinist Scot, resident in England. He published *Justification onely upon a Satisfaction* (London, 1668), which brought friendship with Dr. Owen. His later career as a Whig, Rye House plotter, and rebel with Monmouth was colorful. He rebutted a tract by WP in *An Answer to Mr. Penn's Advice to the Church of England* (1668). *DNB.*

16. Opposed.

17. This is a rather tangled passage. The list of theologians is exactly the list cited by Owen, who said they all upheld the orthodox belief in satisfaction, and its corollary, "that Jesus Christ is therefore our Saviour, because he hath satisfied the justice of God, by which we being sinners deserved to be condemned for all our sins." See Thomas Russell, ed., *The Works of John Owen, D. D.* (London, 1826), 10:ccccclv-vi. Owen, in this epistle, had little to say about God's pardoning sinners without requiring satisfaction, although he appears to admit the possibility, p. ccccclvi.

18. That is, *Innocency with Her open Face.*

19. In *The Sandy Foundation Shaken,* WP had objected to "the vulgar doctrine of satisfaction, being dependent on the Second Person of the Trinity" or "that there was no other way by which God could obtain satisfaction, or save men, then by inflicting the penalty of infinite wrath and vengeance on Jesus Christ the Second Person of the Trinity, who for sins past, present, and to come, hath wholly born and paid it (whether for all or but some) to the offended infinite justice of his Father." *The Sandy Foundation Shaken,* p. 16. An excellent discussion of WP's ideas on justification is in Endy, pp. 175-80.

20. Lev. 16:8-10, 21-22.

21. In *Works* the word "doctrine" is inserted here.

22. *Quakerism A New Nick-Name for Old Christianity* ([London], 1672); *Reason against Railing And Truth against Fiction* ([London], 1673); and George Whitehead, *The Divinity of Christ, and Unity of the Three that bear Record in Heaven* (London, 1669).

23. Rev. 17:5.

77
FROM ROBERT BARCLAY

Urie[1] the 6th of the 1st
Month [March] 1673[/4]

Dear frind W: P

To whom is my deare and tender Love In the truth In which I also salute thee at this present with thy wiffe I have often remembred thee In a Sence of gods Love. who gathered us to be wittnesses for him the excelency of which high and glorious calling is to be prefered and prized before all the wisdome and glory of this world, In the sence whairof I truly rejoiced and was refreshed to feel thee In knowning how needfull it is for such of us who heretofore have had a Share In these things more then others to accompt them all as Losse and dung In respect of the crose of christ In which I travell[2] to be more and more exercised, that thereby every naturall gift and propertie maybe leavened and seasoned with the simplicitie of truth. I spok to thee of the papers of Sir Gideon Scot, who has writt In the defence of truth[3] which I have now ordered to be transcribed and sent to london to be Left for thee at Will Welsh when thou has perused them Let Isack Peningtone see them To whom & his wiffe is my dear Love, I have lately writt about a sheet by way to Theses directed to the clergie comprehending the principl[es] of truth In short propositiones,[4] which paper I may In a few dayes send to Thorntone[5] who is now at London from whom thou {may call for them}, frinds here think it may be of publick service, [illegible deletion] Truth this way prospers very much severall solid substantiall men are come among us within This month. which I know thou and other frinds will be willing to hear of, I should be glad as the lord maikes way for it to see thee In this natione for there is a great openess this way at present. So with my Love to all frinds with you I rest Thy frind

& brother In the Truth
R Barclay

Iff thou finds accesse at anytime to writt to me
Thou may direct thy letters by post for me to be
Left with David Falconar[6] merchant In Aberdeen

Scotland

ALS. Penn-Forbes Papers, HSP. (*Micro.* 1:605). Addressed: For | William Penn at his house In | Rickmunworth | Leav This with William Wels[h] | merchant In puding lane[7] | neer the bridge | London | Docketed: R. Barclay | 6 1st mo—73.

1. Robert Barclay (1648-1690), the chief Quaker theologian of the seventeenth century, lived at Urie (also Ury), an estate near Aberdeen. The son of a prominent Scottish soldier, he received an excellent classical education, became a Quaker about 1667, at the same time as WP, and by 1670 had begun writing in defense of his faith. Barclay first met WP in 1672 or 1673, and the two became close friends. They travelled together through Holland and Germany with George Fox in 1677, and Barclay was appointed governor of East New Jersey by WP and his fellow proprietors in 1683. Barclay is best known for his *Theologiae verae Christianae Apologia* (1676), published in English as *Apology for the True Christian Divinity* (1678), the first systematic defense of the Quaker faith and a work that did much to make Quakerism respectable in scholarly and intellectual circles. This letter is the first extant correspondence between Barclay and WP. *DNB*.

2. Travail or labor at. *OED*.

3. Sir Gideon Scott (c. 1620-1672?), of Highchester, Roxboroughshire, Scotland, a collateral ancestor of Sir Walter Scott, served as sheriff of Roxborough, represented the shire in the Scottish Parliament in 1650, and was knighted in 1660. He was one of the most important of the early Scottish Quakers. His manuscript writings were prob-

ably never published; there are no titles by him in Wing's *Short-Title Catalogue*. In London in June 1674, the Quaker leadership decided not print any works sent to them by Scottish Quakers unless the Scots agreed to take four hundred copies to defray the costs. Sir Gideon Scott's "papers" may well have been among the works that the meeting had in mind. *DNB*, under Sir Walter Scott; Joseph Foster, *Members of Parliament, Scotland* (London 1882), 304, 308; London Yearly Meeting, Minutes, 1672-1693, 16 June 1674, FLL (microfilm).

4. This was *Theses Theologicae* (London, 1675), one of Barclay's earliest systematic theological writings.

5. Samuel Thornton (d. 1685) of Hampsthwaite, Yorks., the Quaker leader and itinerant minister, is probably meant. WP had met him in Ireland in 1669; see doc. 35.

6. David Falconer, a young Scottish Quaker of good family, was a factor for David Barclay, the Apologist's father, and married a sister of Robert Barclay's wife. Braithwaite, *Second Period*, p. 338.

7. The street just east of London Bridge, where the great fire of 1666 began.

78
TO SQUIRE BOWLES

[1674]

To oppress an Innocent Man is so Unrighteous & Dishonourable, that who regards his own Reputation here, & the Judgment of Allmighty God hereafter, would never do it. How far thou[1] art concerned in such a kind of Proceedure (at least by the instigation of others) the story of Thomas Please sufficiently declares.[2] I was willing to let thee know what the King was pleased to say in a case of the like nature to a Justice, that lately disturbed some Meetings in or near Cambridgeshire.[3] The King askt him, By what Authority he gave those Dissenters that Disquiet; he answered, By the Laws. The King replyed, The Execution of them was by him suspended: And further gave this severe Rebuke; I thought, sayes he, There had been but One King in England. He dismist the Justice with this Sort of Entertainement, & I think, the Loss of his Justiceship, reputeing such busy Meddlers the greatest Enemies of his Interest; & the Peace of his Kingdom. 'Tis true, the Declaration is called in; but 'tis as true that the Parliament intended a more Legal & establisht Indulgence, which, though not accomplisht through the multiplicity of other Affaires, yet the Whole was left in the King's Bosom,[4] who has never since declared any dislike or Discontinuance of the Purport of his Declaration. Certainly, nothing but Prejudice, or detestable Avarice could induce any to put their Hands to such Unworthy Work. I do desire thee to let the poor Man have his Goods so Unchristianly & illegally taken from him, restored, or else we shall be necessitated to make our Complaint to the King, which shall be speedily & effectually done. We have been plunder'd & pilledged enough already. The King & Law are ready both to our just Protection & their severe Rebuke that so unhumanly overrun the Property & Priviledge of an Englishman.

I write this in Love to disswade, not to menace or enrage; & if it be received in the same Candor, it will have a good Issue, which I heartily desire, not only for my Friend's sake but thine: for indeed it is beneath the Spirit of a true Gentleman, as well as contrary to that of a true Christian to be at the back of an Ungodly Crew of illegal Informers.

Rickmers: 74 WP

LBC. WP's Letterbook, 1667-1675, HSP. (*Micro.* 1:591). Docketed in WP's hand: To one Sqr. Bowls. wilts.

1. Probably John Bowles (1622-1697) of Burcomb, Wilts., who was loyal to Charles during the Commonwealth, or one of his brothers. Burke's *Commoners* (1836), 1:693; *Nobility and Gentry,* p. 100; Richard Hoare, *The Modern History of South Wiltshire* (London, 1822-1837), 4 (pt.2):36; Maurice Fitch, ed., *Index to Wills Proved in the Prerogative Court of Canterbury, 1694-1700* (London, 1960), p. 47. It is unclear what act of persecution WP is complaining about. According to Besse (2:44), three Wiltshire Quakers had property distrained in 1673 in county court for nonpayment of tithes. Squire Bowles may have served on this court.

2. Thomas Please or Plaice of Edington, Somerset, was imprisoned in 1673 for attending meeting, fined £20, and had his goods distrained. Besse, 1:611; Bristol and Somerset Quaker Register, GSP. The relationship of this case to Bowles is not clear, but no other Thomas Please is mentioned in Besse, nor were there Quakers named Please in Wilts.

3. This incident has not been further identified. In 1671 WP had written at length about Justice Edward Partridge, who disturbed Quaker meetings at Littleport, Cambridgeshire. See doc. 65.

4. In Mar. 1673, after Charles II suspended the Declaration of Indulgence, Commons passed a bill for the relief of Protestant dissenters, but this bill suffered crippling amendments in Lords, and died when the king prorogued Parliament. Dissenters hoped that this bill would be revived and passed in a subsequent session. WP believed that Charles still favored toleration. Instead, the king abandoned the dissenters, and in Feb. 1675 the Privy Council called once again for the suppression of conventicles. Frank Bate, *The Declaration of Indulgence,* pp. 123-41.

79

TO J[OHN]. H[AWTREY?]. AND COMPANION

Rickm. the 31 of the 1st mo. called March: 1674.

To Justice H,[1]

Because you are Justices as well as Neighbours, & reputed Gentlemen; not only Civility, but duty engages me to govern meself with all due respect in this Epistle. Which, as it proceeds out of Love to your persons, & that hearty desire I have, your Actions may not fall short of that Courtesy, Naighbourhood, Conscience, & fundamental Law, that ~~it~~ {it} becomes every man, much more a Gentle-man, & he an English man, & a Justice too, but most of all a true Christian, to square himself by, rather then any sinister End. So I beseech you, give it yr perusal, & serious consideration; & then, if you please, afford me yr answer.

I offer'd, as you may remember, several things, to abate yr proceed with us at Ruslipe;[2] which then it did not please you to hear ~~of~~ enough to embrace. Perhaps a Reiteration may conduce more to yr Satisfaction; at least, it will acquit my Conscience: which, whatever you sayd, or think, is great of Value with me. And those, that have known me better, then you do; are not ignorant, how much I have been thought to stand in my own light, meerly to preserve that unblemisht.

I told you then, that since you affirmed, the report of this meeting to have reached you a month since (which I think, was at least a week ~~since~~ before any such thing was intended) it had been handsom & neighbourly, indeed but natural & just, to give us notice of yr Intentions. For in a County so quiet as this (as where is there now any disquiet?) who could have expected such a Sound or rock to strike upon? Men use to provide Land marks, [space] & such-like tokens for Caution, where danger is, to prevent it; We never heard you to be severe; on the contrary, moderate, men of more candor, ~~&~~ [space] then to express severity, or extend the Letter of the Law upon your Neighbours.

For what else, I beseech you, can I call yr sending for all, that should meet there, to appear before you, without any the least preceeding Intimation of yr displeasure? Again, the Constable could give no Evidence of a meeting, who left the people some in the house, some in the yard, some in the orchard, & severall walking in the highway: no more preach- or praying, then where no people were. When you came, those that the constable saw, were disperst; & had been near an hour we thought, the thing you only aimed at; finding some fire, that remained, either at some repast, or discourse very remote from a Conventicle to your own sence of the word. How fair an opportunity had you, to clear yr hands as Justices & Friends; nothing offensive to the Law in yr hands being present to you. Perhaps we expected to hear you, that you were glad to find the people gone; & that the occasion of any rigour to you unpleasant, was removed; with, it may be, some gentle Caution for the future: that you might quit yr selves, as {well like} men in Power, as kind Neighbours. But truly none of us I dare say, so much as conceiv'd one thought like yr Actions: not that I think them the harshest, that were ever shown; by no means: but exceeding our expectations; the circumstances consider'd, & the door, that was thereby open'd for you to ~~get~~{oe} out at: Especially, when you would not take our words to be gone; but after an untoward manner compelled us out. I further urg'd the general quiet of the Season; the unpleasantnes of these things to the king; his absolute renunciation of all such proceed; that his declaration was a great Instance: that though it be cancelled; yet not the Liberty: for the quarrel lay not against the Indulgence; but grant of it, formaliter: It was not by an Act of Parliamt & an ill president said the Parliamt:

I further added; that the Parliam^{t} had voted Indulgence to the Kings Dissenting Protestant Subjects; & intended to ratifie the former more firmly; at least to all Protestant Dissenters: & that such we are.

I intreat you, to peruse this short Discourse ag^{t} the Papists:[3] to say nothing of the Vast disparity & Antipathy of our Principles & Worship. To these latter Allegations you singly & joyntly answer'd; That the Act[4] was in force, by the Repeal, or Cancelling of the Declaration. True; strictly taken: But don't you know, that there be many Acts meer formally repeal'd, that obtain no force among us; but as much neglected, as if they were abrogated by new Laws? I much question, if that very Law, by which the Protestants were burnt for their Noble Testimonies ag^{t} Room,[5] were ever revoked.[6] This might be sufficient to you, That the King dis-likes it: that the Parliam^{t} declar'd their readiness to repeal the Law, that Countenanceth it: That all are quiet: That the Reason of the Law ceasing; the law, as to its Execution, should cease also: That the King & Counsil in the Preamble to the Declaration have disclaimed all Pretence to better Settlements by Severity upon Dissenters:[7] That you have Work enough to imploy y^{r}selves about, In First living; & then Executing all Laws, that recover & preserve morality, mercy, Justice, Sobriety, & godly living; And lastly, that you had nothing offensive to ~~your~~ {the} Law {before your} eyes ~~at~~, when you came amongst us.

I further urg'd Argumentum ad hominem,[8] the Kings Power in Ecclesiastical Matters: That, if you acknowledg'd him Head of the Church, it seem'd somew^{t} unnatural, that any members shaggle from the Judgm^{t} & divertion from the Head. It was answer'd by one of you; & the best thing sayd, That the King was Head in Civils too: Yet we would not for bear recovering a Debt by Law, though the King should interpose his Civil Headship to prevent receiving it: or words to that Purpose. I sayd then, & now more fully reply; The Case is Vastly differing upon y^{r} own Principles. The Civil ~~law~~ Government of England depends upon Law grounded upon Sincerity, the eternal Law: and its not by the Antient & fundamental Constitution allowable, that meum et Tuum[9] should be overrul'd by any Prince what ever. It is the Glory of the King of Englands Government, that he is a Prince by Right, not Might: by law, not Power. He has Power: but from & according to Law: not that he makes his will & Power Law. This Right is agreeable to human nature so called, & that oeconomy, which God has imprinted upon it. But in Matters Ecclesiastical you say (if old Protestants) That it is inherent to, & inseparable from the Civil Magistrate, so soon as he professeth Christ, to be the head of the Church in his Dominions (upon the strain of the Jewish story, how reasonable soever it be).[10] And upon this very foot was, & is the English Reformation sett; Where all original Compact, all Coronation-oaths, all fundamental law, & legislators too are layd aside. For the King is not Constituted Head of the Church {by common consent} of Lords & Commons, though thereby declared so; but by being a Christian King.

[blank] are but, where the Parliamt Party was in 41 & seen to exchange the Plea, the King must be only so head of the Church (say they), as that Lords & Commons should come in for a Chair;[11] thereby understanding the word, King, not to be his Natural, but Political Person: A distinction forbidden: yet I can see no reason, why you should condemn it in them at that time; & now urge it y^{r}selves.[12] For if I understand any thing, You wholly understand by Head of the Church, King, Lords, & Commons, which make up the Regal Power, or Political King. {# in fine}[13]

Again, I distinguish between Laws. Some are Fundamental; & those are durable, & indissolveable: some are ~~more~~ Circumstantial, & Superficial; & those be Alterable.[14] By the First I mean all those Laws, that Constitute the Antient Civil Government of England, & which make up these two words, English men. By the Latter I understand all Laws suited to State, or national Emergencies; which are pro tempore, & away: they live as long, as the reason of them lives; & then dye often times of themselves. These may be both Civil & Ecclesiastical. Civil, as they act ag^{t} trans-porting of Irish Cattle: a Famine repeals that, by the Antient Law-Maxime: Cessante ratione legis, cessat lex.[15] Ecclesiastical; as this in question. They that made it, had unity; peace & Plenty in their Eye~~s~~: We found upon Tryal, to increase animosities, disturb the peace, & lay waste honest & industrious Families. Thus much the King, whom you confess to be head of the Church, by the Advise of his privy Counsil, men doubtless wiser then any of us, has almost in so many words declared.

Further, let it be weighed, that we came not to our Liberties, & Properties by the Protestant Religion; their Date rises higher. Why then should a Non-Conformity to it purely conscientious deprive us of them? This or that sort of religion was not ~~Anti~~ specified in the Antient Civil Governmt; though the Clergy twisted into the Great Charter: Yet let it be considered, that it was not intended to deny others their Liberty of Conscience; but to secure their Church, Properties, & Revenues from the Kings Seisure. The nature of Body & Soul; Earth & Heaven; this World & that to come differs: their can be no reason to persecute any man in this World about any thing that belongs to the next. Who art thou (says Holy Scripture in this ~~place~~ {case}) that judges another Mans Servant? he must stand or fall to his Master, the Great God:[16] Let Tares & Wheat grow together till the great Harvest.[17] To call for fire from Heaven was no Part of Christs Religion; though the reproved Zeal of some of his Disciples: his sword is spiritual, like his Kingdom. Be pleas'd to remember, that Faith is the Gift of God; & what is not of faith, is sin. We must either be Hypocrites, in doing w^{t} we believe in our Consciences, we ought not to do; or forbearing, what we are fully persuaded, we ought to do. Either give us better Faith; or have us with such as we have: for it seems unreasonable in you to disturb us for this that we have; & yet be unable, to give us any other. O ye do not do to us, as you would be done by: Can it become Protestants to use that Severity to others, they once condemn'd in others. There can be no Pretense of Conscience for limiting other mens, that are Virtuous; & who wish you heartily well. Were we Immoral, or did our religion & worship border upon any impiety; we should blush to Apologize, as we doe: But being no ways conscious of any Affinity with immoral principles or practices; on the contrary, knowing ourselves to be better taught by Gods Grace, that leads to all moral & holy living, how ever different we may be in some particular perswasions; we do take confidence to remonstrate our Case, & so intreat yr serious Consideration of it; That we, yr Country men & neighbours may enjoy ourselves in the Worship of Allmightie God with Quietness, & Security. And I am well assured, it shall less repent you upon your Dying bed, to have acted moderatly, then severely. You can not but know, how fallible Protestants acknowledge themselves to be in Mttrs of Religion; & consequently, with what Caution they should proceed agt any about Religion. You also see, how much more destructive Vice & Intemperance are to Body & Soul; then meer Opinion: & Consquently, how much more reasonable it is, to punish the one; then prosecute the other. Think not, that meer perswasion Damns us; 'tis Sin, whose Wages is Death.[18] I love & honour all Virtuous Persons, that differ from me; & hope, God will have regard to every such one, according to sincerity. And however it shall please you deal with us, at this or any other Time; I pray, God forgive you; open your eyes; tender your hearts, & make you sensible, howmuch more moderation & Virtue are worth yr study, & pursuit; then the Disturbance of Religious- dissenting Assemblies: that, so far as I know of them, desire to honour the King, love their neighbours as themselves, & to do unto all men, as they would have all men do unto them.[19]

Be pleas'd, to Accept this in good part, & with the most favorable Construction, which becomes yr Quality, & is but to do Right to his Intention, that with good wishes for you subscribes himself—

Your Very True Friend
Wm Penn.

P. S. I have sent you a Discourse agt the Papists: & another, of Liberty of Conscience: severall 100s of which were presented to the House, that year it was printed.[20]

{#}[21] I could produce a Dosen presidents to confirm this; & truly, it looks hard upon yr own Principles, That you should give yr Servants Liberty to use their Discretion in Errands; or Constables in the Execution of their Trusts; provided, they Answer the main End, which is Voluntas Magistri, Salusq Regis et Populi.[22] Nay, that you can use sometimes a prerogative y^rselves, et relaxare legem:[23] remembring doubtless, that Summa Justitia (is) Summa Injuria (summum jus summa injuria)[24] as the Old King sayd; And yet, That you should not allow the King a Power to suspend the Execution of but a temporary Law, when the Execution of it is Impracticable, without destroying those very Ends, for which it was first made. I beseech you, call to mind the Antient Veneration of Protestants to Princes Prerogative in Ecclesiastiques,[25] & their Principles about it. In Reigns of H. 8. E: 6. Q E. K.J. & particularly KC. the 1st

LBC. WP's Letterbook, 1667-1675, HSP. (*Micro.* 1:608). Docketed in WP's hand: To J. H. & companion, Justices in Middlesex. The salutation is also in WP's hand. Several blank spaces in the text indicate that the clerk who transcribed this letter had trouble deciphering WP's handwriting.

1. Probably John Hawtrey (c. 1630-1682) of Ruislip and Pinner Hill, Middlx., a Cambridge graduate and a barrister. *Alumni Cantabrigienses; Nobility and Gentry,* p. 57; C. Harold Ridge, ed., *Index to Wills Proved in the Prerogative Court of Canterbury, 1676-1685* (London, 1948), p. 162.

2. Ruislip is a parish in Middlesex about five miles south of Rickmansworth. The confrontation between the Ruislip Quakers and the Middlesex magistrates, about which WP complains in this letter, is not recorded in Besse and has not been further identified.

3. *A Seasonable Caveat Against Popery* (1670). See WP's postscript, below.

4. The Conventicle Act of 1670. See doc. 59.

5. Rome.

6. WP refers to the reestablishment of church courts and restoration of former laws against heresy by the Marian Parliament of 1554. About 300 Protestants were put to death during Mary's reign. David H. Willson, *A History of England* (New York, 1967), p. 275.

7. In the introductory paragraph of the Declaration of Indulgence, Charles stated that "there is very little fruit of all these forcible courses" taken against dissenters since 1660. Frank Bate, *The Declaration of Indulgence,* p. 77.

8. Appealing to (Hawtrey's) personal prejudices.

9. My rights and yours.

10. Anglicans (in WP's term, "old Protestants") claimed that the King of England as Supreme Head of the Church exercises approximately the same ecclesiastical authority as the Jewish kings in the Old Testament.

11. "Share."

12. WP refers to the actions of the Long Parliament, which sought to restrict royal power over the Church of England. In 1641 Anglicans supported the royal prerogative; now, WP argues, in enforcing the penal laws rather than submitting to Charles' abrogated declaration, they are taking Parliament's side. Godfrey Davies, *The Early Stuarts, 1603-1660* (Oxford, 1959), pp. 117-26.

13. At this point WP means to insert the closing paragraph of his postscript. The preceding paragraph is not printed in *Works,* apparently because of the missing word or words at its beginning.

14. WP made the same distinction in *England's Present Interest Discovered* (1675).

15. When the reason for the law is removed, the enforcement of the law must end. The Irish Cattle Act of 1666 forbade the importing of Irish cattle into England, a protectionist measure designed to raise falling English rents. The act was frequently ignored, however, especially following the great London fire, and smuggling was common. Browning, *English Historical Documents,* p. 732; Richard Bagwell, *Ireland Under the Stuarts* (London, 1916), 3 vols., 3:71-77.

16. Rom. 14:4, adapted.

17. WP alludes to Matt. 13:30.

18. Rom. 6:23, adapted.

19. Matt. 7:12.

20. *A Seasonable Caveat* (see n. 3, above), and *The Great Case of Liberty of Conscience* (1670).

21. A marginal sign indicates that this paragraph should be inserted in the main text of the letter; see n. 13, above.

22. The wish of the magistrate and the welfare of the king and people.

23. To relax the law.

24. A too rigorous interpretation of the law is sometimes the greatest injustice.

25. Eccles. 8:2, "I counsel thee to keep the king's commandment, and that in regard of the oath of God."

80
TO CHARLES II

[1674]

Notwithstanding that it pleased the King by his Declaration to dispense with the present Execution of Ecclesiastical Penal Laws, & that the Parliament (though disgusted at the manner of granting that Liberty thereby procured to Dissenters) {ex}~~op~~prest their Likeing of a Tolleration to Dissenters, {&} that a Bill of ease was brought in, & lies now depending till the next setting of Parliament,[1] {yet} some Justices of the Peace in Sommersetshire have been very severe in the Revival & Prosecution of that Act which hath so long slept, nay have out done the sharpest parts of it, by most extrajudicial Procedings; as countenancing of perjured Persons to inform; fineing Persons that were never there; Levying fines without Warrants, (as inferiour Officers say) & that to the breaking open of Locks & Bolts, & take sometimes double, what the Fine itself amounts to; & such as are not able to answer them, send to Prison as Rioters.[2] Several Families are well nigh ruin'd; their Houses laid waste, & their Creditors disappointed of their Dues, though before sufficient to answer all

Particularly there is one H. Steer, Town Clark of Bridg Water,[3] an Uncivil, Envious & Persecuting Man, & as Runegades use to be, worse then all the Town beside. He us'd in O. Cromwell's dayes to be active, & read Proclamations against the King; now none more violent for him, (indeed, against him, & the good of his Kingdom)

One William Bull,[4] & Coll: Stawell,[5] Justices, are also furious to the Ruin of us: They have one or both not only suffer'd, nay encouraged such lewd Persons to act thus unrighteously towards us; But when we would find out the Names of the Informers, to the end they may be punisht for perjurers, in that they swear horrid falsities to be truths, they, or the Clarks withold the Records of Convictions, untill the very last Day of the Sessions, that we may be wronged without remedy.[6] We therefore, with all due Respect, do intreat, that we may have some Letter of check to such Persons, that they may not go unreproved ~~by~~ {of} Superiours, in Actions that not only defy the Kings Clemency, & his well known purpose of Liberty, but the wholesome

Laws of England that are both Jealous & Lawfull of the Property of Englishmen And if it be desired, we are able to produce & prove a long shedul of the illegal Proceedings of these Men.

W P.

LBC. WP's Letterbook, 1667-1675, HSP. (*Micro.* 1:588). Docketed in WP's hand: To the King Ch. 74.

1. The House of Commons had passed a "Bill of ease" for dissenters in Mar. 1673, which died in the Lords. See doc. 78, n. 4. Parliament did not resume action on this bill when it reconvened in Jan.-Feb. 1674, but WP hoped for passage in the next session.

2. WP described two of these incidents in *The Continued Cry of the Oppressed for Justice* (1675), pp. 11-12. Margery Osmond was fined by Justice Francis Pawlett in Somerset for attending a Quaker burial at which she was not present. For preaching at the same burial, John Anderton was fined twice: £20 in his own name, and £24 as the "unknown" preacher. The other incidents remain unidentified.

3. Humphrey Steare (d. 1693) of Bridgwater, Somerset. *Alumni Oxonienses,* 4:1416; Ridge, *Index to Wills . . . 1686-1693,* p. 263.

4. William Bull (d. 1676) of Shapwick, Somerset, justice of the peace under both Charles I and II. On 28 Mar. 1674 he had James Paple of Stawell, Somerset, imprisoned for not paying tithes. This suggests that WP's letter dates from after 28 Mar. 1674. John Collinson, *History and Antiquities of the County of Somerset* (Bath, 1791), 3:428; *Nobility and Gentry;* WP, *The Second Part of the Continued Cry of the Oppressed for Justice* (1676), p. 38.

5. Ralph Stawell (c. 1640-1689) of Cathelstone and Somerton, Somerset, son of a staunch adherent of Charles I, was deputy lieutenant for Somerset and colonel of a militia regiment. In 1675 he was made commissioner for recusants in Somerset, a sign of his loyalty and zeal in promoting the established church. Later he was sheriff and member of Parliament. In 1683 he was created Baron Stawell of Somerton. *Peerage,* 12:265-66; Collinson, *Somerset,* 3:251.

6. In the case of Margery Osmond, n. 2 above, the justice went through elaborate machinations to protect the informant from a confrontation with the accused. WP, *Continued Cry,* p. 11. For the Quakers' difficulties with informers, see Braithwaite, *Second Period,* pp. 78-9, 113, 125.

WORKING WITH GEORGE FOX

1674–1677

In 1674 WP turned thirty years old, but in most respects his life in his early thirties was much like that of the late twenties. He and Gulielma lived at Rickmansworth until late 1676, when they moved to a larger house at Warminghurst in Sussex. Their first child to survive infancy, Springett, was born in January 1675. As before, WP was much absorbed in a wide range of Quaker activities. The chief new development of the mid-1670s was that increasingly he became the trusted lieutenant of George Fox, the founder and leader of the Society of Friends.

Documents 81-82 and 84-86 deal primarily with WP's efforts to free Fox from Worcester prison. The Quaker leader had been arrested in Armscote, Worcester, on 17 December 1673 and sentenced to life imprisonment in July 1674 for refusing to take the oaths of allegiance and supremacy. The letters from August 1674 to January 1675 between Fox and WP illustrate the internal operation of the Society of Friends, as members cooperated or failed to cooperate in their strategies to lessen the effects of persecution. Their correspondence demonstrates the growing bond between the two leaders as they worked together to guide the development of Quakerism in the face of attack by government authorities, members of competing sects such as the Baptists and Presbyterians, and separatists among Friends themselves led by John Wilkinson and John Story.

WP, with other Friends, followed two courses of action to obtain Fox's liberty on terms that the Quaker leader could accept. The first plan, for which WP's connections at court were crucial, was to obtain a release from Charles II. This failed because the king would offer only a pardon; Fox would not accept this because it implied guilt. The second strategy was to appeal Fox's conviction on the basis of technical errors in the bill of indictment. This plan succeeded, and in February 1675 the judges of the King's Bench at Westminster quashed Fox's indictment and freed him by proclamation. Besse, 2:71-76; Fox, 2:265-310; Fox, *Journal* (London, 1709), 2:235-50.

81
FROM GEORGE FOX AND THOMAS LOWER

Worcester goale this 28th of the
6th moth [August] 1674

Deare w p:

To whome is my love, & to thy wiffe & Friends I heare trouble thee with another {letter} Inclosed from Mary lande; ~~& I desire thee~~ by wch thou maist see that an order upon recorde is entred in there assembly bookes: touchinge Freinds yea & nea Insteade of an oath: & they onely stay for an order for confirmation from the olde Baltamoore.[1] when thou goest to speake with him thou may take Sam: Groome[2] with thee: hee knowes the condition of Mary lande; & I desire thee to speake with Tho: moore[3] concerneinge that wch thee & I had in discourse touchinge the errors in the Indictment:[4] & thou gave me a hint, though I did not lay much stresse in the words: howe that J. Story & J: wilkison[5] were willinge to referr there matter to Go: W: & A: P [6] for they to make an end of the strife they have raised amongst Freinds: soe, lett them Judge in truth & righteousnesse: or it will be a fearfull thinge elsce; without respect of person or favor: {& I shall bee glad of it} & beginn with the originall Cause whether It was not my letter that I writt to preserve the unity {of truth} & glory of God. in the north when they first fledd[7] & the noice thereof fled over the nation {& there aunswer} ~~& also y~~ & therer shewinge it to the quarterly meetinge & soe lett them goe downe into the North & with those auncient ministers there with every thinge in order First matters of fact then matters of words lett It be examined togeather with all the partys to the differens that Joynes with them: & had they donne this before I Came into the lande: when they were both downe in the north & in the midst off them especially G: [W?]:[8] they had donne well: soe I shoulde be glad if they woulde take it upon them: & Judge righteously. & lett every thinge have Its Just weight measure & proportion: & when they have donn lett them draw upp an account of there Judgement: & recorde it in there book of there condemnation & Justification: that Coppys of it may be sent to the[m?] whome they have troubled. butt keepe this to thy selfe: & lett It not bee seene ~~but thou~~ except a service of the thinge goes on; but thou maist make use of the words: I shall write a few words to A: P: soe noe more butt my love: {I ausked T:l. to} writt this beinge weake & not able {to} ly in bedd ~~about two~~ {but risse about one} in the morninge: soe noe more butt my love to thee & Freinds

G: F:

Dear w:p:

I have beene with the high Sheriffe,[9] & undersheriffe to ~~Indeavor~~ obtaine from them the graunt of the priviledge of the townde[10] for my Father: {to bee in} whome I founde very loveinge & ready to Comply with our desires: butt that the undersheriffe feared: that some of the Justices woulde Call him in question for it: heereafter: seeinge such flockes of Quakers did resort to him: wch was tolerable whilst in prison: but woulde not when abroade or in townde for says hee they have sent one preacher to prison: & nowe they have a 100 Come into there Country: which vexes them to thinke: that truth is like to Increase: butt In discourse with him & others: I finde; that there Judgement is: that a writt of error: & an arrest of the Judgement or sentence of praemunire:[11] woulde undoe & overthrowe all this worke of theres; wch if soe woulde much more torment & plaugue them: then if my Father were freed from his praemunire by the kinges graunt: butt whether this be as secible as they speake it: I woulde desire thee to be well adviced therein: with some able Councell: before thou enter into the doeings any thinge therein: for if there be not a Certainety of overthroweinge there worke that way & soe bringinge my Father out of: prison over there heads; It were not wisedome to enter into it elsce: but if: upon advice with Councell: & mature consideration: It may be accomplished best: that way: then thou may proceede to effect it: as thou shallt be adviced: butt if not: then for Tho: moore ~~to try~~ {& thee}: to pursue the kinges former promise to him: to free [illegible deletion] {him} whensoever ~~I~~ hee was praemunired & thou maist assist him, & accompany him: in that worke: if you both Judge it fitt: My Father is still weakely & sicke: rather worse then better: & wants aire very much to refresh him: butt cannott gett downe staires & upp: hee is soe weake: Wee have sent to one of the Justices to day: Caled Sr Francis Russell:[12] to try whether wee Can gett him: & Coll: Sands[13] to Consent & Comply: with the Sheriffes grauntinge of him to be att some Freinds house in townde; wch if they will doe then the Sheriffe hath Promised to doe it: what will be the Issue of that endeavor wee leave to the Lorde: whoe turnes the hearts of men as best pleases him: soe desirenge an account from thee of what thou does: or Can doe: in this affaire; by the first opportunity: with the remenbrans off my mothers[14] mine & my Sisters[15] deare love unto thee: & Freinds I rest

Thy dearely & truely loveinge
Freind Thomas Lower

If Tho: moore be not In townde My Father woulde desire thee to ride over to Tho: Moores: & Informe him about the errors & what advice thou receives from Councell upon it: Coun: Stroude[16] was of Councell for us: upon his last removall: It might not be amisse to advice with him againe: Tho: Rudyarde Can Informe thee wch of the Stroudes it was:

AL (written and signed by Thomas Lower for George Fox and himself). Penn-Forbes Papers, HSP. (*Micro.* 1:632). Addressed: For William Penn these | leave this with: | att the signe of the hoode & scarffe | in bowe lane neere Cheape | syde these: | London. Docketed: G. Fox | 6mo 74.

1. Cecil Calvert, the second lord Baltimore (1606-1675), was granted the proprietorship of Maryland in 1632. Charles Calvert (1637-1715), Cecil's eldest surviving son, served as governor of Maryland under his father in 1661-1675, and shortly after this letter succeeded him as proprietor (see doc. 108).

Friends enjoyed considerable toleration in Maryland. Several Quakers served on county courts until 1678, when they rejected further appointments, and a disproportionately high number sat in the assembly between 1660 and 1689. Friends were fined for refusing militia service, however, and their abhorrence of oaths prevented them from administering estates. When the Maryland Quakers asked the assembly to accept affirmation in place of oaths in May 1674, the assembly referred the question to the proprietor, not knowing whether they had the "Power to alter the forme of the Oath Provided by the Lawes of England." Cecil Calvert did not approve, and Friends continued to petition for the change until 1688, when Charles, Lord Baltimore, exempted Friends from swearing. With the Revolution of 1689, oaths were required for all public offices, and Friends no longer participated in government on any level in colonial Maryland. *Peerage,* 1:393-94; Besse, 2:378-88; Lois Green Carr and David William Jordan, *Maryland's Revolution of Government, 1689-1692* (Ithaca, 1974), pp. 198, 212-13; David William Jordan, "Political Stability and the Emergence of a Native Elite in Maryland," *The Chesapeake in the Seventeenth Century: Essays on Anglo-American Society,* ed. Thad W. Tate and David L. Ammerman (Chapel Hill, N. C., 1979), p. 249; Kenneth L. Carroll, "Maryland Quakers in the Seventeenth Century," *Maryland Historical Magazine* 47:297-313; William Hand Browne, ed. *Archives of Maryland, Proceedings and Acts of the General Assembly of Maryland, April 1666-June 1676* (Baltimore, 1884), pp. 355-56.

2. Samuel Groom (d. c. 1684), mariner, of Stepney, Middlx., was a prominent Friend and served as correspondent to Virginia and Maryland for the London Meeting for Sufferings. In 1682, he purchased with WP and ten others the proprietorship of East New Jersey from the estate of Sir George Carteret, and in the same year was appointed surveyor-general and receiver-general of that province. John E. Pomfret, *The Province of East New Jersey, 1609-1702* (Princeton, 1962), pp. 130-31, 203.

3. Thomas Moore, J. P. of Hartswood near Reigate, Sur., was convinced of Quakerism by George Fox in 1655 and jailed in Southwark in 1663 and 1672, though he probably left the Friends before his death. He was able to use his acquaintance with Charles II and other high officials to help imprisoned Quakers, and tried to persuade the king to release Fox from Worcester prison in Aug. 1674. According to Moore, his efforts to obtain a release for Fox were frustrated because several other Friends — Gilbert Latey, Jane Woodcock, and Martha Fisher — had approached the king just a few days before and had accepted a decree that Fox could be released in order to regain his health but must post bond and could be recalled by the jailer or justices at their discretion. On 3 Sept. 1674, Moore wrote to Fox, saying that he would speak with WP as Fox requested, but thought that attempting to gain a release by pursuing errors in the indictment was unwise because the justices could simply tender another oath. Fox, 1:200, 435; 2:268-72, 296-304.

4. The bill of indictment against Fox, which was approved at the quarter sessions in Worcester in Apr. 1674, included mistakes concerning Fox's residence and the date on which he had refused the oath, as well as omitting reference to Fox as an English subject and reference to the king. Fox, 2:288-89.

5. John Wilkinson and John Story (d. 1681), both husbandmen from Westmorland in northwest England, were early Quaker "Publishers of Truth." They traveled together often, primarily in southern and western England, and in 1662 Wilkinson was imprisoned in Bristol for refusing to take an oath. Starting about 1672, the two Johns became increasingly alienated from George Fox, WP, and their allies. Fox accused them and other members of the Preston Patrick meeting in Westmorland of fleeing from persecution, and in turn Wilkinson and Story attacked several disciplinary procedures that had been recently established within the Society of Friends. See the headnote to doc. 91 concerning the controversy and schism that ensued. Norman Penney, ed., *The First Publishers of Truth* (London, 1907), pp. 256, 267-68; Besse, 1:43; Braithwaite, *Second Period,* pp. 295, 323.

6. George Whitehead and Alexander Parker.

7. Fled from persecution. According to the Kendal (or Westmorland) Quarterly Meeting minutes of 3 Apr. 1674, Fox asked members of that quarterly meeting to inquire into the weakness of Preston Patrick Friends in paying tithes and meeting in

the woods, so as to avoid being arrested or fined. He also asked several traveling ministers to question Wilkinson and Story about their dissenting beliefs. Braithwaite, *Second Period,* p. 296; William Rogers, *The Christian-Quaker* (1680), pt. 4, pp. 7-14. It has been argued that Fox provoked persecution in order to be more like the early Christians. In fact, Westmorland Friends had openly defied the new Conventicle Act in 1670 by meeting each Sunday "in force." Wilkinson and Story evidently refused to challenge local authorities in this way and, with many other Quakers, adopted strategies to avoid harassment, such as permitting vicars to take crops from their fields as tithes. See William Wayne Spurrier, "The Persecution of the Quakers in England: 1650-1714" (Ph.D. diss., University of North Carolina at Chapel Hill, 1976), quotation on p. 43.

8. The second initial is overwritten, and appears to be changed from *F* to *W.* From the context, Fox seems to be referring to George Whitehead.

9. Rowland Taylor was the sheriff of Worcester City in 1674. PRO, *List of Sheriffs for England and Wales, From the Earliest Times to A.D. 1831,* PRO Lists and Indexes No. 9 (1898; reprint ed., New York, 1963), p. 228.

10. Since his hearing before the King's Bench in London in Feb. 1674, Fox had been free on his own recognizance until praemunired in July. Edward Pittway (d. 1676) of Bengeworth, Worcs., who had been a magistrate of Evesham until he joined the Friends in 1655, also requested that Fox be given the liberty of the town. In response, Justice Henry Parker, of Worcester, who had first brought charges against Fox and who apparently was his most enthusiastic adversary in this case, in Oct. 1674 directed the jailer, John Harris, to do "What lawful Favour you can do, for the Benefit of the Air for his Health," but did not permit Fox's release. Besse, 2:71-76; Fox, 1:433; Fox, *Journal* (London, 1709), 2:247-48; *CSPD, 1673-1675,* p. 306.

11. The writ of *praemunire facias,* created by statutes passed in 1353, 1365, and 1393 to protect the power of the king vis-à-vis that of the pope, was originally designed to prevent English subjects from taking legal suits to Rome. Henry VIII, Elizabeth I, and James I extended the writ's jurisdiction, and under Charles II, Friends were praemunired for refusing to take the oaths of supremacy and allegiance; see doc. 41, n. 5. The penalty of praemunire was loss of the king's protection, forfeiture of estate, and imprisonment for life or at the king's pleasure. A writ of error, if technical mistakes were proved in Fox's indictment, could reverse this praemunire sentence. *OED;* Cross, *Christian Church;* Braithwaite, *Second Period,* pp. 14-15.

12. Sir Francis Russell (d. 1705), baronet, of Strensham, Worcs., was the son of Sir William Russell, who had been the royalist governor of Worcester during the Civil War. *VCH: Worcester,* 4:205, 456.

13. Colonel Samuel Sandys (d. 1685), M.P., of Ombersley, Worcs., was a strong royalist who governed Worcester during part of the Civil War. According to Fox, in a letter dated 17 Jan. 1674, "one Coll: Sands" sent a letter from London to some of the Worcester justices in support of Fox's release. *VCH: Worcester,* 2: 219, 238; 3:463; Fox, 2:269.

14. Margaret Fox.

15. Probably Susanna Fell (b. c. 1650), the sixth daughter of Thomas and Margaret Fell of Swarthmore, who stayed with her mother at Worcester during Fox's imprisonment (see doc. 83). She married William Ingram (c. 1640-1706), of London, in 1691, but left no children. Fox, 2:452; Fox, *Journal* (London, 1709), 2:244, 251.

16. George Stroud pleaded for Fox before the judges of the King's Bench in Jan. 1674. Fox, *Journal* (London, 1709), 2:232-33.

82
TO GEORGE FOX

5 7th [September 16]74

Dr: & worthely Beloved GF.
In the unalterable love of god, I salute thee, & my spirit visits thee, whom I Cannot but remember with all endeared Affection, {for} that

divine beutys sakc which the lord has shined upon thee, in this his glorious day & which Covers thee as a Garment, that waxes not old to that eye wch Can behold it. Dr: Georg, we gott that evening to Shipston, where we had a precious meeting & much people, the next day one at Banbury,[1] & the 4th evening at Bray Dawlys.[2] the next night I gott home; since then I have stirred In thy business;[3] & I find, that a person of some quality[4] has undertaken it, as wth the K.[5] who will not be known; so as to the K. he desires that none may move for 3 or 4 days more, till he sees wt may be done. As for T. M.[6] I perceive his interest is but flatt; & that the K. does not much like that he should come to him. but this is private. As for the errors, we have travill'd[7] in that also, & I forbear to Mention any thing yet about thos errors till I have taken more Counsellers mind. I love not to give encouragements wth out grounds. some have been Consulted, & they think that thou mayst be releas'd upon a writt of error, at last. more per next. The Baptists have in my & G. W.[8] absence gott a meeting, pronounced T Hicks innocent & reported that we knew of the meeting, but were afraid to meet them, after we had so heavily charg'd him.[9] so that the whole Citty are up against us. it was managed with much levity, & enmity. & all Coffe houses & such like publique places are filld wth the manor of it. o the wickedness of them, but it will turne for good in the end. & the shame of it will returne heavy on their heads. we think to challeng out the Bapts that have cleard T. H. as for J. S. & J. W.[10] they are much cryed up. such is the temper of our Town. the latter gone for Reading,[11] the former goes next secon-day. they talk of Comeing down to thee. Their carriage is smooth, & gaining; though I beleive, they like not those that are for them, yet now is not a time to show themselves. they are for womens meetings &c: {say some}. the lord god preserve peace in his church & a sound & plain heart in friends amen. my Dr: love to M. & S. & T. L.[12] my famely is pritty well. noe more at present.

Thy lover & honorer in Xt Jesus
London 5th 7bre 1674 WP.

ALS. Penn MSS, FLL. (*Micro.* 1:639). Addressed: To Edward Borne[13] in | Worcester | For G. F. Docketed: Will penns | letter to G: F: | 5 day 7 mo 1674.

1. WP had been visiting Fox in Worcester prison; the places he mentions here are on the route from Worcester to his home in Rickmansworth, Herts. Shipston-on-Stour was a market town in Warwick, about thirty miles southeast of Worcester. Banbury, approximately twelve miles east of Shipston, is a municipal borough on the Cherwell in Oxfordshire.

2. Bray D'Oyly (d. 1696) was a Quaker who lived in Adderbury West, Oxford, four miles south of Banbury. He was born before 1634, the son of John D'Oyly, and in 1656 succeeded his father in the manors of Brownes and St. Amonds. He joined WP in preparing a report on Friends' sufferings for Parliament, and he supported Fox against Story and Wilkinson. Fox, 2:446-47.

3. See headnote to doc. 81.

4. Probably Charles Sackville, Earl of Middlesex, whom WP describes in doc. 85

(1 Dec. 1674) as a "Great man" whose uncle had lately died and who had recently married. Middlesex married Mary, widow of Charles Berkeley, Earl of Falmouth, in June 1674, and his uncle died 26 Oct. 1674. In his undated "Account of my life since Convincement" (*Micro.* 6:208), WP wrote that he and William Mead approached the earl of Middlesex, who offered to speak to James, Duke of York, in their behalf. They obtained an audience with the duke, who said he opposed religious persecution and would take their case to the king. Charles Sackville (1638-1706) was the nephew of Lionel Cranfield, Earl of Middlesex, from whom he inherited his title and an estate of £3000 per year in 1674. Upon the death of his father, Richard Sackville, in 1677, Charles also became earl of Dorset. He was M. P. for East Grinstead (1661-1675), Gentleman of the Bedchamber (1669-1685), and envoy to Louis XIV of France in 1669. *Peerage,* 4:425-26; 8:691-92.

5. Charles II.

6. Thomas Moore.

7. Travailed or labored.

8. George Whitehead.

9. See headnote to doc. 83.

10. John Story and John Wilkinson (see headnote to doc. 91).

11. The monthly meeting in this town west of London was split over the Wilkinson-Story controversy by 1677. Several of the weightiest Friends supported the separatists and took control of the meetinghouse, while the majority remained allied to George Fox. The meeting did not reunite until 1716. Howard R. Smith, "The Wilkinson-Story Controversy in Reading," *JFHS* 1:57-61.

12. Margaret Fox, Susanna Fell, and Thomas Lower.

13. Dr. Edward Bourne (d. 1708), of Worcester, a Quaker who was imprisoned many times for attending Friends' meetings, refusing the oath, and speaking in public. He accompanied Fox on a religious visit in Worcester in 1655. Fox, 2:384; Besse, 2:37, 60, 65-70.

83
TO JOHN FALDO

In the autumn of 1674, while working to free George Fox, WP was embattled with the Independent preacher John Faldo and the Baptist Thomas Hicks. WP had been writing pamphlets in answer to the hostile tracts of both men since 1672 (see doc. 74). In them, he defended Friends' beliefs concerning the validity of the Scriptures, the humanity and resurrection of Christ, the afterlife, the sacraments, and the inner light.

The Baptists called a conference at their London meeting place, the Barbican, on 28 August 1674, to discuss Hicks' charges against Friends; WP and George Whitehead, who had collaborated on a pamphlet attacking Hicks, *Reason against Railing, and Truth against Fiction* (1673), could not attend. Faldo was there, however, and presented a list of thirteen charges against the Quakers, offering to debate. Faldo and WP then exchanged challenges, privately and in print, and WP suggested that Faldo speak at the conference scheduled by the Quakers and Baptists for 16 October 1674 at the Friends' Wheeler Street meetinghouse.

Faldo refused to attend, but the conference did take place, with Jeremy Ives, Thomas Hicks, and others speaking for the Baptists, and Whitehead, Stephen Crisp, WP, and George Keith taking the part of the Friends. (For charges made by WP and these other Quaker leaders against Hicks and his allies, see *Micro.* 1:638.) Faldo probably never met WP face to face, but their pamphlet war continued when Faldo reissued his original tract of 1672, *Quakerism no Christianity*, with a commendatory preface signed by twenty-one clerics (see doc. 85). WP responded with *A Just Rebuke* ([London?], 1674). These books inspired WP's encounters with two more illustrious divines, the Cambridge Platonist Henry More (doc. 90) and the eminent Presbyterian Richard Baxter (docs. 94-98). John Faldo discussed the latter stages of his controversy with WP in *XXI. divines . . . cleared* (1675). See also, Fox, 2:305-7, 455; Janney, p. 92; William Sewell, *The History of the Rise, Increase, and Progress, of the Christian People Called Quakers,* "new ed." (Philadelphia, 1832), 2:131-33.

[c. September 1674]

J Faldo.

I received a letter from Thee with a kind of nameless Challenge inclosed.[1] Just before it came, I had seen one at a Booksellers; but thought it not worth my notice; because any body might have pickd up such a Paper for Gain, out of the Contents of thy First Book Twice answerd.[2] But since thou ownst it; I shall give my Answer in Print.[3] For thy Letter, it is Civil; I wish, all thy Procedure has grated no more. I love, & shall at any time convenient embrace (God Assisting) a sober Discussion of Principles of Religion: for truly, I aime at nothing more, then Truths Tryumph; though in my own Abasement. But, First, most, if not all those things mention'd in thy Paper, are now in Controversy between T H.[4] & us. And I freely Consent, that thou shouldst engage us at the same Time, as Confederates in the same Work. Next, As to Personal Reflections, I know not what thou wouldst be at; nor how far thou extendst those Words. If only to meer Personal Criminations, not touching upon Principles, nor bespattering our Profession, I am content, they should be layd aside; at least for the Present. But since we are represented so ridiculous, & Impious by T H, yet but as Real Quakers; which is matter of Fact; & that we have so charged him; & that he, & his Abetters have engag'd to us to come next to that matter of Fact; wee do expect they should fulfil their Promiss: And it is our Present Resolution, to stick there. Our Charge was yesterday read; by that we will abide. No more, but good will to thee & all men.

Thy Friend
W P.

LBC. WP's Letterbook, 1667-1675, HSP. (*Micro.* 1:583).

1. After the 28 Aug. 1674 meeting at the Barbican, Faldo published his thirteen charges in *A Challenge* ([n.d.]), sending a copy to WP enclosed in a letter which has not survived. Joseph Smith, *Bibliotheca Anti-Quakeriana; or A Catalogue of Books Adverse to the Society of Friends* (London, 1873), p. 173; John Faldo, *XXI. divines . . . cleared* (1675).

2. In 1672, Faldo wrote *Quakerism no Christianity*. WP answered in 1673 with *Quakerism A New Nick-Name for Old Christianity* (see *Works*, 2:227-313). Faldo then defended his book, and WP answered again in 1673 in *The Invalidity of John Faldo's Vindication of his Book, called Quakerism No Christianity being a Rejoynder in Defence of the Answer* (see *Works*, 2:314-462).

3. WP did respond in *An Answer to John Faldo's printed Challenge* [(n.d.)]. Smith, *Bibliotheca Anti-Quakeriana*, p. 173.

4. Thomas Hicks.

84
FROM GEORGE FOX AND THOMAS LOWER

Worcester this 10th of the 8th moth [October] 1674

Deare William P:

I received thy letters: & another from Tho: Moore: wherein hee signifyes that It was thy desire hee shoulde be still: In moveinge the kinge as touching my release; thou beinge pretty confident: off effectinge of it by another ~~means~~ {hande}[1] & as for Mudd & his wiffe[2] I woulde not have them any ways Concerned {with them} for they are false: butt I desire thee to acquainte thy selfe with the Earle of ~~Shrewsberrys~~ {Salsburry} younger Son;[3] whoe Commands the troope that L[d] Fretwell[4] had the Commande off: whoe is much familiar with the duke of Munmuth:[5] hee was with mee heere to visitt mee In prison: & staied about two houres: hee tooke a Coppy of the errors In my Indictment: & is Convinced In his Judgement off the truth: hee goes often to bull & Mouth meetinge[6] & his lodgeinges Is In Bartholemew Close[7] hee is of a pretty naturall disposition: & knew thee formerly: It may be thou maist Informe thy selfe ~~by him~~ off some off the officers {of his troope} & troopers that quarters In the townde where thou lives:[8] & some other [illegible deletion] off them In Gilforde:[9] {where hee is} For I woulde have thee acquainte thy selfe with him upon truths account: & what ever other service may occasionally offer: It may be Improved as thou sees [m]eete: And soe If thou canst effect my release: without the title of a [par]don: thou maist: (Concerneinge w[ch] I have written to thee formerly) Soe I leave It to the orderinge of the Lords power & wisedome: & soe remenber my love to thy wiffe: & G: w: & A: P:[10] If In townde: & the rest off Freinds that enquires after mee: & to I: p: & his wiffe,[11] & R: R:[12] when thou sees them: & Th: Lawson[13] if that ways: & It might doe well: If Tho: L: & R: R: did sett upp a schoole In the Country neere London: For if thou didst discourse with Tho: L: thee wouldst understande farther: For I doe not understande that Friends at London Can aunswer R: R:s {way of teachinge} whoe is a man fitt to perfect scollars; rather then to pupill them: butt these thinges I shall leave to themselves: & soe noe more butt my love to thee: I am not very well to write butt my desire is you may be preserved In the power of God & In his seede: In wch dominion wisedome & life is:

G: F:

And keepe over all those contentious
spiritts with there disputes: wch are
men of Corrupt minds: whoe are out of the light life & power of Christ: that the prophetts & Apostles was in with It they all shoulde be Judged & kept out with the sharpe pointe of the sworde of the spiritt wch is as a hammer on the heads of them:
My mother[14] mine & my Sister Susans[15] deare love is remenbred unto thee, & thy wiffe & Freinds that may aske after us: & unto: G: W: & A: P: whose letter my Father received: last weeke

T: L:

AL (written and signed by Thomas Lower for George Fox and himself). Penn-Forbes Papers, HSP. (*Micro.* 1:648). Addressed: For William penn these | Leave this with philippe | Forde att the signe off | the hoode & scarffe | In bowe lane | neere Cheape syde | these | London. Docketed: G. Fox | 8mo 74.

1. See docs. 81 and 82.
2. Thomas and Ann Mudd. See doc. 74.
3. This aristocratic soldier cannot have been a son of James Cecil, third earl of Salisbury (d. 1683), who was married c. 1665 and whose eldest son was born c. 1666. He was possibly William Cecil, son of William, the second earl of Salisbury (d. 1668). *Peerage,* 11:407-9; Burke's *Peerage,* 2:2175; *CPSD, 1673-1675,* p. 133.
4. John Frescheville (c. 1607-1682), who became Baron Frescheville of Staveley, Derby, in 1665. He commanded a regiment of eight troops of horse for Charles I during the Civil War. Frescheville was governor of York and in charge of York Castle when Fox was imprisoned there briefly in 1665. *Peerage,* 5:578-79; Fox, 2:94, 399.
5. James Scott, Duke of Monmouth and Buccleuch (1649-1685), the illegitimate son of Charles II. He was acknowledged in 1663 by his father, whose marriage was childless, and given precedence over all dukes not of royal blood. In 1670, Monmouth became a privy councilor and, despite the opposition of the duke of York, was also made captain-general of all of the king's forces. He later allied with the Whigs, led an abortive rebellion against James II, and was executed in 1685. *DNB;* Ogg, *England in the Reign of Charles II,* 2:644-56.
6. The Bull and Mouth Meeting, also known as the City or London Meeting. The meeting took its name from an inn, known by the sign of the Bull and Mouth, in Aldersgate Street, which Friends secured in 1654 in order to have a place that would hold a large gathering. The building was destroyed in the Great Fire of 1666, but was rebuilt in 1671. Beck and Ball, pp. 134-44.
7. A narrow passage near the church of St. Bartholomew the Great in West Smithfield, or Farringdon Without, London. Cunningham, 1:55, 59.
8. Rickmansworth, Herts.
9. Guildford, in Surrey, twenty-eight miles southwest of London.
10. George Whitehead and Alexander Parker.
11. Isaac and Mary Penington.
12. Richard Richardson (c. 1623-1689), of Bishopsgate, London, was the joint author with WP of *A Treatise of Oaths* (1675). In 1679, he was schoolmaster in Wheeler Street, Spitalfield, and in 1681, with the death of Ellis Hookes, he became the salaried clerk of several Quaker committees and meetings. Fox, 2:498-99.
13. Thomas Lawson (1630-1691), educated at Cambridge and appointed minister at Rampside, Lancs., in 1649. He gave up his living after being convinced of Quakerism by

Fox in 1652 and opened a school in Great Strickland, Westm. Lawson was clerk of monthly meetings for many years, and had goods distrained for nonpayment of tithes. He was learned in Hebrew, Greek, and Latin, and was a noted botanist. *DNB;* Fox, 1:408; Besse, 2:24, 35.

14. Margaret Fox.

15. Susanna Fell.

85
TO GEORGE FOX

[1 December 1674]

Dr: G: F:

My fervent upright love salutes thee: thyn per post, & E. M.[1] I have. for thy business,[2] It becomes me not to say wt I have endeavour'd; but surely I have wth much diligence attempted to gett all done, as I Could desire, & I am yet resolv'd to make one push more about it; so that I cannot write a positive & Conclusive account till next 7th or 2d day, by wt time I hope to have an answear of this Great man.[3] his uncle lately died & left him 3000l per Ano & just married, wch did divert the matter.

I wrote Concerning the writt of error, that it must be receiv'd in open sessions, & the record of the Judgement certefied by the Clark, up to the Judges of the Kings Bench, & if then it appear that there is error to bear an habias Corpus, thou shalt have one:[4] I have ever thought that done in kindness; the King knows not that thou refusest a pardon; only that we chose rather a more clear & suitable way to thy innocency. I am & stay in town to doe my utmost. the Lord god knows I Could come in thy place to release thee; but the lords will be done. Dr: George, things are pritty quiet, & meetings very full & precious, & liveing, blessed be the lord god forever. J. Faldos book twice Answeard by me, is printed, or some think the remainder, unsold, bound up, wth an Epistle in faver of it subscrib'd by 21 Priests[5] as manton,[6] Baxter,[7] bates[8] &c: but it shall be their burden; they will repent them, when they know wt they have done.

As for the sufferings,[9] I have spoaken to G. W.[10] & they say, that there is not stock for such a work, that they have neither press nor materialls for such a Considerable worke, {& that} 1500,l will scarcely doe it for L. Ms.[11] I shall mind that; & Answear as well as I am able thy desires therein. Dr: George, My wife is well; & child,[12] only teeth, she has one Cutt. the name of the Everliveing lord god, be blessed & praised for his goodness & mercys for ever, saith my Soul, he is our blessed rock, the life, joy, & leng[th] of our days, the [illegible deletion] blessed portion of them that beleive & obey. my unchainge-able love flows to thee, Dr: George, & in it I salute thee, thy Dr. wife T. L. & S. F.[13] wth friends, I am

Thy true & Respt friend

Lond: 1st 10mo 1674 W Penn

ALS. Gibson MSS, FLL. (*Micro.* 1:668).

1. Edward Mann, who probably visited Fox at Worcester prison during Oct. or Nov. 1674 (see Fox, 2:305). "Thyn per post" probably refers to a letter to WP from George and Margaret Fox, dated 25 Nov. 1674 (*Micro.* 1:665).

2. See headnote to doc. 81.

3. Charles Sackville, Earl of Middlesex. See doc. 82, n. 4.

4. WP had earlier reported this to Fox in a letter dated 21 Nov. 1674 (*Micro.* 1:660).

5. The second edition of John Faldo's *Quakerism no Christianity*, published in Nov. 1674, had a commendatory preface written by twenty-one ministers. See headnote to doc. 83.

6. Thomas Manton, D.D. (1620-1677), a popular Presbyterian minister, was rector of St. Paul's, Covent Garden, London, from 1656 until 1662, when he resigned his living after passage of the Act of Uniformity. Thereafter he held services at his home in King Street, Covent Garden, until his congregation became too large and the meetings were held elsewhere. He was imprisoned for six months c. 1670. *DNB*.

7. Richard Baxter (1615-1691) was the most prominent Presbyterian divine in England. His endorsement of Faldo's book led to a confrontation with WP in Oct. 1675. See docs. 94-98.

8. William Bates, D.D. (1625-1699), also a Presbyterian, was vicar of St. Dunstan's-in-the-West, London, c. 1647-1662. With Manton and Baxter, Bates attempted but failed in the 1660s and 1670s to reach a compromise with the Anglican bishops; the three also presented, unsuccessfully, a petition to Charles II for "relief of nonconformists." *DNB*.

9. Beginning in 1660, Ellis Hookes, clerk to Friends, kept a record of Quaker sufferings, and many accounts of particular sufferings were printed. Fox evidently wanted a more systematic publication, and in keeping with his wishes it was decided at a conference on sufferings convened by the London Morning Meeting of Ministers on 18 Oct. 1675 to publish the entire collection. The Friends' intent was to present examples of harsh persecution to Parliament. In fact, however, systematic publication was delayed for many years, until Joseph Besse's abstracts appeared in 1733-1738, and his *A Collection of the Sufferings of the People called Quakers* in 1753. See Braithwaite, *Second Period*, pp. 282-85.

10. George Whitehead.

11. London meetings?

12. Margaret Penn. The first three children born to WP and his first wife Gulielma died in infancy. Gulielma Maria was born 23 Jan. 1673 and died less than two months later on 17 Mar. The Penn twins, William and Margaret were born 28 Feb. 1674; William died 15 May of the same year and Margaret died 24 Feb. 1675. Digest of Quaker Registers, Bucks, GSP; Peare, p. 162.

13. Margaret Fox, Thomas Lower, and Susanna Fell.

86
FROM GEORGE FOX

[11 January 1675]

Deare W: P:

To whome is my love & thy wiffe; & the rest of Freindes Will: Meade had a Copy of the inclosed wch hee shewed to the Lt of the Tower[1] & hee was very much affected with it: Soe thou & hee may make use of it as yee see occasion; for w: m: had a Coppy of it if hee has not

lost it; Soe noe more butt my love to him: & Margarett if in townde[2] & the rest of Freindes as though named
worcester prison this 11th of the 11th moth
1674 G F:
T: Ls:[3] deare love is unto thee & thy wiffe

What I Can say Insteade of the oath of Allegiance & supremacy:[4]

This I doe in the truth & presence of God declare; that Kinge Charles is lawfull Kinge of this Realme; & all other his dominions; & was brought in & sett upp kinge over this Realme by the power of God: & I have nothinge butt love & good will to him & all his subjects: & desires his prosperity & eternall goode And I doe utterly abhorr & deny the popes power & supremacy & all his superstitions & Idolatrous Inventions & affirme that hee hath noe power to absolve Sin: & I {abhor &} deny his murderinge of princes or other people by his plotts or contrivances & likewise all plotters & contrivers agst the Kinge or his subjects: Knowinge them to bee the workes of darknes & of an evill spiritt: & agst the peace of the kingdome: & nott from the spiritt of God the fruites of wch is love And I dare not take an oath; because it is forbidden by Christ; & the Apostle butt if I breake my yea or nea; then lett mee suffer the same penalty as them that breake there oaths:

From mee whoe desires the peace & eternall welfare off the kinge & his subjects:

George Fox

This was tenderd to the Judges before
I was praemunired:

And I was Cast into Darby dungeon & there kept six months: because I refused to take upp armes att worcester Fight agst Kinge Charles:[5] & alsoe I was carryed upp as a plotter to bringe in Kinge Charles: before Oliver Cromwell; by the presbyterians & Independants: & there kept prisoner a longe while;[6] & now this oath was tendred to mee in envy by one {Simpson a} turne-coate presbyterian:

AL (written and signed by Thomas Lower for George Fox). Penn-Forbes Papers, HSP. (*Micro.* 2:030). Addressed: For William pen these | Leave this att philippe | Fordes att the Signe | of the hoode & scarffe | in bowe Ally neere | Cheape syde to | bee sent or delivered | as abovesd | London. Docketed: G Fox's Declaration | Instead of an Oath | & his Letter—74.

1. Sir John Robinson.

2. Margaret Fox went to London sometime after 8 Oct. 1674 and, probably in company with Thomas Moore, spoke to Charles II. The king treated her kindly, but refused to free her husband except by pardon. Fox, 2:304; Fox, *Journal* (London, 1709), 2:248, 251.

3. Thomas Lower.

4. In Jan. 1674, Leonard Simpson, presiding justice of the Worcester quarter sessions, had tendered Fox the oaths of allegiance and supremacy, after evidence on the original charge for which he had been arrested (holding a conventicle) proved insufficient. Fox refused the oaths, defending his stand with the arguments that follow. A similar copy of this statement, written by Ellis Hookes and Thomas Lower and endorsed by Fox, is published in Fox's *Journal.* Fox, 2:272-73, 448; Besse, 2:73-74.

5. Fox refers to his imprisonment of 1650-1651 at Derby under the Blasphemy Act of Aug. 1650. While there, he was put into a dungeon because he refused a captaincy in the fight against Charles and the Scottish army at Worcester. Braithwaite, *Beginnings,* pp. 53-55; Fox, 1:11-14.

6. Fox was arrested on 11 Feb. 1655 after Cromwell was informed that Friends and royalists were conspiring to revolt. Fox was imprisoned at Leicester, and on 6 Mar. taken before the Protector, who accepted his assurance that Quakers abhorred violence and were not involved in any plots. Braithwaite, *Beginnings,* pp. 178-80; Fox, 1:166-68.

Five years after his return from Ireland, WP still maintained good relations with the Anglo-Irish nobility. Documents 87 and 88 concern Roger Boyle, Lord Broghill, who had aided WP in 1670. Broghill apparently wanted to buy the command of an Irish troop, and applied to WP for a loan with which to make the purchase. WP could not oblige, but he seems to have found a lender with whom Broghill could deal.

87
FROM LORD BROGHILL

Satturday Morneing. [c. April 1675]

Mr Penn,

I know nott what to say to you, for the trouble I have given you; more then the assurance itt alwayes shall bee acknowledged; & the returne of a thousand thanks for y^r Conscarne for mee; wch I am Confidant hath nott bin small.

Had I acquaintance Enough In any man {of the Citty} (worth 500^l) to gett them to bee security I did nott doubte raiseing the money; butt my seldome being In England, & lesse frequenteing the Citty, is the occasion of my being unprovided of soe good a freind as may Att this time; advance that summ wch I can dispose off soe much to my advantage; considering whatt you have told mee of y^r condition-sion, t'would bee unkind In mee to desier that Kindeness from you; butt If you Could present mee soe to y^r freind[1] to Accept of Bond & Judgm^t from mee; I would Certainely bee punctuall; I doe nott doubt butt too bee as servissable to you In Ireland upon severall other accounts; butt however; you shall alwayes find mee really y^r freind; & willingly Espouse y^r Intrest; though the profitt of a Troope bee Conscciderable yett the Hon^r of such a Command In my owne Cuntry, would bee of more advantage to mee; I thinke I need nott presse you any more; butt If yr freind hath butt a smale proportion of faith hee may oblidge mee mightely; If you please I'll meete you any where about 12 of the clock In the Citty, & bring a Rentroole[2] of the Estate In England & Ireland settled on mee; (You know my fathers[3] hand well Enough to beleeve what I shall shew you to bee true) parte where of will come when itt plaseth God, the rest Is in the possession off

Yr humble servant Broghill

The bearer will find mee wth yr Answer;

ALS. Add. MS 40,856, BL. (Not filmed).

1. Apparently Edward Nelthorpe. See doc. 88, below.
2. Rent roll. Broghill means to assure his prospective creditor that he can meet his obligations.
3. Roger Boyle, Earl of Orrery. See docs. 18 and 19.

88
FROM LORD BROGHILL

April the 27th [16]75

Mr Pen,

I hope you doe nott take itt unkindely I have nott bin wth you soe oftne as I would have done of Late, butt you know (I suppose (& feare) too well by Experiance that who Ever hath buisenesse att Courte must waite both wth dilligance & Patiance as itt hath binn my Case these three months; Else had Certainely come to have returnd you thanks for yr Last Kindeness, wch I am mightely Troubled should bee so Ill requited; I have binn wth Mr Nelthorp[1] to prevent any Trouble happening to you upon my Account; wch I have done by Assureing him the paymt of the money Either this weeke or the Next; I wish itt may Lie In my power to returne this obligation; Noebody would serve you More readily & Cordially then

Yr: humble servant
Broghill

ALS. Penn-Forbes Papers, HSP. (*Micro.* 2:042). Docketed: Broghill | Ap 27. 75. Addressed: For My Esteemed freind Mr. | William Penn att the signe | of the blew anker In Hanshaw- | Streete | London.

1. Probably Edward Nelthorpe, a London banker and wine merchant who supplied the Royal Navy. In 1673 he and his partners received a prize of £10,000 for delivering four Dutch trading ships to the king. In 1676 he was disqualified as a member of the London Common Council when his partnership went bankrupt. WP may have known him through his connection with the Navy. *CSPD, 1672*, p. 61; *CSPD, 1676-1677*, pp. 22, 450; *Calendar of Treasury Books, 1672-1675* (London, 1909), p. 773.

89
TO WILLIAM BURROUGHS

[c. 1675]

W. Burroughs,[1]
Its no Wonder, that a Priest should speak ill of me: but that he should heap up the foulest lyes, & most infamous Slanders, inventable ag^{t} Innocency; & all this unprovokt to, justly surprises me. Thy religious Letters[2] had imprest another Character of thee on my Mind: and I never mentioned thee with Dis-respect, much less insinuated any the least Scandal ag^{t} thee. The E. of Devonshire Steward[3], who I hear, was with thee, heard no such Language of me in Discourse of Thee. What,[4] if it were a Report? Is he a Christian (much les Christs minister) That shall propagate Things of so tender {a} Concern to Reputation; (especially, where there is a Pretence to an higher Point of Vertue, then Ordinary.) unless he knew it to be true. What sordid Envy, what wretched malice is this! God, that lives for ever, will avenge my Cause. Thou a minister of Christ? that art so far from loving thy Neighbour as thyselfe, that thou traducest,[5] & defamest an innocent Neighbour without a Cause. And then to suggest this to Persons, that believed well of me; on Purpose, to defile their minds with foul & false Apprehensions. If thou dost not retract this base, inhospitable & unjust Practice; I shall make my Complaint to those superiors, that have Power & Will enough to punish such Insolence. For the Earl of Middlesex[6] I am going to him, thou shalt suddainly know the Effect of our Acquaintance: who, before he would have treated me at this undecent, yea rude & barbarous Rate, would have denyed his Honour; as thou hast done thy Religion.

For the Impunity, thou tellest me of, I enjoy none: for I offend no Law of God Cognisable before men. I do honeste vivere, alterum non laedere, & suum cuig[7] tribuere. If thou meanest, that I am punishable for my Conscience; I have been, & may again, molested, when such men of Quality, as thyself, shall turn Informers.

But I hereby offer thee a Meeting,[8] wherein I will undertake to prove, that thou art a greater Transgressour of Christs Law, in what thou hast done to me, then I am for a Conscientious Dissent. As if there were no Sin, but that of not Coming to hear such Insolent Persons, as thou art. Wm Burr: were Wm Penn a Lover of this Worlds Glory, & sought it; his Figure in the World would have had other Language from thee. A gilt Coach, & a Title, being a sort of Calf, such as thou art, uses to worship:[9] but a Generous Mind in an Age so debauchd, would value retired virtue, & self-denyal, though Dissenting; & not abuse it. Nay, a wise man would never attaque in those Tearms; that he knowes, the dayly Impietys of too many of his own Gang furnish with invincible matter against him. But Ignorance is the frequent Companion of Malice. I have no more, but to wish thy Repentance, & better Information; that if thou canst not live like a Christian-minister; at least observe the Decency of a sober Heathen; whose Morals are a Reproof to thy Actions. I expect a Line or two, if thou pleasest; if not, I shall Act in the Matter, as becomes a Just Man, & one, that is in the midst of thy Unhandsomnes to thee a Friend—

Wm Penn

I have only this to Add, that what ever I was, I am redeemed from the reigning Evils of this World; & the Days of my Vanity Character'd me more a Son of the Church, then these of my greater Sobriety: which is no Reputation {in}to it in my Opinion. But this know, & an hundred Persons living not of my present Perswasion; yet sober, & of Qualitie, & Credit, will testifie, that from 13 years of Age I have been a sedulous Pursuer after Religion; & of a retired Temper; which never sufferd but one Intermission to please my Relations, & that was no farther then Finery, & Gayty.[10] Make what Use hereof thou wilt; God will Judge us Both.

WP.

LBC. WP's Letterbook, 1667-1675, HSP. (*Micro.* 1:567). Superscribed in WP's hand: To Wm B. parson of Chanys.

1. The "urroughs" was struck through by WP. William Burroughs was the Anglican parson of Chenies, a parish four miles northwest of Rickmansworth. This may have been the same Burroughs who wrote *An Account of the Blessed Trinity,* republished in London in 1694. *VCH: Buckinghamshire,* 3:199-203; Wing, *Short-Title Catalogue,* 2d ed., vol. 1.

2. Burroughs' religious letters, if ever published, have not been identified.

3. WP probably means "the Earl of Devonshire's steward." William Cavendish (1617-1684), third earl of Devonshire, had his principal seat in Derbyshire, but he also owned the manor of Latimer, two miles northwest of Chenies, which his steward probably was visiting. WP perhaps knew the earl through his son, William, Lord Cavendish (1641-1707), the future fourth earl and first duke of Devonshire, who had fought in the battle of Lowestoft in 1665, and who, like WP, would become deeply involved in Whig politics in 1679. Burke's *Peerage; DNB; VCH: Buckinghamshire,* 3:209; and doc. 129 below.

4. This comma was struck out by a later hand.

5. This comma was added by a later hand.

6. For Charles Sackville, Earl of Middlesex, see doc. 82. While the vicarage at Chenies was in the gift of the earl of Bedford, whom WP does not appear to have known well, Sackville's tolerant views were congruent with those of the Presbyterian Bedfords, and his family had roots in Bucks. and was distantly related to the Bedfords. This made Sackville a logical choice to bring WP's complaint against Burroughs. *DNB;* Burke's *Peerage;* WP, "Account of my life since Convincement" [1689?], *Micro.* 6:208; *VCH: Buckinghamshire,* 3:39-41, 202, 329, 453, 455.

7. "Cuig" is probably written for "quique." The phrase, which WP has paraphrased from repeated passages in Cicero's *De Officiis,* may be translated "I live honorably, do no harm to others, and give to each his due." Translation by Prof. Robert E. A. Palmer, Dept. of Classical Studies, University of Pennsylvania.

8. No record of this meeting has been found.

9. See Exod. 32:1-6.

10. See docs. 3-6, above; and Pepys, 30 Aug., 5, 14 Sept. 1664, which place WP's years of "Finery and Gayty" about 1664-1665.

90
FROM HENRY MORE

This long and learned letter from the eminent theologian Henry More to WP is of interest on several grounds. First, it makes clear why even liberal churchmen, and dissenters, thought that the Quakers' total rejection of baptism and communion was Biblically unjustified. Perhaps more important, it shows the difficulty most Christians had in understanding the Quakers' greatly-reduced emphasis upon Christ as a divine entity distinct from, yet of the same nature as, God. Finally, More's letter reminds us that as late as the 1670s, Quakers were still widely identified as the lineal descendants, or at least the close relations, of one of the most extreme dissenting sects of the 1650s, the Familists, and were seen as dangerous radicals by Englishmen of a wide variety of religious views. More's disagreements with and suspicions of the Quakers are especially interesting in light of his own theological liberalism, which was, by the 1670s, leading him to approve several aspects of Quaker belief.

This letter also introduces the reader to a number of learned, religious, and philosophical persons whom WP was coming to know well in the 1670s: George Keith (see docs. 101, 109, and 119), Lady Conway (doc. 101), Francis Van Helmont, and Princess Elizabeth (doc. 119).

[22 May 1675]

S^r^

I[1] have had this long time an intention to write to you, but having this more then ordinarie fitt opportunity of sending, I could now no longer forbear. It is to thank you for your visit att my lodging in Pauls Churchyard,[2] when I was last at London, though I had not the happinesse then to be there, and for your kinde intention of writing to me and sending me some bookes. But that you did neither, I conceive was because you might be afterward informed, that I had bought the very bookes, that you intended to send me (and it was an omission in Mr Kettilby that he did not informe you so at his shop)[3] and so the occasion of writing ceasing you forbore to write.

Indeed the meeting with the little Pamphlett of yours newly come out, wherein some twenty and odd learned and Reverend Divines are concerned,[4] I had the curiosity to buy it and read it; and though I wish there were no occasion of these controversies and contests betwixt those that have left the Church of Rome, yett I found such a tast both of witt and seriousnesse in that Pamphlett, and the argument, that it was about, so weighty, that I was resolved to buy all of J:

Faldo['s] and all of yours touching that subject.[5] But before that little Pamphlett I never mett wth any of your writings. But was the more encouraged to read them, when I mett with them, by a question G. K.[6] putt to me, when he was with me at my chamber in Cambridge. For I taking the liberty of commending his Immediate Revelation,[7] as the best book, I had mett wth amongst the writings of the Quakers, he ingenuously and honestly asked me, Didst thou never read any thing of Will Penns? and I told {him} I had not. And then he gave that character of your writings, that invited me to buy that Pamphlett I mentioned above,[8] so soon as I mett wth it in London. But presently after G. K. had left Cambridge I had a strong instigation to read over againe his Immediate Revelation and made some Remarks upon the first part of it, wch, hoping to see him againe at Cambridge at his returne into Scotland, I intended to communicate to him, and spoke to W. B.[9] on purpose to signify to him, that I should bee glad to see him at his returne. But it seemes he was gone back, before W. B. was aware. And therefore I have sent those very Remarks inclosed to you, hoping that you can convey them safe to him, wth a letter I have writt to him. But upon these occasions it was, that I had prevented your intended kindenesse of sending me those bookes. I mean those two agst J. Faldo,[10] and {hold} myself as much obliged for your good intention as if you had done it. And now I have perused them, I cannot but say thus much that I mett wth severall excellent passages in them, that are very expressive of a vigorous resentment and experience of what appartaines to life and Holinesse, and that I exceedingly rejoice, that the Quakers have emerged above that low beginning of an heartlesse and hopelesse Familisme,[11] that quitting the expectation of a glorious Immortality after this life, quitted also all dependence or relation to our Saviours person as man; beleeving his Soul as mortall as they do the rest, and that there is nothing surviving of him, but that light, that was ever and is common to all men, the eternall word, that lightens every man, that comes into the world. I must confesse, that I have ever an invi{n}cible suspicion, (so far as I can see) that this was the first state of the Quakers at the beginning of their ~~first~~ appearance. Touching wch, since I have said enough for the present in my Remarcks I have sent you, I shall give you no further trouble on this point. But being of this persuasion, you cannot imagine, how much I was pleased wth my converse wth G. K. who so freely and declaredly affirmed to me, that he, (and he putt in the rest of the Quakers) did heartily beleeve the History of the Gospell, or the literall sense thereof, as I finde you also express herein up and down, in your two bookes. And I am very glad that the Quakers have thus far (since for the present we can not gett them into the Church) two such able and faithfull guides, to keep them wthin the maine verges of Christianity And I hope according to the measure of their sincerity, the Quakers faith and practise will grow more ample and articulate, {till} they reach at last the full stature of Christ in the primitive and Apostolick times. And for the present I must confesse, that those charges that J. Faldo layes ag^st^ them (though I do little doubt but that they are all true ag^st^ the Familists, from whence the Quakers may sprung) yett the Quakers themselves, (if they be all of the same minde wth yourself and G. K) are free from the most and cheifest of them. And therefore so far as I can remember (for I have not J. Faldo here by me) the maine difference now betwixt you and your Antagonist is about Baptisme and the Lords Supper. In wch I must ingenuously confesse you seem to me to have given the least satisfaction. Your maine refuge, as I remember, is this, That neither Christ nor his Apostles instituted nor appointed either of these Sacraments, though Christ {celebrated} indeed the Lords Supper wth his disciples, and the Apostles practised baptizing of Beleevers. But neither are commanded or instituted by either.

But as for Baptisme, me thinks, there is an expresse Institution of it. Marc. 16.v.15.16. Go into all the world and preach the Gospell to every Creature, He that beleeves and is baptized, shall be saved, but he that beleeveth not shall be damned. The institution of water baptisme here is plainly implyed, because lesse stresse is layd upon it, then in beleeving. For he that beleeveth not shall be damned. But he does not say, he that is not baptized shall be damned. But if spirituall baptisme were he look't upon, merely and adaquately, wch is regeneration by the Spiritt, he that is not baptized would be certainly damnd. For he that has not the Spirit of Christ is none of his. Nay indeed the very beleeving that Jesus is the Lord and Christ, emplyes the party to be baptized wth the Spirit already, because no man can say that Jesus is the Lord, but by the Holy Ghost, wch is also answerable to that forme of speech, that calls baptisme Lavacrum Regenerationis,[12] intimating what is implyed in the baptisme of the Spiritt, namely our Regeneration, by wch we are {in}abled really and cordially to beleeve and professe that Jesus is the Lord and Christ, wch no man can do, but by the Holy Ghost. And therefore it is here sayd, he that beleeves and is baptized shall be saved, where if baptized were not water baptisme, but the baptisme of the Spirit, it were a Tautologie, whence it is reasonable to conclude, that baptizing there is for a signe of their inward baptisme of the Holy Ghost, wch they have partaked of, whereby they beleeve in the Lord Jesus, as also for a ceremonie of their admission into the congregation of beleevers. Accordingly as St. Peter argues. Acts. 20.47. Can any one forbid water, that these should not be baptized wch have received the Holy Ghost as well as wee. Nor was it needfull in the above cited place of Marck, that it should be sayd, he that beleeves and is baptized wth water, because the very baptizing emplyes so much, that being the usuall sense of the word with the Jewes, nor could our Saviour Christ but foresee, that they disciples would understand it so. W^ch^ is a signe it was also his own meaning. And the Disciples of John the Baptist (John. 3.26.) declares to him, how Jesus whom he bore witnesse to, baptized, and that all came to him. Wch certainly was wth water, and it was the ceremonie of the professing themselves the disciples of Jesus as appeares, John. 4.1. where Jesus is againe sayd πλείονος μαθητὰς ποιεῖν καὶ βαπτίζειν,[13] to make and baptize more disciples then John. Wch though it is sayd there he did it not in his own person, yett being he is sayd to do it, though he did it by others, it is plaine, that they did it by his institution or comission. And John does acknowledge to his own disciples, that Jesus made and baptized more disciples then he, and gives the reason of it, because he was the Messias to whom the gathering of the people should be, but that himself was onely the forerunner of him. etc. It is plaine therefore, that the making of disciples to Christ and entring them into his flock by water Baptisme is an institution of Christ.

And from this passage of John 4. v.1. where Christ is sayd πλείονας μαθητὰς ποιεῖν κὶ βαπτίζειν; to make and baptize more disciples then John, is most easily and naturally understood that precept Christ gives to his Apostles. Math. 28. Goe therefore, μαθητόνσατε [μαθετεύσατε, *or* μαθετούσατε?] i.e. μαθητας ποιεῖτε,[14] make disciples of all nations now promiscuously, as you did of Jews onely at first, baptizing them in the Name of the Father, Son and Holy Ghost. But as you baptized them wth water then to beare my name and to professe themselves my disciples, so now I enjoine the same Sacrament or Ceremonie, but wth a more explicit forme, In the Name of the Father, the Son and the Holy Ghost. Of the Father the Creatour and Originall of all, of the Son, that is the Messias or the Christ of God, in whom the Æternall logos[15] became man, and of the Holy Spiritt, by whose illumination and sanctification, all true Beleevers in the Messias (by virtue of their Regeneration through this Spiritt, wch the Messias promised, should perpetually assist his Church) become the Sons of God. This is the profession, that by the externall Ceremonie of water, all nations, that were converted to Christ were to be baptized into, and I think, no man will be so extravagant as to think, that this forme of words was used wthout the Ceremonie of water Baptisme accompanying it.

And there is no baptisme now that is available to mankinde but this, namely that one Baptisme, that is into this one faith, and one Lord the Christ of God the Father, who has promised all requisite aydes of his Spirit to them that rightly beleeve in him. And in this regard is it sayd there is but one Baptisme, because both the water Baptisme, and that of the Spirit signifyed thereby, terminate in this one point, that is, the profession of that one Faith and that one Lord, namely the Lord Christ, God and man, the Soul and body of the Messias being united wth the logos, and so continuing as a gracious and powerfull Intercessour for his Church with Father, for ever, according as he has promised, behold I am wth you to the End of the world.

But though this Baptisme be truely one in one respect, and that a maine one as I have declared, yett it is not absurd in another sense to say there are two, namely that of the Spirit and that of the water. Flaminis et Fluminis[16] as some have expressed it. And the Authour to the Hebrewes seemes to allude to some such thing. Chap. 6.[17] where he reckons amongst the first Rudiments or Principles of the Christian Religion, the doctrine of Baptismes, this water baptisme and that of the Spirit, plainly acknowledging two in this sense, that one is exteriour and elementary, the other spirituall and interiour, but they drive at one thing, as the sense of a word and the sound of a word, though two thinges, yett are counted one, they reaching at one and the same mark.

But that the Apostles might be the more able administratours of this concrete Baptisme. For any one can doe the Ceremonie of water, Christ promised them wthin a few dayes he would baptize them wth the Holy Ghost. Act. 1. 4. 5. so potent an Intercessour should they finde him with the Father. And that this therefore should be the difference betwixt Johns Baptisme and that his was mere water baptisme in a maner, but the Baptisme to be administred by Christs Apostles and disciples, though the exteriour was water, yett it should to all beleevers, be accompanyed wth the Baptisme of the Spiritt. Wch was accordingly in the Apostles time, even to miraculous gifts of the Spiritt. But that water-baptisme was {included} also in that command Matt. 28. besides those reasons above alledged, is methinkes extremely manifest to any indifferent man, in that the Apostles understood our Saviour in that sense, witnesse their practise. And that they should understand him amisse even after they had received the Holy Ghost is very reproachfull to them, if not to the Holy Spirit they received.

To all wch may be added, That the forme of words in Matthew plainly emply, That Baptisme was to be an externall signe of admission into the Church, and profession of the Authour and Finisher of their Faith, namely Christ, the Messias the Son of God in reference to whom, viz. this Son, the Father is mentioned as also the Spirit; His Illumination, Sanctification and Consolation, being promised by the Messias the Son of God to all beleevers in him. And that Baptisme is a forme of admission into the Church and profession of our Faith in Christ the Son of God, is apparent from Act. 10.48.[18] and other places. But Baptisme being more particularly and especially into the name of Christ, there called κύριος,[19] it is to be noted, that those that would lay aside baptisme, are such especially that would lay aside the Person of Christ, as the Familists do. I mean such a person of Christ as includes the Soul of the Messias in it, wch the Sadducisme[20] of the Familists can not admit. Whence the aversnesse of the Quakers from Baptisme, wch commemorates Christ the anointed of God (when as it is improper for the mere logos[21] to be anointed) seemes to me to be part of the reliques of Familisme in them. Else me thinkes, the Quakers standing so much for the Spirit (in wch they doe well and are highly to be commended for it) they should be in love wth that excellent forme of Baptisme, wch does so plainely make one part of our profession of Christianity, a declaring of our faith in Christ, for the promise of the Spirit, and the allmighty power thereof, for the destroying and mortifying all sin in us, and the renewing us into the glorious Image of the Son of God. So that he that does not beleeve this, may seeme in a maner to renounce his Baptisme. And therefore they lett goe a considerable advantage to oblige men to that wighty point of our Christian faith, and most effectuall for the drawing on that great designe of promoting life and Godlinesse in the world; by laying aside this forme of Baptisme.

And now for the Lords Supper that it was instituted by Christ and declared so to be by St Paul as well as the Evangelists Matthew, Marck, Luke, is evident out of the Scripture. For Matth. 26.v.26.27.[22] There Christ is sayd to break bread and to give it to the disciples and to say, Take eat this is my body, and to take the cup and to say, Drink you all of it, For this is my blood of the New Testament, wch is shed for many for the remission of sinnes. And againe Mark. 14.24. he there calles the cup, His blood of the New Testament, wch is shed for many. And the same in Luke. 22.v.19. This is my body, wch is given for you, and v.20. This cup is the New Testament in my blood wch is shed for you, where in the former verse, touching the breaking of bread, he addes. This doe in remembrance of mee. And lastly by St Paul. 1. Cor. c. 11. It is observable that he commends the Corinthians (in the beginning of the Chapter) for keeping the ordinances, as he had delivered them to them. τὰς παραδόσεις καθὼς παρέδωκεν ἀυτοῖς.[23] Of wch it is plaine, the celebrating the Lords Supper is one. v. 23. For I have received of the Lord what also I delivered to you, ὃ καὶ παρέδωκα ὑμίν.[24] Wch παράδοσις, ordinance or Tradition is this of celebrating the Lords Supper, and he sayes he received this Ordinance or Tradition from the Lord himself, that bread is to be broken and eaten as a signe of the body of Christ broken for us on the crosse. v. 24. and that we are to doe this in remembrance of him, that was thus bruised for our transgression and v. 25. the like he sayes of the cup. That it is the New Testament or New Covenant in his blood, wch he exhorts as often as Beleevers drink of, that they would doe it in Remembrance of him whose blood was shed. For v. 26. this is the end of the celebrating the Lords supper, that we may hereby annunciate to ourselves and all the world the endearing sufferings of our ever blessed Saviour, as the Apostle intimates, never antiquating it, till he come againe and appeare in glorie a~~nd~~ the last day; not in the form of a sinfull Malefactour on the Crosse, but as the glorious judge of the quick and the dead, as the Apostles creed professes,[25] wch is the most famous second coming of Christ and most celebrated in the Church. And to wch I do not at all doubt, but that of Acts. 1. 11. alludes. This same Jesus wch is taken up from you into Heaven shall so come in like maner, as ye have seen him go into Heaven, that is he shall come wth a visible personall appearance, and wth power and great glory. And that also of Hebr. 2.28. makes to this purpose. So Christ was once offered to bear the sins of many, (wch oblation and Passion of his we celebrate in the Lords supper) and unto them, that look for him shall he appeare the second time, wthout sin unto salvation,[26] that is to say, not in the forme of sinfull flesh, being made sin for us who knew no sin, that is being made חטאה, sin or sin offering;[27] but he will come as a glorious judge of the quick and the dead, and will then prove a Saviour to the utmost, changing our vile bodies into the similitude of his glorious body according to the working whereby he is able even to subdue all thinges unto himself. Philip. 3.20.21.

Now from all these places of Scripture me thinkes it is manifest, that the celebrating the Lords supper is an Institution from Christ himself, he intimating such reasons of it as are permanent, and continue so long as Christ shall have a Church upon Earth. For he saying Matth. 26. Drink you all of this, for this is my blood of the New Testament, or New Covenant, wch is shed for many for the remission of sins,[28] this blood of Christ being still in force for remission of sins, there remain~~ing~~s still the same reason of celebrating so great a benefitt. And the same may be sayd of th~~at~~e same passage in Marck.[29] And besides in Luke, c. 22. it is sayd, This is my body, wch is given for you, namely as a propitiatory sacrifice on the crosse, and straitway is added, This doe in remembrance of me,[30] that is of me who gave my body a sacrifice for you to propitiate the wrath of God, and procure remission of sins, and can this be a transient consideration and not continue as long as the Church on Earth, and remembrance is of thinges past not of thinges present, so that there is not the least pretense of laying aside the Lords Supper, it being a celebrating the endearing Passion of Christ past on the Crosse. And last that of St Paul. 1. Cor. 11. where he having commended the Corinthians for keeping the Ordinances or Traditions delivered to them by him, anon he mentions this ordinance of the Lords Supper, wch he declares he received from the Lord. Wch therefore must needs be obligatorie to them and to all succeeding generations after them. And the very forme of words emplyes so much. This is my body wch was broken for you, namely upon the Crosse, This doe in remembrance of me, that is of me that was crucifyed. And so of the Cup. This Cup is the New Covenant in my blood. And be sure you never forgett it is so, when ever you drink thereof, but be mindefull of me, who shed my blood for you, that is, dyed for you according as the Apostle interprets it. v. 26.[31] For as often as you eat this bread and drink this Cup καταγγέλλετε, you carry down the commemoration of the death of the Lord till his second coming:[32] to be understood out of the first of the Acts and the 9th of the Hebrewes above mentioned.[33] Certainly any one freed from all prejudice and præpossession of opinion, will easily acknowledge this to be the naturall sense of these places, touching the Lords Supper, and that the Institution thereof is grownded upon reasons immutable so long as Christ has a Church upon Earth. For the grounds in the Institution is the Passion of Christ on the Crosse at Jerusalem. This alone is mentioned in the Institution it self, and this we are commanded to comemorate, more then once or twice in the forecited Scriptures. And this is of huge importance for the exciting of our Love to Christ, and sincere kindenesse one to another. Nothing more usefull in all the Gospell: and therefore nothing lesse abrogable.[34] For the expresse grownd, alledged by Christ himself in the Evangelists, {and} by St Paul from Christ, in his Epistle to the Corinthians, of celebrating the Lords Supper, is not that it may be a Type of the body and blood of Christ in that sense Christ speakes of John. 6.[35] but that it may be a commemoration of his passion on the Crosse and of that endearing Love he showd to us there in suffering so shamefull and painefull a death for us. That we may thereby be even enforced, by an ingenuous sense of gratitude to be content to mortify our own lusts, be it never so painefull, and to adhere to our blessed Saviour by an unfeigned Love and also to {one} another, according as he himself has intimated. John. 15. Greater Love hath no man then this, that a man lay down his life for his friends. Ye are my frends if ye do whatsoever I command you. And, This is my commandement. That ye love one another as I have loved you:[36] I do in no wise deny, but that there is another Mysterie also included in the Lords Supper, wch takes in the body and blood of Christ, in that sense Christ speakes. John.6. that the bread and wine are also Types of the Celestiall Manna the Divine body of Christ and his Spirit, as I have more largely described in my Remarks on G.K. book,[37] wch also the office of the Communion, in our Church Liturgie wth great piety and judgement taketh in, wch insinuates such a spirituall participating of the body and blood of Christ, that we thereby dwell in Christ and Christ in us, that we be one wth Christ and Christ with us. But it is in the meane time abundantly evident, That the grownd and reason of the Institution of the Lords supper specifyed by Christ himself {at the instituting thereof, is the celebrating his passion, and therefore that ground still remaining, and besides an Institution of Christ being} being abrogable by no power lesse then Divine, It is Evident that the celebrating the Lords supper is not to be layd aside under pretense, that we have arrived to that wch in one sense is signifyed by the bread and wine, viz. the Divine body and Spirit of Christ. For besides that it is not at all absurd, that the signe and the thing signifyed, may continue together (as the Rainebow and the assurance of Gods promise he will never againe destroy the Earth by water)[38] that other grownd, upon wch alone the Lords supper was instituted, still remaines entire. Not to adde that wch I noted above, touching Baptisme, That Peters arguing was this, That because Beleevers had attained the thing therefore they should also receive the signe even Water-Baptisme.[39] And lastly whereas it is alledged, That we are not to celebrate the Lords supper in outward Elements of bread and wine any longer then till he come, namely in the Spirit. Here I demand what autority any one has to make such an exposition, wch is so groundlesse and unwarrantable. For it is agst all reason, to interprett it of any other coming of Christ but such as was notoriously known and received in the Church from the Apostles time to this very day, and of wch amongst other places, those two above cited Acts.1. Hebr. 9.[40] do witnesse. But for his coming in the Spirit it has been alwayes to all true Beleevers, ever since He left us with whom he has kept his promise, as being the faythfull Amen, that cannot lye. He has I say ever sent his Spirit to them to mortify, to sanctify, to regenerate, to comfort and guide them through out their life: But if this will be putt off, by saying it was not in that measure, as is hoped for and experienced by some in this Age. Even to this also it may be sayd: That they obtaine this measure but by degrees and must have time to grow to the highest, and in the meane time at least, the obligation, upon their own concessions, will lye upon them to celebrate the Lords supper in outward bread and wine, and being there will bee allwayes in the Church children as well as old men, this custome, even upon their own grownds must never cease in the Church for ever. Besides, that whatever becomes of their grownds, the grownds our Saviour himself instituted it upon remaine unshaken and unalterable.

Wherefore if I may speake freely wthout offense what I verily conceive to be true. This omission of the Lords supper by the Quakers, is part of that smutt of Familisme that still lyes upon them. For the coming of Christ in the Spirit wth the Familists, is nothing else, but a trick of Infidelity, as touching the personall offices of the Soul of the Messias, wch they think has perished with his body, as they phancy of all mens Soules else, and so being driven to Hobsons choice[41] (if I may use so mean a proverb in so high a matter) they must either professe a coming of Christ according to the Spirit inward onely, or no Christ at all. And therefore they labour hugely to bring back their religion beyond the incarnation of Christ and make it as old as Abraham or Adam himself. They acknowledging no other Christ, then what ever did and ever will inlighten every man that comes into the world. Wch cannot be understood of the Soul of the Messias, whose Incarnation, Passion, Resurrection etc. is the rise and Epocha of the Christian Religion. The Deniall whereof is the coming of Christ in the Spirit to them, and their acknowledging merely the eternall logos for Christ. W^ch yett is a contradiction in the very termes. For the eternall Logos is not the anointed as Christ signifyes, but the Anointer, he that imparts to us the unction of the Holy Spirit, that teacheth us all thinges. But it is this logos in conjunction wth the Divine Soul of the Messias incarnate of the Virgin Mary etc. that is the speciall object of our Christian Fayth, in wch all must beleeve that beleeve the Historie of the Gospell, wch the Familists doe not, and so quitt all relation or dependence on the person of Christ in the orthodox sense, and wholy boast of the coming of him in Spirit, out of a Spirit of Infidelity underneath. But the Quakers through the goodnesse of God having emerged to a greater and more sound measure of fayth, wrong themselves in retaining such thinges as are more naturall appendages to Familisme, then to their own present state and more pure Christian Profession.

But because so great stresse is layd upon that passage of John. 1. 9. The light that lightens every one that comes into the world: wch seeming to denote the eternall logos onely, beares the mindes of the Familists and too many of the Quakers too I feare so high, that they overlook the noble Soul of the Messias, as no part of the Object of their fayth; I will briefly here intimate what I conceive to be the genuine sense of the first part of that Chapter to the 14th verse; such as was suggested to me one night after the reading one of your bookes, having taken up my Greek Testament and impartially perusing this former part of this first Chapter a little before I went to bed; if happily there be any thing awaked in your Spirit, that will close wth what was so clearly and assuredly suggested to mine. W^ch I will briefly hint to you according to the order of the verses.

The Evangelist therefore having in his minde the Divinity of Christ as well as his Humanity, begins wth that first, and wth the four first verses describes the Trinity of the Godhead, under those three appellations of ὁ θεὸς, ὁ λόγος, and ἡ ζωὴ [42] wch answers to what occurrs in his generall Epistle,[43] when he sayes. There are three that beare record in Heaven, ὁ πατὴρ, ὁ λόγος, καὶ τὸ ἅγιον πνεῦμα the Father, the Word and the Holy Ghost. τὸ ἅγιον πνευμα[44] there answering to ἡ ζωὴ,[45] here in the Gospell, and indeed it allwayes seemed strange to me, that the Spirit was not here mentioned as well as the word. But here it occurrs under the name of ἡ ζωὴ, if it had been ψυχὴ[46] Amelius the Platonist might have had more evident occasion of that high asseveration of his Per Jovem barbarus iste cum nostro Platone sentit,[47] and of phansying the mysterie borrowed from him. But to show he had it from an higher and more Divine Fountaine. The Evangelist putts in the third place. ἡ ζωὴ not ψυχὴ, wch is by far the more true and proper expression, for that wch is ordinarily called the 3^d Hypostasis.[48] ψυχὴ emplying a body to actuate but not ζωὴ, and therefore ζωὴ may be eternall but not ψυχὴ, and is elswhere called the æternall Spirit. But this my intended Brevity will not suffer me to insist upon. In the meane time it is manifest that ἡ ζωὴ or the Life, is the same that the Holy Ghost. And thus far of the Deity as in it self. But in latter part of the 4th verse is breifly and in generall declared, that this Holy Ghost was and is τὸ φῶς τῶν ἀνθπώπων. that eminent light or illuminatour of singular and excellent men (for so τὸ and τῶν will by easy criticisme emply, those articles being used ordinarily to signify eminency) in all ages and places of the world; according as is declared thereof in the book of Wisedome,[49] chap. 7.22. For Wisedome there described the ancient Fathers understand of, the Logos or Divinity of Christ, and in her there is sayd to be φιλάνθρωπον πνεῦμα[50] (as here ἐν ἀυτῷ ἡ ζωὴ)[51] wch in all ages entring into Holy Soules maketh them friends of God and Prophets. v. 23. and 29. These singularly illuminated soules therefore become the lights of their respective Ages and Countryes, and are called Lights, as Christ told his disciples, they were the Lights of the world, and he sayes John the Baptist was a burning and a shining light.[52] And thus the minde of the Evangelist being engaged in the consideration of concrete lights, as I may may so speake, that is of noble illuminated Soules that have come into this world, he presently fixes on the most eminent example, namely the Soul of the Messias come into the flesh,[53] that most illustrious light promised of God to come in time, and declared by Simeon, to be the Light to lightens the Gentiles, and to be the glory of the people of Israël.[54] Upon this eminent light therefore the Evangelist fixing his minde considers wth himself the successe of his appearing, and therefore declares in the 5th verse.

That this eximious[55] concrete light, namely the Soul of the Messias come in the flesh, That this Light shines in darknesse (still present by the Historie of his life and personally present before his death) but the darknesse comprehended it not. i.e. few acknowldged him to be what he was, in so much that he wanted the testimonie of John the Bapist to awaken their slownesse of beleif. Nay some of them were more inclined to think John the Baptist might be the Messias rather then he, as appeares from v. 19. 20. 21.

That this is the genuine sense of this 5th verse, is manifest from the 6th. 7. and 8. verses. where it is plaine that John the Baptist is not compared wth the eternall logos but wth the visible person of Christ. He was not that light but he was to beare witnesse of that light, as he does v. 20. and apertly[56] tells the Messengers that he was not the Messias, but that Jesus was he v. 27. Wherefore it is a plaine case that the Soul of the Messias come in the flesh is the light mentioned in the 5th verse, and there is no question in the world, but that it is the same light that is mentioned in the 9th verse, because the light mentioned in the 5th and 9th verses is the same that is mentioned in the 8th wch light being compared wth John the Baptist must be Jesus the Messias.

This came into my minde wth that clearnesse and conviction, that

I could not resist it, though I was otherwise prejudiced agst it by our English Translation[57] and many other Translations, and by my own use of this place (either in private letters, or my publick writings) in a sense, that concerned the logos, not that complex of the logos and the Soul of the Messias together. And therefore looking upon the Greek Text I easily found the genuine and most proper and chief sense, and such as is coherent wth the context both foregoing and following to be this. Johns competitour namely Jesus the Messias, whom the Evangelist had so specially fixt[58] his minde, he was the true light, who being come into the world enlightens every man, as well Gentill as Jew, according as Simeon declares moved by the Holy Ghost, that the child:[59] Jesus was to be a light to lighten the Gentiles as well as the glory of the people of Israël. The Grammaticall consideration of this Text will beare this sense wth all imaginable easinesse, and the coherence of thinges necessarily requires it.

And hitherto Christ is described but onely as the most eminent Prophet that ever came into the world, that Prophet that the Lord their God should raise amongst the Jewes. Act. 3.22.

But the 5. following verses are of an higher straine, and give wittnesse to his Divinity, that he is θεάνθρωπος[60] God as well as man. Else how could the world be made by him, as it is sayd to be v. 10. even that world that knew him not. And his coming to his own, v. ii. may emply his speciall superintendency over the Jewes, before he took flesh. But then v. i2. i3. That as many of the Jewes or others as received him he should give them the opportunity and power of becoming the sons of God, by recovering the Divine Nativity and being borne againe of the incorruptible seed of the body and blood of the son of God, of wch he speakes John. 6.[61] that is, to be borne of the Divine body and to be enlivened of the ζωὴ of the λόγος,[62] or eternall Spirit, wch perfects regeneration to the Soules of the faythfull by operating on the Divine matter wch it unites to the Soul, and actuates the Soul through it, as the Spirit of Nature perfects naturall Generations, working on the common matter of the Universe, This is a power attributed to Christ or the Messias so great towards them that beleeve in him, that it must needs emply his Divinity also. And therefore it coherendly followes. v. 14. καὶ ὁ λόγος σάρξ ἐγένετο. For the word was made flesh (for καὶ[63] will easily signify for) that is, there being that strict union betwixt the Soul of the Messias and the logos the Soul of the Messias taking flesh, the logos is sayd to be incarnate also, though I will not trouble you wth Scholastick termes to expresse it, nor tire you out wth any further enlargement on this matter. You will easily perfect the rest yourself, if you can close wth the maine that I have hinted.

In the meane time it is very clear to me, That that true light mentioned vers. 9. is not (in the cheif sense and that wch will be coherent wth the context) to be understood of the mere logos, but of the Soul of the Messias incarnate and visible person of Christ, who being man as well as God must have an humane Soul as well as a body to be united to the logos. Wch Soul being still in being and in union wth the logos, as also wth its own glorious body, is our great High Priest and Intercessor for his Church with the Father in the Heavens for ever, and that the Christian religion properly so called does not loosen it self into so generall and lax tenure, as belonges to the times before Christ as well as after, but is circumscribed, and bounded by the appearance of the Soul of the Messias in the flesh. Nor does the logos enlighten every man that comes into the world, otherwise, then by having given them a naturall conscience, wch talent if it be well used, then the ζωὴ or æternall Spirit, or Holy Ghost as St John calls it in his Epistle, may further illuminate them, but this is the τὸ φῶς τῶν ἀνθρώπων, that supereminent light of singularly excellent men, in whatever ages of the world. But a gift common to all true Beleevers in Christ, accordingly as he has promised that he that beleeveth on him, out of his belly shall flow rivers of living water. John. 7.[64] But that every reproof of conscience for evill or motion to good, is the operation of the light of the logos, superadded to the light of naturall conscience; This 9th verse of John. 1. affords no co{u}ntenance to such {a} mistake in either Theologie or Philosophy, nor yett to overlook the humane nature of Christ, by pretending that every man is enlightened immediately by the Divine logos, wch were all one as to affirme, that every one is inspired by the Holy Ghost. But the right Apostolick Fayth is not incumbred wth any such needlesse Paradoxes.

But the maine thing of all that I would drive at is this, That the Soul of the Messias united wth the logos become incarnate or appearing in the flesh, is that supereminent and true light mentioned in 9th verse of the 1. St Johns Gospell, and is that universall light intended for all the world Jew and Gentile to be gathered to, who can be no otherwise a light in this sense, but by virtue of the Records and Historie of his life and doctrine, and of the lives and doctrine of his Apostles, whom he promised to be with and to guide into all truth by his intercession wth God the Father and the mission of the Holy Ghost. That this Christ above described is so supereminent and universall a light and such as all the world, as they have opportunity, ought to look after, is manifest even to the mere naturall man, upon the evidence of the History, that this man Jesus was borne of a Virgin, did stupendious miracles in his life, rose from the dead after he was crucifyed, ascended into Heaven visibly in the sight of his disciples, and by his intercession wth God the Father powred upon his disciples according to his promise in a miraculous maner the gift of the Holy Ghost. Wherefore even the mere naturall and unregenerate man is convincible from hence that Jesus is a worthy and safe guide to follow as being a so eminent a messenger sent from God. Of wch there is this notable usefulnesse, That those holy and heavenly precepts of our Saviour wch are even contrary to the naturall man, as self-deniall the unfeigned love of our enemies, and the like, though he have no inward Principle in him that can close wth these as convinced of the lovelinesse of them in themselves, yett by his common naturall reason is so convinced of the excellency of Christs person, and that we ought to follow the commands and guidance of so excellent a Teacher and infallibly inspired of God, that he findes himself obliged to obey these commandements as neare as he can, that is to abstene for the present (he being able to go no further) from the acts of revenge on his enemies, and from satisfying other appetities that are so strong and so dear to flesh and blood, though the lust themselves of pride, concupiscence and revenge, still remaine, and the externall obligation to the contrary as strongly urging. And thus being at a losse in himselfe, Jesus Christ the same yesterday and to day and for ever, that is for ever able and ready to procure the ayde of the Holy Spirit to all that call upon God in his name, if he call upon God the Father in fayth and sincerity, in the name of his Son the Lord Jesus Christ, for the Assistence of the Holy Spirit to Strengthen him agst all the assaults of sin, to mortify and eradicate all inordinate lusts, and to regenerate his Soul into the living Image of {Righteousnesse and true Holinesse} our blessed Saviour that cannot lye he has promised and he will procure it for him. If ye shall ask any thing in my name I will do it. John. 14.[65] And it is the very sense of our Baptisme, wch is the profession of our belief in Jesus Christ the Son of God, from whom he procures the assistence of the Holy Spirit to all them that believe in him.

But in the meane time it is very manifest of what use the doctrines of Christ and his Apostles are, and what obligation they ought to have in us, even before we reach the sense of their innate worthinesse and lovelinesse, by a principle of life wthin, upon the mere externall command of so divine and infallible Teacher as our Saviour. For there are three degrees of the Divine Law taking hold upon us and obliging, one is externall conviction, when we are indeed convinced we ought to follow such a command, but it is onely upon exteriour considerations, that is, from the excellency and infallibility of the person that commands it, and the feare of punishment or hope of reward, wch is competible[66] even to naturall men and unregenerate. The 2d is Internall Conviction, when we arrive to a discoverie, that there is an innate worthinesse Lovelinesse and Reasonablenesse in the commands of Christ, but yett this Conviction is more Imaginarie and rationall then substantiall and vitall, but is accompanyed it may be wth some Rudiments of reall Regeneration. But the 3d is not onely internall Conviction, that we ought to do or be so and so, as being the most perfect and lovely state, but that we finde it to be our naturall joy and pleasure, and the very life of our soul and fullest content of our heart, to be and do as our Saviour has prescribed unto us. Wch is the condition of an higher advance in real Regeneration, when the Spirit of Holinesse is to us, what our naturall Spirit was and we are made partakers to this degree of the Divine nature. Butt in all these degrees it is manifest, that the conviction and obligation lye upon us. And that the Scripture is both obligatorie and usefull to us, even in our first state, before experience and reall Regeneration, wch I thought worth the taking notice of, because if I mistake not some of the Quakers seem to speak to the contrarie, and so dishearten men from reading the Scripture till they be that allready that the Scripture drives at. If it be not a relick of the Familists, who are as affrayd of their Novices meddling wth Scripture {till} they be soundly tinctured wth the principles of their sect as the Romanists are. And indeed the impartiall sense of the the Scripture is even as much repugnant to the one as the other, wch makes them both conspire in the use of the same artifice. These few thinges were suggested to me upon my reading of your bookes agst J. Faldo, but since I came hither to Ragly,[67] I had the opportunity of looking againe into your No Crosse no Crown,[68] wch I look upon as a serious book and very pious and Christian in the maine, yett I question how consistent it is {in}[69] some points wth that generosity and freedome, and charity and kinde compleasancy that one would think did naturally accompanie a truely Christian Spirit. The great and Royall Law wch is to measure all our Christian actions by is, Thou shalt love the Lord thy God wth all thy heart and all thy Soul and thy neighbour as thyself.[70] And one point of our Love to {our}[71] neighbour, is not to give him offense but to comply wth him in thinges of an indifferent nature, as all thinges are that are not of their own nature evill, (and such are all those thinges that are what they are, or signify what they signify, by use and custome and not by nature) unlesse some Divine Law or the Law of our Superiours has bound us. But no Law neither Divine nor humane has bound us, but that we may say, You, to a single Person, nay custome wch is another nature, and Another Law, and from whence words derive their signification, has not onely made You, to signify as well singularly as plurally, (as the verb Love does, in I Love and we Love, when as the Latine sayes Ego amo, nos amamus) but has superadded a signification of a moderate respect used in the singular sense, as it has added to Thou, of the highest respect and reverence (for no man will You God, but use the pronoun Thou to him) or else of the greatest familiarity or contempt. So the proper use of You and Thou is settled by a long and universall custome. And wordes signifying nothing of themselves but as custome makes them, (whence Scripsimus and canimus or the like usually signify no more in Latine writers then scripsi and cano,[72] and the very Greek grammar explaines οἱ ἀμφὶ Σωκράτην.;[73] Socrates) there is not onely no intrinsick evill in the using them in that sense custome has put upon them, but a great deal of Christian kindenese and charity in taking heed how we give unnecessarie offense to our neighbour, by using such a word, as use has made significative of over much familiarity or contempt. Wch would be like the calling of a person of honesty and quality knave, because knave at first had no reproachfull signification.

This short hint is enough for a buisinesse of this nature.

And now for Cap-Honour, and Titular respects, the not complying in these thinges moderately and unaffectedly, methinks is lesse Christian. If the Apostles could comply with the Jewes in some Mosaicall Rites, that the coming of Christ had abrogated, that they might give no offense to the Jewes,[74] how much more ought Christians for the avoyding of offense comply with one another in such customes as no Law neither humane nor divine has yett abrogated: And such is Cap-Honour, and Titular respects. For the first is but a Theticall[75] expression, (and therefore of a nature indifferent) of that respect we beare to creatures of our own mould and shape (whose blood as it is not to be shed, so their persons are not to be slighted but to be respected. For in the Image of God made he man. Gen. 9.6.) and as the Turks bow to one another so we putt off our hatts, but they both signify the same thing, a kinde inclination and readinesse to serve one another. And as for Titles they are usually significative of either offices or orders and dignities in a Kingdome, and if there be these distinctions of orders and dignityes in the body Politick, why may there not be names to them, and if they have names, why may they not be called by them; And it is as naturall in a body Politick that there should be different ranks and orders of men, as in the naturall there should be of members. So that the slighting all these thinges must needs be a riddle to the sober. It is not a thing long to be insisted upon, and yett I cannot omitt to speak something of the places you alledge for the practise of the Quaker. The cheif are Matth. 23. v. 5.6.7.8.9.10.11.12. John 5.44. James 3.1. wch are alledged under Reason. XIII.

To that of Matthew I answer, the 5. 6. and 7. verses are no declaration agst Titles or orders and precedency, but agst the being of so vaine and proud a minde as to please themselves in them and affect them, wch is a signe of a vaine empty Spirit. In wch sense also the 8th verse is to be understood. But be not ye called Rabbi, that is do not affect that title, and pride yourselves in it, as the Scribes and Pharisees did. But this is not agst calling others Rabbi, Master or Doctour, but the being so called ourselves. And the wordes following in this verse, wch gives the reason of the precept, plainely insinuate that to be the sense. For one is your Master or you have one onely Master, καθηγητης, teacher or guide and that is Christ, and you are all brethren that is fellow followers or disciples of him, according as St Paul expresseth himself. Be ye followers of me as I am of Christ, so far and no further. Wch therefore seemes a Propheticall caution agst these infallible dictatours of new forged Articles and uselesse formes and opinions, wch Christ foresaw would sometime be brought into the Church, by them that would pretend to have power to obtrude upon mens[76] consciences such thinges as are not the teachings of Christ and his Gospell, but against expresse Scripture and the indeleble notions of Truth, that Christ the æternall logos has implanted in the soules of men. Wch Prophetick caution is farther carryed on in the very next verse, v.9. And call no man Father upon Earth (wch cannot be understood of Father in a civill or naturall sense, for then it would not be lawfull for a son to call his Father father) but that no Christian is to admit any one so to be his spirituall Father, as to give beleif to him or obey him in such instructions and comands, as are contrary to the instructions and commands of our Heavenly Father, the Father of Lights and Giver of every good and perfect gift. Nothing is more frequent in the mouthes of the Romish Laity to their Priest and Confessours then Mon Pere, My Father, who under pretense of this reverend Title are blindely led by them, into all superstition and Idolatry and are hindred from seeking the truth. And indeed the whole Christian world in a maner is oppressed and prejudiced by a superstitious awe[77] from the names and opinions of severall Ancient Writers, that have gott the Titles of fathers, whose autority must stop mens mouths and obstruct their free enquiry into truth, and our assent to it, evidenced by the clearest reason and Scripture, if any determination of these Fathers seeme to contradict it. But here we are forbid by our Saviour Christ in this sense to call any one Father upon Earth, and to give no ear to their Instructions and commands, no further then they agree wth the minde and will of our Heavenly Father, revealed to us by his Son Jesus Christ. The 10th verse is very like the 8th verse. But καθηγητὴς answering to Rabbi in the 8th verse and Rabbi signifying as well Magnas as Doctor or Magister, that it may not seeme a Tautologie, this is a Propheticall caution agst the affected grandure and Prince-linesse, that Christ foresaw would in time be affected in the Church. (where in the ordinary slight civility of calling Mr such a one and Mr such an one, I conceive is little concerned) intimating there ought to be no dignityes in the Church, but such as emplyed an office correspondently onerous and laborious, wch is emplyed in the 11th verse,[78] that he that ascends the highest in these dignityes, if he have them upon the due terms he ought to have them, he will thereby become the greatest servant and have the most laborious task of all. And the 12th is a Prophesy, of the downfall of the man of sin, who has so many yeares endevour'd onely the magnifying himself and exalting himself, but not the Kingdome of the Lord Jesus.

To John 5.44. How can ye believe that receive Honour one of another and seek not the Honour that cometh from God onely. To this I answer, That this concernes not Cap honour and Titular respects, but esteem and opinion the[79] had of one another, whereby they were bolstered up ag^st the Testimonies and witnessings of Christ. They would not confesse Christ nor entertaine him, because they loved the praise of men more then the praise of God. John. 12.43.[80]

As for that of James 3.1. My Brethren be not many Masters knowing that we shall receive the greater condemnation. The Greek has it μὴ πολλοὶ διδάσκαλοι γίνεσθε Be not many Teachers,[81] what doth this therefore respect, either Cap-honour or Titular respects. But is a sober monition, that men should {not} out of a rash self-conceit take upon them to be teachers of others, before they be fitt for such an employment. For in many thinges sayes he πτούομεν παντες,[82] we all offend or stumble like men in the dark, and he's a perfect man indeed that trips not in his tong,[83] and so he goes on discoursing of that instrument, showing what dangerous use there is of in setting {all} on ~~all~~[84] fire in shisme and dissension in the Church, and concludes wth an Encomium of that wisedome wch is from above that makes an able Teacher, that it is first pure, then peacable etc.

Those Scriptures alledged under Reason. XIV. and XV. are these 2. Sam. 14. 14. Acts 10.35.[85] Ephes. 6.9. Col. 3.25. James 2. v. 1.2. to the 11th vers. Job. 32.22. Revel. 22.8.9.

To the four first of these, there can be nothing concluded, but that God is no respecter of Persons, but rewards every own according to his work. But that he calles none by their Titles, or commands us so, is not true. For in one place he sayes, I sayd Ye are Gods,[86] wch is an high Title. And the word of the Lord to Jeremie[87] is: Cap. 13. 18. Say unto the King and to the Queen. But your most materiall place is that of James. 2. but yett nor does that reach the present controversie. For it is not ag^st Cap-honour, wch the rich ordinarily do to the poor as well as the poor to the rich, nor ag^st Titular respect, but ag^st an unrighteous rating and preferring a gaily deck't unbeliever, and that in an Holy assembly ἐὶς τὴν συναγωγὴν ὑμῶν,[88] before a poor brother rich in fayth. This is that προσωποληψία[89] condemned in verse 9th. That they will so industriously and wth such a deal a doe disturbe the congregation, for the preferring a man wth gay apparell and a gold ring on his finger, before a poor brother {rich in fayth, and an heire of the Kingdome of Heaven, and that in the time of Holy worship or of their Holy assembly, where a poor man rich in etc} rich in fayth, has so much the præeminence before him wth the gold ring and gay apparell. But abroad and on civill affaires, the case will be alter'd, if his civill quality answer to his clothes. This intimation shall suffice for that of St James. And as for Job. 32.22. For I know not to give flattering Titles, in so doeing my Maker would soon take me away. It is evident by the following chapter. That flattering Titles are not there the Titles of Master, S^r, and the like, but the Titles of Just of Innocent etc. wch Elihu out of conscience could not give to Job, as appeares, v. 12. Behold in this thou art not just etc. And lastly, as for Revel. 22. It is manifest it little concernes Hatt-honour, and

Titular-respects. For it was so profound a prostration of himself[90] John was about, and so near approaching to Divine worship, and that hight of humble affection wch we owe to God onely, that the Angel espying it in Johns countenance, forbad him to goe on in that intended worship, more fitt for God then any creature, and therefore he addes worship thou God. But what is this to Hatt-honour and Titular respects, calling S^{r} or M^{r}, or the like, and moving the hatt decently and unaffectedly.

Wherefore I conceive there is no grownd for in Scripture (as I am certaine there is not in reason) for this scrupulosity in the Quakers about Hatt-honour and Titular respects, though they may conscientiously behave themselves as they do out of ignorance and mistake, being, as I do vehemently suspect, abused into it, at the first by some enemies to the Reformation,[91] to make the upshot of it look as ugly and unpleasantly as they could, wch I will forbear to speake of here, having intimated enough in my Remarcks on G. K. Immediate Revelation wch I send you. But as for the rest of your No Crosse no Crown, it is in the maine very sober and good, though it may be over strickt in some thinges, but not unusefull to some sort of men. But to those that are sincere, Christ and the written Gospell will be their faythfull guide in all thinges. And as for your other two bookes agst J. Faldo,[92] what ever passages there be that may not be agreable to my sentiments, you will easily perceive of what nature they are by perusing my Remarks upon G. K.' Immediate Revelation. But there are sundry passages in those two bookes of yours very nobly Christian, and for wch I have no small kindenesse and esteeme for you they being testimonies of that which, I cannot but highly prize, where ever I finde it. And I wish the Quakers would disincumber those excellent thinges they professe and give witnesse to from such things as {make} them seem so uncouth and ridiculous. That the most excellent thinges of the Gospell be not slighted condemned or suspected, by men through the odnesse and indiscretion of such as seem the most zealous professours of them. This intimation is not alltogether unlike that of Paul to Timothy, lett as many servants as are under the yoke count their Masters worthy of *All* honour, that the name of God and his doctrine be not blasphemed.[93] W^{ch} Monition of the Apostle by Analogy will reach a great way, and one of your sincerity and parts will easily improve it. I have nothing more for the present to add but that the trouble I have given you and myself in writing this letter is from mere kindenesse and good will, and that I hope you will take it so. And therefore committing you to God and the gracious guidance of the Spirit of his Son the Lord Jesus Christ. I take leave and rest

Your Affectionate Friend
to serve you
Hen. More

From Ragley. May. 22. 1675.[94]

The bearer hereof is Monsieur Van-Helmont,[95] a person of quality, and Baron of the German Empire, though he loves to live and goe incognito, The first occasion of the happinesse of my being acquainted with him, was his bringing commendations to me from the Princesse Elizabeth,[96] and a letter from a learned friend of his in Germani[a][97] concerning severall points of philosophy. He is not of so plausible a [illegible word] but he has a [sound?] witt and discerning in him and is a great lover of truth and goodnesse and has courage enough to suffer for it. witnesse his 18 moneths in the Inquisition at Rome,[98] this is only to give you a tast of him; the rest, if you both have liesure to converse, you may better observe of yourself. But I thought it not [illegible word] to give you some hint of his character.

LS. Penn-Forbes Papers, HSP. (*Micro.* 2:044).

1. Henry More (1614-1687), the Cambridge Platonist theologian, lived at Christ's College, Cambridge, as a student and as a fellow, from 1631 until his death. He was a prolific writer, and refused all offers to the masterships of colleges or to high clerical office so that he might pursue his studies. During his long writing career, he became an increasingly ardent supporter of the Church of England. His voluminous work is the fullest expression of the rational Christian teachings of the Cambridge Platonists. *DNB;* Frederick J. Powicke, *The Cambridge Platonists, A Study* (London, 1926), pp. 150-73.

2. The street that encircles St. Paul's Cathedral in London.

3. See nn. 5 and 10 below for the WP works to which More refers. Walter Kittilby, a London bookseller from 1669 to 1711, was a noted publisher of works on divinity. Located at St. Paul's Churchyard, he first printed a Henry More tract in 1672, and published More regularly from 1679 to 1686. Henry R. Plomer, *A Dictionary of the Booksellers and Printers who were at work in England, Scotland, and Ireland from 1668 to 1725* (Oxford, 1968), pp. 178-79.

4. *A Just Rebuke to the One & Twenty Learned and Reverend Divines* ([London], 1674).

5. On John Faldo, see doc. 83 above. The key pamphlets in the exchange between WP and Faldo, all presumably published in London, were, in their probable order of composition: WP, *The Spirit of Truth Vindicated* (1672); Faldo, *Quakerism No Christianity* (1673); WP, *Quakerism a New Nick-Name for Old Christianity* (1672); Faldo, *A Vindication of Quakerism No Christianity* (1673); WP, *The Invalidity of John Faldo's Vindication* (1673); [Faldo, *A Curb for William Penn's Confidence,* date unknown]; WP, *William Penn's Return to John Faldo's Reply, called, A Curb for William Penn's Confidence* [1674]; Faldo, et al., *The Epistles of many learned and Worthy Divines* (n.d.); WP, *A Just Rebuke to One and Twenty Learned and Reverend Divines* (1674); and Faldo, *XXI. divines . . . cleared* (1675). Faldo's *A Curb for William Penn's Confidence* is known only from WPs reply to it.

6. George Keith (1639?-1716) was born near Aberdeen, received a good classical education in that city, and became a Quaker about 1662. He and Robert Barclay were the leaders of Scottish Quakerism in the 1670s. Keith had been deeply influenced by More's religious thought since the early 1660s and had known him personally since 1670. In that year More introduced Keith to Lady Conway and Francis Van Helmont (see nn. 67 and 95 below). Keith visited More at Cambridge in the springs of 1674 and 1675 on his annual trips to London to meet with leading Quakers, including WP, whom he had also known since about 1671. Keith would travel to Holland with WP in 1677 (see doc. 119 below) and emigrate to New Jersey and Pennsylvania in the 1680s. There he founded a schismatic movement within Quakerism, and by 1700 he had abandoned the faith completely to take holy orders in the Church of England. *DNB;* Ethyn Williams Kirby, *George Keith (1638-1716)* (New York, 1942), pp. 8-9, 19-21, 25-26, 29.

7. George Keith, *Immediate Revelation, . . . Not Ceased, but Remaining a standing and perpetual Ordinance of the Church of Christ* (1668; 2d ed., with app., 1675 and 1676).

8. See n. 4 above.

9. A London-area Quaker seems called for here. Possibilities include William Beane, host to Quaker meetings in Spitalfield in the 1660s; William Beech of Westminster; William Brend (or Brand, d. 1676); William Blackbury, husband of the Quaker preacher Sarah Blackbury (d. 1665); and William Bingley (c. 1651-1715), later a prominent London Friend, but perhaps not yet living in London in 1675. Fox, 2: 453, 478, 484; Braithwaite, *Second Period,* pp. 42, 105, 450, 488.

10. Probably *Quakerism a New Nick-Name for Old Christianity* (1672), and *The Invalidity of John Faldo's Vindication* (1673). See n. 5, above.

11. The Family of Love was a vehemently anticlerical, radically antinomian, and vaguely communistic and pantheistic sect of Anabaptist origin, founded in Holland in 1540 by Hendrick Niclaes (c. 1502–c. 1580). Niclaes visited England in the 1550s, and his followers survived there underground until the 1640s, and then notoriously in the open. With the Ranters, the Familists were on the extreme left wing of English dissent, both theologically and socially. George Fox recruited many Quakers from among the Familists and the related Seekers and Grindletonians in the North of England in the 1650s. Henry More had first connected the Familists and the Quakers in an anonymous letter signed "Mastix" in 1656, and again in *An Explanation of the Grand Mystery of Godliness* (1660) and in *Divine Dialogues* (1667), no. 5. By 1675, as shown in the present letter, More was distinguishing between the Familists, whom he still despised, and the Quakers. This reassessment continued with his reading of Barclay's *Apology* (1676) and his 1677 meeting with Barclay, Fox, Keith, and WP. In the second edition of his *Divine Dialogues* (1678), pp. 567-75, More stated that he had come to a more favorable view of the Quakers. A further reason for his change of heart was that his patron, Lady Conway, joined the Quakers about 1677. See n. 67, below. Powicke, *The Cambridge Platonists,* pp. 165-69; Cross, *Christian Church;* Hill, *The World Turned Upside Down.*

12. "The baptismal basin of regeneration."

13. Here, as in most of the New Testament Greek passages in this letter, More gives a translation close to that of the King James version (i.e., John 4:1, "Jesus made and baptized more disciples than John."). Wherever More's translation varies from the King James version, or where he supplies no translation of the New Testament Greek, the editors will supply the King James translation. Wherever More's Greek text departs from the New Testament Greek text of his day, the editors will supply this text, using Η ΚΑΙΝΗ ΔΙΑΘΗΚΗ. *Novum Testamentum: ex Utraque Regia, Aliisque optimis editionibus summo studio expressum.* (Amstelodami [Amsterdam], 1639), reprinted in London in 1653, and bound with the Greek Septuagint translation of the Old Testament.

14. "To teach, i. e., to make disciples." See Matt. 28:19.

15. The Greek word *logos* in the New Testament usually means simply the "word" or "message" of Christ and the apostles, but More refers to its particular use by the Evangelist John to mean "the Divine Expression" of God's word in the flesh, that is, Christ himself, in John 1:1, 14.

16. Literally, "of the priest and of the river."

17. V. 2.

18. See Acts 10:45-48.

19. "Lord."

20. The Sadducees, a Jewish priestly sect, rejected the doctrines of the resurrection of the body and of retribution in an afterlife for sins committed on earth, and vigorously attacked the early Christians for preaching Christ's resurrection. Many Familists, Ranters, and other radical dissenters questioned these same doctrines. Cross, *Christian Church;* Hill, *The World Turned Upside Down.*

21. More is evidently contrasting the "Divine Logos" of John 1:1, 14 with the "mere logos," or "message," of God, as given by human interpreters (see n. 15, above).

22. Actually vv. 26-28.

23. "The ordinances, as I have delivered them."

24. "That which also I delivered to you."

25. The Apostles' Creed, developed in the fourth century, became the standard baptismal creed of the Western Church by the ninth century. Both the Apostle's Creed and the related Nicene Creed (c. 325) were modelled on Matt. 28:19, and other New Testament passages. Cross, *Christian Church.*

26. Actually Heb. 9:28.

27. This Hebrew word, phoneticized as "khat-aw-aw" in English, means either an

offense or a sacrifice made to atone for an offense. It appears in Gen. 20:9; Exod. 32:21, 30-31; 2 Kings 17:21; and Ps. 40:6; 109:7.

28. Vv. 26-27.

29. Mark 14:23-24.

30. V. 19.

31. Matt. 26:26-28.

32. Translated "ye do shew the Lord's death till he come," in the King James version.

33. Acts 1:11; Heb. 9:28.

34. Capable of being abrogated. Rare, but used by WP, in this same year, in *England's Present Interest Discover'd*. *OED*.

35. Vv. 48-58.

36. From the word "Savior" to this point in the text (or MS), More quotes loosely, and out of order, from John 15:9-14.

37. See John 6:49-51, 58. George Keith's book was *Immediate Revelation* (1668). The editors have not traced More's critique of Keith's argument, but More may refer to his *Enchiridion Metaphysicum* (1671), of which he gave a copy to Keith in 1674, or to his *Opera Theologica* (1675). See Kirby, *George Keith*, p. 29.

38. Gen. 9:8-17, esp. v. 12.

39. Acts 10:47.

40. Acts 1:11; Heb. 9:28.

41. Thomas Hobson (1544?-1631) was a Cambridge stablemaster who let out each horse in turn, saying "this horse, or none," irrespective of his patrons' desires. His "choice" became shorthand for "Either this, or nothing at all." *DNB*.

42. Literally, "God, the Word, and the Life (or Spirit)."

43. 1 John 5:7.

44. The Holy Spirit (literally, "the holy breath").

45. The life, or spirit.

46. Psyche, or the mortal sentient spirit of animals.

47. Amelius (Amerius Gentilianus) of Etruria was a third-century philosopher, and a pupil of the neo-Platonist Plotinus from 246 to 270. *Oxford Classical Dictionary*. The Latin translates "From God the famous barbarian shares something with our Plato." Translation by Prof. Robert E. A. Palmer, Dept. of Classical Studies, University of Pennsylvania.

48. The third "person" (the Holy Ghost) in the developing Christian creed, a concept that was formalized in the First Council of Constantinople in 381 as three "persons" in one "substance," that is, the Trinity. Cross, *Christian Church*.

49. The Wisdom of Solomon, one of the books of the Apocrypha, had a powerful influence on early Christianity which is especially evident in Paul's letters to the Romans and the Ephesians.

50. "Courteous spirits," the equivalent of "humane spirits." See Wisd. of Sol. 7:23.

51. "In him was life." John 1:4.

52. Matt. 5:14, 16; John 5:35.

53. John 1:14.

54. Luke 2:25-35, esp. v. 32.

55. Eminent. *OED*.

56. Plainly. *OED*.

57. The cause of More's dissatisfaction with the King James translation of John 1:1-14 is not entirely clear here, since the English text does not contradict his argument. Probably he thought, understandably for a Platonist, that an ideal translation should emphasize the distinction between the divine logos and human thought, and between divine light and the light of men, more than the King James version did.

58. "Fixt" may be in another hand, possibly More's.

59. "Child" is definitely in another hand, probably More's.

60. Literally "God-man," or "God-in-man." This Greek word does not appear in the New Testament.

61. Vv. 35-58, esp. 50-58.

62. The (eternal) "life" of the (divine) "word."

63. Usually translated "and."

64. V. 38.

65. V. 14.

66. Appropriate, or applicable. *OED*.

67. Ragley Castle, in southwest Warwickshire, was the seat of Viscount Conway and his wife, Lady Anne Conway (1631-1679), who had studied with More before her marriage in 1651. Lady Conway invited More to visit Ragley whenever he wished and to stay as long as he liked. In the early 1670s she became interested in the Quakers, and sometime in 1675 began corresponding with WP. It was perhaps in an attempt to keep Lady Conway from falling under the Quakers' spell that More became more interested in Quaker ideas. See Powicke, *Cambridge Platonists*, pp. 160-68, and doc. 101, below.

68. Published in London in 1669.

69. This insertion appears to be in More's hand.

70. Matt. 22:37, 39; Mark 12:30-31; Luke 10:27.

71. This insertion appears to be in More's hand.

72. Literally, "we write" and "we sing," and "I write" and "I sing."

73. The Greek literally means "the [men] with (or around) Socrates." The punctuation following the Greek phrase is uncertain.

74. More refers to the decision of the Apostles to follow the Jewish rituals regarding cleanliness of the hands and body before eating while living among the Jews, even though Christ had declared that all of the Jewish laws of ritual cleanliness and diet, particularly as found in Lev., chaps. 10-17, were of no religious significance (Matt. 15:1-20; Mark 7:1-23). An example of the Apostles' behavior is St. Paul's submitting to ritual purification in Acts 21:21-26.

75. Positive or absolute. *OED*.

76. In this sentence, the words "foresaw," "power," and "mens" have been corrected by a later hand, perhaps More's. The words first written are illegible.

77. "Awe" is written in a later hand, possibly More's.

78. Matt. 23:11. "But he that is greatest among you shall be your servant."

79. "They."

80. See also v. 42.

81. "Be not many masters," in the King James translation.

82. In the Greek text, ου is written over other, illegible letters in πτούομεν. The correct New Testament reading is πταίομεν ἅπαντες.

83. "Tongue." See James 3:5-8.

84. The correction and the preceding insert are made by a later hand, probably More's.

85. Actually Acts 10:34.

86. Ps. 82:6; and see John 10:34.

87. Jeremiah.

88. Literally "into your (holy) assembly."

89. "Respect to persons." Different forms of this word are used in James 2:1, and 2:9; More gives the simplest noun form.

90. The "self" has been added in a later hand, possibly More's.

91. More probably had in mind the founders of extreme antinomian sects and movements, such as the Familists, Ranters, and Fifth Monarchists, whom he saw as bringing the moderate, rational Reformation to which he was committed into ill repute.

92. See n. 10, and nn. 3-5 above.

93. 1 Tim. 6:1.

94. This date line, the signature, and the postscript are all in More's hand.

95. Franz (Francis) Mercurius Van Helmont (1618-1699), son of the famous Belgian chemist and physician Jean Baptiste Van Helmont (1577-1644), was, like his father, a scientist, physician, alchemist, and mystic. He lived in England from 1670 to 1679, mostly at Ragley, where he treated Lady Conway, to whom Henry More had introduced him, for her nervous condition and migraine headaches. Van Helmont was a "scholar gipsy," one of the most widely travelled and best-known men in seventeenth-century Europe. Marjorie Hope Nicolson, ed., *Conway Letters: The Correspondence of Anne, Viscountess Conway, Henry More, and their Friends, 1642-1684* (New Haven, 1930), pp. xxiv, 316-17.

96. Elizabeth, Princess Palatine of the Rhine. See doc. 119, n. 62, below.

97. Baron Christian Knorr von Rosenroth, also known as Peganius, a student of the Cabbala who corresponded with both George Keith and Henry More in the 1670s. Nicolson, ed., *Conway Letters*, pp. 323-24, 333; and Kirby, *George Keith*, p. 21.

98. Van Helmont was kept in prison in Rome on the orders of the Inquisition between Nov. 1661 and Apr. 1663. Nicolson, *Conway Letters*, p. 316n.

In 1675, the Society of Friends was embroiled in a serious debate, known as the Wilkinson-Story controversy, concerning the authority of the church. WP and his fellow Quaker leaders were challenged by a faction of Friends led by John Wilkinson and John Story of Westmorland who wanted to maintain the individualistic character of early Quakerism. WP, like George Fox, defended the institution of formal organization and discipline because he believed that the society would fall apart if it did not supervise the beliefs and behavior of its members. During the period from 1674 to 1679, he helped to create a viable church structure within a religion that stressed a personal relationship with God. Thus, while WP thought there was room for a diversity of religious ideas within the society at large, and later established his "holy experiment" in Pennsylvania on this basis, at the same time he believed that heterodoxy should not be permitted within the Society of Friends.

The schism of the late 1670s was the product of long-building tension within Quakerism. Beginning in 1667, Fox had promoted the organization of monthly and quarterly meetings to provide poor relief, discipline members, supervise marriages, and keep written records. The London Morning Meeting of Ministers took on some of the functions of a central executive body, and by 1675 its responsibilities included assigning ministers to meetings for worship, overseeing the publication of Friends' manuscripts, and arbitrating disputes within local meetings. These changes aroused the antipathy of many Friends, such as William Mucklow and John and Mary Pennyman (see docs. 71 and 74). Wilkinson and Story were concerned about the growth of Fox's personal influence in the society, but they primarily objected to recording papers of condemnation, submitting marriages to women's meetings, and disciplining members who paid tithes or worshipped in secret places when threatened with imprisonment.

The Wilkinson-Story controversy first developed in the early 1670s when the Friends of Preston Patrick meeting in Westmorland, led by the two Johns, attacked several of the newly established disciplinary procedures (see docs. 81 and 82). By May 1675, the Wilkinson-Story party had set up its own meeting, separate from the established quarterly meeting, and on 27 May 1675 the London Yearly Meeting of Ministers responded by issuing a fundamental statement of official discipline that addressed the main points of contention (doc. 91). Westmorland and London Friends attempted to heal the breach. A meeting, held at Poolbank and Milnthorpe in Westmorland in July 1675, was unsuccessful because Wilkinson and Story refused to attend. In April 1676, at Draw-well in Yorkshire, Wilkinson and Story signed a paper of regret for their spirit of separation, but then in the summer of 1676 denied that they had fully condemned their behavior and rallied supporters to their side (docs. 107 and 120).

In 1677-1678 the center of controversy shifted to Bristol, where several long meetings were held involving Story and William Rogers, his ardent supporter, on the one side, and WP, Fox, George Whitehead, and William Gibson on the other (doc. 124). No agreement was reached at these meetings, and Wilkinson and many of his adherents remained in opposition for the rest of their lives. John Story, on the other hand, confirmed in 1679 the paper of regret that he and Wilkinson had signed at Draw-well in 1676 (doc. 135), and thus rejoined the Society of Friends.

91
EPISTLE FROM THE LONDON YEARLY MEETING

London, the 27th Day of the 3^{d} Mo [May]: 1675.

At a solemn general Meeting of many faithful Friends and Brethren[1] concern'd in the publick Labour of the Gospell, and Service of the Church of Christ from the most part of this Nation.

Beloved Friends and Brethren;
Upon weighty Consideration had of the Affairs relating to the Church of Christ in our Day, in the Counsell, Wisdom and Orderings of God's holy Spirit, whose Glorious, bright and refreshing Presence was plentifully manifested among us, We do with one consent agree to and conclude upon these following Particulars, seriously recommending them to the Care and Diligence of all Friends and Brethren in the Truth in their respective Places and Services, whether in these or other Parts of the World where this may come; Hoping that upon reading hereof, they will have some sense of that Heavenly Power, Presence and Wisdom of God that filled our Hearts, and gave us Heavenly Unity both in receiving and giving forth of this our Advice and Counsell: And that through a sensible Fellowship in the same Power and Wisdom of God in themselves {they ~~you~~ may} be stirr'd up to put the same in Practice in their several Places, to the Exalting of that Blessed Name in which we have found Salvation, and to the debasing and bringing under whatever hath lifted up itself against that most Holy Name, and lead from the Unity of the Faith and good Order that stands therein.
Forasmuch as we are deeply sensible of the Sorrows and Sufferings that have come upon the Church of Christ in several Places by reason of certain disorderly Proceedings of some Professing the Truth, which have occasion'd many Questions and Debates among some Friends, and our Advice being desired thereupon, We do in the Name

and Counsell of God hereby signifie our Sense Advice and Judgment, as follows:

1. Concerning Marriages of Kindreds.
It is our living sense and Judgment in the Truth of God, that not only those Marriages of near kindred {expressly} forbidden under the Law, ought not to be practiced under the Gospell; but that inasmuch as any Marriage of near Kindred in the times of the Law was in Condescension, and upon such extraordinary Occasions, as upholding their Tribes, and that the nearer their Marriages were, the more Unholy they were accounted, We in our Day ought not to approach our near Kindred in any such respect, particularly first Cousens;[2] being redeem'd out of those Kindreds ~~and~~ Tribes {& unholy lotts} for the upholding of which Marriages within the kindred were {once} dispens'd with, and brought to that Spiritual Dispensation, which gives Dominion over the Affections, and leads to those Marriages, wch are more Natural, and are of better Report. And though some have through Weakness been drawn into such Marriages, which being done must not be broken; yet let not their Practice be any President or Example to any others amongst us for the time to come.

2. Concerning Contracts in order to Marriage.
That such Friends as have with serious Advice, due Deliberation, free and mutual Consent, as in the sight of God and Unity of his blessed Truth, absolutely {agreed espoused or} contracted ~~and spoused~~ themselves upon the Account of Marriage, shall not be allow'd or own'd among us in any Unfaithfulness or Injustice one to another, to break or violate any such Contract or Engagement, which is to the Reproach of Truth or Injury one of another: And where any such Injury, Breach, or Violation of such solemn Contracts is known or complain'd of, or Enmity or Strife occasion'd thereby, we advise and counsell that a few faithfull Friends, both Men and Women, in their respective Meetings, to which the Parties belong, be appointed to enquire into the Cause thereof, and in the Wisdom and Counsell of God to put a stop and speedy End thereto, and bring God's Power and the Judgment thereof over them that have offended in this Case, until they come to unfeign'd Repentance.
And further we advise and exhort that no Engagements made without honest Endeavours to obtain, or due regard first had to the Counsel and Consent of Parents ~~& Friends~~ {relations & Friends} be countenanc'd ~~or allow'd~~ that so all foolish and unbridled Affections, & all ensnaring & Selfish Ends ~~be condemned, and for the future prevented~~ {be not so much as found amongst you on any hand}.

3. Concerning Men & Women-Meetings.
It is our Judgment & Testimony in the Word of God's Wisdom, that the Rise & Practice, setting up & Establishment of Mens & Womens-Meetings in the Church of Christ in this our Generation, is according to the Mind and Counsell of God, and done in the ordering and

leading of ~~God's~~ his Eternal Spirit. And that it is the Duty of all Friends & Brethren {in the ~~gods~~ powr of god} in all Parts, to be diligent therein, and to encourage and further each other in that blessed Work, and particularly that Friends and Brethren in their Respective Counties, encourage their faithfull & grave Women in the Settlement of the said Meetings: And if any professing Truth shall either by Word or Deed, directly or indirectly discountenance or weaken the Hands of either Men or Women in that Work {& the service} of the Lord, let such be admonish'd according to the order of the Gospell; and if they receive it not, but resist Counsell, and persist in that Work of Division, we can't but look upon them, as therein not in Unity with the Church of Christ {& order of the gospell}: And therefore let Friends go on in {the powr of god & in} that Work for ~~God~~ {him,} his Truth and People, and not be sway'd or hindred by them or their Oppositions.

4. Concerning Sighing, [illegible deletion] {Groaning and} Singing in the Church.

It hath been and is our living sense and constant Testimony, according to our Experience of the divers Operations of the Spirit and Power of God in his Church, that there hath been and is serious sighing {sensible Groaning & reverent singing,} breathing forth an Heavenly Sound of Joy with Grace, with the Spirit and wth Understanding in blessed Unity with the Brethren while they are in the publick Labour and Service of the Gospell, whether by Preaching, Praying or Praising God {in the same power and spirit} and all to Edification and Comfort in the Church of Christ, which therefore is not to be quencht or discourag'd by any; but where any do or shall abuse the Power of God, or are immoderate, or do~~th~~ either in Imitation, which rather burdens then edifies, such ought to be {privately} admonisht {unless rebellious} for that Life sprit {& power is} risen in the Church which doth distinguish, and hath Power according to judge.

5. Concerning our Testimony agt Tythes.

That our ancient Testimony agt Tythes wch we have born from the Beginning and from wch many have deeply suffer'd, some {not only the spoiling of their goods, but Imprisonments ~~even~~} even unto Death, be carefully & punctually upheld and countenanc'd {in the powr of god} & that all those that oppose, slight or neglect that Testimony, be lookt upon & dealt withall, as unfaithfull to the ancient & Universal Testimony of Truth, according to Gospell order {as} establisht among us.

6. Concerning [illegible deletion] {our} open Testimony {or publick ~~worship~~ Meetings} in times of Suffering

That, as it hath been our Care and Practice from the Beginning, that an open Testimony for the Lord should be born, and a publick Standard for Truth & Righteousness upheld {in the powr & Spirit of god} by our open and Known Meetings agt the Spirit of Persecution, that in all Ages hath sought to lay waste God's Heritage; and that only through Faithfulness, Constancy & Patience Victory hath been & is obtain'd: So it is our Advice & Judgment, that all Friends {gather'd in the name of Jesus} keep up those publick Testimonies in their respective Places, and not decline, forsake or remove their publick Assemblies, because of Times of Suffering, as Worldly, fearful & Politique Professors have done, because of Informers and the like Persecutors, for such Practices are not consistent with the Nobility of the Truth, & therefore not to be own'd in the Church of Christ.

7. Concerning recording the Churches Testimonies & {the Parties} Condemnations ~~ag^{t} scandalous Walkers~~.
That the Churches Testimonys & Judgment ag^{t} disorderly and scandalous Walkers, as also the Repentance & Condemnation of the Parties restored be recorded in a distinct Book in the respective Monthly ~~&~~ {or} Quarterly Meetings for the clearing of the Truth, Friends and our Holy Profession, to be produc'd or publisht by Friends for that End & Purpose, so far only as in God's Heavenly Wisdom they shall see needful. And it is also our Advice in the Love of God that after any Friend's Repentance & Restoration {(he abideing faithfull) in the truth that condemns the evil} none among you so remember his Transgression as to cast it at him or upbraid him wth it; for that is not according to the Mercies of God.

8. Our Judgment ag^{t} contemptible Names given ag^{t} our Heavenly Order, Care, & Instructions in these Matters.
It is our Sense, Admonition & Judgment in the Fear of God, & the Authority {~~& powr~~} of his {powr &} Spirit to Friends and Brethren in their several Meetings, that no such slight and contemptible Names & Expressions, as calling Mens or Womens Meetings, Courts, Sessions or Synods, that they are Popish Impositions, useless & burdensom. That {faithfull} Friends Papers {(wch wee Testifie have bin given forth from the spirit & ~~the~~ power of God)} are Mens Edicts and Canons; or embracing them, bowing to Man; Elders in the Service of the ~~Truth~~ Church, Popes~~sh~~ or Bishops, with such scornful Sayings be permitted amongst them; but that God's Power be set upon the Top of that unsavory Spirit that uses them.

9. Concerning propounding Marriages.
It is our Judgment, that for better Satisfaction to all Parties, and that there may be due time for Inquiry of Clearness of the Persons concern'd, it is convenient that Marriages be at least twice propounded to the Meetings that are to take care therein (both to the Mens & Womens-Meetings (where both are establish'd) before they are accomplish'd; {And when things are cleared that the marriage be accomplished in a grave & publique assembly of Friends and [illegible deletion] relations.}

10. Concerning Disputes.
That Friends as far as in them lies, in their several Places take great Care not to entangle themselves or others in Debates and Disputes with foreward and contentious Spirits, being men of corrupt Minds

{destitute of the truth ~~some~~} ~~professors and others~~ {whether Proffessors or others}, that the Church be not disturbed by unprofitable Controversie; but that Friends stand over that crooked Envious Spirit in the Dominion of God's Power {& peaceable truth} & place Judgment in that upon their Heads: Yet where Controversies can't with Clearness & Honour to the Truth be avoided, that Friends stand in God's ~~strength~~ {wisdome & powr}, in Defence of the Truth, & those Friends & Brethren, that are engaged in the Defence of the Lord's Truth & their Labours be not discouraged ~~but receiv'd & cherisht according to their~~ [illegible word deleted].

11. Concerning Trading.

That Friends and Brethren in their respective Meetings watch over one another in the Love of God, & Care of the Gospel, {particularly} that they admonish that none trade beyond their Ability, nor stretch beyond their Compass {and that they use few words in Dealing and keep to there Word in all things} least they bring through their Forwardness Dishonour to the pretious Truth of God.

12. Of Friends ancient Testimony agt the Corrupt Fashions & Language of the World.

And lastly, it is much upon us to put Friends in remembrance, to keep to the ancient Testimony, Truth begot in our Hearts in the Beginning agt the Spirit of this World {and for wch many have suffered cruell mockings, beatings & stoneings &c} particularly, as to their corrupt Fashions, Dealings and Language of the World, their Overreachings and vain jestings, that the Cross of Christ in all things may be kept to, wch preserves Friends blameless, and honours the Lord's Name and Truth in the Earth.

These are an Abstract of those things that were propounded, and much more largely & livingly spoaken to & agreed upon, with great Tenderness, Clearness & Unity in the Love {Spiritt} Power and Wisdom of God at the aforesaid Meeting; all which we recommend to the Evidence of God's Holy Witness in the Hearts of his People, resting

Your Faithfull Brethren
in the Love & Labour of the
Gospell & Friends present
att the said Meeting

Alexander Parker
George Whitehead.
~~Wm Penn~~
Thomas Salthouse
John Burnyeat
Stephen Crisp[3]
William Penn

~~Signed on the behalfe {& unity} of the said meeting the rest of whose names are as followeth.~~

DS. Penn vs. Ford, vol. 6, HSP. (*Micro.* 2:094). Docketed: Articles of London Meeting | that are controverted by the | Separates.

1. The London Yearly Meeting of Ministers. This epistle was written by WP and his fellow Quaker leaders to defend the principles and procedures of discipline they had recently established within the Society of Friends. Story and Wilkinson objected to the new requirements for presenting written condemnations to monthly meetings and appearing before both men's and women's meetings for approval of marriages (see secs. 3, 7, and 9). They contended that Fox, WP, and their allies were attempting to establish a "government." Story and Wilkinson also objected to the accusation (see secs. 5 and 6) that they and their supporters were paying tithes and meeting secretly to avoid persecution. In other sections of the epistle, WP and his colleagues made policy statements about less controversial issues, and so this document became the basis for later Quaker statements of discipline. Braithwaite, *Second Period,* chap. 11; William Rogers, *The Christian-Quaker* (1680).

2. See the case of first cousins John Jennings and Mary Arnold in doc. 73.

3. Stephen Crisp (1628-1692), a successful baize maker of Colchester, Essex, was an Anabaptist before his convincement to Quakerism c. 1655. He went to Holland as a missionary in 1663, but his trip was a failure because he required an interpreter. In 1667, he returned to the Continent knowing both German and Dutch, and from then until 1683 spent most of his time establishing and supervising meetings for discipline in Holland and Germany. Crisp's writings were collected and published by John Field in 1694 as *A Memorable Account . . . of . . . Stephen Crisp; in his Books and Writings herein collected.* His sermons were issued as *Scripture Truths Demonstrated* in 1707, and his *Short History of a Long Travel from Babylon to Bethel* was published in 1711. *DNB;* Fox, 2:485-86.

92
TO SIR WILLIAM PETTY

In July 1675 Sir William Petty, WP's friend from his Irish journey, tried to get the English Treasury to reduce the quit rents and back rents due from his lands in county Kerry, Ireland. Petty appealed to WP to use his influence in gaining the reduction, and doc. 92 shows WP's response. Petty had been in frequent conflict with the farmers of revenue in Ireland, and had proposed several reforms in the Crown collection of rents there. On the same day as this letter of WP's, Petty wrote to his wife in Ireland that his efforts to achieve a reduction had gone awry, but that "on Tuesday next [3 August] we shall have another Tug, especially about the arrears." (Edmond Fitzmaurice, *Life of Sir William Petty,* p. 165.) He succeeded, for in November 1675 new patents issued to the farmers of Irish revenues provided for a reduction in quit rents on Petty's lands. (*Calendar of Treasury Books, 1672-1675* [London, 1909], pp. 345-49, 823, 855, 859.)

[30 July 1675]

My old friend,— I have broacht that affaire to the great man.[1] He took it marvellous kindly and desired me to give it him in writeing, promissing to name noe person, but upon assurance to thrive. Now

I entreat thee most earnestly to have in writeing what was read to me of Eng(land) and Ir(eland) as to revenue. The bearer waites wholly for it, for this night I am to goe to him again. I was with him yesterday about my own business, and then fell into discourse about this. Ireland took as well as England. Now is the crisis; therefore pray fail not, and if anything be to be done for the retriveing my business about the Lord Ranalagh,[2] lett me have two words; and what progress is made in our Irish affaires there. I will run, goe, or doe ten times more for thee at any time. Noe more, but once more beseech you not to fail for both our sakes. In great hast.

Thy sinceer friend
Windsor: July 30, 1675.[3] Wm. Penn.

For my old and worthy friend Sir William Petty at his house in Pecedille. Speed and Care.

Printed. Edmond Fitzmaurice, *Life of Sir William Petty, 1623-1687* (London, 1895), pp. 166-67. (*Micro.* 2:114).

1. Possibly James Butler, Duke of Ormonde, who was in London at Charles II's request to answer Ranelagh's scurrilous charges about his handling of the Irish government during his lord lieutenancy. *DNB*.
2. Richard Jones, Lord Ranelagh, was in 1675 vice-treasurer for Ireland and in complete control of collecting revenues there. He participated in the Treasury's negotiations over the new contract with the farmers of Irish revenue which would take effect at Christmas 1675. WP's own business with Ranelagh is unknown, but the urgent tone of this letter suggests that the vice-treasurer was pressing him hard for the payment of back quit rents on his lands in Ireland.
3. Not WP's usual style and perhaps changed by the nineteenth-century copyist.

93
FROM GEORGE FOX

[30 September 1675]

Deare William

I Received thy Letter;[1] & my love to thee & thy wife & the rest of Friends, G: W. & A: P:[2] & all the rest, that Inquires after mee: Now as Concerneinge the things thou writes to mee, about the 2: Johns;[3] and such as has great faith Concerneinge them; Then why would not they seeke them, this 3: or 4: years, & come downe, & Joined with the other Friends, & have had Meettings with them, which it is like they have knowne, how things has beene; And soe have come & seene, & heard, how things was; & not have Judged afarr off.—And as touchinge the Jury men,[4] I doe not understande, that they ever give Judgement, or pronounce sentence, but onely try the matter of fact; But Dr William, I shall not strive with thee about matter of Law, or Law pointes, but they made noe Exceptions against their Jury-men or Judges, nor that they finde any fault with them, or the matters evidenced, onely one Article, as I heare from London, Jno Story protests against; And all they that does thinke, the John's are wronged, & all the others are wronge in their Judgemt, & proceedings agst them, in their Meettings, & yett has putt them upon those Meettings; they themselves has beene the orderers, & setters on of these Meettings, some of them: Therefore it had beene well for them, to have come downe, & done right at first, if they thinke these have done wronge, & not to complaine against that, which many Antient Friends has done; For they have not Concerned mee in the thinge:—And as touchinge any application to them at London, I doe not see any such thinge is done, but onely to Lett them see what was done, because their advice was followed, in the former Meettings as they ordered; and upon their Complainte upon their Judgemt, they did soe farr Condescend to them, that if they thought, the John's were wronged, they might come downe, & have a Meettinge, with the same persons, at the same place, and have a Rehea{r}einge of the matters againe; Not that they wanted Councell or Judgemt, or their Advice in the things; but had sounde Judgemt in themselves; I understand; though many of them, I did not see, that came above 40: Miles, & waited upon them the best part of A weeke: And as for offerringe them another Meettinge, I never hearde they desire any such thinge, or makes any such complainte; Therefore lett them that dos complaine above, Come downe, & not lie frettinge, & troubleinge themselves there; And for mee to profferr A Meettinge, that has not beene Concerned, & time, & place for others, Except I was there my selfe; and to gather upp them, that was there then, off 100: miles Compasse; It would not bee soe proper for mee, as them that did first Concerne themselves: and to doe such a thinge without their desireinge of it, is to bringe a Question upon the proceedings of them, that gave Judgement, who are farr dispersed abroade since, Jno Burnyett for Wales, Thomas Langhorne[5] {T: Robertson}[6] & Jon Graves[7] for London: And J: Burnyett & Rob: Lodge[8] were lately amongst there Meettings, & went through them; But the two John's would not come neare them, to see them, nor to complaine of any wronge done them; But they have had their seperate Meettings from Friends, before the Judgemt was given Agt them; and have drawne upp a paper, subscribed by about 84: names at it,[9] some of wch old Apostates, as Jno Scafe[10] & the like, & others payers of Tythes, and such as were Marryed by Preists, & such as have not come amongst Friends, for severall yeares past, & some boyes; and such are the party they are gatheringe: Neither doe I know, what the Complaintes are that the 2: Jno's writes to G: W: or A: P: about;—Jno Burnyett & Rob: Lodge were speakeinge of writeinge upp to Friends at London, to G: W: & J: Batt, & W: G:;[11] thou mayst enquire of them, for their Letter; —And to make A Nationall businesse of it, they have not beene such publicke persons, in the Nation; But where the facts has been Committed, is the fittest place, to heare it, or neare it; — And all such, as are disatisfied, Whethe^{r} in Citties, Townes, & Country, Its most proper for them, to come who are desireous to heare it againe; & they that ordered the Meettinge first; if they bee not satisfied with the Judgem^{t} & proceedings off Friends, of the Quarterly Meettinge,[12] if they cann gett them out, & if all the others will agree to it, to admitt of such A Meettinge, before they Judge their former Stubbornesse, Lett them doe as they see fitt, if they thinke others has not Judged Equally, they may come & mende the matter if they cann; But I doe not heare, that any of those dissatisfied ones, doe mention any thinge that the two Johns has done amisse, but onely complaines of such as gave Judgem^{t}: — But truely William, the Lords power Reignes over all these things, & his Everlastinge seed; — & I doe not understande but they might have brought their 84: to the Meettinge, if they woulde, that hath subscribed to them; — But these subscriptions was not in the begininge, who brought people to have their names written, in the Lambs booke of life; — Now if any of them came to mee to complaine, they was greived in any of these things, then I knew what to say. And such as does complaine without heareinge or seeinge, as eye and eare wittnesses, yett its like has heard; How they have vindicated, Flyeinge in times of Persecution, and affirmed, that the paym^{t} of Tythes is not Antichristian, & womans Meettings are Reputed Monsters, And Recordinge Condemnations, giveinge the Devill Advantage; and singeinge in Meettings whilst others are prayinge or speakeinge, Confusion, & delusion; & calls Monthly & Quarterly Meettings Courts, & Sessions; — And Now these things are Judged, they call this hard measure: But lett all such as will stand by these things, & thinkes these things are not to bee Judged, they may come downe, & heare them againe proved; And if any will stande by them in these things, Lett them subscribe their names, in their List, & Joine with the rest of them, and make a short worke, & appeare what they are; For these are the things I understande, Friends has Judged them for, and many othe^{r} such like things, though I was not there to heare it: And soe with my Love to all, in the power of God, that is over all these disquieted spiritts.

Swarthmo^{re} the 30th of the 7th moth G: F:
1675:

L. Penn-Forbes Papers, HSP. (*Micro.* 2:121). Addressed: For william Penn these | Leave this with phillippe | Forde att the Signe off | the hood & scarfe in | bow lane neere | cheapesyde these | London. Docketed: G: Fox | 7mo 75.

1. Probably WP's letter of 9 Sept. 1675, of which only fragments remain (*Micro.* 2:115, 117). In that letter, WP told Fox that Friends in London questioned the decision reached on the Wilkinson-Story controversy (see headnote to doc. 91) at Poolbank and Milnthorpe in Westmorland, in July 1675. The nonseparatist Westmorland Friends had invited nine leading Quakers from Cumberland and Yorkshire to Poolbank to arbitrate the dispute with Wilkinson and Story. The dissenters refused to attend because they had not helped to choose the judges. The meeting was held anyway, and, not

surprisingly, the judgment was against the separatists. Braithwaite, *Second Period,* pp. 301-2.

2. George Whitehead and Alexander Parker.

3. John Wilkinson and John Story.

4. The nine Quakers from Cumberland and Yorkshire who attempted to settle the dispute at Poolbank were Thomas Langhorne, Thomas Robertson, John Burnyeat, John Grave of Isell Meeting, John Tiffen of Pardshaw, Hugh Tickell and Thomas Laythes of Portinscale, Robert Lodge of Richmond Monthly Meeting, and Richard Robinson, also of Yorkshire. Braithwaite, *Second Period,* p. 302; John Blaykling, et al., *Anti-Christian Treachery Discovered* (1683), pp. 45-48; *Journals of the Lives and Gospel Labours of William Caton and John Burnyeat,* 2d ed. (London, 1839), pp. 222-23.

5. Thomas Langhorne (d. 1687) of Heltondale, a husbandman, belonged to Strickland Head Meeting in Westmorland. He accepted Quakerism in 1653, became a minister around 1660, preached in northwestern England and went to London often with John Blaykling and Thomas Camm, two Westmorland Friends with whom he was allied in opposition to Wilkinson and Story. In 1686, Langhorne emigrated to Pennsylvania, where he died the next year. Penney, *The First Publishers of Truth,* pp. 271-72.

6. Thomas Robertson (d. 1695), of Grayrigg and Kendal in Westmorland, traveled in the ministry, often in the company of Ambrose Rigge (c. 1635-1705), also of Westmorland. Fox, 1:442, 2:470-71; Penney, *The First Publishers of Truth,* p. 266.

7. John Grave (d. 1675), of Isell Meeting in Cumberland, became a Quaker in 1654 and traveled as a minister in many parts of England and Scotland. Fox, 2:473.

8. Robert Lodge (1636-1690), a butcher by trade, was a resident of Masham, Yorks. He was a Seeker before he accepted Quakerism, and traveled extensively in the ministry throughout England, Ireland, and Scotland. Fox, 2:412-13.

9. This paper, signed by eighty-seven Wilkinson-Story supporters, requested that the power to conduct church business be limited to representatives chosen by each meeting. The orthodox members of the Westmorland Meeting considered it schismatic, but Story denied any intentions to separate. Blaykling, et al., *Anti-Christian Treachery,* pp. 33-35; Thomas Camme, *The Line of Truth* (London, 1684), p. 37; *The Memory of that Servant of God, John Story, Revived* (London, 1683), pp. 40-45.

10. John Scafe was an early publisher of truth from Hutton Meeting in Westmorland. Of "low estate in the world"—he was either a servant or a day laborer—he traveled in the ministry to Somerset and adjacent areas as early as 1654, but subsequently left the Society of Friends. Penney, *The First Publishers of Truth,* p. 269.

11. George Whitehead, Jasper Batt, and, most likely, William Gibson.

12. Kendal, or Westmorland, Quarterly Meeting.

On 5 October 1675, WP held a seven-hour public disputation with Richard Baxter, England's most prominent Presbyterian clergyman. Baxter had been invited to preach in a number of churches in the Rickmansworth area, and challenged WP to a debate at which he hoped to convince local residents of the errors of Quakerism. Baxter wrote two accounts of the meeting; these are not printed here, because Baxter gave little space to WP's statements, while recapitulating his own arguments at enormous length. (See *Micro.* 2:182 for an incomplete transcript of Baxter's shorter account, and *Micro.* 2:197 for a transcript of his very long and detailed report of the debate.) In docs. 94 through 98, the two men pursued their controversy and challenged each other to another debate, but it is unlikely that a second meeting took place. (See Roger Thomas, "Letters of William Penn and Richard Baxter," *JFHS* 48:204-7.)

WP, according to Baxter, began the meeting on 5 October by criticizing Baxter's subscription to the epistle of twenty-one divines that was appended to the recent reissue of John Faldo's *Quakerism no Christianity* (see headnote to doc. 83). WP especially wanted to dispute Baxter's apparent agreement with Faldo's assertion that Quakers believed man's soul was God. But Baxter had planned a more general discussion of Friends' beliefs, and in the debate and correspondence that followed, he accused Quakers of separating from other Christians by clinging to their testimonies against the paid ministry, hat honor, and the use of "you." Baxter thought that all of these beliefs were trivial and wrong, and further attacked Friends' stress on the inner light, arguing that inspiration from God comes from the scriptures as well as from the Holy Spirit. WP, in turn, reminded Baxter that Presbyterians, like Quakers, had also been persecuted separatists since 1662, even if they were working for inclusion within a reformed Church of England. He defended Friends' testimonies, contending that they were divinely inspired through the Bible and the Holy Spirit. WP's central theme in the controversy, however, was his demand for toleration. He argued that the English ministry of the 1650s, including Baxter and many other nonconformists, had eagerly joined Anglicans in suppressing Friends, and predicted that Baxter would again help persecute sects if the Presbyterians were included within the Church.

Docs. 94 through 98 demonstrate that neither man had in any way convinced the other. The debate and the subsequent exchange of letters only confirmed their hostility. To Baxter, WP was a noxious hypocrite who pretended simplicity "while hee swims himselfe in wealth" (doc. 95). To WP, Baxter was not merely a persecutor, but "a Perverter, Traducer and forger" (doc. 97).

94
TO RICHARD BAXTER

[6 October 1675]

Richard Baxter[1]
Though thou hast reprobated the Quakers and their Religion with what Envye, and Artifice thou art capable of, accompanied with the indecent Carriage of thy Landlord[2] (a manifest breach of those Lawes of Conference thou wert soe precise in makeing) and that this entertainment is doubtlesse argument enough of an infirme cause and of as virulent, and imperious a behaviour, yet the Spirit of Christianitye in us[3] inclines us to offer thee Another Meeteing, both to

show that wee are not affraid of our Cause, or thy abilityes, and to prevent those tedious Harangues, and almost unpardonable Evasions and perversions thou wert guilty of, and which wee were obstructed from discovering in any quick returnes, least wee should be clamor'd against, as interrupters and violaters of those rules mutually agreed upon; We desire therefore another meeteing, and that it may [illegible deletion] be on the 7th instant about Eight in the morneing The matters wee offer to debate are

1. Concerning the True and false Ministry

2. Concerning the true and false Church

3. Concerning the sufficiencye of the Light within {all men to eternall Salvation} and what els it shall please the to add.

And to render this desired Conference more distinct, and intelligible, with respect to a perticuler discussion of things, wee offer this Method

1st. That some one of the aforementioned perticulars be throughly debated before any other be insisted on

2. That two or three on each side shall have Liberty to speake butt so as butt one only att a tyme

3. That there shalbe as strict & close keepeing to the matter in hand as may welbe, to prevent impertinent preachmts and trifleing excursions to shun the matter and evade the dint of Argument, and this to be inviolably observ'd on both hands

4. That soe doeing, there shalbe noe interruption of either side

5. name what place thou pleasest but that which I am forbidden[4]

To all which wee desire thy returne by this bearer to thy Freind.

The 6th day Wm Penn
of 8th {Augst}[5] Month

P.S.
I hope at the end of this Conference we may have a little tyme to debate the Meritts of John Faldoes cause and thy subscription,[6] at least in a few perticulars.

LS. Baxter Papers, Dr. Williams's Library, London. (*Micro.* 2:128). Addressed: This | For Richard Baxter.

1. Richard Baxter (1615-1691), preeminent Presbyterian divine and political theorist, received his living first at Bridgnorth, Shropshire, in 1640, and then in Kidderminster, Worcs., in 1641. He sided with Parliament during the Civil War, serving as chaplain in the army in 1645-1647. He joined his fellow Presbyterians in opposing Oliver Cromwell and supporting the Restoration of Charles II, but with the Act of Uniformity was forced to retire to Acton, Middlx., in 1662. Thereafter, he preached when he could, wrote voluminously, and lobbied for the inclusion of Presbyterians within the Church of England. His numerous works include *The Saint's Everlasting Rest* (1650), *The Quaker's Catechism* (1655), and *A Holy Commonwealth* (1659). *DNB;* Richard Schlatter, *Richard Baxter and Puritan Politics* (New Brunswick, N.J., 1957), pp. 3-42.

2. Baxter stayed with Richard Berisford, Esq., Clerk of the Exchequer, of Chorleywood, Herts., who had obtained invitations for Baxter to preach at local parish churches for ten Sundays. See *Micro.* 2:158; J. M. Lloyd Thomas, ed., *The Autobiography of Richard Baxter* (London, 1925), pp. 236, 238.

3. George Keith and other Quakers attended the conference with WP. *Micro.* 2:182.

4. WP may have feared being imprisoned again under the Five Mile Act, which held that no person could preach in an unlawful assembly within five miles of an incorporated town. See doc. 57.

5. Inserted in another hand, by someone who did not understand the Quaker system of dating.

6. Richard Baxter was one of twenty-one divines who signed the preface to John Faldo's *Quakerism no Christianity* (London, 1675). He also probably attended the Wheeler Street meeting on 16 Oct. 1674 concerning the Baptist Thomas Hicks' charges against Friends (see headnote to doc. 83). In early 1675, WP and Baxter exchanged papers in which they debated several of the issues later raised at the Oct. 1675 debate, including the nature of the inner light. In this early 1675 exchange, the two men were more amicable than in docs. 94-98. See *Micro.* 2:170 and Thomas, "Letters of William Penn and Richard Baxter," pp. 204-7.

95
FROM RICHARD BAXTER

[6 October 1675]

I shall stand to the Offer which I made of an other dayes Conference (God willing) but not at yor appoynted time nor at yor rates, I suppose I need not tell you that it was an Extraordinary Case with me to bee able to hold out Seaven howers yesterday[1] & doe you Think seriously, that I can doe the like to morrow, an hower in a day is as much as I can expect to bee able to speake or two at the most (though rarely it fall out otherwise) besides that my nights & dayes being usually spent in paine, Litle doe I know ~~before~~ before hand which will bee my day of ease, (though I have had more in this place then usuall)[2] I told you I think to remove speedily I hope to preach the next Lords day & dare not disable my selfe by another dayes talke with you before it but after, I shall bee ready at the first opportunity (which is not at my Command,) where I shall bee I know not perhapps in the Common Goale where one now lyeth for preaching for mee I am driven to part with howse Goods & books and am going naked out of the world, as I came naked into it,[3] And if you & the Prelates conjunct[?] could have satisfyed mee that I might leave this Calling you would greatly accomodate my Flesh when I meete you I must tell you it will bee with lesse hopes of Candor from you or benefitt to you then yesterday I did for I perceive in you a designeing persecuting spiritt and that you know not what manner of spiritt you are of was it not like a meere designe to choose to meete soe neere to dynner time as thinking I could not have held out fasting till night that you might have the last word & take that for a victory and say as some did to the Anabaptists they run, Is it any better now to call mee to an other bout to morrow that my disability to speake as long as you might seeme to bee yor victory & what hope can I have of that man, that will say &

unsay, as you did & of that man that hath within him, a spirit which judgeth the Ministry which laboured twenty years agoe to bee the most corrupt & persecuting in the world[4] (not excepting the Papists Inquisitors[5] nor (I thinke) the Mahametans and who soe oft pronounceth them noe Ministers of Christ that take Tythes or hyre which is almost all the Christian world not only of this but of all former Ages these 1300 yeares &[6] from the Apostles' dayes alsoe they tooke a constant Maintenance till then though not constreined by Majestrates (because none were Christians) hee that hath a Spiritt which would rid Christ, of almost all his Church & Ministers & say that they are none of his, & would have all people thinke as odiously of them as you by Calumny described them hee that would have all men take all those as soe bad, that is, as hatefull, and then say that hee speaketh for love where there is noe way to preach downe love & preach ~~downe~~ {up} hatred but by perswading men of the hatefull evill of the persons) hee that will soe farre justify, that spirit that at the rise of Quakery soe barbarously rayled at the best of Gods servants that ever I knew in the Land, yea that will soe farre justify James Naylor,[7] whose tounge was bored for blasfemy yea, that can find in his heart, to wish & draw others to wish, that not only all the Ministers of this Age that take Tythes but of all former Ages & places had been disowned & deserted and would have not only the 1800 Nonconformists[8] silenced but all the Setled Ministry of the Land that there might bee none of them to make opposition to ignorance ungodlynes or Popery butt the few woefull Quakers might bee all the Teachers that the Land should have hee that could soe unjustly run over the late horride usurpations rebellions over Turnings & Flatteryes (of which Sectaryes who were much of his owne Spiritt were the great cause) & charge that on the Clergy as a reason to prove them noe Ministers of Christ, which not one of ten or twenty of the now non Conformists nor one of 40 of the Conformists (but such Sectaryes) had a hand in, yea, that which multitudes of the reviled Ministers ventured their Estates & lives against hee that can perswade the People of the Land to soe great Theevery as not to pay those Tythes which they never had property in, nor paid rent for, but by the Law are other mens, as much as their Lands & Goods & calls it Persecution to constraine men soe to pay their debts and give every one his owne yea, and make this requiring of their owne to bee a proofe that they are noe Ministers of Christ & a sufficient cause to degrade & sep[arate?] from almost all the Christian Churches of the world hee that will say that wickednes is more where there is a Clergy then ~~where~~ where there is none (that is among Canniballs & other heathens,) hee that can say that the Christian Religion is o^{r} Conformity to the Spiritt & not to a Catalogue of Doctrines (and soe if that spiritt bee the universall sufficient Light within men that all the heathen & Infidells in the world are Christians & that there are as many Christian Religions as there are men of different Sizes of the spirit or Light) hee that can find in his heart thus to reproach even a suffering Ministry when wee are stript of all & hunted about, for preaching & to joyne them with them that preach without Tythes or any hyre or pay with the rest reproched, & while hee swims himselfe in wealth, to insult over the poore & falsely to professe that he will give all that hee hath to the Needy if they want it more than hee (which the Event I thinke will proove hipocrisy & untrue, hee that dares: joyne with these that he calleth persecutors ~~y~~ yea with Papists Drunkards & ungodly men in reviling & accusing the same Ministry just, as they doe, and when God is love & Christ & his Spiritt is soe much for unity is himselfe soe much for malice & division as to seperate from almost all the Christian world This man is not one, that I can have any great hopes of a faire or profitable Conference with But I will once more meete him (if able) only for two howres Conference, but cannot doe it to morrow or this weeke, Its like enough; that for want of a better Cause hee will tell his poore Followers that this is a Flight & hee might as honestly challenge mee to try the strength of ~~his~~ {oure} Leggs in running a Race with him to know who is in the right {[illegible deletion]} as to doe it by trying the strength of o^{r} Lungs but after the next bout supposing him to continue in his Sin; I will obey the Spirit which saith a man that is an heretick after the first and second Admonition, avoid knowing that hee that is such is condemned of himselfe[9] (he excommunicateth himselfe from the Church & need not be condemned by the Churches excommunicatory Sentence but it must bee that harises arise, that they that are approved may be made manifest I only foretell him, that I greatly doubt that if hee repent not speed[ily] (which is not likely) hee is in great danger of dying a Papist, or an Infidell. As to the Reproach used in your Letter it doth but shew that you are soe much more impatient of plaine Truth & of being contradicted, then other ordinary men, that wee have little reason to beleive that you have more of the Spiritt of humility, meekenes & patience, then those whose Communion you renounce, as not being spirituall, and that they call not for an answer; but for pitty, what you charge my Landlord[10] with, debate it with him I was sorry you began with him & that with soe provoking incivility; but you dreame not sure that I undertooke for any one but my selfe; tho I told you & them what was meete & what was my request: I will say what at o^{r} first meeting I said to you that I suppose you were never acquainted with the Persons whom you revile, other wise I cannot excuse you from downe right malignity, my great acquaintance with abundance of the reviled Ministers & People did cause [one letter deleted] mee to perceive that they lived in Mortification of the Flesh & contempt of such Riches as you possesse few of them having more then meane food & raiment and being therewith content the greatest Adversaryes in a way of Sobriety to worldlynes, sensuality,

Lordly Pride or lazines in Ministers that ever I knew, frequent & fervent in prayer, watching, over the Flocke with love & diligence unweariedly labouring in preaching the antient simple Christianity Faith Patience Repentance obedience love & Concord humbly [illegible deletion] stooping to the lowest & doing good to the Soules and Bodyes of all according to their opportunity & Talents & liveing exemplary in peace among themselves following peace with all, and abhorring usurpations Rebellions, herises & Schisme, and to this day preach for nothing through sufferings with patience I say I know soe much of these that he {that} would perswade mee to hate them or {to} beleive them to bee as odious as you have described them, doth to mee seeme to bee the messenger of Sathan and if I know Gods Spirit speaking in the Scripture, & in mee it teacheth mee to say Gett thee ~~th~~ behind mee Sathan, the accuser of the Bretheren & Reviler of the Servants of the living God And the preacher of hatred to the members of Christ

Yo^r^ Monitor[11]
Ric Baxter

Oct 6th 1675

I would you would studdy what is meant in Scripture by the words hereticks & διαβὸλος trnslated false Accusers.[12]

ALS. Baxter Papers, Dr. Williams's Library, London. (*Micro.* 2:134).

1. The conference on 5 Oct. 1675 (see doc. 94) lasted with no break from 10 A.M. to 5 P.M. WP and Baxter spoke to two roomfuls of people, including one nobleman, two knights, and four Anglican priests. Matthew Sylvester, ed., *Reliquiae Baxterianae: or, Mr. Richard Baxter's Narrative of The most Memorable Passages of his Life and Times* (London, 1696), pt. 3, p. 174.

2. Baxter, tubercular as a young man, was physically weak throughout his life. It should be remembered that Baxter was sixty years old at this time, while WP was only thirty-one. *DNB*.

3. Baxter had recently built a chapel in Oxendon Street, London, but was forced to discontinue services because of threats of distraint of his possessions and imprisonment. He sold his books and goods and went to Rickmansworth, where he still had a license to preach. While he was there, Mr. Seddon, a nonconformist from Derbyshire, preached at Baxter's chapel, was arrested in his place, and jailed for three months. Cunningham, 2:609; Thomas, *The Autobiography of Richard Baxter*, pp. 235-39.

4. Much of the debate between WP and Baxter on 5 Oct. 1675 concerned the Quakers' testimony against the paid ministry. WP argued that the English clergy of 1655, which included Baxter and other nonconforming clerics, could not be distinguished from the conforming Anglican clergy of 1675. (See *Micro.* 2:182, 197, and n. 8, below.)

5. The Papal Inquisition was established in 1232 to root out heresy, and was very active in the prosecution of Protestants during the Reformation. Cross, *Christian Church*.

6. Baxter wrote an ampersand, but probably meant "plus."

7. James Nayler (1617?-1660), Quaker minister of Wakefield, in the West Riding of Yorks. He joined the Parliamentary army in 1642 and became an Independent preacher. Nayler was converted to Quakerism by George Fox in 1651 and became his close associate. By 1656, however, the two men fell out, because Nayler failed to discourage overzealous followers who called him Christ. He was jailed for blasphemy and tried and convicted by Parliament in Dec. 1656. In punishment he was pilloried, whipped, branded with a *B* on his forehead, dragged through the streets behind a

horse, had his tongue bored, and was jailed again. When released in Sept. 1659, he was reconciled with Fox and resumed preaching. Baxter considered Nayler, rather than Fox, to be the chief leader of Friends before WP. *DNB;* Fox, 1:398-99.

8. Approximately 2000 Presbyterian ministers lost their livings in 1662, when they refused to submit to the Act of Uniformity. This law (13 & 14 Car. II, c. 4) required that all clerics accept the Book of Common Prayer and denounce armed rebellion against the king. Cross, *Christian Church.*

9. Titus 3:10-11.

10. See doc. 94, n. 2.

11. One who gives advice to another concerning his conduct. *OED.*

12. Usually translated as "devil" in the New Testament, but translated "false accusers" in 2 Tim. 3:3 and Titus 2:3.

96
TO RICHARD BAXTER

[c. 8 October 1675]

I have received a long Letter[1] from thee which I shall answer with what brevity I can. The first part {of} it contains an Evasion of Meeteing, The last a repeticon of thy old refuted Clamours and both wrapt up in termes only fitt for the Devill, such is the sweetnesse of thy nature, and the great Charity of thy new modell'd Religion. but to the first part thy words are these I shall stand to ~~m~~ the offer {I made} of another dayes conference but not at your time nor Rates. but who concluded thee? not I. tis true I offer'd those things, but so as I left roome for exceptions: yet why should not I have the giveing the Lawes of the second when thou hadst the giveing of the Lawes of the first Conference twas my turne in Equity. But thou art weake and full of paine, if so God help thee: I can't say soe of thy Cause though it's more infirme. well but thou canst not meet me this weeke because of preaching the next Lords day; when then? after it I shall be ready; what day? the first opportunity; who shall judge of that? it is not at my command; nor mine thou hast told me already; who may I aske for Richard Baxter? where may I find him? when will he be at leisure to make good his false Insinuations ag[t] the poore Quakers? In this wood he leaves us or rather hides from us; and then tells the lamentable story of being driven from bookes, house, goods &c O Richard Baxter, and is this a tyme to draw diabolicall pictures of the poore Quakers to render them hatefull and their Religion accursed, and that in the face of Magistracy, whilst thou complainest of persecution for {thy} dissent from others; wher's sweetnesse, meeknesse and charity now? however if I were Richard Baxter no man should goe to prison for me; as one he sayes hath done for him; nor should it be a troubled pulpit, but a troubled Conscience that should make me fly. Goe to London & goe to Gaole, if that must be the Consequenc and learne ~~and learne~~ charity by bonds & thou wilt perhaps practice it better when at Liberty. Well but thou saist I have a designeing wrathfull persecuteing Spirit in me: how am I designeing by comeing {so} neer to dinner time as thinkeing I could not have held out fasting till night: what a prodigious designe was this to blow up poore R. Baxter. but did he really thinke I could stand him so long? doubtlesse his disciples (especially above other gifts In that of patience) fancied nothing lesse then that wee like poore selfe condemned mortalls should cry out, Men and Brethren what shall we doe to be saved? But to holy R. Baxters perception that is as dim here, as his eyes, or his notes were t'other night; I well informe him, that I came late from London the night before the Conference & knew no more of the hour then the unborne Child; nay in the Letter sent from London about the meeteing no tyme was so much as mentioned. what a designeing man was I, R. B. all this while? well but I am wrathfull why? because I take so much paines & am so zealous in discovering & reprehend[ing] his and his Brethrens Cruelty to us. and in what persecuteing? In writing bolder ag^t it (without vanity I say it) then any man In England wittnesse my severall peeces to the parliament,[2] & that impartially, while R. Baxter and his Brethren are for casting us & others to the doggs by a comprehens[ion][3] leaveing us under the Clutches of mercilesse men. thus much [to] the first part of the Letter To the second which containes two sides and a quarter, and all upon this straine, what hope can I have of a man that will say & unsay, that hath a Spirit that judgeth the Ministry that laboured 20 yeares agoe &c I shall by retortion & Inversion, as also by some additionall exceptions give I hope a full & convinceing returne

What hope can I have of him, that subscribes a booke of foulest charges ag^t an whole people,[4] that I have cause to beleive he never read; and yet justifyes it; He that authorizes quotations he never compared; & justifyes Consequences that he never examined; He that sayes wee deny the holy Scriptures to be any meanes of good, when we maintain the contrary, that we set them & the Spirit in opposition, who affirme their exact unity in Testimony, what shall we say of him & what is he that makes us to deny Christ his manhood one while his godhead another while, and that sayes we dispise reject & deny his transactions at Jerusalem for mans salvation when our writeings plentifully mention them wth honour. He that sayes we deny the ministry (because we deny theirs; yea thrice over in the debate, though I warned him of it as a gross abuse) instead of proveing the Ministry of his US and WE the true Gospell ministry. He that makes us to deny a Gospell church, wch we beleive. He that charges us with makeing our Souls God, & so our selves God; He that renders us to deny heaven, & hell, rewards & punishments; & gives these things under his hand, as the doctrines and principles of the Quakers, that are not to be found in any of their writeings, nay that are confest to be butt consequences of his or his freinds drawing never consented agreed or acknowledged by us, but detested & abominated; He that will recommend them after being confuted at least answered without reading our Justification; wch was either by downe right deniall as In some Cases or cleer distinctions as in other places; He that shall maintaine anothers allegations & citations out of mens bookes, that are plainely false & forged; Again he that shall begin a dispute betweene, we and you, & shall require what the you are & refuse to tell what the WE are; He that shall charge his opposer with Studying beforehand that never thought what to say whilst himselfe had writt his matter, & therefore contended for his method, because els he had beene at a losse. He that turnes disputation into preaching, He that Evades Answers, & runs all into reflections, or perversions, He that counted us no Xtians (though he allowed it to papists) yet neither said in what, nor disprov'd our Confession. He that made us to deny any Ministry but that of the Spirit in us only to our selves individually though he prov'd particulerly ~~to~~ the contrary, & that never takes notice of it, but perseveres with dreaming repetitions; He that made me to say I cared not a farthing for Christs Church, that only said it of a persecuteing mercinary Adulterated divorced Church. He that represented me to cry downe Christs ~~Church~~ Ministry; that only deny'd A persecuteing bloody minded Clergy, full of temporizeing & flattery. He that made me accuse Marshall[5] Ward[6] Burgess[7] Edwards[8] &c of fawneing upon O. Cromwell,[9] that only mentioned them as some of those that cryed downe with Baals preists[10] &c on the one side & that most bitterly withstood the Independents &c as shismaticks on the other: calling upon the Civill Magistrates to sweepe the Land of them; on purpose to give proofe of some presbyterian Charity; He that charges shisme upon us & is by his seperate meeteing & flying for doeing so a detected separatist him selfe:[11] He that cryes US and WE takeing in protestants of all sorts & papists too, under some Xtian Qualification but leaveing us out; that hath abetted the beginning of those troubles that are charg'd with sedition & schisme, He that had the Confidence to say he and his freinds, had no hand in separation or persecution, nor daubing of the powers; who writt an holy Commonwealth to An usurper to practice, & raise his new Monarchy upon,[12] & that hath preach't up the use of Civill power to restrain Consciences And Countenanced severity upon Tho. Goodier,[13] so as he had beene kill'd butt for Lt Salsberry, and whose Brethren said at Manchester letts blow up this Quaker at G. Boothes[14] riseing & cry'd Banish them, & for the children doe as the Irish did, nitts will be lice my wittnesses are neere. He that cryes up the Ministry of 1655 for the best in the world and when put close to it, runs of & quitts the field, & of above 9000 preachers with 1800. were the 1800 the ministry & not the 9000?[15] & did none of those call Oliver Moses, the Light of their eyes, & breath of their nostrills. & Rich^{d} [16] the Joshua that was to lead them to the holy Land? did none of these flatter the powers, persecute dissenters? & force their Maintenance?

He that calls this takeing a Malicious advantage of the tymes when God knows I was greived to mention it, but driven to it by such extravigant praises of them as being of the best which I thinke in a sence is corruptest; & to show it must tell their story. He that calls the Law wch forces maintenance from people to a Ministry they own not one of those Lawes of the Land that is the Rule of propertye, & yet denyes the Law that distrains Religious meeteings as agt property. He that makes us deny any Christianity at all to be in any butt our selves, that inferres from our words that all else are Antichristian butt our selves &c because we acknowledge this way to be more excellent as that which has given life to our Souls & in which we have found the redeeming power of Xt in our Soulls; wch we never felt under other ministrys & in other wayes. He that from our declining the [illegible deletion] fashions & Customes of the world in pure Conscience to God, the only token of our esteeming our selves Xtians, & that sayes we goe out of one Extreame into another. He that chargeth us wth maintaineing popery & yet counts {the} papists Xtians, whilst he denyes us to be such, at least questions it. He that admitted not perticular instances to conclude against Generalls, & him selfe draw reflections from J. Naylor uppon the whole people called Quakers & their Faith: He that chargeth me with beleiveing, & bids me repent, of what ~~I~~ never was, but wt if it were, I told him I utterly detested, and that after he was told so, yet sums up his discourse in the same termes without proveing his accusation or takeing {any} notice of my abhorrence of any such thing as that he charg'd: & he that can make a people guilty of such fault as J. N. might committ when they solemnely & in print [renounce & censure it.] He that finds fault with agravateing evill agt persons as a way that tends to destroy Love, & yet practices it by a dull & envious repetition of storyes thrice over not at that tyme to be perticulerly disproved. He that makes it a mark of a false Church in us that we contradict & write one agt another (wch is still false, we never did soe) yet justifyes the Episcopalians[17] presbyterians Independents & Baptists that have done the like & continue to doe so. He that pretends they are all his Brethren & the papists too for he calls them Xtians (which must be by being borne of one Stocke) yet say that this Spirit of Schisme this rending Spirit that leads into these perverse wayes began with those that cryed downe with Baalls preists &c descended thence into the Sectaryes, that is Independents (for so the presbyterians called them) from them to the Anabaptists so to the Rant[ers;] and then to the Quakers. He that can justifye a man in calling the Quakers Light ~~a sinfull sordid & corrupt thing~~ within a sinfull sordid and corrupt thing & yet appeal to it in print & say its but what we have of him & his Brethren. He that reproves us for Rayling that defend our selves In Scripturetearmes rightly applyed as we offer to prove, to both use it & abett it in others. He that can call a man Brother one houre & Divill the [illegible deletion] next; first extoll and Hosanna then debase & crucifye bid me gett me behind him & God rebuke me as If I were a Divel[:][18] He that can doe all these things, I hope I may say, is so far neither a good man, a charitable man, nor a faire disputant. And whether R. Baxter be not this very man I leave it with him seriously to consider [illegible deletion] as he will answer the great God at his tribunall; Ah doe not so harshly represent nor cruelly Character a poore people that are given up to follow the leadings of that Jesus, abundance of you have long told us, has stood even all night at the doore of our hearts knocking that he might come in,[19] who's pure Spirit & fear we desire to be subject to, & waite upon God, when together in true silence from all fleshly thoughts, that we may feel our hearts replenisht with his divine Love & life, in which to forgive our opposers, & those that spitefully use us: in wch deare Love of God R. Baxter I doe forgive thee & desire thy good & felicitye; & when I read thy Letter the many severityes therein could not divert me from saying that I should freely give thee an apartment in my house, & thy liberty therein that I could visitt, & yett discourse thee in much tender Love; notwithstanding this hard entertainment {from thee} I am without harder words

Thy sincere and Loveing
freind Wm Pen

My Master went to London and left me this to Coppy over which I have done I thinke exactly As I could[20]

Original lost. We follow the contemporary copy in the Baxter Papers, Dr. Williams's Library, London. (*Micro.* 2:141). Uncertain or illegible passages have been supplied in brackets from the copy in the hand of Mark Swanner in WP's Le⁺⁺erbook, 1667-1675, HSP. (*Micro.* 2:150).

1. Doc. 95.

2. WP is probably referring to his tracts, *A Treatise of Oaths* (1675); *The Continued Cry of the Oppressed for Justice* (1675); and *England's Present Interest Discover'd* (1675). All three were addressed to Parliament. He was also attending parliamentary sessions at this time. See doc. 97.

3. Baxter advocated a policy of religious "comprehension," authorized by act of Parliament, which would permit the inclusion of nonconformists (especially Presbyterians) within the established Church of England. Presbyterians had supported the Restoration of Charles II in 1660, expecting to remain within the Church, but the Cavalier Parliament of 1662 excluded them with the Act of Uniformity. Quakers advocated bills for toleration rather than comprehension because they believed, with good reason, that Presbyterians would support the Church in persecuting sects. Charles F. Mullett, "Toleration and Persecution in England, 1660-89" *Church History* 18:18-43.

4. Baxter was one of twenty-one divines who signed the preface to John Faldo's *Quakerism no Christianity* (London, 1675). See headnote to doc. 83.

5. Stephen Marshall (1594?-1655) advocated the Presbyterian model of church government, and supported the Parliament during the Civil War. Marshall took an active part in the Presbyterian Westminster Assembly and was appointed one of Oliver Cromwell's "triers," who examined the fitness of local ministers, in 1654. *DNB*.

6. Nathaniel Ward (1578-1652), a Puritan divine who emigrated to Massachusetts in 1634, was the author of *The Simple Cobbler of Agawam* (1647), in which he denounced religious toleration. On returning to England in 1646, Ward supported Parliament,

which was mostly Presbyterian, in its power struggle with the army, which was led by the Independents. *DNB*.

7. Anthony Burgess, vicar of Sutton Coldfield, War., also supported the Parliament in the Civil War and was a member of the Westminster Assembly. He lost his living after the Restoration. *DNB*.

8. Thomas Edwards (1599-1647), appointed a university preacher at Cambridge c. 1623 and minister of St. Botolph's, Aldgate, London, in 1629, supported the Presbyterians during the Civil War. He attacked the Independents furiously, first in *Antapologia* (1644) and then in *Gangraena: or a catalogue* (1646), which listed the alleged heresies of various sects. *DNB*.

9. Oliver Cromwell.

10. Ahab, under the influence of Jezebel, angered Israel's God by setting up altars and graven images to the Syrian god Hadad, called Baal. See 1 Kings 16:31-33 and 2 Kings 10:18-28. Charles M. Laymon., ed., *The Interpreter's One-Volume Commentary on the Bible* (Nashville, 1971), p. 192. In WP's view, the Presbyterians were ardent persecutors: they denounced the Anglican clergy as Baal's priests, and they tried to sweep away all other Protestant churches and sects.

11. See doc. 95, n. 3.

12. Fearful that radicals would destroy English society, Baxter supported Parliament's plea to Oliver Cromwell in 1657 that he become king of England. Cromwell rejected this plea, but did assume the title of hereditary Protector. When Oliver Cromwell died in 1658, Baxter supported his son Richard Cromwell as Protector, and designed for him the government outlined in *A Holy Commonwealth* (1659), which included a divine-right king and a parliament of saints. Schlatter, *Richard Baxter & Puritan Politics*, pp. 11-21, 68-124.

13. Thomas Goodaire (d. 1693) was convinced of Quakerism by George Fox in 1651. Imprisoned frequently, he was jailed for speaking in Baxter's church in Kidderminster in 1655 while making the first Quaker missionary visit to Worcester. WP refers here to a subsequent trip to Worcester in the same year when Goodaire was attacked by parishioners of St. Swithin's for attempting to speak after Baxter's sermon. Goodaire was saved by soldiers who took him home. Baxter neither supported nor opposed Goodaire's persecution. Fox, 1:399; Braithwaite, *Beginnings*, pp. 194-95; Penney, *The First Publishers of Truth*, pp. 274-75.

14. In June 1659, one month after Richard Cromwell's abdication, Quakers presented petitions to Parliament for the elimination of tithes. Afraid that Parliament would agree with the change, Presbyterian clergymen supported the royalist rising of Sir George Booth of Cheshire. Booth's excuse for mustering over a thousand men at Warrington, Lancs., in Aug. 1659, was to put down a rumored Quaker revolt. Braithwaite, *Beginnings*, pp. 458-59.

15. Of England's 9000 parishes, about 2000 were held by nonconformist ministers who were ejected from their livings by the Act of Uniformity of 1662. Cross, *Christian Church*.

16. Richard Cromwell (1626-1712), became Protector upon the death of his father Oliver in Sept. 1658. Not tenacious of power, he abdicated in May 1659 under pressure from the army. *DNB*.

17. The Church of England.

18. Matt. 16:23.

19. Rev. 3:20.

20. See provenance note.

97
TO RICHARD BAXTER

[11 October 1675]

Richd Baxter
I have receiv'd a letter from thee, of the 10th Inst. Just now;[1] being the 11th — & about six at night: In the first place it looks like a designe, I mean, not to meet me, (though it be to offer a meeting)—Such an one as it is) for by the date, it was, for ought I Know, a night and almost halfe a day a comeing less then two miles: A man that had not read thy principles of love, and heard Thee dispute, would thinke that this letter lay legier[2] at Rickmansworth by order, till I Should be gone to London, but I am more charitable: The begining of this unhappy Epistle tells me, *if I have not yet enough;* of what?[3] raylery, Slanders, interruptions, dirty reflections? yea, too much, had R: B: pleasd, but of reason, good language, order, and personall Civility, little or none fell from R: B: I affirme. Well—but *in the vaine ostentation of my forwardness to an other meeting shall be no Cover to my Shame.* I thought I had been Shameless; there's hopes of me I See: But R: B: Why—asham'd, for thy Sensless, headless taleless talke; I profess I was more then asham'd, for I was greiv'd; has my last Kinde letter had noe better Success? I perceive the: Scurvy of the minde is thy distemper; I feare its Incurable: I would Say, I had rather be *Socrates* at the day of Judgement then R: *Baxter,* but that he would tell me, that I am neerer akin to Heathens then Christians; and the truth is, then Such meerly nominall ones, I desire to be.
In the next place, be pleased to Know that I came late {from} London the last Seventh night, and am upon apointments at London this weeke, [illegible deletion] So that time, once mine, is irrecoverably gone till the next 6th day at Soonest vulgarly fryday;—I am also to attend upon the Parliement, as I was all the last Sessions, on the behalfe of many poor and Lamentable Sufferers for pure Conscience;—insomuch as not receiving any Reply to my last, had I not gone So early my wife & part of my familie had Come up wth mee for this Session & Terme.
However, I shall never refuse a day (in my power) to Richard Baxter, but to use his terms, not at his tyme & rates. I shall discourse on either of the points mentioned the other night; or if he will, I shall undertake to prove R: B: a Perverter, Traducer and forger, a Charge Black, but it shall staine me if I dont make it good; so little is he man of true love; next I shall Chuse short argumentation: 3ly that at the Conclusion each of us may have tyme to sum up his sense In a Conscientious manner by way of repetition & Recommandation to the People. 4ly I utterly refuse the limitation of tyme, let the Conference end wth the matter, or by Consent upon [illegible deletion] {the

place}. I am not so flush of my tyme, nor so ill dispos'd of, that I should leav London, my Conscientious Imploym[t] for the releif of poor Sufferers,—Severall apointments not in ~~po~~ my power to undoe (to Say nothing of my owne wordly[4] Concerns that are great) to ride down to Charlewood[5] but for two hours talke wth R: B: besides I cant Confine my Selfe precisely to an hour, as those that are accustomed to notes & hour glasses. I refuse not my neighbours house, Since invited to it, thus much at present from

thy Friend

London the 11th of the *8mo {Augst}*[6] 1675 Wm Penn

LS. Baxter Papers, Dr. Williams's Library, London. (*Micro.* 2:160). An incomplete version is in WP's Letterbook, 1667-1675, HSP (*Micro.* 2:164). Addressed: For Richard Bax | ter at | Charlewood.

1. R. Baxter to WP, [10 Oct. 1675], *Micro.* 2:158. In this letter, Baxter offered to meet WP for two hours on the next Tuesday (12 Oct. 1675). He gave WP a choice of formats: they could continue discussing either Quakerism or the paid ministry, or they could each question the other for one hour, presumably on a wide range of topics.
2. Obsolete form of *ledger*, or resting in a place. *OED*.
3. "Of what?" was first underlined, but the underlining was then scratched out.
4. "Worldly."
5. Chorleywood, Herts., near Rickmansworth.
6. Inserted in another hand, by someone who did not understand the Quaker system of dating.

98
FROM RICHARD BAXTER

[post 11 October 1675]

So much to yo[r] second Letter:[1] To yo[r] last[2] lesse may serve. I wrote to you as its dated: The servant that brought it was required to be early with you: He saith that he was at yo[r] house by nine a clock: I knew not that you had taken horse before he came. Being now at London, I take yo[r] Reasons ag[t] coming hither now, as sufficient, & cast not false suspicions on them, as you did on mine. The rest of yo[r] Letter is but to tell me how farre you are from *Christian humility & patience*, notwithstanding yo[r] oft boastings, of the great works of the Spirit uppon yo[r] heart; when you are not able to heare of yo[r] sin & erro[r], (or at least my reasons so to think of them) without that smart & passion w[ch] you expresse, falsly calling my reasons, *Railery, slanders, interruptions, dirty reflexions*, (as before you calld it *Envie Reprobating* you &c), that I used little or no *Reason, good language, order* or *pers~~o~~nall civility:* w[t] *obeysance* did you expect, who so pleaded agt that w[ch] custome with us calleth civility. I did not *Thou* you; I put off my *hatt:* why did you not name the *Incivility* of *word* or *action*, nor then accuse me of it, nor yet the *Railery*, or *interruption* by me. Yea you have in this short letter of mine, found the symptomes of an *incurrable Scurvy of the mind,* which you have the kindnes to yor selfe to call yor owne last *Letter* (*kind*). And that I may be past doubt whether or no it be a spirit of *Christian Love* that acteth you, You let me know that you had rather be *Socrates at the day of judgmt than R. B;* & that *he is but a meere nominall Christian.* By wch the world may judge of yor accusations of other men. Wt is the crime by wch you have proved me worse than a heathen. Did you charge any thing on me, save my contradicting you & yor way, (& yor false accusation in yor Letter of Countenancing some cruelty agt Tho: Goodier.) when taking tythes or hire was yor proofe that we are no true Ministers of Christ, & I told you I had taken neither these thirteen yeares, you had nothing to say agt me, but that *one swallow makes no summer.* And yet if that one do but tell you why he thinketh you a *heynous sinner,* he is worse than a heathen with you: And yet God saith, Thou shall not hate thy brother in thy heart; Thou shalt in any wise rebuke thy neighbor & not suffer sin uppon him, Lev. 19.17. And Paul Gal. 2. withstood Peter to his face before many, when he was blameworthy;[3] & he tells Timothy that there are mouthes that must be stopped, & some that must be cuttingly reproved.[4] Do you do no worse by us, than tell us of or reall sin, & prove it, & that in order to or amendemt, to hold us in union & concord with Christs church, & not make a heape of false or frivolous accusations to be a Reason of yor dividing separations, & condemning allmost all Christs ministers on earth as none of his, nor such as should be heard, & I hope we shall shew that or patience & humility is more than yors: I can tell you, that R B maketh it not his work to perswade you that he is faultlesse, & he taketh yor condemnation easily, as knowing that as you are not his finall Judge, so it is safe for him to be oft provoked to suspect & try himselfe, nor is it his worke to passe a judgment on the person & finall state of Socrates or you, but only to enquire, *whether yors* into wch you call people from Christs Churches, be really the way of Christ; that I & others may know or duty: wch we cannot do without taking notice of the practices of yor party, because it is yor practicall excellency above other men, by wch you principally endeavor to prove that it is Gods spirit in you by wch you Condemne & divide yorselves from the servants of the Lord, & labor so industriously *to destroy Love & unity,* wherin I hope to resist you to my power while I have life, breath & opportunity.

AL. Baxter Papers, Dr. Williams's Library, London. (*Micro.* 2:177).

1. Doc. 96.
2. Doc. 97.
3. Gal. 2:11-16.
4. Titus 1:11-13. Paul did warn Timothy that it would be necessary to reprove their followers in order to keep them faithful, in 2 Tim. 4:1-5, but Baxter's scriptural reference is from Paul's letter to Titus.

99
ADVICE TO THE SUSSEX QUARTERLY MEETING

A Memoranda of those Generall things discoursed & assented unto by the Late meetings about Sufferings[1] the 18th of the 8th Mo: [October] 1675.

1 That Friends Suffering be laid upon those in Power agreed unto.

2 that the meeting doth not enjoyn, Impose upon or advise any friend in Sufferings to take cours at Law for a remedy, neither on the other hand can wee impose upon any, not to use the Law in any Case, but a freedome is left to the Sufferers to use such means as Consists with the unity of friends & their own peace & satisfaction in the truth, and in the Clearing A faithfull testimony in the truth.

3 That friends doe not Judge or reflect upon one another in these Cases a freedome being Left upon urgent occasions to take Such Course for reliefe, & ease to the opressed as may not be Prejediciall to truth's testimony.

4 That if any friend or friends Aprehend A necessity to endeavour A reliefe by the Law of the land to stop the destroyers &c. they first advise about their Case, with their respective Monthly or Quarterly meetings or at Least with some of their Principall friends Pertaining thereto.

5 That it's Convenient that friends that Suffer beyond the Limits of the Law, have an understanding thereof for divers Causes and especialy to be Capable of laying it on the Heads of their persecutors for exceeding their own Law in Severity, & that they may know in what Cases relief may be had, they Haveing their Liberty in the truth to except thereof or Suffer.

6 That Friends who Suffer are advised not to let out their minds into too much Expectation of outward relief by friends here in poynt of law but that they Patiently & Principally depend upon the Lord & his power to plead their Cause

7 That Truths testimony against Tithes & Friends inocency in Suffering be kept to & though inocent endeavors may be used to save them from being taken away, yet that friends be Carefull of Violent Strugling to detain them when the Adversary Comes to take them by force.

8 That in all {Such} Cases wherein friends want information in poynt of Law they may send up their Questions to Tho: Rudyard or Ellis Hooks to Procure & send them a resolve: both as to such Cases wherein they may have relief & wherein they may not, that they may not remaine, in any Groundless or uncertain expectation

9 Persons nominated to draw up a short Paper of Some instances of most Gross Sufferings to be presented to the Parliament

with Convenient Speed, as also to draw up the book of Sufferings at large as soon as may be as well those upon the late act[2] unprinted as Tithes &c

~~10~~ Steph: Crisp Wm Welch Wm Gibson, Wm Pen, Tho: Rudyard, Arthur Cook,[3] Tho: Elwood Fra: Moore,[4] Bray Doyly.

10 That the Book of Sufferings before the king Came in be transcribed & Reviewed by the severall Countyes Respectively to Inspect & take Care of the Certainty of matters before it be Printed, & when fitted that the Printing of it goe on.

11 That after they are reviewed by the Counties & returned to London Friends of the Second days meeting[5] Advise about the reviewing them over again for their better methodizing in order to a Brief History to be Published.

MBE. Epistles and Advice from Yearly Meetings, Quaker Records 12/1, East Sussex County Record Office. (*Micro.* 2:270). A contemporary copy, nearly identical, is in the Leek MSS, FLL.

1. On 4 June 1675 the London Yearly Meeting called each quarterly meeting to send a representative to London on 18 Oct. to discuss suffering and how to resist it. The 18 Oct. meeting organized the Meeting for Sufferings with twelve members, two from each of the six greater-London meetings. At the beginning of each session of Parliament, representatives from the country meetings would meet with the twelve London members to prepare petitions to the king and Parliament. For a commentary on this document, see Braithwaite, *Second Period*, pp. 283-85, 676-77.

2. The Conventicle Act of 1670. In Feb. 1675 Charles II had issued orders in council to return to strict enforcement of the act. Bate, *The Declaration of Indulgence*, pp. 140-41.

3. Arthur Cook (d. 1699) of Shadwell parish, Middlx., was a currier. In 1672 he was released from Newgate, pardoned after the Declaration of Indulgence. In 1675 he was one of the original members of the Meeting for Sufferings. Later he immigrated to Pennsylvania, where he was a member of the Provincial Council and Chief Justice of the Provincial Court. Besse, 1:437; London Yearly Meeting Minutes, 1668-1693, FLL, 4 4 mo. 1675; *PMHB* 5:157, 33:426; Hinshaw, *Encyclopedia of American Quaker Genealogy*, 2:349; Digest of Middlesex Quaker Registers, GSP.

4. Francis Moore (d. 1679), of Stepney and London, was a merchant and distiller. He was imprisoned in 1670 and had goods confiscated in 1676 and 1677. Besse, 1:439; Digest of Middlesex Quaker Registers, GSP.

5. The Second Day's or Morning Meeting, composed of men ministers, was primarily responsible for supervising the printing of books and for assigning ministers in the London area. Braithwaite, *Second Period*, p. 280.

100
FROM ANTHONY LOWTHER

Maske[1] 18 Oct: [16]75

Deare Brother

Though I cannot excuse my selfe of neglect in omitting to answer your kinde letter[2] I hope you will pardon me and for the future I shall endeavor to amend that fault wch I must confesse I am to often guylty of; but having the happynesse of hearing of your wellfayre and my sisters[3] either by my Lady Penne or my wife has made me continue the longe[r] in it. The pleasant countrey you were pleased to show me when I were at Rickmansworth makes me desirous to try whither any of those trees that thrive so bravely there will come to any thing with us here; in order to wch I desired your Gardiner this being a plentifull yeare for Beeche maste[4] that he would get me six o 8 bushells of itt with some young beeche trees and elmes wch he promised should be donne I thinke he sayde they might be got for 5 shillings the {100} if they will come at that rate I would be glad to have 500 of each but if much dearer then but halfe the number of each but I am more desirous of the elmes then the others because I hope by theire ~~chaff~~ {seedes} to rayse some beech. I desire you to excuse this trouble and to beleive that I am

Your affct Brother & servant
Ant Lowther

My Lady[5] & my wife as well as my selve give our kinde love to you and my sister.

ALS. Penn-Forbes Papers, HSP. (*Micro.* 2:274). Addressed: These | For Mr Penn at | Mr Phillip Fords at | the black skarfe | in Bow lane | London. Docketed: Ant Lowther | 18 8br 75.

1. Marske, Cleveland, Yorks., Lowther's ancestral home. Anthony and Margaret (Penn) Lowther divided their time between Marske and Lowther's uncle's home in Walthamstow.
2. WP's letter to Lowther has not survived.
3. His sister-in-law, Gulielma Penn. Lowther could, however, be referring to his own youngest sister, Hannah Lowther (b. 1654), who might have been visiting her uncle. ACM, vol. 49B.
4. Mast is the fruit of the beech or other forest trees, especially as used for food for swine. *OED.*
5. Lady Penn, who was evidently visiting the Lowthers at Marske.

101
TO LADY ANN CONWAY

This letter to Lady Conway is an interesting personal expression of WP's theory of divine light, and shows how he exhorted the nearly converted. In it, WP suggests that the "light & Spirit of Jesus" bring man to direct knowledge and experience of God, and that this experience, constantly renewed, overcomes the kind of formal, tradition-bound Christianity which is dry, lifeless, and leads to man-made sectarianism. For WP and the Quakers, the divine light within was the true guide to faith. The light helped one to understand what, for example, in all the various interpretations of Scripture, comes from God. The light within could guide a woman like Lady Conway to what was true in all her reading and thinking. However, it was also understood that conversion is a long process, requiring patience, denial of self ("not only the filthyness of flesh, but spirit done away"), and passive acceptance of "the leadings of his eternall spirit." Ultimately, the reward is true peace. For further discussion of WP's ideas concerning divine light and conversion, see Endy, pp. 153-58, 169-75; and Vann, *The Social Development of English Quakerism, 1655-1755*, pp. 32-46.

London 20th 8mo [October] 1675.

My Friend[1]

Not only the generall fame of thy desires after the best things, but thy perticuler kind Invitations, have begotten in me very strong Inclinations to see thee; & since many great difficulties have of late depriv'd me of that satisfaction, & that my own late illness, my Attendence on the Parliamt for the releife of many of our poor distressed friends, wth An unusuall importancy of business now befallen me[2] [two letters deleted] {obstruct} I have been the more [illegible deletion] {earnest} wth the Bearer, my innocent, learned, christian Friend George Keith, to visitt thee, who comes in the Spirit of Jesus; that gathers out of the life, glory, pride, pleasure & honner of this world. o My friend, we preach not our selves, but the light of Xt in the Conscience, wch is gods faithfull & true wittness, that the worldly, pompous church has slain, & made merry over; & all thos that are in a fleshly religion (Insensible of this pur light & spirit of Jesus) they are in Babilon, & wch is wors, of Babilon[3]; That outward Jew, circumcison, christian, that is Born of the fleshly nature in religion[4] (viz) form without eternall life & powr) Persecutes him that is born of the spirit;[5] the one is the whore the other the lambs bride; now that wch gathers to be one of that blessed church, wch is the Lambs spouse (that wares & goes in white linnen)[6] is the light & spirit of Jesus, wch shines in the heart, to give unto people the blessed Knowledge of the glory of god In the face of Jesus Xt. So Dear friend, that thou mayst retire thy mind to that tender spirit of truth wch god hath sent into our hearts to Convince us of sin, of righteousness & of Judgement, that thou mayst be redeemd from lifeless professions that are in the world. I have been acquainted wth Papists, Protestants, Presbiterians, Independents, Baptists; & I know that they have formerly felt some touches of the divine powr, that raises up the Soul above formality; And the Ancient church of Rome receiv'd not the Pope, but the Spirit (Rom. 8.) to be their Rule, the Ancient Protestants, especially the blessed Martyrs were of our mind, & Pleaded for inspiration to be the true foundation of all Right Knowledge, hope, faith. the Puritans did the same, & for the Independents & Baptists, a spring of divine life was among them, that (as I may say) brought them forth to reprove the Lordly, mercinary ministrys; but none of them knew a stay to their minds {where} to waite for a dayly supply of powr & life, but insteed of waiting for less mixture of their own spirits, they became careless; & grew letterall, Earthly, formall; And fell to ~~a~~ mans-worship; & held their faith by Traditions of men & therefore did the Lord god send us forth, in poverty of spirit, much fear & dread, under the operation of the powr of the everlasting god, to Cry down thes dry halts & rests by the way, in wch is not eternall life, & to hold forth A Purer manifestation of truth & life then hath hether to been; & our Testemony is, that all turne their mindes unto the light & spirit of Jesus within them; for their the divil has reign'd & there he must be dethron'd by the brightness of the comeing & breath of the mouth of the Lord; And though I had a great proffession, flourisht wth leaves, & made a fair appearance; yet till I came to be subject to this testemony of god in my heart, to love & obey it, I had noe true peace. this is [one letter deleted] he the Priests have Long told us stands at the doore & knocks, & now they are Angry that we lett him in; for he teaches us, that his gospell is milk & hony with out mony & Price; but the Priests gospell [illegible deletion] is mony & great Price, without milk or hony. My Friend, turn into thy heart, hear his voyce, salvation is comeing to thy house, lett him have the dominion; watch least thou enter not into temptation; & o watch unto heavenly Breathings, prayings, & Praises; for the dead cant, 'tis the liveing (into whom god has again breathed the breath of his pure life) that can acceptably pray, or praise the lord. So that we are desirous [illegible deletion] {thou} mightst be acquainted wth the word neigh thee in thy heart (Rom. 10) that thou mayst hear it & doe it. o the blessed redemption, the heavenly union & dominion that is felt by all such true followers of the lamb; who give {up} to the leadings of his eternall spirit. such shall have a root of life in them selves; & stand upon a Rock; an hope that makes not ashamed, for it is grounded on divine experience. The Lord god of heaven & earth draw, incline, & gather thy spirit Into himselfe, to bear his cross, & wittness, not only the filthyness of flesh, but spirit done away; not only {to} suffer loss of earth, but heaven; I mean that wch is to pass away; that the new & permanent earth & heaven may be wittnessed, in wch dwells righteousness, where the lamb has the victory, & the soul, through his word & testemony. that the comforts & refreshments of his innocent life may abound towards thee. That, a wittness, a living, faithfull & true wittness thou mayst be in thy generation, to his Immediate powr & worke in the soul agst all lifeless, letterall, formall worships, in wch the heavenly fellowship Can not be found. o Thy Crys god will Answear if thou keepest but the lambs word of patience! & thou wilt be patient, if thou watch unto the light of Jesus, & give not way to the roavings & wandrings of thy mind. o this blessed inward yoak, burden & Cross has been my preservation, wth thousands. I cannot But Admire it, speak honorably of it, & earnestly recommend it, as that wch leads back to innocency by redeeming the soul from evill, & strengthening it ag^st^ temptation. This is more noble then Crosses of ~~gold or~~ silver or gold, or dead Religions; this inwardly stays & mortefys, & brings into the fellowship of the [illegible deletion] Mistery of the Death & Resurrection of X^t^ & his assencion too, Into the heavenly place; for the Children of the resurrection, live in heavenly places in X^t^ Jesus.

I have entertained thee wth w^t^ was at present upon my spirit. I pray god affect thee therewith, & the Xtian visit of my friend, that thou mayst be sensible of our Internall travil for thy temporall & ternall felicity. I cannot but signefy wth all due acknowledgements, thy great Kindness to me, In thos friendly Invitations it pleas'd thee to send me;[7] God almighty be more abundantly good to thee then I Can express, In whose presence I am sure there's life, & at whose right hand there is pleasure for ever more; & I had rather be a day in his courts then a thousand elsewhere; & a poor dore keeper in his house Then a great Prince in the Tents of wickedness,[8] for his goodness endures for ever, & of his tender mercys there is no end to his children. God Almighty keep & preserve thee to his eternall Kingdom; so wisheth

Thy Friend in
godly Love & sincerity
Wm Penn

my Father Penington[9] Sends the hi[s] Love & a smal present wth it.

I have been wth H. Moor who is better acquainted wth us then formerly; & will I hope right us to the world;[10] however, our life is hid wth X^t^ in god.

ALS. Add. Ms. 23217, BL. (*Micro.* 2:278).

1. Lady Conway showed an early interest in philosophy and theology, and was one of the most learned women in England. Although largely self-educated, she did study informally with the Cambridge Platonist Henry More, who became one of her closest friends. In the early 1670s she became deeply interested in Quakerism, and she was convinced about 1677, two years before her death. Only one of her works was published, the posthumous *Opuscula Philosophica* (Amsterdam, 1690), translated into English as *The Principle of the Most Ancient and Modern Philosophy* (1692); the German philosopher Leibnitz acknowledged its influence upon him. Nicolson, *Conway Letters; DNB;* and doc. 90, above.

2. The year 1675 was indeed a busy one for WP. Throughout the year he continued several religious controversies, orally and in print, and wrote tracts on oaths and toleration. In October, before the date of this letter, he contended with Richard Baxter, and joined the Quakers' new Meeting for Sufferings in its nationwide campaign to end the persecution of English Friends. See docs. 94 through 99, above.

3. See Rev. 17:1-5, 15-16. The identification of Babylon with the "whore" in Revelation led to the frequent use of the word *Babylon* as a symbol for luxury and wickedness in the church.

4. Rom. 2:25-29.

5. John 3:4-7.

6. See Rev. 19:7-9.

7. No evidence that WP ever visited Lady Conway has yet been found, but Marjorie Nicolson believes that he did, on the basis of "casual references in papers of the Quakers." *Conway Letters*, p. 435.

8. Ps. 84:10.

9. Isaac Penington.

10. In November Lady Conway wrote to More that if he had not actually promised to write something on the Quakers' behalf, there had been an misunderstanding, because they believed that he had. He answered, in December, that he liked some Quakers, and some things about them, but that he had not really changed his mind about their "Familisticalness" and would not write a general testimonial. In Jan. 1676 he said that he might give testimony about some individual Quakers whom he respected and mentioned George Keith and WP, but said again that he would not testify for the whole sect. Nicolson, *Conway Letters*, pp. 409, 416, 418-19.

102
TO GEORGE FOX

Walthamstow: 4th 1mo [March] 1676.[1]

Very Dr: G: F:

And eternally beloved, yea all Ages shall bless thee, & Magnefy the Powr that has guirded, does guird & Crown thee over all envy, pride, darkness, & thy kingdom is not of this world, nor has the spirit wisdom & lusts of it any part therein, for I feel thee to Raign over all such things & spirits. & thy place is very neer that lamb, whos life & Blood takes away the sin of the world; & the not seing Thee in thy true place, nor haveing a sense of thy heavenly commission & Authority, foolish shortsighted & pufft up spirits Intrude & smite & Rebell, & this has been & I fear will be the Loss of many: such, whatever may be the outside of the platter, have inwardly departed from the liveing god, & live Loose from the Cross in the mind, & being Carried with a Tempest of dark stubbornd thoughts withstand & roughly run over the tender shootings of the Immortall Powr & day: well, my soul is in full Confidence of its downfall, & I hope to behold it.

Now Dr: G, I have thy last to me of the 18th 12mo[2] I have given order about the books for R. Fretwell.[3] But some that saw the letter wonder'd, first that thou shouldst be so sharp wth the Js[4] & so kind to him that is, say they, an odd spirited & imperious man. 2ly That thou shouldst Reflect on J. W. for goeing down wth J. Scafe,[5] when, Harwood[6] & Murford[7] were thy companions; Thus they fling of thy words, & they have {place} little wth Such: G. W.[8] is at Bristol & has prevaled wth J. S. to goe down, upon the time apointed to be in the North.[9] W. R.[10] accompanys them; It had been well if this had been 4 months agoe, but better late then never. he writes of good Service

there, & that there is some Tenderness. T. Curtis[11] went down wth him; the Reading Friends are out of Goale, the D. of y. was as good As his word in that matter;[12] I desire & earnestly beseech thee to be ~~there~~ at the meeting; & Because Poor Margt [13] is so much smitt at, & run upon (as I beleive never woman was, for wch god the righteous Judge will Judge, & plead wth them), as if she was the Cause; & of an Implacable temper; without bowels, or the spirit of Reconciliation, to show them that she Can pass by all that past between them that Concerns herselfe; & to make the most of the good or the tender thing, if it arise never so little In either of them, this would be a deadly stroak upon that back biteing spirit, & so Confound them that smite, yea so stop their mouths, that there would be no place for them to hide In: o then would this dark serpents head lye so fair for the Blow; well, I leave it, but earnestly desire it in my own spirit. & Dr George, it would be well to have [illegible deletion] some very weighty friends of that County there, that may keep down the Reasoning spirit, for that pragmatical spirit will doe noe god: that so the Powr may in the Ancient dread of it Arise & determin. I hope to be present wth some from these parts. Dr: J. Burn:[14] goes out 2d day the lord willing. And today, W. Gib.[15] is gone; the Lord of heaven & earth determin this thing clearly among us.
Thy Book committed to me to gett {fitted &} Printed is out, a precious thing, as are all thy papers, friends have great Regard to many of thy late papers & Books, deep & heavenly openings, & great variety of them. that Book was to such as Profess Xt in words & deny him in works; it is Titl'd Possession above Proffession,[16] also Another Call'd Cain gainst Abel,[17] that T. R.[18] brought to the meeting for N. Engd Proffrs Matthew Hide a long opposer is dead, & has left a blessed testemony To Truth & Friends, wch Is gone to the Press, well Attested;[19] at present I have enough to doe: Persecution is coming too, & its an ill time to leav London destitute; the Mayr has sent to frds to come to him, tis {to} warn them not to meet.[20] I think to have some of thy Dantsick letters[21] deliver'd among them. Wm Rogs [22] & I, are in a close combat about things, he is very high indeed, & neer the brink, the lord keep him from falling. N. Colman[23] that saw the Vision of the Angel {ready to} cutt~~ing~~ him off &c: about womens meetings, has recanted it, condemn'd it, calls it the effect of thy threats, & my Insinuations. & is exceeding high, threatning me wth Judgemts & I know not what. I have clear'd my Conscience at our 2ds morning meetings about the Js staying there away thus to stagger & defile; though I have suffer'd hard for it; yea more then ever I had from the greatest Princes of the world before I knew Truth; but the Lord blott out all, swe{e}ten all, & cement all, if it be his blessed will. I Adjourn much till I see thee, wch I shall rejoyce to doe & that famely, to whom is my Dr: love, with my Dr wifes; but beyond all words to

thy selfe, who art in our hearts above all upon Earth in the Eternal; for we know thee; so wth unfeined never dying Love to thee & Dr: Marg. I rest

thy Faithfull sober
W. P.

I desire that Jo: Blaickling[24]
& R. Barrow[25] may have notice.

Dr: T. L.[26] thyn I had wth Dr: G: Fs thy Love is Dr: to me, & mine salutes you all in the blessed Fellowship of the light. I will not say any more till we meet, that I know of; hopeing to have atime to ease my selfe shortly; we are all well, take kindly yr remembrance, & return you our faithfull greetings.

Thy true friend &
Brother in truth W P.

ALS. Luke Howard Collection, FLL. (*Micro.* 2:421). Docketed: W pen to g F | 1: mo: 167[5?].

1. This date in New Style is 4 Mar. 1677, but WP's letter can be dated with certainty as written in 1676. First, WP mentions the death of Matthew Hide, which occurred during the night of 19 Feb. 1676 (N.S.). Second, WP reports that Fox's book, *Possession above Profession*, has been printed; Fox wrote the book in Oct. 1675, and it was printed in the same year. Finally, the meeting in the north that WP wants Fox to attend took place at Draw-well at the beginning of Apr. 1676. *Works*, 1:711-13; Fox, 2:459; Braithwaite, *Second Period*, pp. 304, 679.

2. This letter has not been found.

3. Ralph Fretwell (d. 1686), one of the chief judges of the Court of Common Pleas in Barbados, was removed from office when he converted to Quakerism, following George Fox's visit to that island in 1671. Friends' meetings were frequently held at his house, including at least one attended in 1676 by eighty blacks. Fretwell had many thousands of pounds of sugar confiscated from him for refusing to perform military service or to pay tithes. Fox, 2:192; Besse, 2: 291, 309-10, 318, 331.

4. John Wilkinson and John Story. For a summary of the Wilkinson-Story controversy, see the headnote to doc. 91.

5. John Scafe.

6. John Harwood, a Yorkshire man, was imprisoned in the 1650s as a Quaker activist. Harwood became estranged from the Friends around 1660 when George Fox and others criticized his disorderly proceedings in marriage. Harwood wrote *To All People That Profess* ([London], 1663) against Fox; Fox replied in *The Spirit of Envy, Lying and Persecution* (1663). Fox, 2:314, 461-62; Besse, 2:89-90, 658-59.

7. Thomas Murford (d. 1694), of Somerset, was convinced of Quakerism by John Audland at Bristol in 1654. Though an eminent Friend, he was excitable and overly enthusiastic, and eventually "lost his condition" through immorality. DQB; Penney, *The First Publishers of Truth*, p. 228.

8. George Whitehead.

9. WP here refers to the meeting held at Draw-well in Yorkshire in Apr. 1676 concerning the Wilkinson-Story controversy. See headnote to doc. 91.

10. William Rogers.

11. Thomas Curtis, a woolen draper of Reading, was imprisoned several times for his beliefs. In 1670, the authorities broke up meetings held at his house, took away his possessions, and padlocked the door. Curtis and his wife Anne joined a number of prominent Reading Friends in support of Wilkinson and Story; their meeting split in 1684 after the two sides had quarreled for several years, and did not reunite until 1716. Fox, 1:441; Besse, 1:11-14, 29; Smith, "The Wilkinson-Story Controversy in Reading," pp. 57-61.

12. The duke of York had assured WP that he was against religious persecution

when WP asked his help in releasing George Fox from Worcester prison. Janney, pp. 101-3.

13. Margaret Fox was involved in the Wilkinson-Story controversy as early as 21 Jan. 1673, when, according to William Rogers, she read a paper against John Story in the Westmorland Quarterly Meeting. Her encouragement of women's meetings was probably the principal reason for the separatists' antipathy to her. Wilkinson told Margaret Fox that he opposed women's meetings because there was no example for them in Scripture, but Story thought that women's meetings could consider certain business "most proper for them to inspect into." Both seem to have opposed the new procedure for marriage that included visits on two separate occasions to the men's monthly meetings and approval by the women's meeting. Quotation in William Rogers, *The Christian-Quaker* (1680), pt. 4, pp. 7-14; John Blaykling, et al., *Anti-Christian Treachery Discovered* (1683), pp. 29-31; Ross, *Margaret Fell*, p. 286.

14. John Burnyeat.

15. William Gibson.

16. *Possession above Profession* ([London], 1675) was among the books that Fox wrote while resting at Swarthmore following his Worcester imprisonment. He subtitled it "& how the professors now persecute Christ in spiritt as the Jews persecuted him in the days of his flesh." Fox, 2:312, 459.

17. *Cain against Abel, Representing New-England's Church-Hirarchy, in Opposition to Her Christian Protestant Dissenters* ([London?], 1675), written at Swarthmore and dated 20 Nov. 1675. Fox, 2: 312, 459.

18. Probably Thomas Robertson.

19. In *Saul Smitten to the Ground* (London, 1676), WP told how Matthew Hide had opposed Quakers publicly in and around London for about twenty years prior to his death in Feb. 1676. WP described Hide's deathbed testimony in this tract, relating how Hide told George Whitehead and others that he had been wrong in persecuting Friends. See *Works*, 1:711-13.

20. The Lord Mayor of London in 1675-1676 was Sir Joseph Sheldon. He had been a member of the court at the trial of WP and William Mead in Sept. 1670. Secretary of State Henry Coventry wrote Sheldon, 28 Mar. 1676, denying the rumor that Charles II had decided not to enforce the laws against conventicles and calling on the mayor and aldermen to execute the laws. *CSPD, 1676-1677*, p. 46.

21. Fox wrote this group of letters, a "litle book to the majestrates of Danzicke," while at Swarthmore in 1675. It was dated 3 Nov. 1675 and printed with the title *Christian Liberty Commended and Persecution Condemned* ([London?], 1675). Fox, 2:312, 459.

22. William Rogers became a chief supporter of Story and Wilkinson following the Draw-well meeting in Apr. 1676, which he attended as a representative from Bristol. He drafted the paper of regret that Wilkinson and Story signed at the end of the meeting, but when the other arbitrators called it a condemnation, he joined the two Johns in saying that "there was nothing in it" and that "it was no better than a rattle to please children." Rogers wrote several treatises in defense of the separatists, including most prominently *The Christian-Quaker* (1680). Braithwaite, *Second Period*, pp. 304-7.

23. Nathaniel Coleman, of Sutton Benger in Wiltshire, had rejected the establishment of women's meetings in his county and confronted George Fox over the matter at a meeting in Slaughterford in 1673. As he left this meeting, Coleman believed that he saw an angel with drawn sword, which convinced him that he was wrong in opposing Fox. But as WP states here, Coleman again changed sides. In 1678, Coleman and several others separated from the Wiltshire Quarterly Meeting, taking the minute book with them. Fox 2:262, 446; "Nathaniel Coleman's Testimony" (*Micro.* 14:766); Braithwaite, *Second Period*, pp. 316-17.

24. John Blaykling (1625-1705) lived at Draw-well near Sedbergh in northwest Yorkshire. He traveled extensively as a minister and was often imprisoned for refusing to take an oath or pay tithes and for attending Friends' meetings. Blaykling was a chief opponent of the Wilkinson-Story party; the meeting in Draw-well in Apr. 1676 was held at his house. In 1683 he and a number of Westmorland Friends wrote *Anti-Christian Treachery Discovered* (1683), in response to Rogers' *The Christian-Quaker* (1680). Both books serve as important, though biased, sources of information on the Wilkinson-Story controversy. Fox, 1:403; Braithwaite, *Second Period*, pp. 295, 304-5; Besse, 2:101, 105, 109-10, 136; William Evans and Thomas Evans, eds., *Piety Promoted* (Philadelphia, 1854), 1:269-72.

25. Robert Barrow (d. 1697) of Kendal meeting in Westmorland, was another active opponent of Wilkinson and Story. Barrow accepted Quakerism early in his life, suffered considerable persecution, and traveled extensively as a minister throughout the British Isles. In 1694 he went to America, and in 1696 was shipwrecked and captured by hostile Indians while en route from Jamaica to Pennsylvania. He died shortly after arriving in Philadelphia in 1697. Penney, *The First Publishers of Truth*, pp. 261-63; Besse, 1:326, 474, 2:13, 17-19, 26, 30; *Piety Promoted*, 1:122-24.

26. Thomas Lower. His letter to WP has not been found.

103
ON CREATING QUAKER HISTORY

For a number of years Friends had been collecting accounts of their sufferings. In 1675 the newly organized Meeting for Sufferings petitioned Parliament for relief from persecution, and in 1676 London Friends decided to publish an extensive collection of Quaker sufferings. The following document, drafted by WP, is an appeal to the monthly and quarterly meetings to report all "memorable Sufferings" to London, so that a "full Narrative or History" of early Quakerism could be left to posterity. WP clearly saw a strong parallel between the sufferings of Friends and the martyrdom of the early Christians (see doc. 57). He also believed that the meager account of Christianity's long first generation (c. 33-65 A.D.) found in the Acts of the Apostles and the letters of St. Paul had permitted error, corruption, apostasy, and persecution to warp the Christian message and deform the church. The Quakers, he hoped, could present a fuller historical record. A powerful account of Quaker sufferings would not only shame the persecutors but encourage Friends to hold firm to every part of their testimony, and thus combat the disunity threatened by the followers of Story and Wilkinson (see points 10 and 12 in the present document). Braithwaite, *Second Period*, pp. 281-85; Lloyd, *Quaker Social History*, pp. 11-14; Endy, pp. 133, 138-39.

[c. May 1676][1]

Dearly Beloved Friends & Brethren,[2]
In the ~~everlasting~~ neverdying Truth is our love to you all, greeting you in the sweet & heavenly Fellowship of the same, which is very pretious to our Soules: & we doubt not, but it is the same to you.

Dear Friends, it hath long lain upon the minds of many Faithful Friends, to have a true & punctual Account, so far as can be obtained of the last-breaking-forth & progress of ~~Truth~~ the blessed Truth to this very Day (at least for the first 20 years, that make up by the common Acceptation one full Age) to the end that we may leave to posterity a plain, true, & full Narrative or History of, as well, the most memorable Matters of Fact, as Doctrine: the want of which after the Apostles Decease was the Occasion of much Mischief to the Church. For so it hath happened, that scarcely can we compass one pure peece of Antient Tradition.

It was the Wissdom of God, that lead the Israelites first to write; & then to transmit the several Chronicles contained in the Scriptures, to After-Generations. And something was done of the Apostles Travels in that called The Acts; though very short, & as we may say, imperfect: considering, that much of Pauls Travels & Planting of Churches is omitted; & little, if any thing sayd, of the great & succesful Travels of many other Apostles, & ~~faith~~ Labourers.[3] Not to mention the neglect or loss of any Account of the Churches conversion; divers Sort of Sufferings; their Persecutors; Gods Judgm^{ts} upon them etc. that would have been serviceable to Posterity.

It seems therefore to us very expedient, to Collect on all hands, what we can procure; that may make up such a Relation, as will answer the witness of God in all, & render us prudent & carefull of truths Concerns, respecting our Posterity. We know not of Immediately Digesting any Relations, that we shall get into such an History: onely, that such an Account may be procured, & then lay by as good & able Tools to perform so good a work with.

In Order to this we do in many Friends Name desire, that you would please to let us know, as followeth:

1. Who brought the Testimony first amongst you?
2. When it was?
3. What memorable Sufferings were by such messengers then & there sustained?
4. Who received the Truth first in those parts, & what Fame or the contrary its report had?
5. When you have meetings first setled amongst you; & when your mensmeetings were begun?
6. What Sufferings from year to year attended for the Testimonies sake?
7. By whom inflicted?
8. The Judgm^{ts} of God upon such in any sort?
9. His mercies in turning their hearts: as in some places Informers have pin'd to death; in other places they have repented, & loved Friends: & Friends have contributed to their wants doing good for Evil.
10. Where any fell off; & were followed with Gods Curse.
11. Where any have signally lost all; & God hath wonderfully the Threats of Fathers to their Children: & they have in the End known the Promiss made good an hunderd fold in this life as well as life everlasting.
12. Where bad spirits have risen, & false brethren appear'd,

with y[r] Judgm[t] & their End; either to return; or where any notable displeasure from God hath followed, either by running into the Spirit of this World visibly, notwithstanding their pretences to more self-denying or heavenly things: or where the wrath of God hath taken hold of them, or their family, or Estates.

13. What books came out ag[t] you? & when? & by whom? also by whom answer'd.

14. What Eminent Friends dyed every year; especially if any considerable Testimony fell from them.

In all the Cases we seek only some memorable Instances, because of brevity. Such as have sent up their sufferings already, which is one hears, touchd now upon; we would not trouble them over again in that particular; but will have recourse to E. Hookes, & his Voluminous Account of sufferings.[4] But in all other Cases we intreat y[r] utmost Care of the Truth, & Exactness of y[r] relations, & not less diligence in the dispatch of y[r] enquiry to these matters. We hope the love you have to the Lord & his blessed Truth, & y[r] desires with ours, that his name may be magnified, & his eternal Truth made famous to all Generations, will whet you on to further this good intendm[t] without farther exhortations. The God & Father of our Lord Jesus Christ preserve us all in unity w[th] himself, & one w[th] another, to his eternal praise, & our mutual comfort, world w[th]out End.

Your Loving Friends & Brethren.

LBC. WP's Letterbook, 1667-1775, HSP. (*Micro.* 14:713). Docketed in WP's hand: writt by W.P., signed by many Brethren.

1. This document has been dated by its resemblance to the letter of 18 May 1676 sent by the London Yearly Meeting to every monthly and quarterly meeting in England (*Micro.* 2:341). The present document is perhaps a draft from which the final letter was composed. See London Yearly Meeting Minutes, 1668-1693, 18 3 mo [May] 1676, pp. 29-30 (microfilm); and Leek MSS, pp. 89-90 (*Micro.* 2:341), both FLL.

2. The salutation addresses Quakers in each monthly and quarterly meeting in England.

3. The Acts of the Apostles, together with the letters of St. Paul, were the earliest authentic accounts of the development of the Christian Church. But while the author of Acts was one of the more historically minded writers of the New Testament, his account, and Paul's letters, were composed to meet immediate theological and political challenges from Jews, Gentiles, and Roman officials, with little thought of the need for a comprehensive history of the Church. Laymon, *One-Volume Interpreter's Bible*, pp. 729-30.

4. Hookes had been collecting accounts of Friends' sufferings since at least 1660. The present document was designed to expand and systematize this work. Hookes, like WP, had long seen the connection between the history and sufferings of Friends and of the early Christian martyrs. He published *The Spirit of Christ, and . . . of the Apostles, and . . . of the Martyrs, is Arisen, which beareth Testimony against Swearing Oaths* in 1661, and *The Arraignment of Popery* (with George Fox) in 1667 and at his death had in manuscript the *Spirit of the Martyrs Revived* (1682). His manuscript collection of Quaker sufferings swelled to 1300 folio pages by the time of his death in 1681, and formed the foundation for Besse's *Sufferings* in the next century. London Yearly Meeting Minutes, 1668-1693, pp. 6-7, 11, 13, 24, 26, 29-30, FLL (microfilm); Norman Penney, "Our Recording Clerks," *JFHS* 1:12-22; Fox, 2:402, 454; and see doc. 60, n. 3, above.

104
FROM ANTHONY LOWTHER

[June 1676?]

Deare Brother

It is a greate while to lett yours of the 8th present[1] be thus long unanswered, but I hope you will neither impute it to neglect nor Idlenesse; I am very glad to heare that you are gon through with your concernes in sussex[2] & shall make it my whole busynesse to settle all concernes here to fitt my selfe to wayte on you as soone as I can, though I feare I shall not be well able to put my affayres in that posture I desire before winter, and if so ~~a~~ I must deferre [~~m~~]y ~~Jou~~ our remoovall till the spring and then by Gods permission I shall not fayle coming to ~~p~~ you. As to the tearmes of being with you I shall most willingly agree to what waye you shall thinke most fitt & easye for us both; if wee have all our children, with us wee cannot be lesse then 8 or 9 in family[3] & either 5 or 6 horses of which 3 probably will be constant in the house; but for that I shall sute my selfe as I finde conveniency. And as for what you advice me to considder concerning the circumstances of your religion I have weighed that with my selfe and I am confident that there is nothing on that part will be uneasye for me, and I hope I shall demeane my selfe so as to give no scandall to any I shall converse withall; for I doe as much desire a retirement as parcimony

My wife and I intend the next weeke to visit Sr John Lowther[4] and soone after our returne I shall goe to Billton[5] and put things in the best order I can there; heare[6] all things are so settled that I could at a months warning leave it; till my returne from thence I cannot be able to give a positive resolve whither I shall be able to come up this winter or not; I would desire you if you can by your next resolve us whither you {& my sister}[7] shall spend all the winter in sussex; I must not forgett to returne you my harty thanks ~~you~~ for the charriot you were pleased to present us; we use it often and finde it very convenient All here are very well and give you theire respects as well as doth Your affct Brother

Ant Lowther

ALS. Granville Penn Book, HSP. (*Micro.* 14:680). Addressed: These | For Mr Wm Penne at | Samuell Harsnetts | at the blew ancker | In Fanchurch Streete[8] | London Docketed: Anth. Lowther.

1. This letter is undated, but June 1676 seems probable. WP moved from Rickmansworth in Hertford to Warminghurst in Sussex in 1676, and the number of children in the Lowther and Penn families in 1676 agrees with Lowther's remark below (see n. 3). For June, see n. 2 below.

2. On 3 June 1676, WP and Gulielma sold several hundred acres of land in Sussex for £3000, and on 7 June 1676, they purchased Warminghurst for about £4500. They moved to Warminghurst in September. Doc. 151, below; ACM, vols. 55-56.

3. The "8 or 9 in family" would have included five or six Lowthers: Anthony, his wife Margaret, and their children Margaret (b. 1668), Robert (b. 1672), and William (b. 1675), and possibly Anthony's sister Hannah (see doc. 100, n. 3, above); and three Penns: William, Gulielma, and their son Springett (b. 1675). The next child born in either family was Anna Lowther in June 1677. ACM, vol. 49B; Jenkins, pp. 66-67.

4. Anthony Lowther had two cousins of this name. Sir John Lowther (1643-1706) of Whitehaven, Cumb., was M.P. for Cumberland, 1665-1670, and a wealthy coal magnate. Sir John Lowther (1655-1700), of Lowther, Westm., was M.P. for Westmorland, 1676-1696. Because Anthony did not move to Sussex, as he contemplated in this letter, but stayed in the North and became M.P. for Appleby, Westm., in 1679, it seems likely that one of the Sir Johns persuaded him to remain in the North. Burke's *Peerage*, p. 1589; *DNB*.

5. There are three Yorkshire villages named Bilton: one two miles northeast of Harrowgate; one eight miles west of York; and one five miles northeast of Kingston upon Hull. The first two of these villages were near Lowther family land holdings.

6. Marske, Anthony Lowther's home in northern Yorkshire, on the North Sea. See doc. 100, and ACM, vol. 49B.

7. His sister-in-law, Gulielma Penn.

8. Probably Samuel Hersent, a Quaker tradesman who did much business with WP (see docs. 139-44). There were, however, two Harsnetts living in London in 1638. Fenchurch Street is a major thoroughfare in the eastern end of the City of London. T. C. Dale, ed., *The Inhabitants of London in 1638* (London, 1931), pp. 36, 216; *London Monuments*, 4: endpaper map and index.

The two letters that follow (docs. 105 and 106) show the close, working relationship between WP and Robert Barclay, who were by 1676 among the chief spokesmen of the Society of Friends, and leaders in the effort to end the persecution of their sect. Both letters identify Barclay's, and WP's, contacts at court. The second letter (doc. 106), by illuminating the complex interrelationships between prominent courtiers, helps explain the difficulty Quakers had in checking persecution. Barclay's letters are particularly valuable because no letters from WP to Barclay survive for this period and because few WP letters from the 1670s explain the nature of WP's contacts at court.

105
FROM ROBERT BARCLAY

London the 20 of the 5th Mo [July] 1676.

Dear W.P.

Seeing it falls out so that I am not like to see thee at this time it comes pretty near me I should have parted with thee so abruptly.[1] I have been constantly following my bussinesse since, and have had ocasione to be twice with the Duke[2] since thou art gone. I have found him very generous in keeping his word and I am like to effectuat something by his means.[3] Thy frind Ashtone[4] hath proved wonderfull serviceable to me for which I expect thou will thank him: being at present in great haist I have not time to enlarge. This may let the understand I could not keep the appointment I designed. My dear love is with thee & dear Jo. Burnet.[5] I wish thee successe in thy labour for the truth in which I am one with thee Mind me to Will Rogers, entreat him not to forget my advise at parting.[6] I wish him heartily well. There came as I understand—that was read the last 2nd day, a letter from Kendall Meetting[7] complaining of the Insolency of those there in their opposite procedures. I reckne thou has Intelligence of this from other hands so shall not enlarge. I shall be glad to hear from thee and doe in the mean time continue thy

dear brother in the truth
Barclay.

Transcript. Penn-Forbes Papers, HSP. (*Micro.* 2:356). Addressed: For | William Pen | at Present | at Bristoll | These.

1. WP was in London on 1 July (see doc. 152, below), and then went to Bristol, possibly to combat the growing influence of the dissidents John Story, John Wilkinson, and William Rogers among the Quakers in that city.

2. The duke of York. WP probably introduced Barclay to the duke, directly or by letter. See WP's "Account of my life since Convincement" [n.d., 1689?], *Micro.* 6:208.

3. Barclay was trying to secure the release of his father and several other Quakers from prison in Aberdeen. He had good reason for the optimism that he expresses here, for in June he was civilly received by Prince Rupert and in August he had an audience with Charles II, who forwarded Barclay's petition on behalf of the Aberdeen sufferers to the Scottish Council in Edinburgh, with his express approval. For the disappointing result of this petition, see doc. 106 below. *DNB*; D. Elton Trueblood, *Robert Barclay* (New York, 1968), pp. 64-65; Besse, 2:510-11.

4. John Ashton (d. 1691) was clerk of the closet to Mary of Modena, who had married the duke of York in 1673. He was a faithful servant to Mary and James for over fifteen years, went with them into exile in 1688, and plotted James' return to the throne, for which he was executed at Tyburn. Ashton, who had known WP from the 1660s, helped secure for WP the audience with the duke of York in 1674 that reestablished their friendship. "Account of my life," *Micro.* 6:208.

5. John Burnyeat.

6. Barclay had probably encountered William Rogers in London, or somewhere in eastern England, upon his (Barclay's) return from Holland. Rogers was going around the country giving his version of the meeting of Quakers at Draw-well, Yorks., in April, concerning the Wilkinson-Story controversy. Braithwaite, *Second Period*, p. 307.

7. The quarterly meeting in Kendall, Westm.; see the headnote to doc. 91, above.

106
FROM ROBERT BARCLAY

Edenbrough the 6th of the
5th [7th] Mo: [September] 1676.[1]

Dear W.P.

In the living sence and remembrance of that pretious life wherewith the Lord hath visited us and oftne causes to overflow, doe I dearly salute thee in that desiring to be united with thee and all the children of light for ever. I suppose thou receaved ane accompt at thy retourne[2] of all that, after long labour and attendance, I obtained there,[3] which has here proved inefectual for I presented it here to the Councel yesterday and they have confirmed there former ordinance and ordained the prisoners to remaine till they pay there fines.[4] It is judged that this proceeds from Lautherdails[5] privat Instructions who is willing to crush that way of getting any thing done by the D. of Y. his Influence. I have writ to the D. & Ashtone of it.[6] But leave it to thee to taike thy owne way to inclukate to the D. how much it concerns him not to suffer himself to be so bafled, for would he deal roundly with L. he would yield to him. I leave to J. Swintone[7] who will be shortly there to give thee a more particular accompt of things, to whom iff he medle any thing by the D. in his owne bussinesse I doubt not but thou will give thy assistance. I have received from the Princesse Elizabeth[8] a very refreshing letter wherein she declares her full satisfactione with truth & her desires to be faithfull to it, also a very considerable accompt of things I have from ane other Germane Prince who has invited me to come up to visit him the next Spring: but as to that I reckne thou will receave a particular accompt from B. F.[9] who I here intends to be at London. This maiks me wish thou could maik a step for Holland to put a stop to any unhappy differences may be stiring among them which hinders the general progresse of truth. That about mariadge will be easily quieted by only giving liberty to those that are free to goe to the magistrate to doo it after they have fully satisfied the order of truth which is the scence of divers good frinds and seems also to be G. F.[10] judgment to whom I spok of it.[11] I wish all tenernesse were ussed in the caise for fear of the consequence. I intend this day northwards and doubt not but I may be a prisoner be this come to thy hand.[12] ther does a very glorious power appear in ther meetings in prison to the astonishment of many[13] and the heavenly life overfloes in great abundance and breaks wonderfully through even yong boyes & girles which I beleave is a token for good to this Natione, so that to share with them I goe cherfully to pertaik of ther bonds where it will be very refreshing to me to hear from thee and other of my brethren[14] to whom let these transmitt the tender of my dear love as also thy dear Wyffe

I am thy brother in the truth
that is unchangeable
Barclay

Transcript. ACM, vol. 55, CCHS. (Not filmed).

1. This date was probably erroneously transcribed, for the content of this letter makes it clear that it follows Barclay's letter of 20 July, written in London (doc. 105, above). For reasons given in n. 4, below, the editors date this letter 6 Sept. 1676.

2. WP had returned from Bristol by 18 Aug. See doc. 116, below.

3. At court in Westminster.

4. Barclay presented a petition to Charles II in late July or early August, which the king, on 7 Aug., endorsed and sent to the Scottish Privy Council in Edinburgh. According to Besse, the petition and royal endorsement were presented in Edinburgh on 7 Sept., which event Barclay refers to here as happening "yesterday." This would date his letter 8 Sept. But Besse appears to be mistaken about the date of the Scottish

Privy Council's action, for on 6 Sept. Barclay wrote Princess Elizabeth that the Edinburgh Council had rejected his petition, adding, "I this day take my Journey towards" the Scottish prisoners. This exactly fits his statement in this letter: "I intend this day northwards." Thus 6 Sept. seems the correct date for this letter. Besse, *Sufferings*, 2:510-30; Trueblood, *Robert Barclay*, pp. 65-66.

5. John Maitland (1616-1682), Duke of Lauderdale, was the king's secretary for Scotland and virtual ruler of that nation in royal matters. He was a vigorous opponent of dissent. *DNB*.

6. The duke of York and his servant, Colonel John Ashton. See doc. 105, above.

7. John Swinton (1621?-1679) became the most powerful political figure in Scotland under Cromwell, and at the Restoration he was imprisoned for treason for several years. He became a Quaker in 1657 and wrote several religious tracts in the 1660s. Swinton was a close friend of Robert Barclay's father, David, and played a role in the elder Barclay's convincement to Quakerism in 1665-1666. *DNB*; Braithwaite, *Second Period*, pp. 335-37.

8. Barclay had visited Princess Elizabeth Palatine at her convent at Herford, Germany, earlier in the year. WP had visited Herford in 1671 and would see the princess again in 1677. See docs. 63 and 90, above, and 119, below.

9. Benjamin Furly. See doc. 63, above, and 119, below.

10. George Fox.

11. WP soon took Barclay's advice and went to Holland, with Barclay and other Quaker leaders; see doc. 119, below. On the controversy in Holland over registering Quaker marriages with the civil authorities, see doc. 122, below.

12. Barclay did proceed to Aberdeen, where he was arrested and imprisoned on 7 Nov. 1676, joining George Keith and several other Quakers, including Barclay's father, David. Besse, *Sufferings*, 2:517; Trueblood, *Robert Barclay*, pp. 66-75.

13. Besse, *Sufferings*, 2:510, describes the prisoners preaching through the barred prison windows to the crowds outside.

14. See doc. 109, below.

107
TO JOHN RAUNCE AND CHARLES HARRIS

[11 September 1676]

Jno Raunce & Charles Harris,[1]

My sp^t^ (I can say it in God, who is the day the pure spring & stay of my life) is deeply grieved to behold you & yor work, wch is not that of gathering to but scattering from the Lord in this day of temptation. The Lord stop you by his power, for yor steps lead to Egypt again; if I have any sense of God it is agrutching, factious, mutinous sp^t^ that hath entred; yea a jealous & exalted one. The Lord God of my life save you from it, & bring up the antient tender love, life, faith, hope & fellowship, wch for God I plainly testify {un}to you, ye are now in measure departed from; & in order to see yor selves & yor entanglem^ts^. Consider yor confusion; ye say there is not yet a right understanding between the J's [2] & us, but the day will declare it, & yet ye have only yor information from that side, & notw^th^standing will be thought to be middle-men, moderato^rs^ &c. Ye contradict our sense in the North[3] & despise our travell, & in matters of fact have undertook to plead the J's innocency, wherein we have found them guilty; still ye would be thought unbyassed & impartiall men; nay ye know not how to contradict us, but by wt they & theirs tell you; yor Language betrays you to be of them, & for all yor pretences of impartiality & mediation, wn ye are prest close by us, ye cannot forbear falling upon us wth their declarations; & do ye think that ye are fit men to moderate their spts towards their brethren, & chase away, at least supplant & remove their jealousys of our excercising Lordship, turning Bishops, Popes, Imposters, men going back into the Apostacy, that can like Pennyman, Whitehouse,[4] Mucklow,[5] Boyse & others, lay the like things to our charge? Is not this mediation of yors meer deceit, since it is acting like partys, under the disguise of indifferent men? But God hath discovered yor very inside to us, & yor spts we savor, & whither ye are tending, & our souls mourn for you; & pray that ye may see yor snare, & be delivered. Ah my friends, wt have {we} done to be thus treated at yor hands? Can ye pretend to be our friends & deny to believe us, & yet can ye pretend to be unbyassed men towards the J's & yet reject us & our report because of the J's & the partys insinuations? Is this yor measure, ye have taken to measure us by, & will ye still think ye are wronged, if we call you of their party? Well, but wt is it we have done that deserves so little of yor faith, love & charity? Give me leave to boast for my Brethren, & that in God, where our glorying stands, What have ye done that they have not done? wt have ye suffered, that they have not suffered? yea, wt have ye denied that they have not denied? When have ye laboured for the Lord, & they have not & do not labour for the Lord? Ah my righteous soul is justly offended wth you & all yor Associates, that excell us in nothing that relates to our God & that service & testimony he has committed to us, neither in power, diligence nor suffering. Where then doth our Apostacy lye? in not suffering loose & libertine spts to tread down our hedge, under the specious pretence of being left to the light wthin, as if the Light were inconsistent wth itselfe, or admitted of unity, under not only different but contrary practices in the one family & flock of God? Well, ye have judged us & smitten us, or life, labor & judgemt, wth God I leave it, who will assuredly avenge the cause of his own power, wch we are engaged in, & so to him I leave it, but now I shall a little further expostulate wth you. Ye say ye found things ill at Bristoll,[6] but left them well, wt do ye mean by ill & well? if by ill, ye mean that some were agst the Johns, & by well, that now they are for them I hope ye will not pretend longer to be indifferent men, if ye mean that ye found too many for them, but the number is lessened, & that ye call well, then how comes it about that ye herded & flockt so together, why do ye talk their {jealous} Language, & how comes it that ye so much grieved the tender-hearted for Gods glory, by yor publick & private smites & reflections, as many letters from eye & ear witnesses testify? but if ye mean that ye found them divided, but left them one, then ye prevaricate & tell us a fib, for they are more fixtly opposite than ever, & many reflect upon yor carriage there

& in Wilts.[7] more thanever. Was it yor Indifferency to plead J:S. his innocency, & oppose his going down to make an end of that seperation, wn many Friends desired it as the next {way} for peace, unworthily if not wickedly turning that motion aside, as if it were to send him away by authority of a monthly or quarterly Meeting, that was only a tender entreaty to him, as the next best expedient: but it's usuall wth guilt to dodge & the serpent to hide his head. Again ye tell us that Bristoll said this & Bristoll said thus, & ye left Bristoll so & so. John & Charles, is this common honesty in you so presumptiously to speak & deceive ~~s~~ simple {people?} What is that Bristoll that so said & that ye so left? Come now show yorselves if ye are men. I offer you fair, name me one of yor Bristoll that is not of J:S. & W:R's [8] Bristoll. I say name me one, not pleading their cause & rejecting or report, that is of yor Bristoll; oh, for shame; wt, moderators still, days-men still, nay not commonly honest between man & man to tell yor tales thus equivocatingly! But now ye that cry up love & charity, wheres yors, that makes J: Moon,[9] Ch: Jones,[10] R: Sneed,[11] Ch: Hartford,[12] W: Highfield,[13] Eras. Dole,[14] R: Vickridg,[15] Jer: Hignall[16] &c. & their familys, no part of yor Bristoll? Well, further I ask you, who is there that stood agt J: S. & his ungospell dealings, that ye have brought to say, Amen. Come Charles & Jno: the work of God will be too hard for you & yor devices, & I warn you from God that ye defile not the minds of Gods friends, wth yor poisonous & infectious jealousy's: for ye have already done more then ye can ever answer to God, & bloud will lye at yor door in the day of account, the power will tread you down if ye persist, & God {will} raise poor Lads & Lasses to silence you wth the dread of his own authority, if we should hold our peace; for my part, though these things are like to give a present Exercise, I bless my God I see & behold the downfall of this spt; yea I plainly discern the hidings, dodgings & all the lurking holes of it, & 'tis such dirty {earthly} wisdom & carnall trash, yea such darkness, as at a year old, I comprehended it; & yor talents will God take away, & yor Bishoprick (as saith the scripture in alike place) will he give unto others, if ye bow not to the power which ye are risen up agt, & truly this is an Apostate spt, that having lost the power, & being inwardly cast forth from the enjoimt of the Lords presence, is ~~no~~ {now} wandring in dry places, seeking rest in this transformation & the other, but shall never find rest, for judgemt shall follow it forever: & whereas one, if not both of you, talk much of the day that shall discover all things, know that day is come, & for want of it ye see not, & the temptation that ye warn of, ye have lamentably entred into, & ye are darkened by it; & ye do but talk yor own states. Well, for your souls salvation I pray, as for my own, but never into pure fellowship wth God, nor any faithfull Brethren that know these things, can ye come, till ye have, from the bottom of yor hearts, condemned your words & carriages, & plain seperation from many of yor honest brethren, & from the pure spt of unity, in wch they live & grow to God & in sweet communion one wth another, where W:Rogers's impious reflections (yor Brother in this Schism) can never come to harm us, or ever to make afraid; som that love, wch by righteous judgemt would have you saved, I remain,

Your mourning friend for you

11. of 7. Mon. 1676. Wm Penn.

Copy. Penington MSS, FLL. (*Micro.* 2:369).

1. John Raunce, a doctor, and his son-in-law Charles Harris were two leading Friends of High Wycombe, Bucks. They joined with John Wilkinson and John Story in their dispute with George Fox, WP, and other prominent Quakers (see headnote to doc. 91) and helped establish separate meetings in Buckinghamshire. Braithwaite, *Second Period,* pp. 46, 307, 475.

2. John Wilkinson and John Story.

3. In the Apr. 1676 meeting at Draw-well to settle the Wilkinson and Story dispute, the two Johns signed a paper regretting the controversy, thus seemingly ending the matter. After they left, however, the arbitrators, including George Whitehead and Alexander Parker, drew up a narrative of the meeting that stated that Wilkinson and Story were guilty of schismatic activities and had condemned their separation in the paper. Wilkinson and Story denied this, and prospects for unity were ended. Braithwaite, *Second Period,* pp. 304-7.

4. John Whitehouse, of Staffordshire, was an ardent supporter of the schismatic John Perrot in the 1660s. Braithwaite, *Second Period,* p. 237.

5. William Mucklow (1631-1713) was a London Friend who joined John and Mary Pennyman in the hat controversy in 1671 (see doc. 71).

6. Many supporters of Wilkinson and Story belonged to the Bristol meeting; their leader was William Rogers. They apparently set up no separate meeting, but continued to disrupt meetings occasionally as late as 1696. Braithwaite, *Second Period,* pp. 303, 479-80.

7. A number of Friends in Wiltshire supported Wilkinson and Story. In Apr. 1678, they separated from their quarterly meeting, taking the minute book with them. By 1684, however, the schism there had ended and many separatists rejoined the Friends. Braithwaite, *Second Period,* pp. 316-17, 478-79.

8. William Rogers.

9. John Moone, mercer, of Bristol Monthly Meeting, was imprisoned in 1681 and emigrated to Pennsylvania c. 1683. Mortimer, *Minute Book of the Men's Meeting . . . Bristol,* p. 210; Besse, 1:54.

10. Charles Jones (d. 1714), a soapmaker, was a member of the Bristol Monthly Meeting, jailed in 1663, 1684, and 1685. Besse, 1:45, 69, 73-74; Bristol and Somerset Quarterly Meeting, Births and Deaths, 1657-1729, Friends Historical Library of Swarthmore College, Swarthmore, Pa.

11. Richard Snead (d. 1712), a mercer, was also a member of the Bristol Monthly Meeting. He was incarcerated on several occasions between 1682 and 1685, a period of particularly harsh persecution for Bristol Friends. Besse, 1:59, 67, 73-74; Braithwaite, *Second Period,* p. 104; Mortimer, *Minute Book of the Men's Meeting . . . Bristol,* p. 216.

12. Charles Harford took a prominent role in opposing William Rogers' schismatic activities. Braithwaite, *Second Period,* pp. 104, 480.

13. William Ithield (d. 1697) was an active member of the Bristol Monthly Meeting. Mortimer, *Minute Book of the Men's Meeting . . . Bristol,* p. 205.

14. Erasmus Dole (c. 1635-1717), a pewterer, suffered persecution in 1664 and from 1681 to 1684. He was disowned by the Bristol Monthly Meeting for drunkenness in 1692 and 1698. Besse, 1:54, 59, 69; Mortimer, *Minute Book of the Men's Meeting . . . Bristol,* p. 199.

15. Richard Vickris (d. 1700) was a prominent Quaker merchant of Bristol who was imprisoned in 1683 for refusing to take an oath and was fined and jailed on several other occasions. In two treatises written in 1691 and 1692, he defended Quaker beliefs against the attack of John Norris (1657-1711), the rector of Bemerton, near Salisbury,

in Wiltshire. Besse, 1:55-56, 59, 71-72; Braithwaite, *Second Period*, pp. 107, 392-93; Bristol and Somerset Quarterly Meeting, Births and Deaths, 1657-1729.

16. Jeremiah Hignell (d. 1703), a cooper, was another member of Bristol Monthly Meeting, and was imprisoned several times. Besse, 1:41, 45; Mortimer, *Minute Book of the Men's Meeting . . . Bristol*, p. 203.

108
FROM LORD BALTIMORE

Lond°. 11th xber [December] 1676[1]

Mr Pen

In answer to your letter of this date I {first} returne you many thanks for the visites you have made, and blame my people, that did not acquaint me when you did me that kindnesse, had you thought fitt to have acquainted me where I might have given y° {a} visit, I should have pay'd you those respects {wch} your greate parts challenge from all that know or have heard of you; as to the latter part of your letter, because I will not here enlarge upon a subject, I had rather discourse, then committ to paper,[2] you may be assured that on Wednesday next in the morning about nine or Ten of the clock at our Freind Mr Ri: Langhornes[3] Chambr I will not faile to meete you, and then owne my obligations for yr kindness and Civility, to

Yr freind
Ch. Baltemore

ALS. Penn-Forbes Papers, HSP. (*Micro.* 2:382). Addressed: For Mr William Pen. Docketed: Baltimore | Lond. 11. 10br 76.

1. Charles Calvert, Lord Baltimore, usually resided in Maryland, but visited England briefly in 1676. *DAB*.

2. Probably WP wanted to discuss with Baltimore oath-taking by Friends in Maryland. See doc. 81, n. 1.

3. Like Baltimore, a Catholic, and sometime counsel to Friends. See doc. 37, n. 23.

109
TO GEORGE KEITH AND OTHER SCOTTISH FRIENDS

[c. 1677]

Deare G: Kieth Robert Berkley and the rest of the Brethren Imprison'd at Aberdeen for the Testimony of Jesus[1]

Deare Brethren

Salvation and peace by Jesus xt the Light of the World, our eternall glorious day, be Multiplyed among you, who is the Rock of Safety, and fountaine of everlasting Consolations, from whose pure Life descends Sweet refreshments into the Soules of all that Love him in truth and Sincerity and I doubt not my brethren but you are witnesses of the same; as a letter from our deare brother G: Keith [gives] me with others hereaway to understand[2] which being read among us, broke our hearts and deeply affected our Soules to behold with you the Goodness of the Lord to you in yor tribulations; These Warrs and Rumers of Warrs are certaine forerunners of the Redemption of that Country;[3] and great will their reward be from the Lord that fly nott in this winter time nor on this Saboth day, I feel an Immortall spring of pure life riseing among you, and can say I am with you in Spirit, and behold the Aurora of the day of the Lord over Scottland. And all my brethren be Scattered to and setled in your owne, and waite for the feeling of the power of the Lord that Subjects all to him; and then waite for the Signification of that power and none to quench the Spirit, nor to miss of the Spirits mind that you may now grow Spirituall Souldiers expert, and fitted by these execises, for those Spirituall Conflicts the Lord has for you to goe thorow in the Lambs warr. O these tryalls are blessed Mortifyings to the Sensuall and Worldly man, and for the awakening of the Soule to the things that are beyond time and mortality, O you litle leaven and salt[4] of that Country love the pure power the true and Certaine power and grow in it as trees in winter downwards, that your Root may Spread, so shall you stand in all stormes and tempests and oh blessed are they that firmly believe patiently and Contentedly waite for Gods Salvation to be Compleated God will stay such with his everlasting Arme with flaggons of Love, and in that pure peace Persecutors neither know, nor can take away, My Deare Brethren this Suffering is not strange neither is it for naught; all waite to see the end of the Lord therein and all bow thereto and none resist the Lords purpose, for this is to bring up the seed and the Power into Dominion to make his Righteousness and truth known to the world & his Love and his faithfulness to you; and to keep that downe which for want of exercise might overgrow the truth in the particuler much I see of the Lords wisdome Mercy and goodness in this thing, and it will end for his glory I am perswaded; wherefore I can say be of good Cheere for everlasting strength is with you and in you.

The affaires of truth, here away are very well the Lords Power reignes over Publick and private opposition,[5] our meetings are very large and quiet and friends generally well, yet great Sufferings upon the 1.23.29.35 of Eliz: and the 1:3. of James[6] and I see not but that Sufferings hasten upon us more and more you are in our remembrance to be mentioned with others to the King and Councell and soe leave our Cause with the Lord who will arise in his due time for his poore seeds sake and blessed are they that are not offended in him nor his dealeings dispensations and tribulations many are the troubles of the Righteous but out of them all shall he be delivered in time that is not ours, but the fathers time whose will must be done in Earth as it is in Heaven ~~with~~ which with my endeared Salutation to you all my heavenly kindred & fellow travellers in the narrow way that leades to the eternall rest Concludes this Espistle from

Your faithfull simpathizeing
Friend and brother in the
tribulation and patience of
the Kingdome of Jesus
Wm Penn

Copy. Penn Papers, Ford vs. Penn, HSP. (*Micro.* 2:396). Docketed: An epistle | to Frds in Scotland.

1. George Keith was imprisoned at Aberdeen on 19 Mar. and Robert Barclay on 7 Nov. 1676. Many other Quakers were also imprisoned in this period, most of them between March and May. Keith, Barclay, and several others were set at liberty on 9 Apr. 1677. WP's letter could have been written at any time between Nov. 1676 and early Apr. 1677. Besse, *Sufferings*, 2:503-28.

2. This letter has not been found. The editors have supplied the word *gives*, in brackets, for clarity.

3. Scotland. For the "wars" to which WP refers, see Matt., chap. 24, especially v. 6; Mark, chap. 13, especially v. 7.

4. See Matt. 5:13, 13:33.

5. By "Public opposition," WP probably refers to his four-year controversy with John Faldo, which had recently ended; by "private opposition," to the Wilkinson-Story schism among the Quakers, in which the schismatics were temporarily fairly quiet.

6. WP here refers to several statutes passed against Roman Catholic recusants which compelled any suspected person to take an oath of loyalty to England's monarch or face imprisonment. In the 1670s these laws were widely used against Quakers because magistrates knew that they would not swear to an oath. The laws were passed in the twenty-third, twenty-ninth, and thirty-fifth years of Elizabeth (1581, 1587, and 1593), and in the third year of James I (1605). The last law was the most important, and the most severe. For more details, see doc. 126, n. 7, below.

110
GEORGE FOX TO HENRY SIDON

London the 25th of the 3d moth [May] 1677

Dr Friend[1]
To whome is my love & all the rest of Friends, in the Truth of god, & my desire is, that thou & all the rest may be preserved in gods peacable Truth & in the love of it. now Concerning the thing thou speakst to me of, that Sarah Harris[2] should say to the that wm Mead {& wm Penn} did ware Perrywiggs & call them Periwigg men;[3] first concerning wm Mead, he bid me putt my hand upon his head, & feel, & said he never weare Perriwig in his life, & wonder'd at it, & as for wm Penn, he did say that he did weare a little {civil} border because his hair was Gone of his head, & since I have {seen &} spoak wth wm

Penn, his border is so thin, plain & short, that one Can not well know it from his own hair; w. Penn when but 3 years ould {so} lost his hair, by the small Pox that he woar them then, long, & {about} 6 years before his Convincem[t], he woar one, & after that he endeaverd to goe in his own hair, but when kept a close Prisoner in the Towr next the leads,[4] 9 months, & no barber suffer'd to come at him, his hair shed away; & since he has worn a very short civil thing, & he has been in danger of his life after ~~hea~~ violent heats in meetings & rideing after them, & he wares them to keep his head & ears warm & not for pride; w[ch] is manifest in that his perriwigs Cost him many Pounds a piece formerly, when of the world, & now his Border, but a fwe shillings: & he has lay'd of more for Truth then [three words deleted] her & her Relations and I am sorry the should speak such things, & the did not do well to discours of such things, I desire the may be wiser for the time to come. & so wth my love to thee & thy wife & father & N. Newton[5]

G. F.

And hee's more willing to fling it off if a little hair come, then ever he was to putt it on;

Copy in WP's hand. Port. 10:64, FLL. (*Micro.* 2:441). Endorsed: G F to Henry Sidon, 1677, 25 3 mo.

1. Henry Sidon was one of the earliest and principal Friends in Baddesley Ensor, War., about sixteen miles from Birmingham. Three weeks before writing this letter, Fox had visited Henry Sidon at Baddesley on 5 May 1677 and held a meeting there on 6 May. Fox, *Short Journal,* pp. 230, 357.

2. Perhaps the Sarah Harris of Baddesley Ensor who died in 1726. Digest of Warwick Quaker Registers, GSP.

3. Quakers objected to wigs as violating their ideals of plainness and simplicity. Arnold Lloyd, *Quaker Social History,* pp. 72-73. For a contemporary attack on wigs, see John Mulliner, *A Testimony Against Perriwigs and Perriwig-Making* (1677).

4. The roof. *OED.*

5. Henry Sidon's wife Elizabeth died in 1680. Digest of Warwick Quaker Registers, GSP. N. Newton was Nathaniel Newton (d. c. 1711) of Harshill, War. Fox had visited him on 7 May 1677. Fox, *Short Journal,* pp. 231, 357.

111
ON KEEPING QUAKER PRISON REGISTERS

In the following epistle to Friends in Somerset, WP called upon the local meetings, as he had in doc. 103, to supply the London leadership with better records of Quaker persecution. The new proposal in this letter is that jail registers be established in all towns where Quakers suffered imprisonment.

[1677]

Deare Friends and Brethren

In the Love of our God and father with whom is everlasting Life and Redemption doe we tenderly Salute you desireing with fervency of Spirit that we may all be preserved in the feare of the Lord sensible of his pretious power, and in his universall fellowship that over all that which would draw out of the heavenly Society and unity we may be kept it was desired of us by the Meeting of Sufferings to write to you to let you know that upon a serious discourse of the most Certaine speedy and punctuall way of haveing an account of friends Sufferings it rise in the heart of us me to propose this with which the rest had much unity (viz[t]) that in every towne where friends are and use to be Imprisoned (or the towne or place that you see the most Convenient that is adjacent) there be a Register kept of the names Sufferings Persecutors tryalls &c: that So the Monthly or Quarterly meetings may be the better Informed and we from them as occasion shall require of all the Sufferings of our deare friends, And truely if a Goale Record (for So it is though it ought not to be exposed to the Goale but kept neare it) should be stablisht it Seemes to be the Naturallest way of preserveing an Impartiall account of Persecutions Sufferings tryalls and all appendances so that it is not only to answer the referrence of the Meeting but to express our owne Sence, & soe doe from them and on our owne account recommend it unto you We were alsoe desired by our brethren of the said Meeting to put you in mind of sending up all such sufferings as have not yet been sent up upon any Law or act whatever (especially upon the late act)[1] that were not presented in the last printed book to the Parliament[2] as also what Sufferings have been since that time that we have a fresh account to present the next Session, But more especially be pleased to take Care that there be an exact Catalogue sent up of the Names of all friends Imprisoned In what Cause at whose Suite and how long they have Suffered we entreat your dilligence and brotherly Care in these things and to direct your answer to Ellis Hookes as formerly. And it is further desired that you send us up the Names of witnesses of Such facts and especially as many of the World as you Can because the want of them made a Bishop to retort where is your witness denying the thing

Soe deare brethren the Lords Power is over all in which we believe and in which that we all may be kept witnesses for the Lord in Simplicity and faithfullness is the desire of

Your endeared faithfull
Brethren
William Gibson,
William Penn

Copy. Bristol MSS, Somerset Record Office. (*Micro.* 2:401). Addressed: For Henry Lavor[3] | at Yeovill[4] | in | Somersetshire. Docketed: 1677 | London | To record friends | sufferings in the | Countyes & returne | acc^ts to London.

1. The Second Conventicle Act of 1670. An Order in Council, 3 Feb. 1675, directed the more diligent execution of the Penal Laws. Braithwaite, *Second Period,* p. 86.

2. Probably Ellis Hookes, *For the King, and both Houses of Parliament, Being a brief and general Account of the late and present sufferings of many of the peaceable subjects called Quakers* (1675), or WP, *The Continued Cry of the Oppressed for Justice . . . Presented to the Serious Consideration of the King and both Houses of Parliament* (1675).

3. Henry Lavor (d. 1684) was fined £20 in 1670 for having a meeting in his house in Yeovil. Besse, 1:600; Ridge, *Index to Wills Proved . . . 1676-1685*, p. 207.

4. Yeovil is a market town and parish in Somerset.

PROPRIETOR IN NEW JERSEY

1675–1676

The following group of documents opens the most important chapter in WP's life, his participation in American colonization. WP became a colonizer quite by accident; there is no evidence that he had any interest in America before he was suddenly drawn into the settling of a dispute between two Quakers over land in West New Jersey.

In 1664, the duke of York granted the proprietorship of New Jersey to the courtiers Sir John Berkeley and Sir George Carteret. In March 1674, Berkeley offered to sell his half interest in the proprietorship to his friend Edward Byllynge for £1000 so that Byllynge could sell off the land and recoup his declining fortunes. Byllynge agreed, but because he was bankrupt, he had his fellow Quaker, John Fenwick, purchase Berkeley's interest in trust for Byllynge. Byllynge and Fenwick then quarreled, and Fenwick demanded a share in the New Jersey proprietorship and a cash sum in payment for the £1000 he had spent. Byllynge could not pay the money and did not want to surrender any of his proprietorship. Quaker leaders, fearing that the dispute would go to court and discredit their sect, persuaded Byllynge and Fenwick to submit their differences to an arbitrator; for this role they chose WP.

The three letters from WP to Fenwick, below (docs. 112-14) show the role of the Quaker arbitrator, illustrate the Quaker attitude toward litigation, and reveal the frustration that the dispute caused WP. His last letter to Fenwick (doc. 114) also shows that in 1675 WP regarded colonization as a dubious road to wealth. The agreement that WP negotiated was formalized in a legal indenture whereby Byllynge transferred ten of his one hundred shares in New Jersey land to Fenwick and agreed to pay him £400. The indenture placed the remaining ninety shares in trust with three Quaker proprietors, Gawen Lawrie and Nicholas Lucas, who were creditors of Byllynge's, and WP, who initially had no financial interest in the colony. These trustee proprietors were empowered to sell Byllynge's shares to pay off his debts and return to him any shares remaining when he was again solvent. The indenture, dated 10 February 1675, is summarized in doc. 152.

112
TO JOHN FENWICK

London 20th 11th [January] 1674[/5].

John Fenwick[1]

The present difference betwixt thee & E.B[2] fills the hearts of Freinds wth greife, & a Resolution to take it in 2 dayes into their Consideration, to make a publique deniall of the person, & action that offers violence to the Award made[3] or that will not End it wthout bringing it upon the Publique Stage. God the Righteous judge will Visitt him that stands off. E.B. will Referr it to me, againe If thou wilt doe the like,[4] send me word, & as opprest as I am wth businesse I will give an after noone to morrow or next day to determine, & so prevent the Mischeife that will certainely follow divulgeing it in Westminster Hall,[5] let me know by the bearer thy minde. O John Lett Truth & the honoure of it in this day prevale, woe be to him that causeth offences. I am an Impartiall man

W Penn.

the heads of my Answers, to W.P.[6]

I desire: to performe yr Award, & not to infringe it, but to receive my money securely; &

To Reserve my 2 pts intirely.

To have up all my Writts and my Reputation Repaired, and vindicated. All wch Will. Penn promised he would see performed.

If any other thing be propossed contrary to the Award, it must not be yeild unto for severall Reasons, espetially it will imediately open a doore for a suit in Chauncery

Copy. Harleian MSS 7001, BL. (*Micro.* 2:034). Docketed: the copies of William Penns 1st 2d & 3d letters. These three letters (docs. 112-114) appear to be copies entered into a letterbook kept by John Fenwick.

1. John Fenwick (c. 1618-1683) was born in Northumberland, entered Gray's Inn in 1638, and was commissioned a major in Cromwell's army in 1648. He served in General Monck's cavalry, where he may have known Edward Byllynge, and belonged to an Independent congregation before joining the Friends sometime in the 1650s or early 1660s. By 1665, he was living in Binfield, Berks.; in that year he was imprisoned at Reading for participating in Quaker worship. Following the arbitration of his dispute with Byllynge, Fenwick sailed for New Jersey, where he spent the remainder of his life, embroiled in controversies with his fellow proprietors, with settlers, and with magistrates in New York and in New Castle over his rights to land and to governing authority in New Jersey. *New Jersey Archives,* 1st ser., 1:185; Besse, 1:29, 78; Pomfret, *West New Jersey,* chap. 5.

2. Edward Byllynge (c. 1623-1687) was an officer in Monck's cavalry at Leith, Scotland, in 1657, when he was convinced by George Fox. By 1659 he had moved to London, where he quickly became a leading Quaker and a prosperous Westminster brewer. As a result of the complex legal transactions discussed in the headnote above and summarized in doc. 152, below, Byllynge secured the major interest in the proprietorship of West New Jersey from Sir John Berkeley in 1675. For the next five years, he cooperated closely with his trustees, WP, Gawen Lawrie, and Nicholas Lucas, in pro-

moting the settlement of his colony, and by 1682 he was out of debt and had also become a proprietor, with WP and others, in East New Jersey. In 1680, he arranged with the duke of York to have full governing authority in West New Jersey vested in himself, and promptly sent the first in a series of deputies to America to govern the colony. The last five years of his life were taken up with controversies with the West New Jersey colonists, who disputed his right to govern. *New Jersey Archives,* 1:185; Pomfret, *West New Jersey,* chaps. 5, 6, 8; Fox, 1:297, 305, 452; Braithwaite, *Beginnings,* pp. 273, 352, 455, 471, and Braithwaite, *Second Period,* p. 28; Besse, 1:469-70; Nash, *Quakers and Politics,* pp. 5-6.

3. WP had initially determined that Byllynge should pay Fenwick £900, grant him 2/100 of his interest in the proprietorship of New Jersey, and retain 98/100 of the interest that Fenwick had purchased from Berkeley. London's Quaker leaders did not in fact condemn Fenwick at this time, but in July 1675 they did publicly rebuke him for his haste and greed in founding his own colony in New Jersey, and stated that they had never had any faith in him. Pomfret, *West New Jersey,* p. 68; *The Proceedings of the New Jersey Historical Society* 54:4-5.

4. The comma has been struck out in a later hand.

5. The Court of Chancery at Westminster, to which Fenwick was threatening to take his disagreement with Byllynge.

6. This memorandum is Fenwick's response to WP's letter.

113
TO JOHN FENWICK

[30 January 1675]

J.F.

I am sorrie for thy arreast;[1] E.B. I stopt from any proceede, but for the Lord Berkely,[2] twas not in my power; as to thy Councell, myne[3] has told me that he was wth him, & has stated it quit upon an other foot, giveing as I perceive a Relation wth all advantage for thee. Now I must neede complaine of that proceeding. I tooke care to hide the pretences on both hands, as to the Originall of the thing, because it Reflects on you both, and wch is worse, on the Truth. Therefore I under tooke it; That I might hide yor shame, & serve the truth. & let me tell thee, that it was an unworthy secret piece of undermineing of my Conduct in the matter, to give any such accompt, w^t^ concerned that the present accord. I cannot enough expresse my Resentm^t^ of this thing, I intend to be to morrow Night att London, & designe to make one Essay more, if that will not doe, I intend noe further concerne therein. And for the Award, I say, {that} it is broake in nothing, but that of the way of Raiseing money.[4] & if thou wilt not acquies in that particuler, Rather then come before the world. I am heartily sorry. I wish the true felicity, wch stands in the blessed Truth, and thy conformitie to it

Thy well wishing freind

Rick:[5] 30th 11^th^m 1674[/5] W P.

Copy. Harleian MSS 7001, BL. (*Micro.* 2:037). Docketed: the copies of William Penns 1st 2^d^ & 3^d^ letters.

1. Fenwick, like Byllynge before him, was now in desperate financial straits, and Sir John Berkeley, to whom he may still have owed some of the £1000 purchase price for the New Jersey proprietorship, had him arrested for debt. Pomfret, *West New Jersey*, p. 68.

2. Sir John Berkeley, first baron of Stratton, began his involvement in colonization in 1663, when he became one of the original proprietors of Carolina, joined the Privy Council, and presided over the Council for Foreign Plantations. His brother, Sir William Berkeley, was for over thirty years the royal governor of Virginia. See also doc. 35, n. 281, above. *DNB;* Pomfret, *West New Jersey*, pp. 52, 56-58.

3. No records identify WP's legal counsel at this time, but Thomas Rudyard, an agent for Byllynge's trustees in July 1676 and a signer of the West New Jersey Concessions, is the most likely. Richard Langhorne, who witnessed the 1 July 1676 deed that divided New Jersey (see doc. 152, below), is also a possibility. ACM, vol. 116; Pomfret, *West New Jersey*, pp. 91, 95.

4. See doc. 112, n. 3, above, for the award that WP had made earlier in the month. Fenwick's memorandum to WP's letter of 20 Jan. (doc. 112) suggests that had he been satisfied that he would quickly receive his £900, he would not have sought a larger share in the New Jersey proprietorship. From this letter, it is clear that Fenwick had been publicly expressing doubt that he would get his money, and within the next ten days he would demand, and get, more New Jersey lands. See docs. 114 and 152, below.

5. Rickmansworth.

114
TO JOHN FENWICK

London 13th 12mo [February] 1674[/5]

J.F.

I have upon serious Consideration of the present difference (to end it wth benifitts to you both,[1] and as much quiet as may be) thought my Councells proposalls very Reasonable; indeed thy owne desire, the 8 partes added[2] was not soe pleasant to the other p[ar]tie,[3] that it should be now shrunke from by thee as injurious, & when thou hast once thought a proposeall reasonable, & given power to another to fixe it, Tis not in thy power, nor a discreat, indeede a Civil thing to alter, or to warp from it, & call it a being forced. John I am sorry, that a Toy, a Triffle should thus Robb men of tyme, Quiet, & a more proffitable employ, I have had a good conscience in wt I have done in this affaire. And if thou Reposseth confidence in me, and believest me to be a good & Just man, as thou hast said, thou shouldest not be upon such Nicety, & uncertainty, a Way wth vaine fancys, I intreat thee, & fall closely to thy busines, thy dayes spend On, And make the best of wt thou hast, thy great Grand children may be in the other world before wt Land thou hast allotted will be employed.[4] My Councell I will ans[wer] for it, shall doe thee all right & service in the affaire that becomes him, whom I told thee att first, should draw it up as for myselfe, if this cannot Scatter thy fears, thou art unhappie, & I am sorry.

Thy Sinceer freind
Will Penn

Copy. Harleian MSS 7001, BL. (*Micro.* 2:039). Docketed: the copies of William Penns 1st 2d & 3d letters.

1. John Fenwick and Edward Byllynge.

2. Fenwick had demanded eight more of the one hundred shares of West New Jersey land, in addition to the two that WP had already awarded him in January. Pomfret, *West New Jersey*, pp. 67-69.

3. Edward Byllynge, who wished to abide by WP's first award to him of ninety-eight shares of the one hundred, but reluctantly consented to accept only ninety, to satisfy Fenwick.

4. Fenwick was already fifty-seven, and had several grandchildren who would soon accompany him to America.

115
THE WEST NEW JERSEY CONCESSIONS

In the summer of 1676, WP put his signature to one of the most innovative political documents of the seventeenth century, the West New Jersey Concessions and Agreements. In forty-four chapters, arranged under several topical headings, the Concessions laid out a careful plan for distributing land in the new colony and framed a government with several unusual features. In contrast to the governments of England and nearly all of her colonies, New Jersey's political system vested power primarily in its legislature rather than in its executive branch. Its annually elected assembly held all legislative power, while its annually elected board of commissioners was thoroughly subordinate to that assembly and lacked any prerogative, military, or veto powers. All "inhabitants" could vote, and there was no religious test for civic activity. The extensive rights granted to these inhabitants included trial by jury for all offenses and disputes and freedom from imprisonment for debt. There were no prison fees, and the assembly had the power to legislate capital punishment only for murder and treason.

The authorship of this remarkable constitution cannot be established conclusively. Among the proprietors, Edward Byllynge probably made the greatest contribution; much of the structure and content of the document resembles his republican tract, *A Mite of Affection* (1659). The legal style of the Concessions, and the fact that the manuscript was drafted in an almost chancery hand, suggests that a legal advisor, such as Thomas Rudyard, played some role. WP's share in drafting the document is difficult to determine. The Concessions more closely resemble Byllynge's pamphlets than WP's later Frame of Government for Pennsylvania (1682), but early drafts of the Frame of Government were closer to the Concessions than the final document. Moreover, several chapters of the Concessions echo themes in WP's recent *England's Present Interest Discover'd* (1675): the abolition of imprisonment for debt (chap. 18), the increased judicial power of juries (chap. 19), and the involvement of all inhabitants in the making of law (chaps. 32, 35). In earlier Quaker writings to which he contributed and in his letterbook drafts of laws and petitions, WP repeatedly sought authority from England's ancient constitution, which appears as the benchmark of the Concessions (chap. 39). As a document drawn up without Crown influence for a colony whose only "charters" were a set of legal indentures that said nothing about powers of government, the West New Jersey Concessions could promulgate an essentially republican government. When WP established his own colony, based upon a formal charter from King Charles II, the conditions for colonization had changed, and undiluted Quaker republicanism was no longer tenable.

The origins of the political thought embodied in the Concessions and the document's impact upon subsequent colonial political thought are too involved to trace here. But it is clear that the Concessions set forth several of the principles of colonial government that WP would soon employ in Pennsylvania. And while neither the Concessions nor WP's Frame of Government outlasted the seventeenth century, both constitutions did much to establish the concept of an essentially republican legislature and to shape the colonists' view of the role of law throughout the colonial era.

The best discussions of the Concessions are Pomfret, *West New Jersey*, chap. 6; and *The West Jersey Concessions and Agreements of 1676/77: A Round Table of Historians*, Occasional Papers, No. 1 (Trenton, N.J., New Jersey Historical Commission, 1979), especially the essays by Caroline Robbins (pp. 17-23), Mary Maples Dunn (pp. 24-28), and John M. Murrin (pp. 42-49).

[c. August 1676][1]

The Concessions and Agreements of the Proprietors Freeholders and Inhabitiants of the Province of West New Jersey in America:

Chapter 1

Wee doe consent and agree as the best present expedient that such persons as shall be from time to time deputed nominated and appointed Comissioners by the present Proprietors or the major parte of them by writeing under their hands and seales shall be Comissioners for the time being and have power to order and manage the Estate and affaires of the said Province of West New Jersey according to these our Concessions, hereafter following and to depute others in their place and Authority in Case of Death or removeall and to continue untill some other persons be deputed nominated and appointed by the said proprietors or the Major parte of them to succeed them in that Office and service And the Comissionrs for the time being are to take care for [se]tting forth and dividing all the Lands of the said Province as be allready taken up or by themselves shall be taken up and contracted for with the Natives and the said land soe taken up and contracted for to divide into one hundred parts as occasion shall require that is to say for every quantity of Land that they shall from time to time lay out to be planted and setled upon they shall first for expedition divide the same into tenn equall parts or shares and for distinction Sake to marke in the Register and upon some of the trees belonging to every tenth parte with the letters A B and so end at the letter K[2] And after the same is so divided and marked the said Comissioners are to grant unto Thomas Hutchinson of Beverley Thomas Pearson of Bonwicke Joseph Helmsley of great Kelke George Hutchinson of Sheffield and Mahlon Stacy of Hansworth all of the County of Yorke[3] or their Lawfull deputies or p[ar]ticular Comissioners for themselves and their friends who are a Considerable number of poople and may speedily promote the Planting of the said Province that may have free liberty to make choice of any one of the said tenth parts or shares which shall be first divided and set out being also done with their consent that they may plant upon the same as they see meet and afterwar[d] any other person or persons who shall go over to inhabitt and have purchased to the number of tenn proprieties they shall and may have Liberty to make choice of any of the remaineing Parts or Shares to settle in and all other Proprietors who shall goe over to settle as aforesaid and cannot make up amongst them the number of tenn Proprietors yet nevertheless they shall and may have Liberty to make choice of settleing in any of the said tenth shares that shall not be taken up before and the Comissioners have hereby power to see the said one tenth parte that they shall soe make choice of laid out and divided into tenn proprieties and to allott them so many Proprieties out of the same as they have order for and the said Comissioners are to follow these Rules untill they receive contrary order from the major parte of the Proprietors under their hands and seales

The said Comissioners for the time being have hereby power for appointing and setting out fitt places for Townes and to limitt the bounderies thereof and to take care they be as Regular built as the present occasion time and conveniency of the places will admitt of and that all Townes to be erected and built shall be with the consent of the Comissioners for the time being or The major parte of them And further the said Comissioners are to order the affaires of the said Province according to these concessions and any other instructions that shall be given them by the major parte of the Proprietors untill such time as more or other Comissioners shall be chosen by the Inhabitants of West Jersey as here in these Concessions is mentioned and appointed[4]

And it is further expressly provided and agreed to that whereas there is a contract or agreement granted by William Penn Gawen Lawry And Nicholas Lucas unto Thomas Hutchinson Thomas Pearson Joseph Helmsly George Hutchinson and Mahlon Stacy Dated the second day of the month called March 1676 instant wherein they grant unto the said persons certaine priviledges for a Towne to be built whereby they have Liberty to choose their own Magistrates and officers for executing the Laws according to the Concessions within the said Towne which said Contract or agreement is to be held firme and good to all intents and purposes and we doe by these our Concessions confirme the same

Chapter 2

And that all and every person & persons May enjoy his and their just And equall propriety and purchase of lands in the said Province it is hereby agreed concluded and ordained that the Survey or Surveyors that the said Proprietors have deputed and appointed or shall depute or appoint they faileing that the Comissioners shall depute & appoint or that the generall free Assembly hereafter shall depute and appoint shall have Power by him or themselves or his or their Lawfull Deputie or Deputies to Survey lay out or bound All the Proprietors Lands and all such Lands as shall be granted from any of the Proprietors to the Freeholders Planters or inhabitants and a particuler or Terryor[5] thereof to Certifie to the Register to be recorded

Chapter. 3.

That hereafter upon further settlement of the said province the Proprietors Freeholders and Inhabitants resident upon the said Province shall and may at or upon the five and twentieth day of the month Called March which shall be in the yeare according to the English account One thousand six hundred and Eighty and soe thenceforward upon the five and twentieth day of March yearly by the ninth houre in the morning of the said day assemble themselves together in some publick place to be ordered and appointed by the Comissione[rs] for the time being and upon default of such appointment in such place as they shall see meet and then and there elect of and amongst themselves tenn honest and able men fitt for Government to officiate and execute the place of Comissioners for the yeare ensueing and untill such time as tenn more for the yeare then next following shall be elected and appointed which said elections shall be as followeth that is to say the Inhabitants Each tenn of the one hundred Proprieties shall elect and choose one and the one hundred proprieties shall be divided into tenn divisions or Tribes of Men

And the said elections shall be made and distinguished by ballating trunks to avoid noise and confusion and not by voices holding up of the hands or otherwise howsoever[6] which said Comissioners so yearely to be elected shall likewise Governe and order the affairs of the said Province pro tempore for the good and wellfare of the said people and according to these our concessions Untill such Time as a generall free assembly shall be elected and deputed in such manner and wise as is hereafter expressed and conteined.[7]

Chapter 4

And that the planting of the said Province be the more {speedily} promoted it is consented granted concluded agreed and declared

{1st} **That** the proprietors of the said Province have and doe hereby grant unto all persons who by and with the consent of one or more of any of the proprietors Of the said Province Attested by a certificate under his or their hands and seales Adventure to the said Province of West New-Jersey and shall Transport themselves or servants before the first day of the month commonly called Aprill which shall be in the yeare of our Lord one thousand six hundred seaventy and seaven these Following propsitions viz[t] for his owne person Arriveing Seaventy Acres of Land English Measure and for every Able man servant that he shall carry with him and arriveing there the like Quantity of seaventy Acres of land English Measure and whoever shall send Servants before that time shall have for every able man servant he or they so send as aforesaid and arriveing there the like Quantity of Seaventy Acres And for every weaker servant male or female Exceeding the Age of fourteen years which any one shall send or carry Arriving there Fifty Acres of Land and after the expiration of their time of service Fifty Acres of Land for their owne use and Behoofe to hold to them and their heires forever all such person and persons Freemen or servants and their respective heires and assignes afterwards paying yearely to the Proprietor his heires and assignes to whom the said Lands belong one penny an acre for what shall be laid out in Townes and one halfe penny an acre for what shall be laid out elsewhere the first yearly payment to begin within two yeares after the said lands are laid out.

{2} To every Master or Mistress that by and with such consent aforesaid shall goe hence the second yeare before The first day of the month called Aprill which shall be in the yeare one thousand six hundred seaventy and eight Fifty Acres of Land and for every able man servant, that he or she shall carry or send & arriveing there the like quantity of Fifty acres of Land & for every weaker servant Male or female exceeding the age of fourteen yeares arriveing there Thirty acres of land and after the expiration of their service Thirty acres of land for their owne use and behoofe to hold to them and their heires forever all the said persons and their respective Heires and Assignes yearely paying as aforesaid to the Proprietor his heires and assignes to whom the land belongs one penny farthing the acre for all such lands as shall be laid out in Townes and three farthings the acre for all that shall be laid out elsewhere.

{3} To every Freeman that shall arrive in the said Province within the third yeare from the first day of the month commonly called Aprill in the yeare one thousand six hundred seaventy and eight to the first of the said month called Aprill one thousand six hundred seaventy and nine (with an intention to plant) Forty acres of Land English measure and for every able man servant that he or she shall carry or send as aforesaid forty acres of land of like measure and for every weaker servant aged as aforesaid that shall be soe carried or sent thither within the third yeare as aforesaid twenty acres of land of like measure & after the expiration of his or their time of service twenty acres of land for their own use and behoofe to hold to them and their heires forever all the said persons and their heires and assignes paying yearly as aforesaid to the Proprietor his heires or assignes with whom they contract for the same One penny halfe penny the acre for what shall be laid out in Townes and one penny the acre for what shall be laid out elsewhere All which lands that shall be posessed in the said province are to be held under and according to the concessions and conditions as is before mentioned and as hereafter in the following Paragraph is more at large expressed **provided** alwayes that the before mentioned land that shall be taken up and so setled in the province as aforesaid shall from the date hereof be held upon the conditions aforesaid conteining at least two able Men servants or three such weaker servants As aforesaid for every hundred acres and so proportionably for a lesser or greater quantity as one hundred acres besides what a Master or Mistress shall possess which was granted for his or her owne person in failer of which upon notation to the present occupant or his assignes there shall be three yeares given to such for the compleating the said number of servants and for their sale or other disposure of such part of their lands as are not so peopled within which time of three yeares if any person holding any land shall faile by himselfe his agents executors or assignes or some other way to provide Such number of persons unless the Generall Assembly shall with respect to poverty Judg it was impossible for the partie so faileing to keep his or her number of servants to be provided as aforesaid in such case the Comissioners are to summon together twelv men of the neighbourhood upon such inquest verdict and Judgment past of such default they are and have power of disposeing of soe much of such land for any terme of yeares not exceeding twenty yeares as shall not be planted with its due number of persons as aforesaid to some other that will plant the Same reserveing and preserveing to the Proprietor or his lawfull assignes the rents to become due and owing for or in respect of the same according to the tenure and effect of these concessions And further that every proprietor that goeth over in person and inhabitt in the said Province shall keep and maintaine upon every lott of land that they shall take up one person at least and if the lot shall exceed two hundred acres he shall keep and maintaine for every two hundred acres the like quantity of one person at the least

And for all other proprietors that Doth but go over in person and inhabit in the said province shall keep and maintaine upon every lot of land that shall fall to them one person at the least and if the said lott exceed one hundred acres then upon every hundred acres that fall to them as aforesaid they shall keep and maintain one person at the least and if any neglect or deficiency shall be found in any of the proprietors of their keeping and maintaineing the number of persons before mentioned that then and in that case the Comissioners are to dispose upon the said lands for any terme of yeares not exceeding twenty To any person or persons that will keep and maintaine upon the said lands the number of persons as before is mentioned reserving alwaies unto the said proprietors the rents that shall fall due for the same as before is reserved and appointed to be so Alwaies provided that the keeping and maintaineing of the said number of persons upon the severall lots and number of acres before mentioned is to continue for ten yeares from the date of the concessions and no longer except wher there have been any deficiency so as the comissioners have lett the lands for a longer time to any person Or persons they are to enjoy the same dureing the term granted them by the Comissioners any thing in this last proviso to the contrary notwithstanding.

Chapter 5

And for the regular laying out of all lands whatsoever in the said province this method is to be followed by the Register & Surveyor

That the Register to be appointed as aforesaid having recorded any grant from any of the Proprietors to any person for any quantity or quantities of acres shall make out a Certificate to the surveyor or his deputie enjoying him to lay out limit and bound Acres of land for A B out of the severall Lots of C D one of the Proprietors in the proportions following that is to say part thereof in the lott of the said C D in which the Surveyor or his deputie shall lay out limitt and bound accordingly and shall certifie back to the Register on what point of the Compass The severall limitts thereof lie and on whose lands the severall parcells Butt and bound which last certificate shall be entered by the said Register or his deputie in a booke for that purpose with an Alphabeticall table of the

Proprietors names and the name of the planter or purchaser referring to the said Certificate shall by the said Register be endorsed on the back of the grant with the folio of the booke in which it is entered and his name subscribed to the said Indorsement.

And that the Comissioners for the time being are hereby impowered to acertaine the rates and fees of the publick Register Surveyor and other officers as they shall see meet and reasonable how much or what every one shall pay for Registering any conveyance Deed lease specialty Certificate or other writeing as also what shall be paid by every proprietor for surveying divideing and laying out of any lands in the said province which said Register Surveyor or other officer is not to exact or demand any more or greater rates as shall be established as aforesaid

Chapter 6

Wee doe also grant convenient Portions of Land for High waies and for streets not under one hundred foote in breadth in Citties Townes and Villages.

And for wharfes Keys Harbours and for publick houses in such places as the Comissioners for the time being (untill there be a generall assembly) shall appoint and that all such lands laid out for the said uses and purposes shall be free and exempt from all rents taxes and other charges and duties whatsoever as also that the Inhabitants of the said Province have free passage through or by any Seas Bounds Creeks Rivers Rivoletts in the said Province through or by which they must necessarily pass to come from the maine Ocean to any part of the Province aforesaid as also by Land in waies laid out or through any Lands not planted or enclosed.

That all the Inhabitants within the said Province of West Jersey have the Liberty of Fishing in Delaware River or on the sea coast and the Liberty of Hunting and Killing any Deer or other wild beasts the Liberty to Shoot or Take any wild Fowles within the said Province provided alwaies that they do not Hunt Kill Shoot or Take any such Deer wild Beasts or Fowles upon the Lands that is or shall be surveyed taken up inclosed sowen and planted except the owners of the sd lands or their Assign[s]

Chapter 7.

The Comissioners are to take care that Lands quietly held planted and possessed seaven yeares after it's being first duely Surveyed by the Survey or surveyors his or their Lawfull deputies which shall be appointed by the said Proprietors and Registered in manner as aforesaid shall not be subject to any review resurvey or alteration of bounds upon any pretence or by any pretence or by any Person or Persons whatsoever

Chapter 8

The Comissioners are to take care that no man if his cattel stray range or graze on any ground within the said province not actually approprieted or set out to particular persons shall be lyable to pay any trespass for the same provided that custome of Commons be not thereby pretended to nor any person hindred from legally takeing up and appropriating any land so grazed upon.

Chapter. 9.

The Comissioners are to see that all Courts established by the Laws and Constitutions of the Generall Assembly and pursuant unto those Concessions doe execute their severall duties and offices respectively according to the laws in force and to displace or punish them for violateing the said Laws or acting contrary to their duty and trusts as the nature of their offences shall require and where they see cause after condemnation or sentence past upon any person or persons by any Judg Justice or court whatsoever the said Comissioners have power to reprieve and suspend the execution of the sentence untill the Cause be presented with a Coppie of the whole Tryall proceedings and proofs to the next generall assembly who may accordingly either pardon or command execution of the sentence on the offendor or offendors (who are to be kept in the meane time in safe custody untill the sense of the Generall assembly be knowne therein

Chapter 10

To act and doe all other thing or things that may conduce to the safety peace and well Government of the said Province and these present concessions and that all inferior officers be accountable to the Comissioners and they to be accountable to the generall Assembly The Commissioners are to take care that the Constables of the the said Province shall collect such of Proprietors rents who dwell not in the said province but in England Ireland or Scotland and shall pay it to the receiver that they shall appoint to receive the same unless the Generall assembly shall prescribe some other way whereby they may have their rents duely collected without charg and trouble to the said Proprietors.

Chapter 11

They are not to impose or suffer to be imposed any Tax Custome or Subsidie Tollage Assesment or any Other duty whatsoever upon any colour or pretence how specious soever upon the said Province and Inhabitants thereof without their owne consent first had or other then what shall be imposed by the authority and consent of the Generall Assembly and that only in manner and for the good ends and uses as aforesaid.

Chapter 12

That the said Comissioners Registers Surveyors and all and every other publicke officers of trust whatsoever already deputed and chosen are hereafter from time to time to be deputed and chosen shall subscribe (in a booke or bookes to be provided for that purpose that they will truely and faithfully discharge their respective trusts according to the law of the said Province and Tenour of these Concessions in their respective offices and duties and doe equall Justice and right to all men according to their best skill and Judgment without Corruption favour or affection And the names of all that shall subscribe to be entered in the said booke And whosoever shall subscribe and shall violate breake or any wise falsify his promise after such subscription shall be lyable to be punished or fined and also be made Incapeable of any publick office within the said Province.[8]

The Charter or fundamentall Laws of West Jersey agreed upon

Chapter 13

That these following concessions are the common Law or fundamentall Rights of the province of West New Jersey

That the common Law or fundamentall Rights and priviledges of West New Jersey are Individually agreed upon by the Proprietors and freeholders thereof to be the foundation of the Government which is not to be altered by the Legislative Authority or free Assembly hereafter mentioned and constituted But that the said Legislative Authority is constituted according to these fundamentalls to make such Laws as agree with and maintaine the said fundamentalls and to make no Laws that in the least contradict differ or vary from the said fundamentalls under what pretence or allegation soever.

Chapter 14

But if it so happen that any person or persons of the said free Assembly shall therein designedly willfully and Malitiously move or excite any to move any matter or thing whatsoever that contradicts or any wayes subverts any fundamentall of the said Laws in the constitution of the Government of this province it being proved by seaven honest and reputeable persons he or they shall be proceeded against as Traitors to the said Government.[9]

Chapter 15

That these Concessions Law or great Charter of fundamentalls be recorded in a faire table in the assembly house and that they be read at the begining and disolveing of every Generall free assembly And it is further agreed and Ordained that the said Concessions Common Law or great Charter of fundamentalls be writt in faire tables in every Common Hall of Justice within this Province and that they be read in sollemn manner foure times every yeare in the presence of the People by the chiefe Magistrates of those places.

Chapter 16

That no Men nor number of Men upon Earth hath power or Authority to rule over mens consciences in religious matters therefore it is consented agreed and ordained that no person or persons whatsoever within the said Province at any time or times hereafter shall be any waies upon any pretence whatsoever called in question or in the least punished or hurt either in Person Estate or Priveledge for the sake of his opinion Judgment faith or worship towards God in matters of Religion but that all and every such person and persons may from time to time and at all times freely and fully have and enjoy his and their Judgments and the exercise of their consciences in matters of religious worship throughout all the said Province.

Chapter 17

That no proprietor Freeholder or Inhabitant of the said Province of West New Jersey shall be deprived or condemned of Life limb Liberty estate Property or any wayes hurt in his or their Priveledges Freedoms or Frachises upon any account whatsoever without a due tryall and Judgment passed by twelve good and Lawfull men of his neighbourhood first had and that in all causes to be tried and in all tryalls the person or persons araigned may except against any of the said Neighbourhood without any reason Rendred (not exceeding thirty five and in case of any vallid reason alledged against every person nominated for that service.

Chapter 18

And that no proprietor Freeholder Free denison or Inhabitant in the said Province shall be attached arrested or imprisoned for or by reason of any debt dutie or other thing whatsoever (cases fellonious criminall and treasonable excepted) before he or she have personall summon or summons left at his or her last dwelling place if in the said Province by some legall Authorized Officer constituted and appointed for that purpose to appear in some Court of Judicature for the said Province with a full and plaine account of the cause or thing in demand as alsoe the name or names of the person or persons at whose suite and the Court where he is to appeare And that he hath at least fourteen dayes time to appeare and answer the said suite if he or she live or inhabitt within forty Miles English of the said Court and if at a further distance to have for every twenty miles two dayes time more for his and their appeareance and So proportionably for a larger distance of place.

That upon the recording of the summons, and non appeareance of such person and persons a writt or attachment shall or may be issued out to arrest or attach the person or persons of such defaulters to cause his or their appeareance in such Court returnable at a day certaine to answer the penalty or penalties in such suite or suites and if he or they shall be Condemned by legall tryall and Judgement the penalty or penalties shall be paid and satisfied out of his or their reall or personall Estate so Condemned or cause the person or persons so condemned to lie in execution till satisfaction of the debt and damages be made **Provided** alwaies if such person or persons soe condemned shall pay and deliver such Estate Goods and Chattells which he or any other person hath for his their use and shall solemnly declare and averr that he or they have not any further Estate Goods or chattells wheresoever to satisfy the person or persons (at whose suite he or they are Condemned) their respective Judgments and shall alsoe bring and produce three other persons as Compurgators[10] who are Well knowne and of honest reputation and aproved of by the Commissioners of that division where they {dwell} or inhabitt which shall in such open Court likewise sollemnly declare and averr that they believe in their Consciences such person and persons soe Condemned hav not werewith further to pay the said condemnation or condemnations he or they shall be thence forthwith discharged from their said imprisonment any Law or custome to the contrary thereof heretofore in the said Province notwithstanding and upon such summons and default of appeareance recorded As aforesaid and such person and persons not appeareing within forty dayes after it shall and may be lawffull for such Court of Judicature to proceed to tryall of twelve Lawfull men to Judgment against such defaulters and issue forth execution against his or their estate real and personall to satisfie such penalty or penalties to such debt and damages soe recorded as farr as it shall or may extend

Chapter 19

That there shall be in every Court three Justices or Comissioners who shall sitt with the twelve men of the Neighbourhood with them to heare all causes and to assist the said twelve men of the neighbourhood in case of Law and that they the said Justices shall pronounce such Judgment as they shall receive from And be directed by the said twelve men in whom only the Judgment resides and not otherwise And in case of their neglect and refusall that then one of the twelve by consent of the rest pronounce their owne Judgment as the Justices should have done And if any Judgement shall be past in any case civill or Criminall by any other person or persons or any other way then according to this agreement And appointment it shall be held null and void and such person or persons soe presumeing to give Judgment shall be severely fined and upon complaint made to the generall Assembly by them be declared incapeable of any office or trust within this Province[11]

Chapter 20

That in all matters and causes civill and Criminall proofe is to be made by the sollemn and plaine averrment of at least two honest and reputable persons And in case that any person or persons shall beare false witness and bring in his or their evidence contrary to the truth of the matter as shall be made plainly to Appeare that then every such person or persons shall in civill causes suffer the penalty which would be due to the person or persons he or they beare witness against And in case any witness or witnesses on the behalf of any person or persons indicted in a criminall cause shall be found to have borne false witness for feare gaine Mallice or favour and thereby hinder the due execution of the Law and deprive the suffering person or persons of their due satifaction That then and in all other cases of false evidence such person or persons shall be first severely fined and next that he or they shall forever be disabled from being admitted in Evidence or into any publick office employment or service within this Province

Chapter 21

That all and every person and persons whatsoever who shall prosecute or preferr any indictment or information against others for any personall injuries or matter Criminall or shall prosecute for any {other} Criminall cause [(]Treason Murder and Fellony only excepted) shall and may be Master of his owne process and have full power to forgive and remit the person or persons offending against him or her selfe only as well before as after Judgment and Condemnation and pardon and remitt the sentence fine and punishment of the person or persons offending be it personall or other whatsoever.

Chapter 22

That the tryalls of all Causes Civill and Criminall shall be heard and decided by the vardict or Judgment of twelve honest men of the neighbourhood only to be summoned and presented by the Sherriffe of that division or propriety where the fact or trespass is Committed and that no person or persons shall be compelled to fee Any Attorney or Counceller to plead his cause but that all persons have free liberty to plead his own cause if he please And that no person nor persons imprisoned upon any account whatever within this Province shall be obliged to pay any Fees to the officer or officers of the said prison either when committed or discharged

Chapter 23

That in all publick Courts of Justice for Tryalls of causes Civill or criminall any person or persons inhabitants of the said Province may freely come into and attend the said Courts and heare and be present at all or any Such tryalls as shall be there had or passed that Justice may not be done in a corner nor in any Covert manner (being intended and resolved by the help of the Lord and by these our Concessions and fundamentalls that all and every person and persons Inhabiting the said Province shall as farr as in us lies be free from oppression and slavery.

Chapter 24

For the preventing of frauds deceits collusions in bargaines sales trade and traffick and the usuall contests quarrells debates and utter ruine which have attended the people in many nations by costly tedious and vexatious Law suites And for a due settlement of estates

It is agreed concluded and ordained that there be kept a Register at London within the nation of England and also another Register witin the Province of New West Jersey and that all deeds evidences and conveyances of land in the said province of New West Jersey that shall be executed in England may also be there registred and once every yeare the register of the said deeds and conveyances so registered shall be duely transmitted under the hands of the Register[12] and three proprietors unto the comissioners in New West Jersey to be enrolled in the publick Register of the said province as also that the cheif Register which the said Proprietors have deputed or chosen or shall depute or choose faileing that the Comissioners shall depute or choose or which the Generall assembly of the said Province hereafer mentioned shall depute or choose shall keep exact entries and Registries in faire bookes or rolls for that purpose to be provided of all publick affaires and therein shall record and enter all grants of land from the proprietors to the planters and all Conveyances of land house or houses from man to man as alsoe all assignments Mortgages Bonds and specialties whatsoever and all leases for land house or houses made or to be made from Landlord to Tennant and from person to person which conveyances Leases Assigments Mortgages Bonds and Specialtes which shall be executed in West New Jersey shall be first acknowledged by the granter Assignor and obligor before the said Comissioners or two of them at least or some two of their lawfull deputies for the time being who shall under hands upon the back side of the said deed Lease Assignment Mortgage or specialty Attest the acknowledgment thereof as aforesaid which shall be a warrant for the Register to record the same & such Conveyance or specialty if sealed executed acknowledged before three proprietors in the nation of England or Ireland and recorded or registred there within three months after the date thereof or if sealed executed and acknowledged in the said Province or elsewhere out of England and recorded or registered within six months after the date thereof shall be good and effectuall in Law and for passing or transferring of Estates in Lands Tennements or hereditaments shall be as effectuall as if delivery and seizin[13] were executed of the same and all other conveyances Deeds Leases or specialties not recorded as aforesaid shall be of no force nor effect and the said Register shall doe all other thing or things the said Proprietors by their instructions shall direct or the Comissioners or Assembly shall ordaine for the good and welfare of the said Province

Chapter 25

That there may be a good understanding and friendly correspondence between the proprietors freeholders and inhabitants of the said province and the Indian Natives thereof

It is concluded and agreed that if any of the Indian natives within the said province shall or may doe any wrong or injury to any of the

Proprietors Freeholders or inhabitants in person estate or otherwayes howsoever upon notice thereof or Complaint made to the comissioners or any two of them they are to give notice to the Sachum or other chiefe person or persons that hath authority over the said Indian native or natives that Justice may be done and satisfaction made to the Person or persons offended according to Law and Equitie and the nature and quallitie of the offence and injury done or committed And also in case any of the Proprietors Freeholders or Inhabitants shall any wise wrong or injure any of the Indian natives there in person estate or otherwise the Comissioners are to take care upon complaint to them made or any one of them either by the indian natives or others that Justice be done to the Indian Natives and plenary satisfaction made them according to the nature and quallitie of the offence and Injury And that in all tryalls wherein any of the said Indian Natives are concerned the tryall to be by six of the neighbourhood and six of the said Indian Natives to be indifferently and impartially Chosen by order of the Comissioners and that the Comissioners use their endeavour to perswade the Natives to the like way of tryall when any of the Natives doe any waies wrong or injure the said proprietors Freeholders or inhabitants that they choose six of the Natives and six of the Freeholders or Inhabitants to judge of the wrong and injury done and to proportion satisfaction accordingly.

Chapter 26

It is agreed when any land is to be taken up for settlements of townes or otherwayes before it be Surveyed the Comissioners or the major part of them are to appoint some persons to goe to the chiefe of the natives concerned in that land soe intended to be taken up to acquaint the Natives of their Intention and to give the Natives what present they shall agree upon for their good will or consent and take a grant of the same in writeing under their hands and seales or some other publick way used in those parts of the world which grant is to be Registered in the publick register allowing alsoe the Natives (if they please) a coppie thereof and that noe Person or persons take up any land but by order from the Comissioners for the time being

Chapter 27

That no shipp Master or commander of any Shipp or vessell shall receive into his shipp or vessell to carry unto any other Nation Country or plantation any person or persons whatsoever without a Certificate first had and obtained under the hands and seales of the Comissioners or any two of them that the said person or persons are cleare and may be taken on board signifieing that the said person or persons name have been put in three publick places of the Province Appointed by the Comissioners for that purpose for the space of three weekes giveing notice of his or their intention to transport themselves

Chapter 28

That men may peaceably and quietly enjoy their estates

It is agreed if any person or persons shall steale Robb or take any goods or Chattells from or belonging to any person or persons whatsoever he is to make restitution two fold out of his or their estate and for want of such estate to be made worke for his theft for such time and times as the nature of the offence doth require or untill restitution be made double for the same or as twelve men of the neighbourhood shall determine being appointed by the Comissioners not extending either to Life or Limb.

If any person or persons shall willfully beat hurt wound assault or otherwayes abuse the person or persons of any man woman or child they are to be punished according to the nature of the offence which is to be determined by twelve men of the neighbourhood appointed by the Commissioners

Chapter 29

For secureing estates of persons that die and taking care of orphans

{1} **If** any person or persons die the Comissioners are to take care that the will of the deceased be duely performed and security given by those that prove the will and that all wills or Testaments be registered in a publick Register appointed for that purpose and the person and persons that prove the same to bring in one true Inventory under their hands of all the estate of the deceased and to have a warrant under the hand of three Comissioners and the publick seale of the Province Intimateing that they have brought in an Inventory of the Estate and given securitie then and not before are they to dispose upon the Estate

{2} **If** any person die intestate leaveing a wife and children the Comissioners are to take security from the person that shall Administer to secure two parts of the Estate for the Children and the third to the Wife if there be any and if ther be no Child then halfe to the next of Kin and the other to the Wife

{3} **If** the parents of Children be dead and no Will made then the Comissioners are to appoint two or more persons to take the charge of the Children and Estate and to bring in an Inventory of the Estate to be registered and that the said persons are to make good to the children what part of The Estate shall come unto their hands and to give a true account of their receipts and disbursments to be approved of by the Comissioners

{4} **If** parents die leaving Child or Children and no estate or not sufficient to maintaine and bring up the said Child or children in that case the comissioners are to appoint persons to take care for the child or Children to bring them up in such manner as the Comissioners shall appoint and the charges thereof to be borne by the publick stock of the Province and if none be established then by a tax to be leavied by twelve men of the neighbourhood with the consent of the Comissioners or the maine part of them

Chapter 30

In cases when any person or persons kill or destroy themselves or be killed by any other thing

It is agreed if any man or woman shall willfully put hand and kill him or her selfe the Estate of such person or persons is not to be forfeited but the kindred heires or such other as of Right the estate belongs to may enjoy the same or if any Beast or Shipp Boat or other thing should occasion the death of any person or persons nevertheless the said Beast Shipp Boat or other thing is not to be forfeited but those to whom they belong may enjoy the same **provided** alwayes that the said Beast did not willfully kill the said person or hath been knowne to attempt or addicted to mischief or hath been found to hurt or kill any person then the said beast is to be killed.

Chapter 31

All such person or persons as shall be upon tryall found guilty of Murder or Treason the sentence and way of execution thereof is left to the Generall Assembly to determine as they in the wisdome of the Lord shall Judg meet and Expedient

The Generall Assembly and their Power

Chapter 32

That so soone as divisions or Tribes or other such like distinctions are made that then the inhabitants Freeholders and Proprietors resident upon the said Province or severall and repective Tribes or Divisions or Distinctions aforesaid doe yearely and every yeare meet on the first day of October or the Eighth month and choose one Proprietor or Freeholder for each respective Propriety in the said province(the said Province being to be divided into one hundred Proprieties) to be deputies Trustees or Representatives for the benefitt service and behoofe of the people of the said province which body of deputies trustees or Representatives Consisting of one hundred persons chosen as aforesaid shall be the generall free and supream Assembly of the said province for the year ensueing and no longer And in Case any member of the said assembly dureing the said yeare shall decease or otherwise be rendred incapeable of that service that then the Inhabitants of the said Proprietie shall elect a new member to serve in his Roome for the remainder of the said yeare[14]

Chapter 33

And to the end the respective members of the yearely assembly to be chosen may be regularly and impartially elected

That no person or persons who shall give bestow or promise directly or indirectly to the said parties electing any meat drink money or moneys worth for procurement of their choice and consent shall be capeable of being elected a member of the said Assembly And if any person or persons shall be at at any time corruptly elected and sufficient proofe thereof made to the said Free Assembly such person or persons soe electing or elected shall be reckoned incapeable to choose or sitt in the said Assembly or excute any other publick office of trust within the said province For the space of seaven yeares thence Next ensuing and also that all such elections as aforesaid be not determined by the common and confused way of cries and voices but by putting balls into ballating boxes to be provided for that purpose for the prevention of all partiallity and whereby every man may Freely choose according to his owne Judgment and honest intention

Chapter 34

To appoint their owne times of meting and to adjourne their sessions from time to time (within the said yeare to such times and places as they shall thinke fitt and convenient as also to assertaine the number of Their Corum provided such numbers be not less then one halfe of the whole in whome (or more) shall be the full power of the Generall assembly and that the voates of two thirds of the said Corum or more of them if assembled together as aforesaid shall be determinative in all cases whatsoever comeing in question before them Consonant and Conformable to these Concessions and fundamentalls

Chapter 35

That the said Proprietors & Freeholders at their choice of persons to serve them in the Generall and Free Assemblys of the Province give their Respective Deputies or Trustees their instructions at large to represent their grievances or for the improvement of the Province and that the persons chosen doe by indentures under hand and seale Covenant and oblidge themselves to act nothing in that capacity but what shall tend to the fitt service and behoofe of those that send and employ them and that in case of failer of trust or breach of Covenant that they be questioned upon complaint made in that or the next Assembly by any of their respective Electors

And that each member of the assembly Chosen as aforesaid be allowed one shilling per day dureing the time of the sitting of the assembly that thereby he may be knowne to be the servant of the people which allowance of one shilling per day is to be paid him by the inhabitants of the propriety or division that shall elect him

Chapter 36

That in every generall Free Assembly every respective member hath Liberty of speech that no man be interupted when speakeing that all questions be stated with deliberation and Liberty for amendments that it be put by the chaire man by them to be chosen and determined by plurallity of voates also that every Member has power of entering his protest and reasons of protestations And that if any member of such assembly shall require to have the persons names registered according to their II[s] and Noe's that it be accordingly done and that afte[r] debates are past and the question agreed upon the doores of the house be sett open and the people have Liberty to come in to hear and be witnesses of of the voate[s] and the inclinations of the persons voating

Chapter 37

And that the said Assembly doe elect Constitute and appoint tenn honest and able men to be Comissioners of Estate for manageing and carrying on the affaires of the said Province according to the Law therein established dureing the Adjournments and dissolutions of the said Generall Free Assembly for the conservation and tranquillitie of the same

Chapter 38

That it shall be lawfull for any person or persons dureing the session of any generall Free Assembly in that Province to address remonstrate or declare any suffering danger or grievance or to propose tender or request any priveledge profitt or advantage to the said Province they not exceeding the Number of one hundred persons.

Chapter 39

To enact and make all such Laws Acts and Constitutions as shall be necessary for the well Government of the said Province (and them to repeale) provided that the same be as neare as may be conveniently agreeable to the primitive antient and Fundamentall Lawes of the nation of England **provided** alsoe that they be not against any of these our Concessions and Fundamentalls before or hereafter mentioned[15]

Chapter 40

By Act as aforesaid to Constitute all Courts together with the limits powers and Jurisdictions of the same (consonant to these concessions) as also the severall Judges Officer and Number of Officers belonging to each court to continue such time as they shall see meet not exceeding one yeare or two at the most with their respective Sallaries Fees and perquisites and their appellations with the penalties that shall be inflicted upon them for the breach of their severall and respective duties and Trusts And that noe person or persons whatsoever inhabitants of the said Province shall susteyn or beare two offices in the said Province at one and at the same time.

Chapter 41

That all the Justices and Constables be chosen by the people and all comissioners Of the publick seales Treasuries and chief Justices Embassadors and Collectors be chosen by the Generall Free Assembly

Chapter 42

That the Comissioners of the Treasury of the said province bring in their account at the end of their yeare unto the generall Free Assembly there to be seen and adjusted and that every respective member carry a coppie thereof unto that hundred or propriety he serves for to be Registred in the Capitall publick court of that Propriety

Chapter 43

By Act as aforesaid to lay equall Taxes and Assesments and equally To raise moneys or goods upon all lands or persons within the severall proprieties precincts Hundreds Tribes or whatsoever other divisions shall hereafter be made and established in the said Province as oft as necessity shall require and in such manner as to them shall seem most equall and easie for the inhabitants in order to the better supporting of the publick charge of the said Government as alsoe for the publick benefitt and advantage of the said People and province

Chapter 44

By Act as aforesaid to subdivide the said Province into Hundreds proprieties or such other divisions and distinctions As they shall thinke fitt and the said Divisions to distinguish by such names as shall be thought good as also within the said Province to direct and appoint places for such and so many Townes Citties Ports Harbours Creeks and other places for the convenient lading and unlading of Goods and merchandise out of the Shipps Boates and other Vessells as shall be expedient with such Jurisdictions priveledges and Franchises to such Citties Ports Harbours Creeks or other places as they shall Judge most conduceing to the Generall Good of the said Province and people thereof and to erect raise and build within the said Province or any parte therof such and soe many Market Townes and villages and also appoint such and soe many Martes and faires and in such place and places as they shall see meet from time to time as the Grant made and assigned unto the said Proprietors will permitt and admit

IN TESTIMONY and witness of our consent to and affirmation of these present Laws Concessions and Agreements WEE the Proprietors Freeholders and Inhabitants of the said Province of West New Jersey whose names are under written have to the same voluntarily and freely set our hands dated this third day of the month commonly called March in the yeare of our Lord one thousand six hundred seaventy six

E: Byllynge[16]
Richard Smith
Edw. Nelthorp
John Penford:
Daniell Wills
Thomas Ollive
Tho Rudyard
William Biddle
Robert Stacy
John Farrington
Witt Roydon
Richard Mew
Percivall Towle
Mahlon Stacy
Thomas Budd
Sam[ll] Jenings

John Lambert
William Heulings
George Deacon
John Thompson
Edward Bradway
Richard Guy
James Nevill
W Cantwell:
Fospe [?] Ontstont
Machgyel Baron
Casp: Herman
Turrse [?] Plase
Robert Kemble
John Cornelise
Gerriet [?] Van Junne
William ⊗ Gill Jonson [?]
Mickaell ⊗ Larkerouse
Markas ⊗ Algus
Everit ⊗ Aldricks
Hendrick ⊗ Everson
Jillis Tomesen
Paul Doequet [?]
Claus Jansaln [?]
Richard Morgan [?]
Christopher ⊗ White
John Maddocks
John Forrist
James Viccary

Gauen Laurie
WM Penn
William Emley
Joshua Wright
Ni[c]ho Lucas
William Haig
William Peachee
[erased name]
Ricd: Mathews
John Harris [?]
Francis Collins
M
William Kent
Benjamin Scott
[erased] Lambert[17]
Thomas Hooton
Henry Stacy[18]

Hert. [?] ⊗ Jansen
John Surige [?]
Thomas Smith
Jeams Pearce
Edward ⊗ Web
John Pledger
Ric: ⊗ Willkison
Christopher ⊗ Sanders
Reneare ⊗ Vanhurst
William ⊗ Johnson
Charles ⊗ Bagley
Samuel Wade
Tho: Woodrofe
John Smith
Thomas Peirce
William Warner [?]
Joseph Warne
Isaac Smart
Andrew Thompson
Thomas Kent [?]
Henry Jenings
Henry ⊗ Stubbens
W[m] ⊗ Willis
George Haselewood
Rodger Poderick
William Hughes
Abraham ⊗ vanhighst
Hipolitas Lefever

William Rumsey
Richard ⊗ Robison
Marck Reeve
Thomas ⊗ Watson
Samuell Nicholson
Daniel Smith
Richard ⊗ Daniell
William ⊗ Penton
William Danniel
Robert Zane
Wallter ⊗ Peiterson
Anthony Page
Andrew ⊗ Bartleson
Woolley ⊗ Wollison
Anthony Dixson
John Denne
Thomas Benson
John Paine
Richd Buffington
Samll Lovet
Barnard Devenish
Thomas Stokes
Thomas French
Isaac Marriott
John Butceer [?]
Geo. Hutcheson
Thomas Gardner
Thomas Eves
John Borton
John Paine
Richard fenimore
Tho Scholey
Eliazer Fenton
Samuell Oldale
William ⊗ Black
Anthony Woodhouse
Daniel Leeds
John Pancoast
Francis Beswicke
William Luswall
John Snowden
Gruna Jacobson [?]
William Wilkinsin
Andrew ⊗ Shennek
Lause ⊗ Cornelious
Sam^{ll} Hedge
William Masster
John Grubb
John Worlidge
E. [?] Mijer [?]
Thomas Barton
Robert Powel
Thomas Harding
Mathew Allen
R. Wright
Godfrey Hancock
John Petty
Abraham Heulings
John Newbold
John White
Jno ⊗ Roberts
John ⊗ Wood
John Gosling
Thomas Revell

DS. The West New Jersey Proprietors, Burlington, New Jersey. *Micro.* 2:405, reproduces an eighteenth-century transcription, as reprinted in *New Jersey Archives*. 1st ser., 1:241-70, which varies widely from the original.

1. The Concessions were completed and signed in London by mid-August 1676, as the trustees state in docs. 116 and 117, below. James Wasse then took the Concessions and the "Instructions" (doc. 116) to America, departing London by 26 Aug. (doc. 117), arriving in Virginia at the end of October, and then proceeding to Maryland and New Jersey. The date given at the close of the document, 3 Mar. 1677, was presumably that on which the first commissioners, Wasse, Richard Hartshorne, and Richard Guy, were to read the document to the assembled colonists in West New Jersey, at which time the colonists could add their signatures to those of the Londoners. See n. 16, below.

2. On the development of West New Jersey's complex system for locating the shareholders' plots of land, see docs. 116 and 152, below.

3. These five Yorkshire Quakers acquired ten of the one hundred shares in the proprietorship of West New Jersey by an indenture dated 1 Mar. 1677 (see below in this chapter of the document), whereby they agreed to pay all claims against Edward Byllynge in Yorkshire. The claims amounted to about £3500, which was the purchase price for ten shares set by the proprietors. On 2 Mar. 1677, the proprietors granted the Yorkshiremen permission to use their shares to found a settlement of Yorkshire Friends wherever they chose in the colony. The "Yorkshire tenth" was set out in the fall of 1677 as a distinct plot of ground adjoining the "London tenth" (the area settled by the other principal group of colonists) on the north side, but the two groups of Friends united to form the town of Burlington, whose main east-west street was the border between the two tenths.

Thomas Hutchinson and Mahlon Stacy were tanners; George Hutchinson was a distiller; Joseph Helmsley and Thomas Pearson were yeomen. Joseph Helmsley, and Mahlon Stacy's brother Robert, named commissioners for the Yorkshire proprietors, arrived in New Jersey in August 1677. Helmsley had returned to England by 1680, and Pearson never went to America, but George Hutchinson, Thomas Hutchinson, and Mahlon Stacy soon emigrated and became leaders of the new colony. Hansworth and Sheffield are in southernmost Yorkshire, close to the border with Derby; Beverly, Bonwick, and Great Kelk are in eastern Yorkshire, north of Hull and close to the North Sea coast. Pomfret, *West New Jersey*, pp. 88-89, 288.

4. See chap. 3, below.

5. A "terrier" is a register of landed property, or a rent roll. *OED*.

6. The system of electing officials by dropping small balls (ballots) into boxes, which originated in Venice in the sixteenth century, strongly appealed to such English Whigs as Milton and Neville in the seventeenth century. The Quakers' use of this device in West New Jersey was one of its earliest applications in the English-speaking world. *OED*.

7. See chaps. 32-44, especially chap. 33, below.

8. The subscription book provided for here was the proprietors' device for holding magistrates responsible to their duties without requiring the oaths which Quakers could not take.

9. These two chapters, absolutely forbidding the alteration of the Concessions, stand sharply at odds with the flexible, legislature-centered government created by this mostly pragmatic document. WP and his fellow proprietors believed that England possessed an inviolable, unchanging constitution which the persecuting Parliaments of their own day insisted on twisting and destroying. Hence they describe the Concessions as West New Jersey's "common law." WP regarded the Great Charter of 1225 as the core of England's common law, which the Parliament of his day had no right to alter. See n. 15, below.

10. One who swears to another's innocence or credibility; a character witness. *OED*.

11. The proprietors' decision to elevate the jury to judicial supremacy in West New Jersey grew out of the Quakers' repeated confrontations with persecuting justices and badgered juries in England. The most famous, and best documented, of these confrontations was the Penn-Mead trial. See docs. 46-51, above.

12. The proprietors use "register" indiscriminately in this chapter to mean both a register book and a registering official, and capitalize the word upon each use at whim.

13. "Seisin" means legal possession. *OED*.

14. Annual elections were an important item in WP's agenda for parliamentary reform in the 1670s. He connected this practice with the uncorrupted Parliament of the fourteenth century, and Pennsylvania, whose government he would establish six

years after the composition of the Concessions, had annual legislative elections throughout the colonial period. See doc. 126, below.

15. Note that the proprietors state that laws should be conformable to "the primitive antient and Fundamentall Lawes" of England, not to current English law. WP and his colleagues appear, as in chaps. 13 and 32, to be drawing a distinction between the uncorrupted English constitution of the thirteenth and fourteenth centuries and the corrupted statutory accretions of the persecuting sixteenth and seventeenth centuries. See nn. 9 and 14, above; and note WP's conception of Magna Carta in doc. 48, n. 6, above, and in doc. 126, below; see also *The People's Ancient and Just Liberties Asserted* (1670), in *Works,* 1: 12, 18, 23-32.. This chapter also suggests that the Concessions, unlike most colonial charters, were drawn up entirely without the influence of crown lawyers or parliamentary committeemen. Indeed, the chapter's final clause establishes the Concessions, rather than English law, as the controlling framework of West New Jersey law.

16. The editors have not attempted to identify the one hundred fifty-one signers of this copy of the Concessions, but two observations about them are in order. First, most if not all thirty-one signers on the first manuscript page signed the document in London in July or Aug. 1676, before James Wasse took it to America. Most if not all of the one hundred twenty signers on the second, third, and fourth manuscript pages signed in West New Jersey, beginning in the winter of 1676-1677. The break between the first and second manuscript pages is marked below. Second, twenty-eight signers were illiterate, or nearly so, and employed a variety of marks, usually placed between their first and last names. These individuals are indicated by the symbol ⊗ placed after their first names. Flourishes, the phrase "his mark," and other extraneous marks have not been reproduced here. Information on these men can be found in Pomfret, *West New Jersey,* and in *New Jersey Archives,* 1st ser., especially vols. 1 and 21.

17. *New Jersey Archives,* 1st ser., 1:268, has "Thomas Lambert."

18. The first manuscript page, containing the signatures fixed in London, ends here.

The next three documents illustrate the colonizing techniques employed by WP and his colleagues to develop West New Jersey as a Quaker community. In May and June 1675, when the quarrel between Edward Byllynge and John Fenwick had seemingly been resolved, WP, Byllynge, Gawen Lawrie, and Nicholas Lucas arranged with Fenwick that all lands to be patented should be distributed by lot. Fenwick was to have the disposal of ten plots of ground in every one hundred, town by town; WP, Lawrie, and Lucas, serving as Byllynge's trustees, were to have the disposal of the other ninety. The following month Fenwick, desperate for funds, mortgaged his tenth to two other Quakers, John Edridge and Edmond Warner. In August he sailed for New Jersey with a shipload of settlers. There, against the wishes of Byllynge and the trustees, he laid out all the land that he had sold in one area, around Salem on the Delaware River, and promptly claimed full rights of government. Although the trustees opposed Fenwick's land policies, soon they, too, were selling off lands in distinct areas dominated by clusters of colonists from different parts of the British Isles, first a "London tenth" and a "Yorkshire tenth" and later an "Irish tenth." See doc. 115, above, and Pomfret, *West New Jersey,* p. 88.

In Fenwick's absence, WP and the other trustees in England

made their own plans. In June 1676, they allied with John Edridge and Edmond Warner to secure legal control of Fenwick's tenth in order to negotiate with Sir George Carteret the formal division of New Jersey into two distinct colonies, West New Jersey and Carteret's East New Jersey. This partition was completed on 1 July (see doc. 152). In August 1676 the trustees named James Wasse of London, Richard Hartshorne of East New Jersey, and Richard Guy of the Salem colony in West New Jersey to act as their commissioners in America, and gave them a set of instructions (doc. 116), supplemented by a letter to Richard Hartshorne (doc. 117). These two pieces illustrate the trustees' hopes for their new colony and their determination to stop John Fenwick's separatism. They also issued a promotional pamphlet, *The Description of West New Jersey* (London, c. July 1676), which was probably written by WP. This tract encouraged colonization so enthusiastically, however, that several Friends questioned whether the promoters were tempting Quakers to shirk their Christian duty to bear up under persecution at home. The trustees responded with a brief apology that defended New Jersey's merits, while urging all Friends to weigh the impact of their departure upon their English communities before deciding to emigrate (doc. 118).

116
TO THE WEST NEW JERSEY COMMISSIONERS

London the 18th 6mo Called Augst 1676

Wee whose names are heer under Subscribed doe give full Power Commission & Authority unto James Wase[1] Richard Harthorn[2] & Richd Guye[3] or any tuo of Them to Act & doe for us According to the following Instructions, and wee doe Ingage to Ratifie & Confirm whatsoever They shall doe in Prosecution of the Same.

(1) Wee desire yow to get a me{e}ting wth John Fenwick and the People that went wth him (but Wee wold not have yow tell your busines) untill {you} gett Them together Then shew & read the deed of Partition with George Cartwright[4] alsoe, the Transactions between William Penn, Nicholas Lucas,[5] Gawen Laury[6] John Elridg[7] & Edmond Warner,[8] and then read our Letter to John Fenwick, & the rest and shew John Fenwick He hath noe Power to sell any Land theer without the Consent of John Elridg and Edmond Warner.

(2) Know at John Fenwick, if He will be willing peacably to lett the Land hee hath taken up of the Natives be devided in a 100 parts according to our and his Agreement in England. Casting lotts for the Same Wee being willing that Those whoe being Setled and have

Cultivated ground now wth him shall Injoy the Same without being turned out {although They fall into our lotts alwayes Provided that wee be reamburst the like value & quantatie in goodnes out of Jo^n Fenwicks Lotts} and wee are alsoe Content to pay our 90th parts of what is paid to the Natives for the Same. And for what James Wass hath purchassed of Jo^n Fenwick and He setting out the same unto him not being in a Place to be alotted for a Towne upon a River but att a distance, & the sd J^on Fenwick allowing us like-value in goodnes in some other {of the} lotts Wee are willing hee shall posses the same from any clameing by or under Us And for the Towne lots wee are willing hee Enjoy the same as freely as any Purchasser {buyes of Us}

(3) Take Information from some that knoues the soundings of the River & Creeks and that is acquaint in the Country and when James Wase is in Maryland hee may Inquire for one Agustin[9] whoe as wee hear did sound most part of Dalwer River & the Creeks He is an able surveyer see to agree with Him to goe with you up the River as farr as over agamst Newcastell or further if yow can soe farr as a vessell of 100 Tun can goe for Wee intend to have a way cut Cross the Country to Sendy hook[10] soe the further up the River the way will be the shorter and therupon some Creek or bay in some halthy Ground find out a Place fitt to make a Setlment for a Towne and then goe to the Indians[11] and agree wth Them for a Track of Land about the said place of Tuenty or Therty myles long more or less as yee see met, and as broad as yow see meet If it be to the midle wee care not only Enquire if George Cartwright have not purchased some there already that soe yow may not buy it over againe.

(4) Then Lay out four —— or five[12] Thousand Akers for a Towne and if Agustine will undertake to doe it reasonably lett him doe it for He is the fittest Man and if He think he cannot Survey soe much being in the winter time then let him lay out the less for a Towne at present If it be but two[13] Thousand Akers and let him devide it in a hundred parts & when it is done lett John Fenwick if He pleas be There however lett him have Notice but houever lett some of yow be there to see the Lotts cast fairly by One Person, that is not Concerned —the Lotts are from N° 1 to a hundred and put the same numbers of the Lotts on the Partition Trees for distinction.

(5) If John Fenwick and Those Concernd with him be willing to Joyn with yow in those Things as above which is just & faire then He or any of them may goe a long with yow in yor busines & lett them pay their Proportion of what is paid to the Natives wth other Charges and soe hee and They may dispose[14] of their lotts with Consent of John Elridge & Edmond Warner. which lotts are 20:21:26:27:36:47: 50:57:63:72:[15]

(6) If John Fenwick and his People refuse to lett the Land They have taken up of the Natives be devided & refuse to joyn with Yow Yow may lett the Country know in what Capasity John Finwick stands

That He hath noe Power over the Persons or Estates of any Man or Woman more then any other Person.

(7) What Land Thow takes of the Natives lett it be taken in our Names viz Nynty parts for the use of William Penn Gawen Laury & Nicholas Lucas and Ten parts for J^on Elradge & Edmond Warner.

(8) After yow have taken up land as above and devided for a Town or setlment and cast Lotts for the same as above Then If any have a mynd to buy one or more Proprietyes sell them at two hundred £: piece They takeing Their lotts as others doe paying to yow in hand the value of fifty pound in part of a Propriety & the rest on sealing there Conveyance in London, and soe they may presently setle when any of the Lotts falls to ws that i[s] to say Hee that buyeth a Propriety may setle on any one Lott of nynty parts which said persons that buyes and what lotts falls to Them There They may setle and acquaint ws what Numbers they are and If any will take Land to Them & their heires for ever for every Aker taken up in a Place laid out for a Toune Acording to the Concessions They are not to have above what shall fall by Lott to a Propriety in a Towne

(9) What Charges James Wase is at by takeing up the Land of the Natives Wee doe obleidge to pay the same unto him again wth what proffitt is uswall there upon English Goods & hee may [torn]pois[16] upon two Lots one {in} each Towne If they be taken up before that comes away to his own proper use for his trouble & pains and we[e do]e alsoe Engage to alow & pay what Charges any of our Comission^rs shall disburst In Executeing these our Instructions to t[he]m or their Assignes.

(10) Lett ws be advised by the first Shipe that Cometh for England of all Proceedings herupon and writt to the friends at Sandy hook Leting them know how things are and that Wee have devided w[i]th George Cartwright and that our devision is all along on Dalwer River[17] and that Wee have made Concessions[18] by o^r selves which wee hope will Satisfye Friends there If John Fenwick or any of the People wth Him desire a Coppye of the deed of Partition let them have it.

(11) Wee desire that our Origonall deed[19] may be keept in yor own Custodie that it may be ready to shew unto the rest of the Comission^rs which wee intend to send over in the Spring with full Power for setling things and to lay out Land & dispose upon it, and for the setling some method of Government according to the Concessions.

(12) If yow cannot gett Agustin to goe wth yow or that hee be unreasonable in his demands then Send a Man to Thomas Bushroods at Esex Lodge in yorke River for Willi[am] Elliot[20] whoe writt to Gawen La[ury] this year and offerd himself to be a surveyer and tell him yow had Orders from sd Laury to send for him and take him wth yow Hee will be willing to be there all winter & will survey & doe other things He had a good Plantation in Virginia but was not able to keep

it He is a fair Conditioned sober Man let him stay there all winter and ord[r] Him some thing to live upon
(13) If the said Elliot goe wth yow give him directions what to doe if yow cannot stay till a place for a Towne be surveyed yet wee thinke yow may stay untill yow have not only pitched upon a Place for a Toune but alsoe upon a Place for a second Towne & Setlment {and have marked out the Place round about there} and lett William Elliott devide both which noe doubt but He may doe before the spring that Wee send over more Comoss[rs] and People and if J[o]n Fenwick be willing to goe on joyntly wth yow there his surveyer may goe a long & help ours & the Charges shall be brought in for both proportionably on all, Mynd this & speak to Rich[d] Gay or Rich[d] Hartshorne & leave ord[r] wth Them to lett William Elliot have provisions for himself till spring And wee shall Order Them satisfaction for the same And if there be noe house neer the Place yow take up for the surveyors to Lodge in Then let there be a Cotadge built for Them on the Place and Wee will alow the Charges.
(14) And whereas there is Tackling their already for fitting of a Sloop as Wee Judge in the Custodie of Rich[d] Gay Wee alsoe give yow Power if yow see meet & that it be of necessary use & advantage for the wholl Consern yow may Order those ship Carpint[rs] to build a sloop sutable for those materials & apoint Them some provisions for their food & for the rest of their wages Thy shall either have it in a part of sloop Or be otherwayes satisfyed in the spring of the yeare, The sd sloop to be ordered & disposed[21] upon by you untill more Comissioners come over wth further Instructions.
(15) For the [illegible deletion] goods Wee have sent over wth Ja: Wase, are to be disposed upon for purchassing Land from the Natives or otherwayes as need is giveing us Acco[tt] thereof.

Edmond Warnor	E: Byllynge	Wm Penn
Nicho. Lucas	Gauan laurie	

DS. New Jersey Historical Society, Newark. (*Micro.* 2:358).

1. James Wasse, a Quaker surgeon and a citizen of London, began his involvement with West New Jersey in July 1675 when he bought 5000 acres from John Fenwick. In Aug. 1676 he left England for Virginia and Maryland, then went to East New Jersey, and finally to Salem in West New Jersey, bringing a copy of these "Instructions" and of the "Concessions and Agreements" (doc. 115, above) with him. Wasse took up his land between Cohanzey and Alloways Creeks, an area straddling the present Salem and Cumberland counties. "Salem No. 1," fol. 135, in *New Jersey Archives* 21:564; Pomfret, *West New Jersey*, pp. 77, 92.

2. Richard Hartshorne (c. 1641-1722) was born in Leicestershire and emigrated to eastern New Jersey in 1669, where he took up land in Middletown. George Fox stayed with Hartshorne when he visited New Jersey in 1672. In Nov. 1675 Hartshorne wrote an enthusiastic letter describing the colony that was printed in *A Further Account of New Jersey* ([London], 1676). Hartshorne became a member of the East New Jersey council in 1684 and served as speaker of the East New Jersey legislature from 1686 to 1693, and again from 1696 to 1698. Hartshorne's brother, Hugh, became an East New Jersey proprietor in 1682. Fox, 2:211, 435; *New Jersey Archives* 1:220, 366.

3. This name appears to be corrected from "Gay." Richard Guy, a Quaker cheese-

monger in Stepney, was imprisoned from 1670 to 1672. In 1675 he bought 10,000 acres of West Jersey land from John Fenwick and accompanied him to America. "Salem No.1," fol. 72, in *New Jersey Archives* 21:561; Besse, 1:429, 437; Pomfret, *West New Jersey*, pp. 77, 83.

4. Sir George Carteret (1610?-1680), born on the Channel island of Jersey, became treasurer of the Navy and one of Admiral Penn's colleagues at the Restoration. In 1663 he joined the Privy Council's committee on trade and plantations and became one of the eight proprietors of Carolina. In 1664 the duke of York granted New Jersey, named in Carteret's honor, to Carteret and Sir John Berkeley; Carteret governed the eastern half of the colony through deputies until his death, despite opposition from the duke of York's deputies in New York. *DNB*.

5. Nicholas Lucas (1607-1688) was a maltster in Hertford and a prominent Friend, imprisoned from 1664 to 1672 for holding Quaker meetings in his house. He was also one of Byllynge's creditors and a trustee of West New Jersey. Besse, *Sufferings*, 1:241, 244-46, 248-50; *VCH: Hertford*, 4:356-57n.; Pomfret, *West New Jersey*, p. 68.

6. Gawen Lawrie (d. 1687) was a London merchant, a Quaker, and one of Byllynge's creditors. In addition to his role as a trustee, he purchased two shares in the proprietorship of West New Jersey. Lawrie later became a proprietor and deputy governor of East New Jersey and died in that colony. Pomfret, *West New Jersey*, pp. 68-69, 85, 87-88, 91.

7. John Edridge, a tanner from St. Paul Shadwell, Middlx., was arrested as a Quaker in 1665. He purchased 10,000 acres of West Jersey land from John Fenwick in 1675. For his relationship to Fenwick and to the trustees, see the headnote to docs. 116-118 above, and doc. 152 below. "Salem No.1," fol. 44, in *New Jersey Archives* 21:560; Besse, *Sufferings*, 1:407.

8. Edmond Warner was a poulterer, a citizen of London, and a Quaker; he purchased 10,000 acres of land from Fenwick in 1675. On Warner's role in West New Jersey, see the headnote to docs. 116-118 above, and doc. 152 below. "Salem No.1," fol. 76, in *New Jersey Archives* 21:561.

9. Probably Augustine Herrman (c. 1623-1686), the famous surveyor of the Chesapeake region. Herrman was born in Bohemia but raised in Holland and came to New Amsterdam in the 1640s as a clerk for the Dutch West India Company. In 1659 he traveled along the Delaware River, en route to Maryland, where he settled in 1660. Lord Baltimore granted him an estate named Bohemia Manor on the Eastern Shore in return for a detailed map of Virginia and Maryland, on which Herrman worked for ten years; it was published in London in 1673. He continued to reside at Bohemia Manor, on which, in 1684, he settled a colony of Labadists. WP corresponded with Herrman and his son Ephriam between 1681 and 1683. The trustees apparently did not secure Herrman's services. Augustine Herrman, *Virginia and Maryland as it is Planted and Inhabited this present year 1670* (London, 1673); Jeannette D. Black, *The Blathwayt Atlas*, 2 vols. (Providence, R.I., 1975), 2:75, 78, 90, 93, 103-5, 110-11, 116; *Micro.* 3:287, 635, 4:194.

10. The trustees, and many other Englishmen, supposed that the distance across New Jersey between the Delaware River and the mouth of the Hudson River was quite short.

11. The word "Indians" appears to have been first written "Ingians."

12. The line after "four" appears to fill in an erasure, while the "five" may be corrected from another word.

13. Here the copyist has entered a long dash with a flourish, perhaps to fill in a space left for another word expressing quantity, or to cover an erasure.

14. Corrected from "despose."

15. These were the randomly selected lot numbers that John Fenwick received in the agreement that he struck with Byllynge and the trustees on 7 May 1675. See doc. 152, below.

16. Perhaps "repose" is meant here.

17. One of the purposes of the partition agreement with Carteret was to secure title to all of the land on the east bank of the Delaware River. See Pomfret, *West New Jersey*, p. 74.

18. See doc. 115.

19. Probably either the Berkeley-Fenwick-Byllynge deed of 18 Mar. 1674, or the Fenwick-Byllynge-Penn-Lawrie-Lucas deed of 10 Feb. 1675. See doc. 152, below.

20. Thomas Bushrod (c. 1604-1676), emigrated from England to Massachusetts,

and then to Virginia, where he married a Quaker widow, Mary Hill, sometime before 1661, and lived thereafter at the Hill plantation, Essex Lodge, near Yorktown. In 1661 he strongly defended Virginia's Quakers against attacks by Anglican clerics, although it is not known whether he became a Friend. William Elliott was perhaps the William Elliott, Esq., of "York Buildings" who became an associate of Governor Spotswood in an ironworks in the eighteenth century. *Tyler's Quarterly Historical and Genealogical Magazine* 1:264-69, 3:300-1; *William and Mary Quarterly*, 1st ser., 11:30-33; Lillie Du Puy Van Culin, ed., *Colonial Men and Times* (Philadelphia, 1916), pp. 480-83; *Virginia Magazine of History and Biography* 13:95-96.

21. Corrected from "desposed."

117
TO RICHARD HARTSHORNE

London, 26th of
the 6th month [August], 1676.

Richard Hartshorne.

We have made use of thy name in a commission and instructions, which we have sent by James Wasse, who is gone in Samuel Groome's ship[1] for Maryland; a copy of which is here inclosed, and also a copy of a letter we have sent to John Fenwick, to be read to him in presence of as many of the people that went with him as may be; and because we both expect, and also entreat, and desire thy assistance in the same, we will a little shew things to thee, that thou may inform not only thyself, but friends[2] there; which in short is as follows.

1st. We have divided with George Carteret, and have sealed deeds of partition, each to the other; and we have all that side on Delaware river from one end to the other; the line of partition is from the east side of little Egg Harbour, straight North, through the country, to the utmost branch of Delaware river; with all powers, privileges, and immunities whatsoever: ours is called *New West-Jersey*, his is called *New East-Jersey*.

2d. We have made concessions by ourselves, being such as friends here and there (we question not) will approve of, having sent a copy of them by James Wasse; there we lay a foundation for after ages to understand their liberty as men and christians, that they may not be brought in bondage, but by their own consent; for we put the power in the people, that is to say, they to meet and choose one honest man for each propriety, who hath subscribed to the concessions;[3] all these men to meet as an assembly there, to make and repeal laws, to choose a governor, or a commissioner, and twelve assistants, to excute the laws during their pleasure; so every man is capable to choose or be chosen: No man to be arrested, condemned, imprisoned, or molested in his estate or liberty, but by twelve men of the neighbourhood: No man to lie in prison for debt, but that his estate satisfy as far as it will go, and be set at liberty to work: No person to be called in question or molested for his conscience, or for worshipping according to his conscience; with many more things mentioned in the said concessions.

3. We have sent over by James Wasse, a commission under our hands and seals, wherein we impower thyself, James Wasse and Richard Guy, or any two of you, to act and do according to the instructions, of which here is a copy; having also sent some goods, to buy and purchase some land of the natives.

4. We intend in the spring to send over some more commissioners, with the friends and people that cometh there, because James Wasse is to return in Samuel Groom's ship for England: for Richard Guy, we judge him to be an honest man, yet we are afraid that John Fenwick will hurt him, and get him to condescend to things that may not be for the good of the whole; so we hope thou wilt ballance him to what is just and fair; that John Fenwick betray him not, that things may go on easy without hurt or jar; which is the desire of all friends; and we hope West Jersey will be soon planted; it being in the minds of many friends to prepare for their going against the spring.

5. Having thus far given thee a sketch of things, we come now to desire thy assistance, and the assistance of other friends in your parts; and we hope it will be at length an advantage to you there, both upon truth's account, and other ways; and in regard many families more may come over in the spring to Delaware side, to settle and plant, and will be assigned by us to take possession of their particular lots; we do intreat and desire, that thou, knowing the country, and how to deal with the natives; we say, that thee, and some other friends, would go over to Delaware side, as soon as this comes to your hands, or as soon as you can conveniently; and James Wasse is to come to a place called New-Castle, on the other side of Delaware river, to stay for thee, and any that will go with him; and you all to advise together, and find out a fit place to take up for a town, and agree with the natives for a tract of land; and then let it be surveyed and divided in one hundred parts; for that is the method we have agreed to take, and we cannot alter it;[4] and if you set men to work to clear some of the ground, we would be at the charges; and we do intend to satisfy thee for any charge thou art at, and for thy pains: This we would not have neglected; for we know, and you that are there know, that if the land be not taken up before the spring, that many people come over there, the natives will insist on high demands, and so we shall suffer by buying at dear rates, and our friends that cometh over, be at great trouble and charges until a place be bought and divided; for we do not like the tract of land John Fenwick hath bought,[5] so as to make it our first settlement; but we would have thee and friends there, to provide and take up a place on some creek or river, that may lie nearer you, and such a place as you may like; for may be it may come in your minds to come over to our side, when you see the hand of the Lord with us; and so we can say no more, but leave the thing with you, believing that friends there will have a regard to friends settling,

that it may be done in that way and method, that may be for the good of the whole; rest thy friends,

Gawen Lawrie,
William Penn,
Nicholas Lucas,
E. Byllinge,
John Edridge,
Edmond Warner.

Printed. Samuel Smith, *The History of the Colony of Nova-Caesaria, or New Jersey* (Burlington, N.J., 1765), pp. 80-83. (*Micro.* 2:364).

1. Possibly the *Globe*, of London, which Groom and his son sailed to Maryland in 1679. On Groom's career, see doc. 81, n. 2, above. The present document is the first evidence of Groome's involvement with New Jersey. ACM, vols. 119-20.

2. Both the recipient of this letter and all six of its signers were Quakers. The proprietors' aspiration for West New Jersey to become a Quaker community is evident throughout this letter.

3. A *propriety*, as the term is used here, was one of the one hundred shares in the proprietorship of West New Jersey. Thus a person might purchase and retain one whole share to himself and become an assembly member, or sell his share in parcels to many persons, who could then elect a representative for their propriety. The full assembly would have one hundred members. For details, see doc. 115, chap. 32, above.

4. Byllynge, Lawrie, Lucas, and WP had legally committed themselves to this arrangement in their 7 May 1675 indenture with John Fenwick, and John Edridge and Edmond Warner had pledged to observe it when they signed a mortgage agreement with John Fenwick on 17 July 1675. See doc. 152, below.

5. WP and his fellow trustees thought that Fenwick's Salem was too far down river. They preferred a site as far up the Delaware as ocean-going ships could navigate, as they suggest in doc. 116. This consideration led them to establish a settlement at Burlington, just a few miles below the first falls on the Delaware at Trenton.

118
TO PROSPECTIVE SETTLERS IN WEST NEW JERSEY

[c. September 1676]

Dear friends and brethren,

In the pure love and precious fellowship of our Lord Jesus Christ, we very dearly salute you: Forasmuch as there was a paper printed several months since, entitled, *The description of New-West-Jersey,*[1] in the which our names were mentioned as trustees for one undivided moiety of the said province: And because it is alledged that some, partly on this account, and others apprehending, that the paper by the manner of its expression came from the body of friends, as a religious society of people, and not from particulars, have through these mistakes, weakly concluded that the said description in matter and form might be writ, printed and recommended on purpose to promp and allure people, to dis-settle and transplant themselves, as it's also by some alledged: And because that we are informed, that several have on that account, taken encouragement and resolution to transplant themselves and families to the said province; and lest any of them (as is feared by some) should go out of a curious and unsettled mind, and others to shun the testimony of the blessed cross of Jesus, of which several weighty friends have a godly jealousy upon their spirits; lest an unwarrantable forwardness should act or hurry any beside or beyond the wisdom and counsel of the lord, or the freedom of his light and spirit in their own hearts, and not upon good and weighty grounds: It truly laid hard upon us, to let friends know how the matter stands; which we shall endeavour to do with all clearness and fidelity.

1. That there is such a *province* as *New-Jersey,* is certain,

2. That it is reputed of those who have lived and have travelled in that country, to be wholesome of air and fruitful of soil, and capable of sea trade, is also certain; and it is not right in any to despise or dispraise it, or disswade those that find freedom from the *Lord,* and necessity put them on going.

3. That the duke of York sold it to those called lord Berkeley, baron of Stratton, and sir George Carteret, equally to be divided between them, is also certain.

4. One *moiety* or half part of the said *province,* being the right of the said lord Berkeley, was sold by him to John Fenwick, in trust for Edward Byllinge, and his assigns.

5. Forasmuch as E. B. (after William Penn had ended the difference between the said Edward Byllinge and John Fenwick) was willing to present his interest in the said *province* to his creditors, as all that he had left him, towards their satisfaction, he desired William Penn (though every way unconcerned)[2] and Gawen Lawrie, and Nicholas Lucas, two of his creditors, to be trustees for performance of the same; and because several of his creditors, particularly and very importunately, pressed William Penn to accept of the trust for their sakes and security; we did all of us comply with those and the like requests, and accepted of the trust.

6. Upon this we became trustees for one moiety of the said *province,* yet undivided; And after no little labour, trouble and cost, a division was obtained between the said sir George Carteret and us, as trustees: The country is situated and bounded as is expressed in the printed description.

7. This now divided moiety is to be cast into one hundred parts, lots, or proprieties; ten of which upon the agreement made betwixt E. Byllinge and J. Fenwick, were settled and conveyed unto J. Fenwick, his executors and assigns, with a considerable sum of money,[3] by way of satisfaction for what he became concerned in the purchase from the said lord Berkeley, and by him afterwards conveyed to John Edridge and Edmond Warner, their heirs and assigns.

8. The ninety parts remaining are exposed to sale, on the behalf of the creditors of the said E. B. And forasmuch as several friends

are concerned as creditors, as well as others, and the disposal of so great a part of this country being in our hands; we did in real tenderness and regard to friends, and especially to the poor and necessitous, make friends the first offer; that if any of them, though particularly those that being low in the world, and under trials about a comfortable livelihood for themselves and families, should be desirous of dealing for any part or parcel thereof, that they might have the refusal.

9. This was the real and honest intent of our hearts, and not to prompt or allure any out of their places, either by the credit our names might have with our people throughout the nation, or by representing the thing otherwise than it is in itself.

As for the printed paper sometime since set forth by the creditors, as a description of that province; we say as to two passages in it, they are not so clearly and safely worded as ought to have been; particularly, in seeming to limit the *winter* season to so short a time; when on further information, we hear it is sometime longer and sometime shorter than therein expressed;[4] and the last clause relating to liberty of conscience, we would not have any to think, that it is promised or intended to maintain the liberty of the exercise of religion by force and arms; though we shall never consent to any the least violence on conscience; yet it was never designed to encourage any to expect by force of arms to have liberty of conscience fenced against invaders thereof.[5]

10. And be it known unto you all, in the name and fear of Almighty God, his glory and honour, power and wisdom, truth and kingdom, is dearer to us than all visible things; and as our eye has been single, and our heart sincere to the living God, in this as in other things; so we desire all whom it may concern, that all groundless jealousies may be judged down and watched against, and that all extremes may be avoided on all hands by the power of the Lord; that nothing which hurts or grieves the holy life of truth in any that goes or stays, may be adhered to; nor any provocations given to break precious unity.

This am I, William Penn, moved of the Lord, to write unto you, lest any bring a temptation upon themselves or others; and in offending the Lord, slay their own peace: *Blessed are they that can see, and behold him their leader, their orderer, their conductor and preserver, in staying or going: Whose is the earth and the fullness thereof, and the cattle upon a thousand hills.*[6] And as we formerly writ,[7] we cannot but repeat our request unto you, that in whomsoever a desire is to be concerned in this intended *plantation,* such would weigh the thing before the Lord, and not headily or rashly conclude on any such remove; and that they do not offer violence to the tender love of their near kindred and relations; *but soberly and conscientiously endeavour to obtain their good wills, the unity of friends where they live; that whether they go or stay, it may be of good savour before the Lord (and good people) from whom only can all heavenly and earthly blessings come.* This we thought good to write for the preventing of all misunderstandings, and to declare the real truth of the matter; and so we commend you all to the Lord, who is the watchman of his Israel. We are your friends and brethren,

William Penn,
Gawen Lawrie,
Nicholas Lucas.

Printed. Samuel Smith, *The History of the Colony of Nova-Caesaria, or New-Jersey* (Burlington, N. J., 1765), pp. 88-91. (*Micro.* 2:367). The original, a printed broadside (London, 1676, title unknown), has not been found.

1. This promotional broadside, which was probably written by WP, is entitled *The Description of the Province of West-Jersey in America: as also, Proposals to such who desire to have any Propriety therein* ([London], 5th Mo: [July], 1676); it is reprinted in *Proceedings of the New Jersey Historical Society* 54:8-11. Wing, 3:31.

2. WP, unlike Lawrie and Lucas, was not one of Byllynge's creditors, nor had he invested any money in West New Jersey; thus he had no rights to land there as a proprietor, but was only a trustee for Byllynge. He did not invest in West New Jersey until 1682-1683, when he bought Fenwick's tenth from Edmond Warner and John Fenwick.

3. £400. See doc. 152, below.

4. *The Description of the Province of West-Jersey* stated that "The Dayes [in New Jersey] are about two Hours shorter in the *Summer,* and as much longer in the *Winter,* than ours here in *England;* the *Winter* being generally not above six Weeks." *Proceedings of the New Jersey Historical Society* 54:9.

5. *The Description* stated: "But it's intended (with the first [settlers]) to send over *Commissioners,* to see that every Man have the right done upon the place when he comes there. Being resolved (by the help of *God*) that every individuals *Property,* as also *Liberty of Conscience;* both as Men, and Christians, shall be inviolably preserved (to all Intents, and Purposes) from all manner of Invasions, and Valuations whatsoever." *Proceedings of the New Jersey Historical Society* 54:11.

6. Ps. 50:10.

7. The reference is obscure; WP is not referring to *The Description of the Province of West-Jersey,* which gives no such cautionary advice.

IN HOLLAND AND GERMANY

1677

119
AN ACCOUNT OF MY JOURNEY INTO HOLLAND & GERMANY

This account of WP's second journey into Holland and Germany gives us a portrait of the seasoned traveler and mature missionary. He celebrated his thirty-third birthday shortly before he returned to England; he was healthy, vigorous, and full of energy. The journal is eloquent testimony to a kind of restlessness and love of movement which were important characteristics of the man. He enjoyed recording the details of travel—how far he went in a day, how he traveled, whom he met, the towns where he stopped. It is easy to plot his exact itinerary.

This journey, like WP's trip to the Continent in 1671, was a religious mission. He traveled with a group of prominent Quakers, including George Fox, Robert Barclay, Thomas Rudyard, and George Keith. They were trying to heal divisions among Dutch Friends caused by differences about religious discipline and to spread the Quaker message more widely in Germany. WP appears to have been in an exalted state during much of his journey. The intensity with which he sought spiritual communion is only matched by his endurance during hours of prayer and preaching. He gave much thought to his own religious life and to the spiritual state of the people whom he met. We have, therefore, several extremely interesting accounts in WP's journal of his conversion, and details of his relations with his family after he became a Quaker. We also have glimpses—brief, but clear—of the Christians he encountered along the way.

By and large, WP sought out people with whom he had something in common: Protestants with some leaning toward pietism, or Quakers. He mainly travelled in areas where he could find such kindred spirits; he was uncomfortable in Paderborn, a Catholic town, and quickly moved on. Because Holland had become a haven for fugitives from religious persecution, it was a fertile soil for new sects like the Quakers, who traced their history in Amsterdam back to 1655. The Rhineland was highly particularized and autocratic; the ruler of each little state decided on the local religion. Some, like the electors of the Palatine and of Brandenburg, had been rather tolerant, and WP spent a good deal of time in their territories. He also spent considerable time in old commercial cities of the Hanseatic League, cities with histories of independent governance, cosmopolitan toleration, and early acceptance of the Protestant Reformation.

WP met a variety of people along the way, but perhaps it was characteristic of his social attitudes that we hear most about the well-born and well-connected. When he arrived in a new place, he followed Christ's exhortation to his disciples (Matthew 10:11) to find out who was "worthy." He was asking after a certain religious receptivity, but "worth" seems to have implied status as well. It is also striking how many upper-class women he met, women with whom he shared spiritual experiences and with whom he kept in touch by letter during his journey.

While this journey was invigorating to WP's soul, it would also prove important in his colonization schemes. It was certainly no accident that he later mounted an intensive advertising campaign for colonists in precisely the areas that he had visited on this trip. He had made important contacts, which he used to spread the word; people whom he met in 1677 would invest in Pennsylvania. All in all, this journey was a significant event in his life.

In the preface to the first printed edition, WP said that when he returned from the Continent he had copies of his journal made for friends. The manuscript used here is a contemporary copy which once belonged to Granville Penn, a grandson of WP, and is now in the HSP. It was made by the same clerk who copied most of the second half of WP's letterbook of 1667-1675. This clerk was probably the German Mark Swanner, who came to England sometime after 1676. On 2 November 1677, immediately after WP's return from Holland and Germany, Philip Ford made a cash payment of five shillings to "the German that writes for thee" (see doc. 145). On 19 November, Ford made another payment to "Marke the German" (see doc. 146). The HSP copy of WP's journal was probably the first to be made. It contains several insertions in another hand (which appear in braces in this edition) that were made either by WP himself or at his direction. A number of quite long letters are inserted in the manuscript which break the pagination and sometimes disrupt the chronological order. The copyist put in guide marks and marginal notes to show the proper sequence of entries. This sequence has been followed in the present edition, and the copyist's guide marks are also indicated.

We can be reasonably sure that this HSP copy was only one step from the original, since another clerk's copy, a "fair copy" of the journal, also survives in the Albert Cook Myers Collection, CCHS. This fair copy was written in five sixteen-page stitched booklets (one of which is now missing) by the same clerk, and incorporated almost all of WP's corrections from the HSP copy. However, several letters which were included in the HSP copy were not entered into the fair copy.

One of the friends who received copies of WP's journal was Lady Conway. When she died, her copy turned up among her papers, and Francis Mercurius von Helmont urged WP to publish it. Probably the HSP copy used here supplied the text for the first printed edition, *An Account of W. Penn's Travails in Holland and Germany* (London, 1694), since the letters and corrections inserted into the HSP copy all appear in the printed edition. Moreover, both the HSP copy and the first printed edition use New Style dating for the general meeting held in Amsterdam on 2 August 1677 (O.S.), whereas in the fair copy of the journal this meeting is double-dated 2/12 August. On the other hand, there are also several differences between the HSP manuscript and the first printed edition. The first published edition contains letters and essays not in the manuscript. However, one of these essays, addressed *To the Churches of Jesus Throughout the World*, had been published separately in 1677 and was simply reprinted along with the journal in 1694, with its 1677 title page. The HSP manuscript copy of the journal also lacks the final section of the printed edition, which details WP's return to England and includes his closing letter of 24 October 1677 to Friends in Holland and Germany.

A second impression of the *Account of W. Penn's Travails*, also issued in 1694, advertises itself as "Corrected by the Author's own Copy, with some Answers not before printed." WP probably corrected his own copy of the first published edition and added letters from Princess Elizabeth. In this second printed version, the date of the Amsterdam meeting is changed to 2/12 August, but that alteration is not inserted in the HSP manuscript copy.

WP's journal has been printed many times since 1694, but no later edition has been based on the manuscript. Reprints issued between 1694 and 1726 were made from the first edition of 1694, and later printings were taken from Joseph Besse's edition of the journal in *Works*. None of these editions is annotated. However, one modern scholar, William I. Hull, worked extensively on the history of seventeenth-century Friends in Germany and Holland, and took a particular interest in WP's experience there. We have relied heavily on his work.

In annotating this journal, we have drawn repeatedly on the following sources, which have not been specifically cited in the footnotes: Fox, *Journal;* Fox, *Short Journal;* Hajo Holborn, *A History of Modern Germany, 1648-1840* (New York, 1964); William I. Hull, *Benjamin Furly and Quakerism in Rotterdam* (Swarthmore, 1941), *The Rise of Quakerism in Amsterdam, 1655-1665* (Swarthmore, 1938), *William Penn and the Dutch Quaker Migration to Pennsylvania* (Swarthmore, 1935), and *William Sewel of Amsterdam, 1653-1720* (Swarthmore, 1933); and Ernest F. Stoeffler, *The Rise of Evangelical Pietism* (Leiden, 1965). Josef Engel, *Grosser historisches Weltatlas* (Munich, 1962), has been the primary geographical source; the spelling of place names in the notes has been standardized according to *Webster's Geographical Dictionary,* rev. ed. (Springfield, Mass., 1969).

In this edition, the manuscript directions for internal rearrangement are given in footnotes. A few difficult readings are enhanced in the notes by the reading of the fair copy. The dates and places, in the margins in the original, are inserted in braces and treated as lines of text, for ease of composition. In the manuscript, the copyist wrote the dates in the inner margins and the places in the outer margins of the book. We have standardized the arrangement by placing all dates on the right and all places on the left.

An Account of my Journey into
Holland & Germany.

[22 July-12 October] 1677.

{at Worminghurst in Sussex} {I. 22 5m. [22 July]}

The 22st day of the 5th month, 1677. being the First day of the week I left my Dear Wife & family in the love & fear of god, & came well to London that night.

{London Essex} {II. 23 5m [23 July]}

The next day I employed myself on Friends behalf, that were in suffering, till the evening: & then went to my own Mothers in Essex.[1]

{Colchester} {[III. 24] 5m. [24 July]}

The next morning I took my journey to Colchester,[2] & met George Watts[3] {of london} upon the way; who {return'd &} wth me came well to that town that evening. We lodged at John Furley's the Elder;[4] but had a blessed meeting at Jonathan Furley's[5] house that night.

{Harwich} {[IV. 25] 5m. [25 July]}

The next morning early I left Colchester, & came to Harwich about Noon; accompanyed with G. Watts, & John Furley the elder, W[m]

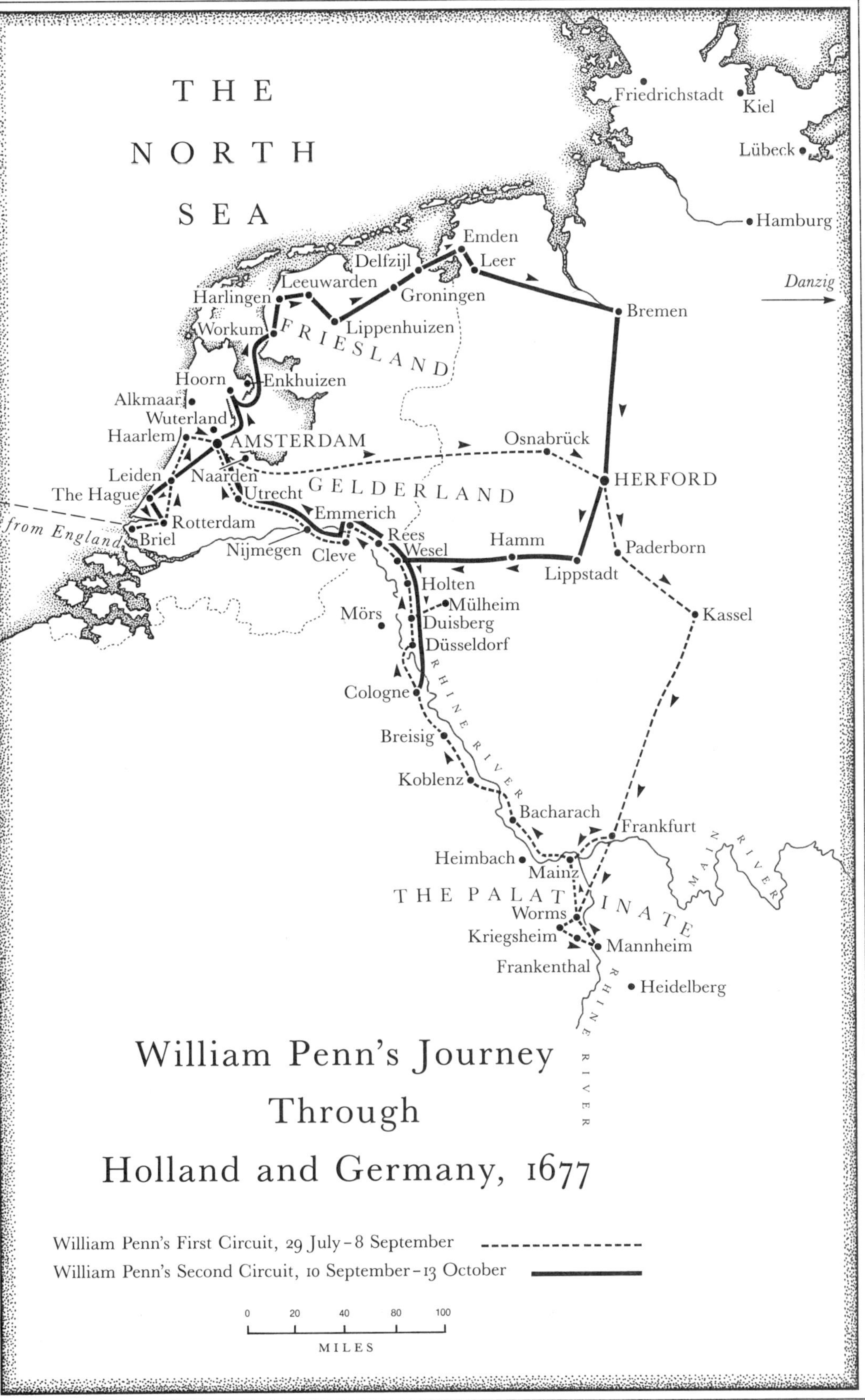
THE NORTH SEA
Friedrichstadt
Kiel
Lübeck
Hamburg
Danzig
Emden
Leer
Delfzijl
Leeuwarden
Groningen
Harlingen
Bremen
Lippenhuizen
Workum
FRIESLAND
Hoorn
Enkhuizen
Alkmaar
Wuterland
Haarlem
AMSTERDAM
Osnabrück
Leiden
Naarden
HERFORD
The Hague
Utrecht
GELDERLAND
Emmerich
Rotterdam
from England
Briel
Rees
Hamm
Paderborn
Nijmegen
Cleve
Wesel
Lippstadt
Holten
Mülheim
Kassel
Mörs
Duisberg
Düsseldorf
Cologne
RHINE RIVER
Breisig
Koblenz
Bacharach
Frankfurt
MAIN RIVER
Heimbach
Mainz
THE PALATINATE
Worms
Kriegsheim
Mannheim
Frankenthal
Heidelberg
RHINE RIVER
William Penn's First Circuit, 29 July–8 September
William Penn's Second Circuit, 10 September–13 October
0 20 40 80 100
MILES

William Penn's Journey Through Holland and Germany, 1677

Talecote,[6] & G. Whiterly[7] of Colchester: where we found Dear G F.[8] at John van de Walls[9] house, with many more Friends.

After dinner we went all to the meeting, where the Lord gave us a blessed earnest of his love & presence, that should be with us in this voyage. For his holy overcoming refreshing power did open all our hearts, & many of our mouths in ministry, prayer & prayses, to the magnifying of his own name, & truth in that place.

The meeting done, we return'd to John van de walls house, where we took our leave of Friends, that is to say, of the Friends of that place, ~~G. Barnadiston,~~[10] ~~R. Duncon,~~[11] ~~G. Whiterly, S. Bolton, & Job Bolton~~[12] with others that came wth us, or met us there: & so went on board of the Pacquet=boat: Where by the special favour of the Master of the Pacquets {to me haveing formerly serv'd under my father,} we had the best accommodation given to us. Many of the Friends accompanyed us to the Ship, not leaving us, till all was fix'd: And then we parted in the fellowship of Jesus.

Those that came over, were G[eorge]. Fox. G. Keith.[13] R. Barclay.[14] G[eorge]. Watts. J[ohn]. Furley. Wm Talecote. I. Yeomans.[15] E. Keith,[16] Myself, with two of our servants.

{Briel} {V. 26 5m. [26 July]}

We sett sayl about 3 in the morning, being the 5th day of the week; & got the 6th day at night within half a league of the Briel.[17]

{VI. 27 5m [27 July]}

We had good service these two days in the ship with several passengers, French & Dutch; & though they seemed at first to be shey of us, and to slight us; yet {at last} their hearts were much open'd in kindnes towards us, & the universal principle had place.

{VII. 28 5m. [28 July]}

The next morning Friends were fetch'd on shoar by a boat of Rotterdam, which some Friends of that city came in to the Briel to meet us. The Friends that came, were A. Sonmans,[18] B. Furley,[19] & Sim. Johnson Vettekeucken;[20] with 3 young men that live at Benj. F[urly's]. house.

{Rotterdam}

After we had eaten, we took boat immediately for Rotterdam, where we arrived about Noon, & where many Friends came to see us, among whom we were comforted.

{I. 29 5m. [29 July]}

The next day, being the First day of the week, we had two meetings at B[enjamin] F[urly].^{s} house, whither resorted a great Company of people; some of them being of the considerablest note of that citty: & o! blessed be that True Word of life, that never faileth them, that rest upon it, & abide in it! The Gospel was preach'd, the dead were raised, & the living comforted; & god, even our god bore heavenly

Record to his only begotten son in us: and truth is honorable in the eyes of several in that place.

{II. 30 5m. [30 July]}

The next day, being the 2d day of the week, we spent in visiting Friends from house to house, not in one company; being lodg'd in several quarters of the city. All our Visits were pretious meetings; for indeed, for that end god brought us into this land. Several of us dined & supped that day at two great mens houses, where we had blessed oportunitys to make known unto them, wt was the hope of our glory: that mystery, which to the Gentiles is now revealing, even Christ Jesus, the light & life of the world manifested in us.

{Leyden} {III. 31 5m. [31 July]}

The next day, being the third day of the week, G[eorge] F[ox]. J[ohn] Furley, W[illiam]. Talecote, Is[abel]. Yeomans, {& my Selfe} after having broke our fast at A[rent]. Sonmans, took boat for Leyden,[21] where we came that night, in order to be at Harlem[22] next day at a meeting appointed by G[eorge] F[ox]. & myself from Rotterdam; being accompanyed with J. Roeloffs,[23] J. Arents,[24] & Jo. Clauss,[25] that came from Amsterdam on purpose to conduct us thither.

{Haerlem} {IV. 1 6m. [1 August]}

At Haerlem we arriv'd about the 11th hour, & went to the house of a good old man, that long waited for, & is now come to behold the consolation & salvation of Israel.

After we had a little refresht ourselves, we went to the meeting, where the Lord gave us a blessed oportunity, not only with respect to Friends, but many sober baptists & professors, that came in, & abode in the meeting to the end: blessed be the name of the Lord.

{Amsterdam}

The meeting done, we went to Amsterdam in company with several Friends of that city, & of Alckmaer,[26] & Embden,[27] who met us at the meeting at Haerlem: & we were lodg'd at Gertruyt [illegible deletion] Diriks house.[28]

G[eorge] K[eith]. & his wife & R[obert] B[arclay]. stay'd over the 4th day's meeting at Rotterdam; & so came not till the next day; which was the day of the General meeting of Friends in this countrey.

{V. 2 6m [2 August]}

The 5th day of the week at G[ertrude] D[irick's]. house the General meeting was held, both of men & women; & the Lord, who is setting up his own Kingdom by his own power, owned us with his own blessed presence, & open'd us in that wisdom & love, that all things ended, with great concord & comfort; many things being spoken, especially by our Dear Friend G[eorge] F[ox]. that were of good service, & I hope, will dwell with them forever.

These several things agreed upon, being of
good favour & report, I thinck fit here to insert them.

At a General Meeting of Friends at Amsterdam
the 12th of the 6th month 1677. etc.[29]

---

1. Be it Known to all, that the power of god, the gospel, is the authority of all our men & womens meetings; & every heir of that power is an heir of that Authority: & so becometh a living member of right of either of these meetings, & of that heavenly fellowship & order, in which they stand; which is not of man, nor by man.

2. That each monthly meeting have a collection apart. And also, that there be another collection quarterly at Amsterdam from each meeting for general services: & that it be not disposed off, but by the consent of the sd quarterly meeting.

3. It is agreed upon, that henceforth a yearly meeting be held here at Amsterdam, unto which Friends in the Palatinate,[30] Hamb.[31], Lubeck,[32] & Fredrichstadt[33] etc. be invited; of which meeting there shall be ~~given~~ notice {given} ~~of~~ to Friends of the yearly meeting at London; to be kept always on the 5th day of that week, which is ~~fully~~ the third week following after the yearly meeting at London.

4. This also agreed upon, that henceforth this general meeting [illegible deletion] be chang'd into a quarterly meeting: & that the first quarterly meeting hereafter, shall be held on the second 5th day of the 9th month following. And so forth every quarter on the second 5th day of the month. This 11th of the 9th month is to be this first quarterly meeting.

5. It is also [illegible deletion] {agreed} that henceforth a monthly meeting in Vriesland[34] should be establisht: as also at Rotterdam; & that on the second 2d day of each month: & at Harlingen[35] upon the 3d third day of the month.

6. Further, that in the Interim the Friends of Alckmaer, & Haerlem & Waterland[36] are to have their monthly meeting with Friends at Amsterdam: & to begin the sd meeting the 6-7 [illegible deletion] Month, & so forth, always upon the first second day of the first week of the month, the 8th hour.

7. And further concerning Gospel order, though the Doctrine of Xt Jesus requireth his people to admonish a brother or sister twice, before they tell the Church; yet that limiteth none, so as that they shall use no longer forbearance, before they tell the Church: but that they shall not less then twice admonish their brother or sister, before they tell the Church. And it is desired of all, that, before they publiquely complain, to wait in the power of god to feel, if there is no more required of them to their brother or sister, before they expose him or her to the Church. Let this be weightily considered.

8. And further, when the Church is told, & the party admonisht by the Church again & again, & he or she remain still unsensible, &

unreconciled; let not final Judgment go forth ag^{t} him or her, till every one of the meeting have cleared his or her conscience: that if anything be upon any further to visit such a trangressor, they may clear themselves; if possibly the party may be reach'd & saved.

And after all are clear of the blood of such an one, let the Judgm^{t} of Friends in the power of god go forth ag^{t} him or her, as moved, for the Lords honour & glory's sake; that no reproach may come or rest upon gods holy name, truth & people.

9. As much as possible can be, let all differences be ended by some honest Friends; & ~~not~~ trouble {not} the monthly or quarterly meetings with them: And if that will not do, proceed to your particular monthly meetings. But if they be not there ended neither; then take aside 6 honest Friends out of the quarterly meeting, & let them hear & determine the matter. And in case any person or persons be so obstinate, as that they refuse the sense & love of Friends, & will not comply with them; then to proceed towards them, according to the way of truth in such cases.

10. That all such, as behold their brother or sister in a transgression, go not in a rough, light, or upbraiding spirit to reprove or admonish him or her. But in the power of the Lord, & spirit of the Lamb, in the wisdom & love of the truth, wch suffereth thereby, to admonish such an offender. So may the soul of such a brother or sister be seasonably & effectually reach'd unto, & over come; & have cause to bless the name of the Lord on their behalf: & so a blessing may be rewarded into the bosom of that faithful & tender brother or sister, that so admonisheth.

11. {And} Be it known unto all, we cast out none from among us: for if they go from the light, & spirit, & power, in which our unity is, they cast out themselves. And it hath been our way to admonish them, that they may come to the light & spirit of god, which they are gone from; & so come into the unity again. For {our} fellowship standeth in the light, that the world hateth; & in the spirit that the world grieveth, vexeth & quencheth. And if they will not hear our admonitions ~~as before~~, the light condemneth them, & then goeth our testimony out against them.

12. That no condemnation is to go farther, then the transgression is known. And if he or she return, & give forth a condemnation ag^{t} himself or herself (which is more desirable, then that we should do it) this is a testimony of his or her repentance & resurrection before god, his people, & the whole world: As David Psalm 51. When Nathan came to admonish him.

13. That no testimony by way of condemnation be given forth ag^{t} any man or woman, what ever crime they commit, before admonition; & till such time, as they have had gospel order, according to X^{ts} doctrine.

14. And if any brother or sister hear any report of any brother

or sister, let him or her go to the party, & know the truth of the report: & if true, let the thing be judg'd. If false; go then to the reporter, & let him or her be judg'd. And if any should report it at a second or 3^{d} hand, without going to the party, of whom the report goeth; let such be brought to Judgment: for thou shalt neither raise, nor suffer a report to lye upon my people, saith the Lord: for they are to be holy, as he is holy: & just, as he is just.

15. And if any controversy or weakness should appear in either men or womens meetings, let it not be told out of your meetings; because such speeches tend to {the} defaming of such persons & meetings, & to the hurt of the common ~~society~~ {Unity}, & breach of the heavenly society & priviledge.

This is an Account of w^{t} past in this General meeting.[37]

{VI. 3 6m. [3 August]}

Next day, notice being already given, we had a large publique meeting, in wch the sound of the everlasting Gospel, testam^{t} & covenant went forth: & the meeting ended with a sweet & weighty sense.

That evening we had a more select meeting of Friends, then the day before; in which the nature of marriage, & the practice of Friends relating to it, & other things were very weightily & closely discoursed. The resolutions were these following:

---

1. A Scruple concerning the Law of the Magistrate about marriage being proposed & discoursed of in the fear of god among Friends in a select meeting, It was the Universal & Unanimous Sense of Friends, That ~~the~~ Joyning in Marriage is the work of the Lord ONLY, & not of Priest or Magistrate.[38]

For 'tis gods ordinance, & not mans: And therefore Friends cannot consent that they should joyn them together. For we marry none: 'tis the Lords work; & we are but witnesses.

2. But yet, if a Friend through tenderness have a desire, that the magistrate should know it; and (after the marriage is performed in a publique meeting of Friends & others according to the holy order & practice of Friends in truth throughout the world, the manner of the holy men & women of god of old) to go, & carry a copy of the Certificate to the magistrate, they are left to their freedom herein. But for priests or magistrates to marry, or joyn any in that relation, it's not according to scripture: & our testimony & practice have been always ag^{t} it. It was Gods work before the Fall; & it is gods work only in the Restoration.[39]

3. If any Friend have it upon him to reprint any book already printed & approved either in England or here; they may do it upon their own charges.

4. It is also agreed, that the care of reading & approving books

be layd upon some of every meeting, to the end, no book may be publisht; but in the unity: Yet any other faithful Friends not so nominated are not thereby excluded. Though in all those cases it is desired, that all would avoyd unnecessary disputes about words, which profitt not; but keep in the love, that edifyeth.

5. It is further concluded, that the General Stock of the quarterly meeting be not disposed off, but by the consent of the quarterly meeting. But if betwixt times there should be a pressing necessity concerning the Publique; let that monthly meeting, where it shall fall out, lay down the money, & give in an Accompt at the next quarterly meeting in order to their relief; if it appear, that they are thereby over charged: And let all things be done without favour, Affection, Relation or any Respect to persons, even for the Lords sake, & his blessed everlasting truth; that god may bless & prosper his people. And let all things be written down, both as to your monthly & quarterly meeting— Collections, w^{t} you receive, w^{t} you disburse; that all may be fair & clear to the satisfaction of all that may desire to see & examine the books.

So the Lord be with you, & bless you, & Keep you in his life, love, power & wisdom for ever & evermore.[40]

And the Lords Fear & power ~~was~~ & life was over all; in which the Lord Jesus preserve his for ever.

{VII. 4 6m. [4 August]}

The next day, being the 7th day of the week, was employed in visiting of Friends, & preparing themselves for a further journey; that is to say, G[eorge] K[eith]. R[obert] B[arclay]. B[enjamin] F[urly]. & myself.

{Finding letters here from the Friends of Danzig,[41] complaining of their heavy sufferings, they underwent, informing us also that the King of Poland[42] was there, asking advise about an Address to him, it fell upon me, to write the following letter in the name of the Friends of Danzig. (B)}[43]

(B)

To the King of Poland.

Great Prince,

Actions of Justice, Mercy & truth are worthy of all men; but in a most excellent manner, of the serious consideration of kings & princes. We certain Inhabitants of the city of Danzig have been long great sufferers not for any wickednes committed ag^{t} the Royal Law of God, or any breach of those civil laws of this city, that relate to the well-governm^{t} of it in all natural & civil things; but purely & only for the Cause of our tender Consciences towards god. This severity being by us represented to the magistrates of this city, we could not as yet receive from them any relief; some expressing, as if easing the burden of our oppressions should give thee o King, an occasion of dissatisfaction, agt them, who art our Acknowledg'd Protector.

Being thus necessitated, & in a manner driven to make this address unto thee, so be it not amiss, that we with that humility & patience, that becometh the servts & followers of Jesus, & with all manner of Christian respect, & sincerity of mind, briefly relate ~~un~~to Thee, the most Fundamental Principles most surely believed by us; which we hope thou will believe, deserve not those punishmts that are inflicted upon us as Evil doers.

1. We do reverently believe, that there is one god & Father, one Lord Jesus Xt & one holy Spt; & these Three are One. Ephes. 4, 6.[44]

2. We believe the scriptures of the old & new testament to have been given forth by divine inspiration; & that they are profitable for doctrine, for reproof, for correction, for instruction in righteousnes, able to make the man of god wise unto salvation through faith, which is in Jesus Xt 2 Tim. 3, 25, 26.[45]

3. That these holy scriptures are not to be understood, but by the discoverys, teachings & operations of that eternal spirit, from whome they came.

4. We believe, that all Mankind through disobedience to the Spirit of god are fallen short of the glory of god; & in that state are under Condemnation. But that god out of his infinite goodnes & Kindnes hath sent his son a light into the World, that whosoever believeth & obeyeth this light, should not abide in darkness, but have the light of eternal life.

5. We believe, This gift of light & grace through Jesus Xt to be universal, & that there is not a man or woman upon Earth, that hath not a sufficient measure of this light, & to whom this grace hath not appeared to reprove their ungodly works of darknes; & to lead them that obey it, to eternal salvation. And this is the great condemnation of the World at this day under all their great professions of god, Xt, Spt, & Scriptures, that though Xt hath enlightened them, yet they will not bring their deeds to the light; but hate the light, & love their dark Customes & practices rather then the light, because their deeds are evil.

6. We do believe in the birth, life, doctrine, miracles, death, resurrection & Ascencion of Jesus Xt our lord & that he layd down his life for the ungodly; not to continue so, but that they should deny their wickednes & ungodlines, & live soberly, righteously, & godlikely in this present evil world, as the saints of old did, that were redeemed from the earth, & sat in heavenly places.

7. We do believe that as the devil through mans disobedience brought sin into mans heart; so Jesus Xt through mans belief in, & obedience to his holy Spt, light & grace cleanseth the heart of sin, destroyeth the works of the devil, finisheth transgression, & bringeth

in everlasting righteousness. That as the devil hath had his kingdom of darkness in man, so X^{t} may have his Kingdom of light, life, righteousnes, peace & joy in the holy ghost, in the heart of man. And not, that X^{t} Jesus saveth men from wrath, & not from sin; for the wages of sin is death, in whose heart forever it liveth: but the gift of god is eternal life to all that believe & obey, through Jesus X^{t}.[46]

8. We do believe, that all true ministry & worship only stand in the experimental sense, operations, & leadings of this holy light, sp^{t} or grace, that is shed abroad in the hearts of men & women to conduct them in the holy way of regeneration unto life eternal. This was the Antient Apostolical Doctrine; they spoke, w^{t} they had seen, tasted & handled of the word of god. And this is our faith, doctrine & practice in this day.

And be not displeas'd with us, o King, we intreat thee, if we give this for the reason of our absenting ourselves from the publique & common ministry or worship, namely, that we have no taste or Relish, no sense or Evidence, that their ministry & worship are authorised or performed by the Apostolical power & Sp^{t} of Jesus; but rather that they are the Inventions, studys & powers of mans nature: all which are but strange fire, & therefore cannot kindle a true & acceptable sacrifice to god. For it is not mans spirit & degenerate nature speaking & professing the words of gods Sp^{t} that giveth acceptance with the Lord, or administreth heavenly edification to men: nor can we believe, that where pride, passion, wrath, malice, persecution, Envy & strife, lusts, wantonnes, vanity, & worldly-mindednes have such sway & power, that the true Christian Spirit, life, & doctrine can be heartily rec'd & followed.

And as this is the reason in the sight & presence of that god, that made heaven & earth, & will Judge quick & dead, wherefore we cannot joyn in the common & publique worship of these parts; so doth the same light & sp^{t} of god lay an holy necessity upon us with a meek & quiet spirit to come together after the manner of the Antient Christians, that were the True followers of Jesus: & with godly fear, & a retired mind to wait upon god, & meditate in his holy law of life, that he hath writ in our hearts, according to his New-Covenant promise that he may feed us, teach us, strengthen us, & comfort us in our inward man. And as by this holy Sp^{t} according to the practice of the Churches of old, any are inclined or moved to reprove, exhort, admonish, praise or pray, we are found exercised in these holy practices.

Now, o Prince, give us, poor Christians, leave to expostulate with thee. Did X^{t} Jesus, or his holy followers endeavour by precept or Example to set up their religion with a carnal sword? Called he any troops of men or Angels to defend him? did he encourage Peter to dispute his Escape with the sword? but did he not say, put it up?[47] Or did he countenance his over-Zealous disciples, when they would have had fire from heaven to destroy those that were not of their mind?

No: but did not Xt rebuke them, saying; ye know not, wt spt you are of?[48] {Yes,} And if it was neither Xts spt nor their own spt that would have fire from heaven; oh, wt is that Spirit, that would kindle fire on earth to destroy such, as peaceably dissent upon the Acct of conscience! If we may not wish, that god should smite men of other Judgmtts, because they differ from us (in which there is no use of carnal weapons) can we so far deceive ourselves, as to esteem ourselves Xrns, & followers of Xt, whilst we encourage men with wordly weapons to persecute such as dissent from us?

O King, when did the true religion persecute? When did the true church offer violence for religion? Were not her weapons prayers, teares, & patience? did not Jesus conquer by those weapons, & vanquish Cruelty by Suffering? Can clubs, & staves, & swords, & prisons & banishments reach the soul, convert the heart, or convince the understanding of man? When did violence ever make a true Convert, or bodily punishmts a sincere Christian? This maketh voyd the end of Xts coming, which is to save mens lives, & not to destroy them; to perswade them, & not to force them. Yea, it robbeth gods Spt of his office, which is to convince the world: That is the Sword, by which the antient Christians overcame. It was the Apostles testimony, that their weapons were not carnal, but spiritual; but the practice of their pretended successors proveth that their weapons are not spiritual, but carnal. Suppose we are tares, as the true wheat hath always been called; yet pluck us not up for Xts his sake, who saith, Let the tares & the wheat grow together until the harvest, {that is} ~~un~~til the end of the world.[49] Let god have {his} ~~the~~ due as well as Caesar;[50] the Judgmt of conscience belongeth to him: & mistakes about religion are best known to him.

And here give us leave to mind thee of a noble saying of one of thy ~~progenitors~~ {Ancestours}, Steven, King of Poland;[51] I am king of men, not of Conscience; King of bodys, not of souls. And there have been found, & still are among the Emperours, Kings, princes & States of the world, some, that have had that noble spirit of indulging their conscientious dissenting subjects; & not only with Gamaliel[52] & Gallio[53] not to persecute, but also eminently to protect & defend them from the hatred & violence of their Enemys. Be not thou less noble then they: Consider how quietly & comfortably our Friends live under other Governments.

And indeed, we conceive it to be the prudence of the kings & states of the world: for if the wise man say{th} true; The Glory of a prince is in the multitude of his people. But this practice saith, No: the Glory of a prince is in the Conformity of the people to the Canons of the Clergy: which seemeth to strike at all civil Society, wch consisteth in men of virtue, parts, arts, & Industry.

But let men have never such excellent abilitys, be never so honest, peaceable, & industrious; all which render them good & profitable subjects to the prince: yet they must not live within their native Country, unles they will sacrifice the peace of their conscience by an hypocritical submission to the Canons & fashons of the Church. *Is not this, o ~~King,~~ Prince, to set the Church above the state; the bishop above the King; to waste & give away the strength & glory of a Kingdom?*

O that thou mayst be wise, even in thy Generation, & use the power, that god hath given Thee, for god, & truth, & righteousnes; that therein thou mayst be like unto god, who, Peter tells us, accepteth of all that fear him & work righteousnes, throughout the world: whose sun shineth upon all, whose rain cometh upon all.[54]

And least any should be so injurious to us, as to render us enemys to civil Government, Be it known unto thee, o King, That we honour all men in the Lord; not with the vain Invented honours of this world; but with the true & solid honour, that cometh from above: but much more Kings, & those, whom god hath placed in authority over us. For we believe, Magistracy to be both lawful & useful for the terrifying of all evil doers; & the praise & encouragem[t] of those that do well.

The premises duely considerd we intreat thee, o prince, to take our suffering Case into thy serious regard, & by that power & influence, thou hast with the magistrates of this city, to recommend our suffering condition, to their serious consideration, that we may no longer lye under these, not only unchristian, but unnatural severitys; but receive that speedy & effectual relief, which becometh Christian magistrates to give to their own sober & Christian [illegible deletion] people.[55]

{I. 5 6m. [5 August]}

The first day of the week being come, the meeting began about the 11th hour, & held till about the 4th hour in the afternoon. There was a mighty concourse of people from several places of this country, & that of several perswasions; presbiterians, socinians, baptists, seekers[56] etc. & god was with his people, & his word of life & power, of wisdom & strength covered them; yea, the hidden things both of Esau & Jacob, the mystery both of iniquity & godliness were opened & declared in the demonstration of the eternal spirit that day.[57] And O blessed & magnifyed be the name of the Lord, that hath not {only} left ~~only~~ himself, but his servants not without a witnesse! O he is worthy to be loved & feared, & obeyed, & Reverenced for ever!

{Naerden} {II. 6 6m. [6 August]}

The next day G[eorge] K[eith]. R[obert] B[arclay]. B[enjamin] F[urly]. & myself, having taken our leave of Dear G[eorge] F[ox]. & Friends, took boat for Naerden;[58] where we arrived about the 2[d] hour in the afternoon.

And after having eaten, we took our leave of those Friends, that had accompanyed us thither; & began our Journey in the common

{Osnabrug} {III. IV. 8 6m [8 August]}
post-waggon to Osnabrug:[59] where we came the 4th day following in the evening.

We past through a very dark country to that place; yet I felt not so great a weight & suffering in my spirit, as 6. years ago, when I went through the same places.

At Osnabrugg we had a little time with the man of the Inn, where we lay; & left him several good books of Friends [illegible deletion] in the ~~of~~ low and high duch tongues[60] to read & to dispose of.

{Herwerden.} {V. [9] 6m. [9 August]}

The next morning, being the 5th day of the week, we set forward to Herwerden;[61] & came thither at night. This is the city, where the Princesse Elisabeth Palatine hath her Court;[62] whom, & the Countess[63] in company with her, it was more especially upon us to visit: & that upon several Accounts.

First, In that they are persons seeking after the best things.

2^{ly}, That they are actually Lovers & Favourers of those, that separate themselves from the world for the sake of righteousness. For the Princess is not only a private supporter of such; but gave protection to de Labadee[64] himself, & his company: yea, when they went under the reproachful name of Quakers about 7 years since. This man was a French man, that being dissatisfyed with the loosness & deadness of the French Protestants, even at Geneva itself, left them, & came for Holland; & so vehemently disclaimed ag^{t} the Apostacy of the priests & people there~~to~~, that the clergy were enraged ~~agt him~~, & stirred up the magistrates ag^{t} him; & the rather, because many followed him, & several women of great quality.[65] Upon this the Princess giveth them an Invitation: & they came, & were protected by her. But since {some} miscarriages falling out {in that place} ~~they they not walking answerable to their pretenses~~ she {in good measure} withdrew there upon {her} favour from them; ~~&~~ they removed into an other place.

I was moved to visit this man {& his company} 6 years ago, & did see him, & his two great disciples;[66] but they would not suffer me to see the people, which I labourd for. I in that day saw the Aireness & unstableness of the mans spirit; & that a sect master was his name. And it was upon me both by word of mouth & writing to let them know, that the enemy would prevail ag^{t} them to draw them into inconvenient things, if they came not to be stay'd in the light of Jesus Christ, & {to know} ~~into~~ the holy silence: & that at last they would come to fall out one with another, & moulder away: which is in {some} ~~good~~ measure come to pass. {as I feared;} For I clearly perceived, that though they had rec'd some Divine Touches, there {was a danger they would} run out with them, & spend them like prodigals; not knowing {then} where to stay their minds for daily bread. Yea, though they were something Angelical, & like to the celestial bodys yet ~~they~~

{if they} kept not their station; {they would prove fallen stars.} They moved not in the motion of him, that had visited them: but were filled with gross mixtures, & thereby brought forth mixed births, that is to say things not natural, but monstrous. {in fine they were shy of us, they knew us not.} Yet I beleived well of some of the people. for a good thing was stiring in them.

And in this Case was the Countess[67] commendable, in that she left all, to have joyn'd with a people, that had, a pretense at least, to more spirituality & self denyal, then was found in the national Religion, she was bred up in: for god had reachd her (as she told me) about nine years ago {& that by an extreordinary way.}

Now, it seemed great pity to us, that persons of their quality in the world should so willingly expose themselves for the false Quaker, the reprobate silver,[68] the mixtures; & that they should not be acquainted with the life & testimony of the true Quaker.

Now, about a year since R[obert] B[arclay]. & B[enjamin] F[urly]. took that city in their way from Fredrichstadt to Amsterdam, & gave them a Visit: in which they informed them somew^{t} of Friends principles, & recommended the testimony of truth to them; as both a ~~more~~ nearer & {more} certain thing, then that utmost of De L'abade's doctrine. They left them tender & loving.

Soon after ~~this~~ Gertruyt Diricks & Elisab[eth]. Hendricks[69] from Amsterdam visited them, & obtained a meeting with them; improving that little {way} ~~entrance~~ God by his providence had made, more closely to press the testimony. And though they, especially the Countess, made some objections in relation to the ordinances, & certain practices of Friends; yet she seemed to receive {at that time,} satisfaction from them. These visits have occasion'd a correspondence by way of letter betwixt them, & several of us; wherein the mystery of truth hath been more clearly open'd to their understandings: & they have been brought nearer into a waiting frame, by those heavenly directions, they have frequently rec'd by way of Epistles from several of us.

This digression from the present history, I thought not altogether unnecessary {or unpleasing.}

But to return. Being arrived at this citty, part of which is under her Governm^{t}, we gave her to understand it; desiring to know, what time next day it would be most proper for us to visit her? She sent us word, She was glad that we were come; & should be ready to receive us the next morning about the 7th hour.

{VI. 10 6m. [10 August]}

The next morning being come, wch was the 6th day of the week, we went about the time she had appointed us. We found both she & the Countess ready to receive us: which they did with a more then ordinary expression of kindness. I can truly say it, & that in gods fear, I was very deeply & reverently affected with the sense, that was upon my spirit, of the great & notable day of the Lord, & the breaking in of his eternal power upon all nations; & of the rising of that slain witness to judge the world: who is the treasure of life and peace, of wisdom & glory to all, that receive him in the hour of his judgm^{t} {& abide with him}. The sense of this deep & sure fundation, wch god is laying as the hope of eternal life & glory for all to build upon, fill's my soul with an holy testimony to them; which in a living sense was followed by my brethren: & so that meeting ended about the 11th hour.

The Princesse intreated us to stay & dine with her; but with due regard both to our testimony & to her, at that time we refused it; desiring, if she pleased, another oportunity that day: which she with all chearfulnes yeilded to, she herself appointing the second hour. So we went to our quarters: & sometime after we had dined, we returned.

The meeting soon began; there were several present, besides the princess & countess: It was at this meeting, that the Lord in a more eminent manner began to appear. The eternal word show'd itself a Hammer this day, yea, sharper ~~as~~ {then} a two edged sword, dividing asunder between the soul & the spirit, the joynts & the marrow.[70] Yea, this day was all flesh humbled before the Lord: It amased one, shook another, broke another. Yea, the noble Arm of the Lord was truly awaked; & the weight & work thereof bowed & tenderd us also after an unusual & extraordinary manner; that the Lord might work an heavenly sign before them, & among them: that the majesty of him, that is risen among the poor Quakers, might in some measure be known unto them, w^{t} god it is we serve; & w^{t} power it is, we wait for, & bow before. Yea, they had a sence & a discovery that day, what would become of the glory of all flesh, when god shall enter into Judgment. Well; let my right hand forget its cunning, & my tongue cleave to the roof of my mouth, when I shall forget the loving kindnes of the Lord,[71] & the sure mercys of our god to us his travelling servants {that day.} O Lord, send forth thy light, & thy truth, that all Nations may behold thy Glory!

Thus continued the meeting, till about the 7th hour. Which done, with hearts & souls fill'd with holy thanks-givings to the Lord for his abundant mercy & goodnes to us, we departed to our Lodging; desiring to know, whither our coming the next day might not be uneasy or unseasonable to her, with respect to the Affairs of her Government, it being the last day of the week, when we were informed, she was most frequently attended with Addresses from her people. But with a loving & ready mind she replyed, That she should be glad to see us the next morning; & at any time, when we would.

{VII 11 6m. [11 August]}

The next morning, being the 7th day, we were there betwixt 8 & 9. where, R[obert] B[arclay]. falling into some discourse with the

Princess, the Countess took hold of that oportunity {& whisperd me to withdraw,} to get a meeting for the more inferior servants of the house; who would have been bashful to have presented themselves before the princess. And blessed be the Lord, he was not wanting to us: but the same blessed power, that had appeared to visit them of high, appeared to visit them of low degree also: & we were all sweetly tender'd & broken together. For Virtue went forth of Jesus that day, & the life of our god was shed abroad amongst us, as a sweet savour: for which their souls bowed before the Lord, & confest to our Testimony. Which did not a little please that young Noble woman to find her own report of us, & her great Care of them, so effectually answer'd. O what shall we say! is there any god like to our god, who is glorious in holiness, fearful in praises, working wonders! To his eternal name, power & Arm be the glory forever.

The Meeting done, the Princess came to us, expressing much satisfaction, that we had that good oportunity with her servants: telling us, she much desired, they should have a true & right Character of us: And that therefore she chose to withdraw, that they might have freer access; & that it might look like their own Act:[72] or words to that purpose.

The 12th hour being come, we returned to our Inn, letting them understand, we purpos'd (the Lord willing) to visit them sometime that afternoon.

I must not here forget, that we found at our Inn the first night at Supper a young merchant of a sweet & ingenuous temper belonging to the City of Bremen,[73] who took occasion from that nights discourse the 6th day at Dinner & Supper, & the 7th day also to seek all opportunitys of Conference with us. And, as we have reason to believe, he stay'd 24 hours in that city on our Account. We open'd to him the Testimony of Truth; I know not that in any one thing he contradicted us. At last he plainly discover'd himself unto us to be a follower of a certain minister in Bremen, that is even by his fellow-ministers & Protestants reproach'd with the name of Quaker, because of his singular Sharpnes ag^{t} the Formal, lifeles ministers & Christians in the world. We layd fast hold upon this, & asked him, in case any of us should visit that city, If he would give us the opportunity of a meeting at his house? which he readily granted us. So we gave him some books recommending him to the true & blessed Testimony of X^{t} Jesus the Light & Judge of the world, & life of them that receive him, & believe in him & ~~we~~ parted.

It being about 3 in the Afternoon, we went to the Princesses, where being come, after some little time, the Princesse & Countesse put me in remembrance of a promise I made them in one of my letters out of England, namely, that I would give them an Acc^{t} at some Convenient Time of my First Convincem^{t}, & of those tribulations & consolations, wch I had met withal in this way of the Kingdom, wch God hath brought me to. {After som pause} I found myself very free & prepared in the Lords love & fear to comply with their request: & so after some {silence} ~~pause~~ began. But before I had half done, it was Suppertime; & the Princesse would by no means let us go, we must Sup with her. Which Importunity, not being well able to avoyd, we yeilded to, & sat down with her to Supper. Among the rest present at these opportunitys, it must not be forgotten, that {there was} a Countesse, Sister of the Countesse, then come to visit her, & a French woman of Quality;[74] the first behaving herself very decently, & the last often deeply broken, & from a light & slighting Carriage towards the very name of a Quaker she became very intimately & affectionately kind & respectful to us.

Supper being ended we all return'd to the Princesses ~~bed~~ Chamber: where making us all sit down with her ~~under her Canopy of State~~, she with both the Countesses & the French woman prest {from me} the Continuance of my Relation {but none more then the Countess's sister}. Which though late, I was not [illegible deletion] unwilling to obliedge them ~~in~~; because I knew not when the Lord would give me such an opportunity {& I found them affected}. It continued till about ten at night: yet many particulars omitted, partly through forgetfulnes, & partly for want of Time. Howbeit, I must needs say, they heard me with an Earnest & tender Attention: and I hope & believe, the Lord hath made it profitable to them.

This done {& some discourse they had upon it,} we spoke about a meeting for the next day, being the first day of the week; & that we might have not only as many of her own family, but of her Town, as would willingly be there. She yeilded to it; & appointed the meeting to begin at the 2^{d} hour. So we parted, being near the 11th hour at night.

{I. 12 6m. [12 August]}

The next morning we had a meeting among ourselves in our Chamber, wherein the Lord refresht us. And there was a great travel upon our spirits, that the Lord would stand by us that day, & magnify the testimony of his own truth by us; that he might have a seed & people in that place to lift up a standard for his name.

At Dinner there were several strangers, that came by the post waggon that day: among whom there was a young man of Bremen being a student at the Colledge at Duysburgh,[75] who informed us of a sober & seeking man of great note in the City of Duysburgh: to him we gave some books. There was one more ~~of them rather more~~ {who was} tender & enquiring; to whom also we gave some books.

The second hour being at hand, we went to the meeting; where there were several as well of the town as of the family. The meeting began with a weighty Exercise & Travail {in prayer} that the Lord would glorify his own Name that day; And by his own power he made way to their Consciences, & sounded his awakening trumpet in their

Ears; that they might know that he was god, & that there is none like unto him. O the Day of the Lord livingly dawned upon us: the searching life of Jesus was in the midst of us. O the word that never faileth them, that wait for it, & abide in it, opened the way, & insealed the book of life. Yea, the quickning power & life of Jesus wrought & reach'd to them; & Virtue from him, in whom dwelleth the God-head bodily, went forth, & blessedly destilled upon us his own heavenly {life} [illegible deletion] sweeter then the spices with pure Franckincense; yea then the sweet smelling myrrh, that cometh from a far Country. And as it began, so it was carryed on, & so it ended: Blessed be the name of the Lord, & confided in be our god for ever.

As soon as the meeting was done, the Princesse came to me, & took me by the hand (which she usually did to us all coming & going) & went to speak to me of the sense she had of that power & presence of god, that was amongst us; but was stopd: & turning herself to the window broke forth in an extraordinary {passion}, [illegible deletion] crying out, *I can not speak to you, my heart is full; clapping her hand upon her breast.* It melted me into a deep & calm tendernes, in wch I was moved to minister a few words softly to her. And after sometime of silence she recover'd herself; {And as I} was taking my leave of her, ~~which~~ she interrupted {me} thus; will you not come hither again? pray call here, as you return out of Germany. I told her, we were in the hand of the Lord; & being his, could not dispose of ourselves. But the Lord had taken care, that we should not forget her, & those with her: for he had raised & begotten an heavenly Concernm^{t} in our souls for her & them: & we loved them all with that Love, wherewith god hath loved us: with much more to that purpose.

She then turned to the rest of the Friends, & would have had us all to go down to supper with her: but we chose rather to be excused: we should eat a bit of her bread, & drink a glass of her wine, if she pleased, in the Chamber, where we were. At last we prevailed with her to leave us. The Countesse, the French woman, & the Countesses waiting woman stayed with us; & we had a very retired & seasonable opportunity with them.

After the Princess had supped, we went all down, & took our solemn leave of her, the Countess, her sister, the French woman, with the rest of the Family whose hearts were reach'd & open'd by our Testimony: recommending unto them, holy silence from all will worship & the workings, strivings & Images of their own mind & spirit: that Jesus might be felt of them in their hearts, his holy teachings witnessed & followed in the way of his blessed Cross, that {would} crucify~~eth them~~ them unto the world, & the world unto them. That their Faith, Hope & Joy might stand in x^{t} in them the heavenly prophet, shepheard, & bishop; whose voice all, that are truly sheep, will hear & follow, & not the voice of any stranger whatever. So we left them in the love & peace of god, praying that they might be kept from the evil of this world. So we returned to our lodging, having our hearts fill'd with a weighty sense of the Lords appearance with us in that place. And being late, towards the ninth hour, we prepared to go to rest.

{II. 13 6m. [13 August]}

The next morning being the second day of the week, G[eorge] K[eith]. B[enjamin] F[urly]. & myself got ready to begin our journey towards Franckford;[76] which by the way of Cassel[77] is about 200 English miles. R[obert] B[arclay]. prepared himself to return by the way we came, directly back to Amsterdam. But before we parted, we had a little time together in the morning in our Chamber; whither came one of the Princesses Family, & one of the town. The Lord moved me to call upon his great name, that he would be with them that stay'd, & with them that returned also; & with us, that went forward {~~ward in wild~~} {in wild & untrodden places.} And his blessed love & life overshadow'd us; yea he filled our Cup together, & made us drink into one spirit, even the cup of blessings in the Fellowship of the everlasting seed:[78] in which we took leave of one another. And after having eaten ~~a bit~~, it being about the 7th hour, we departed the city.

{Paderborn}

We came to Paderborn[79] that night 6 German miles, which is about 36 English. It is a dark Popish Town, & under the Governm[t] of a Bishop {of that religion}. Howbeit, the woman where we lodged, was an Antient, grave, & serious person; to whom we declared the testimony of the light, showing her the Difference betwixt an outside — & an Inside — Religion: which she rec'd with much kindnes. We left some books with her, which she took readily.

There was also at supper with us a Lutheran, that was a Lawyer, with whom ~~we~~ I had very good service, in opening to him the great loss of the power of godlines, as well among them, {who} ~~as~~ separated from Rome, as in the Roman Church: which he confessed. ~~We~~ I directed him to that Principle of Light in his conscience, that let him see the Lifeles state of the false Christians; & if he turn'd his mind to that principle, & waited there for power, he would receive power to rule & govern himself according to true Godlines. And that it was the Loss of Christendom, that they went from this Principle, in which the Power standeth; that conformeth the soul ~~in~~to the Image & Likenes of the Dear son of god: And thither they must come again, if ever they will have the true Knowledge of god, & enjoy life & Salvation. With much more to that purpose: All which he rec'd lovingly.

{Cassel} {III. 14 6m. [14 August]}

The next morning we set forth towards Cassel: but through great foulnes of weather, & having only naked Carts to ride in, the waters being also high with the rains, we got not to Cassel till the next day,

{IV. 15 6m. [15 August]}

{wch was} ~~being~~ the fourth day of the week. It being late, we made little Enquiry that night, being also wearyed with the foulnes of the ways & weather.

{V. 16 6m. [16 August]}

But the next day we made our usual enquiry {viz,} who was worthy in the city? & found some that tenderly & lovingly rec'd us: To whom we declared the visitation of the light & love of god. Among the rest was Duræus,[80] our Countryman, a man of 77. years of Age, who had learned in good measure to forget his learning, Shool=divinity, & priest-craft: & for his Approaches towards an inward Principle is reproachfully saluted by some with the honest Title of Quaker. 'Tis much better then papist, Lutheran, or Calvinist; who are not only ignorant of, but enemys to quaking & trembling at the word of the Lord, as moses & others did.[81]

{VI. 17 6m. [17 August]}

Upon the 6th day of the same week about noon we set out towards Franckford, having left several books behind us; which hath been our practice in our journey.

{Frankfurt} {VII. I. II. 20 6m. [18-20 August]}

At Franckfurt we arrived the second day about noon, being just a week from Herwerden, And having from thence {and Cassel} made known our Intentions of coming to that city, two considerable persons came & met us about one half german mile from the city, informing us of several well-affected in that town. Upon which we told them the end of our Coming, & desired to have a meeting with them in the Afternoon. Which we easily obtained at the house of a mercht,[82] one of the two that met us. The persons that resorted thither, were generally people of considerable note, both of Calvinists & Lutherans: & we can say, they rec'd us with gladnes of heart, & embraced our Testimony with a broken & reverent spirit; thanking god for our Coming amongst them, & praying that he would prosper this work in our hands. This engaged our hearts to make some longer stay in this city.

{III. 21 6m. [21 August]}

We therefore desired another meeting the next day, which they chearfully assented to: where several came, that were not with us the day before. And the Lord, that sent us into this Land, was with us, & by his power reached to them, insomuch, that they confess'd to the truth of our Testimony. Of these Persons there were two women, one a virgin, the other a widdow, both noble of birth;[83] who had a deep sense of that power & presence of god, that accompanyed our Testimony: & their hearts yearned strongly towards us. The virgin giving us a particular Invitation to her house the next morning: where we

{IV. 22 6m. [22 August]}

had the most blessed opportunity of the three. For the Lords power so eminently appeared, that not only those that had been with us before, were more effectually reached; but a certain student, residing in the house of a Lutheran minister (sent for by that young woman) was broken to peeces; & magnifyed that blessed power, which appeared. Also there came in a Doctor of Physick[84] accidentally, who unexpectedly was affected, & confest to the truth; praying god to prosper us. This was the blessed Issue of our Visit to Franckfurt.

But there is one thing more not unfit to be mentioned. Among some of those, that have inclinations after god, a fearful spirit, together with the shame of the Cross hath entred: ag^{t} which our Testimony in part striking, we took notice, it was as life to these noble women. For that was it, as they told us, which had long opprest them, & obstructed the work of the Lord amongst them. Therefore, sayd the young Virgin, *Our quarters are free for you, let all come that will, & lift up your voices without fear: for (sayd she) it will never be well with us, till persecution come, & some of us be lodg'd in the Stadthouse,* that is, *the prison.* We left the peace of Jesus with them; & the same afternoon we departed out of that city, being the 4th day of the week.

{Worms Crisheim} {V. 23 6m [23 August]}

The fifth day we arrived by the way of Worms[85] at ~~this Village of~~ Crisheim[86] in the Palsgraves Country,[87] where we found to our great joy a meeting of tender & faithful people. But it seemeth, the Inspector of the Calvinists {~~came next day~~} hath enjoyned the Faut {Voght.} or cheif officer not to suffer any preaching to be among our Friends: who, poor man fearing the indignation of the Clergy

{VI. 24 6m [24 August]}

{came next day} ~~hath been {wth them} here this morning~~, to desire Friends not to suffer any preaching to be amongst them, least he should be turnd out of his place. To whom we desired Friends to say, that if he pleased, he might apprehend us, & carry us to the Prince,[88] before whom we should give an Acc^{t} of our Testimony. But blessed by the Lord, we enjoyed our meeting quietly & comfortably; of which a Coachful from Worms made a part. Among whom was ~~the~~ a Governour of that Country, & one of the chief Lutheran priests.[89]

It was upon me in this place to salute the Princess & Countess with this following Epistle:

My worthy Friends,

Such as I have, such I give unto you, the dear & tender salutation of light, life, peace & salvation by Jesus Christ, the blessed Lamb of god, with the unspeakeable joy, of which, he hath replenisht my soul at this time, that my cup overfloweth; which is the reward of them, that chearfully drink his cup of tribulations; that love the cross, & triumph in all the shame, reproaches & contraditions of the world, that do attend it. My god take you by the hand, & gently lead you through all the difficultys of regeneration: & as you have begun to know & love his sweet & tender drawings, so resign the whole conduct of {your} ~~their~~ life to him.

Dispute not away the pretious sense, that you have of him, be it as small, as a grain of mustard seed, which is the least of all seeds; there is power in it (if ~~th~~ you do but believe) to remove the greatest mountains of opposition.[90] O pretious is this faith! yea, more pretious then the gold & honour [of] this world, that perisheth: it will give Courage to go with Christ before [illegible deletion] Caiphas & Pilate; yea, to bear his cross without the Camp, & be crucifyed with him; knowing, that the spirit of god & {of} glory shall rest upon them. To the Inheriters of this faith is reserved the eternal Kingdom of peace & joy in the holy ghost.

O be you of that little flock, unto whom Jesus sayd, Fear not; for it is my Fathers good pleasure to give you a Kingdom.[91] And to be of this flock, you must become as sheep; & to be sheep you must become harmles; & to become harmles, you must hear, & follow the Lamb of god, as he is that blessed light, which discovereth & condemneth all the unfruitful works of darknes, & maketh harmles as a dove: which word, All, leaveth not one piccodillo or circumstance undiscover'd, or unjudged. And the word (Darknes) taketh in the whole night of Apostacy: & the word unfruitful, is a plain judgm^t ag^t all these dark works. Wherefore out of them all come, & be you separated; & god will give you a crown of life, which shall never fade away.

O the Lowness & meanness of those spirits, that despise or neglect the joys & glorys of immortality for the sake of the things that are seen, which are but temporal; debasing the nobility of their souls; abandoning the governm^t of the divine Spirit; & embracing with all ardency of affection the sensual pleasures of this life! But such, as persevere therein, shall {not} enter into gods rest forever.

But this is not all that hindereth, & obstructeth in the holy way of blessednes. For there is the worlds fear, as well as the worlds joy, that obstructeth many; or else Christ had not sayd, Fear not, to his little flock. The shame of the cross is a ~~yoke too~~ yoak too uneasy, & a burthen too heavy for flesh & blood to bear. 'Tis true; but therefore shall flesh & blood never enter into the Kingdom of god. And not to them that are born of the flesh, but to those, that are born of the spirit, through the word of regeneration, is appointed the Kingdom, & that throne, which shall judge the 12 Tribes of Israel, & all the world.[92]

The Lord perfect, w^t he hath begun in you, & give you dominion over the love & fear of this world.

And, My Friends, if you would profit in the way of god, despise not the day of small things in yourselves: know this, that {to} desire

& sincerely to breath after the Lord, is a blessed state. You must seek, before you find. do {you} believe? make not haste. Extinguish not those small beginnings by an over-earnest or impatient desire of victory: Gods time is the best time. Be you faithful; & your conflict shall end with glory to god, & the rewards of peace to your own souls.

Therefore love the Judgmt, & love the fire: start not aside, neither flinch from the scorchings of it; for it will purify & refine you, as gold 7 times tryed.[93] Then cometh the stamp & seal of the Lord upon his own Vessel, Holiness to him forever: which he never gave, nor will give to reprobate silver;[94] the state of the religious worshippers of the world. And herein be comforted, that Zion shall be redeemed through Judgmt, & her converts through righteousness. And after the appointed time of mourning is over, the Lord will give beauty for ashes; the oil of joy for mourning; & the garment of praise for the spirit of heaviness. Then shall you be able to say, who is he, that condemneth us? god hath justifyed us: there is no condemnation to us, that are in Xt Jesus; who walk not after the flesh, but after the spirit.

Wherefore my Dear Friends, walk not only not after the fleshly lusts, but also not after the fleshly Religions & worships of this world: for that, that is not born of the spirit, is flesh; & all flesh shall ~~wither~~ wither as the grass; & the beauty of it shall fade away, as the flowr of the field[95] before gods sun, that is risen, & rising. But the word of the Lord, in which is life, & that life the Light of men, shall endure forever; & give life eternal to them, that love & walk in the light.

And I intreat you by the Love you have for Jesus; have a Care, how you touch with fleshly births, or say Amen, by word or practice to that, which is not born of the spirit. For god is not to be found of that in yourselves, or others, that calleth him Father, & he hath never begotten it in them: that Latitude & conformity is not of god; but secretly grieveth his spirit, & obstructeth the growth of the soul in its acquaintance & intimate communion with the Lord. Without me, saith Jesus, you can do nothing; & all that came before me, are Theives & robbers.[96] If so, O what are {they} that pray, preach & sing without Jesus, & follow not him in those dutys; but even in them crucifyd him! O that I may find in you an ear to hear, & an heart to perceive & embrace these truths of Jesus!

And I can say, I have great Cause to hope & patiently to wait; till the salvation of god be farther revealed to you, & the whole family; with whom (I must acknowledge) I was abundantly refresht & comforted, in that god in measure made known the riches of his grace, & operation of his celestial power among you: & his witness shall dwell with you (if we never see you more) that god magnifyed his own strength in our weaknes. With him we leave our Travails; affectionately commending you to his holy spirit of grace, that you may be conform'd to the image of his own dear son, who is able & ready to preserve you. O, stay your minds upon him, & he will keep you in perfect peace, & abide with you forever.

The Allmighty take you into his holy Care & protection now & forever. I am

Your True Friend
ready to serve you
with fervent love
in the will of
God
W P.

My dear Companions
G[eorge] K[eith]. &
B[enjamin] F[urly]. do with me give you the dear salutation of unfeigned love, & those in the family, that love & desire to follow the Lord Jesus in sincerity & truth without wavering.

{There was a postscript by way of narrative of our Travail since we left Herwerden, wch I omit because it is before exprest (turn 2 pages back after the cross)}

We are this evening bound towards Manheim[97] the Court of the Prince Palatine. {& travell'd about 12 English miles on foot that night.}

{Franckenthal. Manheim.} {VII. 25 6m. [25 August]}

We lodged at Franckenthal[98] ~~this night~~; & got the next morning, being the 7th day of the week to Manheim. But were disappointed of our design, wch was to speak with the prince: for he was gone the day before to Heydelbergh,[99] his chief city, about 15 miles English from that place. And considering, that by reason of the meeting next day with Friends at Crisheim, already appointed, we could neither go forward, nor stay, till he return'd; & yet being not clear to come away, as if we had never endeavoured to visit him; it was upon me to write him this following letter {to lett him know we had been there, & briefly our end in comeing.}[100]

Great Prince,

It would seem strange, that I, both a stranger, & a subject should use this freedom to Address to a Prince, were he not one, whose Actions show him to be of a Free Disposition, & easy of Access to all: Would to God, all Princes were of that mind! But I have not chosen this way of Application; I am driven to it by the disappointm^t^ thy Absence from this Court gave me; & the necessity I am under, to expedite my Return. And though I cannot so fully, & consequently, not so clearly express by letter the grounds inducing me to attempt this Visit; yet this being all the way, that is left me, I shall declare them as well as I can.

In the first place I do with all sincere & Christian Respect acknowledge & commend that Indulgence thou givest to all people professing religion, dissenting from the national Communion: For it is in itself a most natural, Christian, & prudent thing. Natural, because it preserveth nature from being made a sacrifice to the savage fury of fallible yet proud opinion, outlawing men of parts, arts, industry & honesty, the grand requisites of humain society; & exposing them & their familys to utter ruine for meer nonconformity not to Religion, but modes & fashons in religion. Christian, since the contrary expresly contradicteth both the precept & Example of Christ; who taught us to love enemys, not to abuse our Friends, & triumph in the destruction of our harmles neighbours. He rebuk'd his disciples, when they called for fire from heaven upon dissenters, it may be opposers: certainly, then he never intended, that they should kindle fire on earth to devour men for Conscience. And if Christ, to whom all power was given, & his holy Apostles refused to employ humain force & Artifice so much as to conserve themselves;[101] 'tis an Arrogancy every way indefensible in those that pretend to be their followers, that they assume an Authority to superceed, controul, & contradict the precepts & examples of Christ, & his Apostles: whose kingdom not being of the nature of this ambitious violent world, was not erected or maintain'd by those weapons, that are carnal; but spiritual & intellectual, adequate to the nature of the soul, & mighty through god to cast down the strong holds of sin, & every vain Imagination exalted in man above the lowly meek fear of god; that ought to have the preeminence in the hearts of the Sons of men. Indulgence is prudent, in that it preserveth concord: No Kingdom divided ag^{t} itself, can stand.[102] It encourageth Arts & Parts & Industry to show & improve themselves: which indeed are the ornam^{t}, strength & wealth of a Country. It encourageth people to transplant into this land of liberty, where the sweat of the brow is not made the forfet of the conscience. And lastly, it rendreth the Prince peculiarly safe & great. Safe, because all Interests for Interest {sake} are bound to love & court him. Great, in that he is not govern'd or clogg'd with the power of his clergy: which in most Countrys is not only a Coordinate power, a kind of Duum-viratship[103] in governm^{t}, Imperium in Imperio,[104] at last an Ecclips to monarchy; but a superior power, & rideth the prince to their Designes, holding the helm of the Governm^{t} & steering not by the Laws of civil freedom; but certain Ecclesiastical maximes of their own to the maintenance & enlargement of their wordly empire in their Church. And all this villany acted under the Sacred, peaceable & alluring names of Christ, his ministers, & church; though as remote from their nature, as the woolf from the sheep, & the Pope from Peter.

The next thing I should have taken the Liberty to have discourst, would have been this; what encouragm^{t} a Colony of virtuous &

industrious familys might hope to receive from thee, in case they should transplant themselves into this country?[105] which certainly of itself is very excellent respecting Taxes, Arms, Oaths etc.

Further, to have represented the Condition of some of our Friends, & thy own subjects: who, though they are lyable to the same tax as mennists etc.[106] (not by part, the case of other Dissenters) yet the Faut of the town where they live, came yesterday to forbid all preaching amongst them: which implyeth a sort of contradiction to the indulgence given.

And in the last place, that for as much as all men owe their beings to something greater then themselves, to which, it's reasonable to believe, they are accomptable: from whence followeth reward, or punishment. I had an earnest {desire} to have spoken of the nature, truth, use, benefit & rewards of religion, & therein as to have discourst, What is Christian Religion in itself (freed from the~~se~~ unreasonable garbs, some make it to wear, so justly offensive to Wise & thinking men) so to have proved the principles & life of that people in scorn called Quakers, to have been sutable to the true followers of holy Jesus. But as the particulars would swell a Letter to a book, I shall take the freedom to present thee upon my return with some Tracts treating upon all these subjects.

Prince, my Soul is filled with love & respect to thee & thy family; I wish you all true & lasting felicity. And earnestly desire, that you may never forget your Afflictions; & in the remembrance of them, be dehorted[107] from these lusts & impietys, which draw the vengeance of heaven upon the greatest familys on earth: that god may look upon you with the favorable eye of his providence. And blessed is that man, whose god (by profession) is the Lord (in reality) viz: that is ruled & govern'd by the Lord, & that liveth in subjection to his grace; that having a divine sense of god in his heart delighteth to retain that sense & knowledge of him, & that meditateth in his noble royal law, that converteth the soul to god, & redeemeth man from the sensual pleasures of this world to the true satisfaction of the intellectual & divine life. O the meanness & Lowness of their spirits, that abandon themselves to the Governm^t^ of sense, the animal life; thereby debasing their natures, rejecting the divine light, that shineth in their hearts, saying; Let us eat & drink, for tomorrow we shall dye:[108] forgetting, whence they are descended, & not considering the peace & joy of the virtuous. I desire, that the Lord would put it into thy heart, to think of thy latter end; & with the light of X^t^ in thy conscience examine, how it standeth with thy soul: that thou mayst know & diligently watch to do those things, that belong to thy eternal peace.

One thing more give me leave to recommend to thee, & that is, To be very careful of inculcating a generous, free, & righteous principle into thy son, who is like to succeed thee; that, when thou art gone, the reputation of the Country may not sink by contrary practices, nor the people of divers Judgments, now thy subjects, be disappointed, distress'd, or ruin'd. Which {with} sincere desires for thy temporal & eternal good concludes this from

Thy unknown but
sincere
Friend
W. Penn

Manheim
etc.

{Worms Crisheim.} {I. 26 6m. [26 August]}

Which being done, & having refresht ourselves, we return'd that night by the Rhyn[109] to Worms. From whence we, the next morning, being the first day of the week, walked on foot to Crisheim: wch is about 6 English miles from Worms.

We had a good meeting from the 10th hour till 3, & the Lords power sweetly open'd to many of the Inhabitants of the town, that were at the meeting. Yea the Faut, or chief officer himself stood at the dore behind the Barne, where he could hear, & not be seen; who went to the priest, & told him, that it was his work, if we were hereticks, to discover us to be such: but for his part, he heard nothing but what was good: & he would not meddle with us.

In the evening we had a more retired meeting of the Friends only; very weighty & tender; yea, the power rise in an high operation {among them}. And great was that love of god, that rise in our hearts at the meeting to visit them: & there is a lovely, sweet, & true sense amongst them. We were greatly comforted in them; & they were greatly comforted in us. Poor hearts, a little handful, surrounded with great & mighty Countrys of Darknes: 'Tis the Lords great goodnes, & mercy to them, that they are so finely kept, even natural in the seed of life. They were most of them gathered by Dear Wm Ames.[110]

{Worms.} {[II. 27] 6m. [27 August]}

The next morning we had another meeting, where we took our leave of them & so came accompanyed by several of them to Worms. Where having refresht ourselves we went to visit the Lutheran priest, that was at the meeting the 6th day afore at Crisheim. He rec'd us very kindly, & his wife, not without some sense of our Testimony. After we had discourst about an hour with him of the true & heavenly ministry, & worship, & in what they stood; & wt all people must come unto, if ever they will know {how} to worship god aright, we departed: & immediately sent them several good books of Friends in high dutch.

{Mentz}

Immediately we took boat, being about the 3d hour in the afternoon, & came down the river Rhyn to Mentz;[111] where we arrived about the 5th hour in the morning. And immediately we took an open

Charrot for Franckfurt, where we {came} ~~arrived~~ about the first hour in the Afternoon.

{Franckfurt.} {[III. 28] 6m. [28 August]}

We presently informed some of those people, that had rec'd us the time before, of our return to that city; with desires, that we might have a meeting that afternoon. Which was readily granted us by the Noble Women; at whose house we met: whether some resorted, that we had not seen before. And the Lord did after a living manner open our hearts & mouths amongst them; which was rec'd by them, as a further Confirmation of the coming of the Day of the Lord unto them: yea, with much joy & kindnes they rec'd us. The meeting held till the 9th hour at night. They constrained us to stay, & eat wth them; which also was {as} a blessed meeting unto them. Before we parted, we desired a select meeting the next morning at the same place, of those that we felt more inwardly affected with Truths Testimony, & that were nearest unto {the state of a} silent meeting: which they joyfully assented to.

{IV. 29 6m [29 August]}

We went to our Lodging; & the next morning we returned unto them; with whom we had a blessed & heavenly oportunity: for we had room for our life among them. {it was as among faithful friends, life run as oyle, & swom[?] a top of all.}

We recommended a silent meeting unto them that they might grow into an holy Silence into themselves; that the mouth, that calleth god Father, that is not of his own birth, may be stopped, & all Images confounded. That they might hear the soft voice of Jesus to instruct them, & receive his sweet life to feed them, & to build them up.

About the 9 hour we parted from that place, & went to Van de Walls, where the meetings were the time before; & there we had a more publique meeting of all that pleased to come. The Lord did so abundently appear amongst us, that they were more broken, then we had seen them at any time. Yea, they were exceeding tender & low; & the Love of god was much raised in their hearts to the Testimony. In this sensible Frame we left them; & the blessings & peace of our Lord Jesus Christ with {& among} them.

{Mentz}

And after having refresh't ourselves at our Inn, we took boat down the Mayn[112] to Mentz: where we arrived about the 5th hour. 'Tis a great city, but a dark & superstitious place according to the popish way; & is under the Governmt of a Popish Bishop. We stayed not longer there, then till our boat was ready; which might be better then half an hour.

{Hampach}

From Mentz we went on our way down the Rhyn, {6 German miles} [illegible numeral deleted] ~~German miles~~ {& came} that night to Hampach.[113]

{Bacherach Coblentz Treissig} {V. 30 6m.[30 August]}

From thence the next morning we went by Bacherach,[114] Coblentz,[115] & other places upon the Rhyn to Treissig[116] that night, being about 11. German miles.

{Cölln} {VI. 31 6m. [31 August]}

Next day being the 6th day of the week we got to Cölln,[117] a great Popish City, about the 3d ho{ur} in the Afternoon.

We gave notice to a sober mercht[118] in that town, a serious seeker after god, that we were there arrived: who presently came to us. We sat down, & had a living & pretious oportunity with him; opening {un}to him the way of the Lord, as to us it hath been manifested: {entreating} ~~desiring~~ him, that if he know any ~~of~~ {in} that city, who had desires after the Lord, or that were willing to come to a meeting, that he would please to inform them of our being here, & of our desire to meet with them. He answered, that he would readily do it.

This night, when we were in bed, came the Resident of several Princes (a serious & tender man) to find us out. we had some Discourse with him; but being late promis'd to see us next day.

{VII. 1 7m. [1 September]}

The next Day morning came {the} aforesaid merchant informing us, that it was a busy time, several preparing for the miss[119] or great fair at Franckfurt; yet some would come: & he desired, it might be at his house in the Afternoon about 3.

In the morning we went to visit that Resident; whom we met coming to see us: but he return'd, & brought us to his house. We had a good time with him; for the man is an Antient Seeker, opprest wth the Cares of this world: & he may be truly said, to mourn under them. His heart was open'd to us, & blessed god that he had lived to see us. We gave him an Acct how the Lord appeared in the Land of our Nativity, & how he had dealt with us: which was as the cool & gentle showers upon the dry & scorched Desert.

About noon we returned home; & after we had eaten, we went to the merchts house to the meeting. Where came 4 persons, one of which was the presbiterian priest {who} preacheth in private to the protestants of that place: for they are no ways allowed in that city. Surely, the true Day & power of the Lord made known itself to the Consciences of them present; yea, they felt, that we were such, as had been with Jesus; & that had obtained our testimony through the sufferings & travails of the Cross. {they were tender.}

The Resident & Mercht conducted us to our Inn, & from thence to the boat; being about 7. at night.

{Duysbergh.}

We set out towards the City of Duysbergh of the Calvinist way, belonging to the {Elector} ~~Duke~~ of Brandenburgh;[120] in & near to which we had been informed, there were a retired & seeking people.

{l. 2 7m. [2 September]}

We arrived there the next day about noon, being the first day of the week. The first thing we did, after we came to our Inn, was to enquire out one Dr Mastricht[121] {a civilian in[?]} for whom we had a Letter to introduce us, from a mercht of Colln. Whom quickly finding, we informed him, wt we came about; desiring his assistance: which he readily promis'd us. The first thing we offerd, was an Access to the Countess of Falchenstein, & Bruch.[122]

He told us, she was an extraordinary woman; one, in whom we should find things worthy of our Love: That he would write to her to give us an oportunity with her, That the fittest time was the present time, in that we might find her at the ministers[123] of Mullheim,[124] on the other side of the river from her Fathers Castel;[125] for that she used to come out the first day morning, & not return till night. That we must be very sh~~e~~y {of} making ourselves publique, not only for our own sakes, but for hers; who was severely treated by her Father[126] for the sake of these religious inclinations, that appeared in her: although her Father pretended to be of the protestant Religion.

We therefore dispatchd towards Mullheim, having rec'd his letter; & being also Accompanyed by him about ⅓ part of the way. But being 6 miles English, & afoot, we could not compass the plâce, before the meeting was over: for it was past 3, before we could get out of Duysbergh. And following that way, which lead to the Back-side of the {Grave} Graffe's Castell & Orchard (which was also a common way to the town; though if we had known the country, we might have avoyded it) we met with one Henry Smith, Schoolmaster & Catechiser of Spelldorp;[127] to whom we imparted our business: & gave the letter of Dr Mastricht of Duysbergh to introduce us to the Countess. He told us, he had just left her, being come over the water from the worship: but he would carry the Letter to her, & bring an Answer suddainly. But not withstanding stayed near an hour. When he came, he gave us this Answer: she would be glad to meet us, but she did not know, where: but rather inclined, that we should go over the water at the ministers house; whither if she could, she would come: but that a strict hand was held over her by her Father.

After some more serious discourse with him concerning the witness of god in the conscience, & the discoverys, testimony, & Judgmt of the true light unto which all must bow, that would be heirs of the Kingdom of god, recommending him to the same, we parted, he returning homewards, & we advancing to the town. But being necessitated to pass by her Fathers Castel, who is {seignieur} ~~souverain~~ of the Country, it so fell out, that at that very instant he came forth to walk. And seing us in the habit of strangers, sent one of his Attendants to demand, who & whence we were? & whither we went? {calling us to him & asking us the same questions} ~~And answering that~~ we answeard we were English men, come from Holland, going no further in these parts, then his own Town of Mulheim; ~~without~~ {But not} showing him or paying him that worldly homage & respect, which was expected from us, some of his Gentlemen asked us, If we know, whom we were before? & if we did not use to deport ourselves after another manner before noblemen, & in the presense of Princes? we answered, we were not conscious to ourselves of any disrespect or unseemly behaviour. One of them sharply replyed, why don't you pull off your hats then? Is it your Respect to stand cover'd in the Presence of the Souverain of the Country? We told them, it was our practice in the presence of our prince, who is a great King: & that we uncover'd not our heads to any, but to the Allmighty god. Upon which the Graffe called us Quakers, saying unto us, we have no need of Quakers here; get you out of my dominions: you shall not go to my town. We told him, that we were an Innocent people, that feared god, & had good will towards all men; & that we had true respect in our hearts towards him: we would be glad to do him any real good or service. And that the Lord had made it matter of conscience to us, not to conform ourselves to the vain & fruitles customes of this world: or words to this purpose. However, he commanded some of his soldiers to see us out of his territory. To whom also we declared some w^{t} of the reason and intention of our coming to that place in the fear & love of god, {who were civil to us.}

We parted with much peace, & comfort in our hearts. And as we passed through the village, where the shoolmaster dwelt, yet in the dominions of that Grave, we called upon him; & in the sense of gods power & kingdom opend to him the message & testimony of truth: which the man rec'd with a weighty & serious spirit. For under the Dominion of that Graffe there is a large congregation of protestants called Calvinists, of a more religious, inward, & zealous Frame of Spirit, then any body of people we ~~are~~ met with, or heard of in Germany.

After we had ended our testimony to him, we took our leave, desiring him not to fear, but to be of good courage; for the day of the Lord was hastening upon all the workers of iniquity: & to them, that feared his name {wherever} scattered throughout the earth, he would cause the sun of righteousness to arise, & visite them with healing under his wings. And to remember us with true kindnes & love to the Countess, daughter to this Graffe, & to desire her, not to be offended in us; nor to be dismayed at the displeasure of her Father. But eye the Lord, that hath visited her soul with his holy light, by which she seeth the vanity of this world, & in some measure the emptiness & deadnes of the religions that are in it; & he would preserve her from the power of the wrath of man, that worketh not the righteousness of god.

So we left the peace of Jesus with him, & walked on towards

Duysbergh; being about 6 English miles from thence, & near the eight hour at night. The Lord was with us, & comforted our hearts, as we walked {without any outward guide} through a tedious & solitary wood about 3 miles long, with the joy of his salvation, giving us to remember & to speak one unto another of his blessed witnesses in the days past, who wandred up & down, like poor pilgrims & strangers in the earth, their eye being to a city in the heavens, whose builder & maker is god.

Betwixt 9 & 10 we reachd the walls of Duysbergh; but the Gates were shutt. And there being no houses without the walls, we layd us down together in a field, receiving both natural & spiritual refreshment, {blessed be the lord.}

{II. 3 7m. [3 September]}

About 3 in the morning we rose, sanctifying god in our hearts, that had kept us that night. And walked till 5, often speaking one to another of the great & notable day of the Lord dawning upon Germany, & of several places of that land, that were almost white unto harvest.[128]

Soon after the clock had struk 5, they opend the gates of the city. And we had not long got to our Inn, but it came upon me with a sweet yet fervent power to visit this persecuted Countess with a Salutation from the love & life of Jesus, & to open unto her more plainly the way of the lord: which I did in this following Epistle:

My Dear Friend,

Jesus the Immaculate Lamb of god (griev'd & crucifyed by all the workers of Iniquity) illuminate thy understanding, & bless & be with thy Sp^t forever.

Though unknown, yet art thou much beloved for the sake of thy desires & breathings of soul after the living god, the report whereof {from} ~~of~~ some in the same state hath made deep impressions of true kindnes upon my Spirit, & raised in me a very singular & fervent Inclination to visit thee. And the rather, because of that suffering & tribulation thou hast begun to endure for the sake of thy zeal towards god, myself having from my childhood been both a seeker after the Lord, & a great sufferer for that cause from parents, relations, companions, & the magistrates of this world: the remembrance whereof hath so much the more endeared thy condition {un}to me, & my soul hath often in the sweet sense & feeling of the holy presense of god, & the pretious life of his dear son in my heart with great tenderness implored his divine Assistance unto thee; that thou mayst both be illuminated to do, & made willing to suffer for his names sake; that the sp^t of god & of glory may rest upon thy soul.

And truly, I can say, I felt the good will of god, his holy Care, & heavenly visitations of love to extend unto thee. But one thing more especially lay upon my Sp^t to have communicated unto thee, which made me the more pressing for an oportunity to speak with thee; & that was this: That thou shouldst have a true, right & distinct knowledge of thy own state, & wt that is, which hath visited thee, & in wt thy faith, patience, hope & salvation stand~~eth~~, where to wait, & how to find the lord, & how to distinguish between that wch is born of god, & that which is not born of god; both with respect to thyself in all the motions & conceptions of thy heart, & with respect to others in their religious worships & performances; to the end, that thou mayst not be deceived about the things relating to gods Kingdom & thy eternal peace: this is of greatest weight.

Now know certainly, that which hath discoverd unto thee the vanitys of this world, the emptines, & the fading of all earthly glory, the blessednes of the righteous, & the joy of the world that is to come, is the light of Xt Jesus, wherewith he hath enlightned thy soul. For in him was life, & that life is the light of mankind, Joh. 1, 4, 9. Thus god promised by the prophet Isaiah[129] to give him, viz. for a light to lighten the Gentiles, & for his salvation to the ends of the Earth. So that Xt the Light is gods gift, & eternal life is hid in him; yea, all the treasures of wisdom & Knowledge, who is the light of the Gospel temple, true believers, Revel. 21. And all that receive this light into their hearts, & bring their deeds to it, to see, in wt ground they are wrought; whether in god, or in the evil one; & make this blessed light the guide of their life, fearing with a holy fear to do anything that this light manifesteth to be evil; waiting & watching with a godly care to be preserved blameless before the lord; I say, all such become children of light, & witnesses of the life of Jesus. O blessed wilt thou be forever, if in the way of this holy light thy mind walketh to the end!

Let this that hath visited thee, lead thee, this seed of ~~life &~~ light & life, which is the seed of the Kingdom. Yea, 'tis Xt the true & only seed of god, that visited my soul in my young years, that spread my sins in order before me, reproved me, & brought godly sorrow upon me, making me often to weep in solitary places, saying within my own soul, O that I knew the lord, as I ought to know him! O that I served him, as I ought to serve him! Yea often was there a great concern upon my Spt about my eternal Estate, mournfully desiring, that the lord would give my soul rest in the great day of trouble. Now was all the glory of the world as a buble, yea nothing was dear to me, that I might win Xt: For the love, friendship, & pleasure of this world were a burthen unto my soul.

And in this seeking Estate I was directed to the testimony of Jesus in my Conscience, as the true shining light, giving me to discern the thoughts, & intents of my own heart. And no sooner was I turned unto it, then I found it to be that, which from my childhood had visited me; though I distinctly knew it not. And when I rec'd it in the love of it, it shewed me all that ever I did, & reproved all the unfruitful works of Darknes; judging me as a man in the flesh, & laying Judgmt to the line, & righteousness to the plummet in me.[130] And as by the brightnes of his coming into my soul he discovered the man of sin there upon his throne; so by the breath of his mouth, which is the two edged sword of his spirit,[131] he destroyed his power & kingdom. And having made me a witnesse of the death of the Cross, he hath also made me a witness of his resurrection: so that now my soul can say {in good measure} I am justifyed in the Spt. And though the state of condemnation unto death was glorious; yet Justification unto life was {& is} more glorious. In this state of the new man all is new; behold, new heavens & new earth; old things come to be done away, the old man with his deeds put off.[132] Now new thoughts, new desires, new Affections, new love, new friendship, new society, new kindred, new faith, even that which overcometh this world, through many tribulations; & now hope, even that living hope, that's founded upon true experience, which holdeth out all storms, & can see to the glory, that is invisible to carnal eyes, in the midst of the greatest tempests.

Now, 'tis the same blessed seed of light, life & grace, that from god the Father is sown in~~to~~ thy heart, & hath moved & wrought there that change which thou hast witnessed, from the Spt of this world. Turn to it, watch in it, that by it thou mayst be kept from all that it discovereth to be contrary to god: but especially from thyself; from thy own runnings, willings, & strivings. For wtsoever is not born of the Spirit, is flesh; & that inherits not the kingdom of god: & all that sow to it, shall inherit corruption.[133] By this thou wilt come to feel not only all sin to be a burthen, but all thy own righteousness, yea all mans righteousness to be a burthen. Thou wilt see the difference betwixt the dutys & prayers which thou begittest, & the dutys & prayers which in thy true silence from all self-activity of mind, the Lord begetteth in thee. O that thou mightst know the mystery of the new Birth; & wt that is, that can truly call god Father, even that, that is begotten of him, which liveth & breatheth, & hath its beginning & being in that life, which is hid with Xt in god; & by which it hath been quickned to the knowledge & worship of Xt & god. And this thou shalt not fail to know & enjoy, as thou patiently sufferest the lord to work his own work in thee, by his own blessed Spt, & that which will give thee to discern & savour the right motions & conceptions, dutys & performances in thyself from the false, will give thee to discern & savour that, which is right in others from that which is false; that which is of god, from that which is of man. Have a Care of gathering of sticks, & kindling a fire of thy own; & then compassing thyself about the sparks of the fire, which thou hast kindled; for the end of this state is to lye down in sorrow; because the heavenly fire is absent, wch maketh the sacrifice acceptable. Yea the Lord may sturr in thy heart, & thou mayst bring forth; but he that giveth to conceive, he bringeth to the birth, & he giveth power to bring forth: for without X^{t} we can do nothing. And blessed are they, that stur not, before the Angel moveth the waters; that goeth not before X^{t}, but is led by him; & that awaketh not her beloved, till he please; in whose hand the times & the seasons are. O blessed are they, whose eys are open'd to see him always present, a god always nigh at hand, whose hearts are stay'd upon his holy appearance in them, & they are thereby translated into his likenes: whose faith & hope is in X^{t} in them, the hope of Glory.

My dear Friend, weigh these things with a serious, retired, sweet & tender spirit, & the god that hath called me, & that hath called thee by the light of his dear son, open thy understanding to perceive the truth, as it is in Jesus; & w^{t} is the mystery of the ~~saints~~ fellowship of the saints in light. So to the Lord I recommend thee, the watchman & keeper of Israel: the Lord strengthen thee, & be thy holy comforter, & speak peace to thee, & never leave thee, nor forsake thee, till he hath conducted thee through all tribulations to his everlasting kingdom of rest & glory. O Dear heart, be valiant, & stay thyself upon X^{t} Jesus the everlasting rock, & feel him a fountain in thy soul: Feel his blood to clense, & his blood to drink, & his flesh to eat. Feed upon him, for god hath given him for the life of the world.

I had seen thee, had not thy Fathers strange sort of severity hindred. I confess, I do not use to be so treated in my own Country, where the Lord hath raised up many hundreds of meetings, that he hath gathered out of all sorts & professions, to worship him, not in their spirits nor wills, but in his will, sp^{t} & truth: And we are generally (after much affliction & suffering) in good esteem, even with the great ones of this world. And this let me add for thy particular comfort, that though I have been a man of great anguish & sorrow, because of that scorn & reproach, that hath attended my separation from the world, having been taught of Jesus to turn my back upon all for the sake of that glory, that shall be revealed: yet to gods honour I can say it, I have a 100^{d} Friends for one: yea, god hath turn'd the hearts of my enemys towards me; he hath fulfill'd his promise, to turn the hearts of the parents unto the children. For my parents, that once disown'd me for this blessed Testimonys sake (of the Jew, Christian, Circumcision & baptisme inward ag^{t} the fleshly Christian) have come to love me above all, {~~& have left me all,~~} thinking they could never do {& leave} enough for me. O how good is the Lord, yea the ways of his mercy are even past finding out.

Wherefore, my dear Friend, trust in the Lord forever: & the God of Abram, Isaac, & Jacob, the god of the Prophets & of the Apostles, the god of all the holy martyrs of Jesus, illuminate, fortify, & preserve thee steadfast, that in ye end thou mayst receive the reward of life & eternal salvation. To whom be glory & to the Lamb that sitteth upon the throne, one god & one Lord blessed & magnifyed forever & ever, Amen.

Thy great & faithful
Lover for the blessed
& holy Truths sake
William Penn.

Duysbergh the 13-7mo.
n. st. 1677

P S. My dear Brethren & Companions George Keith, & Benjamin Furley with me salute thee in the dear love of god. The inclosed I rec'd from a religious young woman at Franckfurt.[134] We have had a blessed oportunity in this town with some, that have a desire after the Lord, in which we are abundantly comforted. We have just now rec'd thy message & salutation by H V. which hath exceedingly refresht & relieved us; for our trouble was not for ourselves, but for thee. And we hope, our love will not turn to thy disadvantage; For we mentioned nothing of thy name, nor of the name of any other person; only that we desired to speak with the Minister of Mulheim: & that was only to the soldier. The Lord made us a good bed in the fields, & we were very well satisfyed. We are going this afternoon out of the town towards Wesel, from thence to Cleave,[135] & thence to Herwerden (the Lord willing). So, farewell in the Lord.

{Here followeth a Letter to her Father, the Graffe of {Brûch &} Falchenstein.}[136]

To the Graffe of Bruch & Falchensteyn
Friend,

I wish thy salvation, & the Lord reward thee good for the evil that thou ~~shewdst~~ shewedst unto me & my Friends the last night, if it be his will. But since thou art but a mortal man, one that must give an Accompt in Common with all to the immortal god, let me a little expostulate with thee.

By what law on Earth are men, not scandalous, under no proscription, harmless strangers, about lawful occasions, & men not vagabonds, but of good quality in their own Country, stopt, menaced, sent back with soldiers, & that at sun-set, expos'd to the night in an unknown Countrey, & therefore forc'd to lye in the Fields; I say, by w[t] Law are we judged, yea, thus punished before heard? Is this the Ius Gentium, or Germanicum? Naturale, or Christianum?[137] O! Where's nature? Where's civility? where's hospitality? but where's Christianity all this while?

Well, but we are Quakers. Quakers? w[t]'s that for a name? is there a law of the empire ag[t] that name? {No.} ~~But what;~~ did we own it? no. But if we had; the Letters of that name neither make up Drunkard, Whoremaster, Thief, Murtherer nor Traitor. Why so odious then? w[t] harm hath it done? why could Jews pass just before us, that have crucifyed X[t], & not Quakers that never crucifyed him? ~~& the false Christian, & the false Jew have one Father~~ {but Ignorance} is as well the mother of persecution as devotion; & the false Christian, & the false Jew have one Father.

But Argumentum ad hominem,[138] my Friend, bear with me a little. Art thou a Christian? how canst thou be rude, uncivil, & persecute then? Thou art to love Enemys, not abuse Friends, harmles strangers. Well, but thy life is dead; this Doctrine antiquated; Jesus Christ turnd out of dores I perceive: What are thou for a Christian? a Lutheran? yes. Cans thou so lately forget the practices of the papists; & with what Abhorrance thy Ancestors declared ag^t^ such sort of entertainment? were they not despised? mocked, & persecuted? & are their children treading in the steps of their old enemys? Friend, it's not reformed words, but a reformed life, that will stand thee instead: 'Tis not to live the life of the unregenerate, & wordly minded, & wicked, under the profession of the saints words, that will give an entrance into gods rest. Be not deceived; such as thou sowest, such must thou reap[139] {in the day of the Lord}. Thou art not come to the Bereans[140] state, that tryed all things; & therefore not noble in the Xristian sense. The Bereans were noble, for they judged not, before Examination.

And for thy saying, We want no Quakers here, I say under favour, you do. For a true Quaker is one, that trembleth at the word of the Lord; that worketh out his salvation with fear & trembling; & all the days of his appointed time waiteth in the light & grace of god, till his great change cometh; & that taketh up the daily cross to his will & lusts, that he might do the will of god manifested to him by the light of Jesus in his conscience; & according to the holy precepts and examples in the holy Scriptures of truth layd down by Jesus & his followers for the Ages to come. Yea, he is one, that loveth his enemys, but never feareth them; that blesseth those that curse him; & prays for them that despitefully treat him;[141] as god knoweth, wee do for thee. And o! that thou wert such a Quaker! then wouldst thou rule for god, & act in all things, as one that must give an Accompt to god for the deeds done in the Body, whether good or evil. Then would temperance, mercy, justice, meeknes, & the fear of the Lord dwell in thy heart, & in thy family & countrey.

Repent, I exhort thee, & consider thy latter end; for thy days are not like to be many in this world. Therefore mind the things, that make for thy eternal peace; lest distress come upon thee, as {an} armed man, & there be none to deliver thee. I am

Thy well wishing
Friend
Wm Penn.

Duysbergh
etc.

This being done we went to D[r] Mastricht to inform him of w[t] had past: who though of a kind disposition, & very friendly to us, yet seemed surprised with fear (the disease of this Country) crying out, w^{t} will become of this poor Countess? her father hath called her *Quaker* a long time, behaving himself very severely to her; but now he will conclude, she is one indeed: & he will lead her a lamentable life. I know, sayd he, you care not for suffering; but she is to be pittyed. We told him, that we both loved her, & pittyed her; & could lay down our lives for her, as X^{t} hath done for us, in the will of god, if we could thereby do her good: but that we had not mentioned her name, neither was the letter, that he gave us to her, so much as seen, or known of her Father. But still he feared, that our carriage would incense the graffe so much the more ag^{t} both his Daughter, & all those serious enquiring people up & down his Country. We answer'd with an earnestnes of spirit, That they had minded the incensings, & wrath of man to much already; & true religion would never spring or grow under such fears: & that it was time for all, that felt anything of the work of god in their hearts, to cast away the slavish fear of man, & to come forth in the boldnes of the true Christian life. Yea, that sufferings break & make way for greater liberty; & that god was wiser & stronger then man. We asked him, if there were any in that city, who enquired more diligently after the way of the Lord. He recommended us, (as we had already been informed in another place) to the family of the Praetor, or Chief Governour of the Town, whose wife & sister more especially, were seeking after the best things.[142] So we parted with him in love; & by the help of his daughter we were conducted to this Family.

We had not been long there, before a School-master of Dusseldock,[143] & withal a minister came in, enquiring after us; having heard at Mulheim, where he preachd the Day before to that people, or else by the way, of our attempt to visit that place, & the entertainmt we rec'd at the hands of the *Graffe* {Grave}. He sat down with us: & though we had already had a sweet oportunity; yet feeling the power to rise, the meeting renewed. And o! magnifyed be the name of the Lord, he witnessed unto our Testimony abundantly in all their hearts & Consciences, who were broken into much tenderness. And certainly, there is a blessed power & zeal sterring in that young man: yea he is very near the Kingdom. So we took our leave of them, leaving the Lords peace & blessing upon them.

It was now something past the 12th hour of the Day, in the way to our lodging we met a messenger from the Countesse, a pretty young tender man near to the Kingdom;[144] who saluted us in her name with much love, telling us, That she was much grieved at the entertainm^{t} of her Father towards us: advising us, not to expose ourselves to such difficultys & hardships; for it would grieve her heart, that any, that came in the love of god to visit her, should be so severely handled: for at some he setteth his dogs ~~upon them~~; & ~~at others~~ {upon others} he putteth his soldiers to beat them. But what shall I say, that itself must not hinder you from doing good, sayd the Countesse.

We answered him, That his message was joyful to us, that she had any regard to us & that she was not offended with us. We desired the remembrance of our kind love unto her, & that he would let her know, that our concern was not for ourselves, but for her. We invited him to eat with us; but he told us, he was an Inhabitant of Meurs,[145] & was in haste to goe home. So, we briefly declared our principle & message, commending him to X[t] the true light in his conscience: & parted. So we went home to dinner, having neither eaten nor drank, since first day morning, & having lain out all night, {in the field}.

We had no sooner got to our Inn, but the man {was constrain'd to} come after us, & sat down with us, & enquired concerning our Friends, the rise, principles, & progress. And in all things, that he desired satisfaction about, he declared himself satisfyed.

{Holton.}

Dinner being done, & all cleared, we departed that city, being about the 4th hour in the Afternoon: & for want of Accommodation, were forced to walk on foot 8 English miles ~~that night~~ to a town called Holton,[146] where we rested that night.

{Wesel} {III. 4 7m. [4 September]}

The next morning we sett out for Wesel[147] & got thither at noon.

The first thing we did, as had been our Custome, was to enquire, who was worthy? Particularly {for} 2 persons recommended to us by the Countesse of Horn, that liveth with the Princesse Elisabeth. But upon enquiry, one of them was come to Amsterdam with his wife, who had been formerly a preacher: but being conscientiously dissatisfyed with his own preaching, layd it down; & is now in a seeking state. But in lieu of him we found out three more, with the other person, that had been recommended to us.[148] We bespoke a meeting amongst them after dinner: which accordingly we had at a womans house of good note in the town, who told us, That she had long been in a solitary Estate, dissatisfyed with the religions generally profest in that country, waiting for salvation: & she hoped, that now the time was come, & that we were the messengers of it.

The Lord was with us in the meeting, & their hearts were open'd by the Word of god, to receive our Testimony, as glad tydings of salvation.

Meeting being done, we immediately returned to our lodging, desiring we might see them together in the same place the next morning to take our leave of them. To which they readily assented.

{IV. 5 7m. [5 September]}

Next morning we came, & had a pretious meeting with them, & there were some present, that were not there the night afore.

{Rees.}

So, we left them in much love, & went to our Inn; where, after having refresht ourselves, we went to Rees,[149] where we met with a Counseller of Gelderland,[150] with whom we had a good oportunity to declare the testimony of Jesus; who rec'd it, & parted with us in much Kindnes.

{Emmerick}

From thence we went to Emmerick,[151] & there called upon an Eminent Baptist-Teacher, recommended to us by one of Wesel. We spent some time with him, opening to him the way of life, as in the light it is manifested to all, that come & obey the light: & of that more spiritual & pure ministry, that from the living word of god is rec'd by many true witnesses in this day. The man was somew[t] full of words; but we felt, the living visitation of the love of god reached to him.

{Cleve}

And so we left him; making all the haste we could, to get Cleve that night, which accordingly we did, though late; being forced to walk a third part of the way a foot. That night notwithstanding one of us went to a certain Lady,[152] to whom we had recommendations from the princesse; & that was particularly known to one of us: informing her, that we were come to that city, desiring to know, w[t] time next day we might give her a Visit. She appointed 8 in the morning.

{V. 6 7m. [6 September]}

About that time we went to see her; she rec'd us considering her quality & courtship, far from any appearance of offense at our deportm[t]. We told her, Our message & visit was to those of the city, that had any inclinations or desires, hunger or thirst after the true & living Knowledge of god: for that end we had left our own country, & had wandred up & down in several parts of germany. She told us, that some there were, that searched after god; but she feared, the name of Quaker would make them shey: because they were called Quakers themselves by people of the same profession {only} for being more serious & retired in their conversations.

We replyed, That it was an honour to the name, that all sobriety throughout Germany was called by it; this ought to make the name less odious: yea, it will make the way the easier for those, that are truly called so, or that are quakers indeed: It will take off much of the wonder, & it may be, of the severity of the places, where we come, that the name is gone before us, & {hath} received a dwelling place in their towns & citys. In fine, to all such God hath committed to us, the word of life to preach; & such we seek out in all places, where the Lord bringeth us. And hitherto we can say it to the prayse of our god, he hath vindicated our service & testimony by his own blessed power shed abroad in their hearts, to whom we have been sent. So, she told us, she would send for an Attorney at Law {one} that was more then ordinarely eminent, having deserted the Church, & being therefore reproach'd with the name of Quaker.

In this Intervall we had close discourse with her, a woman certainly of great wit, high notions, & a very ready utterance; so that it was hard to obtain a true silence, a state, in wch we could reach to her. But through some travil of spirit more then ordinary we had a sweet time of refreshmt, & the witness was raised in her, & we really & plainly beheld a true nobility; yea that which was sensible of our testimony, & did receive it.

By this time the person she sent for, came; & a blessed sweet time we had. For the power & presence of the Lord, our staff & strength, unto which our eye hath been throughout all our travils, that we might be only acceptable in that, plentiously appeared amongst us (the Lord have the glory of his own work) both confessing to the truth of wt had been sayd; & the Attorney to the living sense, in which the truth had been declared.

We would have return'd to our Inn to eat, according as we had appointed in the morning; but she layd a kind of violent hands upon us, & necessitated us to stay & eat with her: which we did. And we had no sooner sat down, then her brother in law, a man of Quality & Employmt in that Court of the {Elector} ~~Duke~~ of Brandenburgh, came in, who dined with us. As we sat at meal, we had a good meeting; for the time was much taken up about the things of god, either in answering their questions, or our ministring to them about the true Christian nature & Life. In all which her brother behaved himself with great sweetnes & respect.

After Dinner we took our Christian Leave of them in the fear of god, recommending unto them the light of Xt Jesus, that bringeth all that receive it, into the one spirit, to live in holy peace & concord together. Particularly & alone speaking to the Lady, & the Attorney, wt was upon us as to their states.

{Nimmegen Utrecht} {VI. 7 7m [7 September]}

And so we departed, & soon after took waggon for Nimmegen.[153] Where arriving about 7. that night, we immediately took waggon for Utrecht,[154] & got thither about the tenth hour the next morning. We hear, there is a people in that city, but had not time now to visit them, referring it to another oportunity.

{Amsterdam}

About the 1st hour in the Afternoon G[eorge] K[eith]. & B[enjamin] F[urly]. took waggon for Rotterdam, & I took waggon for Amsterdam; where I safely came ~~the last~~ that night about 6 in the evening. & ~~where~~ I found Friends well; though it is a sickly time in this Country: the meeting house is much enlarged, ~~& the good news of~~ {& there is} a fresh Enquiry among many people after truth, & great desires to hear the testimony & declaration of it.

I also understand, that Dear G[eorge] F[ox]. is returned from Fredriks-stadt, & Hamborgh into Friesland, whither Thomas Rudyard & Isabel Yeomans are gone from this city to meet with him. He hath had a hard time of travail with respect to the weather; yet {I hear} is in good health, through the Lords power, that hath kept him.

{VII. 8 7m [8 September]}

This day at night {beeing the 7th day of the week} came John Hill[155] from Vriesland to the house of G[ertrude] D[iricks]. in Amsterdam.

{I. 9 7m [9 September]}

The next day being the 1st day of the week we had a very blessed & large meeting, larger then ordinary, because a great Addition of room since our Journey into Germany. Indeed, there was a great Appearance of sober professing people, yea, several of the chief of the baptists, as Galenus etc.[156] The lords heavenly power was over all, & the meeting blessedly ended about the 4th hour.[157]

{Horn Enckhuysen Worckum} {II. 10 7m. [10 September]}

That night after supper (having taken my leave in a sweet little meeting among Friends) I took boat for Horn,[158] ~~about the 7th hour at night~~, Peter Hendricks accompanying me, about the 7th hour at night; & got thither about two in the morning. where laying down till about 6. we took waggon for Enck-huysen,[159] ~~where~~ we came {thither} a little after 8. in the morning; where having refresht ourselves, about the 9th hour we took ship for Worckum[160] {in Vriesland}; ~~where we~~ & arrived about 1. And thence immediately took waggon for Harlingen, where we arrived about 6.

{Harlingen}

There we met with Dear G[eorge]. F[ox]. & I[sabel] Yeam[ans]. T[homas] Rudy[ard]. J[an] Clauss & his wife.

{III. 11 7m. [11 September]}

The next day we had two blessed meetings: one amongst Friends, being the first monthly meeting, that was setled for Vriesland, Groningen[161] & Embden. The other a Publique meeting, where resorted both Baptists, Collegiants, & others: And among the rest a Doctor of Physick & a presbiterian priest.

All sat with great Attention & sobriety; but the Priest, & Doctor more especially. The priest having a Lecture-sermen to preach that evening, went away; but notwithstanding speedily returned, G[eorge] F[ox]. still speaking. But as a man in pain to be gone, yet willing to stay, sat at the Dore, till G[eorge] F[ox]. had done; & then stood up, & pulling off his hat, looking up to Heaven in a solemn manner, & with a loud voice, spoke to this purpose: The Allmighty, the Allwise, Omnipotent Great God, & his son Jesus Christ, who is blessed forever & ever, confirm his word, that hath been spoken this day. Apologysing, that he could not longer stay, for that he was a minister of the reformed Religion, & was just now going to preach; where all that would come, should be wellcome. And so left the meeting.

The Physician also was called away, but returned, & stayed, till the meeting ended. Just as the meeting ended, came the same priest again, who sayd in the hearing of some Friends, that he had made his sermon much shorter then ordinary, that he might enjoy the rest of the meeting.

At night came the Physician to see me; who after a serious & Christian discourse, expressing great satisfaction in most things[162] relating to Friends, left me, w^th^al telling me, that if I had not been to go the 4th hour next morning, he would either have stay'd longer with me, or come again. He also remembred the priests love to us, & told me, that if it had not been for fear of giving offence, or coming too much under the observation of the people, he would have come to have seen us: adding, that it was great pity, that this people had not printed their principles to the world. To which the D^r^ answered, that he had some of our books; & he would lend him them. Blessed be the Lord, his pretious work goeth on, & his power is overall.

It being about the 10th hour at night, I took my leave of G[eorge] F[ox]. & Friends.[163]

[11 September 1677]

Dear Friend, J E M.[164]

My dear & tender love, which god hath raised in my heart by his living word to all mankind: but more especially unto those, in whom he hath begotten an holy hunger & thirst after him, saluteth thee; & amongst those of that place, where thou livest,[165] the remembrance of thee with thy companion[166] is most particularly & eminently at this time brought before me. And the sense of your open heartednes, simplicity & sincere love to the testimony of Jesus, that by us was delivered unto you, hath deeply engaged my heart towards you; & often raised in my soul heavenly breathings to the God of my life, that he would keep you in the daily sense of that divine life, wch then affected you. For this know, it was the life in your selves, that so sweetly visited you by the ministry of life through us.

Wherefore love the divine light & life in yourselves: be retired & still: let that holy seed move in all heavenly things, before you move. For no one ~~other~~ receiveth anything (that truly profiteth) but w^t^ he receiveth from above: thus saith John to his disciples.[167] Now that, that stirreth in your hearts, draweth you out of the world, slayeth you to all the vain glory & pleasure, & empty worships, that are in it. This is from above, the heavenly seed of god, pure & incorruptible, that's come down from heaven to make you heavenly; that in heavenly places you may dwell, & witnes with the saints of old this heavenly t~~h~~reasure in earthen Vessels. O stay your minds upon the Appearance of Jesus in you, in whose light you shall see light. It will make you of a weighty considering spirit more & more that you may see, how the mystery of iniquity hath wrought, & how mankind is corrupted in all things. And w^t part you yet have, that belongeth not to the paradyse of god, that you may lay it all down at the feet of Jesus, & follow him; who is going up & down, doing good to all that believe in his name.

So, possess your souls in the sensible feeling of his daily divine visits, shinings, & breathings upon your spirits; & wait diligently, & watch circumspectly, least the enemy surprise you, or your lord come {at} unawares upon you, & you be unprepared to receive his sweet & pretious visitations. That so these holy beginnings, which thou art a witness of with thy companions, may not be lost; or as if they had never been. But that you may from day to day feel the growth of his light, life, power & Kingdom in your souls, that you may be able to say, the Kingdom of God is come; yea, it is given to the saints.

And w^t I say unto one, I say unto all, that rec'd our Testimony in that city; to whom thou mayst give, if thou pleasest, the remembrance of my dear love, who travel in the spirit for their redemption; that they may be brought into the glorious Liberty of the sense of god. Particularly salute me to the young woman, that met with us at thy lodging;[168] the Lord Jesus Christ, the prince of peace, dwell amongst you, keep your hearts steadfast in his holy light without wavering all the days of your appointed time, untill your great & last change shall come, when he will receive his ~~sheep~~ own sheep into his own everlasting Kingdom, from the power of the Foxes & the Wolves, & all the devouring beasts & birds of prey: when he will wipe away all tears from their eyes, & sighing & sorrowing shall be no more: & when it shall be sayd, there is no more death, no more night, no more time.

{Ceulon}

So Dear JEM, know, that the Lord hath brought us well to Amsterdam, not without good service by the way. For at Ceulon[169] we had a pretious meeting, & were rec'd with much gladness of heart.

{Duysbergh Mulheim}

We also went to Duysbergh, & from thence towards Mulheim, being the first day of the week, hoping to get an oportunity with the Countess of Bruch, & to deliver thy letter. But her Father, who is a Cruel & severe man, meeting us near his Castel, stopt us: & after some little time, finding w^t we were, sayd, there wanted no Quakers there: & sent us with some of his soldiers out of his Territory: It was about sunset, so that we were forced to return towards Duysbergh. But the Gates of the city being shut, & there being no houses without it, we were forced to lye in the fields all night, where the Lord made us a good & comfortable bed. We told the Grave at parting, we were men, that feared the Allmighty god, we desired the good of all men; & we came not thiter for any evil designe. But he would not hear; the Lord, if he please, forgive him. Nevertheless, we had a good meeting at Duysbergh, where we had our hearts desire; the blessed power & life of god making its own way in the hearts of those that heard our testimony. I also writ a large & tender letter to the Countess, & rec'd a sweet & loving message from her: & I have great hopes, that all things will work for the best.

{~~Wesel~~}

From Duysbergh we went to Wesel, where we enquired out, who was worthy. Where we found out 4 or 5 separated from all congregations, waiting for the Consolation of Israel.[170] With whom we had 2 pretious meetings. And leaving the peace of Jesus with them,

{~~Emmerick~~}

went to Emmerick, where we visited the chief Baptist teacher; who confest to our Testimony, & rec'd us lovingly. We directed him to that gift of god in himself, that pure & eternal word in the heart, that he might know the pure ministry of that from the Ministry of Mans spirit; which cannot profit, or give life to the soul.

{Cleve}

From thence we went to Cleve; where, at a Ladys house, belonging to that Court, we had a pretious meeting. And we found some, that had deserted the publique ministry, as not being anointed of god to preach, neither knowing by a true experience the way & travil of the new birth; but are made & maintained by men. We sounded the joyful gospel amongst them. And from thence by the way of Nimmegen

{~~Nimm: Utrecht. Amst.~~}

& Utrecht we came last 6th day to Amsterdam, wch was the 7 of the 7th month, This last First day I had a great & blessed Meeting at Amsterdam, almost of every quality & religion: the Lords heavenly power, that is quickning people into a living sense of him, that they may say, *The Lord liveth, & he liveth in me,*[171] reigned that day over all. In the evening I took boat for Horn; and from thence came last night,

{~~Horn Harlingen~~}

being the 2d day of the week, to this city of Harlingen: where we met with some of our brethren, that had been up at Hamborough & Fredrichstadt, And this day are we to have two meetings in this city: the one among our Friends; the other publique for the town. It is upon me to visit de L'abade's people, that they might know him in themselves, in whom their salvation standeth; for these simple people are to be pittyed. From thence I think to visit Leuwarden, Gronnigen, Embden, Bremen, Herwerden, Wesel, Emmerick, Cleve, Utrecht; & so return to Amsterdam, the Lord enabling me by his own power.

This ariseth in my heart to thee; Give not thy bread to dogs; spend not thy portion: feed not the serpent, neither hearken to him. Abide with Jesus, & he will abide with thee; that thou mayst grow in wisdom & in righteousnes through the Cross, that crucifyeth thee to the world, & the world to thee.

So in that love, which overcometh the world, that is divine, & from above, & leadeth all thither, that receive it into their hearts, I take my leave of thee, with thy Companions, & all the rest of that city, known to us; remaining

Thy Faithful Friend,
& the Lords Day-Labourer
WP.[172]

Harlingen,
etc.

{~~Leuwarden~~} {IV. 12 7m [12 September]}[173]

Next morning about the 4th hour I took boat for Leuwarden;[174] John Clauss, who had been at Fredrichstadt with G[eorge] F[ox]. went with me. G[eorge] F[ox]. I[sabel] Y[eamans]. & T[homas] R[udyard]. with P[ieter]. Hendrichs return'd that day towards Amsterdam.

{Leuwarden}

At Leuwarden we came about 9, & began the meeting about 10; which we enjoyed with peace & refreshmt: several being there (as in other places) that were never at a meeting afore.

{Wiewart}

The meeting done, & having refresht ourselves with food, we took waggon for Wiewart; the mansion house of the family of the Somersdyke's where De Labade's company resideth: it being strong upon my spirit, to give them a visit.[175]

We got thither about 5. & as we were walking over a field to the house, we met a young man of that company, who conducted us in. I asked for Ivon the pastor, & Anna Maria Shuermans.

Ivon presently came with his Co-pastor,[176] who rec'd us very civilly: However, they seemed sh~~e~~y of letting me speak with A[nna] M[aria] S[churman]. objecting her weaknes, Age, taking Physick etc. But putting them in mind, how unhandsomely I was used at Herwerden 6 years ago by de Labade, their Father, who though I came a great journey to visit him & his people, suffered me not to speak with them. They presently complyed, & went in to let her know, that such a person desired to speak with her; ~~who presently~~ {& quickly} returned, desiring me to come in. But fore-seing, my time would be too short for my message, the sun being near setting, & having two English miles of unknown way to our *lodging* {on foot}, desired them,

{Osterwirdum.}[177]

that they would give me an oportunity the next morning: which they readily complyed with ~~me~~. So I took my leave of them: who in a Friendly manner brought us a little on our way.

{~~Osterwirdum.~~}

That night a great weight was upon my spirit; & especially the next morning: yet my faith was in the power of god. And I had a plain sight, that I should have a good service among them: however, I should clear my conscience, & my peace should rest with me.

{V. 13 7m. [13 September]}

The next morning I return'd to them, & J[an]. Clauss along with me. So soon as we came, we were brought {in}to A[nna] M[aria] Shuermans chamber: where also was with her one of the three Somerdykes.

This A[nna] M[aria] S[churman]. aforsaid is an Antient maid above 60 years of Age, of great note & fame for learning in Languages & philosophy; & hath obtained a considerable place among the most learned men of this age.

The Somerdykes are Daughters to a Nobleman of the Hague, people of great Breeding & Inheritances.

These with several other persons being affected with the zealous Declamations of De Labade ag^{t} the dead & formal Churches of the world, & awakened to seek after a more spiritual fellowship & society, separated themselves from the common calvinist Churches, & followed him in the way of a refined Independency. They are a serious plain people, {& are} come~~ing~~ nearer to Friends as to Silence in meetings, women speaking, preaching by the Spirit, plainness of garb, & furniture in their houses, then {formerly more then} any other people I know ~~living~~.

With these two we had the Company of the two pastors, & a Doctor of Physick. After some silence I proposed this question to them: what was it, that induced them to separate from the common way, they formerly lived in? I desired them, that they would be pleased to be plain & open to me, as to the ground of their separation {for I came not to cavil, but in a Xtian Spi^{t} to be informed.}

Upon this, Ivon, the chief pastor gave us the history of de Labade'^{s} Education, how he was bred among the Jesuits, & deserted them; & embraced the protestant Religion: & finally of his great dissatisfaction with the {Protestant} Churches of France, how he, & the other pastor joyned themselves with him in the same dissatisfaction, & resolution to separate themselves from the Churches of France: And that, if God would not give them a purer church, ~~that~~ they 3 would sit down by themselves: resolving nevermore to mixe themselves amongst the babilonish assemblys of the world. Adding, several solemn Appeals concerning the simplicity & integrity of all their hearts in these things.

Ivon having done, A[nna] M[aria] Shuermans began in this manner: I find myself constrained to add a short Testimony— She told us of her former life, of her pleasure in learning, & her love to the religion she was brought up in: but confessed, she knew not God or Christ all that while. And though from a child god had visited her at times; yet she never felt such a powerful stroak, as by the ministry of de Labade. She saw her learning to be Vanity; & her religion like a body of death. She resolved to despise the shame; desert~~ing~~ her former way of living & acquaintance; & to joyn herself with this little family, that were retired out of the world: among whom she desired to be found a living sacrifice offerd up intirely to the Lord. — She spoke in a very serious & broken sense, not without some trembling. These are but short hints of w^t she sayd.

After she had done, one of the Somerdyks began in a reverent & weighty frame of mind, & in a sense, that very well suted her ~~suffering~~ contempt of the world she told us, how often she had mourned from her young years, because she did not know the Lord as she desired ~~it~~: often saying within herself, If god would make known his way to me, I would trample upon all the pride & glory of the world. She earnestly exprest the frequent anguish of Spirit, that she had because of that deadnes & formality of those Christians she was bred amongst, saying to herself, O the pride, O the lusts, O the vain pleasures, in which Christians live! Can this be the way to Heaven? is this the way to glory? are these {the} followers of Christ? O no. O God, where is thy little flock; where is thy little family, that will live intirely to thee, that will follow thee? make me one of that number.

And when the servant of the Lord de Labade came into Holland, I among others had a Curiosity to hear him; & among several others was deeply affected by him. He spoke the very Thoughts of my heart; me thought, my heart was prick'd when I heard him: & I resolved by the grace of god to abandon all the glory & pride of this world to be one of those that should sit down with him in a separation from the vain & dead worships of this world. I count myself happy, that I ever met with him, & those pastors; who seek not themselves, but the Lord. And we are a family, that live together in love, of one soul, & one spirit, intirely given up to serve the Lord: & this is the greatest Joy in the world.

After her, de Lignon, the other Pastor, gave us also an Account of his inducements to embrace J[ohn]. de Labade, {but not so lively.}

After him the Doctor of Physick, that had been bred {for} a Priest, but voluntarily ~~deserted~~ {refused} that Calling, exprest himself after this manner: I can also bear my Testimony in the presence of god, that though I lived in as much reputation at the University, as any of my Colleges[178] or Companions, & was well reputed for my sobriety & honesty; yet I never had ~~any~~ {such a} living sense of god, ~~till~~ {as when} I heard the serv^t of the Lord, de Labade: adding, ~~that~~ the first day ~~he~~ I heard him, ~~he~~ I was so struck & affected, that ~~he~~ I can truly say, through the good grace of god, & the conduct of his holy spirit, ~~that~~ it was to ~~him~~ {me}, as the Day of ~~his~~ {my} Salvation, He did so livingly touch my heart with a sense of the true Christian worship. Upon which I forsook the University, & resolved to be one of this family: And this I can say in the fear of god.

Ivon concludeth; This is w^{t} we have to say concerning the work of god amongst us.

All this while, I minded not {so} much their words; but I felt & had unity with a measure of Divine sense, that was upon them. Certainly, the Lord hath been amongst them: yea, I had a living sense in my heart, that somew^{t} of the breath of life had breathed upon them. And ~~they~~ though they were in great mixtures; yet that gods love was towards them.

After some time of silence, I began on this wise: I come not to judge you, but to visit you; not to quarrel or dispute, but to speak of the things of gods Kingdom: And I have no prejudice, but great love & regard in my heart towards you. Wherefore hear me with Christian patience & tendernes.

I do confess & believe, that god hath touch'd your hearts with his divine finger, & that his work is amongst you: that it was his spirit that gave you a sight of the vanity & folly of this world, & that hath made you sensible of the dead religions, that are in the world. 'Tis this sense I love & honour; & I am so far from undervaluing or opposing this tender sense I feel upon you, that this it is, I am come to visit, & you for the love of it. And as for the reproaches that may attend you on the score of your separation, with all the reports, that therefore goe concerning you, they {are} w^{t} I respect you for, being well acquainted with the nature & practice of this world towards those that retire out of it. Now since I have with patience, & I can truly say, with great satisfaction heard y^{r} Acc^{t} of y^{r} experiences, give me the like Christian Freedom to tell you mine; to the end you may have some sense of the work of god in me. For those who are come to any measure of a divine sense, they are as looking-glasses to each other, seing themselves in each other, as face answereth face in a glass.

Here I began to let them know, when & how the Lord first appeared unto me, which was about the 12th year of my age, Anno 1656. how at times betwixt that & 15. the lord visited me; the divine impressions he gave me of himself, of my persecution at Oxford; how the Lord sustained me in the midst of that hellish darknes & debauchery; of my being banisht the Colledge. The bitter usage I underwent when I returned to my Father, whipping, beating, & turning out of Dores, in 1662. Of the Lords Dealings with me in France; & in the time of the great plague in London: in fine the deep sense he gave me of the vanity of this world; of the irreligiousness of the religions of it. {Then} Of my mournful & bitter cryes to him, that he would show me his own way of life & salvation; my resolutions to follow him, whatever reproach or sufferings should attend me: & that with great reverence & brokennes of Sp^{t}. How after all this the glory of the world overtook me, & I was ever ready to give up myself unto it; seing no such thing, as the primitive sp^{t} & church in the earth;

And being ready to faint concerning my hope of the restitution of all things, {and} that it was at this time, that the lord visited me with a certain sound & testimony of his eternal word through one of those the {world} called a Quaker. I related to them the bitter mockings, & scornings that fell upon me; the displeasure of my parents; the invectivenes & cruelty of the priests; the strangnes of all my companions, w[t] a sign & wonder they made of me: But above all, the great Cross of resisting & watching ag[t] my own inward vain Affections & thoughts. Here I had a fine oportunity to speak of the mystery of Iniquity & ungodlines in the root & ground, & to give them an Acc[t] of that power & presence of god, w[ch] attended us in our publique testimonys & sufferings; after an indirect manner, censuring their weaknesses by declaring & commending the contrary practices among Friends, too large to be here related. And notwithstanding all my sufferings & tryals by magistrates, parents, companions, & above all from the priests of the false religions in the world, the lord had preserved me to this day, & had given me an 100[d] fold in this world, as well as the Assurance of life everlasting. Informing them of the tendernes of my Father to me before & at his death; & how through patience & long suffering all opposition was conquered. Then beginning my exhortation unto them, which was on this wise:

That therefore god hath given me & them a divine sense of him, that our eye might be to him, & not to man; that we might come more into a silence of ourselfs, & a growth into that heavenly sense: that this was the work of the true ministry, not to keep people to themselves ever teaching them; but to turn them to god, the new Covenant Teacher {& to X[t] the great Gospel-teacher.} Thus John did, & thought it no dishonour, that they left him to go to X[t]. *Behold, the Lamb of god* saith he, *that taketh away the sins of the world:*[179] And even Johns disciples left him to follow X[t]. Nay, John testifyeth of himself, that he was to decrease, & that X[t] was to increase. Wherefore I prest them to have their eye to X[t], that taketh away the sin; that is from heaven, heavenly, to see, that he increase in them. Yea, that hence forward they should know no man after the flesh; no, not X[t] himself; that their knowledge of, & regard & fellowship with one another should stand in the revelation of the Son of god in them, which is gods great prophet, by whom god speaketh in these latter days. And if their ministers be true ministers, they will count it their glory to give way to X[t]; & that they decrease, & X[t] increase: that the Instrum[t] giveth way to him that useth it; the serv[t] to the Lord, which though it seemeth to detract from the minister; yet it was {& is} the glory of a true minister, that god & X[t] should be all in all, & that his will should be fulfilled. For the day of the Lord was come, & all people must look to him for salvation. That all people must now come to keep gods great Sabbath, to rest from {meer} man, & the Sp[t] of man; & all mans thoughts, words & works: And that, if they were true believers, they were at least entering into the rest. I closely recommended that to them, that they might not be of those, that begin ~~with~~ {in} the spirit, & end in the flesh: for that those, that should so do, & thereby break gods Sabboth day, should be stoned to death, by that stone, that is cut out of the mountain without hands; yea, that should fall upon them, as a millstone, & should grind them to powder.[180] Therefore let X^{t} have his honour; let him preach & speak amongst you: & you in him, & by him only to sigh, groan, pray, preach, sing, & not otherwise; least death come over you: for there the Apostacy came in {their going before X^{t} instead of X^{ts} going before them.} And wait in the light & sp^{t} of judgm^{t} that hath visited you, that all ~~might~~ {may} be wrought out, that is not born of god. So will you come to be born of the incorruptible seed of the word of god, that liveth & abideth forever: that you may be an holy priesthood, that offereth up a living sacrifice with gods heavenly fire; that god may have his honour in you all, & through you all by Jesus X^{t}.

And turning myself towards the Somersdyks with a serious & tender spirit I exprest myself thus: That you should be pilgrims in the Inheritance of y^{r} Father, I have a deep & reverent sense of: O that you might dwell with him forever, & exalt him, that hath so visited you! with whom are the rewards of eternal Blessednes.

So I left the blessing & peace of Jesus amongst them, departing in the love & peace of god. And I must needs say, they were beyond expectation tender, & respectful to us; all of them coming with us, but the antient A[nna] M[aria] S[churman], (who is not able to walk) to the outward dore, giving us their hands in a very Friendly manner, expressing their great satisfaction in our Visite. And being come to the porch, & meeting several persons of the family, I was moved to turn about, & to exhort them in the presence of the rest, To keep to X^{t} that had given them a sence of the spirit of this world; & had raised desires in them to be delivered from it: & to know no man after the flesh, but in X^{t} to have their fellowship, union & communion with god, & one with another. That all their worship & performances might stand in him, that he might be all in all; desiring, that the Lord might keep them in his fear all the days of their appointed time, that they might serve him in their generation, in his own universal sp^{t} to his glory: who is blessed for ever.

The 2 pastors & the Doctor came with us a fields length, where we took waggon, And the chiefest of them took occasion to ask me, if the truth rise not first amongst a poor, illiterate & simple people? I told him, yes, that was our comfort, & that we owed it not to the learning of this world. Then, sayd he, let not the learning of this world be used to defend that, which the sp^{t} of god hath brought forth. For schollars now coming amongst you, will be apt to mixe shool learning amongst your simpler & purer language, & thereby obscure the brightnes of the testimony. I told him, it was good for us all to have a care of our own spirits, words & works; confessing, w^{t} he sayd, had weight in it: telling him, it was our care to write & speak according to the divine sense & not humain Invention.

The Lord comforted my soul in this Service: yea, all that is within me, magnifyed his holy name, because of his blessed presence, that was with us. O let my soul trust in the Lord, & confide in him forever! O let me dwell & abide with him, that is faithful & true, & blessed forevermore.

So, in a very sober & serious manner we parted, being about 12 at noon.

{Lippenhusen}

This night about 10. we got to Lippenhusen,[181] where there is a little meeting of Friends, being about 25 English miles.

{VI. 14 7m. [14 September]}

The next morning we had a blessed meeting among Friends, Many of the world came in, were very serious, & well affected; one whereof was a magistrate of the place. The Lord pleadeth his own cause, & crowneth his own testimony with his own power. There is like to be a fine gathering in that place.

{Groningen}

After Dinner we took waggon for the city of Groningen; where we arrived at 8 at night, being about 25 English miles.

{VII. 15 7m. [15 September]}

The next morning we had a meeting among Friends of that city; whither resorted both Collegiants, & Calvinist students; who behaved themselves soberly. The Lords power was over all, & his testimony standeth.

When meeting was ended, they went out; & as I was concluding an Exhortation to Friends, came in a Flock of students to have had some conference with us. But having set the time of our leaving the city, we recommended them to the universal love of god; promising them {some} books of our principles. With which they exprest themselves satisfyed; & ~~very~~ civilly parted from us.

{Delfzyl}

After Dinner we took boat for Delfzyl,[182] & came there about 6 at night.

{I. 16 7m. [16 September]}

The next morning about 7 we took boat for Embden; which is about 3 leagues.

On board of that Vessel it came upon me to write a letter to Friends {in England} concerning the present Separatists,[183] & their Sp^{t} of Separation, which had several times been opend unto me, & had remained some days upon my Sp^{t}. The Letter followeth:

To
Gods Friends everywhere,
concerning the present
Separatists
& their Spirit of
Separation
This came upon me in the Ship between
Delfzyl and Embden
Upon the 16-7 month {1677} to send amongst you.

Friends & Brethren,

By a mighty hand, & by an outstretched Arm hath the Lord god everlasting gather'd us to be a people, & in his own power & life hath he preserved us a people unto this day: & prayses be to his eternal name, not one weapon, that hath yet been formed ag[t] us either from without or from within, hath prospered. Now this I say unto you, & that in his counsil, that hath visited us; whoever goeth out of the unity with their brethren, are first gone out of unity with the power & life of god in themselves, in which the unity of the brethren standeth. And the least member of the body in the unity standeth on the top of them, & hath a Judgm[t] ag[t] them; unto which Judgm[t] of both great & small amongst the living family, that in the unity are preserved, they must bow, before they can come into the unity again. Yea, this they will readily do, if they are come into unity with the life & power of god in themselves, which is the holy root that beareth the tree, the fruit & the leaves; all receiving life & virtue from it, & thereby are nourished, unto gods prayse.

And let all have a Care, how they tamper with the Judgm[t] of the Power; & how they weaken that, or bring that under their exaltation & high Imagination {of those}, that it is revealed ag[t]. For I feel, that unruly Sp[t] is tormented under the stroak & Judgm[t] of the power, & in its subtilty is seeking occasion ag[t] the Instruments, by whom the power gave it forth: let all have a Care, how they touch with this Sp[t] in those workings. For by being one with this Sp[t] in Judging those, that have been faithful according to that gift of wisdom they have rec'd of god, they will feed it, & fortifye it, & in the end come to be one with them agt the power itself; & at last run out, & become open enemys & despisers: for whom is reserved the blacknes & darknes forever.

Wherefore all that labour for the restoration of those that are out of unity with the brethren, let them be such as are of a sound mind themselves; else what will they gather from? or w[t] will they gather to? And let them labour in the simplicity, integrity, love & zeal of the power, that first gatherd us to god. For that which is rightly gotten, will endure; but that which is obtained by the Contrivance, Interest, & perswasions of men, getteth no further then man {&} is of the flesh, & wt is of the flesh, is fleshly, & shall never inherit the Kingdom of god.

Therefore let none look out of the seed for help, for all power is in it, & there the true light & Judgmt stand forever; & that seed only god hath ordained to bruise the serpents head:[184] They that would save it, & those that would bruise it by any other thing, are both breakers of gods great ordinance, & fly to Egypt for strength. For 'tis David the stripling, that shall be too hard for Goliah, the Giant: & that not by {Sauls} armour, but with gods living little stone cut out of the mountains without hands,[185] without mans Invention & contrivance. O this hath wrought all our mighty works in us & for us to this day! Wherefore let us be still, & trust & confide therein forever. Let none look back, faint, or consult; for if they do, they will darken their pure eye, & loose their way: & into the eternal rest of the flocks of the Companions will never come.

Brethren, the Judgmt gone forth agt this Spt & all those that have resisted our love, & forbearance, & *that are joyned to it,* must stand; & all that are out of unity with that Judgment, are judged by it before god & his people, ~~that are joined to it~~. Therefore as all would stand clear before the lord & his people, let not this Spt be reason'd withal: Enter not into proposals & Articles with it: but feed it with Judgmt, that is gods decree: so may the souls that are deceived, come by the right dore into the heavenly Unity.

My Brethren, look forward, & lift up your eyes, for the fields are even white unto harvest[186] up & down the nations. Remember the great name of the lord, & behold the great work that he is doing before all people: whose saving health is visiting the world, & whose eternal word & testamt must from amongst us go forth to gather the nations. Let that that will be unjust, be unjust still; let the dead bury the dead: ~~To his appearance the Kings & Kingdoms of the Gentiles shall bring their glory.~~ Let us all, who have rec'd the gift from god, wait in deep humility to be raised up & impowred by him more & more, to eye & prosecute his universal service in the world {to whose appearance the Kings & Kingdoms of the Gentiles shall bring their glory.} which noble work, had those that are gone into the Separation, but layd deeply to heart, they would never have sat at home murmuring, fretting & quarreling agt the comely & godly order & practice of their brethren; but love, peace & joy had fill'd their hearts, & not the troubler & Accuser of the Brethren; who hath opend an evil eye in them, & begotten them into a discontented, self separating mind: & this image they bear; & the pure eyes sees it.

O let none tempt the Lord; let none provoke the eyes of his Jealousy. Let us all dwell in that divine sense that he hath begotten in us: where our love, as a fresh & pure stream will always flow to god, & unto one another. Here all his ways are pleasantnes, & all his paths are peace: For where he keepeth the house, who is Prince of peace, he will keep all in his heavenly peace. We are but as one Family, & therefore we have but one Lord & Master: We are but as one floch, & we have but one heavenly shepherd to hear, who goeth before us, & giveth us eternal life, that follow him. And if any are offended in him, or in his, it is their own fault; if they faint, & grow weary, we are truly sorry; {If through unwatchfulnes the enemy hath enter'd, (begetting coldnes to the brethren, & carelesnes of embracing the oportunitys, by wch the unity is rendered & increased; so that what's done by the brethren without them, is lookd upon first with a slight eye, & then with an evil eye: which begetteth distance, & this distance in time a separation; & separation continues, enmity; and this enmity death itself) we are in etc.} our hearts ~~are~~ truly griev'd for them. However the Judgm^{t} of god must stand agt them, & that Spirit that leadeth them; in which they gather not to god, but to themselves. And we to them, that strengthen their hands, & despise counsil; they will have much to answer for before the Lord. I feel a slighting, scornful, haughty Spirit often flying at me with its venemous sting; but the seed of life is over it, & the lord god will distress it.

Wherefore friends, in all places, where this Spirit hath had entrance, keep sound Judgmt upon it, if you will keep your garments clean; And enter not into disputes & Contests with it; 'tis that it seeketh & loveth. But go on in your testimony, & business for the lord, in the lords {peaceable} power & spirit; & his blessings & presence of life shall be with you, & in multiplying he shall multiply you: for no good thing will ~~be~~ he withhold from you. We can say it of a truth, god is good to Israel, & to all that are of an upright heart.

And let us be of good chear; for 'tis gods determination, that the house of David shall grow stronger & stronger; & his branch shall encrease, & spread, & of his government, Kingdom & Dominion there shall never be end.

Your Faithful
Friend & Brother in
the Service of our
dear Lord
WP

From {on} Board
the Passage-boat
between Delfzyl
& Embden
16—7mo. 1677.

Gods Blessed work increaseth & prospereth in these lands: magnifyed be his everlasting name.

{Embden.}

We arrived at Embden about the 11th hour. This is that city, where Friends have been so bitterly & barbarously used, the like hath scarcely been known in any place, where truth hath broke forth in our day; they having been banish'd some 30 & some 40 times, & above. The first family that rec'd truth in this city, was Doctor John Willem Haesbaert[187] & his wife; at whose house also the first meeting was set up among friends to wait upon the Lord by way of publique testimony: they are now both dead; but the memory of ~~the righteous~~ their fidelity is as pretious ointmt amongst the righteous. They were with me at a meeting 6 years agoe in {this} ~~that~~ city; & I remember, the power had that sweet operation upon them, that I sayd {to B[enjamin]. Furly & Thos. Rudiard then wth me} It will not be long, before they will [illegible deletion] publiquely own, & bear {a} testimony in this place. And in about three months after he came forth; & she about a year after him: & from their fidelity & integrity, notwithstanding all the sore & bitter tempests of persecution, a fine meeting sprang. But at this day they are scattered, being still sent away, as fast as they return. We visited his mothers family, where we found 3 of his sisters in the love of truth; his 4th sister being also a friend, & is the wife of John Claus living at Amsterdam. We had a little sweet, comfortable meeting with them: After it, returning to my lodging, as I was writing to Doctor Andreas, president of the Councel of state (who is reported to have been the Author of this cruelty to our Friends) a burden came upon me, my writing would not serve turn) but I must go myself; & in the name & fear of the Lord, to plead the innocent & suffering cause of our Friends with him. So, away we went to his house. He was at first astonisht to see, w^{t} manner of men we were; but after a little time, he comported himself with more kindnes, then we expected at his hand. {I Askt him if he & the Senat had not receiv'd a letter in latin from an englishman about 2 years since ~~about~~ {concerning} their severity towards the people called Quakers, he told me he had, I replyed I was the man;[188] & I was constrain'd in conscience to visit him on their behalf. & I could not see how he being a commonwealths man & a Protestant could persecute.} ~~We~~ I pleaded with him the unnaturalness, the Inchristianity, & imprudence of such proceedings, & pressed our reasons earnestly, but tenderly upon him. He assaulted us with several objections; but blessed be the Lord, they were mostly fic{ti}tious; & therefore easily removed & answered. He also promised me, That if I would write to the Senate a remonstrance of the Case of our Friends, & express my request to them, & enclose it to him, he would both present it, & get it to be read; & make it appear, that he was not so much our enemy, as we lookd upon him to be. I promised to send him some books containing a defense of our principles; which were accordingly put into the hands of Elisab. Haesbart[189] to deliver him in my name.

{Lier}

Having taken our leave of the old woman & her daughters, & a man friend residing in that citty, & left the blessings & peace of our god amongst them, we took ship for Lier;[190] where we arrived the next morning.

{Bremen.} {II. 17 7m. [17 September]}

Thence we took waggon for Bremen, where we came safe {III. 18 7m. [18 September]} through the Lords goodnes the next day; there we met our friends & companions G[eorge]. Keith & Benjamin Furley, who were come theith{er} some hours before us from Amsterdam. In this city there is a work of the Lord begun, though yet obscurely: we had a travail upon our spirits, that the blessed & pretious truth of our dear Lord & master might find a place to rest its foot upon. To that purpose we writ to two ministers under some suffering from their brethren, {IV. 19 7m. [19 September]} because of their great zeal agt the formality & deadnes of the so called reformed Churches.[191] This we sent by a mercht who{m} we formerly met at Herwerden; With some difficulty we got to them: but the person chiefly struck at, was sh~~e~~y to speak with us. His reason was this; It was known, that we were in town; & it was one of the Accusations agt him, that he was a fosterer of all the strange religions, that came through the town. Also, he was then actually under process;[192] & that the people, that ~~h~~ad=heard ~~of~~ {to} the innocency of his cause, conceiving a prejudice agt our name, though it might be without cause; he could not at present conferr with us. And sayd, he was sorry for it, with all his heart: but wt we should say to his brother, should be the same, as if it had been sayd to him: to whom he referred us. However, I took hold of his arm, & sayd; I have this message to deliver {to} thee, that I may disburden myselfe before the Lord, which was this: mind that, which hath touched thy ~~own~~ heart; let that guide thee: do not thou order that. Consult not with flesh & blood, how to maintain that cause, which flesh & blood in thy enemys persecuteth thee for. He answered, Rather then I will betray that cause, or desert Xt, by gods strength they shall pull off the flesh off my bones. So he left us in his house. And truly we had a good time with his companion, the other minister, almost {three} hours; testifying unto him, That the day was come, & coming, in which the Lord would gather out of all sects (that stand in the oldnes of the letter) into his own holy spirit, life & power; & that in this the unity of faith, & bond of peace should stand. And therefore that he & all of them should have an eye to the principle of god; that being turned to that, they might speak from {it}. & that therein they would glorify god, & be edifyed. So we parted; leaving the man in a sensible & savoury frame.

We visited the mercht twice, & had a very good time with him. The man is of a loving & sensible spirit; & the love of god opened our hearts to him {often}.

We also visited *Doctor Johannes Sophrony Cosack,* an odd Composition of a man. He hath had great & strange openings. He hath writ several hundred Tracts; some of them now are printing at Amsterdam. He is a great Enemy to the priests, & in society with none: of a merry, yet of a rough disposition, without any method, or decency in his cloaths, food, furniture, & entertainm^{ts}. He wanteth but 3 of 4 score; yet {of} a wonderful vigor, & pregnancy. We were twice with him; & we have reason to think, he was as loving to us, as to any body. And truly, he did show at parting some serious & hearty Kindness: but we could fasten little upon him, as to gods power, or any inward sense of us or our testimony. Yet we had little to object ag^{t} w^{t} he sayd too; nay, some things were very extraordinary.

From him we went to Doctor Bollingham, an English Physitian, a man of a lowly & tender spirit; who rec'd us in much love; lamenting, when we left him, that he had no more time with us.

At the Inn we had frequent oportunitys to declare the way of truth; & we must needs say, we were heard with patience & sobriety. Particularly a D^{r} of Law, who lodg'd at the house, & an Antient sober man, of Kiel in Holstyn.[193]

{V. 20 7m [20 September]}

We left books amongst them all; & in the love & fear of god we took our leave of them on the 5th day after dinner, & began our Journey towards Herwerden, ~~where is~~ the Court of the Princess,

{VI. [21 September]}

~~Palatine Elisabeth:~~ where we arrived on the 7th day in the morning every way well, through the mercys of the Lord.

{Herwerden.} {VII. 22 7m. [22 September]}

We sent to her to ~~let~~ {informe} her ~~know~~ of our Arrival; & {to know} w^{t} hour it would be convenient for us to visit her? who returnd us this answer: That being then employed in the business of her Governm^{t}, it would be the 2^{d} hour {after noon} before she could be at leasure.

The time being come, we went to visit her; & found both her & the Countess[194] ready to receive us: which they did, with much love & tenderness. I observed them to be much lower then ever; & that our former blessed oportunitys had had a blessed effect upon them.

That afternoon was employed in the narrative of our travails; which they heard wth great attention & refreshm^{t}: The whole discourse ended with a pretious little meeting.

The house being clear of strangers, they both earnestly prest us to sup with them: which not being well able to decline, we submitted.

At supper the power of the Lord came upon me; & it was a true supper to us. For the hidden manna was manifested among us; yea, a blessed meeting it proved to us. O the reverent tendernes, & lowly frame of spirit, that appeared this evening both in the princess & Countess!

The French Woman[195] we found greatly improved both in her

love, & in her understanding: yea, she is very zealous, & very broken: she was always with us in these occasions.

After supper, we return'd to the princesses Chamber; where we stay'd, till it was about ten at night. At parting, I desired, the Princess would give us such another oportunity the next day (being the 1st day of the week) as we had the last time we were with her. She answered me; *With all my heart: but will you not come in the morning too?* I replyed; yes, willingly: wt time wilt thou be ready to receive us? She answered, at seven.

{I. 23 7m. [23 September]}

About 7 the next morning we came there: about 8, the meeting begun, & held till 11. Several persons of the city, as well as those of her own family being present. The lords power very much affected them; & the Countesse was twice much broken {as we spoak.}

After the people were gone out of the chamber, it lay upon me from the Lord, to speak to them too, (the princess & countess) with respect to their particular conditions, occasioned by these words from the princess; I am fully convinc'd; but O my sins are great!

Whilst I was speaking, the glorious power of the lord {wonderfully rise, yea after an awfull manner &} had a deep entrance upon their spirits; especially upon the Countesse, that she was broken to peeces: God hath {raised & I hope} fixed his own testimony in them.[196]

We returnd presently to our Inn; & after dinner we came back to the 2d meeting upon that day, wch began about the 2d hour afternoon. And truly, the reverend blessed pure word of life was divided aright; the pretious sense of truth was rais'd in the meeting. There came more of the city, then in the morning; & we were much comforted in the Lords power, that was with us. For the truth had passage, & the hungry were satisfyed & the simple hearted deeply affected. This day at both meetings was one of the princesses women, that never was at meeting before; & she, though very shy of us, the last time became tender & loving to us. She was truly reached: O magnifyed be the name of the Lord, whose presence was with us, & whose arm stood by us.

After meeting the princess prest us to stay & sup with her; pleading the quietness of the family, & that they were alone at supper, as the night before. It was upon me to commemorate the goodness of the Lord, his daily providences, & how pretious he is in the Covenant of light to the dear children & followers of the light. Great was the reverence & tendernes, it was upon the spirits of both princess & Countess {at the instant.} After supper we returned to the princesses Chamber, where we spent the rest of our time in holy silence or discourse, till about the 10th hour: then we repair'd to our quarters.

{II. 24 7m. [24 September]}

Next morning about 8. we return'd to the Court; where Princess

& Countess were ready to receive us. The morning was employed in very serious Conference relating to the Affairs, practice & sufferings of Friends in England; with wch they seemed greatly affected: When about the 11th hour a ratling of coach interrupted us. The Countess immediately stept out to see w^t was the matter; & returnd with a countenance somew^t uneasy; telling us, that the young Princes, nephews to the Princess, & the Grave of Donaw[197] were come to visit her. Upon which I told them, we should withdraw, & return to our Lodging; but entreated, that forasmuch as we were to depart that night with the postwaggon, we might not be disappointed of a farewell-meeting with them; & the rather, for that I had a great burden upon my Spirit. Which they readily complyed with, telling me, These persons would only dine, & be gone. As we went to the dore, the Countess stopt before us, & opend it for us: & as I past by, she lookd with a weighty Countenance upon me, & fetchd a deep sigh, crying out, O the Cumber & Entanglements of this {vain} world! they hinder all good. Upon which I replyed, looking her stedfastly in the face; O Come thou out of them then—.

After we had dined at our Lodging, something being upon me to write to the Professors of that Countrey, I went up to my Chamber, that I might be the more retired. Just as I was about the conclusion of the paper, cometh the Steward of the house to the princess with this message, That the Princess entreated us to come to her, for the Graffe of Donaw had a great desire to see us & speak with us. This brought a fresh weight & Exercise upon us: but committing all to the Lord, & casting our care upon him, we went.

Being arrived, the Graffe approacheth us in french; at first took no great notice of our inceremonious behaviour:[198] But proceeded to enquire of us our success in our Journey, & w^t we found answering our Journey & inclinations. Then we fell to points of religion, & the nature & end of true Christianity; & w^t was that way that leadeth to the eternal rest. After some short debate about compleat sanctification in this life we both agreed, That Self-denyal, mortification & Victory was the duty, & ought to be the endeavour of every sincere Christian. From this I fell to give him some Accompt of my retreat from the world; & the inducements I had thereto; & the necessity of an Inward work: with which he seem'd much pleased. After this he fell to the hat etc. this choaketh; & the rather, because it telleth tales; it telleth w^t people are; it marketh men for Separatists. It's blowing a trumpet, & visibly crossing the world: & that the fear of man (greatly prevalent with too many serious people in that land) can not abide, starteth at, & runneth away from. Howbeit, the Lord enabled me to open the thing to him, as that it was no plant of gods planting; but a weed of degeneracy & Apostacy; a carnal & earthly honour; the effect & feeder & pleaser of pride & of a vain mind: that no advantage redounded to mankind by it. And how could they, that ought to do all to the glory of god, use that vain & unprofitable Custome; which cannot be done to the glory of god. I entreated him seriously to consider with himself the rise & end of it; whence it came? & wt it pleased? & wt that was, that was angry, that it had it not. I also told him of that sincere & serviceable respect, which truth substituteth in place thereof: & exhorted him to simplicity & poverty of spirit; to be like that Jesus, he profest to be his saviour, whose outside as well as doctrine pleased not the Jews. And so we parted: he took his leave of the Princess & then of us with great Civility.

After he was gone, the princess desired us to withdraw to her bedchamber; & there we began our Farewell meeting. The thing lay weightily upon me, & that in the deep dread of the Lord: & eternally magnifyed be {the name of} the Lord, that overshadow'd us with his glory. His heavenly, breaking, dissolving power richly flowed among us, & his ministring Angel of life was in the midst of us. Let my soul never forget the divine sence that overwhelm'd them all at that blessed fare-well I took of them. Much opend in me; of the hour of Christs temptation; his watchfulnes, perseverance & victory; about the ten virgins; wt the true virgin was, the true oil & lamp; wt that bridegrom, his dore, chamber, & supper. And in conclusion that torrent of heavenly melting love; that we were all deeply affected.[199] I fell on my knees, recommended to the Lord, cryed with strong cryes for their preservation; beseechd the Lords presence with us, & so ended.

After some pause I went to the princess, & took her by the hand; which she received & embrac'd~~d~~ with great signes of a weighty kindness, being much broken. I spoke a few words apart to her; & left the blessings & peace of Jesus with & upon her. Then I went to the Countess, & left a particular exhortation with her; who fervently beseechd me to remember, & to implore the Lord on her behalf. From her I went to the French woman, & bid her, be faithful & constant to that which she knew: she was exceedingly broken; & took an affectionate & reverent leave of us. Then I spoke to the rest, & took leave severally of them: my companions did all the like. They followed us to the outwd room: & there it was upon me to step to the Countess, & once more to speak to her, & take my leave of her: Which she rec'd & return'd with great sense, humility & love. So turning to them all, my heart & eye to the Lord, I prayed, that the fear, presence, love & life of god with all heavenly blessings might descend & rest with & upon them, then & forever.

Hence we went to our Lodging; supp'd, clear'd the house, exhorted the family, left books: & then took waggon for Wesel, about 200 English miles from Herwerden.

{III. 25 7m [25 September]} {IV. 26 7m. [26 September]} We rid 3 nights & days without lying down on a bed, or sleeping, otherways then in the waggon; which was only cover'd with an old ragged sheet. The company we had, with us made 12 in number, which much streigthened us. They were often, if not always vain, yea, in their religious songs; which is the fashon of that countrey, especially by night: they call them Luthers songs; & sometimes Psalmes.[200] We were forc'd often to reprove & to testify ag[t] their hypocrisy; to be full of all vain & often profain talk one hour, & sing Psalmes to god the next: We show'd them the deceit & abomination of that.

{Lipstadt. Ham. etc.}

We passed through several great towns by the way, as Lipstadt,[201] Ham[202] etc. many discourses we had of truth & the Christian Religion & Worship; & all was very well: they bore, w[t] we sayd.

But one thing was remarkable, that may not be omitted. I had not been 6 hours in the waggon, before an heavy weight & unusual oppression fell upon me, yea, it weigh'd me almost to the Grave; that I could almost say, my soul was sad, even unto death. I knew not at present the ground of this exercise: It remain'd about 24 hours upon me. Then it open'd to me, that it was a travail for the seed, that it might arise over all in them I had left behind; & that nothing might be lost, but the son of perdition. o the strong Crys, the deep Agonys, many tears, & sincere bowings & humblings of soul before the Lord! that his holy sense, which was rais'd in them, might be preserv'd alive in them, & they forever in it! That they might grow, & {spread as} heavenly plants of righteousnes to the glory of the name of the Lord.[203]

(These following is taken out of a letter
from Amsterdam. {To the Countess of Horn.})

{Wesel.} {V. 27 7m. [27 September]}

The Lord brought us well to Wesel on the fifth day, after we left Herwerden, having some service by the way. At Wesel we had a good time with Doct. Shuler, & Rosendael, & the woman,[204] we mentioned to thee. But the Taylor was shy & fearful of coming to us at the Doctors.

{Duysbergh} {VI. 28 7m. [28 September]}

The next day we went towards Duysbergh,[205] We visited the Schult[206] {or cheif governour} that night, whom we found at home: he rec'd us with much Kindnes. His wife & sister, we fear, have been shaken in their good belief of our testimony, since we were last there: some fowls of the aire have devoured the seed that was sown. O that sweet & tender frame, in which we left them the time before! However, the entrance we had upon the Spirit of the Schult, a little consolated us. Hence we sent ~~a~~ Maria Martha's Friend[207] a letter, desiring him, to let us have his answer the next night at Dusseldorp inclos'd to Neander, when & where we might see him, either at Dusseldorf, Mulheim, or Duysbergh; & if it were possible, we would gladly visit the Countess of Bruch.

{Dusseldorp.} {VII. 29 7m. [29 September]}

We got early to Dussledorp next day, being the last day of the week: Neander was gone to Mulheim in order to preach on the morrow; so that we were disappointed of our Intelligence.[208]

{Ceulon.} {I. 30 7m. [30 September]}

Next morning we went towards Ceulon,[209] & there arrived that evening.

{Van den Enden} {II. 1 8m. [1 October]}

The next day we had a good oportunity wth *van Dunando,* & Docemius,[210] at the house of the latter; & that afternoon took boat for Dusseldorp.

{Dusseldorp} {III. 2 8m. [2 October]}

Where arriving next morning, we presently sent for Neander; who came to us, & 3 more in company. We had a blessed meeting with them: & one of the three, that came wth him, our souls were exceedingly affected with.

The meeting done, they went away; but Neander returned. And first of our letter to Mulheim; we found by him (as also at our return to Duysbergh) that Kuper was so far from endeavouring our Visit to the Countess, that he would not meet us himself, neither at Dusseldorp, Mulheim, nor Duysbergh. Nay, it did not please him to send us an Answer, much less any the least salutation. I confess, it griev'd us; ~~but from hence my Fr. Friend may learn a profitable lesson, at best to rest where she is.~~

Now for Neander, the young man hath a zeal for god, & there is a visitation upon him; my soul desireth, that it may not be ineffectual. But I have a great fear upon me; for this I know certainly from the Lord god, that liveth forever, & I have a cloud of witnesses to my brethren, That retiremt & silence before god is the alone way for him to feel the heavenly gift to rise, & come forth pure & unmixt. This only can preach for god, pray to god, & beget people to god, & nothing else. But alas! his office in that family is quite another thing: namely: to perform set dutys at fixt times; pray, preach & sing, & that in the way of the worlds appointmts. His very office is Babilonish, namely, a Chaplin; for 'tis a Popish Invention. In the good old times godly Abraham, that was a Prince, & Joshua a great General, & David a King, with many more, instructed their familys in the fear & knowledge of god; but now people are too idle, or too great to pray for themselves: & so they worship god by Proxy. How can a minister of the Gospel be at the beck of any mortal living; or give up his soul & conscience to the time & appointmt of another? the thing in itself is utterly wrong, & agt the very nature & worship of the new & everlasting Covenant. You had better meet to read the Scriptures, the book of Martyrs[211] etc. if you cannot sit & wait in silence upon the Lord, till his Angel move upon your hearts, then to uphold such a formal, limited, & cerimonious worship: this is not the way out of

Babilon. And I have a deep sense upon my soul, that if the young man strive beyond the talent god hath given him, to answer his office, & fill up his place, & wait not for the pure & living word of god in his heart to open his mouth; but either studyeth for his sermons, or speaketh his own words, he will be utterly ruin'd. Wherefore ô Dear friend, have a care that you be no snare to him, nor he to you: mans works smother & stifle the {true} life of Christ. What have you to do, but to look to Jesus, the Author of the holy desires, that are in you; who himself hath visited you. Tempt not the lord, provoke not god. What should any man preach from, but Christ? & w^{t} should he preach people to, but X^{t} in them, the hope of glory? Consider, nothing feedeth that which is born of god, but that which cometh down from god, even the bread of god, wch is the son of god; who giveth his life for the world: feel it, & feed on it. Let none moch god, nor grieve his eternal spirit, that is come to seal them up from the mouth of man, that hath deceived them; that Jesus the anointing may teach them, & abide with them forever. Be stedfast & immoveable, & this will draw the young man nearer to the Lord, & empty him of self, & purge away mixtures: And then you will all come to the divine silence. And when all flesh is silent before the Lord, then is it the Lords time to speak: & if you will hear, your souls shall live. O my soul is in great pain, that you may be all chastly preserved in that divine sense begotten in your hearts by the eternal word of god, that abideth forever; that nothing may ever be able to extinguish it. But more especially, that thou my Dear Friend, mayst be kept in faithfulnes: for the Lord is come very near to thee, & thou must begin the work; the Lord god expecteth it at thy hand: if one sheep break through, the rest will follow. Wherefore watch, ô watch, that thou mayst be strenghtned & confirmed, & strenghten all, that is begotten of god in that family by thy weighty, savory & circumspect life. O how is my soul affected with thy present condition! it is the fervent supplication of my heart, that thou mayst through the daily obedience of the Cross of Jesus conquer, & shine, as a bright & glorious star in the firmament of gods eternal Kingdom. So let it be, Lord Jesus! Amen.

We tenderly, yet freely spoke our hearts to him, before we parted. Which done, in gods love we took our leave of him and Dusseldorp; & got that night to Duysbergh, being the 3^{d} day of the week.
{Duysbergh}

We first visited Doctor Mastricht, a man of a good natural temper, but a rigid Calvinist. I perceived by him, that they held a Consultation about seing us at Bruch; but they all concluded, it was best to decline meeting with us, because of the Graffe; he being ready to fling our name in reproach upon them in his displeasure. And this would confirm him in his Jealousys of them.

This might excuse the Countess; but by no means K~~oo~~{u}per:

and if I had any sence, Mastricht was there with them upon designe to frustrate the hopes we had conceived of meeting with her. We from that descended to other things of weight; & in love & peace parted.

From his house we return'd to our Inn; & after supper we visited the Schult, who wth much civility & some tendernes rec'd us. His sister also came to us, & we had a good little meeting with them; & our god was wth us, & his pure tender life appeared for our justification, & pleaded our innocent cause in their consciences. And so we parted with them, Leaving our masters peace among them.

{Wesel.} {IV. 3 8m. [3 October]}

The next day we came to Wesel, being the 4th day: Where we understood by Doctor Schuler, that thy sister desired we would be so kind, as to see her, when we returned. Upon that we went, & visited her; she rec'd us very kindly. Thy brother-in-laws & two sisters were present; we stay'd with them at least two hours. Many questions she put to me & which I was glad to have an oportunity to answer; for it made way for a meeting. She intreated us to come again, if we stay'd; & told us, our visit was very grateful to her: adding, that because we past her by the last time, she concluded with herself, we had no hopes of her: with more to that effect.

From thence we went to Doct[r] Schulers, who freely offered us his house for a meeting next day: & indeed the man is bold after his manner.

{[V. 4] 8m. [4 October]}

The next day about 7. I writ a Billiet {in french} to thy sister,[212] to inform {her} of the meeting to begin about 8. She came, & her two sisters with her; there was Rosendale Co[ll] Copius & his wife, & about 3 or 4 more. And to our great Joy the Lord god Allmighty was with us, & his holy power reached their hearts; & the Doc[t] & Copius soberly confess'd to our testimony.

The meeting lasted about 3 hours. Being ended, we took our leaves of them in the spirit of Jesus; & so returned to our Inn. The Taylor all this while afraid of coming to our Inn, or to the Doct[s] to the meeting. Great fears have overtaken him; the poor man liveth but in a dry land.

After Dinner we visited Copius & Rosendale: & at Copiuss we had a blessed broken meeting; he, his wife, Rosendale, his wife, & another woman, wife to one Doctor Willicks's brother,[213] present. They were extreamly affected & overcome by the power of the Lord: 'twas like one of our Herwerden meetings. Indeed, much tenderness was upon all their Spirits.

This done, & having left books both there, & with thy sister, we left Wesel with hearts ful of joy & peace: And let me say this, that more Kindnes & openess we have scarcely found in all our travails. O that this blessed sense may dwell with them! A seed there is in that place, god will gather; yea, a noble people he will find out: & I doubt not, but there will be a good meeting of Friends in that city, before many years go about. My love is great to that place. O how good is our dear Lord to us, who helpeth our Infirmitys, & carryeth through all opposition, & feedeth us with his divine presence, in which is life. His candle hath hitherto rested on our tabernacle, & he hath made us glad in his own salvation: eternal glory to his excellent name!

{Cleve.} {VI. 5 8m [5 October]}

We immediately took a post-carr, & came next day about 2 in the afternoon to Cleve, where we had a very pretious meeting at an honest procurators house, who rec'd us with much love. Four or five more were present, all grave & tender: our hearts were greatly affected with their love & simplicity.

We also visited the Lady Hubner {who was kind to us.} ~~by whom I had a letter informing me of the good news of being plundered of several of my cattle, upon the accompt of a certain meeting I was at just before my coming into this land; blessed be the name of the Lord.~~

{Nimmegen Utrecht} {VII. 6 8m [6 October]}

Next morning we set out for Nimmegen, & thence immediately to Utrecht, where we arrived that night; & took the night boat for Amsterdam; because of a pressure upon my spirit to be next day at the meeting: & the rather, having intimated as much from Ceulon.

{Amsterdam.} {I. 7 8m. [7 October]}

We arrived in the morning at Amsterdam, where we found our Dear Friends generally well; the city much allarmed, & great Curiosity in some, & desires in others to come to the meeting: we had a very great meeting, & many people of note resorted. Gods Gospelbell was rung; the great day of the great god sounded, & the dead was raised; & much tenderness appeared in several. O blessed be the name of the Lord, whose work & testimony prospereth.

{[II.] 8 8m. [8 October]}

The next day was spent in divers affaires relating to the truth:

{III. 9. 8m. [9 October]}

And the Day following we had a meeting wth Galenus Abrahams (the Great Father of the Socinian-Mennists in these parts) accompanyed with several preachers, & others of his Congregation; divers of our Friends were also present. It continued about 5 hours: He affirmed in opposition to us, That there was no Christian Church, Ministry, or Commission Apostolical now in the World. But the Lord assisted us with his wisdom & strength to confound his Attempts.[214]

For Anna Maria De Hornes, stiled,
Countess of Horn.

[10 October 1677]

My Dear Friend,

O that thou mayst forever dwell in the sweet & tender sense of that divine love & life, which hath visited thy soul, affected & overcome thy heart! O tell me, hath it not sometimes rais'd thy spirit above the world, & fill'd thee with fervent & passionate desires, yea, holy resolutions to follow Jesus, thy blessed Saviour: who hath given his most pretious blood for thee, that thou shouldst live not to thyself, but to him that hath so dearly purchas'd thee! O the retired, humble, reverent frame, that I have beheld thee in, when this blessed life hath drawn thee into itself, & adorn'd & season'd thee with its own heavenly virtue; beautifying thy very Countenance beyond all the vain & foolish ornaments of the wanton daughters of Sodom & Egypt (for therein are charms not known to the children of this world.)

O that this holy & chaste life may be always pretious with thee! & that thou mayst be forever chastely kept in the love & fellowship of it; that out of this Worlds nature, sp^{t} & practice thou mayst be redeemed by him, who is the way, the truth & the life: who, as then watchest with holy vigilance, will not only daily manifest the devices of the Enemy to thee; but save thee from him. For X^{ts} work in thee is thy Sanctification, as it is in him his Fathers will; as he sayd of old to his disciples, This is the will of god, even your sanctification.[215]

O my dearly beloved Friend, be stedfast, immoveable without wavering & work out thy great Salvation with fear & trembling.[216] And lose not that sweet & pretious sense, that the Lord hath begotten in thee; it's soon lost, at best weakned: but hard to recover.
—Wherefore let not the spirit of the world in any of Its appearances, vain company, unnecessary discourse, or wordly affairs prevail upon the civility of thy nature; for they will oppress the innocent life, & bring grievous weights & burthens upon thy soul, & prolong the coming of the Lord, whom thou lookest for; & putt the day of thy redemption afar off. O beware of this complaisance! Let me put thee in mind of that sensible resolution so frequently & so passionately repeated, *il faut que Je rompe, il faut que je rompe.*[217] Ah! this speaketh a weight; this weight a sense; & this sense a strong conviction. Now, be assured, that till obedience be yeilded to that present manifestation & conviction, the good things desired & thirsted after can never be enjoy'd.

Wherefore my Dear Friend, be faithful, & watch ag^{t} the workings of the spirit of this world in thyself; that the nature & Image of it in all things may be crucifyed: that thou mayst know an entire translation with holy Enoch, & walk with god.[218] Jesus the holy light is this cross, the power of god, that killeth & maketh alive: & he is the heavenly vine too; if thou abidest in him, thou wilt bring forth fruit. But if thou abidest not in him, thou wilt not bring forth that fruit in which his heavenly Father only can be glorifyed.[219]

O see w^{t} thy mind daily abideth in!—
— O my soul is even ravisht with the sense of that holy & quiet habitation! In me, saith he, you shall have peace; but in the world

trouble: however be of good chear, I have overcome the world. I am not of the world: as if he had sayd; I am not of the worlds ways, worships, customes, nor fashons. For w^{t}ever is of the nature & spirit of this world, hath no part in me: & as I am not of the world, neither are you of this world; for I have chosen you out of the world, out of the~~ir~~ Inventions, out of the~~ir~~ Worships & fashons {of the world.} You are to leave them all, to come out of them all, & live & walk as pilgrims in the world; that is, strangers to what? to the life & practice of the world, not using but renouncing the vain customes & ceremonys, yea, the whole conversation of the world: remembring, That the Friendship of this world is enmity with god. And w^{t}, if the world hateth you; it hated me first: & the disciple is not greater then his master, nor the servant, then his Lord. If you were of the world, the world would love you, & not reproach & persecute you: for the world loveth its own.[220]

—O my dear Friend, mayst thou be perfectly sensible, w^{t} it is; not to be of this world!

But there is yet a farther ~~a~~ mystery in these words, not discern'd even of many, in whom some tenderness & enquiry is begotten, much less of the wordly Christians. This world hath a false [illegible deletion] earth, & a false heaven; a false foundation, & a false joy; not only gross wickedness, but iniquity in a mystery, inwardly & outwardly. The whore, false prophet, & dragon, & all their offspring are here concern'd: this is their world, that must be burnt with fire; that X^{t} is not of, nor his true disciples.[221] O the light of Jesus discovereth it; & he is that spiritual salomon, that giveth true Judgment, & that saveth the living child, the true birth, giving it to the right Mother, & not to the false pretender.[222] And all that ~~hear~~ hear his voice & follow him, shall receive true sight, discerning & Judgm^{t}, to whom all Judgm^{t} is given: they shall know his voice from mans.

There are two trees of differing natures; that have contrary fruits & leaves. The one is the tree of life, that is X^{t}; the other the tree of death, & that is Satan. The fruit of the one giveth life; the fruit of the other bringeth death.[223] The leaves of the first heal; the leavs of the last poysen. Many that discern the tree, cannot clearly distinguish the branches: & those that see many Arms & branches, cannot distinctly behold the fruit; & much less the leaves. This cometh by the gradual discoverys & revelations of the light of Jesus, the word of god, as it is daily rec'd, & daily obey'd. Yea, & that word is the ax & sword of the Allmighty to cut it down: daily feel the strokes of this eternal searching light & word at the very root of this corrupt tree, this evil one, & his corrupt nature, works~~eth~~ & effects~~eth~~. For which end Jesus Christ is come; & therefore is called a saviour: which is little known in truth to the Christians of this world.

Ah my dear Friend, thou knowest this word; yea, thou hast felt it: o! hide it in thy heart; treasure it up in thy soul; & love it, & abide with it forever. Alas! whither shouldst thou go? this hath, & is, the word of eternal life. Daily therefore watch & wait, that thou mayst be grafted more & more into it; that thou mayst live & grow by the virtue & life of it; & that it may grow in thy heart, as it grew among the first Christians, the holy followers of the persecuted Jesus. And when it searcheth thy wound, & cutteth away thy dead flesh; yea when it separateth between the soul & the spirit of this world, & divideth between joynts & marrow;[224] when it cutteth off the right hand, & plucketh out the right eye; O watch unto prayer, & pray, that thou mayst endure. O Keep the holy patience of this pure & living word; & this very word will keep thee in the hour of thy sharpest tryals, & sorest tribulations. O all virtue is in it! O [illegible deletion] 'tis a tryed word, a sure refuge; the staff & strength of the righteous in all ages. 'Twas Davids Teacher & Buckler; a light to his feet, & a Lanthorn to his paths: walk thou in the light thereof, & thou shalt not stumble. In this word is life, as in the root; & this life is the light of men: they that receive & love the light of it, will therein receive {~~that~~} divine life from it to live to god. This is the bread of god, that cometh from god; & feedeth & leadeth up to god: By this only, that which is born of god, liveth, & is nourished. This is that Carcass, to which the wise Eagles gather: see, thou gatherest to no other, nor feedest on no other: This is that hidden manna, that cometh from heaven; that feedeth gods Israel.[225] The world hath a manna, but it perisheth: but this endureth forever. For it is not of man, nor from man, but immortal, & from god; hid from the knowledge of all the vain Christians in the world. So that the Israel of god can say to the children of this world, & that in truth & righteousness, We have a bread you know not of. For this manna wait daily, that thou mayst be strengthned in thy Wilderness=Travail to the Land of Eternal Rest.

Wherefore labour not for the bread that perisheth, that is, the bread of mans inventing & making, which cometh from below, & profiteth not; because it giveth not life Eternal. But labour thou my dear Friend, for the bread that never perisheth; that endureth forever: O! that giveth eternal life to all that feed upon it. O cast thy care upon this word, love it, & dwell with it; wait daily upon it. Hear its voice only, & follow it; for it bringeth the soul to the eternal habitation of rest & glory. Yea, when all flesh shall wither, & the beauty thereof fade away; this word, & they that are grafted into it, shall abide forever. O that this may be thy choice! & it shall be thy ~~diadem~~ diadem, & thy eternal Crown & glory.

These are the fervent desires, & these the daily prayers of my soul to the god of my salvation for thee, not only, that nothing [illegible deletion] in thee may be lost, besides the son of perdition; but that thou mayst cast off every weight & burden, & that sin, that doth so easily beset thee, that grieveth, boweth, & oppresseth thee; under the heavy weight~~ed~~ of which, thou groanest & sighest, that the redeemer would come from Zion to deliver thee. O give not heed to the enemy, the false Accuser; that seeketh to devour that, which is begotten of god in thee. Neither look upon thy own sin, Burdens, or Weaknes; but lift up thy head, & look to Jesus, the Author of thy blessed visitation, & holy hunger & thirst after him the Spiritual Brazen Serpent, that healeth & relieveth all, that in faith & full assurance look to him. Want of looking to him, hearing & obeying him, & having true faith in him, is the cause both of all the presumption & despair, that ~~is~~ {are} at this day: he did no mighty things of old in those places, where they believed not.

O faint not; look not back. Remember the holy Antients, the holy Pilgrims of Faith, the Royal Generation of Heaven, Hebr. 11. Thou believest in god; believe also in him for the works sake, that he hath already wrought in thee: he will minister to thee, as he was ministred unto by his Fathers Angel in the hour of his abasement, & great temptation.[226] O Watch, & be faithful; & thou shalt be a Noble Witness for the Lord.

Once more let me expostulate with thee. Wouldst thou overcome the Enemys of thy Souls peace, & enjoy the delightful presence of the Lord with thee; then keep nothing back: let nothing be withheld, that he calleth for. Remember, that Saul of old lost his Kingdom for keeping that alive, which he should have slain: Thou knowest, w[t] befel Ananias & Saphira outwardly.[227] But be thou like the poor widdow of old, that therefore gave more into the treasury, then all the rest, because they reserv'd the greatest part to themselves; but she gave all she had.[228] O blessed are they, that make no bargains for themselves, that have no reserves for self, neither consult with flesh & blood, nor in any sense conform to the least Cerimony, which is born of them; but that submit their wills in all things to the Lords; that they may be made perfect throug sufferings, as X[t] was.

Read me in the mystery of life. I speak not of deserting or flinging away all outward substance: but that thy heart may reign above all visibles, & make god its treasure: & never rest~~ing~~ in anything of this lower world, or short of Christ, the eternal rest of all the seed of faith.

[The Lord brought us well to Wesel etc. as in the ~~journal~~ narrative from the 27 7m to the 10 8m.][229] {this followed w[t] is their mention'd in the letter to the Countess.}

I intend a visit to the Hague, to the La[dy] overkirk, Sister of the Somerdikes,[230] & some others, that have sober characters of truth & Friends. And thence to Rotterdam, where I have much to do, both with respect to meetings, & the press: G[eorge] F[ox]. & B[enjamin] F[urly]. goe with me.

Thus, my Dear Friend, have I given thee a tedious Narrative, yet I hope, not altogether unpleasant: perhaps the brevity of my letters hereafter may best Apologize for the Length of this. However, I consider two things; one is, that thou hast time enough, one time or other to look over it: & next, that I have plentifully {answeard thy request and} demonstrated, I have not forgotten the. O Dear Friend, let us live, & remember one another now absent, in that divine sense, in which the Lord God dissolv'd our spirits, when together. O the Unity of this faith! the purity of this love, & the bond of this peace! The Lord Jesus be with thy Sp^t^ & keep thee in this the hour of thy temptations; that thou mayst come forth as gold 7 times tryed, so shall thy testimony shine for the god, that hath called thee: & he will reward thee with honour, glory & eternal life. Amen.

Thus saith the Lord, I remember thee, the Kindnes of thy youth, the love of thine espousals; when thou wentest after me in the Wilderness, in a land that was not sown. Jerem. 2, 2. Dear Friend, consider this. Yet again: The way of the just is uprightnes: thou most upright, dost weigh the path of the just.

Yea, in the way of thy Judgm^ts^ O Lord, have we waited for thee, the desire of our Soul is to thy name, & to the remembrance of thee.

With my soul have I desired thee in the night: yea, with my sp^t^ within me will I seek thee early: for when thy Judgm^ts^ are in the earth, the Inhabitants of the world will learn righteousness.

Lord thou wilt ordain peace for us; for thou also hast wrought all our works in us.

O Lord our god, other Lords besides thee have had dominion over us; but by thee only will we make mention of thy name.

Lord, in trouble have they visited thee; they poured out a prayer, when thy chastning was upon them.

Like as a woman with child, that draweth near the time of her delivery, is in pain, & cryth out ~~of~~ {in} her pangs; so have we been in thy sight o Lord.

We have been with child, we have been in pain, we have as it were ~~brought~~ brought forth wind; we have not wrought any deliverance in the earth, or either have the Inhabitants of the world falln.

Thy dead men shall live, together with my dead body shall they arise: awake, & sing ye that dwell in the dust; for thy dew is, as the dew of herbs: & the earth shall cast out the dead.

Come my people, enter thou into thy chambers, & shut thy dores about thee: hide thyself, as it were for a little moment, until the indignation be overpast.

For behold, the Lord cometh out of his place, to punish the inhabitants of the earth for their Iniquity; the earth also shall disclose her blood, & shall no more cover her slain. Isa. 26, 7, 8, 9, 12, 13, 16, 17, 18, 19, 20, 21.

So come, Dear Lord Jesus, that was dead, but is alive, & liveth forever, Amen.

Very dearly farewell.
Thy Friend, that
Faithfully travaileth
for thy redemption.
WP.

Amsterdam,
the 10th 8 mo.
1677.

{[III.] 9 8m. [9 October]}[231]

The next day (wch is this day) we had a blessed publique meeting never to be forgotten: O the majesty, glory & life, that the Lord attended us with! our hearts were deeply affected wth his presence. Tomorrow we have another meeting with Galenus & his Company; for they are the most Virulent & obstinate Opposers of truth in this Land.

(Thus much out of {a} letter from Amsterdam, dated the 10—8mo.—followeth part of a letter from the Briell, dated the 20—8mo. 1677. viz:)

{[IV.] 10 [8m. 10 October]}

Since my last we had a blessed meeting at Amsterdam; being the next day after the date of my last; great reverence & brokenness were over the meeting, more then I had seen. The meeting ended; we were opposed by a preacher, who was closely pursued by several merchants etc. (not of us) that cryed out, he was rude & ignorant: & offerd to dispute in our defense. But the Priest run away: they followed him, till they hous'd him.

{[V.] 11 [8m. 11 October]}

Next day we had a meeting with Galenus; the success thou mayst perhaps see suddainly in print; & therefore I may differ the narrative: only in general, our dear Lord, our staff & strength was with us, & truth reigned over all.

{Leyden}

That night we went to Leyden, where we visited some.

{Hague} {VI. 12 8m. [12 October]}

Thence next day to the Hague; where also we had a little meeting. O the lust & pride of that place! thou camest into my mind, as I walked in the streets; & I sayd in myself: Well, she hath chosen the better part. O be faithful, & the Lord will give thee an eternal recompence.

{Rotterdam.}

Thence we came to Rotterdam, where the Lord hath given us several heavenly oportunitys in private & publique.

{Briel}

We are now come to the Briell, & wait our passage. The Lord Jesus be with you that stay, & with us that go; that in him we may live & abide forever. etc. God Allmighty overshadow thee, hide thee under his pavilion, be thy Shield, Rock, & Sanctuary forever;[232] farewell, farewell!

Thy Friend & the Lords
servant.

Briel, 20—8mo.
1677.

WP.[233]

{IV. 10 8m [10 October]}[234]

The {same} ~~next~~ day we had a blessed publique meeting never to be forgotten: O the majesty, glory & life, that the Lord attended us with! our hearts were deeply affected with his presence. Great reverence & brokenness was over the meeting, more then I had seen. The meeting ended, we were opposed by a preacher; who was closely encounter'd & pursued by several merchants etc. (not of us) that cryed out, he was rude & ignorant; & that they had a testimony for us: who offered to dispute in our defence. But the priest run away; they followed him, till they hous'd him. etc

It was upon me this {day} ~~afternoon~~ to engage Galenus Abrahams to a 2d conference, that we might more fully & clearly debate & confute his grand objection agt the present dispensation of truth, & the heavenly Ministry witnessed among Friends. ~~Which he yeilded to Th time fix'd was the 5th day in the morning about 8. being the 11th of the month,~~ He refused not my offer of a 2d meeting, but send me word; his business would not give him leave to let it be anytime this day. Upon wch the next morning was fix'd for the Conference, to begin at 8. which

{V. 11 8m. [11 October]}

accordingly it did; & held till One. The most impartial acct of both these conferences, that I am briefly able to give, followeth.

A Brief Relation of the most Substantial passages in two Conferences held at Amsterdam, between Galenus Abrahams, & William Penn, in the presence of a ~~large &~~ free {& large} Auditory[235]

Copy. Penn MSS, HSP (*Micro.* 2:446). This copy is primarily in the hand of one clerk, Mark Swanner, with corrections by another.

1. At Walthamstow.

2. Colchester is also in Essex, about forty-five miles northeast of Walthamstow.

3. George Watts (d. 1688) was a London Friend who lived in Aldersgate. He was presumably fairly well-to-do, since he had a country house in Enfield. He returned to Holland in 1684, and entertained Dutch Quakers in England.

4. John Furly (1618-1686) the second, Colchester's leading merchant in the 1660s. The Furlys, prominent linen-drapers, had become Quakers in the 1650s and suffered

frequently from persecution. This John Furly was the elder brother of Benjamin Furly of Rotterdam.

5. Probably John Furly (1644-1693?) the third, son of John Furly (see n. 4, above). Also a Colchester Quaker, he went to Holland in 1669 and would go again in 1693.

6. William Talcot (c. 1622-1697) was another wealthy Colchester merchant, a close friend of John Furly the second, and father-in-law to John Furly the third.

7. George Weatherley (1624-1686), a maltster, and a Friend by 1660, when he was imprisoned for refusing to take the oath of allegiance. He was also acquainted with Friends in Holland.

8. George Fox. In subsequent entries of initials only, names will be completed in brackets.

9. John Vandewall (1646-1707), of Harwich, Quaker merchant and baker of Dutch ancestry. The Vandewalls were intermarried with the Furlys.

10. Giles Barnardiston (c. 1624-1680) spent six years studying for the ministry, joined the army, and in 1661 was converted to Quakerism by George Weatherley. He accompanied John Furly the third on a missionary trip to Holland in 1669.

11. Robert Duncon, a tanner, and a Friend since 1654.

12. Samuel and Job Bolton. Job was a Friend by 1670, when he was tried for attending the meeting that led to the Penn-Mead trial. He was fined 20 marks. In 1674 and 1678 Job was distrained of goods in lieu of tithes, as was Samuel in 1677. Both were prosecuted in ecclesiastical courts in 1686. Besse, 1:426-28, 438-39, 482.

13. George Keith.

14. Robert Barclay.

15. Isabel Fell Yeamans.

16. Elizabeth Johnston Keith, a Scotswoman who married George Keith in 1672. Her father was a professor at the University of Aberdeen.

17. Briel, or the Brill, a Dutch seaport fourteen miles west of Rotterdam.

18. Arent (Aaron) Sonnemans (d. 1683), a Rotterdam merchant and Quaker. He and Benjamin Furly translated and published WP's works in Dutch and French. WP stayed with Sonnemans in Rotterdam. Sonnemans later became a proprietor of East New Jersey. A close friend of Robert Barclay, he moved to Scotland and was killed there by a highwayman.

19. Benjamin Furly (1636-1714), a leader among Dutch Quakers, was born in Colchester, convinced in 1655, and settled in Rotterdam about 1658. He became a prominent merchant and an active scholar and translated a number of WP's tracts into Dutch. During this visit of the leading English Quakers, Furly frequently acted as interpreter. He was also interested in English politics and corresponded with many prominent Whigs; WP consulted with him on the frame of government for Pennsylvania.

20. Sijmon Jans Vettekeuken (died c. 1679), a prominent Friend of Rotterdam. In 1675, when the Dutch Quakers published an appeal from WP against persecution in Emden (see *Works* 1:609-11), there was mob violence against the Friends in Rotterdam, and Vettekeuken joined Furly in appealing to the Dutch government for protection. Vettekeuken's widow left a considerable sum to Rotterdam Friends for a meeting house.

21. Leiden, a major city in south Holland, and a university town. About twenty miles southwest of Amsterdam.

22. Haarlem, a town in north Holland, about twelve miles west of Amsterdam.

23. Jan Roelofs van der Werf may have been the son of a Mennonite from Hamburg. He was an early convert to Quakerism (1659) and a prominent controversialist. He visited England in 1686.

24. Jacob Arents, a Quaker of Oudesluis, a village near Alkmaar.

25. Jan Claus, an Amsterdam merchant, was converted to Quakerism in England, where he was sentenced to transportation to Jamaica for seven years in 1664. He survived this punishment, returned to Holland, and became a leading figure in Dutch Quakerism. He was WP's guide, companion, and translator on this journey.

26. Alkmaar, a town in north Holland, about twenty miles northeast of Amsterdam.

27. Emden, a town on the North Sea in East Friesland in Germany, near the Dutch border, was a free city in the seventeenth century. It was located about 100 miles northeast of Amsterdam.

28. Gertrude Diricks (or Deriks) van Losevelt Crisp (d. 1687), was an early Quaker convert and one of the Quaker leaders in Amsterdam in the 1670s. Her house became the principal meeting house, and was so used for more than one hundred years. She went to England at the end of this tour, returned to the Rhine in 1678, and in 1685 married the English Quaker Stephen Crisp.

29. The clerk used the continental New Style of dating. By the English Old Style calendar, this meeting was held on 2 Aug.

30. The Palatinate incorporated the scattered territorial holdings of the Palatine elector, Carl Ludwig (1633-1680). Quakers were no doubt attracted to the Palatinate because of its longstanding Protestant tradition, the presence of Pietists, and a degree of toleration.

31. Hamburg, a Hanseatic city in northern Germany, had accepted the Reformation in 1521-1529.

32. Lübeck, another German Hanseatic city, on the Baltic Sea, northeast of Hamburg.

33. Friedrichstadt, a port in Schleswig founded by Dutch emigrants in 1621, is on the North Sea, about seventy miles northwest of Hamburg.

34. West Friesland was a Dutch province, fifty miles northeast of Amsterdam; East Friesland was a German province on the Dutch border.

35. Harlingen, a small port in West Friesland, on the Wadden Zee.

36. Wuterland, a low-lying region just north of Amsterdam.

37. This is the same system of church government and discipline that Fox had instituted in England in the late 1660s. The following resolutions concerning marriage, Friends' publications, and finances were also in accord with English practice.

38. Directions here in the manuscript text read "(turn over 8 pages. For 'tis etc.)" Actually, one turns over fourteen pages to find the continuation of the record of this meeting. The text here moves from fol. 9 to fol. 19, but also moves across ten inserted sheets which are (in a later hand) given separate sets of numbers.

39. Directions in the text at this point read "(turn about)," but the continuation in the original is simply on the overleaf.

40. Directions here read "(See back again 9 pages: And etc.)." This line, therefore, comes from fol. 20, the following one from fol. 9.

41. Danzig is a major port on the Baltic Sea, over 600 miles east of Amsterdam. This was probably the eastern extremity of Quaker activity in the seventeenth century.

42. John III Sobieski (1624-1696). He was elected king of Poland in 1674.

43. This insertion is written in the margin in the manuscript, on fol. 10. It is clearly intended that the letter to the king of Poland should follow. The *B*s are given as guide marks in the original, and direct the reader to the letters which are located on fols. 11A - 18A.

44. WP's reference here is puzzling. 1 John 5:7 is more appropriate.

45. The correct citation is 2 Tim. 3:15-16.

46. Rom. 6:23.

47. John 18:10-11.

48. Luke 9:54-56.

49. Matt. 13:25-30, 36-40.

50. E.g., Matt. 22:17, 21.

51. Stephen (István) Báthory (1533-1586), elected king of Poland in 1575.

52. Gamaliel was a prominent rabbi who counselled the Jews to tolerate St. Peter and the early Christians in Jerusalem. Cross, *Christian Church.*

53. Lucius Junius Gallio was the Roman proconsul of Achaia in Greece, c. 52, who refused the request of local Jewish leaders to stop St. Paul from preaching there. Acts 18:12-17; Cross, *Christian Church.*

54. Matt. 5:45.

55. In the manuscript, a letter to Anna Maria van Hoorn follows immediately after the letter to the king of Poland. This letter is dated 10 Oct. 1677, and carries a separate set of folio numbers (1B - 11B) written in a later hand. It has been moved by the editors to the appropriate point in the journal.

56. Seekers believed that there was no true church, and that God would found one in his own time. During the Commonwealth the term was used loosely to describe people dissatisfied with existing churches, and WP may have used it here in that sense.

57. Gen. 25, 27, 32-33.

58. Naarden, a small town in south Holland on the IJsselmeer (Zuider Zee), about fifteen miles east of Amsterdam.

59. Osnabrück, a town in northwest Germany, about 120 miles east of Amsterdam. The Peace of Westphalia (1648) was signed there.

60. That is, both Netherlandish and German.

61. Herford, in the Electorate of Brandenburg, in northwest Germany, about 150 miles east of Amsterdam. Princess Elizabeth's nunnery was on top of a hill, the town at its foot.

62. Elizabeth, Princess Palatine of the Rhine (1618-1680), whose parents were Frederick V, Elector of the Palatine, and Elizabeth, daughter of James I of England. At the age of sixteen she refused to marry the king of Poland because she could not accept his Roman Catholicism. She studied at Leiden with Descartes and became his lifelong friend and correspondent. In 1667, Princess Elizabeth became the head of the Abbey of Herford, and used her position to protect the Labadists, whom she invited to settle in Herford (see doc. 63). Elizabeth was sympathetic to Quakers and corresponded with WP until her death. As abbess, she had imperial status but no power. Herford at this time was in economic decline. See G. Benecke, *Society and Politics in Germany, 1500-1750* (London, 1974), pp. 105-8.

63. Anna Maria, Countess van Hoorn (also styled de Hornes), canoness of the abbey chapter at Herford. She was the lifelong companion of Princess Elizabeth and shared her sympathy for Quakers. She translated Isaac Penington's *The Way of Life and Death* (1658) into Dutch before 1661. Countess van Hoorn was present when Elizabeth interviewed Barclay in 1676 and WP in 1677; she later corresponded with both.

64. John de Labadie.

65. De Labadie's followers included Anna Maria van Schurman; Anna, Maria, and Lucia Sommelsdijk; and Luise Huyghens. The three Sommelsdijk sisters were the daughters of Cornelis van Aersens, Lord of Sommelsdijk, perhaps the richest man in the Netherlands. They inherited from their mother, Lucia van Waltha, the estate and castle of Thetinga, located in Wieuwerd in Dutch Friesland. The Labadist colony moved there in 1675. Luise Huyghens of Rijsbergen was another prominent Hollander converted by the Labadists.

66. See doc. 63. The two disciples were probably Pierre Yvon and Pierre DuLignon. Pierre Yvon apparently assumed leadership of the Labadists following the death of de Labadie in 1674; he married Maria van Sommelsdijk after the group abandoned its vow of celibacy at Herford. Pierre DuLignon married Magdalena van der Haar.

67. Countess van Hoorn.

68. Jer. 6:30.

69. Elizabeth Hendricks, an active Quaker preacher, missionary, and author. She was writing tracts as early as 1660 and was one of the chief leaders of Dutch Quakerism in the 1670s. She was married to Pieter Hendricks, a button maker, who was also a leading Quaker.

70. Heb. 4:12.

71. Ps. 137:5-6.

72. In the manuscript, the rest of this folio (20) is taken up with the completion of the entry from fol. 9 (see above, under 3 Aug. 1677). At this point in the text there is a notation, "(see the next page)." The next page, however, begins a letter to Johanna Eleanora von Merlau, which we have placed under its appropriate date, 11 Sept. 1677. This letter occupies four unnumbered sheets; following the letter, on fol. 21, the entry for 11 Aug. continues.

73. Bremen, a Hanseatic seaport on the Weser river, about 170 miles northeast of Amsterdam.

74. We have not identified the sister to Countess van Hoorn. The Frenchwoman of quality was Mlle. de Reneval, who later married Reiner Kuper (1645-1693), Elizabeth's court preacher from 1674 to 1677.

75. Duisburg, a city at the confluence of the Rhine and Ruhr rivers, about 110 miles southeast of Amsterdam. Its university was founded in 1655.

76. Frankfurt, a German commercial city on the Main river, about 240 miles southeast of Amsterdam.

77. Kassel, a town in the landgraviate of Hesse-Kassel, Germany, about 225 miles southeast of Amsterdam.

78. 1 Cor. 10:16.

79. Paderborn, a town in Germany, the seat of the bishop of Paderborn; about 190 miles east of Amsterdam, and about 28 miles from Herford.

80. John Durie (1596-1680), especially noted for his advocacy of the "union of all Evangelical churches." In behalf of this cause, he travelled throughout western Europe, making Kassel his headquarters from 1662 to 1680.

81. Acts 7:32. In the margin is a deleted comment on this paragraph: "These are taken out of a letter from the Palatinate."

82. Jacobus Vandewalle, a pottery merchant, became a member of the Frankfort Company and an important landowner in Pennsylvania. The Frankfort Company was a German-based group that received land grants from WP in Germantown. At most, two of its members immigrated to Pennsylvania. Stephanie Grauman Wolf, *Urban Village* (Princeton, 1976), pp. 12, 27; Naaman H. Keyser, et al., *History of Old Germantown* (Germantown, 1907), p. 28.

83. Johanna Eleanora von Merlau (1644-1724), who married Dr. Johann Wilhelm Peterson in 1680, and Juliane Bauer van Eysseneck. Both women belonged to the circle of the prominent Lutheran Pietist, Philipp Jakob Spener.

84. Probably Dr. Johann Wilhelm Peterson, who married Johanna Eleanora von Merlau. He later became a member of the Frankfort Company.

85. Worms, an imperial city on the Rhine river, and seat of the bishop of Worms; about 260 miles southeast of Amsterdam.

86. Kriegsheim, a town in the Palatine electorate, was an early center of the Protestant Reformation in the Rhineland; it is about 8 miles west of Worms and 260 miles southeast of Amsterdam. *Pfalzatlas* (Speyer, 1974), map no. 82.

87. "Pfalzgraf's country," i.e., territories of the Palatine elector.

88. Karl Ludwig (1633-1680), Elector of the Palatinate and brother of Princess Elizabeth.

89. In the left margin of the manuscript text is a deleted comment: "Thus far the letter from the Palatinate." In the right margin are two guide marks, indicating the insertion of WP's letter to the princess and countess.

90. 1 Cor. 13:2.

91. Luke 12:32.

92. Matt. 20:28.

93. Ps. 12:6; Mal. 4:2-3.

94. Jer. 6:30.

95. Isa. 40:7-8.

96. John 10:8.

97. Mannheim, a Palatine city at the confluence of the Neckar and Rhine rivers; about 270 miles southeast of Amsterdam.

98. Frankenthal, a small town in the Palatinate, on the way from Kriegsheim to Mannheim.

99. Heidelberg, in the Palatinate, a university town on the Neckar river, about 12 miles southeast of Mannheim and 280 miles southeast of Amsterdam.

100. Directions in the manuscript text at this point (fol. 28) are "(turn over 2 pages)." The next 4 folios are numbered 29A to 32A, and contain a letter to Princess Elizabeth and Countess van Hoorn. See above, under 24 Aug. 1677. They are followed by fol. 29, where the letter to the prince begins.

101. Luke 9:54-56.

102. Luke 11:17.

103. Duumvirate, or government by two men. *OED*.

104. State within a state.

105. The question refers to settlement opportunities for persecuted Quakers. The elector of the Palatinate had previously granted privileges to sectarian immigrants like the Mennonites in order to repopulate the Palatine territories after the devastation of the Thirty Years War. WP later reversed this process, drawing immigrants from the Palatinate to Pennsylvania.

106. Mennonites.

107. Dissuaded. *OED*.

108. Isa. 22:13.

109. The Rhine river.

110. William Ames (d. 1662) was the first Quaker missionary in Holland, Den-

mark, and Germany.

111. Mainz, city and seat of the archbishop of Mainz, at the confluence of the Main and Rhine rivers, about 235 miles southeast of Amsterdam.

112. The Main river.

113. Heimbach, on the Rhine river, about 220 miles southeast of Amsterdam.

114. Bacharach, on the Rhine river, about 12 miles from Heimbach and 215 miles southeast of Amsterdam.

115. Koblenz, a town in the archbishopric of Trier, at the confluence of the Moselle and Rhine rivers, about 25 miles from Bacharach and 195 miles southeast of Amsterdam.

116. Probably Breisig, on the Rhine, about 12 miles from Koblenz and 180 miles southeast of Amsterdam. The text is difficult to read, but "Treissig" is clear in the fair copy.

117. Cologne, a city on the Rhine, and seat of the archbishop of Cologne, about 40 miles from Breisig and 140 miles southeast of Amsterdam.

118. David van den Enden, a Cologne merchant.

119. *Messe*, the German word for "fair."

120. Friedrich Wilhelm, the Great Elector (reign: 1640-1688), creator of the Brandenburg-Prussian state.

121. Gerhard von Maastricht. He later became a member of the Frankfort Company, but did not settle in Pennsylvania.

122. Countess Charlotte Auguste von Dhaun-Falkenstein of the House of Broich, who was known for her piety and ridiculed as a Quaker. Princess Elizabeth knew of the countess (see Elizabeth's letter to WP dated 4 Sept. 1677, *Micro.* 2:540), and probably mentioned her to WP during his visit at Herford. WP attempted to visit the countess on his second circuit through Germany, but was again unsuccessful. See below, 28 Sept. 1677.

123. Either Reiner Copper (Kuper) (1645-1693), who was suspended as a Reformed minister in 1683 and joined a Labadist house; or Arnold Sibel, who preached in the Reformed church in Mülheim (1672-1687) and married Countess Charlotte Auguste von Dhaun-Falkenstein.

124. Mülheim, a town on the Ruhr river in the duchy of Cleve; about 6 miles east of Duisburg and 110 miles southeast of Amsterdam.

125. In the duchy of Cleve, a part of the Brandenberg territories.

126. Count Wilhelm Wirich von Dhaun-Falkenstein of Broich.

127. Heinrich Schmidt. Spelldorp was Château Heltorf, five miles from Duisburg, just outside Mülheim.

128. John 4:35.

129. Isa. 49:6.

130. Isa. 28:17.

131. Rev. 1:16.

132. Col. 3:9-10.

133. 1 Cor. 15:50.

134. Probably Johanna Eleanora von Merlau.

135. Cleve, in the duchy of Cleve, in the Brandenburg territories; close to the Dutch border, about seventy miles southeast of Amsterdam. William Ames had visited this town in 1661.

136. The directions in the manuscript here read "(over against: see ⊗ ⊗.)" In fact, the letter to the Graf, similarly marked, occupies the last two sheets of the volume, which are not paginated.

137. Law binding the world; German law; natural law; or Christian law.

138. An argument to the man, or to one man, that derives its strength from its personal application.

139. Gal. 6:7.

140. Acts 17:10f.

141. Matt. 5:44.

142. Directions in the manuscript text here (at the end of fol. 50) read "(turn over 2 pages)," but in fact fol. 51 follows immediately, and whatever once intervened has been removed.

143. Düsseldorf, on the Rhine, in the dukedom of Berg; about 240 miles southeast of Amsterdam.

144. Probably Joachim Neander (1650-1680), a Pietist and a great hymn writer, who became rector of the Latin School of the Reformed Church in Düsseldorf in 1674. He was increasingly influenced by the Labadists and lost his living in the spring of 1677. He was then appointed chaplain to the count of Dhaun-Falkenstein's court, and two years later became a pastor in Bremen. See also WP's reference on 2 Oct. 1677, below.

145. Mörs, northwest of Duisburg, about 100 miles southeast of Amsterdam.

146. Holten, a village in the duchy of Cleve, about six miles from Duisburg.

147. Wesel, a fortified town in the duchy of Cleve, at the confluence of the Lippe and Rhine rivers, about 15 miles from Duisburg and 100 miles southeast of Amsterdam.

148. See below, n. 213.

149. Rees, in German Geldern, on the Dutch border, about ninety miles southeast of Amsterdam.

150. Geldern.

151. Emmerich, a town on the Rhine in the duchy of Cleve, close to the Dutch border, about seventy-five miles southeast of Amsterdam.

152. Perhaps Lady Hubner, whom WP visited later on 5 Oct.

153. Nijmegen, a town in Geldern, Netherlands.

154. Utrecht, an ancient cathedral and university town, twenty miles southeast of Amsterdam.

155. John Hill was an English Friend in Holland on a missionary journey with Roger Longworth (c. 1630-1687), a Quaker minister who visited Holland six times during his career.

156. Galenus Abrahams (1622-1706), a physician and leader of the Collegiants, a Dutch sect that recognized no organized church or ministry. The Collegiants also had no confession of faith, although they did administer baptism by immersion each year when they gathered for worship at Rynsburg, near Leiden. Cross, *Christian Church*. WP, who met Abrahams several times on this journey, had difficulty in defining his religion.

157. Directions in the text here read "(~~turn over 4 pages.~~)." The deletion is in a contemporary hand. The text continues on the next page without interruption.

158. Hoorn, a town in north Holland on the IJsselmeer; about twenty miles northeast of Amsterdam.

159. Enkhuizen, about ten miles northeast of Hoorn and thirty miles northeast of Amsterdam.

160. Workum, in West Friesland; about fifty miles northeast of Amsterdam.

161. Groningen, a Dutch town in West Friesland; about 100 miles northeast of Amsterdam.

162. A deleted entry here reads "This day it came upon me to write a Letter to JEM. [Johanna Eleanora von Merlau] the noble young woman at Franckfurt: as followeth." This is followed by the direction "(turn over 4 pages)." The copyist or WP decided, however, to insert the letter to von Merlau a few lines later, at the close of the entry for 10 Sept. See n. 163.

163. Guide marks at this point in the manuscript on fol. 59 direct the reader to the last page of an unnumbered section inserted between fols. 20 and 21. The note on this page reads "This day it came upon me to write a Letter to Johanna Eleonora Meermannin, the Noble young Woman ~~of~~ at Franchfurt: as followeth: (turn back 4 pages.)." The letter to von Merlau begins four pages before this note in the manuscript.

164. Johanna Eleanora von Merlau.

165. Frankfurt.

166. Juliane Bauer van Eysseneck, with whom Johanna Eleanora von Merlau lived in Frankfurt.

167. John 3:27.

168. Juliane Bauer van Eysseneck?

169. Cologne.

170. That is, waiting for the Messiah. See Luke 2:25. Laymon, *One-Volume Interpreter's Bible*, p. 676.

171. See Gal. 2:20.

172. On the reverse side of the last page of this letter in the manuscript is written "next morning etc. See overleaf after the line."

173. The manuscript text now resumes on fol. 59.

174. Leeuwarden, a Dutch town in West Friesland, about twelve miles from Harlingen and ninety miles northeast of Amsterdam.

175. In fact, a return visit. See doc. 63. The Sommelsdijks' castle was in Wieuwerd, Dutch Friesland.

176. Pierre DuLignon.

177. Overwerden, a Dutch town in West Friesland; about ninety miles northeast of Amsterdam.

178. "Colleagues."

179. John 1:29.

180. Dan. 2:45.

181. Lippenhuizen, a Dutch town in the province of Groningen, about one hundred miles northeast of Amsterdam.

182. Delfzijl, a Dutch town in the province of Groningen, about 120 miles northeast of Amsterdam.

183. WP refers here to the Wilkinson-Story controversy. See headnote to doc. 91.

184. Gen. 3:15.

185. Dan. 2:45.

186. John 4:35.

187. Jan Willem Haasbaart, the first Quaker convert in Emden. WP wrote to him on 22 Nov. 1672, but no answer from Haasbaart is preserved. See *Micro.* 1:439.

188. WP's letter of protest to the council and senate of Emden, written 14 Dec. 1674, was published in Amsterdam in 1675. It is translated in *Works,* 1:609-11.

189. Perhaps one of Jan Willem Haasbaart's sisters?

190. Leer, a German town, about 14 miles southeast of Emden and 135 miles northeast of Amsterdam.

191. One of these ministers may have been Theodor Undereyck (1635-1693), among the foremost early Reformed Pietists in northwestern Germany.

192. "Legal prosecution or suit." *OED.*

193. Kiel, a port on the Baltic Sea, in Holstein.

194. Anna Maria van Hoorn.

195. Mlle. de Reneval.

196. A small cross-hatched mark at this point in the manuscript on fol. 80 directs the reader to fol. 80A, where the text continues. Four sheets numbered 81 through 88 intervene.

197. Donau, or Danube, a division of Württemberg in southern Germany.

198. That is, they did not remove their hats.

199. Matt. 25:1-13.

200. Martin Luther (1483-1546) wrote many hymns that he patterned after the secular music of the Middle Ages. Metrical versions of the Psalms, rather than hymns, were sung in most English churches during the seventeenth century. Quakers did not sing in their meetings for worship. Cross, *Christian Church.*

201. Lippstadt, a town in the territories of Brandenburg, about twenty-six miles south of Herford.

202. Hamm, a town in the county of Mark, in Brandenburg, about sixty-five miles southwest of Herford by way of Lippstadt.

203. Instructions at this point in the manuscript, on fol. 86A, read: "(These following etc. turn back 3 pages)." Actually, one turns back six pages in the manuscript to pick up the narrative of WP's journey. The entries from 27 Sept. through 9 Oct. (fols. 80-86 in the manuscript) are taken from a letter dated 10 Oct. 1677 to the Countess van Hoorn. See below after 9 Oct. 1677 for the first part of this letter, and *Works,* 1:101-8.

204. Perhaps the wife of Dr. Thomas van Wijlick's brother. See n. 213 below.

205. Duisburg.

206. Mayor.

207. Probably Mlle. de Revenal's friend, Reiner Kuper.

208. Directions in the manuscript here read "(turn over 4 pages)," but in fact the text continues in correct order.

209. Cologne.

210. J. Docenius, resident for the king of Denmark in Cologne. He apparently later wished to immigrate to Pennsylvania, but his wife did not, and so they stayed in Europe.

211. John Foxe, *Actes and Monuments of matters happening in the Church* (London, 1563), recounted in graphic detail the martyrdom of Protestants executed during Mary's reign; his book was popularly known as *The Book of Martyrs*.

212. That is, the sister of the Countess van Hoorn.

213. Dr. Schuler, Rosendael, Col. Copius and his wife, Dr. Wijlick's sister-in-law, and Countess van Hoorn's sister and her in-laws, were the "worthy" people with whom WP met in this area. See 27 Sept. and 3 and 4 Oct.

214. Directions in the manuscript text read "[Here followeth {~~another~~ 2[?] Letter to AM de H [Anna Maria van Hoorn]: etc}." In fact, this letter appears much earlier in the manuscript, on fols. 1B through 11B. See above, n. 55.

215. 1 Thess. 4:3.

216. Phil. 2:12.

217. "I must break off."

218. Heb. 11:5.

219. John 15:1-16.

220. John 15:18-19; Matt. 10:24.

221. Rev. 12, 18-19.

222. 1 Kings 3:16-27.

223. E.g., Matt. 7:16-20.

224. Heb. 4:12.

225. This passage, beginning with "'Twas Davids Teacher," contains a series of Scriptural fragments and is typical of WP's style. See Ps. 91:4; 2 Chron. 23:9; Matt. 24:28; and Exod. 16:14-35. A "buckler" is a small, round shield; the word is used figuratively to mean protector. *OED*.

226. Matt. 4:1-11.

227. Acts 5:1-11.

228. Mark 12:41-44; Luke 21:1-4.

229. The brackets here are WP's.

230. See n. 65, above.

231. The text from this point is crossed out with a large cross drawn over each page.

232. Ps. 27.

233. The crossed-out section ends here.

234. The closing entries, 10-11 Oct., are on fols. 11B and 12B in the manuscript.

235. The manuscript text ends abruptly at this point. In the first printed edition of the journal (1694), there are further entries from 12 Oct. to 1 Nov., recounting WP's final days in Holland and his return to England.

THE WHIG POLITICIAN

1677–1679

In the two years after WP returned to England from Holland and Germany, he experienced a time of challenge which had lasting impact upon his career. In March 1678, he entered more actively into politics than previously, and lobbied at Parliament for religious toleration (see docs. 125-26). Six months later, the brazen perjurer Titus Oates declared that he had discovered a horrible Popish Plot: the Jesuits, according to Oates, were plotting to assassinate Charles II in order to place his Catholic brother James on the throne. These false charges were believed, and they fomented a wild anti-Catholic witch hunt. The king was forced to dissolve Parliament in 1679 and to call new elections; his brother was forced into exile. WP had close ties to the Stuarts, but at this critical juncture he joined the king's political enemies, the Whigs, in the hope of achieving toleration for all Protestants and civil liberties for all Englishmen. In 1679, he campaigned actively for a Whig victory in the parliamentary elections, writing such tracts as *England's Great Interest in the Choice of This New Parliament* (1679), and supporting the candidacy of the republican theorist Algernon Sidney (see doc. 129).

WP's rewards for these efforts were mostly negative. Sidney was defeated in two elections. The Whig challenge to Charles II and James eventually collapsed, and in 1680-1681 the Stuarts regained political control. WP's hope of religious toleration for Quakers and other dissenters, and a broadening of political representation and of civil rights, was dashed. WP's attorney, the Catholic Richard Langhorne, became one of Titus Oates' victims; he was tried and executed on a false charge of treason in 1679 (see doc. 131). WP himself was labeled as a papist both before and during the Popish Plot hysteria; the rumor spread among Quakers that he was in hiding or had fled the country (see docs. 121, 125, and 128). And WP faced other grave problems in 1678-1679. He was unable to prevent a final breach within the Society of Friends between Fox and members of the Wilkinson-Story faction (see docs. 124, 135). Increasingly, he experienced financial pressure; having bought a big house at Warminghurst that he could not afford, he sold much of Gulielma's land, and contracted large loans (see the headnote to doc. 139, and doc. 151).

The following five documents (120-24) are dated between October 1677 and February 1678, before the Popish Plot crisis began. They illustrate several of the problems WP was coping with immediately after his return from Holland and Germany. In doc. 120, Margaret Fox comments on the intensification of the Wilkinson-Story controversy. In doc. 121, WP shows his discomfort at the anti-Quaker persecution he faced in Sussex. In doc. 122, WP's euphoria over the success of his continental mission work evaporates as he argues sharply with Dutch Friends over marriage procedures. In doc. 123, WP is proud of his young son Springett and worried about Gulielma, close to term with their next baby. In the final weeks before Letitia was born, WP could not stay with Gulielma at Warminghurst, for he had to travel to Bristol in order to negotiate with William Rogers and other supporters of the Wilkinson-Story faction. These negotiations failed. Doc. 124 shows why they failed, for Rogers' "dissatisfactions" with the leadership of Fox and WP were great indeed.

120
FROM MARGARET FOX

[October 1677]

W: P.

Dear & Faithfull: whom the Lord hath Chosen, & owned, & honoured with his everlasting Truth, who hath manifested thy selfe to be a true follower of the Lamb, Blessed art thou for ever, that hath Chosen that Good part, that never shall be taken from thee, but in it thou wilt Live, & Grow, & thrive, & be Cloathed with beauty, Glory, & majesty: my heart, & souls Love, is dearly Remembred unto thee & my spirit doth Rejoyce, in thy Faithfullness, & deligence, in the Lords work, & service, who art a Noble, & faithfull Instrument, in the hand of the Almighty: for the spreading abroad of his Truth, & for the exaltation of his Kingdome, O thy Name will be had in everlasting Remembrance, with all the Faithfull, as they Come into that same spirit of Grace, & Life, & power, by which thou art Acted, & Carryed & for the Good service that thou dost for the Lord, & for his Truth & the Gathering of his elect seed, he will Reward it a hundred fold into thy bosome, O: Beautifull is thy feet, that preaches Glad tideings to the poor, & Libertie to the Captives, Children yet unborne will bless the Lord for thee, — I Received thy sweet, &

blessed Letter, which was much Joy to mee, & many more, to hear of that Good service for the Lord, the day that it Came to my hand here was a meeting: & I was moved of the Lord, that it should be Read in the meeting & It was Great Comfort, & Joy, & Gladness to the hearts of Friends, to heare of thy Good service, & of the Truths prospering, Oh, blessed, & honoured be the holy Lord for ever, who is enlargeing the Borders of his sanctuary — & spreading abroad his Truth, & Blessed are the Publishers of it, — Wee have also Received, a very pretious paper of thine, Concerning the seperate meeting[1] — & yester night we Received another from My Husband[2] {writt from Amsterdam:} very pure & pretious, & to the same purpose; But we doe not know that either of them, will be gott Read amongst them, for Friends hath endeavoured to get thine to them, but they have not done it yet For they will not Receive any to Read them, themselves, & now Friends are seperated from them,[3] & meets apart, & they by themselves so that they will hardly suffer any Friend to Come amongst them — {to Read a paper} for when they mett amongst Friends, they would hardly suffer any thing to be Read quietly, that they Looked upon was against themselves some of them growes more hard, & obstinate then ever; others that is more simple, is troubled, & Tormented, we waite in hope, for the Returne of such: Friends meetings more pretious, powerfull, fresh, & Lively since they went from them, then they have been many years before —

Tho Langhorne is now hear, who gives mee a very Good account of their perticuler meetings, & Generall meetings, & men, & womens meetings, all furnished, with the Lords power, & Liveing presence, praysed, & honoured be the powerfull God, so that {now} all is well, as our hearts Can desire: yet Friends is moved of the Lord to goe amongst them To bear their Testimony ag^{st} them: James Fletcher[4] & Richard Johnson[5] is to be with them to morrow at John wilkinsons house & Rich: Ray[6] a scotch Friend is to be with them on the first day he is moved to Goe amongst them, as to a priest in a steeplehouse {to deliver his Testimony: & so Come away.} Its to be feared, they will be very Rough, & boisterous with them but the Lords power is over them, which will bruise them, & break them — Dear w: Friends are very much Gladed, & Refresh'd in the Lord, hereaways on thy behalfe, for that thou hast had a tender Care over Friends, in this thy Great travells, & Journeys, but it is neither sea, nor Land, height nor depth, that Can seperate from the Love of God, which is in Christ Jesus our Lord, which he hath shedd abroad in the hearts of his people — Thy printed epistle was very serviceable, & very dearly Received amongst Friends — $Rememb^r$ my very dear, & eternall Love, to thy dear wife whom I honour in the Lord for her Faithfulness, & Constancy, & Inocency The Arme of the Almighty preserve, & keep you {both} in that bond & Covenant of Love, & Life; that never Can be broken — My daugh[ters] Sarah[7] Susannah, & Rachells[8] Love, is dearly, & Faithfully Remembered unto you both, & so I know it is with my sonn, & daughter Lower[9] but they doe not know of my writeing now. Robt widd[ers][10] was here this day, whose dear Love is to thee,—And Tho Langho[rne] also Remembers his dear Love unto thee,—

And so dearly beloved this is all that I have at present but my ne[ver] dyeing Love Remaines with thee, & that I am thy

dear Friend & sister in the
Lord M F

I would desire a Coppy of thy Journall[11] {at} this time for I would have it Recorded here.
The 8o moth 1677.

Copy. Port. 36, FLL. (*Micro.* 2:558). Docketed: A Coppy of M: Fs: Lett. | to Willm Penn the 8o moth | 1677.

1. While traveling on the Continent in Sept. 1677, WP wrote to English Friends concerning the Wilkinson-Story schism (see doc. 119, 16 Sept. 1677), encouraging them to set aside their differences. His letter was read at Bristol, where the controversy was now centered. Braithwaite, *Second Period,* p. 313.

2. George Fox wrote on 5 Aug. 1677 and again on 25 Sept. 1677 from Amsterdam concerning the separation. He sent at least one of these letters to Bristol, where it added to the strife between William Rogers' group and the orthodox Friends. Both Fox and WP were in Bristol by Feb. 1678. WP participated in several meetings there in an attempt to heal the schism (see doc. 124). Fox, *Journal* (London, 1709), 2:289, 310-13; Braithwaite, *Second Period,* pp. 313-14.

3. On 6 July 1677, the Westmorland Quarterly Meeting separated completely from the Wilkinson and Story party. Robert Barrow, of Kendall meeting, described to WP the circumstances of the schism in Westmorland at about this time. "As concerning Story's sect, or the scismatical spirit, which is chiefly headed or managed in the North by his yokefellow J. W.—that party grows very insolent, many of them, though they are scattering: now & then one who comes out of their scattered state home into the ancient fold; but they look like men frighted with death, & almost overcome therewith. Those that owned their condemnation before the last Yearly Meeting are now pretty well restored. . . . And whereas, before J. W. & his party did only keep their Mens' Meeting apart from the members of their Monthly & Quarterly Meeting, in opposition thereunto; they have now separated themselves from us wholly, both first days & week days, at the place which is called by the name of Underbarrow Meeting: & there is now two meetings. & at Preston two meetings; & at Hutton where J. W. dwells, he hath the whole meeting to himself, but they are but in all about ½ a dozen families, & under thirty persons, & they confess they are all tithe-payers. Its but now three first days since they thus clearly separated from us: they aim to drive on their design to the largest extent, & they are risen to the height, but their fall is suddenly coming, because of their desperate design & wilful apostacy. . . . However, our God is good & kind to us, for our meetings are much more fresh since they went than before, & the glorious presence of our God doth more abundantly shine forth, & in some respect we are greatly eased, for the weight of the dark spirit & the enmity that proceeded from it did often burden us." Robert Barrow to WP, n.d. (*Micro.* 14:673); Braithwaite, *Second Period,* p. 310.

4. James Fletcher, of Lancs., was imprisoned several times for preaching between 1654 and 1656 and had goods distrained in 1679 for nonpayment of tithes. Besse, 1:303, 323.

5. Richard Johnson (1630-1686), a husbandman of Ormskirk, Lancs., traveled in the ministry in England and Ireland and was imprisoned in 1663, 1666, 1674, and 1685. Fox, 2:414; Besse, 1:311, 317, 320, 329-30.

6. Richard Ray (or Ree), of Edinburgh, was among the earliest Scottish Quaker ministers. Besse, 2:494; Braithwaite, *Second Period,* p. 533.

7. Sarah Fell (c. 1643-1714), the fourth daughter of Thomas and Margaret Fell

of Swarthmore, studied Hebrew and was the clerk of several women's meetings. Her accounts of the household at Swarthmore for 25 Sept. 1673 to 15 Aug. 1678 were published in Norman Penney, ed., *The Household Account Book of Sarah Fell of Swarthmoor Hall* (Cambridge, 1920). In 1681 she married William Mead and moved to the south of England. Their only son, Nathaniel (1684-1760), became a lawyer, left the Society of Friends, and was knighted. Fox, 2:386, 491.

8. Rachel Fell (1653-1732), the youngest child of Thomas and Margaret Fell, was a constant companion to her mother and continued to live at Swarthmore after her marriage to Daniel Abraham (1662-1731) in 1682. Fox, 2:452, 490.

9. Thomas and Mary Lower. Mary Lower (c. 1644-1719) was the fifth daughter of Thomas and Margaret Fell and the second wife of Thomas Lower. She married Lower in 1668 and lived with him at the family mansion called Pennance, in Creed, Cornwall. They had ten children, of whom five were still living in 1701. Fox, 2:421.

10. Robert Widders (c. 1618-1686), of Upper Kellet, Lancs., was convinced by George Fox in 1652, served as a traveling minister, and was imprisoned on several occasions. He accompanied Fox to Scotland in 1657, and to America in 1671. Fox, 1:395-96; William Evans and Thomas Evans, *Piety Promoted,* 2 vols. (Philadelphia, 1854), 1:97-99; Besse, 1:305, 307, 315.

11. WP's "Account of My Journey to Holland and Germany," 22 July-23 Oct. 1677 (doc. 119). We know that WP distributed a number of manuscript copies of his journal. Margaret Fox's request indicates that WP told friends about his journal before he got back to England, and that he planned to have copies made soon after his return.

121
TO THE EARL OF MIDDLESEX AND DORSET

[17 November 1677]

My worthy Friend[1]

Being also an enemy to Leggs in writeing,[2] I present my request without any other Apology. There are two gentlemen {in} Sussex, that are pleasd to endeavour to make my liveing there uneasy, & to obtain that end, take advantage of my non conformity in point of religion, their names are, Henry Goreing Justice of Peace, the father,[3] & Colonel Alford,[4] also a Justice of Peace; I never saw one of them but once, & the other never; I never had to doe wth them in any sense; all other Partys are at quiet, & our friends every where else but by me. this perticuler displeasure I understand not; Reflections It becomes me to forbear, yet their conduct on my regard gives great occasion; for the thing it selfe, viz, forcd conformity 'twere to loos time to urge reasons here ag{st} it. the freeness of thy own temper, & Judgement Is[5] enough in the Case, & thy nature as well as understanding are strongly & justly byast an other way. I therefore omitt to render their attempts unreasonable & rediculous. That wch rests, is this, to Implore that powr thou hast, & the influence of it, by that way wch in thy own Judgement may be most effectuall, & Prudent to thy Circumstances, in order to allay their heat, ~~&~~ that haveing as good a stake in the Country as either of them, & being as ready to Improve my little abilitys & interest in the Country to a publique good, I may possess, with my estate, the Common quiet of the Country. give me leave, by the way to observe one passage ~~by the way~~, that of all sussex, there can be found but two Papists fitt for conviction, & by an ~~way~~ [?] ugly misfortune they happen to be both quakers;[6] I say: nothing, but admire at the skill of the chusers, & their profound care of Protestancy. not that I would excite unkindness to the Papists, or that I am so ill natur'd as to make company in [illegible deletion] suffering any abate [?] to the tr{o}uble of it, only to evince the Justice of some People, & how closely they keep to the Title of their office. w^t ever is the Consequence of this address, my Inclination, besides thy manyfold obleigations will allways make me

Thy faithfull
& ready friend to
all Just Services
Lond: 17:9bre 77 Wm Penn

ALS. Lilly Library, Indiana University. (*Micro.* 2:582). Addressed: For my worthy | Friend the earl of | Dorset & Middlesex.

1. Charles Sackville, third earl of Middlesex and sixth earl of Dorset, had assisted WP at court in 1674; see doc. 82, n. 4, above. Sackville's family seat was at Buckhurst in northern Sussex, near one of WP's Springett estates, "The Rocks."

2. WP is saying that in correspondence, as in face-to-face relationships, he eschews all deferential formality, whether "bending the leg," removing the hat, or employing flattering phrases.

3. Sir Henry Goring (1622-1702), of Highden, Sussex, about five miles south of Warminghurst, belonged to one of the county's most eminent families. The Gorings had estates all over south-central Sussex. Sir Henry sat in Parliament as knight of the shire in 1660, and for Steyning, near Warminghurst, from 1661 to 1679. In 1678 he was made a baronet. WP calls Goring "the father" to distinguish him from his son, Captain Henry Goring (1646-1687). Burke's *Peerage*.

4. John Alford (c. 1647-1691) of Offington, Sussex, about ten miles south of Warminghurst, was M.P. for Midhurst (1679-1681), and for Bramber (1688-1689). In 1675, along with Sir Henry Goring, he was named a commissioner for recusants in Sussex. *Calendar of Treasury Books, 1672-1675* (London, 1909), p. 697; *Alumni Oxonienses.*

5. "Is" is written over another, probably incomplete, word that appears to begin "ag."

6. WP is complaining that the only "popish recusants" Goring and Alford can find to prosecute in Sussex are WP and Gulielma. In Mar. 1679, WP was listed with seventeen other Sussex Quakers who "are prosecuted as Popish Recusants but in reality [are] true Protestants." Most of these "papist" Quakers lived within ten miles of Warminghurst, and perhaps belonged to the meeting that was held regularly at WP's house from 1676. See *Calendar of Treasury Books, 1676-1679* (London, 1911), p. 1257; ACM, vols. 55-56; Fox, *Short Journal*, p. 235.

122
TO PIETER HENDRICKS

[19 November 1677]

Dear Friend P. H.

Blessed are they, that are Kept by the Lord, it shall goe well with them, & this all have dayly need of, whom the lord has visitted in this day; others can Say now as ever In days past, that Such are preserved in perfect peace, & live in a quiet habitation. the lord Stay the minds of his people every where upon him, & keep them in the hour of tryall. I perceive by thy two letters how things have been; & my Soul has been made Sad by reason of that Jumble that was among you.[1] I have written to B. F.[2] about it, his letter will Satisfy thee how plainly I dealt wth him, & tould him, that a Short, brittle Spt will never do gods work, adviseing him that he would come into that weighty live, wch can bear & suffer, & is not So easy to be provoaked[.] I read his letters, & myn to him, to Dr. G. F.[3] In Short, I over look all thos aggravateing expressions & bury them by the powr of god, & you must do the like & be patient, & Long suffering, & committ yr cause to the lord. as to the Paper of R. B.[4] I know not where it is; next twas only memorandums, & Signefyed not much, it was [t]oo abrupt. furthermore, as to the thing it selfe, this G. F. & I agreed I [sh]ould write. first that if any out of Tendernesse of Conscience (after haveing perform'd the order among friends (yet before marriage Solemnized) desired to Inform the Magistrate of their Intentions in order to manifest their cleerness, they were left to their liberty, with out being Judg'd or censur'd by friends yet that they might not Censure friends that keep their first practice.

2ly that after the marriage is Solemniz'd if any desire to carry or Send the magistrate a coppy of the certificate they have their freedom so to do. these two things I remember, & if the paper were Short must such vehement reflection & Indignation be conceiv'd or Shown, for such omission. o this is not weighty enough for truth; but I hope the Lord will preserve you all in his wisdome & love, that you may Keep the Seemless garment without rent,[5] & feel yourselves covered with the Same. my dear Salutation in the life of Jesus Xt our Lord is to thee & the Brethren & all friends. o my dear friends keep low [&] tender in the holy Seed that has visitted you, that your joy may be encreased, & your peace Sweetly & deeply flow [as] a pure river. o my Soul ~~ren~~ remembers, with pure prayers, the Ag[e?] of the lord that was with us in that land & Countrye. wt ever comes of the work your day is Sounded, & the lords controversy is declared, & all shall work together for good to them that keep their eye to the lord. lett me hear from thee Sometimes. expect Suddainly, the lord permitting, an accompt of the debate between us & Ga[l]. Abr.[6] So dear Peter, in dear Brotherly kindness, that is easy to be Entreated I rest

Thy faithfull Friend & Bror

Lond: 19th 9mo 1677. Wm Penn

Dr: Peter, & Friends

Keep in the Seed & powr of god that was before all, & will out last all, in wch you will all be preserved in peace & quietness. & so wth my love to them you all, in Holland & Friesland & elswhere.

G F

ALS. Quaker Collection, Haverford College. (*Micro.* 2:589). Addressed: This | For Peter Hendricks | Button=Maker on the | Caesars Graft in | Amsterdam. Endorsed: 1677 9/m 19 London. van W. P. en G. F. This document is torn and the edges frayed. We have supplied some words in brackets from the printed version in the *Bulletin* of the Friends Historical Society of Philadelphia 4:5-7.

1. WP refers to the controversy over the reporting of Quaker marriages in Holland to the Dutch magistrates. At a meeting on 3 Aug. 1677 attended by WP (see doc. 119), Dutch Friends agreed that after a marriage was performed in meeting, those who wished could report it to the magistrates. This was also WP's position. But some Dutch Quakers (such as Benjamin Furly) wanted all marriages reported, as required by the Dutch government, and others wanted no marriages reported. For a commentary on this dispute, see William I. Hull, *Benjamin Furly and Quakerism in Rotterdam* (Lancaster, Pa., 1941), pp. 60-67.

2. Benjamin Furly. Neither WP's letter nor Furly's letter survives.

3. George Fox.

4. Robert Barclay.

5. WP alludes to Matt. 9:16.

6. Galenus Abrahams; see doc. 119, n. 156. For WP's account of his debate with Abrahams, see doc. 119, 9, 11 Oct. 1677.

123
TO MARGARET FOX

[8 January 1678]

My dearly Beloved Friend M. F.

In dear & everlasting kindness, I do Salute & embrace thee, acknowledgeing thy great love & regard to me, wch hath often refresht my soule in the remembrance of it. & blessed be the pure god of all heavenly riches & goodness that hath given me a name among the liveing, & a place in {the} hearts of his righteous & honorable ones: & truly sweet & precious is the holy fellowship that our dear lord hath given us together in his own pure eternall Spirit, that hath quickened us, & made us neer & very dear, above the life, spirit & friendship of this Corrupt world. o that we may forever be kept in the sweet & tender powr of the lord; for there is {no} preservation out of it, & that this day will {declare}, & hath declared already. Truly it is a time of exercise in many respects, but all workes together for good to those that are sinceer, & have their eye to the Lord: verely, the [illegible deletion] chaff shall be seperated from the wheat;[1] & all these things are for cleansing & brightening the faithfull more & more; that the pure Seed may raign above & over all its oppressors. I shall forbear Perticulers, referring thee to thy dr. daughter,[2] who has had a reall service both in this & other nations. thy dr: & hon^{d} husband is well, & in the Service of the great God & King, whos Angell & speciall messenger he is, & woe to them, that rise up agst him in his Lords Service.[3] In generall, the Powr springs & raignes over all, & the lord god of life renowns it day by day. o it comforts the righteous, & will plague the ungodly & unstable that leave their integrety.

My dear wife was well yesterday & my son, a large & active child, my wife is bigg, & expects to lye in the first week in the first month, lett her condition be remembred by thee.[4] Thy son and daughter Rous & their children[5] were well the other day; I have been lately very ill, opprest in body & spirit, but blessed be the god of my life I am finely recover'd. o we are bound up to-gether in everlasting love, precious & Sweet is our heavenly kindred & relation; o how neer & dear are we to one another; o the Powr makes weigh, we cannot forgett one an other, noe time Can wair out, noe distance seperate, noe waters quench our love & union, our dear & tender regard to each other. o this is my life, my Joy, & my Crown; it excells the wisdom & glory of the world; yea Prophesy shall cease & miracles shall Cease, but this more excellent way shall endure for ever. I Could not lett thy daughter goe without this short testemony of my love, & due regard to thee, & thy remembrance of me in thy two last letters, very dear to me; as I hope they will always be. salute me dearly to thy dear Son Lowr & daughter, & Daughter Sarah, Sus: & Rachell, & the lord god all mighty have you all ever in his Protection. I am in endless bonds of heavenly friendship, & fellowship.

Thy endeared
friend & faithfull
Brother
Wm Penn

Bucks: 8th 11mo 1677
I know my dear [wifes]
dear love is to thee & thyn.
Salute me to Dr: L.F. J.Bl. R.W. R.B. T.L.[6]

ALS. Quaker Scrapbook, vol. 1, HSP. (*Micro.* 2:602). Addressed: For my very dearely | Beloved Friend Margt | Fox at Swarthmore.

1. WP alludes to the parable of the tares, Matt. 13:24-30.
2. Isabel Yeamans, who traveled with WP in Holland and Germany. See doc. 119.
3. George Fox had met with the dissident Quakers John Raunce and Charles Harris on 7 Dec. On the day this letter was written, WP joined Fox at Thomas Ellwood's house at Hunger Hill, near Beaconsfield, Bucks., and Isabel Yeamans joined WP and Fox at a meeting at Hedgerly, about two miles from Beaconsfield. Fox, *Short Journal,* p. 261.
4. Letitia Penn was born on schedule, 6 Mar. 1678. The son mentioned here was Springett (1675-1696).
5. Fox had just spent more than two weeks with John and Margaret (Fell) Rous at Kingston-on-Thames, and was doubtless WP's source of information. Only four of the twelve Rous children survived infancy. Fox, *Short Journal,* pp. 260-61; DQB.
6. Leonard Fell, John Blaykling, Robert Widders, Robert Burrow, and Thomas Lower.

124
THE DISSATISFACTIONS OF WILLIAM ROGERS AND OTHERS

Bristoll the 1st of 12th Moneth [February] 1677[/8]

Propositions agreed between William Pen & William Rogers on behalfe of ~~themselves~~ {ourselves} & others concerned, in order to a meetinge[1] for the endinge some differences dependinge between them and also others in the Citty of Bristoll and elcewhere interested, and for satisfaction of any freind or freinds in the things they are dissatisfyed

1st It is agreed by and between the persons abovementioned that each may have a scribe to take all those passages in the Conference which to them severally shall seeme meet, and that before any one head bee left, or a new matter begun, all that each party hath thought fitt to have written be first read, if in anythinge defective amended & finally agreed by both persons to bee a true record, Minute, or memoriale of the Conference & if anythinge bee writt, or exprest short or beside the meaninge of the speaker, that the said speaker hath liberty to Correct, & helpe the said expression.

2ly That all things so written by both scribes, & so agreed upon to bee recorded, shalbee at the end of every meetinge subscribed by both parties & by at least six credible persons of each side & by as many more as shall please to signe the same as witnesses of what is so recorded and the said six respectively to bee named before the meetinge begin, & they then to declare thate they are free to it, but if in anythinge they are dissatisfied with what there passeth, that though they Subscribe the narrative as wittnesses that the same is a true narrative, yet that they have power & liberty in case of dislike, to declare or write their protestation against the same.

3ly That if any freind present hath anythinge upon him, or her, to say or offer to the matter in hand, that such hath his or her Christian liberty to speake his or her minde & that every such thinge said by freinds on either side if the freinds that speake or either of the two persons whose names are hereunto subscribed shall desire it bee also recorded.

4ly That matters or subjects to bee debated on by each party bee first written downe & respectively delivered to each other

5ly That the meetinge begin & beheld at the 9th hour in the mourninge on the 4th day of this instant be[ing] on the 2d day of the weeke & at the house of Richard Sneed

6ly That this agreement bee written in the head of the narrative to bee made in persuance of this agreement

William Pen on behalfe of himselfe
& other freinds concerned

William Rogers on behalfe of
himselfe and other freinds concer[ned]

The meetinge by Consent was ~~adgree~~ held in the publick Meetinge house—

In persuance of the above written agreement wee William Rogers & William Ford,[2] Arthur Eastmead[3] & John Ma[e?]Traverse[4] [illegible deletion of 1½ lines] doe lay downe [illegible deletion] pa[rt] of our dissatisfactions. viz

{1st dissatisfaction.}

Wee are not satisfied that George Fox ~~of~~ hath of late been guided by the spirit of truth in all such matt[ers] relatinge to the truth wherein of late hee hath concern'd himselfe; neither are wee satisfied that those who have of late looked upon him as a man Worthy of double honour & own'd him in all such matters, have had therein a spirituall deservinge, neither are wee satisfied that the beare esteeminge of him as one that hath [not?] of late in all things kept his place & habitation in the truth cann bee the fruit of a dark spt.

The Reasons as to the above dissatisfactions as to George Fox are in part [illegible deletion] as followeth.

That diverse passages in his booke intituled this is an encouragemt unto all womens meetings in the World[5] are are either unsound or impertinently quoted

The 1st quotation

"Page 43 of sd booke tis thus said and was not Micahs mother a virtuous woman, read Judges the 17th & see what shee sd to her son"[6]

The words of the scripture are these. And there was a man of mount Ephraim, whose name was Micah, & hee said unto his mother the 1100 shekells of silver that were taken from thee aboute which thou Cursedst & spakest of also in mine eares behold the silver is with mee, I tooke it, & his Mother said blessed bee thou of the Lord my son, And when hee had restored the 1100 shekells of silver to his mother his Mother said I had wholy dedicated the silver unto the Lord from my hand, for my son to make a graven image & a molten image, now therefore I will restore it to thee yet, hee restored the mony to his mother & his mother took 200 shekells of silver, & gave them to the Founder who made thereof a graven image, and a molten image & they were in the house of Micah and the man Micah had an house of gods.[7]

The quotation is enough to shew that shee was an Idolatrous woman & though it may bee sd tis but a question askt, yet in answer it may bee said that if Geo. Foxes [illegible deletion] reall judgemt bee so, that shee was not a virtuous woman hee hath manifested thereby a scoffinge spirit, but to manifest that such an answer appeares but a meer shift, the reader may observe that about 13 lines followinge hee thus saith, [such] & such women are recorded to posterity for their wised[om] & their Virtue:

The 2d quotation.

"Page 43 And the woman of Tekoa see what a sermon shee preached to kinge David the 2d of Sam: 13: 14"[8]

The scripture quoted informes us that the woman was a subtile woman whome Joab caused to faigne herselfe as a mourner & goe to Kinge David with a lying Story in her mouth wch accordingely shee did, for wh[en] Kinge David askt herr is not the hand of Joab with thee in all this, Shee Answered Joab putt all these words in her mouth so that if it were really so then Shee had been the occasion of pacifying King Davi[d's] wrath, yet it might bee more truely sd that shee deceived kinge David by her lyes than convinced him. Besides though the Story was framed by Joab for the sake of Absolam who slew his brother Amnon & therefore fled, yet appeares that King David was appeased as to his son Absolam as in the 2d Sam: 13: [39?] before the woman came to him with lyes in her Mouth[9]

Wee now Comend to the Consciences of all to consider how this lyinge story can bee called a good and convincinge sermon & bee an evidence of a virtuous Woman for in a very few lines after its said (as before) These & such woman are recorded to posterity for their wisdome & their Virtue:—

The 3d Quotation.

"Page 23. And the woman had their assemblyes in the dayes of the Judges & the Kings. Now old Ely was not against the assemblyes of the women who assembled by troops as you may see in the 1st Sam 2. 21:22: Though some men nowadayes may bee against womens meetings or assemblies in the gosple times. and against womens speakinge & prophecyinge."[10]

The Scripture quoted tells us thus. so Ely was old & heard all that his sons did unto all Israel & how they lay with the women who assembled at the doare of the tabernacle of the congregation which onely proves that there was an assembly of men and women at the doare of the tabernacle of the congregation who Comitted Evill together.[11]

At first veiw this seem'd so abominable a quotation to prove the assemblies of purified women under the gosple distinct from purified Men to bee necessary which is the End. wherefore twas (as wee doe take it) quoted that wee were concerned to informe our ~~self~~ selves from the Scriptures to what end women assembled before the doare of the tabernacle of the congregation — & wee finde by a marginall note in the Scriptures that it was (as the Hebrewes write) after their travell when they came to be purified as in Leviticus the. 12: & 6 where its thus said, now when the dayes of her purifying are fullfilled shee shall bringe to the preist a lamb of one yeere old for a burnt offeringe, and a younge pigeon or a turtle dove for a sin offeringe unto the doare of the tabernacle of the congregation which gives us occasion thus to query.[12]

How can womens cominge in order to their purification with a sin offeringe & to the doare of the ~~take~~ tabernacle of the congregation when defiled by the men that there accompanyed them bee a proof for purified women under the gosple to assem[ble] together distinct from purified men.

The 4th quotation.

"Page 32. And likewise you may see Rachell & Leah their councell to Jacob, who answered Jacob & said unto him, is there yet any portion or inheritance for us in our fathers house are wee not accounted of him as strangers for hee hath sold us and hath quite devoured also our mony, for the Riches that god hath taken from our father that is ours and our childrens & now theirfore whatsoev[er] god hath said unto thee doe, this was Rachells & Leahs councell unto Jacob, and was not these three a church then, and did hee forbid them from speakinge in the Church. See Genesis. 31. 14. 15. 16."[13]

This wee take to bee a quotation to evince womens speak[ing] in the Church to bee accordinge to truth, but yet wee cannot owne it to bee much better (if any thinge at all better) argumt for womens speakinge in the Church of God, when the Church is met ~~together~~ to worship the lord in his spirit, than womens dis[course?] with their husbands aboute their outward estates doth almost every day produce amongst us, and were it so that no better argument could bee produced for the justification of womens Speakinge in the Church of God in the sence wee have understood speakinge in the Church wee might bee ashamed of our principle & their practice.

The 5th quotation.

"Page 42. And the daughters of Israel went yeerely to Lament the daughter of Jeptha. judges. 11th. so here they had an yeerly meetinge on this occasion."[14]

Jeptha made a vow unto the Lord & thus said — if thou shalt deliver the children of Ammon into ~~mine~~ my hand then that thinge that cometh out of the doares of my house to meet mee when I come home in peace From the Children of Ammon, shalbe the Lords & I will offer it for a burnt offeringe and so it happened that his onely child beinge a daughter came out to meet him with timbrells & daunces and when he saw her he rent his clothes and said, Alas, my daughter but yet at the end of two moneths did unto her accordinge to his Vow; havinge given her two monethes time to goe to the mountaines with other Virgins to bewaile her Virginity wch afterwards became a custome in Israel to goe yeerly to the Mountaines to bewaile the daughter of Jeptha.[15]

This occasions us to query whether such a meetinge occasioned on the untimely death of a Virgin (for ~~that~~ Jeptha's vow was a rash vow) cann bee any evidence of the matter ~~that~~ which is taken {by us} to bee intended {viz} either for womens speakinge in the church, or womens meetinge distinct from men on account of Worship to God or performing acts of govermt relatinge to Church discipline.

Severall other passages are contaynd in said booke which wee take to bee in order to prove either womens speakinge in the Church when solemnly mett together to waite upon the Lord and worship him in the spt, or womens distinct meetings on account either of worship or exercise of discipline in the Church of god as in diverse places of sd booke may appeare, but yet wee are dissatisfyed that they are pertinent to the purpose.

Wee finde by a paper given forth by George Fox that hee thus writes. "Freinds to you all this is the word of the Lord—"

"Take heed of judginge one another, and judge not one another I command you in the presence of the Lor[d] neither lay open one anothers weeknes, behinde one ano[ther's] backes for thou that dost so art one of Hams family whi[ch] is under the Curse, & that there bee no back bitinge behind one anothers backes, but love, & so the same that doth condemne behind the backe is for ~~com~~ condemnation with the light.[16]

This brings to our remembrance what Paul writ unto the Romans the 2d chap: 1 v.

Therefore thou art inexcusable, oh, man whosoever thou art that judgest another, for wherein thou judgest another thou condemnest thyselfe, for thou that judgest dost the same thinge, but wee are sure that the judgemt of God is accordinge to truth. against them that committs such things & thinkest thou this oh. man that judgest them ~~that~~ {wch,} doe such things ~~th~~ and dost the same that thou shalt escape the judgment of god[17]

From hence wee observe.

1st That unles George Fox plead's that hee is more than a man, and ~~that~~ on that foote ~~he claimes~~ claimes a priveledge that hee may give instructions to others {as aforesaid} & yet bee justified in actinge contrary thereto himselfe & when he hath so pleaded prove such a priveledge to act accordinge to truth, wee are wholy dissatisfyed that hee can escape the judgemt of god

2ly Wee are not satisfied that all those whome wee take George Fox to owne & who have appeared against John Story & John Wilkinson, ~~&~~ have acted in many things relating thereto, (& wherein wee take George Fox also to owne them) accordinge to the aforesaid councell of George Fox and that may bee esteemed as persons worthy to bee judged accordinge to the judgemt given by George Fox. & by the Apostle paul also; and therefore wee desire that George Fox and the freinds who have prest this meetinge will declare whether or no what George Fox hath written as aforesd bee sound & whether hee himselfe & every {one} elce ~~that~~ if they have acted contrary thereto bee condemnable, and when they have so don wee shalbe ready to come to a faire & equall hearinge to manifest the reasons of our dissatisfactions in this case; but unles the freinds who have urged this Meetinge will so doe, wee shalbee ready to conclude that they are not willinge that the things occasioninge the difference amongst freinds & the continuation & increase thereof should be brought to light ~~&~~

~~so~~ nor yet are willinge to come to the touch, though they themselves have been ready to reflect on us as declininge a meetinge & not willinge to Come to the touch—

{2 dissatisfaction}

Though it hath been asserted that the order of the gosple ~~hath been~~ {is} established throughout the whole nation & {(in a booke approved by the 2d dayes meetinge in London) given forth by R. Barclay[18]} that the antient Apostallick order of the Church of Christ is re-establisht on its right basis & foundation & that the way to distinguish that Church gatherings or assembly of People whereof Christ truely is the head from such as falcely pretend thereto, is by consideringe the principles & grounds upon which they are gathered together the nature of that Hierarchy & order they have amongst themselves, the way & Method they take to uphold it,[19] yet notwithstandinge wee are not satisfyed that all the ~~aforsd~~ aforementioned assertions & ~~method~~ {way} of consideration are sound & reasonable in the sense wee take them to bee spoken ~~by the~~

By the aforesd expressions [illegible deletion] {consideringe} the scope of ~~the papers~~ the writings from whence they are Collected wee understand to bee imported

1st That meetings at set places and tymes are the Church & that [illegible deletion] the meetings hinted at as the Church are ~~the yer~~ monethly quarterly yeerely & other set meetings.

2ly That there are principles upon which they are gathered

3. That they have an Hierarchy & order amongst them

4. That they have a way & method to uphold this Hierarchy & order.

5. That the order of the gosple is established throughout the whole nation.

These 5 particulars occasions us to desire an answer to these 5 queries for our information & satisfaction

1 Q. Since the members of the church of christ are onely such as are circumcised in heart, & have an answer of a good conscience toward god & so are such as are sanctified in christ jesus and called to bee Saints, how can it in truth bee asserted that meetings {with respect to all the members thereof} at set tymes & places where none are exempted from cominge who are under the profession of truth & their conversations n[ot] outwardly scandalous (though not certainly knowne to bee circumcised in heart & sanctified in Christ Jesus) are the Church of christ.

2ly Since the Saints in light have been by the power & spirit of God gathered and baptized into one body how comes it to passe that if there {be} principles upon which the body is gathered that some or other of the meetings at Set tymes & places have not set forth what are these principles ~~as a dem~~ upon which they have been gather[ed] as a demonstration that all who beleive contrary thereto are without the pale of their Society & Church fellowship

3ly Since the power of god hath been declared to bee the order of the gosple, & so received beleived & own'd, on wch ground freinds have often met together & waited upon the Lord in expectation that this power in which their faith stood would bee sufficient to instruct them to bringe forth some outward forme on every diversity of occasion whereon they should have need, how comes it to passe that now an Hierarchy & order which wee take to bee outward must bee one way to distinguish the Church of Christ from such who falcely pretend thereto, especially since it hath been testified in the scripture, Sathan himselfe is transform'd into an angell of light.[20]

4ly Since accordinge to the principle of truth wee are not to expect the appearance of Xt at this day otherwise than by his spirit in the heart, where his spirituall law is written, ~~wh~~ & where hee hath & will come to raigne to governe & to rule, how comes it to passe that an outward Hierarchy & order comes to bee layd downe as the order of the governmte of the church of Christ, and {that} the method of [illegible deletion] upholdinge thereof is one way to distinguish the Church of Christ from such ~~who~~ {as} falcely pretend thereto

The consideration thereof occasions us to desire to bee inform'd & satisfied what that method is that is necessary to uphold the aforesaid Hierarchy & ordr

5ly Since it is so that the order of the gosple is the power of god & so hath been asserted by the opposers of John Wilkinson & John Story, (wch power is of ability to establish man, but man not of ability to establish it) wee desire to bee informed [illegible deletion] whether it can bee asserted on the foote of truth. that the order of the gosple is established throughout the whole nation, & if so, by whome it is established & from whence such establisher or establishers had their power If ~~so bee there~~ any there bee that pretend thereto.—

{3d Dissatisfaction}

Wee are not satisfied that many of those who as wee reasonably take it are accounted Governours, or at least take upon them so to bee, have acted in some things wherein they have been concern'd accordinge to the principle of truth & light of Christ Jesus, & therefore such their actions have had no answer in our consciences

The matters on which this dissatisfaction is grounded are in part as followeth.

John Story and John Wilkinson have been rendered men of bad spirits, and when Thomas Speed of this Citty who solemnly professed hee was of no party, but desired plainely to bee inform'd did at a meetinge held at Richard Sneed's house occasioned by William Pen and others, ask't this sober question, or a question to the like import, what is that good that John Story & John Wilkinson are departed from; & what is that evill they are joined to, Wm Pen as answer referred him to the articles meaninge the 44 articles of accusation drawne up as wee have also been informed on the behalfe of the Church, which are the matters for which John Story and John Wilkinsons sp^{ts} are judged {the} said Articles were signed by Robert Barrow & 26 persons more,[21] wee therefore doe proceed to lay downe a few of those articles of accusations amongst severall others of like nature for which they have been condemned, & leave it to the consciences of unprejudiced ~~readers~~ {hearers to consider} whether such things deserve so severe censure & condemnation as hath been published agst them.

The matter of fact contained in the 5th article against John Story is in these very words viz.

Jno Story speakinge amongst many friends of the danger of formes because of the consequences that might follow said that amongst the Christians of old the diferences that did arise were about formes,

Wee now say that since tis an undoubted truth that some differences did arise aboute formes, wee cannot in conscie[nce] conclude him to bee an offender had hee so said. but hee affirmes his words were spoke with respect to some differ[ences] & not all differences.

The 7th Article thus saith, when there came a paper from the yeerely meetinge at Lond^{o} (when George Fox was beyond ~~the~~ sea) wch intimated that every county should ~~send~~ take care to send {up} one or two freinds to the s^{d} ~~yeerely~~ meetinge yeerly; & that this epistle of theirs should bee written in our booke. John Story did use words severall times to hinder the recordinge of it in our booke[22]

The hearers may now Take notice that severall doe Testify from their owne Knowledge that the yearely meeting intimated did at their meeting the first yeare discontinue the s^{d} meeting and soe noe such constituted meetings have since [then] been held,[23] which clearly shews that where s^{d} ~~meeting~~ paper is recorded, there is a record which the yearly meeting [then] constituted approved not of to be Observed, Amongst the s^{d} 44 articles the subscribers thereof doe thus say that the Brethren agreed to gether at the quarterly meetinge that a Testimoney of Every ones Judgment and Practice in the case of Tithes should bee brought {in} in writing to the next quarterly meeting and one this occation, The 2 next following accusations are [illegible deletion] Inserted in the Articles (viz)

That John Story and John Wilkinson said. They had rather mens actions shewed their faithfullness then their writings which is part of the matter of fact conteined in the 11th article and are savory words That John Wilkinson said, Wee saw little ~~good~~ good could bee done that way, But concerning Tithes freinds must[24] be left to the publick Exhortations and preachinge of the word of life & no other way hee would consent to bee used in this matter this is contained in the 18th article & wherein this should bee an offence wee understand not.

The 19th Article is thus layd downe; when a couple had propounded their mariage at a quarterly meetinge & beinge desired {by some} to goe to the womens meetinge to acquaint them with it. John Wilkinson & John Story objected, what need is there for goinge to them with it is all the mariages that have been before now imperfect, or must they bee maried over againe,

In the 43 Article tis thus said. When wee asked them if they owned the things themselves contayned {in} George Foxes directions to freinds concerninge the afors^{d} matters {note the aforesd matters are: aboute monethly & quarterly meetings women's meetings & testimonies agst tithes & recording of condemnations—} John Story said hee was dissatisfied with somethinge but would not tell what and with our management of them. ~~as to this~~

As to this last accusation tis fitt the hearers should consider, whether it naturally followes from the principle of truth that John Story must bee of a wrong spirit, if hee bee dissatisfied with some things given forth by George Foxes touchinge womens meetinge &c and the managem^{t} thereof by Robt Barrow & the other 26 subscribers of the afores^{d} 44 articles, truely the aforesaid Query is the more observable for that it seemes to us a discovery of the secret cause from whence all these Contentions doe arise & brings to our remembrance two things.

The one is that Robert Barrow & 9 other persons all of them subscribers to the 44 articles have in answer to Jno Storyes & Jno Wilkinsons answer to the 44 Articles they repeated John Storyes words. viz—

John Story further saith that hee did not beleive that George Fox entended any such thinge that they should with severity bee urged upon any of Gods faithfull people, but as instructions or directions recommended them to the Churches leaving the effect thereof to god & his leadinge grace in his people to make up thereof as he should manifest a need of such direction, councell or advice to which one part of the answer is thus, truely John Story thy darknes & blindnes is easy to bee felt & they must bee very dimm of sight that sees the not or [?] the Confusion thy darke spirit is in,

On this wee thus observe that such an answer doth not answer gods wittnes in our consciences & that wee never understood ~~that~~ from the words of George Foxes Mouth; but that what was upon his sp^{t} to deliver to freinds convinced of the truth relating to faith or discipline among the members of the Church of X^{t} was recommended fro his Measure of him who is the fullnes that filleth all things unto our Consciences {that ~~is~~} ~~that~~ thorough the answer of our consciences enlightened by a measure of him who is the fullnes wee might bee att unity therewith. but if it bee really so that George Foxes intention was otherwise than by our sense wee now Expresee wee cannot but ingenuously confesse wee were wholy mistaken in our sense of his intentions, & therefore that the truth may bee manifested & all occasions of Stumblinge & differences removed amongst brethen wee desire that the two questiens proposed {at Drawell}[25] may now bee answered by George Fox & not onely by him but ~~by~~ also by those other publicke persons {now} in this Citty who have by writinge under their hands testified aganst John Story & John Wilkinson as persons of a separate spt or to that Effect by wch wee[26] take theire meaning to be as if they were Seperat from the truth, and the reason why, wee doe desire, that these questions may be in all manner of plainness without any equevacation [illegible letter or symbol] or reservations, answarded is this, wee have a sence that the Answare therof according to the truth may be a great meanes to allay the differances amongst frindes if not affterwards deviated therfrom,

The 2d Questions are as followeth,

1 Query whether or noe wee and all gods people ought not to be left, in all mattrs of faith and discyplien, soe farr as the disiplien becomes matter of {faith} to the manifestation of gods Spt {& truth} in or owne hearts and to speak and act therin as wee are therby Instructed and perswaded and not otherwise

2 Q Since there are diversitis of Tallents and giffts given by the Spt of god, and received by men whether the Judgmt of truth itselfe, given forth through a part of the members of xt body cann become a bonde upon any othr part of the saide body farther then theire undrstandings are Illuminated therby, the other thing is this the said Robert Barrow, and the other 9 persons wrighting about marriages, comeing before womens meetings said this was that, ~~that~~ wch George Fox exhorted to in the begining, and Blessed be the Lord, the faithfull Sees a nesesetie and Cause to propose, the marriages to the Faithfull men and womens meetings, and whether theire Sight is not dark that Sees not the [illegible deletion] nesesetie of proposeing theire Marriages to the Faithfull men and women in theire destinkt meetings, from hence wee observe that it may be reasonablie suposed that theire Confidence Inquering as afforsaid Springs from a presumption that Georg Fox exhorted soe in the begining, & that therfore it must be darkness in all that sees not A nesesetie, to act in that outward Concerne of Accomplishing Marriages according to that very forme and order that Georg Fox directed,

It may allsoe be observed that the darkness of these 10 persons is soe great, as not onely to reflect on ~~the many of the {many frein~~ many} freinds of this Cittie as unfaithfull and darke seighted but allsoe on ~~the~~ {many} [illegible deletion] freinds of Divrs Counties ~~of~~ {in} England beseids—if not at the time of the one wrighting on all freinds in places afforsaid [?] And many publike labourd allsoe who nevr yet saw a necesetie to proposs marriages to the Womens destin[ct] meetings. and in perticular on Georg Foxs Marriage allsoe for that his marriage was not proposed in the womens destinkt meetinge in this Cittie — where it was accomplis[h]ed, though a womens destin[ct] meeting was Severall yeares before held in this Cittie,[27] as by Suffis[t]ient

Testimony of the truth hear[of?] arriseing from amongst the freinds in this Cittie is mannifested, many other observations might [be] made on Said Articles, to manifest that the Contriv^{rs} therof, acted not according to the truth, for the manif[est]ation wherof, wee refere the hearers to the Articles themselves,

Wee now Come to take notice of the pap^{r} Datted From Elias Hooks Chamber in London, the 12th of the 4th mo 1677 ag^{ts} John Wilkison and John Storrie,[28] wch Some of the subscribers vindicatte as A paper from the yearly meeting,

on wch wee observe that if therby Jno Storrie & John Wilkins are Condemned for the matters alleged against them at Drawell, that Seemes Impertinent, because they have beene at a large Ratte Condemned, for that before, but if any shall say as by reportt {it is sayd} that J. W: & J: S: have disowned that paper wch is termed theire paper of Condemnation,[29] and that therfore the paper afforsaid from Elias Hooks Chamber, was given forth to this wee may say, truth cannot owne such a pretence for if it were really soe that they soe did, wch wee doe not beleive because wee have hard J: S owne the same according to the Common exceptations of the Words therin layd downe, yet they ought not to have been Condemned, by such who nither hard them Speak for themselves, nor yet Endeav^{r}ed that they might have opportunetie Soe to doe and if this be not soe wth respect to many if not all, that Signed that paper, wee descire it may be made appeare, to the Contrary—for wee doe knowe that Sev^{r}all in our Cittie who subscribed the same, was not able to manifest to o^{r} Consciences that they were free from guilt

In that Case, and for a further manifestation, of the Reasonableness of our dissatisfacktion, touching that paper from Elias Hooks Chamber wee refer the hearers to an Answare therto, given from this Cittie and allsoe from Wiltshire,[30] both which wee now desire may be read amongst the freinds in this meeting, the next thinge wee come to take notice of, is a paper datted Kendal the 2th of 9mo 77: Subscribed by Robert Barrow and 15 persons more, in answare to a Letter sent by us and other freinds to the number of 62 wch was onely to accompanie a paper sent by Jno Storry to the freinds in the north at varience, as an expedient for peace[31] Concerning wch paper, in Answare to o^{rs} ~~that~~ wee are not Sattisfyed, that the Same is given forth, according to the Sp^{t} of truth, ~~and~~ {nor yet} made use of according to gosple for that it was not sent to us {concerned} but to oth^{rs} and by them read in a meeting ag^{ts} us before given to us [illegible deletion] and for as much as it Came from theire monthly meeting in Kendall therfore wee descire, that o^{r} Letter to wch it is writt as an Answare may be read, togather wth John Storries Epistle, for reuniting the meetings, the paper from Kendall in Answare to o^{rs} and our Answare therto, that soe the hearers may be Informed, rightly of the state of that matter, and soe leave it to theire Consciences to waye and Consid^{r}, whether, the pap^{r} from Kendall Can be the fruitt of the pow^{r} of god, since by the Scoap of theire paper, they would have it soe und^{r}stood, wee now come to Consid^{r}, whether it is according to the truth for these Assemblies hinted {at} to be the Church to take upon them that jurisdiction, wch the Second daies meeting in London, by approveing Robert Berclays Booke alloues them to doe, on this accassion as ~~a the~~ a reason of o^{r} dissatisfaction, wee observe as followeth (viz that the Seconde dayes meeting have allowed, that wch we are not Sattisfyed {can} stand Justifyed in truth wee shall at present name this one perticular, Robt Bercley speaking of the order of the Gov^{r}m^{t} thuse saith In the Second place this ord^{r} reacheth the takeing up and Composing of differances, as to outward thinges &c and a little after Sayth, wee doe bouldly aver as a people gathered togather ~~from~~ by the Lord, unto the same faith, & disstinguished ~~by~~ {from} all others, by o^{r} Joynt Testimonie And Suff^{r}ings, that wee have po[wer] and Authoretie, to deside and remove these thinges Amonge o^{r} selves this as wee take it,[32] Impleing a Juriesdiction over outward thinges, wch christ himselfe Refuesed to take, though descired by one partie as may appeare Luke the 12th 13.14 when a Certaine man Said Master bid my Broth^{r} Devide the Inheritance with me, and Christ Said who made me a Judg and Devider over yo^{u} [33] tis allsoe to be observed that Robt Bertcley['s?] Intent could not be that the Church hath pow^{r} onely when the differing parties, give up theire Case as to outward thinges to them, because that is power given by man, to them, and not Inherant in them as A Church, who as a Church have noe power Inhere[nt] in them, but what they receive from and is given them of god, if the Powers of the Church in outward things According to Robt Berclayes Intentions be noe more then what is given them by Assent of parties then it may truly be said that any Heathen man, may Justly Claime as much pow^{r} in that respect, when tis Soe given to him,—

William Rogers
William Forde
Arthur Esmead
John Matravers

DS. Bristol MSS V., B. R. O. Ref. SF/C1/1(a), Bristol Archives Office. (*Micro.* 2:608).

1. This meeting on 1 Feb. was the first of three meetings held in Bristol in Feb. 1678 between William Rogers, John Story, and their supporters, on the one side, and WP and his supporters on the other, in an effort to end the Wilkinson-Story controversy (see headnote to doc. 91). William Rogers planned to read the paper that follows, but was unable to do so before the meetings adjourned. William Rogers, *The Christian-Quaker* (1680), pt. 5, pp. 11-12. For accounts of the other meetings, see *Micro.* 2:390 and 2:648.

2. William Ford (d. 1709), a serge weaver and an active member of the Bristol Monthly Meeting, was imprisoned in 1654 for no assigned cause and in 1664 for unlawful assembly and resisting arrest. Mortimer, *Minute Book of the Men's Meeting . . . Bristol*, p. 200; Besse, 1:41, 50.

3. Arthur Ismeade, of Wiltshire, was imprisoned in 1660 for refusing to take an oath. With Nathaniel Coleman, John Jennings, and John Matravers, all adherents of Wilkinson and Story, he was disowned by the Wiltshire Quarterly Meeting on 4 Oct. 1680 for "indevors to scattar, devid." See testimony printed in "Wilkinson-Storyism in Wiltshire c. 1680," *JFHS* 16:143-44; Besse, 2:40; Braithwaite, *Second Period*, p. 317.

4. John Matravers, of Wiltshire, also supported the separatists and was disowned by the Wiltshire Quarterly Meeting. See n. 3, above.

5. George Fox, *This is an Encouragement to All the Women's Meetings* ([London], 1676).

6. Fox, *This is an Encouragement*, p. 43. In the manuscript, whenever a passage is quoted, the scribe has placed quotation marks at the beginning of each line. The editors have followed modern convention here and have placed quotation marks at the beginning and close of each quoted passage.

7. Judg. 17:1-5.

8. Fox, *This is an Encouragement*, p. 43.

9. 2 Sam. 13-14.

10. Fox, *This is an Encouragement*, pp. 23-24.

11. 1 Sam. 2:22-23.

12. This scriptural passage refers to purification after childbirth. Lev. 12:1-8.

13. Fox, *This is an Encouragement*, pp. 31-32; Gen. 31:14-16.

14. Fox, *This is an Encouragement*, p. 42.

15. Judg. 11:29-40.

16. See Fox's epistle, "To Friends, concerning Judging," dated 1653 and published in George Fox, *A Collection of Many Select and Christian Epistles, Letters and Testimonies*, (London, 1698), 2:47-51. Fox's reference to Ham is from Gen. 9:22-27.

17. Rom. 2:1-3.

18. Robert Barclay, *The Anarchy of the Ranters* ([London], 1676). The preface was dated Ury, 17 Oct. 1674. Barclay said that he knew nothing of the Wilkinson-Story controversy when he wrote the book. Braithwaite, *Second Period*, p. 340.

19. Barclay, *Anarchy of the Ranters*, sect. 4.

20. 2 Cor. 11:14.

21. The forty-four articles were issued by members of the orthodox Westmorland Quarterly Meeting and were answered by Wilkinson and Story at the Draw-well meeting in Apr. 1676. Rogers, *The Christian-Quaker*, pt. 4, pp. 26, 37-40; *The Memory of that Servant of God, John Story, Revived* (London, 1683), pp. 37-38.

22. The manuscript is written by three different hands. The first clerk stopped at this point.

23. In June 1672 Friends decided that delegates from each county should meet annually in London, but in 1673, when the first representative London Yearly Meeting took place, they decided that future Yearly Meetings should be composed only of ministers. In 1678 the representative meeting started up again, and has continued ever since. Braithwaite, *Second Period*, pp. 276-77.

24. The first clerk began to write again at this point.

25. The meeting held in Apr. 1676 at Draw-well near Sedbergh in Yorkshire.

26. The third hand starts here.

27. A women's meeting was established in Bristol in 1667. George Fox and Margaret Fell were married in Bristol on 27 Oct. 1669. Their intentions were published at three meetings in Bristol: at a meeting on 18 Oct. 1669 attended by men and women, at a men's meeting on 21 Oct. 1669 also attended by women, and at a public meeting on 22 Oct. 1669. Fox, 2:116; Mortimer, *Minute Book of the Men's Meeting . . . Bristol*, pp. 24-25.

28. This paper, issued from Ellis Hookes' chamber on 12 June 1677, was a strong condemnation of Wilkinson and Story. It was signed by sixty-six Friends, after some of the ministers who had gathered for the London Yearly Meeting of Ministers had departed. The paper was printed in John Blaykling, et al., *Anti-Christian Treachery Discovered* (1683). Braithwaite, *Second Period*, p. 309.

29. See doc. 135, n. 2.

30. According to William Rogers, there were two replies to the paper issued from Ellis Hookes' chamber: one signed by John Jennings and seventy other Friends from Wiltshire, and another signed by Thomas Goldney, William Ford, William Rogers, and sixteen others from Bristol. Rogers, *The Christian-Quaker*, pt. 4, p. 109.

31. On 30 Sept. 1677, John Story wrote a conciliatory letter to Friends in Westmorland, calling on both sides to reunite. The members of the orthodox meeting rejected his proposal and, in their paper dated 2 Nov. 1677, offered only to receive confessions from the separatists. Story's letter is printed in *The Memory of . . . John Story*, pp. 40-45. See also, Braithwaite, *Second Period*, pp. 310-11.

32. Barclay, *Anarchy of the Ranters*, sect. 5.

33. Luke 12:13-14.

125
TWO SPEECHES TO A COMMITTEE OF PARLIAMENT

The next two documents show WP making a more vigorous and risky plea for religious toleration than ever before. When WP appeared before a committee of Parliament in March 1678 as a spokesman for the Meeting of Sufferings (doc. 125), he complained of being branded "an Emissary of Rome & in pay from the Pope." Yet he had the courage to argue that Catholics, like Quakers, should not be persecuted for matters of conscience. This was a daring position to take on the eve of the Popish Plot. And it was probably at this time that WP drew up several drafts of bills on toleration to be passed by Parliament; two of these drafts are printed in doc. 126. In the first of these toleration bills, WP calls for the repeal of the penal laws under which the Quakers had long been fined and imprisoned. In the second bill, WP proposes a series of declarations to replace the Test oath, to be taken by Protestant dissenters, by candidates for parliamentary election, and by their electors.

[22 March 1678]

William Penns 2 Speeches before a Committee in the parliam^{t} house the 22nd of the month called March 1678. Upon occasion of a Complaint made by him & his friends (called Quakers) that they suffered not only by Laws made ag^{t} them, but by Laws made ag^{t} Papists. And their presenting (upon the demand of the Committee) a discrimination of themselves from Papists.[1]

The first Speech.

If we ought to believe that it is o^{r} duty, according to the doctrine of the Apostle to be always ready to give an acc^{t} of the hope that is in us, & that to every sober & private enquirer; certainly much more {ought we} to hold o^{r}selves obliged to declare wth all readiness (w^{n} called to it by so great an authority) w^{t} is not o^{r} hope, especially w^{n} o^{r} very safety is eminently concerned in so doing; & that we cannot decline this discrimination of o^{r}selves from Papists, wthout being conscious to o^{r}selves of the guilt of o^{r} own sufferings: for that must every man needs be that suffers mutely under another Character, then that wch truly & properly belongs to him & his belief.

That wch gives me a more then ordinary right to speake at this time & in this place, is the great abuse that I have rec^{d} above any other of my profession. For of along time I have not only been supposed a Papist, but a Seminary, a Jesuit, an Emissary of Rome & in pay from the Pope, a man dedicating my $endeavo^{rs}$ to the Interest & advancement of that party.[2] Nor hath this been the report of the rabble, but the jealousy & insinuation of persons otherwise sober & discreet: nay some zealous for the Protestant Religion have been so far gone in this mistake, as not only to think ill of us & to decline o^{r} Conversation, but to take courage to themselves to persecute us for a sort of concealed Papists.[3] And the truth is, w^{t} wth one thing & w^{t} wth another we have been as the Wool-sacks & common-whipping-stock of the kingdom: all laws have been let loose upon us, as if the design were not to reform but to destroy us, & that not for w^{t} we are, but for w^{t} we are not. Tis hard that we must thus bear the stripes of another Interest, & be their Proxy in $punishm^{t}$; but its worse, that some men can please themselves, in such a sort of administration.

I would not be mistaken: I am far from thinking it fit that Papists should be whipt for their Conscience, because I declaim ag^{t} the injustice of whipping Quakers for Papists, No. For though the hand pretended to be lifted up ag^{t} them hath (I know not by w^{t} direction) litt heavily upon us, & we complain; yet we do not mean, that any should take a fresh aim at them, or that they must come in o^{r} roome for we must give the Liberty we ask, & cannot be false to o^{r} Principle, though it were to relieve o^{r}selves. For we have good will to all men, & would have none suffer for a truly sober & conscientious dissent on any hand: & I humbly take leave to add, that those Methods ag^{t} persons so qualified do not seem to me to be convincing or indeed adequate to the reason of mankind: but this I submit to yor consideration.[4]

To Conclude, I hope we shall be {held} excused of the men of that Profession, in giving this distinguishing declaration, since it is not wth design to expose them, but first to pay the regard we owe to the Enquiry of this Committee. And in the next place to relieve o^{r}selves from the daily spoil & ruin, wch now attend & threaten many hundreds of familys by the execution of Laws (that we humbly conceive) were never made ag^{t} us.

The Second Speech.

The Candid hearing our Sufferings have rec^{d} from this Committee, & the fair & easy $entertainm^{t}$, that you have given us, obligeth me to add w^{t}ever can increase yor satisfaction about us. I hope ye don't believe, I would tell you a lye, I am sure I should chuse an ill time & place to tell it in; but I thank God, it is too late in the day for that; there are some here, that have known me formerly, I believe they will say, I never was that man; & it would be hard, if after a voluntary neglect of the Advantages of this world I should sit down in my Retiremt short of common truth.

Excuse the Length of my Introduction, 'tis for ye I made it. I was bred a Protestant, & that strictly too: I lost nothing by time or study; for years, reading, travail & observation made the Religion of my education the Religion of my judgemt. My alteration hath brought none to that belief; & though the Posture I am in may seem odd or strange to you, yet I am Conscientious, & (till ye know no better) I hope yor Charity will rather call it my unhappiness than my crime. I do tell you again, & here solemnly declare in the presence of Almighty God, & before you all, that the Profession I now make, & the society I now adhere to, have been so far from altering that Protestant judgemt I had, that I am not conscious to myself of having receded from an Iota of any one principle maintained by those first Protestants & Reformers in Germany, & or own Martyrs[5] at home agt the Pope or See of Rome.

On the contrary I do wth great truth assure you, that we are of the same Negative[6] Faith wth the antient Protestant Church, & upon occasion shall be ready (by Gods assistance) to make it appear, that we are of the same belief, as to the most fundamentall positive Articles of her Creed too.[7] And therfore it is we think it hard that though we deny in common wth her those doctrines of Rome so zealously protested agt (from whence came the name Protestant) yet that we should be so unhappy as to suffer, & that wth extream severity, by those very Laws on purpose made agt the maintainers of those doctrines we do so deny. We choose no suffering, for God knows, wt we have already suffered & how many sufficient & trading families are reduced to great Poverty by it. We think orselves an Usefull People, we are sure, we are a peaceable people; yet if we must still suffer, let us not suffer as Popish-Recusants, but as Protestant-Dissenters.

But I would obviate another Objection, & that none of the least that hath been made agt us, viz. That we are enemys to governmt in generall, & particularly disaffected to this we live under. I think it not amiss but very seasonable yea my duty, now to declare to you (& that I do wth good Conscience in the sight of Almighty God) First, that we believe govermnt to be Gods ordinance. And next, that the present govermnt is establisht by the providence of God & law of the Land; & that it is or Christian duty, readily to obey it in all its {just} laws, & wherin we cannot comply through tenderness of Conscience, in all such cases not to revile or conspire agt the governmt; but wth Christian humility & patience tire out all mistakes about us, & wait their better information, that we believe, do as undeservedly as severely treat us. And I know not wt greater security can be given by any people, or how any governmt can be easier from the subjects of it.[8]

I shall conclude wth this, that we are so far from esteeming it hard or ill, that the house hath put us upon this discrimination, that on the contrary we value it (as we ought to do) for an high favo^r (& cannot chuse but see & humbly acknowledg Gods providence therin) that ye should give us this fair occasion to discharge o^rselves of a burden we have not wth more patience than injustice suffered but too many years under. And I hope o^r conversation shall always manifest the gratefull resentment of our minds for the Justice & Civility of the opportunity. And so, I pray, God direct you.

Copy. Penington MSS, FLL. (*Micro.* 2:651). Inscribed in margin: Wm Penns 2 | Speeches in | Parliam^t.

1. The mounting anti-Catholic agitation of the late 1670s directly affected Friends, because the law of 1605 (3 James I, cap. 4), designed to suppress Roman Catholics, permitted justices to administer an antipapal loyalty oath to persons who absented themselves from Church of England services, with no provision for affirmation in place of swearing. Those who refused to take the oath were subject to the penalty for *praemunire facias*. See also docs. 81, 126. The Meeting for Sufferings was very concerned about this development. On 17 Jan. 1678, WP reported that he and other Quakers had addressed the king and council on the subject, and that the king had agreed that it was "very unreasonable" that Friends be persecuted as recusants. However, the king and council told Friends that they had to look to Parliament for relief. Therefore, on 7 Mar. 1678, WP, George Whitehead, and William Gibson were delegated to draw up a paper on Friends suffering under the statute against recusants, to be presented to Parliament. See Minutes of the Meeting for Sufferings, vol. 1, FLL.

2. This charge was brought against WP on a number of occasions, most seriously during the Popish Plot. See docs. 121 and 128.

3. Not only were Friends persecuted under laws against recusants, but they were confused with recusants. Until 15 Feb. 1679 they answered such charges, but on that date the Meeting for Sufferings decided to "respite giveing out any publique writing concerning the Scandalls against friends as papists in generall," a decision no doubt influenced by the fact that elections for a new Parliament were going forward. Minutes of the Meeting for Sufferings, vol. 1, FLL.

4. WP made the same point in *A Seasonable Caveat Against Popery* (1670), and in a letter to Richard Langhorne (doc. 61). In 1675, in *England's Present Interest Discover'd,* he maintained that Roman Catholics, a minority interest, could be contained in a free society (see *Works,* 1:698). The Popish Plot, however, influenced him, and in 1679, in *England's Great Interest in the Choice of this New Parliament,* he warned voters against disguised papists (those who laughed at the plot), and called blind obedience to the papal interest "that Fatal Mischief Popery brings with it to Civil Society." *Works,* 2:681. In *One Project for the Good of England: that is, Our Civil Union is our Civil Safety* (1679), he urged a new test (a declaration, rather than an oath) which would allow Quakers to unite with all other Protestants against the papists. *Works,* 2:689.

5. The Marian martyrs, or Protestants burned as heretics during the reign of Mary Tudor.

6. "Negative" is used here to mean the faith in opposition to the Roman Church.

7. WP's audience was probably not convinced. In Jan. 1679, Edward Conway, Viscount Conway, a communicant of the Church of England, wrote to his wife, Lady Anne Conway, who had just been convinced to Quakerism: "Geo. Gregson presented me lately with two speeches of William Pens to a Committee of Parliament in March last. In one of them he says, They are of the same principles of Faith with us in the most fundamental Articles, if so then the Difference is only in matters of practice, and if I should agree that theirs is better then ours, I think I should loose the use of my reason." Nicolson, *Conway Letters,* p. 446.

8. WP frequently argued that dissent was not necessarily bad citizenship. See his cogent statement of this position in *One Project for the Good of England: that is, Our Civil Union is our Civil Safety* (1679).

126
TWO TOLERATION BILLS

[1678?][1]

An Act for the Preserving of the Subjects Properties, & for the repealing of Several penal Laws, by which the lives & properties of the subjects were subject to be forfeited for things not in their power to be avoyded.

{a form of a Preamble to a Bill of Tolleration.}[2]

Whereas the Governmt & antient Laws of this Kingdom, whilst they continued to consider the preserving of property, as a fundamentall of Governmt, and as that sure and solid Ground, on which the honour, safety, & wealth of our Kings & Kingdome did depend, were so dear unto, & so highly esteemed by all the subjects of this Kingdom, & by strangers also. That, albeit warrs & contentions sometimes hapned in relation to the Title of[3] the Crown of this Realm; yet none were ever found to contrive any change or Alterations in the Laws or Govnmt. Nor were any of the subjects of this Kingdome ever tempted to transplant themselvs into other Contries, though strangers were frequently invited to come & settle here, where they were secured by a lasting Experience, that all persons without Exception should be protected in the enjoymt of their Properties untouchd, so long as they should take care not to offend agt or break any of those Laws, by which property was to be maintained & preserved. And whereas of late times, & by reason of several unhappy differences hapning in this Kingdom in the mattrs of Religion, several severe penal Laws & statutes have been made; which, albeit that they ~~were~~[4] {might be} devised with Good Intent, to compose the sayd Differences, & to reduce all persons to a conformity to the[5] Religion now established by Law in this Kingdom. Neverthelesse, for that the same have been found to intrench upon, & make such notable Alterations ~~of &~~[6] in those our antient laws, by which the subjects Properties stood fenced, & guarded, as that the Estates & Fortunes of all men & the lives of many are by the said late penal laws & statutes subjected to be lost & forfeited, whensoever by any mistakes in Judgmt, or misguidance of their Consciences they shall be unable to close with the Religion here established by Law:[7] The said penal-laws & statutes have not been able to produce those good effects, which were expected from them. But on the contrary, many whole Families of the industrious & trading subjects of this Kingdom for the preserving of their properties, & avoyding of the grivous penalties of the before mentioned Statutes, have been induced to forsake this Kingdom, & to go, & plant themselvs with their Estates & fortunes ~~&~~ in other Countries, & others to[8] the Intent to free themselves from the same penaltyes have beene Tempted To Endeavour & Contrive the Alteracon of the soe long established Governmt of this Kingdome To the Great impoverishing and depopulacon of this Countrey And strangers & forraigners have beene discouraged from comming into and settling themselves amongst us where they apprehend that they and their Children after them ~~ea~~ [?] cann be no Longer secured in the Injoyment of their propertyes Then they shall be able to prevayle with their Consciences to beleive That the Religion which Our Lawes shall at ~~any~~ {all} times approve Is undoubtedly True and the way of Worshipping of God which shall at all at all times be by our Lawes Enjoyned is and shall be more agreeable To the will of God Then any other way in which God is Worshipped in this World Wherefore To the Intent The said Inconveniencyes may be removed And for that it is Clearely Evident That forceable Courses Cannott begett True Fayth which is only from the Grace and Guift of Allmighty God And those who are in Errour are rather to be pyttyed and used with Kindness Then putt to death or deprived of their propertyes because they doe not beleive aright Which is not in the power of Man to doe before Allmighty God is pleased to give them his Grace for that purpose And forasmuch as there is this Great Difference Betweene Truth and Error Error will of it selfe perrish and come to Nothing Whilst Truth beeing of God will stand by virtue of its owne strength And Needs not the Weake and feeble props of humayne Lawes or the force of the sword to support it And for that the principles of the Religion Now Established by our Lawes were never understood to require us To stripp the Dissenters from that Religion of their lives or propertyes because they have not as yett received Faith from God to beleive & Conforme[9]

An other Form of Bill for the better Preserving, & maintaining English Property, being the true Fundation of English Government.

FORASMUCH as Property (by which is understood Right of Ownership, Legislation, & Judgmt by Peers, according as is repeated in the 14 & 29 Cha. of the Great Charter, The petition of Right, & above 30 other Laws)[10] is the Fundation of the English Governmt, and that the preservation of it hath ever been as well the Interest of the King, as the Security of the people; which is the great end of Governmt

And since in after-Ages several laws have been made upon occasion of Dissent in matters of Religion to compell an uniformity to that Religion now Established, that in the Execution of them have provd destructive to Property by an imprisonmt of persons, and a seisure of their Estates for only refusing Conformity to the establisht Religion: not because of any enormity committed agt the civil Authority, or any of those laws made to maintain Property, & that the consequences thereof are pernicious, in as much as the free people of England becomes uncapable by the aforesaid laws upon a meer religious dissent of quietly enjoying their natural Inheritances, however otherwise well qualified, which is a violation upon the antient Governmt of this Kingdom in making the necessary qualification to a Good Subject Not-Conformity to the laws of the Governmt; but the Laws of the Church. And since by long Experience it is found, that this Course ~~th~~ doth not obtain the end designd & desired; but on the contrary that it tends to the encreasing animosities, raising Tumults, impoverishing the Inhabitants, depopulating the Country, & great decay of trade, & that it is so far from inviting, that it justly deters strangers from coming, & setling amongst us. Be it therefore Enacted, and it is hereby enacted by the King etc.— —

That no person or persons within this Kingdom shall be molested, damnified, or any way prejudiced for or because of his or their dissent or non-Conformity to the Religion establisht by or in pursuance of any Laws or Statutes made, or that are in force to that purpose, viz. — —nor any ways hurt, punisht, or destroy'd for the Exercise of his or their Conscience in a different way, then is establisht by law within this Realm; provided allways, That every such Dissenter shall solemnely, and as in Gods presence,[11] before the Justices of the Kings peace in open Sessions repeat & subscribe this following Declaration & Engagemt

> I (AB) do hereby declare, that I have no dependance upon the Bishop or Pope of Rome, nor any other Prince or Power on Earth, then that——of England according to Law: That I do detest, & abhor that wicked Position, that any Pope can absolve me of my due Allegiance to the King & Governmt of England: And I do promiss by Gods Assistance to live a sober, peaceable, & industrious life under the present Government, as establisht by Law.
>
> AB.

I (AB)[12] do hereby promiss & declare to the people & Inhabitants of the Burrough of— that if it shall so come to pass, that they, the said people or Inhabitants shall please to choose, nominate, or appoint me AB. to serve them in Parliamt as their Truste Delegate, Representative, or Servant: That I the sayd AB. will neither directly nor indirectly, for fear, favour, or reward, or upon any other Score or Account whatever, vote, abett, consent, or agree to any Speech, Proposition, Question, Act or Law, that may, or shall be made, that relates to force any Kind of Conformity upon them about matters of Religion, whether it be in points of Faith, worship, or discipline; or to disturb them in, or trouble them for the Exercise of their consciences in the way of worship, wch they sincerely believe most agreeable with the mind & will of God. And I do hereby further promiss & declare, That I will neither directly nor indirectly for fear, favour or reward, or upon any other score w[t]soever vote, abett, consent, or in any Kind agree to any Speech, proposition, question, bill, Act, or Law, that shall or may be made in any Kind by this present Parliam[t] infringing, violating or subverting of the common Law of this Land the Rights, or Priviledges of the people thereof repeated in the Great Charter, & confirmed by sundry statutes of this Realm; especially by the petition of Right in the 3 of Charles 1st: But that in all such Cases I shall diligently, faithfully, & publiquely oppose, withstand, & protest against the same in the name of the free people of—

And I do further promiss & declare, that I will not for fear, favour, or reward hide, abscond, or decline my Attendance during the respective Sessions of this Parliam[t]. In witnesse whereof I do this day of ; here unto sett my hand & Seal.

AB.

We underwritten,[13] being Free People & Inhabitants of the Burrough & Corporation of — having by the common Law, & Fundamental Rights of this Realm of England a Right to chuse, nominate or appoint some one person to serve for us in Parliam[t] as our Delegate & Representative in, & for our Benefit, & behoof: We the said Free People, & Inhabitants do hereby declare, that we do chuse, nominate, & appoint AB. to serve us in Parliam[t] in the Capacity of our Delegate & Representative; in our name, & by our Authority, in all civil things to Act for us, & in our behoof, & for our benefit according to the Common Law, & Fundamentall Rights of this Realm, as they are repeated in 14 & 29 Chap. of the Great Charter, & confirmed by sundry other Statutes, especially the petition of Right; & not otherwise. And for as much, as divers Inconveniences have happened by the Execution of certain Penal Laws made to disturb Religious dissenters, as[?] to force on grievous punishm[ts] their conformity to the Religion & Worship establisht in this Land: We do hereby declare, that we have not given, nor do we give the sayd AB. any power or Authority, neither hath he any power or Authority to contrive, aid, abet, or in any wise countenance or connive at the making of any Law or Laws, that may lead to compell Conformity to the Religion & worship establisht, or to disturb any dissenters in their quiet Exercise of their Consciences in that way they sincerely believe, God requires them to worship him in. And we do hereby declare, that this Election shall not exceed the term of one whole year from the first day of the next Session, according to the good Laws of Edw. the 3, 4, & 36[14]. in which is enacted, That a Parliam[t] shall be held once a year.

LBC. WP's Letterbook, 1667-1675, HSP. (*Micro.* 1:559). This letterbook text is fragmentary. It contains an incomplete version of the preamble of the first bill, up to footnote number "8" in the edited text above; and the preamble, text, and oaths of a second bill, which appears to be complete. The editors have supplemented the letterbook text with another version of the preamble of the first bill, entitled "An Act for the preserveing of the Subjects Propertyes," a contemporary copy in Penn MSS, Chartes and Frames, vol. 8, fols. 65-67, HSP (hereafter called "An Act for the preserveing," no. 2). In addition to these texts, there is a very rough autograph draft of the preamble of the second bill, entitled "Bill for Preserving of Property," in an extra illustrated edition of John Galt's *The Life, Studies and Works of Benjamin West, Esq.*, vol. 1, p. 36, MSS Department, HSP.

1. These undated drafts could have been written at any time between 1673, when WP began his lobbying efforts at court and with Parliament to check religious persecution, and 1678, the date of the latest items from his 1667-1675 letterbook (see pp. 11-12, above). Because a major purpose of these bills was to stop the persecution of Quakers as Catholic recusants, and because WP, his Sussex neighbors, and other English Quakers were being persecuted exactly in this way in 1677-1678 (see doc. 121, n. 6), the editors believe that WP wrote them at about the time he addressed a parliamentary committee in Mar. 1678 (doc. 125).

2. This title appears in the right margin in the manuscript.

3. Corrected to "to" in WP's second draft, "An Act for the preserveing," no. 2.

4. "Were" stands in "An Act for the preserveing," no. 2.

5. "True" is added here in "An Act for the preserveing," no. 2.

6. "Of &" stands in "An Act for the preserveing," no. 2.

7. The most important parliamentary statute concerning religion which infringed upon the property rights of Englishmen was 3 James I, cap. 4 (1605), widely used against Quakers as well as Roman Catholics after the Restoration. See doc. 125, n. 1. All who refused to take the antipapal loyalty oath contained in this 1605 statute were construed to be denying the supremacy of the king, and were thus subject to the penalty for *praemunire facias* (see doc. 81, n. 11). The penalty for *praemunire* was the confiscation of all chattel goods, the deprivation of all income from real property, and imprisonment for life or at the king's pleasure. Restoration judges also used the more recent Uniformity (1662), Conventicle (1664, 1670), and Corporation, or Five-Mile Acts (1665) to attack other dissenters, particularly Presbyterians, Independents, and Baptists, but against Catholics and Quakers nothing was so effective as the *praemunire* provision of 1605. See Danby Pickering, ed., *The Statutes at Large, from Magna Carta to 1806* (Cambridge, England, 1762-1807), 2:72-74 (27 Edward III, stat. 1, cap. 1 [1353]); 6:332-35 (23 Elizabeth I, cap. 1 [1581], secs. 5-7, 11); 6:394-95 (29 Elizabeth I, cap. 6 [1587], secs. 1, 4, 7); and 7:150-62 (3 James I, cap. 4 [1605], secs. 11, 13-15, 27).

8. Here the letterbook draft of this first bill breaks off; from this point the text follows "An Act for the preserveing," no. 2.

9. Here the text of "An Act for the preserveing," no. 2, abruptly ends. The final page or pages of this manuscript draft are missing.

10. WP refers here, as he did at the close of the Penn-Mead trial (see doc. 48, and *The People's Ancient and Just Liberties Asserted,* in Penn, *Works,* 1:18), to the Great Charter of 1225, as restated in the Petition of Right (3 Charles I, cap. 1 [1628]), which WP here cites, and as interpreted in Sir Edward Coke's *Second Treatise* (1642). Chapter 14 of the Charter declared that "A freeman shall not be amerced [fined] . . . except in proportion to the measure of the offence, saving his contenement [his freehold, or sufficient goods to permit him to secure his livelihood]; . . . and none of the aforesaid amercements shall be imposed except by the oaths of honest and lawful men of the neighborhood." Chapter 29 declared: "No freeman shall be taken or imprisoned or deprived of any freehold, or liberties, or free customs, or outlawed, or banished, or in any other way destroyed, nor will we go upon him, nor send upon him, except by the legal judgment of his peers or by the law of the land. To no one will we sell, to no one will we deny, or delay right of justice." These two chapters were considered by seventeenth-century Englishmen to be the heart of the Great Charter, and the liberties in chapter 29 were seen, by 1600, as the origin of the guarantee to a trial by jury. William Sharp McKechnie, *Magna Carta, A Commentary on the Great Charter of King John* (Glasgow, 1905), pts. iv-v, and pp. 334-51, and 436-63; William F. Swindler, *Magna Carta, Legend and Legacy* (New York, 1965), pp. 292-94, 316-21; George Burton Adams and H. Morse Stephens, eds., *Select Documents of English Constitutional History* (New York, 1901), pp. 44, 46, 339-40.

11. Note the similarity here to the phrasing in WP's second speech in doc. 125: "I do . . . solemnly declare in the presence of Almighty God."

12. WP evidently wished this second declaration to be required of all candidates for election to the House of Commons, in order to prevent further persecuting legislation by Parliament.

13. WP evidently wished this third declaration to be required of all freeholders who voted in parliamentary elections.

14. The Cavalier Parliament, elected in 1661, was continued from session to session by Charles II until 1679. WP, in common with many critics of the court, greatly disliked this avoidance of parliamentary elections. His plan recalled the Levellers' plea in 1647 for annual parliamentary elections. The West New Jersey Concessions of 1676 (doc. 115, chap. 32, above) also provided for the annual election of the legislature. In 1679, when a new Parliament was finally elected, the Whigs introduced a bill providing for elections every two years. For the texts of the Edwardian statutes to which WP refers, see Pickering, *Statutes at Large*, 1:438 (4 Edward III, cap. 14 [1330]), and 2:154 (36 Edward III, cap. 10 [1362]). J. R. Jones, *The First Whigs: The Politics of the Exclusion Crisis, 1678-1683* (London, 1961), pp. 53-54.

127
FROM GEORGE HUTCHINSON

When Edward Byllynge and his trustees made provisions for the government of West New Jersey in the summer of 1676 (docs. 115-16, above), they had lacked any legal authority to do so; the duke of York, who had received title to the region in 1664, had never granted the right to govern West New Jersey to anyone. By 1678 this problem had become critical; the Quaker settlers at Burlington and in Fenwick's Salem colony were having difficulties with the duke's governor in New York, Sir Edmund Andros, who claimed the right to govern all of New Jersey. When George Hutchinson, of West New Jersey's Yorkshire tenth (see doc. 115, n. 3, above), wrote this letter to WP, he hoped that the duke's agents were on the point of accepting the Quaker colonists' claim to the right of government. But the Popish Plot interrupted negotiations, which were not completed until August 1680.

Lond: 7th 4th mo [June 16]78

Deare Friend

These shew thee that with much labor & toile day after day at last on the 3d day they promist without faile to set ~~the next~~ {this} 7th day a part to draw up their ~~depart~~ report & doe what lyes upon them to doe viz. Sr {Jno} Churchill[1] & Cousr Finch[2] And Sr Jno Wordin[3] also promist possitively not to let it lye at his[4] door after it came there but would dispatch it forthwith. we had an expectation of thy being here before this according to thy intention when here else had written before now tis Judged there is an absolute necessity of thy being here o'th 2d day[5] & thy absence to day will occasion my longer stay from my family & concerne which I now exceedingly long to be withall, if it have noe worse effect as to the main tis well, Gawin[6] is away also, I suppose (& that not without ground) on purpose soe that I now see as has been generally said, theres noe help to be expected from him, Geo: Whitehead bid me tell thee thou was desired here with what speed thou could therefore on both these acc^ts^ desires thou may not faile being here next 2^d^ day [illegible letter] hopeing if soe things may goe well, I haveing got something in to all the 3 concerned in the report, & got Finches edge taken of by a letter I writt him, not else but my very deare love to thee [?] & thyne unknown I rest

Thy Friend in truth Geo: Hutchinson

ALS. Society Collection, HSP. (*Micro.* 2:669). Addressed: To William Penn | These ddr[7] | Leave this at John Martins[8] | of Stenning in Sussex to | be delivred as above directed | wth care. Docketed: From | George Hutsinson.

1. Sir John Churchill (d. 1685) was attorney-general to the duke of York, and M.P. for Dorchester (1661-1678), and later became master of the rolls. He was a distant cousin of the more famous John Churchill, the future duke of Marlborough, who in 1678 was also in the duke of York's employ. *DNB*.

2. Heneage Finch (1647?-1719) the younger, son of Lord Chancellor Heneage Finch (d. 1682), became king's counsel in 1677 and was made solicitor-general in 1679. He was a nephew of Lady Conway (see docs. 90 and 101, above).

3. Sir John Werden (1640-1716), politician, diplomat, and barrister, was secretary to the duke of York, and M.P. for Reigate, Surrey. *DNB*.

4. Sir John Werden's. Werden had pledged to send the agreement along to the duke of York.

5. The Ford accounts (doc. 146) show that WP was at the London house of William Haige, a West Jersey land purchaser, on 23 May 1678, and again on 10 June.

6. Gawen Lawrie.

7. Probably "directed."

8. John Martin (1653-1695) was a Quaker merchant of Steyning, about five miles southeast of Warminghurst. Digest of Sussex Quarterly Registers, GSP; Besse, 1:717, 721, 723.

128
FROM JOHN GRATTON

In September 1678, Titus Oates announced that he had discovered a Popish Plot to kill Charles II. For the next three tumultuous months, while popular frenzy was mounting, and Parliament was investigating the plot, and Catholic suspects were being rounded up, tried, and executed, we have little evidence of WP's activities. In November he composed a somber epistle from Warminghurst "To the Children of Light in this Generation," in which he bemoaned the sad state of England and called upon the Quakers to mediate with God for their country's deliverance from evil (*Micro.* 2:686). A few weeks later, he received the following letter from a Derbyshire Friend, John Gratton, with its disturbing message that he was widely rumored to have turned Catholic and fled the country. Such a rumor was no laughing matter in December 1678. WP had faced earlier charges that he was a papist or a Jesuit (see docs. 121 and 125), and the reports would persist into the 1680s. Gratton's reference to WP's hiding at this time is rather puzzling because WP had been in London as recently as 22 November 1678. We do know that WP was in some peril in early 1679, and he may have sought refuge at Warminghurst briefly during February of that year. His name appeared on a Treasury Office list of "Quakers that are prosecuted as Popish Recusants" dated c. 7 March 1679, and the London Meeting for Sufferings, on 20 February 1679, was concerned about the "Great Scandall cast on Wm Pen," fearing that "his Absence adds to the same." WP did not stay away from London for longer than two months at any time between October 1678 and the summer of 1679, however, and during that time was in public view as a principal lobbyist against the persecution of Quakers and as one of the primary supporters of Algernon Sidney in the election of February 1679. See docs. 147-49; Minutes of the Meeting for Sufferings, vol. 1, 1678-1679, FLL; Peare, pp. 199-200; Braithwaite, *Second Period*, pp. 146-47, 665; *Calendar of Treasury Books, 1676-1679*, p. 1256-57.

[19 December 1678]

Dear Friend

In the pretious seed of life Eternall in which my unfained love is truly and really great unto thee doe I dearly salute thee in which pretious seed thats pure and without mixture thou art neer mee and of great value with mee as one of the nob[le] race & linage which is begotten and born of god in this the day of life light love & glory which in thee and many is thororo[1] they power of the most high dawned and broken foarth the glory wherof doth far exceed all the glory of Egipt and hath wonn many and afected many hartes and wayned[2] us of from all visible things glory to our god over all amen amen and blesed bee the lord who hath made thee a large partaker of they liveing mercyes of this day and hath raised thee up as a star to shine in the life and power of his sonn and as a sonn of thunder in this great day of battle: between the lamb and his followors and the dragon and his Angells in which the they lamb hath gott great victory blesed over all and magnifyed be his name which is becomn as ointment powered foarth: oh it is in the pure streaming foarth of this pure oyll of gladnes that my soull doth truly love and live with thee: and the unity and sweett fellowship in spirit that I often feell in the rememberanc of thee doth often refresh mee in my inward man and I can bles the lord even on thy behaulfe when I consider the great things that god hath don for thee above many and in that liveing seed of life I question not but thou art right sencible of my love in the truth unto thee and at this time in the waighty senc of gods love it was in my harte to write unto thee: to aquaint thee that heer is in this Country a very malitious ly and fals acusation Cast upon thee and soe foarcablely afirmed for a truth and that by the great ones and magistrates heer amongst us that it greived mee in spirit to behould and to hear it soe that I thought it might doe well to have a line or 2 from thee conserning it; the thing is this: they say thou art turned to bee a Jesuit and doth hide thy self or art fled thy Country; a thing soe far from thee as East and west: and tho I was loath to give thee the trouble of it: yet; by reason of their audatious feirc abetting of this thing for a reall truth, yea say they Confirmed too us by noe mean hands: and much more then I Can mention that I could not Easily forbear: therefore for the stoping the mouth of lyes and for truths sake which they take great corage upon this ocation sorely touching and bespattor in our markets and many places; I would have thee if thou see and find it with thee soe to doe; to write as speedily as thou Can to mee or willm stors of Chestorfeild[3] that wee may shew it to some who seem to beleeve it reall[?]. and in this beleeuf of it seems to bemoan us for poore deluded men & women and in thy letter I desire thee to send mee a Copy of that test[4] against poperey which was given in to they parllament soe in dear love unfained to thee thy dear wife and all that love our lord Jesus Crist in sincearity doe I remain thy ashured Frend & bro thoro mercy in my little measure of his blesed truth

monyash 19th
10 month 1678.
darbysheir

Joh gratton[5]

ALS. Penn Papers, HSP. (*Micro.* 2:698). Addressed: To | My belloved Frend | William penn this | with Care I pray | delivor | leave this with my | Frend Thomas Rudyard | at his house in georg | yard in lumbard street | to be delivored as is | above dyrected | London. Docketed: Jno Gratton | 19—10mo—78.

1. "Through."

2. "Weaned."

3. William Stors, member of Chesterfield Monthly Meeting in Derby, was imprisoned for three months in 1665 and fined over £75 in 1670 for attending Friends' meetings. He married Sarah Sykes in 1669. Digests of Quaker Records, Derby and Nottingham, GSP; Besse, 1:139-41.

4. Testimony. *OED*. Gratton is perhaps referring to WP's speeches to a committee of Parliament on 22 Mar. 1678 (see doc. 125).

5. John Gratton (1641-1712), of Monyash in Derby, was converted to Quakerism about 1672, and travelled in the ministry in England, Scotland, and Wales. He was excommunicated and sent to Derby prison in 1680, and though not released until 1686, he was able to go home for visits and to hold meetings in jail. Gratton's writings include *John Baptist's Decreasing, and Christ's Increasing witnessed* (1674) and *A Treatise concerning Baptism, and the Lord's Supper* (London, 1695). His journal was published in 1720. Fox, *Short Journal*, p. 343; *DNB*.

When Charles II dissolved the Cavalier Parliament in January 1679 and called the first general election since 1661, WP immediately plunged into the campaign. Barred from entry to the House of Commons by his Quakerism, WP supported the candidacy of his radical republican friend Algernon Sidney for a seat at the borough of Guildford, Surrey. Sidney lost this election to a courtier, Thomas Dalmahoy. The new Parliament, known as the first Exclusion Parliament because of its effort to exclude the duke of York from the throne, was quickly dissolved by the king. A second round of elections took place in the summer of 1679. WP again supported the candidacy of Algernon Sidney, who was now seeking a seat at the borough of Bramber, Sussex, near Warminghurst. Sidney was again defeated, this time by his brother Henry. In 1680 and 1681 Algernon Sidney lost further elections, but WP seems no longer to have supported him actively. In 1683 Sidney was tried and executed for alleged complicity in the Rye House Plot.

Documents 129 and 133-34 supply almost all of the surviving evidence of WP's electoral support for Sidney in 1679. Document 129 shows WP's reaction to the defeat at Guildford and his willingness to lobby personally on Sidney's behalf with Shaftesbury and the other chief Whigs. Documents 133-34 show WP's strenuous efforts to avoid a second rebuff at Bramber. Just why WP worked so hard for Algernon Sidney is something of a mystery. He had known the Sidneys for many years (see doc. 43), and he shared some of Algernon's experimental republican principles. But WP did not share Algernon's enthusiasm for rebellion against tyrants nor his eagerness for a warlike state. On the differences between the two men as political theorists, see Caroline Robbins, "Algernon Sidney's Discourses," *William and Mary Quarterly*, 3rd ser., 4:267-96; Mary Maples [Dunn], "William Penn, Classical Republican," *PMHB* 81:138-56.

129
TO ALGERNON SIDNEY

1st, 1st Month, [March 16]79

Deare Friend,[1]

I Hope you gott all well Home, as I by Gods Goodness have done. I reflected upon the Way of Things past at Guildford, and that which occurs to me, as reasonable, is this: That so soon as the Articles or Exceptions are disgested, show them to Sergeant Maynard,[2] and gett his Opinion of the Matter; Sir Francis Winington,[3] or Wallope,[4] have been used in those Occasions too. Thou must have Councel before the Committee, and to advise first upon the Reason of an Address or Petition, with them, in my Opinion, is not imprudent, but very fitting. If they say, that, the Conjuncture considerd; thy Qualifications, and Alliance, and his Ungratefulness to the House, they beleive all may amount to an unfair Election; then I offer to waite presently upon the Duke of Buckingham, Earl of Shaftsbury,[5] Lord Essex,[6] Lord Halifax,[7] Lord Hollis,[8] Lord Gray,[9] &c. to use their utmost Interest in reversing this Business. This may be done in five Dayes, and I was not willing to stay till I come, which will be with the first. Remember the Nonresidents on their Side, as Legg,[10] &c. I left Order with all our Interest to bestirr themselves, and watch, and transmitt an Account to thee dayly. I bless God I found all well at Home. I hope the Disapointment so strainge (140 Pole Men[11] as we thought last Night considerd) does not move thee; thou (as thy Frends) had a conscientious Regard to England; and to be putt aside, by such base Ways, is really a Suffering for Righteousness; thou hast embarqu't thy selfe with them, that seek, and love, and chuse the best Thing: and Number is not Weight with thee. I hope it is retrieveable, for to me it looks not a fair and clear Election. Forgett not, that Soldiers were made free[12] 3 Weeks agoe, in Prospect of the Choice (and, by the Way, they went, we may guess, for Delmahoy's[13] Sake) and thy selfe so often putt by, a Thing not refused to one of thy Condition. Of the Lower House, the Lord Cavendish, and especially Lord Russell,[14] Sir Jo. Coventry,[15] Powell,[16] Saychevrill,[17] Williams,[18] Lee,[19] Clergis,[20] Boskowen,[21] Titus.[22] Men, some able, some hott, and fitt to be neerly engaged in the Knowledge of these Things. 'Tis late, I am weary, and hope to see thee quickly. Farewell.

Thy faithfull Friend,
William Penn.

Printed. Arthur Collin, ed., *Letters and Memorials of State in the Reigns of Queen Mary, Queen Elizabeth, King James, King Charles I, part of the Reign of Charles II, and Oliver's Usurpation* . . . , 2 vols. ([London], 1746), pp. 154-55. (*Micro.* 2:713).

1. Algernon Sidney (1622-1683), second son of the earl of Leicester, fought for Parliament in the Civil War, and served in the republican governments of 1649 to 1653 and 1659 to 1660. After the Restoration, he lived in exile on the Continent until 1677. Although he was blocked from entry to Parliament in the elections of 1679 to 1681, he worked actively in opposition to Charles II, and became a Whig martyr when he was tried and executed in 1683. His chief book, the *Discourses concerning Government*, was published posthumously. *DNB;* Philip Sidney, *The Sidneys of Penshurst* (London, 1901), chap. 9; Caroline Robbins, *The Eighteenth-Century Commonwealthman* (Cambridge, Mass., 1959), pp. 41-47.

2. Sir John Maynard (1602-1690), barrister and judge, was the king's serjeant. He appeared for the crown at most of the Restoration trials and at most of the Popish Plot prosecutions. In politics he steered a middle, ambiguous course, sometimes asserting the royal prerogative, and at other times recognizing Parliament's power. *DNB*.

3. Sir Francis Winnington (1634-1700), former solicitor general, lost this position in Dec. 1678 when he voted to impeach the king's chief minister, the earl of Danby. As M.P. for Windsor, he supported the Exclusion Bill. *DNB*.

4. Richard Wallop (1616-1697), antiroyalist lawyer and judge, frequently served as counsel against the government in state trials during the reigns of Charles II and James II. *DNB.*

5. Anthony Ashley Cooper (1621-1683), first earl of Shaftesbury, was the leader of the Whig opposition to the king and the duke of York. Having forced Charles to dismiss Danby and to dissolve the Cavalier Parliament, Shaftesbury was delighted with the electoral returns for the new Parliament which would meet on 18 Mar. 1679. Nearly half of the M.P.'s were new men, and Shaftesbury calculated that the opposition outnumbered the court party in the House of Commons by 302 to 158. Since Shaftesbury disliked Algernon Sidney, he was probably not greatly bothered by Sidney's defeat at Guildford. K. H. D. Haley, *The First Earl of Shaftesbury* (Oxford, 1968), pp. 500, 508; Jones, *The First Whigs,* chap. 3.

6. Arthur Capel (1631-1683), Earl of Essex, had opposed Danby and supported the Popish Plot story. A Whig and a partisan of the duke of Monmouth, he was accused in 1683 of complicity in the Rye House plot to assassinate the king and the duke of York. He was arrested and confined in the Tower, where he was found with his throat cut. *DNB; Peerage,* 5:145.

7. George Saville (1633-1695), Viscount and later Earl and Marquis of Halifax, member of the reformed Privy Council of Feb. 1679, had opposed the Test Acts and was a friend of Shaftesbury's. Later in 1679 he broke with Shaftesbury and became a favorite of Charles II. In his *Character of a Trimmer* (1688), he argued that the ship of state should be trimmed or ballasted, and by this principle he supported at one time or another Monmouth, James II, and William of Orange. *DNB.*

8. Denzell Holles (1599-1680), Baron Holles of Infield, a leading opponent of Charles I, sometime privy councilor under Charles II, and ambassador to Paris, 1662-1667. He had opposed the Test Act and endorsed the dismissal of Danby, but found Shaftesbury's policy too radical in 1679. *Peerage,* 6:545-47.

9. Ford Grey (1655-1701), Baron Grey of Warke, a Whig peer, and close associate of Shaftesbury. In 1685 he joined Monmouth's Rebellion against James II. *Peerage,* 6:169-70; Ogg, *Charles II,* 2:642.

10. WP is complaining here about nonresidents at Guildford who participated in the Guildford election against Sidney; one of these was George Legge (1648-1691), later Lord Dartmouth, a favorite of the duke of York. He had been M.P. for Ludgershall, Wilts., from 1673 to 1679, though he was governor of Portsmouth during the same years. In 1679 he was elected from Portsmouth. Under James II he commanded the fleet which failed to challenge William of Orange's invasion in 1688. After the Revolution he was stripped of all offices and committed to the Tower, where he died. *DNB; Peerage,* 4:87-88.

11. Poll men, or voters.

12. WP means that the soldiers were made free citizens of Guildford, and so were able to vote in the parliamentary election.

13. Thomas Dalmahoy (d. 1682), Sidney's opponent in the Guildford election, was master of the buckhounds to Charles II. He served in Parliament for Guildford, from 1664 to 1679. *Baronetage,* 4:309.

14. William Russell (1639-1683), Lord Russell, M.P. for Tavistock, was a leading member of the country party. He was later put to death for his supposed role in the Rye House plot. *DNB.*

15. Sir John Coventry (d. 1682), M.P. for Weymouth, had been a royalist, and Charles II made him a knight of the Bath in 1661. After court hooligans assaulted him and slit his nose in 1670, he was firmly aligned with the opposition. *DNB.*

16. Henry Powle (1630-1692), M.P. for Cirencester and a barrister, identified himself with opponents of the court in Charles II's reign, leading the attack on Danby and advocating the Dutch alliance. In 1689 he became speaker of the Convention Parliament, one of William III's most trusted advisors, and master of the rolls. *DNB.*

17. William Sacheverell (1638-1691), M.P. for Derbyshire, took a leading role in investigating the supposed Popish Plot, opposed Danby, and supported the Exclusion Bill. William III made him Lord of the Admiralty. *DNB.*

18. William Williams (1634-1700), M.P. for Chester, was a leading advocate of Commons' privileges and opposed to any extension of the royal prerogative. Later he became speaker of the house, solicitor-general, and a baronet. In 1682 he was Algernon Sidney's counsel in his treason trial. *DNB.*

19. Sir Thomas Lee (d. 1691), M.P. for Aylesbury from 1661 to 1681, frequently sided with the opposition and was a well-known debater. *DNB*.

20. Sir Thomas Clarges (d. 1695) had been George Monck's agent in the maneuvers leading to the restoration of Charles II in 1659-1660. He entered Parliament in 1666 and, being strongly anti-Catholic, joined the opposition on many issues. But in the Parliaments of 1679 to 1681 he supported the court against Shaftesbury's exclusion policy. *DNB*.

21. Probably Edward Boscawen (1628-1686), a "rich Turkey merchant" who represented Truro, Cornwall, in several parliaments of Charles II. In 1678, Edward and his brother William Boscawen were returned for Truro's two seats. *DNB;* J. L. Vivian, *Visitations of Cornwall* (Exeter, 1887), p. 47; George Lipscomb, *The History and Antiquities of the County of Buckingham* (London, 1847), p. 448.

22. Silius Titus (c. 1623-1704), formerly an ardent royalist, was a Presbyterian and an M.P. for Herts. He was one of the strongest believers in the Popish Plot, and supported the Whigs' exclusion policy. *DNB*.

Documents 130 and 132 show how WP was continuing to fight against the persecution of Quakers while he was campaigning for Algernon Sidney. In 1678 and 1679 the ecclesiastical courts frequently identified Friends as recusants (see docs. 121, 125, and 128) and obtained writs of excommunication against them; the civil magistrates then sentenced the excommunicants to long imprisonments and the payment of heavy fines. In doc. 130, found among the papers of a Lancashire Quaker, WP was writing on behalf of the Meeting for Sufferings, looking for ways to block the Anglicans' power of excommunication. In doc. 132, WP asked Friends to circulate copies of his tract, *An Address to Protestants Upon the Present Conjuncture,* in which he called upon the magistrates to spend their time punishing vice, rather than trying to impose religious beliefs by force.

130
TO FRIENDS IN LANCASHIRE

The 11 of the 1mo [March 16]79[1]

Deare frinds & Brethren

My deare love in the one holy unchangeable truth of our god Salutes you desireing that we may all fathfully serve the Intrest there of in our day that peace may be our portion wth the lord for ever; The busines I have to write to you upon this {1st} to desire you that wth all Conveniant speed you {would} send me up A list of your most troublesome & persecuting Justices[2] about wch pray be very Carefull—2nd wth the same diligence & exactness in forme your selves of the excomunicated persons that are not frds especialy if they be Church goers (as they Call them) who are often so handled in the office of Churchwardens[3] and for other reasons When not Coming to publick worship & if you find any such to know whether they are willing to put the Bishops power of Excomunication upon A legal tryal, provided it be not at theire Cost others will sustaine that this is of great weight keep it from noise & observation as much as you Can but it is not improbable that in a little time you may have some thing Extrordinary upon this subject: no more but that I am In & for the truth your friend to do you service.

Wm penn

Copy. Pemberton Papers, HSP. (*Micro.* 2:662). Docketed: William Penn | 1 mo 11. 1679. This letter was copied onto the blank portion of a letter from Thomas Camm at Camsgill, Westm., to Phineas Pemberton, a Quaker at Bolton, Lancs.,[4] dated 13 Apr. 1678. It is in a contemporary hand, but neither Camm's nor Pemberton's. Camm's letter was addressed: For Henery Coward Iron- | monger in Lancaster | these | To be delivered to Phenias | Pemberton wth Care.

1. The date of this letter could be interpreted as 11 Mar. 1680, but it was more likely written in 1679. On 20 Mar. 1679, the London Meeting for Sufferings agreed to distribute an epistle that had been drawn up by WP. It was at this time that the London meeting was most concerned about the excommunication of Friends as recusants. Minutes of the Meeting for Sufferings, vol. 1, 1675-1680, FLL.

2. Justices of the Peace had enormous power over Quakers. The oath could be administered by a single justice, who could also convict under the second Conventicle Act (1670). Lloyd, *Quaker Social History,* pp. 87, 100.

3. Churchwardens presented offenders against church law to the ecclesiastical courts. Cross, *Christian Church.*

4. Pemberton was fined in 1679 for attendance at a Quaker meeting in Bolton. In 1682 he immigrated to Pennsylvania. Besse, 1:324; Fox, 2:469.

131
RELEASE OF PAPERS FROM RICHARD LANGHORNE'S CUSTODY

Richard Langhorne was one of WP's lawyers: he had witnessed Admiral Penn's will in 1670, exchanged letters on Catholicism with WP in 1671, was employed by WP on New Jersey and Maryland business in 1676, and was paid by WP in April 1678 (see docs. 37, 61, 146, and 152). Langhorne was a Catholic, and in October 1678 he was arrested for alleged complicity in the Popish Plot. In doc. 131, WP sought the return of papers that were in Langhorne's possession. Philip Ford's accounts show that on 14 April 1679 WP visited Westminster, perhaps to lobby for the release, and on 22 April he went to the Temple, probably to receive the papers from Langhorne's chambers (see doc. 148). On 9 June 1679, WP visited Newgate when Langhorne was still there awaiting trial; on 14 June, Langhorne was tried and condemned; in early July WP bought several published descriptions of Popish trials, including the trial of the five Jesuits who were accused by Titus Oates of working with Langhorne (see doc. 149). On 14 July Langhorne was executed. We should note that the Popish Plot affected the Privy Council as well, for five days after WP's petition was considered, Charles II restructured the council in order to make room for his Whig critics. Only eight of the members present on 16 April continued as councilors after 21 April. Ogg, *Charles II*, 2:585; Turner, *The Privy Council*, 1:424-30.

At the Court at Whitehall.
this 16th Day of Aprill. 1679.

Present.
The Kings Most Excellent Maty

His Hss Pce Rupert.
Lord Chancellour,[1]
Lord Privy Seale[2]
Lord Chamberlain.[3]
Earle of Bridgwater[4]
Earle of Northampton.[5]
Earle of Peterborough.[6]
Earle of Clarendon,[7]
Earle of Essex.
Earle of Craven.[8]
Earle of Ailesbury[9]
Earle of Carbery[10]
Viscount fauconberge[11]
Viscount Newport.[12]
Lord Bp: of Durham,[13]
Lord Berkeley.[14]
Chancellour of the Excheqr [15]
Mr Seymer,[16]

Upon reading this Day at the Board the Petition of William Penn praying liberty to have some Writeings (wch concerne his Estate, and wth Wch he was entrusted) and were left in the Custody of Mr Richard Langhorne, delivered to him out of the Sayd Langhornes Chamber. His Maty was pleased to Order And it is hereby accordingly ordered, That Sr Thomas Hanmer Knight Treasurer of the Temple,[17] doe cause the Writeings that really concerne the Sayd Wm Penn, & wth wch he was entrusted, & were by him, or his order, delivered to the Sayd Langhorne to be taken out of the Chamber of the Sayd Mr Langhorne, at present under his care, and delivered to the Petr or whom he Should appoint, takeing first a Schedule of, and a Receipt, for the Same.

MBE. Privy Council Register, PC 2/67/157, PRO. (*Micro.* 2:716). Docketed: Mr Pen to have his Writeings out of Mr Langhornes Chambr.

1. Heneage Finch (1621-1682), an ardent supporter of Charles II, was appointed lord chancellor in 1674. He was created earl of Nottingham in 1681. *DNB;* Edward Raymond Turner, *The Privy Council of England in the Seventeenth and Eighteenth Centuries, 1603-1784*, 2 vols. (Baltimore, 1927), 1:424.

2. Arthur Annesley (1614-1686), Earl of Anglesey, was treasurer of the navy in 1667-1668, and lord privy seal from 1672 until 1682, when he was dismissed for criticizing the king's government. *DNB; Peerage*, 1:133-34; Turner, *The Privy Council*, 1:424.

3. Robert Bertie (c. 1630-1701), Earl of Lindsey, was a privy councilor from 1666 until 1679, and was sworn again in 1682. He was also gentleman of the bedchamber (1674-1685). *Peerage*, 8:21-22; Turner, *The Privy Council*, 1:424.

4. John Egerton (1623-1686), Earl of Bridgwater, was appointed to the Privy Council in 1667. He was lord lieutenant of Bucks. from 1660 to 1686, and high steward of Oxford University from 1663 to 1686. *Peerage*, 2:312-13.

5. James Compton (1622-1681), Earl of Northampton, a longtime supporter of

Charles II, served as privy councilor from 1673 to 1679, constable of the Tower from 1675 to 1679, and lord of trade in 1677. *Peerage*, 9:681-82.

6. Henry Mordaunt (1623-1697), Earl of Peterborough, had fought in the Civil War and in the Dutch Wars, and was a privy councilor from 1674 to 1679 and from 1683 to 1689. He was impeached for high treason in 1689 after having converted to Roman Catholicism in 1687. *Peerage*, 10:497-99.

7. Henry Hyde (1638-1709), son of Edward Hyde the first earl of Clarendon (d. 1674), and brother-in-law to the duke of York, was privy councilor in 1679 and from 1680 to 1689. He served James II in Ireland between 1685 and 1687, deserted the king in 1688, but did not hold office under William and Mary. *Peerage*, 3:266-67.

8. William Craven (1608-1697), Earl of Craven, gave Charles II at least £50,000 during his exile. Craven was a lord proprietor of Carolina, and served on the Privy Council (1666-1679 and 1681-1689). *Peerage*, 3:500-1.

9. Robert Bruce (c. 1626-1685) was created earl of Ailesbury in 1664 for his support of the Restoration. He was appointed privy councilor in 1678 and lord chamberlain of the household in 1685. *Peerage*, 1:58-59.

10. Richard Vaughan (1600?-1686), Earl of Carbery, served as lord president of Wales from 1660 to 1672, and as privy councilor from 1661 to 1679. *DNB; Peerage*, 3:7-8.

11. Thomas Belasyse (1628-1700), Viscount Fauconberg of Henknowle, had served as ambassador to Venice, Turin, and Florence in 1669, and became a privy councilor in 1672. *Peerage*, 5:264-65.

12. Francis Newport (1620-1708), created viscount Newport in 1675 and earl of Bradford in 1694, was a privy councilor between 1668 and 1679 and was resworn in 1689; he was also treasurer of the household from 1672 to 1687 and from 1689 to 1708. *Peerage*, 2:274; 9:555.

13. Nathaniel Crew (1633-1721), a favorite of the duke of York, became dean of Chichester in 1669 and bishop of Oxford in 1671. After solemnizing the duke's marriage to Maria d'Este in 1673, Crew received the wealthy see of Durham in 1674, and was appointed privy councilor in 1676. *DNB*.

14. George Berkeley (1628-1698), created earl of Berkeley in 1679, was a member of the Royal African and East India companies, and was governor of the Levant Company from 1673 to 1696. Berkeley was a privy councilor in 1678-1679 and from 1685 to 1689. *DNB; Peerage*, 2:139-40.

15. Sir John Ernle, of Wiltshire, a firm supporter of Charles II, was comptroller of stores in the navy from 1671 to 1676, and a commisssioner of the admiralty in 1677. Turner, *The Privy Council*, 1:425; *VCH: Wiltshire*, 5:158; J. R. Tanner, ed., *Samuel Pepys's Naval Minutes* (London, 1926), p. 257.

16. Sir Edward Seymour (1633-1708) was elected speaker of the House of Commons in 1673 and appointed to the Privy Council in the same year. By 1679 he was critical of the king and the duke. At the Glorious Revolution Seymour opposed the removal of James II, but he later served under William and Mary as lord of the treasury. *DNB*.

17. Sir Thomas Hanmer was knighted by Charles II, and named solicitor to Queen Catherine. He died young. Thomas Watton, *The English Baronetage*, 5 vols. (London, 1741), 1:415.

132
TO FRIENDS IN KENT

[29 April 1679]

Dear Friends

My endeared love salutes {you} in the truth of God: having Lately been drawn forth to write an Address to Protestants upon the present great Conjuncture of Affairs:[1] it was in my hearte to recommend it to you; that in greate towns you give one to the Chiefe Magistrate and one or two in each County to the most noted of those in Authority; for the matter thereof Comes neare to there doors; and is a Condescention and visitation to them: in this doe as it is with you; I have only expressed my ~~mind~~ sense to you: I have disposed of several to the members of both houses; and am Like to do more; so dear Friends & bretheren in the ancient universall Love of God I again salute you and remaine

your Friend & brother in the truth
William Penn

London the 29th of 2d month 1679—

Copy. ACM, vol. 20, p. 26. (Not filmed). Endorsed: For friends at their monthly Meeting in Kent. A variant modern copy of this document, which appears to be less accurate, is in Port. 41, FLL. (*Micro.* 2:718).

1. *An Address to Protestants Upon the Present Conjuncture* ([London], 1678), was reprinted in 1679 and 1681, and again in 1692 with a new title: *An Address to Protestants of all Persuasions: More Especially the Magistracy and Clergy, For the Promotion of Virtue and Charity*. See Dunn, *William Penn* (Princeton, 1967), pp. 26-27, 47.

133
FROM SIR JOHN PELHAM

Horsham[1] July the 25th [16]79

Sr

Scince I came to this place (wher both those[2] who have appeared at Branber[3] now are) I doe find that the difficulty will be much greater to gett your friend[4] chosen then then Sr John Fagg[5] or you apprehend. for Mr Percy Goring[6] was not only borne in the Cuntry but all the subsistance left by his father lyes not farr from that place, he served for that Towne 17 yeares and as I have heard sent during that time some thing to the Towne yearly to treat them, and twas generally said that had he appeared an hour before the election the last time Mr Eversfeild[7] had not bin chosen. Ther is another thing now (besides the little advantage wch my appearing ther can bring) wch renders it in some kind indecent (if what I heare from Captaine Goring[8] be true) that my brother Harry Sydney[9] is now proposed ther to stand, so that till I have some assurance that this report is groundlesse I must beg your excuse for {not} appearing ther. If Sr John Fagg had bin here as I with others did expect our farther proceedings in this might have bin carryed on with the mor unanimity, and certainty. I am

Your humble Servant
J. Pelham[10]

The meeting of the Parlmt was by the Counsell yeasterday (as Mr Goring tells me who was ther) putt off to the 17th of Oct.

ALS. Penn-Forbes Collection, HSP. (*Micro.* 2:731). Addressed: For Mr Penn | at Worminghurst. Docketed: July 79.

1. Horsham, Sus., is about 13 miles north of Bramber, and 10 miles north of WP's house at Warminghurst.

2. Probably Percy Goring and Mr. Parsons (see doc. 134, n. 4). Neither of them won a Bramber seat in this election. For background on the Bramber contest, see the headnote to doc. 129.

3. Bramber, Sus., five miles southeast of Warminghurst.

4. Algernon Sidney.

5. Sir John Fagg (d. 1701) sided with Parliament in the Civil War, but supported the king's restoration in 1660. From 1661 until his death he was M.P. for Steyning, Sus., and had earlier been elected from both Bramber and Horsham. He acquired Wiston, Sus., from the heirs of Sir Thomas Shirley, and successfully defended this acquisition in a protracted dispute in the House of Lords. *DNB;* Dudley G. C. Elwes, *A History of the Castles, Mansions, and Manors of Western Sussex* (London, 1876), pp. 266-67.

6. Percy Goring was elected from Bramber in 1661 and served until Feb. 1679. In 1675 he was a commissioner for recusants in Sussex. Apparently in Feb. 1679 he stood for Horsham, but was defeated by Anthony Eversfield. See n. 7, below. *Returns of the Names of Every Member Returned . . . in Each Parliament,* 2 vols. ([London], 1878), 1:528, 544, 550; *Calendar of Treasury Books, 1672-1675,* p. 697.

7. Anthony Eversfield (c. 1621-1695) was elected from Horsham in Feb. 1679. He had received a B.A. from Oxford in 1640. *Alumni Oxonienses;* Fitch, ed., *Index to Wills . . . Canterbury, 1694-1700* (London, 1960), p. 138; *Returns of the Names . . . in Each Parliament,* 1:538.

8. Captain Henry Goring. See doc. 121, n. 3.

9. Sir John Pelham had married Lucy Sidney (d. 1685), daughter of Robert Sidney, Earl of Leicester, and sister of Algernon and Henry Sidney, in 1647. *Baronetage,* 1:9. Henry Sidney, who was not on friendly terms with his brother Algernon, stood for Bramber in the fall 1679 election and was seated with the support of the royalists. *Returns of the Names . . . in Each Parliament,* 1:544; Peare, p. 207.

10. Sir John Pelham (c. 1623-1703), of Halland, Laughton, Sus., served as M.P. for Sussex in nearly every Parliament from 1645 until 1698. Like his son Thomas, he seems to have been a Whig. *Baronetage,* 1:9; *DNB.*

134
TO ALGERNON SIDNEY

Wiston,[1] 29th 5th Month, [July 16]79.

I Am now at Sir John Faggs, where I and my Relations dined. I have pressed the Point with what Dilligence and Force I coulde; and to say true, Sir John Fagg has been a most zealous, and, he beleives, a successfull Friend to thee. But, upon a serious consideration of the Matter, it is agreed that thou comst down with all Speed; but that thou takest Hall-land[2] in thy Way, and bringest Sir John Pelham with thee, which he ought the less to scruple, because his haveing no Interest, can be no Objection to his Appearing with thee; the commonest Civility, that can be, is all desired. The Burrough has kindled at thy Name, and takes it well; If Sir John Temple may be credited, he assures me it is very likely; he is at Work dayly.[3] An other, one Parsons,[4] treats to Day. But for thee, as well as him selfe, and mostly makes his Men for thee, and perhaps will be perswaded, if you two carry it not, to bequeath his Interest to thee, and then Captain Goreing[5] is thy Collegue; and indeed this I wish, both to make the Thing the easier, and to prevent Offence. Sir John Pelham sent me Word, he heard that his Brother, Henry Sidney, would be proposed to that Burrough, or already was, and till he was sure to the Contrary, it would not be decent for him to appear; of that thou canst best inform him. That Day you come to Bramber, Sir John Fagg will meet you both; and that Night you may lye at Wiston, and then, when thou pleasest, with us at Worminghurst. Sir John Temple has that Opinion of thy good Reasons to perswade, as well as Quality to influence the Electors, that, with what is and will be done, the Business will prosper; which, with my true good Wishes that it may be so, is all at present, from

Thy true Friend,

Sir John Fagg salutes thee. W. Penn

Printed. Arthur Collin, ed., *Letters and Memorials of State in the Reigns of Queen Mary, Queen Elizabeth, King James, King Charles I, part of the Reign of Charles II, and Oliver's Usurpation* . . . , 2 vols. ([London], 1746), pp. 154-55. (*Micro.* 2:734).

1. See doc. 133, n. 5.
2. Halland, in the parishes of Laughton and East Hoathly, Sus., was Sir John Pelham's principal residence. Thomas Walker Horsfield, *The History, Antiquities, and Topography of the County of Sussex*, 2 vols. (Lewes and London, 1835), 1:352, 358.
3. Sir John Temple, solicitor general of Ireland, had an estate in East Sheen, Sur., and perhaps some property near Bramber. WP had called upon him in Dublin, 23 Nov. 1669. See doc. 35.
4. Possibly John Parsons, who had been defeated by Percy Goring at Bramber in 1661. Like Percy Goring, Parsons was unsuccessful in 1679. The two candidates returned from Bramber in this election were Henry Goring and Henry Sidney. *Returns of the Names of Every Member Returned . . . in Each Parliament*, 1:529, 544.
5. Captain Henry Goring. See doc. 121, n. 3.

The next two documents (135-36) illustrate WP's position during the closing months of 1679, just before he petitioned Charles II for the grant of a colony in America. Among his fellow Quakers, some of the friction of 1677-1678 had subsided. With doc. 135, John Story ended his separation from WP and the other London leaders, though John Wilkinson, William Rogers, and other separatists remained permanently estranged. In doc. 136 WP addressed Dutch Friends far more amicably than he had two years before (see doc. 122). In this letter, WP's enthusiastic account of the latest turns in the Popish Plot makes it clear that he fully accepted Titus Oates' year-old charges against the Catholics. Yet very soon WP would be turning to Oates' chief adversary, the duke of York, for help in promoting his new colony of Pennsylvania.

135
JOHN STORY'S APOLOGY

at Ellis Hooke's Chamber Lond^{o} the 20th 8 mo [October] 1679
being the 2^{d} day's Morning Meetin[1]

I John Story doe hearby declare that I doe owne the Paper given forth by mee and John Willkinson at drey well the 2^{d} month 1676[2] ~~and that~~ according to the common and plaine sence & signification of the said Paper with out any Reservation or Equivocation what ever and whereas I John Story did Alleadg to Wm Gibson Before Jno Bu{r}nyeat and William Penn two scriptures Namely that of gods Tempting Abraham and that of the Apostle James about temptation[3] in order to lessen the sence and Authority of the said Paper given forth by mee and John Willkinson at drey well as a foresaid I do allso ~~hearby~~ Acknowledge & Confess that it was not well done of mee soe to speake & I am sorry for it and I doe desire freinds to pass it by & that they would forgive mee

Assented unto in the
presence of

John Osgood
Alexander Parker
William Gibson
William Taylby[4]
James Parke[5]
F: C—[6]
Richard Needham[7]
Geo: Watts
Thomas: Green
Will meade
Wm Penn
John Elson[8]

DS. Penn Papers, HSP. (*Micro.* 2:737).

1. The London Morning Meeting of Ministers, which assumed a number of executive functions in the Society of Friends, such as overseeing Quaker publications and settling disputes in local meetings. Braithwaite, *Second Period,* pp. 280-89.

2. In Apr. 1676, Friends from London and Bristol met with nonseparatist Westmorland Quakers and John Wilkinson and John Story to attempt to settle their dispute. The two Johns signed a paper that expressed regret for the differences between the two factions (see *Micro.* 2:329). When the arbitrators subsequently announced that the dissidents had fully condemned their own actions, however, Wilkinson and Story repudiated their "submission." Despite Story's apology of Oct. 1679, he remained in discord with nonseparating Friends in Westmorland until his death in 1681. John Wilkinson never apologized. Braithwaite, *Second Period,* pp. 306-7, 320-23.

3. The paper signed at Draw-well began with the phrase, "Wee are sensible that in the hour of temptation," and John Story, in denying the importance of the statement, told Gibson, Burnyeat, and WP that the word *temptation* did not imply guilt. He attempted to support his argument by citing Gen. 22:1-14, which describes how God

tested Abraham's loyalty by asking him to sacrifice his son Isaac, and James 1:12, which states, "Blessed is the man that endureth temptation: for when he is tried, he shall receive the crown of life, which the Lord hath promised to them that love him." The London Morning Meeting censured Story for using these two scriptural passages in this way. Braithwaite, *Second Period,* pp. 307, 320-21.

4. William Tileby was included in 1686 on a list of "worthy and valiant" sufferers and testimony bearers from London and its vicinity. Besse, 1:484.

5. James Parke (1636-1696), of Horslydown, Southwark, London, probably originated from Lancashire and was at one time in fellowship with Welsh Independents. He served as a Quaker minister in London, examined manuscripts for the London Morning Meeting, and wrote numerous pamphlets. Fox, 2:495; Fox, *Short Journal,* p. 319; Braithwaite, *Second Period,* p. 224.

6. Most likely Francis Camfield (1628-1708), a London Quaker minister who spoke at Fox's funeral in 1691 and who set up a trust in 1706 for poor ministers of the Society of Friends. Braithwaite, *Second Period,* p. 450; Fox, 2:495.

7. Richard Needham, a London Friend, was imprisoned in 1683 for attending a meeting at Devonshire House and was fined in 1684 for preaching in the street. Besse, 1:455, 462.

8. John Elson (c. 1624-1701), a carpenter, lived at the Sign of the (Baker's) Peel in Clerkenwell, London, which was the site of the Peel meeting as early as 1656. His wife Mary (c. 1623-1706) was a Wiltshire woman and an approved minister. Fox, 2:457; Beck and Ball, pp. 192-93.

136
TO PIETER HENDRICKS AND JAN CLAUS

Lond: 27 9 mo [November 16]79

Peter Hendricks &
John claus— } My dear Frds

In the everlasting truth of our god that has begotten us again to a life & hope that are Incorruptible, do I dearly salute you, your dr: wives & all my endeared Frds & Brethren in that citty {& country}: to whom o that the god of all my comforts & Blessings would multeply grace mercy & Peace, that an heavenly famely & holy society to him you there & we here may be & continue till our last great chainge shall come, when all mortality wth us shall be swallow'd up of life. It is long since I heard from you, & longer I beleive since you heard from me. but surely our love remains in that wch noe distance or time can extinguish or ware out; & I know {not} that I have ever been drawn forth of god In prayer In publiq that you have not been brought liveingly to my remembrance & indeed you are as an epistle writt upon my soul. & tenderness often overtakes m~~y~~e ~~soul~~ in secreet that truth may Spring among you, o the precious meetings that We have had together, lett my soul never forgett the goodness of the lord. things here are well as to Truth, blessed be god, but many Frds drop off {by sickness}. 'tis a sickly time with us. as to the Publiq, the discovery of the Plott & Plotte[rs] goes on notwithstanding all arts to smother it. the Mock-Plott cast on the Presbiterians[1] turn[ed] to good. & oats[2] has lately detected 3 Persons suborned to Sware buggery ag^st him.[3] & it falls on the late Tresurer & the Popish lords.[4] So that now all seem to beleive the Plott but thos that knew it before we did. for they cannot say any more, *do you think we would do this or that as oats &c: says;* for now wors was proved, then ever was conceived. and Truly the lord works wonderfully for the preservation of this nation; & therefore I hope he will save it from the devices of the wicked. Just now a great man tells me the d. of Mon:[5] is arrived, the king bids him be gon. he refuses, & claims an english right {to stay} & referrs himselfe to the Law but stirrs not. the bells Ring, the Fires Burn, & the people are extreamly agitated. but the lord is our choice & his peaceable Kingdom, & in him is our trust & Joy forever. who by all thes things will exalt his truth & Break in upon the spirits of People & begin his work in them. no more, but that I should rejoyce to hear from you of yr wellfair & Truths Prosperity who am

Your faithfull Frd & Bro:
Wm Penn

Salute me to vantougre[6]
J: Rolofs & wife,[7] the Schole
master, J. Claus & & J. L. &c:
you would do well to write somtimes to the 2d Days
meeting how things are.

ALS. Quaker Collection, Haverford College. (*Micro.* 2:744). Addressed: For Peter Hendricks | Mert In | Amsterdam. Docketed: 1679. | Willm Penn ae | vrienden in hollandt.

1. In Sept.-Oct. 1679 a group of Catholics concocted a fictitious Presbyterian Plot, alleging that the Whigs were planning to rebel against the king; they thus hoped to counter the Popish Plot. The chief conspirators were Mrs. Celier, a midwife, Thomas Dangerfield, a professional criminal, and the Countess of Powis, whose husband had been sent to the Tower by Titus Oates (see below). Their plot became known as the Meal Tub Plot when some of Dangerfield's forged papers were found in Mrs. Celier's meal tub. Dangerfield was arrested on 27 Oct. 1679, and confessed that his plot was a sham. To save himself, he then "revealed" a new Catholic plot, also fictitious, to assassinate Shaftesbury. John Pollock, *The Popish Plot* (London, 1903), pp. 204-13; Haley, *The First Earl of Shaftesbury*, pp. 554-55.

2. Titus Oates (1649-1705), perjurer, fabricated the Popish Plot with his associate Israel Tonge in 1678. He told his story with much circumstantial detail to a magistrate, Sir Edmund Berry Godfrey, and repeated it in greater detail to the Privy Council and to the House of Commons. When Godfrey was found murdered in Oct. 1678, the public assumed that the Catholics were responsible. In the next eighteen months, Oates enjoyed tremendous popularity; he appeared as chief witness in the trials and judicial murders of some thirty-five men. With the Whig collapse in 1681 he was discredited, and in 1685 James II had him tried for perjury; he was imprisoned and brutally flogged. After the Glorious Revolution he was freed, but not restored to official favor. *DNB.*

3. William Osborne and John Lane, former servants of Titus Oates, and Thomas Knox, a servant in the earl of Danby's family, testified that Oates was a sodomite. Osborne fled, and Lane and Knox were convicted of perjury on 25 Nov. 1679. Pollock, *Popish Plot*, pp. 338-39.

4. The "late Tresurer" was the earl of Danby; when Oates accused Danby of murdering Godfrey (see n. 2, above), Danby was sent to the Tower for five years. The Popish lords were the earl of Powis, Viscount Stafford, Lord Petre, Lord Belasyse, and Lord Arundell, who were all arrested in Oct. 1678 on Oates' information for complicity in the Popish Plot. Stafford was executed in 1680, Petre died in the Tower in 1684, and the other three were liberated with Danby in 1684.

5. The Duke of Monmouth, Charles II's illegitimate son, was using the Popish Plot to advance his claim to the succession in place of the duke of York. The king had ordered him to go to Holland in Sept. 1679, but he returned to London without permission on 27 Nov. As WP reports, the Londoners staged a mammoth celebration in his honor, but Charles was furious and never restored Monmouth to favor. Haley, *First Earl of Shaftesbury*, pp. 558-59.

6. Barent von Tongeren, an Amsterdam Quaker. Hull, *William Penn and the Dutch Quaker Migration*, pp. 353, 382.

7. Jan and Debora Roelofs were Amsterdam Quakers. WP had seen them in 1677. See doc. 119, n. 23.

APPENDIX

WILLIAM PENN'S BUSINESS RECORDS

WP's principal surviving business papers for the 1660s and 1670s are presented in this appendix. They are grouped here because they differ in character from the other documents in this volume, and because readers interested in WP's property holdings or in his income and expenditures will wish to examine these records collectively. Each document, or group of documents, in the appendix is described in a headnote. The editors have not supplied footnotes because of limitations of space, but most of the persons and places mentioned in these records are identified in previous footnotes and can be traced through page references set in boldface type in the index. These documents represent only a fragment of the business papers WP collected during the 1660s and 1670s. Document 137 is a catalogue of a boxful of records for these years which are now lost. At least five of the accounts submitted to WP by his steward Philip Ford during this period are also missing; the surviving twelve Ford accounts are printed during this period as documents 139-50. The losses are regrettable, but readers will find that the surviving Ford accounts, together with the property records printed or abstracted in documents 138, 151, and 152, are well worth close scrutiny, for they provide considerable evidence about WP's business transactions and spending habits in the fifteen years before he acquired title to 45,000 square miles of land in Pennsylvania.

137
LIST OF MISSING BUSINESS RECORDS, 1649-1699

WP kept most or all of his business papers relating to property in England, Ireland, and New Jersey in a wooden box. Document 137 lists the contents of this box: fourteen (or possibly fifteen) bundles of papers, and a number of loose parchments, ranging in date from 1649 to 1699. About half of the papers in this box were inherited from WP's father and concerned Admiral Penn's property in Ireland in the 1650s and 1660s. The remaining papers were collected by WP and mainly concern his Irish and English lands in the late 1660s and the 1670s. A few papers date from the 1680s and 1690s. The inventory of these papers was probably prepared in 1699, when WP's clerks were organizing their master's collection of papers in preparation for his departure for Pennsylvania. Unfortunately, the box and its contents disappeared, perhaps in 1870, when the Penn family papers were vandalized and scattered (see pp. 6, 11, above). Only the catalogue remains; it was acquired by the British Museum when WP's surviving papers were auctioned in 1870-1871.

Document 137 gives a tantalizing glimpse of lost business records that any interpreter of WP's career would love to examine closely. The first records itemized, an unbundled group of deeds ranging in date from 1671 to 1695, mainly concerned WP's and Gulielma's property in England. WP entered into complex transactions with Sir James Rushout in 1676-1678 when he bought Warminghurst and sold some of Gulielma's land; duplicates of several of the Rushout deeds, found in the Public Record Office and in the Duke of Norfolk's archives, are abstracted in doc. 151, below. Four items, marked in the margin with diamonds, were New Jersey deeds. Another of the loose parchments was WP's settlement with his second wife, Hannah Callowhill, in 1695. Bundles no. 1, 2, and 3 were mainly papers collected by WP's father concerning his Irish lands in county Cork. Included in these three bundles were rent rolls of the Penns' tenants and business papers from WP's visits to Ireland in 1666-1667 and 1669-1670. Bundle no. 4, bonds payable to WP, cannot be further identified. Bundle no. 5, another collection of Irish papers from the 1660s, included a list of the Penns' tenants which gave the total of their annual rents as £1152 2s. 11d. Bundle no. 6, John Fenwick's papers, concerned the New Jersey property transactions discussed in documents 112-18 and 152. Bundles no. 7, 8, and 9 contained further Irish papers, including correspondence with WP's steward Philip Ford and his Cork agent William Morris. Bundle no. 10 contained business papers of Gulielma's father, Sir William Springett. Bundle no. 11 is a mystery; Thomas Elliot and Jos. Boyl have not been identified. Bundle no. 12 is also a mystery, since WP's marriage referred to here may be the one to Gulielma Springett in 1672 or the one to Hannah Callowhill in 1696. Bundles no. 13 and 14 contained still more Irish papers, including Colonel Peter Wallis' lease of Shanagarry at £110 per annum, and "Irish Excheqr Business," which may have concerned WP's payment of back quit rents (see doc. 92). The final item in the catalogue, bundle no. 13 (perhaps a mistake for 15) is another mystery; the records here could have belonged either to Gulielma's or to Hannah's estate. The next-to-last item in the catalogue listed WP's lands in east Cork and west Cork; for another version of the this list, see document 138, below.

A Catalogue of Parchmts and Papers
in a small Deal box N: A.

Lease of the Frieth
Bishop of Killalow's Release of Lands
Sr Wm Penn's Grant of Lands to Bp: of Killalow
W: Penn's Release of the Equity of Redemption of Worminghurst, &c.—78
Counterpart of Henry Bigland's Grant & Release to Sr James Rushout, &c. —76
{1677—} Counterpart of Sr James Rushout's Defeazance upon W: Penn's Security for 498l
Indenture Tripartite, between Sr James Rushout, Wm Garrett & Abigail Cullen—76
{1671—} One part of the Settlemt of W: Penn upon his Intermarriage wth G: M: Springett
One part of the Settlemt of W: P. upon his Intermarriage wth Gulielma Maria Springett, wth Covent to acknowledg a Fine & Recovery—1671
Counterpart of the Release of Lands called the Frieth—1678
Counterpart of W: Penn's & his Wife's Appointment to Sr Ja: Rushout—76
{☞} G: M: Springett her Release of Lands settled on her Mother for her Dower. Not sealed
{◇} Edward Byllynge's East-Jersey Deed
Wm Petit & Thomas Langhorn's Sale of Lands to Sr Richard Ruth & Sr Wm Pool—79
{◇} Wm Penn's Sale of Lands to Wm Haige—1676
One part of the Settlemt of G: M: Springett upon her Intermarriage wth W: Penn 1671
Duplicate of W: Penn's Settlemt of his present Wife's Jointure.—1695
{◇} James Duke of York's ~~Sale~~ Deed to W: Penn—1682
{◇} W: Penn's Gawen Lowry's &c. Deed to Wm Haige 1676

{In Bundle N: 1.}

Articles between Lord Braughall & W: Penn Esqr.
Part of Ld Breyhill
Copy of Genll Penn's Letter of Attorny to his Wife. Anno 1654
Particulars of Lands that Genll Penn is to be put in Possession of
Genll Penn's Lease
Abstract of the Civil Survey
A Draught for Leases
Dr Callaghan's Lease of Clonfadda
Dr Callaghan's Oath of Performance of Seneschalls Office

Counsellor Fisher's Advice about Court for the Mannor
Mc Crump Papers
Capt Ruddocks Papers
John Pettie's Letters
Benjamin Cross's Receipts
Copy of L^{d} of Breyhill's Deed of Release
O: C's Patent to Gen^{ll} Penn—Anno 1656
O: C's Grant to Gen^{ll} Penn

{In a Bundle N: 2}

Acc^{ts} of S^{r} W: Penns Estate in Ireland
Acc^{ts} of Papers belonging to W: P's Wifes Estate
T: ~~M~~ Amory—66
Copy of S^{r} W: Penn's Order
Copy of the Schedule of Lands view'd by the Com^{rs} for S^{r} W: P's Reprisal
Additionall List of Lands for S^{r} W: Penn's Reprisal
T: Elliot's Letter
Instructions about S^{r} W: Penn
Copy of a Letter to S^{r} W: Penn, in answer to his Royal Highness's Commands in 166[ ]
About the Custodium Rent—1663
Copy of the Com^{rs} Return to the E. of Owrey in S^{r} W: Penn's Business—1660
Draught of a Petition to his Maj^{ty} about Lands in Ireland—1663
An Order of the Lords Justices of Ireland—1661
Joss: Boyl
Copy of the King's Order ab^{t} the Quitrent—1666
Lands for Sr Wm Penn—how sett in 40 & 41
Copy of the K's Letter for S^{r} W: Penn's Proviso, &c. to Lord Lieu^{t} of Ireland
S^{r} W: Penn's Petition to K. Charles 2^{d} about his Irish Estate
S^{r} W: Penn's Clause in the Bill

{In a Bundle N: 3.}

Ireland Rent-Rolls
Papers concerning Affairs in Ireland—1660
Certificate of Lands taken out of Thomas Elliot's Office
Col: Osbourn's Letter—67
Copy of the K's Letter
S^{r} W: Penn's Case
P: Elliot's Letter about S^{r} W: Penn's Estate
Irish Business
John Fitz-Gerald
Petition of S^{r} W: Penn ab^{t} the Irish Business—1663
Of the Irish Business under S^{r} W: Penn's own hand
Irish Letters & Acc^{ts}—68 & 69
Thomas Elliot's Certificate for some Lands
R: Fitzmaurice
Ibawne Ten^{ts}
Thomas Franckland
~~Ibawne~~

Thomas Roomcoyl's Sale of a Ship to Sr Denis Gawden
R: Southwell's Letter abt Sr W: Penn's Business
Sr W: Penn's Case wth the Bishop of Killalow
Bill of Exchange
A Bond for Mr Middleton &c
Sr W: Penn's Memorandums
T: Franckland's Acct
Bishop Worth

{[In a Bundle] N: 4}

Divers Bonds payable to W: Penn

{In a Bu[ndle N]: 5}

Clause of the Act of Settlemt
Copy of the Letter of Attorny to the Lady Penn
A Provisoe
An Order by the Lords Orrery & Montroth abt the Lands of Shangerry
Irish Concerns
A List of the English Tenents
Sr W: Penn's Petition to the King—1663
Reasons why Sr W: Penn should be inserted in the Settlemts of Ireland
Copy of a Petition of Sr W: Penn to the K. about the Irish Concerns
Sr W: Penn's Letter of Attorney to ~~Sr~~ W: Penn—1669
Sr W: Penn's Letter
Paper about the Irish Concerns
Petition to the D. of Ormond, & the K's Letter thereupon—1664
The K's Letter to the Lieut of Ireland.
Sr W: Penn's Provisoe
Col. Wallis's Petition to the Lord Lieut
A Clause desired to be inserted into the Bill transmitted from Ireland, Reasons, &c.
Copy of the particular of Lands granted in Custodium to Sr W: Penn, &c
Acct of Lands, Old Proprietrs, &c in Ireland
Philip Ford to W: Penn Esqr
King's Letter to the Court of Claims
A List of forfeited Lands
Sr W: Penn's Petition to the King
A Provisoe in the Act of Settlemt for Sr W: Penn
Copy of the D. of York's Letter to the Lord Lieut—Anno 1664
Donagh Earl of Clancarty restor'd
Copy of D. of York's Letter to the Lord of Orrery in behalf of Sr W: Penn
Duke of York's Letter to the D. of Ormond
A List of the English Tenants, & wt they pay, vizt 1152l:2s:11d
A Paper about the Irish Concerns
Sr W: Penn's Clause in the Bill
W: Penn Esqr to his Tenants
W: Penn to his Father

{[In a Bundle] N: 6}

John Fenwick's Papers

{[In a Bundle] N: 7}
Copy of Sr W: Penn's Patent for the Lands in Ireland

{[In a Bundle] N: 8}
Philip Ford, Ireland—1670-71
W: Penn's Protest—1669
Wm Morris—1671
Wm Bird—1671
Peter Steers

{[In a Bundle] N: 9}
Difference of
An Order of Council
Sr W: Penn's Petition to the King—Anno 1661
A Petition & Provisoe for the Irish Estate
Lands, Proprietrs, &c. about Reprize
Sr W: Penn's Paper
The Address of the house of Commons in Ireland
Copy of Petition to the Commissioners of the Genll Revenue
Kingston—By the Commissioners for executing the K's Declaration—1661
Sr W: Penn's Provisoe-paper
Sr Wm Penn's Order, to have the full Benefit of the Lord Kingston's Order
Lord Kingston's Engagemt about the Reprize—1661
The Improvemts allowed by the Commissioners
Edward Roberts from Dublin about Lands, 1661
Majr Morgan's Draught of a Provisoe for Sr W: Penn—61
Provisoe in the last Act of Settlemt
Sr W: Penn's Copy of the King's Letter into Ireland
Sr Wm Penn's Paper, &c
Lists of Lands for Reprisal
Sr W: Penn's Petition to the King
Sr W: Penn's fiat.

{[In a Bundle] N: 10.}
Bonds & Bills of Sr Wm Springetts

{[In a Bundle] N: 11.}
Thomas Elliot's & Jos: Boyl's Papers

{[In a Bundle] N: 12}
Agreemts, Notes, Bills, Bonds, &c. before & since Marriage

{[In a Bundle] N: 13.}
Covents between Sr W: Penn, & Col. Wallis 61
Col. Wallis's Lease of Shangarron for One Whole Year—110l—1663
Col. Wallis's Lease of Ditto—110l—1664
Sr W: Penn, & Col. Wallis Report—1666
Heads of Agreemt between Coll. Wallis & W: Penn Esqr—66
Certificate at the great Island near Ross agt Coll. Wallis—66
Lord Lieuts Certificate touching the great Island—1666
Articles between Sr Wm Penn & Col. Wallis—67
Lease to Col. Wallis–1668
Sr W: Penn's Case stated wth Col. Wallis

Answers to Col. Wallis Pretensions
Sr W: Penn's Letter of Attorny genll — 1665
King's Letter to the Earl of Orrery — 1660
Lord Orrery's Commission abt Shangerry, &c — 1660
Two Petitions of Sr W: Penn
Sr W: Penn's Reprizes — 1661
W: P's Acct of Ireland to his Father
Copy of the K's Letter to reprize Sr W. Penn in Shangerry &c 1660
Sr W: Penn's Case
Copy of Lords Justices Letter to the Comrs at the Court of Claimes — 1661
Sr W. Penn's Brief for Mr Whitfield
John Gaw
Return of the Jury for the Valuation of the Lands of Immokilly, &c
Irish Concerns

{[In a Bundle] N: 14.}

Irish Excheqr Business, &c.

{[In a Bundle] N: 14}

Sr Thomas Clutterbuck
Dr Worsly
Sr Denis Gawden
Capt Rowse
Acct of Monies in Cevil's hands — 1670
Sr Richard Ruth — 66
Robt Southwell Senr. 68
Thomas Turner's Bill for 249l — 1649
Receipt & Value of Admll Penns Prizes — 1652 - 67000 pieces of 8
Some odd Papers
Receipts of -96-97, 98, 99.

Counterpart of Thomas Reynold's Lease — 97.
Quantity of Lands in the Barony of Imokilly & Ibawme

{[In a Bundle] N: 13}

Papers belonging to W: P's wifes Estate

D. Egerton MSS, 2168, BL. Docketed: A Catalogue of Parchments | and Papers in a small Deal | Box No. A.

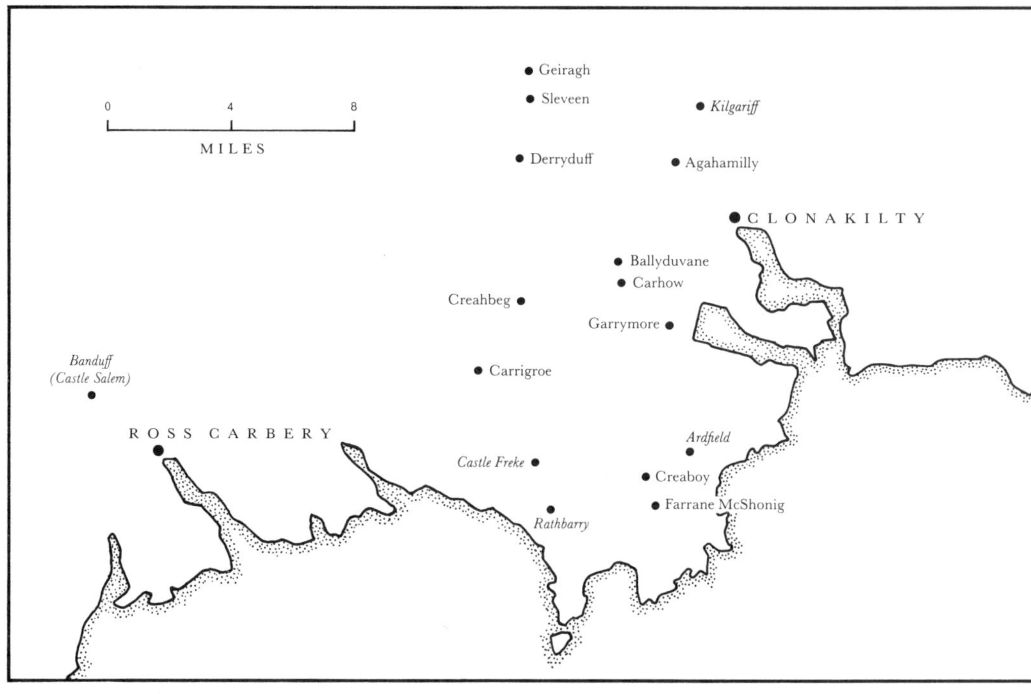

Penn Lands in the Barony of Ibaune and Barryroe, West Cork.

138
PENN'S LANDS AND TENANTS IN IRELAND, 1667-1670

Under the Act of Settlement, Admiral Penn received over 12,000 acres English measure (nearly 7500 acres Irish), in the baronies of Imokilly and Ibaune and Barryroe, county Cork. The intent of the settlement was to provide the Admiral with £1000 per year in rental income. WP secured these lands from the court of claims on his first trip to Ireland, in March and April 1667 (see doc. 13, n. 2), and made leases with his father's tenants in 1667 and again in 1669-1670. Sixty percent of Admiral Penn's lands lay in Imokilly, east Cork, and our data on these tracts is more complete than for the Penn properties in west Cork. For 1669-1670, the Penns leased 3397 acres (Irish measure) in Imokilly for £545, or about 3s. 3d. per acre. Prorating the remainder of the Imokilly land adds another £176, bringing the total for east Cork to approximately £721. In west Cork we know that WP contracted for rents of £106 on 868 Irish acres, or about 2s. 5d. per acre. Prorating the rest of the Ibaune and Barryroe land adds another

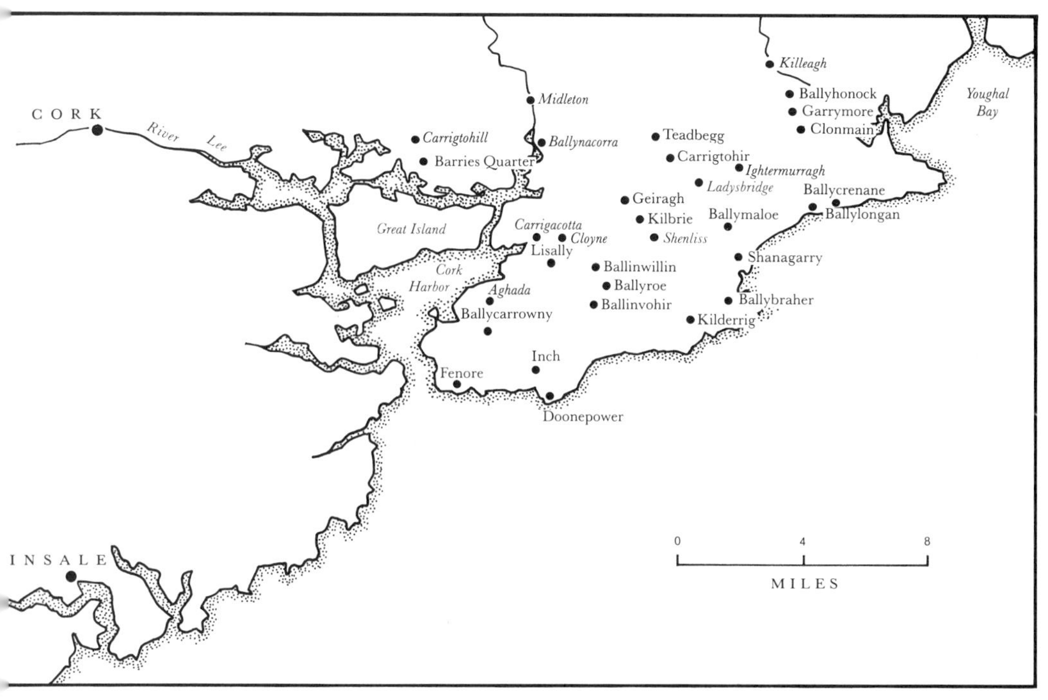

Penn Lands in the Barony of Imokilly, East Cork.

£258, for a total of approximately £364 in west Cork. In all, we estimate that WP's rents for Irish lands in 1669-1670 came to about £1085, a figure that correlates well with the £1152 reported in an undated rent roll from the 1660s (see headnote to doc. 137). Of this amount, WP owed just over £113 to the crown in quit rents—£68 5s. 6¾d. on Imokilly lands and £45 11s. 2½d. on Ibaune and Barryroe lands—a sum he probably found difficult to pay (see doc. 92, n. 2).

The following list is a composite from several sources. The names of Irish lands confirmed to Sir William Penn by the court of claims are printed in the *Fifteenth Annual Report of the Record Commissioners* (Dublin, 1825). We have compared this with the Book of Survey and Distribution for County Cork, PRO, Dublin. We have added a list of the Penns' tenants in 1669-1670, at the time of WP's second Irish trip. Where known, we have indicated the amount of rent agreed to. Irish place names have been standardized to the modern spelling adopted in the notes to WP's Irish Journal (doc. 35). In determining the names of tenants and the lands they leased from the Penns, we have relied heavily on WP's Irish Journal, eighteenth-century Penn deeds and indentures in the Registry of Deeds, King's Inns, Dublin, on document 137, and on the researches of Albert Cook Myers.

Land	Acres	Roods	Perches	Tenant
IMOKILLY (EAST CORK)				
Shanagarry 1 plowland	266			
Kilmaghen including Ardnashiney	116			
Killkeagh	42			
Ballynamony	66	2		
Ballygannybegg	60	2		
Ballingogannigg	60	2		Peter Wallis at £110 per year in 1661, 1663, 1664; at £142/8/8 per year for 99 years in 1667 (including Ballyhinan, below)
Ballingarrane	81			
Ballylongan and Ballingarrane	271			
Ruskemore	48			
Ruskaghbegg	30	1		
Ballymallobegg	93			
Barries quarter	25			Samuel Rolle
Killgillhen	49	3		Francis Smith
Ballyronahane	108			
Ballybraher	161			
Coolenodigg	26	2		Michael Gayle at £82 per year
Carrigkilter	82			
Rathcully	15	2		
Kilderrig	103	2		Thomas Franckland
Lisally	82	2		Richard Bent
Ballyhonick	132	1		Richard Smith at 4s. 6d. per acre (£45 total)
Ballyline	68			
Clonemane	236			Garrett Fitzgerald at £44 per year
Garrymore	157			John Rowse at £38 per year
Curroghticloghy	79	2		John Wakeham at £90 per year (including Fenore, Ballycarrowny, Acredoan, Seskens, and probably Ballincohiskeene)
Condon's acres	42			
[Knockne]geiragh and Knocknegappule	120			Francis Smith, at £42 per year for the first year and £40 thereafter (including Killgillhen)
Kilbrie	115	2		
Sheanless	118	2		Thomas Boles at £62 per year (including Ballyvillin and Ballinvohir)
Carrigtoghir	70		20	
Teadbegg	43	1	20	
Inch	218	2	8	
Doonepower	197			
Lissally	82	3		
Ballinicoll and Ballyshane	124			Andrew Woodley
Lisaknockane	30			
Mucky	27	2		
Ballynatra	33	2		
Ballyvillin	76			Thomas Boles
Seskens	43	1	10	John Wakeham

Land	*Acres*	*Roods*	*Perches*	*Tenant*
Ballincohiskeene alias Ballyhimikin	27	2		John Wakeham?
Tullyplenebegg	26	3		Andrew Woodley
Ballinwillin	83	2		Samuel Rolle
Fenore and Knocknagihy	279			John Wakeham
Ballycarrowny	93			John Wakeham
Ballyhinan	53			Peter Wallis
Ballelowrace and Ballyroe	64			Samuel Rolle
Acredoan	38			John Wakeham
Ballinvohir	27			Thomas Boles
IBAUNE AND BARRYROE (WEST CORK)				
Aghamilly	192	3	8	Abel Guilliams
Carhow [North Carhow?]	309	3	8	Philip Maddox?
Ballidtane alias Ballydowane	134	3	8	Philip Maddox?
Curroe [South Carhow?]	183	2	16	John Southwell? see doc. 35, n. 244
Creaghmore	138	1	24	
Derryduff and Kilronane	386			Adam Clark at £24 per year
Knocknephonery	94			
Creaghbeg	129			David German
Killeleine	100			William Freke at £22 per year
Carrigroe	219			Earl of Barrymore at £20 per year
Garranegoline	31	2	16	Edward Clarke at £40 per year
Kilkerranmore alias Gortneshamroge	89	2	32	Edward Clarke at £40 per year
Gortnekerry	41	2	16	Edward Clarke at £40 per year
Bally McRedmond	133	3		Randall Warner?
Ardquoky	65			John Wood?
Courleigh	75			Walter Harris
Keile and Derryvoreene	114		16	Edmund Nuce?
Maugh	44			Edmund Nuce
Sleiveene	93		32	William Freke?
Sleveene		3	8	William Freke?
Geiragh, Inchicarr, Cnockelloage and Dyrrinreene	172 180			Edmund Nuce?
Creaboy	32			Edmund Nuce?
Farrane McShonig	40			Edmund Nuce?

Total acreage:

Imokilly

4496 acres, 18 perches plantation acres (Irish acres)
7272 acres, 1 perch English statutory measure (English acres)

Ibaune and Barryroe

3000 acres, 24 perches plantation acres (Irish)
4859 acres, 3 rods, 3 perches English statutory measure (English acres)

The next twelve documents are WP's accounts with his steward Philip Ford, who handled much of his money and performed many services for him in the 1670s. The series starts immediately after WP's marriage. Accounts nos. 1-6 (docs. 139-44) cover the span from 19 April 1672 to 7 July 1674. The next five accounts are missing. Accounts nos. 12-17 (doc. 145-50) cover the span from 27 April 1677 to 9 March 1680; of these, account no. 12 is incomplete. The series probably continued into the 1680s, but later accounts have not been found. Ford kept these reckonings in standard double entry form, first listing WP's debts or expenditures, then listing his credits or income. For example, account no. 1 (doc. 139) states that WP had an initial cash balance on 19 April 1672 of £444 18s. 6d. During the next two months, Ford paid out £541 4s. 4d. on goods and services for WP, and received £246 5s. on WP's account in cash and bills of exchange. When Ford closed account no. 1 on 25 July 1672, he calculated that WP's balance was reduced to £149 19s. 2d. Ford then carried this figure over to his next account, stating in account no. 2 (doc. 140) that WP had an initial cash balance of £149 19s. 2d.; he continued to follow the same procedure through this series of accounts.

Philip Ford had first worked for WP in Ireland in 1669-1670, helping him to manage the family estates near Cork (see docs. 35 and 44). By 1672 Ford was WP's London business manager. Operating from his shop at the sign of the Hood and Scarf in Bow Lane, Ford paid WP's bills to tradesmen, paid wages to some of WP's servants, posted and received WP's letters, and sent large quantities of household supplies to Rickmansworth. Whenever WP visited London, Ford paid his master's coach hire or boat hire and other incidental expenses, as on 4 May 1673 (doc. 143), when Ford dispensed one shilling to the poor folk who were begging at the Bull and Mouth Friends Meeting. Ford sometimes traveled with WP to collect rent from Gulielma's tenants in Kent and Sussex (see 10-13 July 1672 in doc. 140); generally Ford went by himself to collect the rent (see 25-29 Nov. 1672 in doc. 142). Ford also frequently supplied WP and Gulielma and WP's mother with pocket money, as on 26 April 1672 (doc. 139), when he tucked £30 into a roll of white frieze cloth he was sending to Rickmansworth. According to accounts nos. 1-6, Ford received £4,256 on WP's account and paid out £4,676 in the space of twenty-seven months during 1672-1674. Part of the payment was to himself; Ford received £295 in salary and business expenses in 1672-1674, and he also had the continuous use of several hundred pounds in WP's cash balance.

It is regrettable that Ford's accounts nos. 7-11, for 1674-1677, are lost. During this period WP moved from Rickmansworth to a larger and far costlier establishment at Warminghurst. WP paid £4,450 for his new house and lands, and in order to obtain the necessary funds for this transaction he sold some of Gulielma's land and contracted a number of loans. Ford's missing accounts, if they could be correlated with WP's real estate transactions of 1676 (see doc. 151), might explain WP's financial status at the time he moved to Warminghurst. Accounts nos. 12-17 (docs. 145-150) indicate that in 1677-1680 Ford was doing considerably less business for WP than he had done in 1672-1674. In thirty-six months Ford received £2,670 on WP's account and paid out £2,999. In other words, Ford received and spent about £1,000 per year for WP in the late 1670s, as against £2,000 per year in the early 1670s. Warminghurst was considerably farther from London than Rickmansworth, so WP probably dealt more with local suppliers in 1677-1680. He no longer asked Ford to collect rent from the tenants in Kent and Sussex, and he no longer paid Ford a salary. When Ford closed account no. 17 (doc. 150) on 9 March 1680, he calculated that WP's cash balance was wiped out, and that WP owed him £107 16s. 8d. This debt was not large, but since WP kept drawing on his steward for further expenses without paying him, and since Ford charged compound interest on what WP owed him, in the next few years WP's debt grew rapidly. When WP sailed for Pennsylvania in 1682, Ford reckoned that WP owed him £2,851. By 1687 Ford claimed that WP owed him over £5,000. By 1696 he claimed £10,447. When Ford died in 1702, WP had made no settlement with him, and Ford's widow and children sued WP for £20,000. The case was heard in Chancery and in the Court of Common Pleas and dragged on for years. In 1708 WP was sent to debtors' prison, and he was finally forced to sell Warminghurst and to settle with the Fords by paying them £7,600 (Peare, pp. 237, 315, 353, 396, 398, 402, 404).

Ford's accounts of 1672-1680 reveal little about the debt which became such a destructive issue in WP's later career. Nor do these accounts disclose WP's full income or expenditures during the 1670s, since Ford only handled part of WP's business. But documents 139-150 do suggest that WP was living well beyond his means. The income from WP's property in Ireland and Gulielma's property in England seems to have been modest; Ford collected about £200 per annum in English rents and £500 per annum in Irish rents. This Irish income was less than half the annual rents WP arranged with his tenants in 1669-1670. The Irish rent money all came from William Morris, who was WP's agent in Cork. It may be that another agent sent additional rents directly to WP, or it may be that WP's tenants were defaulting. The Ford accounts do show that WP contracted sizable loans throughout the 1670s. In 1672-1674 WP was paying 6 percent interest on £2,000 borrowed from six creditors, including his mother and sister.

By 1677-1680, three of these six loans were repaid, but WP had contracted fifteen new loans totaling £3,200. In 1676-1678 WP sold over a thousand acres of Gulielma's land in Sussex for £5,800 (doc. 151), reducing future rental income. As of 1678 he had not paid back any of the money he had borrowed in 1676 to buy Warminghurst. Thus the evidence suggests that WP was under considerable financial pressure in the late 1670s, and that he was badly in need of fresh sources of income when he decided to petition the king for land in America.

The Ford accounts supply detailed information about WP's living habits in the 1670s. Though most of the bills to tradesmen are not itemized, Ford specifies many purchases of food, clothing, and furniture. WP seems to have kept a good table, for Ford sent him barrels of oysters and scallops; shipments of venison, salmon, sturgeon, partridges, larks, capons, and lamb; such fruit and vegetables as gooseberries, strawberries, cherries, carrots, potatoes, "sparrow grass" (asparagus), and "hartechokes;" not to mention vinegar, oil, anchovies, saffron, and "chuckelett"; and brandy and "usqubaugh" (whiskey) to wash it all down. Ford frequently sent rolls or large pieces of frieze and serge cloth, and such items of clothing as shoes, hoods, scarfs, bodices, pettycoats, silk stockings, and a pair of "golosies." There were also books for WP, and toys for his young children. The London coachmaker Robert Gawthrop built three coaches for WP in 1672-1674. The accounts show that WP dealt with a largely Quaker network of London shopkeepers and craftsmen. They show how much Ford paid to post or receive WP's letters (or batches of letters): 476 payments in 1672-1674, and 232 payments in 1677-1680. They also show how very frequently Ford paid porters to haul WP's goods or carry his letters.

Finally, the Ford accounts document some major events in WP's life, such as the death and funeral of his brother Richard (see 7-25 April 1673 in doc. 143). They indicate his visits to London and disclose something of his activities in the city. There were excursions to the pleasure gardens at Vauxhall (called "Fox Hall" by Ford), and business trips to WP's lawyers at the Temple, to sessions of Parliament at Westminster, or to the royal court at Whitehall. WP shopped at the booksellers for the latest tracts written by his religious adversaries and paid the Quaker printer Andrew Soule for publishing his own tracts. At the opening of Parliament, WP several times bought the king's speech. During the Popish Plot hysteria, WP frequently bought newspapers and reports of treason trials. On 9 June 1679 (doc. 149) WP visited Newgate prison; one wonders whether he was visiting his lawyer, the Catholic Richard Langhorne, who had been sent to Newgate in October 1678 and would be tried for treason on 14 June 1679. On 17-19 September 1679 (doc. 149), WP was lobbying on behalf of Algernon Sidney's parliamentary election (see headnote to doc. 129). And on 23-27 February 1680 (doc. 150) WP was searching the Prerogative Office for the inventory of his father's estate: perhaps he was preparing his case for the largest effort of his life, his petition of 1 June 1680 to Charles II for a royal grant to start a new colony in America.

Documents 139-50 were entered as evidence into the Penn-Ford chancery suit of 1706 over WP's debt to Ford, and were retrieved by WP after the case was closed. They are now owned by the HSP, and are printed here for the first time, exactly as Philip Ford presented them to WP.

139
PHILIP FORD ACCOUNT NO. 1
23 APRIL 1672–24 JUNE 1672

2/mo 1672	An Acc^t of Disbusm^ts Since the 19th 2/mo is Debt^r as Follows	£	s	d
23	It: To Cash pd postig letters per Ireld		2	
	It: To Cash pd postig letters to severall places		1	8
26	It: To Cash pd thy self per Carrier in w^t Frize to Basing house	30		
	It: To Cash pd for ½ Reame paper		2	
	It: To Cash pd portig Brandy & glasses			6
	It: To Cash pd portig a baskitt from J Bullock			6
	It: To Cash pd portig trunke to S H: & to W G		1	
	It: To Cash pd to Bodyes Maker			6
27	It: To Cash pd Ldy Penns Coach man	1	1	
	It: To Cash pd thy self in Gould	3	4	6
	It: To Cash pd porter for taylor			6
	It: To Cash pd letter to Basing house			2
	It: To Cash pd for a purse			6
	It: To Cash pd for a p^r Bodys	1		
28	It: To Cash pd S: Maths in full 3/mo Interest due the 13th Ditto	2		
	It: To Cash pd the Ldy Penn	20		
	It: To Cash pd Stephen Crisp per order John Vanduall	3		4
29	It: To Cash pd Musterd pott Mending		1	
	It: To Cash pd John Jenner in pte Joyner worke	10		
	It: To Cash pd for a Bell qt. 4^lb 2 ounce		6	
	It: To Cash pd for a Reame large paper		5	6

		£	s	d
	It: To Cash pd 5 p^{r} stockins per Ld Penn		4	6
	It: To Cash pd for a piece Frize per Ld Penn	1	12	6
	It: To Cash pd for a piece Frize per R Penn	4		
30	It: To Cash pd John Alder per Order Cp^{t} Poole	50		
	It: To Cash pd thy self in Gould & silver	2	1	6
	It: To Cash pd the Lady Penn the Ballance her Acct	45	1	2
	It: To Cash pd Gawthrop for Ldy Penns Coach	22		
	It: To Cash pd Ditto in full his Odd Accts per yee	3	11	6
	It: To Cash pd Ditto in pte thy new Coach	10		
	It: To Cash pd Atturney Pettis bill	8	1	
	It: To Cash pd for a stone Morter		5	8
	It: To Cash pd for a puter Cullinder		4	2
3/mo	It: To Cash pd for 6/mo Interest for 200^{l} to M L per R Rudyard to the 24th ist Month	6		
ist	It: To Cash pd Tho Rudyard for a Jacke	3	18	3
	It: To Cash pd for a pestill		1	8
	It: To Cash pd Rich Dyton per shoose & boots	1	4	8
	It: To Cash pd postig lett^{r}			6
2	It: To Cash pd Samuell Conniers per thy Order	10		
	It: To Cash pd for 1 Doz: Brushes		4	3
	It: To Cash pd for hooks per Glass & hangings 5:9		5	9
	It: To Cash pd thy self sent per Rickmansworth Carrier	20		
	It: To Cash pd for hamper & Coard		2	8
	It: To Cash pd portig severall goods		1	10
3	It: To Cash pd Exchange 84:17^{s}:6^{d} spanish Gould	2	3	6
	It: To Cash pd for 36 yrds w^{t} Frize	2	8	
	It: To Cash pd for wrapper & Coard		1	2
	It: To Cash pd for Frize for R: Penn	1	18	
4	It: To Cash pd Andrew Sowle for printing	8	15	4
	It: To Cash pd Capt: Poole per Haberdashay	33	2	
	It: To Cash pd Exchange 28 Carralusis		14	
	It: To Cash pd Edw: Man for the use of J H	30		
7	It: To Cash pd lett^{r}			6
7	It: To Cash pd lett^{r} & porter per Coach			6
8	It: To Cash pd postig lett^{rs}		1	6
9	It: To Cash pd Edw: Man on the Acct John Hull	20		
	It: To Cash pd postig lett^{s}			9
	It: To Cash pd portig lett^{r}			2
10	It: To Cash pd portig fish to Carrier			8
	It: To Cash pd per p^{r} brass Scales 3^{s}: w^{ts} 6^{s} is		9	
	It: To Cash pd Exchange Bell qt 17^{lb} ¾		18	6
	It: To Cash pd for 6 velvett Rubbers		1	
11	It: To Cash pd lett^{r} per Coach			6
	It: To Cash pd postig lett^{s}			8
	It: To Cash pd for Needles		1	
	It: To Cash pd for a lett^{r}			6
		361	6	6

3/mo 1672	Debt[r]: as Follows	£	s	d
	It: To Cash pd as on the other side	361	6	6
15	It: To Cash pd Ann Whitehead for grosery	2	7	2
	It: To Cash pd the Barbers note	1	19	6
	It: To Cash pd for Oyle Viniger Runlitt & bottle		12	
	It: To Cash pd for Carrig A: P goods left at white harte Coart			4
	It: To Cash pd porter to the Coach			6
	It: To Cash pd postig lett[r]			6
	It: To Cash pd R: Fisher for Geo: Winkfld	25		
	It: To Cash pd Exchange per brass Scales		3	
16	It: To Cash pd porter to Coach			6
	It: To Cash pd to thy self sent in the brass Scales	5		
18	It: To Cash pd porter lett[r] from Carrier			2
	It: To Cash pd per 10 p[r] shoose & slippers	1	12	6
	It: To Cash pd John Jenner in pt work	5		
	It: To Cash pd porter			6
	It: To Cash pd for lett[r] & porter			5
20	It: To Cash pd Tho Clayre per thy Order		5	
	It: To Cash pd porter & lett[r]			6
	It: To Cash pd postig lett[r]			6
	It: To Cash pd william Russells bill in full	22	19	9
	It: To Cash pd Exchange 19 Jacob		9	6
	It: To Cash pd portig lett[r]			2
21	It: To Cash pd for Gooseberryes		1	
	It: To Cash pd for sparrow grass & baskett		3	8
21	It: To Cash pd porter			6
23	It: To Cash pd postig lett[r]			6
	It: To Cash pd postig lett[r]			6
24	It: To Cash pd portig lett[r]			2
	It: To Cash pd for 2 Firkins sope Capers & Olivs	1	6	6
25	It: To Cash pd porter			6
	It: To Cash pd porter to Eslington to the taylor		1	
	It: To Cash pd postig letters		1	
27	It: To Cash pd John Bolesowers bill	7	6	
	It: To Cash pd John Furley in full		14	6
28	It: To Cash pd postig lett[r]			3
29	It: To Cash pd postig lett[r]			3
	It: To Cash pd Rich Mew for Biskitt		11	10
	It: To Cash pd thy self		15	
30	It: To Cash pd Coach & porters with J: Jacob		2	2
	It: To Cash pd thy self sent per J: Jacob	10		
	It: To Cash pd Geo: Gamble per Mugletons book		10	6
31	It: To Cash pd M: Masons Order	6		
4/mo	It: To Cash pd portig box to Carrier—glasse		1	
1st	It: To Cash pd Rich Rodgers in pte wages	4	4	9
2	It: To Cash pd for a Coate per Ditto Rich	1	11	10
	It: To Cash pd portig letts[s]			6

		£	s	d
	It: To Cash pd for 17 & ½ yrds bumbasine	2	9	7
3	It: To Cash pd portig lett^{r}			2
	It: To Cash pd for p^{r} silke stockins		13	
	It: To Cash pd for hearbs		1	6
	It: To Cash pd for a Gazett			1
4	It: To Cash pd postig lett^{r}			3
	It: To Cash pd Tho Bennett per 4 & ¾ yrds Cloth per M Mason bought in the 11/mo last past	1	15	
	It: To Cash pd Exchange 5 peces Jacob: & ½ a Car:		2	9
	It: To Cash pd A: w: for starch blew & Indico		6	4
5	It: To Cash pd for a leather Jack & Inke bottle		4	
	It: To Cash pd for Inke		1	
	It: To Cash pd for postig lett^{rs}		5	6
6	It: To Cash pd portig Jack & Inke to Coach			6
	It: To Cash pd portig lett^{r}			2
7	It: To Cash pd S Hersant in full house Acct	6	14	
8	It: To Cash pd thy self in Exchange gould		9	
	It: To Cash pd the French pewterrer	6	12	3
	It: To Cash pd Exch 4 broad peices gould		2	
	It: To Cash pd for stroberrs Cherres Carratts & portig		4	11
	It: To Cash pd postig letts		1	6
		480	16	5

1672	Debt^{r} as Follows	£	s	d
4/mo	It: To Cash pd as on the other side	480	16	5
10	It: To Cash pd portig lett^{r}			2
	It: To Cash pd Expences with the Atturney			6
	It: To Cash pd William Costers note of Expences		11	5
13	It: To Cash pd thy self	1		
	It: To Cash pd thy wife at temple barr		5	
	It: To Cash pd for Cherres			4
	It: To Cash pd Expences with Atturney		2	9
14	It: To Cash pd postig lett^{rs}		1	6
	It: To Cash pd Coach to Smiths the solisit^{er}		1	
	It: To Cash pd Coach to Ditto Smiths		1	
	It: To Cash pd for a Dinner		2	8
	It: To Cash pd Coach to thy horse		1	7
	It: To Cash pd for horse			4
15	It: To Cash pd to thy self		10	
	It: To Cash pd thy Broth^{er} R: Penn	3	4	6
17	It: To Cash pd John Baker in full per books		10	
	It: To Cash pd S Hersant Man per lett^{rs}		2	5
	It: To Cash pd for boate to Fox hall & back with Expences that night		2	9
	It: To Cash pd for a lett^{r} per Coach			6

18	It: To Cash pd for a lett^r			2
	It: To Cash pd Councill Maisters Clarke	7	5	4
	It: To Cash pd bringing box writings		1	
	It: To Cash pd postig lett^r		1	
19	It: To Cash pd S: H in pte Money owing	18	6	
	It: To Cash pd for a lett^r			6
21	It: To Cash pd postig lett^r			6
	It: To Cash pd postig lett^r Holland			6
	It: To Cash pd for p^r boots		11	
22	It: To Cash pd the Coach to Rickmansworth		3	6
	It: To Cash pd for p^r Bodys for S Her		18	
	It: To Cash pd for p^r bodys for Ld Penn	1	2	
	It: To Cash pd to thy self	20		
24	It: To Cash pd Rich Clipsham to the 24 7/mo 1672	5		
		541^l	4	4
	Due to Ballance.	149	19	2
		691	3	6

Accepted per mee Wm Penn

1672 2/mo	Per Contra Cridit	£	s	d
19	It: By Cash Remaining in My hands at our Accting	444	18	6
3/mo ist	It: By Cash of Isaac Jacobsen of Amsterdam per Bank Money	7	10	
	It: By Cash of Capt Moore per bill Exchange on Silvester Cross per the use of John Hull	30		
4	It: By Cash of Simon Clement per bill Exch on Rich Scott in pte wooll Consigned to John Penington	60		
29	It: By 90 Guines Received of thy self at 1:1:6^d per guine is	96	15	
	It: By Exchange for 40^l for John Hull: p^d Ed: M	2		
639:3:6				
4/mo 21	It: By Cash Received of John Banning per Order H: Springett	50		
		691	3	6
	It: pd as on the other side	541	4	4
	Rest Due to Ballance this Acct the 25th 4/mo 1672	149	19	2

Errors Excepted
per me Philip Ford

ADS. Philip Ford Accounts with William Penn, Penn Papers, HSP. (*Micro.* 1:379). Docketed: P. F.^s Acc^t 1672 | 2-3-4 Mo. | N^o (1).

140
PHILIP FORD ACCOUNT NO. 2
25 JUNE 1672–14 AUGUST 1672

An Acc^{t} of Disbursem^{ts} Since the 25th 4/mo 1672

1672	Debt^{r}	£	s	d
4/mo				
26	It: To Cash pd Coach from Rickmanseworth		3	6
	It: To Cash pd postig lett^{rs}		1	6
	It: To Cash pd Alex: P: for Carrig bedd & other things from white=heart Coart		4	10
	It: To Cash pd lett^{r} to Greenwish			4
27	It: To Cash pd Richard Penn	2	17	
	It: To Cash pd porter to bodys Maker			4
	It: To Cash pd boatig to & from Fox hall		2	
28	It: To Cash pd portig suger to Carrier			6
	It: To Cash pd S: Hersant in pte his bill	10	8	7
	It: To Cash pd William Talby for Jesticore, petty coat & wast	1	6	5
29	It: To Cash pd John Jenner in pte	12	15	
5/mo				
ist	It: To Cash pd for letters		1	
	It: To Cash pd william Welch for lett^{rs}		2	
	It: To Cash pd for lett^{rs} out of Ireland		1	
3	It: To Cash pd postig lett^{rs}			6
	It: To Cash pd postig lett^{rs}			8
4	It: To Cash pd thy self with Tho: Haytor		15	
	It: To Cash pd Coach to Victuling Office		1	6
	It: To Cash pd for pint sacke with Ditto Haytor		1	
	It: To Cash pd Coach from Temple, from S^{r} D: G		1	
	It: To Cash pd qrt Clarrid at S: Hersants		1	
	It: To Cash pd the Lady Penn per Ld Lawson on the Acct the Const Frindship 5:^{l} & 10^{s} lent her is	5	10	
	It: To Cash pd the Lady Penn at S: Hersants	4	10	
	It: To Cash pd Cherres & baskett		1	
	It: To Cash pd Geo: Winkfeild per thy Order	10		
	It: To Cash pd porter with bodys			4
5	It: To Cash pd porter			4
	It: To Cash pd for lett^{r}			6
	It: To Cash pd postig with hornes			4
	It: To Cash pd porter with portmantle			4
	It: To Cash pd porter with wastcoat to Taylor			4
6	It: To Cash pd lett^{rs}			6
	It: To Cash pd postig lett^{r}			6
7	It: To Cash pd Tho: Tantons bill	4	14	
8	It: To Cash pd R: Hodson for silke Laces for thy sister	2	3	
9	It: To Cash pd thy wife		10	

		£	s	d
	It: To Cash pd thy wife more	1		
	It: To Cash pd Rich Penn	2	10	
	It: To Cash pd william Coster his bill given thee		18	6
	It: To Cash pd for a hatt case for thy self		4	2
10	It: To Cash pd a poore Man on the Road to Tunbridg			6
	It: To Cash pd at the Bull & bush River head per horses		5	4
	It: To Cash pd the house bill 14^{s}: 8^{d} & to the Ostlers		15	8
11	It: To Cash pd at Tunbridge	1	16	6
	It: To Cash pd for a lett^{r}			2
	It: To Cash pd at Stone Crowch		10	6
	It: To Cash pd the Man had his house burnt		2	
	It: To Cash pd the Carpenters at John Fullers			6
	It: To Cash pd the Man serv^{t}		1	
	It: To Cash pd the Maide serv^{t}		1	
12	It: To Cash pd the bill at Battell & to the serv^{ts}	1	17	11
	It: To Cash pd thy self at Stone Crouch	24		
	It: To Cash pd the house at Stone Crouch	1	4	10
13	It: To Cash pd at Tunbridg my Expences		2	9
	It: To Cash pd on the Road to London			2
	It: To Cash pd postig lett^{r}			6
	It: To Cash pd letters			5
15	It: To Cash pd Rich Penns Man per his Order	2	10	
	It: To Cash pd for lett^{r}			6
	It: To Cash pd postig lett^{rs}		1	
	It: To Cash pd for a lett^{r}			2
	It: To Cash pd boatig to Fox hall & back to Tower		2	
	It: To Cash pd boate to Fox hall & back the same day		2	
		95	3	11

1672 D^{r}: as Follows

		£	s	d
5/mo	It: To Cash pd as on the other side	95	3	11
15	It: To Cash pd Mapp Carrig from westchester		2	9
	It: To Cash pd for a lett^{r}			2
18	It: To Cash pd Rich Penn	10		
	It: To Cash pd for 2 barr Oysters & portig		5	2
	It: To Cash pd for a Mus million		1	4
	It: To Cash pd Carrig pemuenta from Bristoll		7	
	It: To Cash pd the land waiters		2	6
	It: To Cash pd for a lett^{r}			2
19	It: To Cash pd thy self going to Tunbridg		15	
	It: To Cash pd for a deale box for the books		1	
20	It: To Cash pd Samuell Conyers in pte	10		
	It: To Cash pd portig box books			6
21	It: To Cash pd for a lett^{r}			2

22	It: To Cash pd for a lettr			2
	It: To Cash pd for letts		1	
	It: To Cash pd for a lettr			2
	It: To Cash pd for a Coard			2
23	It: To Cash pd Rich Penn in full for 3/mo Interest per 4000l till the ist 5/mo 1672	45	5	
	It: To Cash pd portig hamper wine		1	
	It: To Cash pd for one nights grass per S Herst horse			8
	It: To Cash pd for a lettr			4
24	It: To Cash pd for two letts			4
25	It: To Cash pd for two letts more			4
	It: To Cash pd S Hersant in full all Accts	25		7
	It: To Cash pd Capt Pooles wife in pte 200l	50		
26	It: To Cash pd for a lettr			4
	It: To Cash pd for a hamper from Rickmansworth			6
	It: To Cash pd portig Ditto to South:			6
	It: To Cash pd John Skidmore per Order Rowland Holt & thy self being for a qrt: rent for Basing house	10	5	
	It: To Cash pd Ditto Skidmore per Order Geo: winkfd	16		
	It: To Cash pd for a lettr			6
	It: To Cash pd for a lettr			2
27	It: To Cash pd postig letts		1	
	It: To Cash pd for lettr			2
29	It: To Cash pd Ann whitehead in full for Grosery	4	8	4
	It: To Cash pd william Penington for lettr			8
30	It: To Cash pd for a lettr			6
	It: To Cash pd for a lettr			2
31	It: To Cash pd for letts			6
6/mo				
ist	It: To Cash pd for lettrs			4
2	It: To Cash pd portig & Carrig baskitt Safforn		1	8
	It: To Cash pd for a lettr			2
	It: To Cash pd for lettrs			6
	It: To Cash pd Carrig baskitt Saffron to Carrier			8
	It: To Cash pd lettr to Southwarke			6
	It: To Cash pd a smale parcell for thy wife			4
	It: To Cash pd John Ginner in full his Acct 6l	6		
3	It: To Cash pd S Hersant per Grace Fletcher Southwark	7		
	It: To Cash pd for a lettr			2
	It: To Cash pd for a lettr & smale parcell			4
5	It: To Cash pd John Jenings the Mcer	1	13	9
	It: To Cash pd william Chandler the Fish Monger	3	18	11
	It: To Cash pd for a lettr		1	2

	It: To Cash pd for lett^{r}			2
	It: To Cash pd for hemp & cannary seeds & bagg		3	
	It: To Cash pd porter			6
6	It: To Cash pd for lett^{r}			2
	It: To Cash pd for lett^{r}			2
7	It: To Cash pd for lett^{rs}			6
		287	10	9

1672	Debt^{r}: as Follows	£	s	d
6/mo	It: To Cash pd as on the other side	287	10	9
9	It: To Cash pd Samuell Conyers in full	6		
	It: To Cash pd for a lett^{r}			4
	It: To Cash pd for a baskitt & lett^{r}			6
	It: To Cash pd portig Ditto to Southwark			6
	It: To Cash pd for 3 p^{r} shoose per thy wife		8	
	It: To Cash pd postig lett^{rs}		1	9
	It: To Cash pd for lett^{rs}			6
	It: To Cash pd william Phillips in full for wine hamper & bottles to Tunbridg	2	15	
	It: To Cash pd for lett^{rs}			6
10	It: To Cash pd for lett^{r}			4
	It: To Cash pd for porter to Walthamstow		2	6
	It: To Cash pd Robt: Gawthrop in full new Coach	27		
	It: To Cash pd his bill in full all Accts	3	8	
	It: To Cash pd Tho Noake per 4 garden potts etc.		17	6
	It: To Cash pd Ralph Rudyard in full his bill with Consideration	103	15	
	It: To Cash pd for lett^{rs}			11
12	It: To Cash pd Capt Pooles wife in full, Considration per the 200^{lb} to the 25th 6/mo 72 & 16:16^{s} pd for Rich Penn in the straites is	24	3	
	It: To Cash pd for lett^{r}			6
	It: To Cash pd Mary Lawrance bill & Consideration	52		
	It: To Cash pd the Lady Penn she to discont	31		
13	It: To Cash pd Mary Peningtons Order per Money Due from thy wife	100		
14	It: To Cash pd My self with Considr^{r} per 7/mo	155	5	
		794	10	7
	Due to Ballance the 14th of 6/mo 1672	482	18	11
		1277	9	6

Errors Accept.
per me Philip Ford

1672	Per Contra: Criditr	£	s	d
4/mo				
25	It: By Cash Remaining in My hands at our last Acct	149	19	2
	It: By Cash Recd from the Ld Lawson per Ld Penn on the Acct: the Ship Constant Freendship disconted	5		
5/mo	It: By Cash Recd of John Osgood that was Miss Cound	1		
12	It: By Cash Recd of Katherine Busse in full ½ yrs Rent due the 25th 1/mo 1672: 1l:8s:6d in taxes 1:6d is 30s	1	8	6
	It: By Cash Recd of Constance Radford in full ½ yrs Rent due the 25th 1/mo 72: 4lb:16s:- for taxes 4s is 5l	4	16	
	It: By Cash Received of John Ven in full ½ years Rent due the 25th 1/mo 72 5l:12s:11d Allowed for the poore 30s per woods subsidy 37s:6d house & land 9s:6d: 32s:1d: 8s frith Charge is in all	5	12	11
	It: By Cash Recd of John Martin ½ years Rent due the 29th 7/mo 1671 in full	4		
	It: By Cash Recd in pte Ditto Martins ½ yeare Rent Due the 25 1/mo 1672: 3:10:6 & 9s:6d in bills is	3	10	6
	It: By Cash Recd of Marke Guy in pt his Rent of 12:10s:- per annum	6	10	5
	It: By Cash Receivd for whip stocks 1:13:6: apreke 7s: is	2		6
23d	It: By Cash Recd of Sr D: Gaudin in pt Money owing	60		
	It: By Cash Charged per haberdasher wares per Capt Poole in former Acct that paymt Contidid	33	2	
6/mo	It: By Cash Received Charges pemienta		9	6
13	It: By Cash of Nicolas Cooke per Charles Duncum	1000		
		1277	9	6
		1277	9	6
		149	19	2
		1127	10	4

ADS. Philip Ford Accounts with William Penn, Penn Papers, HSP. (*Micro.* 1:392). Docketed: P. Fs' Acct 1672 | 4: 5: 6. Mo | No (2).

141
PHILIP FORD ACCOUNT NO. 3
14 AUGUST 1672–29 OCTOBER 1672

1672 6/mo	An Acc^{t} of Disbursemts since our Accting the 14:6/mo:1672 is D^{r}:	[£]	[s]	[d]
14	It: To Cash pd John Jenner in full	14	4	
	It: To Cash pd per bill to thy self for Storkey on Charles Duncum Goldsmith	100		
	It: To Cash pd the Smiths noate		17	8
30	It: To Cash pd portig the Mapps			4
	It: To Cash pd Geo: Winkfeild per thy Order	18	7	
7/mo	It: To Cash pd Samuell Hersant	1		
	It: To Cash pd for lett^{s} at my Returne to Londn		1	9
4	It: To Cash pd Rich Healey per Harness	4	14	6
	It: To Cash pd for a lett^{r}			3
	It: To Cash pd S Jenings per Order M: Penington per Money lent thy wife	5		
	It: To Cash pd porter			5
	It: To Cash pd Sarah Hersant	1		
	It: To Cash pd S M for 3/mo Interest for 100^{l} to the 13th 5/mo 1672	2		
	It: To Cash pd for Close stoole & pann		13	3
	It: To Cash pd Tho: Webb per viniger Oyle & Anchovy	2	1	8
	It: To Cash pd Carrig groseryes to Carrier		1	
6	It: To Cash pd for lett^{s}			2
	It: To Cash pd Carrig the tyles			6
	It: To Cash pd 4 boxes Cakes & Carrig		11	
	It: To Cash pd for a lett^{r}			3
	It: To Cash pd Gerrat Roberts per Order	130		
9	It: To Cash pd porter & lett^{r}			6
	It: To Cash pd porter with lining & baggs			4
	It: To Cash pd S Hersant	1		
	It: To Cash pd thy self per william Gosnell	1		
	It: To Cash pd the Lady Penn per Coachman	2		
	It: To Cash pd thy selfe	1		
	It: To Cash pd postig lett^{rs}		2	
	It: To Cash pd for portemantle pillion strapps & etc.	4	4	2
10	It: To Cash pd a note for Lady Penn per 44 Ells Fust	7	14	10
	It: To Cash pd William Welch per Captive per thy Ord^{r}	2		
	It: To Cash pd Deb: Dunford per Bill	1	3	
	It: To Cash pd thy self going to Kent	5		
11	It: To Cash pd per the Horses & Ostler		9	8
	It: To Cash pd Bridgets Maide		1	
	It: To Cash pd Will Gosnells Boy		2	
	It: To Cash pd porter			4

		£	s	d
	It: To Cash pd per p^{r} horses		3	6
	It: To Cash pd for a lett^{r}			2
	It: To Cash pd portig lett^{r}			4
12	It: To Cash pd John Allin in full for Glasses & tyles	6	5	8
	It: To Cash pd for 2 barr Oysters & portig		5	6
	It: To Cash pd for 4 Iron backs qt 1^{gal} 3^{qrt} 24^{gills} at 13^{s} per ^{gal}	1	5	6
	It: To Cash pd portig to Carrier Iron backs & Oysters		1	
	It: To Cash pd postig letts			6
	It: To Cash pd porter & lett^{r}			6
	It: To Cash pd porter & lett^{r}			6
	It: To Cash pd postig lett^{r}			4
	It: To Cash pd postig lett^{rs}		1	
14	It: To Cash pd for a lett^{r}			4
	It: To Cash pd Ann Whitehead for Grosery	3	14	10
16	It: To Cash pd for a lett^{r} & porter			6
	It: To Cash pd Rich Clipsham in full qrt Rent Due the 23^{d} 10/mo	5		
	It: To Cash pd for a lett^{r}			8
	It: To Cash pd for a lett^{r}			2
17	It: To Cash pd for lett^{r} & porter			4
15	It: To Cash pd Eliz: Games in full all Accts	22	15	
	It: To Cash pd postig lett^{rs}		1	
	It: To Cash pd lett^{r} & porter			5
	It: To Cash pd for a lett^{r}			2
	It: To Cash pd Tho Langhorne his note & porter	5	7	6
	It: To Cash pd the Clarks note for Ingroseing	2	12	
20	It: To Cash pd the Lady Penn in full a qrts rent Due the 16th 10/mo & 6 weekes from the Death of S^{r} w: p to the ist 9/mo with 6/mo Interest per 300	54	8	
	It: To Cash pd for a lett^{r}			2
	It: To Cash pd Tho: Willitt for a hatt & Case per thy self		16	4
	It: To Cash pd thy wife sent per Tho: willitt per her Ord^{r}	50		
	It: To Cash pd for a hatt & Case per Tho: Shipard	1	18	
	It: To Cash pd for p^{r} silke stockins per his wife		14	
	It: To Cash pd for a portemantle per Dittos Cosen		4	6
		458	10	0

1672 7/mo	D^{r}: as Follows	£	s	d
21	It: To Cash pd as on the other side	[458]	[10]	[0]
	It: To Cash pd postig lett^{rs}			10

23	It: To Cash pd per lett^{s}			7
	It: To Cash pd Ben Alder per thy Order	16		
24	It: To Cash pd for lett^{r}			2
	It: To Cash pd per Returne the bill Exchange from S C being placed to Acct	20		
	It: To Cash pd for lett^{rs}			11
	It: To Cash pd for lett^{s}			6
	It: To Cash pd for lett^{s}		1	6
26	It: To Cash pd portig Frize in & out the Cart			8
	It: To Cash pd boatig to & from Fox hall		2	
	It: To Cash pd for a lett^{r}			6
	It: To Cash pd lett^{r} & porter		1	2
28	It: To Cash pd R Rudyard for a silver standich	1	12	
	It: To Cash pd for a lett^{r}			2
8/mo	It: To Cash pd lett^{r} & porter			4
	It: To Cash pd William Welch per a lett^{r}		1	
1	It: To Cash pd for lett^{r}			6
	It: To Cash pd for lett^{rs}		1	8
	It: To Cash pd for lett^{rs}		1	5
	It: To Cash pd portig sope & lett^{s}			9
	It: To Cash pd R Rudyard per Interest 200^{l} to the 24th 7/mo 1672 per M L	6		
	It: To Cash for lett^{rs}		1	4
8	It: To Cash pd Jonathan Chambers per a Cloke	8	13	
	It: To Cash pd lett^{r} & porter			6
	It: To Cash pd boatig to & from Fox hall		2	
	It: To Cash pd for a p^{r} stockins for thy self		5	
6	It: To Cash pd for lett^{rs}			6
15	It: To Cash pd for 2 barr Oysters		3	8
	It: To Cash pd per ½ Doz: partirig at 14^{d} per		7	
16	It: To Cash pd per 2 Doz: larks		1	6
	It: To Cash pd Geo: Winkefeild per thy Order	10		
	It: To Cash pd thy wife 20^{s} & the same time thy self 10^{s} is	1	10	
18	It: To Cash pd R: R: per the Ostelers & Gameses		2	6
	It: To Cash pd R Rodgers his bill 2^{l}:-^{s}:6^{d} & 10^{s}: for making & triming his Coate is	2	10	6
	It: To Cash pd William Mackitt per the Value at Dover	5		
	It: To Cash pd Carrig & portig shoose out of Kent		1	8
19	It: To Cash pd the Nurse of Baskers Child^{r}	1		
	It: To Cash pd thy self	1		
	It: To Cash pd Edw Raynor per thy order	1	10	
	It: To Cash pd Carrig 6 Roles Frize From Bristo with portig Carrig & to waters	2	7	
28	It: To Cash pd for lett^{rs}		1	6
	It: To Cash pd for a lett^{r}			6
	It: To Cash pd for a lett^{r}			6
91.18.10^{d}	It: To Cash pd unroling the Frize		2	

		£	s	d
	It: To Cash pd S M: for 3/mo Interest per 100l to the 13th Instant	2		
	It: To Cash pd the Lady Penns note Due to S Mathewes per Children Cloots	10	11	6
		550	8	10
	Due to Ballance this Acct stated the 27th 8/mo in London	76	3	4
	Totall	626	12	2
	Errors Excepted Philip Ford			
		458	10	00
		91	18	10
		453	8	10

	Per Contra Criditr	£	s	d
6/mo				
14	It: By Cash to Ballance at our Accting	482	18	11
14	It: By Cash of Abraham Dickson in pte wooll Consigned to him	36		
7/m[o]				
4	It: By Cash of John Banning in pte wood sold at the Frith	57		
14	It: By Cash for the 1/6 pte of 173lb pemento & 260lb Indico is	10	13	3
17	It: By Cash of Simon Clement in pte wooll Consigned to John Penington	20		
8/mo				
16	It: By Cash of Simon Clement in full the bill Returned	20		
		626	12	2

ADS. Philip Ford Accounts with William Penn, HSP. (*Micro.* 1:398). Docketed: Ph Fords' Account 1672 | 6. 7. 8 Mo. | No (3).

142
PHILIP FORD ACCOUNT NO. 4
29 OCTOBER 1672–14 FEBRUARY 1673

1672 8/mo	An Acct of Disbursmts since ~~Our Acct~~ the 29th 8/mo 1672 Accts then stated	£	s	d
30	It: To Cash pd Philip Forrest per Order	5		
31	It: To Cash pd lettr per porter			6
9/mo				
1	It: To Cash pd Stephen Crisp per Charges on books		5	6
	It: To Cash pd postig lettr			9

	It: To Cash pd postig letts		2	
	It: To Cash pd for a lettr			2
	It: To Cash pd S Hersants bill	9	14	6
2	It: To Cash pd S Hersant the Lady Penns bill	9	9	8
	It: To Cash pd lettr & porter			6
	It: To Cash pd S Mathews that she lett thee	10	5	
	It: To Cash pd Ann Whitehead in full for grosey	4	12	9
	It: To Cash pd thy self per gardiner	10		
6	It: To Cash pd portig severall things from S Hersants & boxes sugar to Carrier		1	4
7	It: To Cash pd for letts		2	
	It: To Cash pd for lettrs & porter			6
8	It: To Cash pd for lettrs			6
9	It: To Cash pd Tho: Willtts bill	2	9	6
	It: To Cash pd postig lettr		1	
13	It: To Cash pd S Mathews bill in full	8		1
	It: To Cash pd for letts			3
14	It: To Cash pd portig Frize to Tho Bennt			4
	It: To Cash pd for a lettr			4
	It: To Cash pd for a lettr			3
16	It: To Cash pd postig letts		1	3
	It: To Cash pd for lettr			2
18	It: To Cash pd for two Firkins sope		17	6
	It: To Cash pd Orringes lemmons & baskitt		2	8
	It: To Cash pd for a Reame paper		6	4
	It: To Cash pd for a lettr			2
19	It: To Cash pd porter to Carrier			4
20	It: To Cash pd Barr: Oysters & portig		2	10
	It: To Cash pd portig letts		1	
21	It: To Cash pd porter to the Coach			4
	It: To Cash pd Math: Bowmans bill	6	11	6
	It: To Cash pd for a lettr			4
22	It: To Cash pd porter the horse bringing			4
	It: To Cash pd deale box			6
	It: To Cash pd thy self in Money sent in a box to R	15		
	It: To Cash pd porter			4
23	It: To Cash pd Custom & Fright Hatt to Hamburgh		2	4
	It: To Cash pd Male pillion Cropr & gearths		2	4
25	It: To Cash pd 3 nights hay & 3 & ½ pecks Oates		4	4
	It: To Cash pd Expences at Tunbridg		1	
26	It: To Cash pd Expences at Rocks		1	6
	It: To Cash pd Expences at How			6
	It: To Cash pd horse shoos			9
28	It: To Cash pd Expences at Phimwell		3	3
	It: To Cash pd horse shooe			5
29	It: To Cash pd Expences at Phimwell		3	8
10/mo				
2	It: To Cash pd thy self going to walthomstow	1		

		£	s	d
	It: To Cash pd postig lett^{s}		1	6
	It: To Cash pd the Kentish taylo^{rs} bill	2		4
	It: To Cash pd horse hay & Oates 3 Days		3	
3	It: To Cash pd S Hersants bill	1	7	
	It: To Cash pd porter			6
6	It: To Cash pd per lett^{s} & box			4
	It: To Cash pd for a deale box		1	2
	It: To Cash pd portig Frize			6
	It: To Cash pd portig box Clothes			4
	It: To Cash pd thy self sent in the Role Frize	20		
	It: To Cash pd Richard Clipsham to the 23^{d} 1/mo a qrts r^{t}	5		
	It: To Cash pd portig box to walthamstow Coach			6
	It: To Cash pd the Carrig to walthomstow			4
	It: To Cash pd lett^{s}			6
	It: To Cash pd Capt Pooles wife ~~to~~ 3/mo interest to 25th 9/m	1	10	
7	It: To Cash pd William Markeham in full a legacy left his son Geo: per S^{r} W P	5		
	It: To Cash pd for a lett^{r}			6
	It: To Cash pd for a Lock			6
9	It: To Cash pd Rich Penn per thy Order	60		
	It: To Cash pd for a bond		1	
	It: To Cash pd for procuration & Carrig		11	
		181	12	1
			11	5

1672	Debt^{r} as Follows	£	s	d
	It: pd as on the other side	181	12	1
9	It: To Cash pd porter			4
	It: To Cash pd Henry young in full thy note bering date the 21st 12/mo 1671	10		
10	It: To Cash pd Tho: Robinson per looking glases		7	2
	It: To Cash pd for lett^{s}			6
11	It: To Cash pd Geo: Winkefeild per Ord^{r}	7		
	It: To Cash pd my self a years sallary	80		
	It: To Cash pd for a lett^{r}			6
	It: To Cash pd for a lett^{r}			6
	It: To Cash pd for a white woosted Rugg	2	6	
	It: To Cash pd for p^{r} slipp^{rs}		2	6
	It: To Cash pd thy self sent per John Jenn^{er}	3		
	It: To Cash pd for a lett^{r}			6
	It: To Cash pd porter for a lett^{r}			4
	It: To Cash pd S Math^{s} bill	7	7	6
	It: To Cash pd portig Frize & books			10
	It: To Cash pd for a lett^{r}			2
	It: To Cash pd for a lett^{r} & pcrtig			6
	It: To Cash pd for a Screane		9	

	It: To Cash pd for letts		1	
10/mo	It: To Cash pd lettr & porter			4
	It: To Cash pd Orringes & baskitt		3	
30	It: To Cash pd porter & lettr			6
	It: To Cash pd porter to Carrier			4
	It: To Cash pd Robt Scots bill for Books	32	7	
	It: To Cash pd for a lettr			2
	It: To Cash pd S Maths bill disbursmts	2	18	5
11/mo	It: To Cash pd Coach hire per Betty Camball		4	
1	It: To Cash pd lettr & portig pan		1	
	It: To Cash pd ernest the Coach to Rickmansewth		3	6
	It: To Cash pd postig lettr		1	
	It: To Cash pd Chuckelett		8	
	It: To Cash pd the Lady Penn at severall times	17	6	3
3	It: To Cash pd the Lady Penn in full the ⅓ pt rent in Ireland to the ist 3/mo 1673 & per a qrts Interest per 300l to the 16th 10/mo 1672 pd in full	30	9	
	It: To Cash pd postig letts		1	
6	It: To Cash pd thy self sent per B Kemball	40		
	It: To Cash pd for Oyle & Sampler		7	4
	It: To Cash pd boatig to & from fox hall		2	
	It: To Cash pd porter			6
	It: To Cash pd 1 ounce Assafittida & powdr		1	
	It: To Cash pd lettr			2
7	It: To Cash pd porter to Carrier			4
	It: To Cash pd porter & lettr			6
	It: To Cash pd postig lettr			3
	It: To Cash pd postig letts		1	
9	It: To Cash pd Stephen Crisp more per the books		5	8
	It: To Cash pd porter with frize to Carrier			4
	It: To Cash pd for lettr			2
10	It: To Cash pd James Beach his bill	6	1	6
	It: To Cash pd boate to & from Fox hall		2	
	It: To Cash pd porter & lettr			6
	It: To Cash pd for lettr			6
	It: To Cash pd John Coller the Appothacary his bill	2	7	
	It: To Cash pd postig letts			6
	It: To Cash pd for letts			2
	It: To Cash pd for lettr & parcell			3
	It: To Cash pd for a gally pott			1
	It: To Cash pd porter			4
	It: To Cash pd lettr & porter			4
	It: To Cash pd thy self in Guines sent per Carrer	10	15	
13	It: To Cash pd William Bartlett per Nicholas Cooks Order in full 6/mo Interest for 1000l due the 12 11/mo 72	30		

		£	s	d
	It: To Cash pd postig lett^{r}			6
14	It: To Cash pd Walter Shaller his bill per seeds	2	12	5
	It: To Cash pd postig lett^{r}			6
		469	13	9

1672	D^{r}: as Follows	£	s	d
11/mo				
14	It: To Cash pd as on the other side	469	13	9
	It: To Cash pd Carrig w Morris Caster to Bristoll		1	4
	It: To Cash pd lett^{rs}			6
	It: To Cash pd lett^{r}			2
17	It: To Cash pd portig Frize			4
	It: To Cash pd porter & lett^{r}			6
	It: To Cash pd S M 3/mo Interest to the 13th Ditto	2		
18	It: To Cash pd Tho: Coopers bill	6	2	6
20	It: To Cash pd postig lett^{r}			3
	It: To Cash pd 3 files per papers			9
21	It: To Cash pd lett^{r} & porter			4
	It: To Cash pd postig lett^{r}		1	
	It: To Cash pd lett^{r}			2
25	It: To Cash pd Barr Sope & portig	1	14	
26	It: To Cash pd lett^{r}			3
	It: To Cash pd lett^{r} & porter 6^{d}			6
27	It: To Cash pd postig lett^{r}			3
	It: To Cash pd Ph: Theo^{r}		10	
	It: To Cash pd lett^{r}			2
	It: To Cash pd porter to Carrier			4
	It: To Cash pd w welch for a lett^{r}		1	4
	It: To Cash pd lett^{s}		1	
	It: To Cash pd porter with books			5
29	It: To Cash pd porter wth severall things to Car			6
	It: To Cash pd Carrig an end of serges from London		11	6
30	It: To Cash pd Geo: Winkfeild per Ord^{r}	10		
	It: To Cash pd porter & lett^{r}			4
31	It: To Cash pd John Skidmore his bill	16		
12/mo	It: To Cash pd Jane Bullock R: Woollmd^{s} wag^{s}	3		
1	It: To Cash pd J B in pt a Cradle		10	6
3	It: To Cash pd for a lett^{r}			6
4	It: To Cash pd Samuell Hersant his bill	11		
4	It: To Cash pd P Poore	5		
5	It: To Cash pd for a Caster, leather Case 5 hoods & 5 Scarves per william Morris wife & Child^{r}	3	16	6
6	It: To Cash pd for a lett^{r}			2
	It: To Cash pd lett^{r} & porter			4
	It: To Cash pd for Tho: Muncks booke		1	

		£	s	d
	It: To Cash pd for a lettr			8
7	It: To Cash pd for a lettr			6
8	It: To Cash pd portig fish			6
	It: To Cash pd the K speach			6
	It: To Cash pd for a lettr			3
	It: To Cash pd postig lettr			6
8	It: To Cash pd John Ketelby the post fine per land past in Sussex per thy wife to thee	7	10	
10	It: To Cash pd portig hat case & Frize			6
	It: To Cash pd over Reckned in former Accts		10	
13	It: To Cash pd for a lettr		1	
14	It: To Cash pd to Joan Darby per Order	1	10	
		550	5	7
	Due to Ballance	113		2¾
		663	5	9¾

Errors Excepted
Accepted
Wm Penn

Errors Excepted in London the 14th 12/mo 1672
Per me Philip Ford

	Per Contra Criditr	£	s	d
	It: By Cash Remaineing in My hands at our last Accting the 29th 8/mo 1672	76	3	4
9/mo				
3	It: By Cash of Simon Clement in pt wooll Consigned to John Penington	3		6
	It: By Cash of William Morris per bill Exchange in pte Rent due the ist 3/mo last past	100		
	It: By Cash of S Mathew had of thy wife			4
18	It: By Cash of William Morris per bill Exchange on F Bellers & Cumpany in pt Rent due the ist 3/mo last past	70		
21	It: By Cash Received of Abraham Dickson in pt wooll Consigned	50		
	It: By Cash of John Fullr in full ½ yrs Rent & quit rent with 20s Allowed Raines per Coart	42		
	It: By Cash of the widdow Martin in full ½ yr	10	8	4
	It: By Cash of John Venn in full ½ yrs Rent	11	10	
	It: By Cash of Constance Redford in full	5		
	It: By Cash of Katherine Buss in full	1	10	
	It: By Cash of Marke Guy in pte	2		
	It: By Cash of the widdow Chandler in full	21	10	
	It: By Cash of John Buning in full 1220 Coards	137	10	
10/mo	It: By Cash of John Allaway in pte wooll Consigned to William Allaway	40	15	
9	It: By Cash Received of Hen: young in full a bill			

		[£]	[s]	[d]
	Exchange on Bartholomew Collyer per 107:10:—the ⅙ pte amots to 17:18:4d Recd	17	18	3¾
25	It: By Cash Received of S Heron in full the ⅙ pte 8 hoggsheads suger qt neat 47:–:21l the which sume being 55:4:8d	9	4	
	It: By Cash Received of Simon Clement in full wooll Consigned to John Penington per bill Exchange on Nath: Holton	12		
	It: By Cash Recd of Bridges per R Penn	50		
	It: By Cash pd Mary Westfeild per S. Clement	2	16	
	Totall	663	5	9¾

Errors Excepted
Accepted
Wm Penn

Errors Excepted in London the 14th 12/mo *1672*
per Philip Ford

143
PHILIP FORD ACCOUNT NO. 5
14 FEBRUARY 1673–9 DECEMBER 1673

	An Acct of Disbursmts s[ince the] 14th 12/mo 1672/3	[£]	[s]	[d]
12/mo				
14	It: To Cash pd S Mathew per M Cooprs [torn]	2	6	[ ]
15	It: To Cash pd S Maths bill	5	16	[ ]
	It: To Cash pd thy self sent per R: Rodgers wth 10s pd thee at S H	20		
	It: To Cash pd for ½ pecke Cannary seeds		2	
	It: To Cash pd the Lady Penn	10	13	
17	It: To Cash pd S Hersts bill	3	9	6
	It: To Cash pd Edw: Man for Chamber Rent	5		
	It: To Cash pd Andrew Souls bill	4	6	6
	It: To Cash pd portig the 300l		1	
	It: To Cash pd porter & lettr			4
18	It: To Cash pd william Browne in full his bill	22	10	11
19	It: To Cash pd letts & porter		1	
21	It: To Cash pd per 2 Capons & a side of Lamb		10	
	It: To Cash pd porter			6
	It: To Cash pd porter			3
	It: To Cash pd porter & Carrig frize to walthamstow			8
	It: To Cash pd for a lettr			3
	It: To Cash pd John Jenners bill		18	5
24	It: To Cash pd for a lettr			6
	It: To Cash pd lettr & porter			[ ]

	It: To Cash pd thy self at S Hersants 1l	1		
25	It: To Cash pd william Allaways Acct on woosteed	6	5	6
	It: To Cash pd porter to Sr D G		1	8
26	It: To Cash pd John Webb	17		
	It: To Cash pd James Claypoole per thy Coate	1	10	
1/mo				
1	It: To Cash pd Capt Pools wife in full	101	11	
	It: To Cash pd thy self at S Hersants		5	
3	It: To Cash pd to Robert Thomson of Kalerden	1	10	
	It: To Cash pd postig letts		1	
4	It: To Cash pd postig letts			9
6	It: To Cash pd Capt Keene	12		
	It: To Cash pd for a lettr			3
	It: To Cash pd porter			6
	It: To Cash pd with Oysters			4
	It: To Cash pd for peice Canvas			8
	It: To Cash pd S Hersants bill in full	5	2	2
7	It: To Cash pd porter to Clapham		1	6
8	It: To Cash pd lettr & porter			6
10	It: To Cash pd portig Frize			2
	It: To Cash pd portig lettr			4
	It: To Cash pd the widdow Crosby per a pasty per Ldy Pen		9	
	It: To Cash pd for a lettr			3
	It: To Cash pd the Lady Penn	4		
13	It: To Cash pd for a lettr			2
14	It: To Cash pd for a lettr			6
	It: To Cash pd for a lettr			4
	It: To Cash pd for lettrs			6
17	It: To Cash pd for lettr			2
	It: To Cash pd for lettr			6
19	It: To Cash pd William Walkers bill	3	10	
	It: To Cash pd for lettr			4
	It: To Cash pd william Pettits bill		18	4
	It: To Cash pd porter to Sr D Gauden		1	6
	It: To Cash pd the Lady Penn ¼ Interest per 300 to the 16 1/mo Calld Mch 1672/3	4	10	
	It: To Cash pd for a lettr			4
	It: To Cash pd postig lettr			6
	It: To Cash pd Robt Gawthrop in full	9	12	8
	It: To Cash pd porter to Sr D G		2	
	It: To Cash pd postig lettr			3
	It: To Cash pd Geo: Winkefeild per Order	25		
	It: To Cash pd postig lettr			6
	It: To Cash pd Perce Poore per Order	3		
	It: To Cash pd the Lady Penn	10		
	It: To Cash pd thy self at S Hersants	20		
	It: To Cash pd per severall things & taylors bill per James Bradshaw	2	11	3
		306	7	11

	[Dr] as Follows	£	s	d
	It: To Cash pd as on the other side	306	7	11
29	It: To Cash pd Doctr Forrest per Order	1		
	It: To Cash pd postig letts			6
	It: To Cash pd porter to Sr D G		2	
2/mo	It: To Cash pd for Oringes Lemmons & baskitt		4	4
	It: To Cash pd postig lettr			6
3	It: To Cash pd postig lettr		1	
4	It: To Cash pd postig letts		1	3
	It: To Cash pd for a Cheap for thy Cane		1	
	It: To Cash pd for a pr Shoose per R P Man Geo:		3	10
7	It: To Cash pd for a hatt		8	
	It: To Cash pd for 4½ yrds black Cloth at 11s per yd	2	9	6
	It: To Cash pd for a lettr			3
	It: To Cash pd Messenger to Sr D G		1	6
	It: To Cash pd to thy self sent per R Penns Man Geo with 11 Rings	12		
	It: To Cash pd porter			4
8	It: To Cash pd letts			6
	It: To Cash pd Priss a years wages to the 2d 10/mo 1672	5		
9	It: To Cash pd porter			6
	It: To Cash pd lettr			3
10	It: To Cash pd porter to Clapham		1	6
	It: To Cash pd John Cottington per 10 horse & herse	6	15	
	It: To Cash pd porter			4
	It: To Cash pd postig letts			9
	It: To Cash pd Coach hire per Ld Penn		1	
12	It: To Cash pd Coach hire per Ld Penn more		3	
13	It: To Cash pd 17 Doz buttons 2½ ounce silke 12 yrd staying tape per Ld Penn		9	10
	It: To Cash pd porter			1
	It: To Cash pd to thy self	1		
14	It: To Cash pd for Lone Morning Clothes		16	
	It: To Cash pd per 5 yrds dyd lining 2 slives 1 Doz: buttos for the Lady Penn		5	8
	It: To Cash pd the Lady Penn	5		
	It: To Cash pd Coach hire to & from Suff: street per Ld Penn		2	
	It: To Cash pd thy wife	1		
17	It: To Cash pd william welch for a lettr			8
18	It: To Cash pd for brass Kettle & driping pan	2	9	
	It: To Cash pd porter to Sr D Gauden		1	6
	It: To Cash pd Priss Shipard per Order a guinie	1	1	6
	It: To Cash pd to thy self per Priss Shipard	5		
	It: To Cash pd porter to Clapham		1	6
19	It: To Cash pd per proving the will	1	16	4

		£	s	d
	It: To Cash pd postig lett^{r}			6
	It: To Cash pd postig lett^{r}			6
	It: To Cash pd lett^{s}			6
	It: To Cash pd william welchs bill in full	10	10	
	It: To Cash pd 44 p^{r} gloves 5 hoods & Scarf per Ldy	4	17	6
	It: To Cash pd for 2 yrds taffity & 1 hood per thy wife		19	
	It: To Cash pd the Smiths note per Shooing		6	4
	It: To Cash pd per 15½ yrds Searge & Shallaune at 3: per yrd is	2	6	10
21	It: To Cash pd thy self at S Hersants		2	
22	It: To Cash pd thy self delivd to thy wife	20		
	It: To Cash pd James Bradsha	1		
	It: To Cash pd Tho Willitt on the Acct R Penn	1	13	10
	It: To Cash pd Ditto for thy self a Caster per dres		16	
	It: To Cash pd Tho willitt on his note to pay the 22^{d} 6th Month	5		
	It: To Cash postig lett^{r}			3
	It: To Cash pd porter to Clapham		1	10
25	It: To Cash pd the Lady Penn per the preist & Sexton of walthamstow	2	15	2
	It: To Cash pd for a lett^{r}			4
	It: To Cash pd porter & lett^{r}			6
26	It: To Cash pd Tho Rudyard in full 6/mo interst per 200^{l} per M L	6		
		411		
		410	19	11

	[Dr] as Follows	£	s	[d]
[2/mo]	[It: To Cash pd] as on the other side	411		
26	[It]: To Cash pd. for 1 Doz: S T Vindicated & 2 Doz Mugletons sent per Ireland		18	
	It: To Cash pd John Hannons Mother	5		
	It: To Cash pd for a lett^{r}			2
	It: To Cash pd for a lett^{r}			4
28	It: To Cash pd S Hersants 2 bills	8	16	9
	It: To Cash pd postig lett^{s}			6
29	It: To Cash pd porter to S^{r} D G		2	
	It: To Cash pd postig lett^{r}			6
	It: To Cash pd Carrig 2 barr Irish w^{t} from B		5	4
30	It: To Cash pd postig lett^{r}			3
	It: To Cash pd for a baskitt			4
3/mo				
2	It: To Cash pd portig barr & baskitt to Carr			4
	It: To Cash pd the Lady Penn	10		
3	It: To Cash pd the Lady Penn more at same time in the Rent Land at walthamstow	11		

	It: To Cash pd the Lady Penn per land her son Rich held	8		
	It: To Cash pd Rich Clipsham to the 23^{d} 4/mo	5		
4	It: To Cash pd the Poore at Bull & Mouth		1	
5	It: To Cash pd porter to S^{r} D G		1	6
5	It: To Cash pd N Patridge Order	15		
6	It: To Cash pd Katherine pearce per Ja: Bradshaw	2		
7	It: To Cash pd Eliz Jones per Order	1		
	It: To Cash pd S Hersant in full his Chaire	9		
	It: To Cash pd postig lett^{r}			3
	It: To Cash pd porter			4
	It: To Cash pd thy self	2		
11	It: To Cash pd postig lett^{r}			6
	It: To Cash pd the Lady Penn per Cure horse & grass	4	10	
	It: To Cash pd postig lett^{r}		1	
14	It: To Cash pd porter to S^{r} D G		1	6
	It: To Cash pd postig lett^{r}			6
	It: To Cash pd Geo: Winkefeild per Ord^{r}	10		
	It: To Cash pd for lett^{s}			4
	It: To Cash pd postig lett^{s}		1	
	It: To Cash pd the Ldy Penn sent per the Boy	5		
	It: To Cash pd postig lett^{s}		1	
22	It: To Cash pd William Markham per Ord		10	
26	It: To Cash pd the Lady Penn in pt a Picture	3	10	
	It: To Cash pd for a hood per thy wife		5	6
	It: To Cash pd thy self	25		
	It: To Cash pd John Webbs Order in full his 30^{l} Recd per Geo Sevell	13		
	It: To Cash pd the ballance of Geo: Sevell acct	1		
28	It: To Cash pd Geo: Hammon his bill	2	2	4
	It: To Cash pd Tho Goggins Sister	2	10	
	It: To Cash pd William Clarke per trimig	1	11	6
29	It: To Cash pd Lucke Howard per Ord^{r}	3	9	6
	It: To Cash pd S M 3/mo interest to the 13th 3/mo	2		
30	It: To Cash pd S Mathew bill	16	2	1
31	It: To Cash pd Philip the German	2	10	
	It: To Cash pd postig lett^{r}			6
4/mo				
2	It: To Cash pd the Lady Penn per her boy	4		
	It: To Cash pd John Skidmore per Ord^{r}	10		
	It: To Cash pd porter & prince Rup^{ts} lett^{s}			5
3	It: To Cash pd horse Meate		1	6
	It: To Cash pd Expences at Groombridge			10
4	It: To Cash pd Expences at Layton		1	
5	It: To Cash pd John Full^{r} per the poore tax per one yeare from the 12th 1/mo 1672	1	7	
		598	5	7

	Dr	a[s Follows]	[£]	[s]	[d]
4/mo	It: To Cash pd as on the oth[er side].		598	[5]	[7]
5	It: To Cash pd Expences at How			[ ]	[ ]
	It: To Cash pd K: Buss the Kings tax			3	3
6	It: To Cash pd John Venns Bill per Cutting the Fright & other taxes		16	5	8½
	It: To Cash pd Expences at Phimwell			5	4
	It: To Cash pd Expences on the Road				1
7	It: To Cash pd Expences at Tunbridge one night			1	6
	It: To Cash pd per the horse meat at London				6
	It: To Cash pd the Returne of the horse				6
	It: To Cash pd the Lady Penns weaver		1	3	
	It: To Cash pd John Webbs Ordr in full his 30l Recd per Geo: Sevell		13		
9	It: To Cash pd Ellin Greene for severall things thy wife had of her			14	6
	It: To Cash pd postig lettr			1	
	It: To Cash pd postig lettr				6
14	It: To Cash pd the Lady Penn in full a qrts Rent of the lands in Ireland to the ist 6/mo 73		12	11	
	It: To Cash pd the Lady Penn in full a qrt interest for 300 to the 16th 4/mo 1673		4	10	
	It: To Cash pd for silks per M Lowther in pt the 20:–:–owing her per her bro Rich		1	1	6
648:4:3½					
15	It: To Cash pd postig lettrs			1	6
	It: To Cash pd thy self per Geo:		2		
	It: To Cash pd the Lady Penns watch Mending			2	6
18	It: To Cash pd Tho: Bridges 6/mo Interest per 50l R P had to the 2d 4/mo		1	10	
19	It: To Cash pd Geo: Ball per thy Ordr		24	7	4
20	It: To Cash pd William Markeham in pt R Penns acct		2	10	
20	It: To Cash pd thy self at Tho Roberts		10		
21	It: To Cash pd Rich Clipsham in full to the 23d 7/mo September		5		
	It: To Cash pd for two Releases			2	
	It: To Cash pd postig lettr			1	
693:18: 7½					
	It: To Cash pd postig lettr				2
	It: To Cash pd the Lady Penn		10		
26	It: To Cash pd for letts				5
	It: To Cash pd lettr & porter				6
27	It: To Cash pd Philip Theor		1	5	
	It: To Cash pd for a lettr				6
	It: To Cash pd for a lettr				2
	It: To Cash pd lettr for Lady Penn				6
28	It: To Cash pd botig to & from fox hall			2	
	It: To Cash pd postig lettr				6
30	It: To Cash pd porter to Sr D G			1	2

	It: To Cash pd Philip Leman		10	
5/mo				
1	It: To Cash pd S Mathews bill	2	16	6
2	It: To Cash pd for letts			2
	It: To Cash pd thy self sent to Rickmanse	10		
	It: To Cash pd porter			2
2	It: To Cash pd Halligwells book		1	
3	It: To Cash pd Samll Hersant	5		
	It: To Cash pd per a deale box wth 10lb pr			3
4	It: To Cash pd for a lettr			2
	It: To Cash pd for a lettr			3
4	It: To Cash pd boatig to & from fox hall		2	
5	It: To Cash pd for lettr			4
		724		[4½]

	[Dr] as Follows	[£]	[s]	[d]
[5/mo]				
[5]	[It:] To [Cash pd] as on the other side	724		4½
	[It:] To Cash pd Ph: Lemon		5	
	It: To Cash pd porter to Sr D G		1	2
11	It: To Cash pd for letts			6
	It: To Cash pd for letts			2
	It: To Cash pd for letts			6
	It: To Cash pd to thy self sent per Carr	10		
	It: To Cash pd the Lady Penn	10		
	It: To Cash pd for a lettr			2
12	It: To Cash pd william welch postig			8
	It: To Cash pd postig lettr			6
	It: To Cash pd Antoney Peniston per Saffron & baskitt 6s: a pr gloves 2s		8	
	It: To Cash pd for 2¾ gallons brandy & bottles		10	6½
	It: To Cash pd porter to Carrier			4
14	It: To Cash pd Nicholas Cooks Order in full to the 12th 5/mo	30		
	It: To Cash pd postig letts		1	
	It: To Cash pd Andrew Soule in full	8	12	11
15	It: To Cash pd postig lettr			3
	It: To Cash pd postig lettr		1	
	It: To Cash pd for 3 hatts per the Ldy Penns servts & Geo: H		19	
18	It: To Cash pd S Hersant in full	4	9	4
	It: To Cash pd Ph: Lemon		5	
	It: To Cash pd Geo: Hammon	1		
	It: To Cash pd postig lettr			3
	It: To Cash pd John Tysers wife Exch pr shoose		2	
	It: To Cash pd the Lady Penn sent per Dockter Witles Coach Man	5		
19	It: To Cash pd My Sallary to the lst 4/mo	20		
25	It: To Cash pd thy wife at Bristoll	1		
	It: To Cash pd for a hood for Ditto		5	6

	It: To Cash pd postig lett^{s}			3
	It: To Cash pd for two hoods & 1 p^{r} gloves		10	10
30	It: To Cash pd thy self	1		
	It: To Cash pd 3 p^{r} Child & 2 p^{r} womes glovs		6	6
	It: To Cash pd 1 p^{r} Girles Kidd		1	
	It: To Cash pd James Claypooll per thy wife	1	11	6
	It: To Cash pd Sarah Hersant		10	
	It: To Cash pd thy self	1		
	It: To Cash pd thy wife	1		
	It: To Cash pd thy wife	2		
	It: To Cash pd Sarah Hersant		10	
	It: To Cash pd postig lett^{s}		1	6
	It: To Cash pd William Penrice in full 8¾ yd Cloth	3	12	11
	It: To Cash pd S Mathew in full 3/mo Intst: to the 13 5/mo	2		
	It: To Cash pd postig lett^{s}		1	6
	It: To Cash pd the Lady Penn	5		
	It: To Cash pd the Lady Penn	4		
	It: To Cash pd for 4 lett^{s} for Ditto		1	2
	It: To Cash pd the porter for Ditto			4
6/mo	It: To Cash pd the porter for Dittos Firkin & lett^{s}			10
15	It: To Cash pd Geo: Hicks in full the ⅛ pt 360^{l} Cost of the Constant Frindship bought at Amsterdam 32:10:- & 12:10^{s}:- the ⅛ pte 100^{l} Due from Tower	45		
16	It: To Cash pd the Lady Penn in full 3/mo Rent in Ireland to the ist 9/mo 1673 Exchange & interest Deducted	39	3	2
18	It: To Cash pd thy self sent to Rickmansworth per Carrier	30		
	It: To Cash pd porter to Carrier wth H: Springett portmantle			6
	It: To Cash pd postig lett^{s}			3
	It: To Cash pd postig lett^{s} Ld Penn			3
	It: To Cash pd postig lettr^{s}		2	6
	It: To Cash pd postig lett^{r}			6
21	It: To Cash pd william Crouch per Order S Crisp 6/mo int per 300^{l} Due the 17th Instant	9		
	It: To Cash pd W: Penington per thy wifes Ord^{r} per Suger	1	11	6
		965	11	2

	D^{r}: [as Follows]	£	[s]	[d]
6/mo	It: To Cash pd as on the other side	965	[11]	[2]
23	It: To Cash pd Coach to the temple		[ ]	[ ]
	It: To Cash pd a poore Man per Ord^{r}			2
	It: To Cash pd portig the Returne of H Springett portmantle			6

	It: To Cash pd postig lett^{r}			6
	It: To Cash pd to thy self at S Hersants		6	
26	It: To Cash pd P: Lemon		10	
	It: To Cash pd w welch postig lett^{rs}		4	8
	It: To Cash pd Barr Oysters		3	
	It: To Cash pd portig			4
28	It: To Cash pd S Hersant per w Russell per Malt stored	2	6	
	It: To Cash pd postig lett^{s}			6
30	It: To Cash pd paper & portig		3	8
7/mo				
1	It: To Cash pd the booke sell^{r} of Oxfford in full	9		
	It: To Cash pd for lett^{rs}		1	
2	It: To Cash pd for William Smiths primer			10
	It: To Cash pd postig lett^{rs} to w welch		1	
	It: To Cash pd postig lett^{r}			6
	It: To Cash pd Money from Bristoll the Carrig		2	
	It: To Cash pd Exchange 100^{l} from Mine=head	1		
5	It: To Cash pd S Heron per Money	5	5	4
	It: To Cash pd per lett^{r} per Ld Penn			3
7	It: To Cash pd Richard Gunton sadler in pte	6		
	It: To Cash pd postig lett^{r}			3
9	It: To Cash pd porter & lett^{r}			5
10	It: To Cash pd the Lady Penn in full ¼ interest per 300^{l} to the 16 Ditto	4	10	
	It: To Cash pd the Lady Penn in full her pte 3/mo Interest from S^{r} D G to the ist 8/mo	10		
	It: To Cash pd postig lett^{r} per Lady Penn			6
	It: To Cash pd thy self & wife at S M		15	
	It: To Cash pd for a Barr: sope	2	15	8
15	It: To Cash pd John Floyd for John Edlin	15		
	It: To Cash pd in full per 2 picturs per Ldy Penn	1		
16	It: To Cash pd Geo: Hammon		15	
	It: To Cash pd thy wife		10	
	It: To Cash pd William Mkeham in full	2	10	
17	It: To Cash pd William Browne in full	14	15	
	It: To Cash pd thy wife	3		
	It: To Cash pd porter to S^{r} D G		1	6
	It: To Cash pd Exchange 100^{l} drawne on w Morris payable to Geo: Rogers	7		
	It: To Cash pd Richard Barker per Order on R:P: acc^{t}	18	13	9
	It: To Cash pd postig lett^{r} per Ldy Penn			3
	It: To Cash pd postig lett^{r}			3
19	It: To Cash pd Edw: Darby in Money & Apparrell	7	11	10
20	It: To Cash pd S Hersant Mans bill		7	2
	It: To Cash pd postig lett^{s}		1	
	It: To Cash pd porter to Stone Cutt^{r}			3
	It: To Cash pd Priss Shipard		10	

		£	s	d
22	It: To Cash pd Rich Clipsham to the 23[d] 10/mo 73	5		
	It: To Cash pd Barr: Oysters to Walthomstow		2	
	It: To Cash pd W: W: postig lett[r]			8
23	It: To Cash pd postig lett[r]		1	
	It: To Cash pd porter to S[r] D G		1	6
	It: To Cash pd postig lett[r]			4
	It: To Cash pd Barell Oysters to J Claypools		2	6
	It: To Cash pd thy self		10	
	It: To Cash pd Barrell Oysters to Rickmansworth		2	
	It: To Cash pd porter			4
	It: To Cash pd porter to S[r] D G		1	6
	It: To Cash pd porter from lane end			2
	It: To Cash pd postig lett[rs] per Ldy Penn			3
	It: To Cash pd Tho: Webbs bill per Vinigar &c	2	15	6
	It: To Cash pd porter to S[r] D G		1	6
	It: To Cash pd Ann Stratfords bill in full all Accts	7	14	
	It: To Cash pd the Lady Penn	10		
	It: To Cash pd porter to S[r] D G		1	6
	It: To Cash pd thy wife		3	
	It: To Cash pd porter to Walthamstow per Ldy Penn		2	6
	It: To Cash pd porter to Stone Cutt[r]			4
		1102	16	10

	De[bt[r]] as Follows	£	s	d
[8/mo]	It: To Cash pd as on the other side	1102	16	10
	It: To Cash pd Tho Stanton the Stone Cutt[r] in pte	3		
2	It: To Cash pd Mary Penington in pte 100[l]	20		
	It: To Cash pd William Walker in full his note	1	1	
3	It: To Cash pd Geo: Winkfeild in full his note	24		
	It: To Cash pd postig lett[r] to w welch			8
4	It: To Cash pd the Councellor Coach to Bow lane		1	
	It: To Cash pd lett[r] per Ldy Penn			3
	It: To Cash pd postig lett[r]			2
	It: To Cash pd Ben Antribus per Order	2	3	
	It: To Cash pd postig lett[r]			3
6	It: To Cash pd Tho Twinborrow in full per 9 weeks & 2 Days joyner worke at 2:6	7		
	It: To Cash pd Rob[t] Gawthrop per the Mourning Char[t]	10		
	It: To Cash pd John Hammon in full all demand the plow land of Clonemarne	5		
	It: To Cash pd William Chandler fish Monger	3	4	5
6	It: To Cash pd Sarah Mathews note in full	15	17	9
	It: To Cash pd the Lady Penn	1		

8	It: To Cash pd thy wifes gould Cheane Mend		2	
	It: To Cash pd thy self at S M	1	9	
9	It: To Cash pd W Browne per the Cruss Covers		9	6
	It: To Cash pd lettr for Lady Penn			3
11	It: To Cash pd postig lettr			3
	It: To Cash pd the Herrald paintr in full	8		
	It: To Cash pd lettr & porter to Lady Penn			5
	It: To Cash pd the Lady Penn	9		
	It: To Cash pd John Osgoods note per lining	1	18	9
13	It: To Cash pd postig lettr from Holland		1	4
	It: To Cash pd lettr			2
14	It: To Cash pd porter to ship per Ldy Penn			4
	It: To Cash pd lettr & porter			6
	It: To Cash pd Ann Whitehead in full	13	14	
15	It: To Cash pd Edw Mann in full R P acct		18	11
	It: To Cash pd for a lettr			2
	It: To Cash pd for 7¼ yards searge per Coach mans Cloake		15	9
	It: To Cash pd Philip Lemon		5	
17	It: To Cash pd postig lettr			3
18	It: To Cash pd postig lettr Lady Penn			3
	It: To Cash pd the Ldy Penn for 2 bottles Cordiall Water R P had of one Turner	2		
	It: To Cash pd porter for Lady Penn to ship			4
18	It: To Cash pd Richard Gunton sadler in full	6	10	
1240 12 6	It: To Cash pd porter to Bridg house			4
	It: To Cash pd lettr & porter to Lady Penn			6
	It: To Cash pd postig letts Lady Penn			6
21	It: To Cash pd to John Brooking per lettr Capt Brō	10		
	It: To Cash pd postig letts			9
	It: To Cash pd postig lettr			3
	It: To Cash pd to thy self		15	
	It: To Cash pd the Oastler a place Keeping in Coach			4
23	It: To Cash pd to William Lamball that was had of Hen Cooke	3		
24	It: To Cash pd Geo: Winkfeild per Order	10		
	It: To Cash pd postig lettr 6d			6
	It: To Cash pd lettr per Ldy Penn			3
	It: To Cash pd porter to Bridg house			3
	It: To Cash pd Tho: Rudyard per M L 6/mo Interst per 300l to the 24th 7/mo last past	6		
25	It: To Cash pd Ph: Lemon		10	
	It: To Cash pd Lobdy the Shoomaker in full R P acct	2	3	6
	It: To Cash pd porter to Sr D G		1	6
27	It: To Cash pd porter twise to bridgehouse with sturgon		1	9
	It: To Cash pd postig lettr to W W			8
	It: To Cash pd the Kings speach			4

		£	s	d
28	It: To Cash pd porter to Bridgehouse per Ldy Penn			3
	It: To Cash pd lett^{r} Lady Penn			3
30	It: To Cash pd lett^{r} Lady Penn			3
	It: To Cash pd the Lady Penn per my wife	6		
		1279	9	8

	[Debt^{r}] as Follows	£	[s]	[d]
[9/mo]	[It: To Cash pd as o]n the other side	1279	9	8
	[It: To] Cash [pd porte]r twise to bridg house per Ld Pen			6
	[It: T]o Cash pd porter to S^{r} D G		1	6
4	It: To Cash pd thy self in fleet street		10	
	It: To Cash pd Arthur Winds Execut^{r} in full	1	19	6
	It: To Cash pd for a Release per w M per 562:12:8		1	6
6	It: To Cash pd the Lady Penn sent per her boy	4		
7	It: To Cash pd lett^{r} per Lady Penn			3
	It: To Cash pd lett^{r}			3
8	It: To Cash pd porter to S^{r} D G		1	6
	It: To Cash pd Theo: Harris M Lowthe^{s} Ord^{r}	20		
8	It: To Cash pd Tho Wight for 8 gallons usqubaugh	2	2	4¼
	It: To Cash pd postig lett^{s}		1	6
10	It: To Cash pd Expences from London to Phimwell		1	1
	It: To Cash pd Messinger for the tenn^{ts}			6
11	It: To Cash pd Expences at Phimwell		7	6
	It: To Cash pd horse shooing			4
	It: To Cash pd the widow Buss Kings tax		3	9
	It: To Cash pd the Kings tax 6/mo for Fright	4	13	9
	It: To Cash pd John Venns K tax 6/mo	1	3	9
	It: To Cash pd power tax for fright	1	3	4
	It: To Cash pd Malita tax		4	1½
	It: To Cash pd John Venn halfe yeare wages	2	10	
	It: To Cash pd the widow Radford 12/mo K: tax & Malita	1		4
	It: To Cash pd the Widow Mtins 12/mo K: tax & Malita	2	8	4
	It: To Cash pd her More for Mending the pond per thy Order		4	
	It: To Cash pd John Bennt 6/mo K: tax for the Fright	4	12	6
	It: To Cash pd him more for lett^{s}			10
	It: To Cash pd Mke Guies 6/mo tax for Gawthurst		15	
	It: To Cash pd Ditto 12/mo tax for Hawcurst		7	6
	It: To Cash pd Ditto 6/mo tax for Tisehurst		2	
	It: To Cash pd Ditto 3 poore taxes		12	4

	It: To Cash pd Ditto per Esheates for high way			9
	It: To Cash pd towards Bowton Bridge			3
12	It: To Cash pd Expences at Harteley Cross		1	
13	It: To Cash pd Expences at How		1	2
	It: To Cash pd John Fuller per 9/mo Kings tax	6	6	9
	It: To Cash pd John Fuller per John Raynes Coart	1		4
	It: To Cash pd Ditto for a Malita tax		5	
	It: To Cash pd John Fullr per his jorney to Chitchistr	1		
	It: To Cash pd Expences at Chitingly		2	6
	It: To Cash pd 3 Days horse hire		9	
	It: To Cash pd Geo Hammen per my wife	1		
	It: To Cash pd John Skidmore	10		
	It: To Cash pd Ben: Clarke 7l:9s:-	7	9	
15	It: To Cash pd william Hide per Order	6		
	It: To Cash pd lettr for Lady Penn			3
17	It: To Cash pd thy wife at S Hersants	20		
	It: To Cash pd Robt Gawthrop his bill	4	7	
	It: To Cash pd postig lettr			3
	It: To Cash pd the Lady Penn	4		
19	It: To Cash pd John Game in pte	10		
	It: To Cash pd for a lettr			3
	It: To Cash pd Ph: Lemon	5		
	It: To Cash pd porter to Clapham		1	6
	It: To Cash pd for a lettr			2
21	It: To Cash pd for powder & shott		2	
	It: To Cash pd for 4 quire paper		3	
	It: To Cash pd porter to Carrier			4
	It: To Cash pd Andrew Soule in pte	10		
	It: To Cash pd lettr for Lady Penn			3
	It: To Cash pd lettr			2
22	It: To Cash pd Oringes Lemons & baskitt		7	1
	It: To Cash pd for Plimt-Voats & P Ruperts papr			6
		1416	17	7¾

	Debtr *1673* [as Follows]	£	[s]	[d]
9/mo	It: To Cash pd as on the other [side]	141[6]	[17]	[7¾]
24	It: To Cash pd Daniell Wight for Bodys		[ ]	
	It: To Cash pd porter to Walthomstow		2	
	It: To Cash pd porter to Coach for H S			4
27	It: To Cash pd the Lady Penn	8		
	It: To Cash pd Carrig woosteed from Exon		3	9
	It: To Cash pd porter			6
	It: To Cash pd porter with lettr			4
	It: To Cash pd porter to Sr D G		1	6
28	It: To Cash pd porter to Carrier H S box			4
	It: To Cash pd porter with Nailes			4
	It: To Cash pd for 10000: of Nailes	1		
	It: To Cash pd for a lettr for Lady Penn			3

	It: To Cash pd for a lett^{r}			3
	It: To Cash pd Carrig & portig 8 p Searge from Tanton		9	2
29	It: To Cash pd Walter Shaller per seeds	1	8	6
	It: To Cash pd postig lett^{r}			3
	It: To Cash pd the Lady St Jones		6	
10/mo	It: To Cash pd porter with hamp^{r}			4
2	It: To Cash pd Theo: Harris M Lowthers Order	3		
3	It: To Cash pd S Mathews bill	25	18	6
5	It: To Cash pd porter			4
	It: To Cash pd for lett^{r}			2
	It: To Cash pd for quills		1	
	It: To Cash pd porter			4
	It: To Cash pd for R Penns pistolls		14	
	It: To Cash pd lett^{r} for Lady Penn			3
6	It: To Cash pd porter to ship for Lady Penn			4
	It: To Cash pd the Lady Penn per her Maide	1		
	It: To Cash pd Isaac Hemmins per a Cheese bought per John Speed qt 64^{lb} at 5^{d} per ^{lb} & 1^{s} Over	1	7	8
6	It: To Cash pd for lett^{rs}		1	
	It: To Cash pd Ro^{t} Bridges per 6/mo interst per 50^{l} per R P	1	10	
	It: To Cash pd Dying & Cottning 347 yrds Frize	4	16	
8	It: To Cash pd a poore woman			4
	It: To Cash pd prison^{rs} at Ludgate			6
	It: To Cash pd my Sallary to the ist 10/mo 1673	20		
		1489	8	10¾
	Rests Due to Ballance this 9th 10/mo 1673	53	9	
	Summe totall	1542	17	10¾

Errors Excepted Philip Ford

[167]2/3	Per Contra [Credit^{r}]	[£]	[s]	[d]
12/mo	It: By Cash Remaining in [my hands] at our last Meeting the 14th 12/mo 1672	11[3]		[2¾]
17	It: By Cash Received of Stephen Crisp	300		
2/mo				
4	It: By Cash Remaining in my hands of R P	20		
	It: By Cash Received of Tho Wight	17		
	It: By Cash Received of P Shipard per a Role wt frize sold thee & Returned her	2	8	
	It: By Cash Received of P Shipard per the Guine	1		
	It: By Cash Recd of Abraham Dickson the ballance of his Acct of wooll Consigned	11	14	
3/mo				
3	It: By Cash Recd of the Lady Penn for one years			

		£	s	d
	Rent Due the 24th 1/mo 1672/3 for the Lands at Walthamstow	19		
	It: By Cash Received of William Morris the Ballance of his Acct of the half yrs Rent ending the 1 3/mo 72	7	6	10
	It: By Cash Recd of W Morris in pte the ½ years rent ending the 1 2/mo 1672	12	13	2
	It: By Cash Received of Sr D G in full the qrts return for 4000 Due to R P the 1st 2/mo 73	60		
	It: By Cash Received of Geo Sevills Expence on John webb act		5	
	It: By Cash Received on brothr Gosnlls acct per G S exp		6	1
	It: By Cash Recd of John Fullr in full to the 25th 1/m last past for ½ yeares Rent	35		
	It: By Cash Received of John Fullr per a Herriot due from the widdow Fareway	1		
	It: By Cash Received of John Fuller per ½ year rent per the house on the Common		17	6
	It: By Cash Recd in full ½ yrs Rent of J Venn	11	10	
	It: By Cash Received of John Venn for whipstow	1		
	It: By Cash Recd of the widdow Martin in full ½ yeares Rent Due the 25 1/mo	12		
	It: By Cash Recd of Kath: Buss in full ½ yrs Rent	1	10	
	It: By Cash Received of Marke Guies in full ½ years Rent due the 25 1/mo	6		
	It: By Cash Received of John Venn in full Marke Guies Old Arrears	14	5	
	It: By Cash Received of the widdow Redford in full ½ years Rent the 25 1/mo	5		
672:3:5				
	It: By Cash Recd of the widdow Chandler in pt her rent Due the 25 1/mo 73	19	7	8
	It: By Cash Recd of Sr D G in full per 3/mo Interest for 4000l to the 1st 5/mo 1673	60		
5/mo				
19	It: By Cash Received in full Tho. Barrons act	24	7	10
	It: By Cash Recd of William Morris in pte Rent Due the ist 9/mo 1672 drawne per bill Exch on Rich Benson of Bristoll	100		
	It: By Cash Recd of Geo: Hicks the ⅛ pte of the 100l Due from the tower to the Const Frindship for the fright of Gunns	12	10	
7/mo 5	It: By Cash Received of W Morris per bill Exchange on Tho: Potter of Mine=head in pt Rent due the ist 9/mo 1672	100		
5	It: By Cash Received of Samuell Heron in full the ⅙ pte the neate proceede of 23 hogsheads suger from Jamica per the Charles James Taylor Mr on the Acct the Arcana Mcht	24	18	4

	It: By Cash Recd of W Morris per bill Exchange on Edw: Debins of Mine-head in pte Rent due the ist 9/mo 1672	100		
19	It: By Cash Recd of W Morris per bill Exchange on Edw Dymon of Tanton in full per Rent due the ist 9/mo 1672	82		
30	It: By Cash Recd of W Morris per bill Exchange drawne per Lt Colonel John Widinham on John Welcum nere Exon in pte Rent due the 1st 3/mo 1673	100		
	It: By Cash Recd of Will Morris per bill Exch drawne payable to Geo: Rogers of Corke in pte Rent due the 1 3/mo 73	100		
		1375	19	7¾

1673	Per Contra [Criditr]	[£]	[s]	[d]
8/mo	It: By Cash Received as on the [other side]	[1375]	[19]	[7¾]
2	It: By Cash Recd of Humphrey Bowden in pte woosted Consigned to him	20		
9/mo				
8	It: By Cash Recd for friz sold to sevell	11	16	8
11	It: By Cash Recd of the widow Buss in full ½ years Rent Due the 29th 7/mo	1	10	
	It: By Cash Recd of Ditto Kings tax 2d per shilling			6
	It: By Cash Recd of John Venn in full ½ years Rent due the 29th 7/mo	11	10	
	It: By Cash Received of Ditto 2d per shilling K: tax	7	11	
	It: By Cash Recd of the widow Rodford in full ½ years Rent Due the 29th 7/mo 1673	5		
	It: By Cash Recd of Ditto 2d per shilling K: tax		3	4
	It: By Cash Recd of the widow Mtin in full ½ years Rent due the 29th 7/mo	12		
	It: By Cash Recd of Ditto 2d per shilling K: tax		7	11
	It: By Cash Received of Mke Guies in full his half years Rent Due the 29th 7/mo	6		
	It: By Cash Recd of Ditto 2d per shilling K tax		1	
12	It: By Cash Recd of John Fuller in full his halfe years Rent due the 29 7/mo	35		
	It: By Cash Recd of Ditto for the house on the Common in full the same halfe years		17	6
	It: By Cash Recd of Ditto for a Heriott of Deane Thomas widdow of Chitchtr	2		
	It: By Cash Recd of Ditto 2d per shilling Kings tax		16	3
13	It: By Cash Recd of the widow Chandler per the hands of w Chandr in pte halfe years Rent Due the 29th 7/mo 1673 Rests Due 9s: 7d ~~all taxes discount~~	19	2	2

1502l:12s:10¾d

		£	s	d
25	It: By Cash Recd for 20 Searges at 38s per p in pte wooll Consigned to John Allaway	38		
25	It: By Cash Recd of John Allaway in full wooll Consigned & all Accts	2	5	
		1542	17	10¾

Errors Excepted
the 9th 10/mo *1672* in London
Philip Ford

ADS. Philip Ford Accounts with William Penn, HSP. (*Micro.* 1:507). Docketed: P. F.s Acct 1672/73 12/mo | from the 1st to the 8th/mo inclus. | No (5).

144
PHILIP FORD ACCOUNT NO. 6
9 DECEMBER 1673–7 JULY 1674

10/mo	The Acct of Disbursmts Since the Acct stated the 9th Day of the 10/mo *1673*	£	s	[d]
9	It: To Cash pd thy self at S M	2		
	It: To Cash pd thy self for James Bradsha		10	
	It: To Cash pd the Osteler 1s & 1s per a pint sack		2	
	It: To Cash pd Tho: Tanton in full	1	14	
	It: To Cash pd for a lettr			4
	It: To Cash pd Geo: Winkefeild	14		
	It: To Cash pd Geo: Winkefeild	20		
	It: To Cash pd Councillor Langhorne per Merryland	1	1	6
10	It: To Cash pd Geo: Hamon		10	
	It: To Cash pd postig lettr		1	
11	It: To Cash pd for lettrs			2
	It: To Cash pd for lettrs			4
	It: To Cash pd porter to ship for Lady Penn			4
13	It: To Cash pd James Bradsha	7	10	
	It: To Cash pd porter to ship for Lady Penn			4
	It: To Cash pd porter to Sr D G			8
14	It: To Cash pd porter to ship for Lady Penn			4
	It: To Cash pd lettr for Lady Penn			3
	It: To Cash pd postig letts			6
17	It: To Cash pd the Lady Penn	6	10	
	It: To Cash pd quire paper for windows		1	
19	It: To Cash pd for lettr			2
20	It: To Cash pd Martha Samson	2		
	It: To Cash pd for papr for windows			6
	It: To Cash pd lettr for Lady Penn			3
	It: To Cash pd lettr			3
	It: To Cash pd porter			3
	It: To Cash pd for a pr Geldings for R Vicrig	29	10	

		£	s	d
	It: To Cash pd fright hamper for Lady P		2	10
23	It: To Cash pd porter twise to ship per Ldy Penn			8
	It: To Cash pd porter with wharfig hamp^{r}		1	
	It: To Cash pd Tho Rudyard Clarke per Expediton Articles for wood sold		1	
27	It: To Cash pd for lett^{r}			2
	It: To Cash pd the Boy Riding R V horses		2	
28	It: To Cash pd porter with hamp^{r} Cheese for Lady Penn			8
	It: To Cash pd postig lett^{s} from Holland		1	
29	It: To Cash pd porter to S^{r} D G		1	
30	It: To Cash pd porter to Coach			3
11/mo	It: To Cash pd lett^{r} for Lady Penn			3
2	It: To Cash pd S M 3/mo interest to the 15 11/mo	2		
	It: To Cash pd Tho R for lone 30^{l}		3	
	It: To Cash pd M S for ¼ 100 needles for thy wife		2	3
	It: To Cash pd for a lett^{r} from Councll Langhorne			6
	It: To Cash pd lett^{r} to Coach			3
	It: To Cash pd Richard Clipsham to the 23^{d} 1/mo 73	5		
	It: To Cash pd the Apothecarys bill J Gleine		15	
	It: To Cash pd lett^{s} for Lady Penn			3
	It: To Cash pd Scrivoner for lett^{rs} for G F		3	
5	It: To Cash pd porter to S^{r} D G twise			8
	It: To Cash pd William Iles for Books	2	5	
	It: To Cash pd porter & lett^{r} to H Springat			6
	It: To Cash pd for lett^{r}			2
7	It: To Cash pd porter to Councillor Langhorne			4
	It: To Cash pd porter to Councillor Langhorne & lett^{r}			6
	It: To Cash pd the Lady Penn per her boy	7		
	It: To Cash pd for a lett^{r}			3
10	It: To Cash pd lett^{r} Lady Penn			3
	It: To Cash pd porter to S^{r} D G			8
12	It: To Cash pd the Lady Penn in full the ⅓ pte Rent in Ireland all Charges deducted to the ist 12/mo next 71^{l}:10:- & 9^{l}:-:- for 6/mo Interest to the 16th 10/mo last past also 20:-:- in full for 6/mo Interest from S^{r} D G to the last day 10/mo 1673	33		4
		136	18	1

	Debt^{r} 1673 as Follows	£	s	d
[11/mo]	It: To Cash pd as on the other side	136	18	1
13	It: To Cash pd porter to S^{r} D G			4
	It: To Cash pd postig lett^{rs}		2	6

13	It: To Cash pd William Bartlett for Nicholas Cooke to the 12th Instant	30		
14	It: To Cash pd thy self a bill Exchange on John Cooke 11^{l}:12^{s}:6^{d}	11	12	6
14	It: To Cash pd thy self sent per my Maide to S M	5		
	It: To Cash pd postig lett^{r}		1	
12/mo	It: To Cash pd postig lett^{s}			6
4	It: To Cash pd John Floyds wages	6		
11	It: To Cash pd porter to S^{r} D G twise			8
	It: To Cash pd Carrig & portig Runlett lent		4	
13	It: To Cash pd thy self in fleet street		5	
	It: To Cash pd postig lett^{s}			6
16	It: To Cash pd thy self at thy lodging		5	
	It: To Cash pd thy self at Reb: Travises	14	6	
	It: To Cash pd w w postig lett^{s}		1	4
	It: To Cash pd postig lett^{r}			6
	It: To Cash pd porter & lett^{r}			4
	It: To Cash pd S Mathews note to the 16th 12/mo	10	10	8
	It: To Cash pd porter to S^{r} D G			4
18	It: To Cash pd Major Gurlwin per Order	10		
19	It: To Cash pd Geo: Winkefeild	30		
	It: To Cash pd lett^{r} to Coach			2
	It: To Cash pd postig lett^{r}			6
20	It: To Cash pd postig lett^{r}		1	6
	It: To Cash pd Tho: R per S Crisps Order 6/mo interest for 300^{l}	9		
21	It: To Cash pd postig lett^{r}			6
	It: To Cash pd porter			3
	It: To Cash pd lett^{r} & porter			6
22	It: To Cash pd postig lett^{r}			2
	It: To Cash pd lett^{s} & porter			8
	It: To Cash pd for a barrell Oysters		2	6
	It: To Cash pd porter to Carrier			4
	It: To Cash pd postig lett^{r}			3
	It: To Cash pd lett^{r}			2
23	It: To Cash pd porter to S^{r} D G			4
	It: To Cash pd lett^{r}			2
26	It: To Cash pd postig lett^{r}			6
	It: To Cash pd lett^{s}			8
27	It: To Cash pd thy self sent per Lady Penn	20		
	It: To Cash pd postig lett^{r}			9
28	It: To Cash pd postig lett^{r}			6
1/mo				
2	It: To Cash pd lett^{r} & porter to Carrier			6
3	It: To Cash pd lett^{r}			6
	It: To Cash pd postig lett^{r}			3
4	It: To Cash pd porter & lett^{r}			6
5	It: To Cash pd lett^{r} & porter			6
5	It: To Cash pd thy self sent in Guines	10	10	

		£	s	d
	It: To Cash pd for a lett^r			2
	It: To Cash pd porter to S^r D G			6
	It: To Cash pd porter with 2 Cheeses			6
	It: To Cash pd Articles peace with holland			2
	It: To Cash pd for lett^r			2
12	It: To Cash pd for a Reame paper		4	
	It: To Cash pd porter			4
	It: To Cash pd postig lett^r			3
14	It: To Cash pd James Bradsha		10	
	It: To Cash pd porter & lett^r			6
	It: To Cash pd porter with fish & Money			6
	It: To Cash pd thy self sent in the fish baskitt	10		
	It: To Cash pd postig lett^r		1	
16	It: To Cash pd porter twise to Sr D G		1	
		306	17	8

1/mo	Debter 1673/4 as Follows	£	s	d
	It: To Cash pd as on the other side	306	17	8
[1]6	It: To Cash pd porter & lett^r			4
	It: To Cash pd lett^r			2
	It: To Cash pd lett^r			2
	It: To Cash pd lett^r			2
	It: To Cash pd lett^r & porter			6
	It: To Cash pd lett^r & porter			4
	It: To Cash pd thy self per my wife		10	
20	It: To Cash pd the Lady Penn at severall times as per Acct given her in full the ⅓ pte Rent Ireland to the ist 3/mo 1674 in full Interest for 300^l to the 16th 1/mo last past & in full Interest from S^r D G to the ist 2/mo 1674 all Charges Deducted Amots to the summe of	90	1	
26	It: To Cash pd thy self at thy lodging	6		
	It: To Cash pd Rich Clipsham to the 23^d 4/mo	5		
	It: To Cash pd a poore woman at S H dore			6
	It: To Cash pd for a Case Knifes		13	
	It: To Cash pd porter twise to S^r D G		1	
	It: To Cash pd Robt Gawthrop in pte	2		
27	It: To Cash pd postig lett^r			6
	It: To Cash pd thy watch stringing & dry		2	
	It: To Cash pd postig lett^s			4
2/mo				
2	It: To Cash pd porter & lett^r			3
	It: To Cash pd lett^r & porter			6
	It: To Cash pd porter 3 times to S D G		1	
3	It: To Cash pd porter to Carrier			4
	It: To Cash pd porter to S^r D G			6
	It: To Cash pd Carrig yarne from Exon		2	6
	It: To Cash pd for lett^r			2
	It: To Cash pd porter to S^r D G			6
	It: To Cash pd lett^r			2

	It: To Cash pd thy self a bill Exch on John Skidmore	8		
6	It: To Cash pd thy self per my wife at Rick		5	
	It: To Cash pd postig lettr			6
	It: To Cash pd for pr Childrens Shoose			6
10	It: To Cash pd for letts			8
	It: To Cash pd John Edlings Order	6		
	It: To Cash pd for a lettr			2
	It: To Cash pd postig lettr			6
11	It: To Cash pd porter twise to Sr D G		1	
12	It: To Cash pd porter to Bridge house			4
13	It: To Cash pd thy self at my house		10	
15	It: To Cash pd R Beresford in full his Rent for Rickmanseworth house & land to the 25 1/mo 1674	10	1	
15	It: To Cash pd Andrew Soule in full his Acct of 13:11:-d	3	11	
	It: To Cash pd postig lettr		2	
	It: To Cash pd postig lettr			2
16	It: To Cash pd William Bakers bill Mantle furring	1	6	4
	It: To Cash pd for pr Shoose per Girle			6
	It: To Cash pd postig lettr			6
17	It: To Cash pd postig letts			9
18	It: To Cash pd S Mathews bill	7	11	5
	It: To Cash pd S Mathews in full 3/mo interest to the 15 2/mo 1674	2		
20	It: To Cash pd postig lettrs			6
	It: To Cash pd for lettr			3
	It: To Cash pd porter to Bridge house			4
22	It: To Cash pd postig letts			6
	It: To Cash pd for lettr			2
24	It: To Cash pd postig lettr		1	
	It: To Cash pd for lettr			2
25	It: To Cash pd porter			4
		45l	9	2

2/mo	Debtr as *1674* Follows	[£]	[s]	[d]
	It: To Cash pd as on the other side	45l	9	[2]
26	It: To Cash pd Candlestick Retard			[ ]
	It: To Cash pd lettr & porter			[4]
	It: To Cash pd porter to ship			4
	It: To Cash pd porter to Sr D G			4
28	It: To Cash pd william Costerd going to how	1		
29	It: To Cash pd J Claypooll for a lettr			3
3/mo	It: To Cash pd postig letts			6
	It: To Cash pd lettr to Sr D G			4
1	It: To Cash pd fright & portig 2 bar fish		2	6
	It: To Cash pd porter to Rick Coach			4
3	It: To Cash pd postig letts			9

		£	s	d
	It: To Cash pd lettr			2
	It: To Cash pd lettr & porter			4
4	It: To Cash pd Johanna		5	
	It: To Cash pd for a lettr			3
6	It: To Cash pd 6lb Anchoves & pott		9	4
	It: To Cash pd lettr			2
7	It: To Cash pd letts			8
	It: To Cash pd lettr & porter			6
8	It: To Cash pd porter wth Anchoves to Co			4
	It: To Cash pd 2¾ yrds Cloth & 4½ yd Shalloon with buttons silke & Making the Coate	2	11	4½
9	It: To Cash pd Carrig friz with Money to walthamstow		8	
	It: To Cash pd for pr stockins for R R		2	10
10	It: To Cash pd for lettr			4
	It: To Cash pd porter twise to Sr D G			8
	It: To Cash pd porter to Coach			4
11	It: To Cash pd for lettr			2
	It: To Cash pd Badnells Executors in full	4	15	
	It: To Cash pd porter to Sr D G			4
	It: To Cash pd thy wife sent in R R cart	5		
12	It: To Cash pd porter to Sr D G			4
	It: To Cash pd for lettr			3
	It: To Cash pd porter twise to Sr D G			8
13	It: To Cash pd for lettr			6
	It: To Cash pd John Skidmore per N Parteig	20		
14	It: To Cash pd porter to Sr D G to Clapham		1	6
	It: To Cash pd for letts		1	
15	It: To Cash pd lettr			2
	It: To Cash pd lettrs			4
16	It: To Cash pd porter to Sr D G		1	6
18	It: To Cash pd lettr			3
	It: To Cash pd R R for 6/mo interst per 200l per M Lo due the 24 1/mo last past	6		
19	It: To Cash pd thy self going home to Rickmanseworth	1		
	It: To Cash pd for a silver Cupp for the Child		9	3
22	It: To Cash pd Geo: Winkefeild 2 bills in full	30	17	
	It: To Cash pd for a lettr & porter			6
	It: To Cash pd for Oringes & Lemons		4	
25	It: To Cash pd thy self with Oringes	10		
	It: To Cash pd 10½ qrts wormewood Renish & bott		18	7
	It: To Cash pd porter to Carrier twice		1	
27	It: To Cash pd 2 Ounce Creame tarter			8
	It: To Cash pd postig letts			6
	It: To Cash pd letts			8
	It: To Cash pd postig lettr			6
28	It: To Cash pd lettr			2
	It: To Cash pd porter to Sr D Gauden			8
		536	10	9½

[3/mo]	Debtr 1674 as Follows	£	s	d
	It: To Cash pd as on the other side	536	10	9½
	It: To Cash pd thy self going to Rickmanseworth	1		
28	It: To Cash pd lettr & porter			4
	It: To Cash pd thy self sent per Gardinr	10		
	It: To Cash pd John Mahoney per Ordr	2		
29	It: To Cash pd lettr			2
	It: To Cash pd porter to Sr D G		1	6
	It: To Cash pd postig letts		4	4
4/mo				
1	It: To Cash pd 1 Doz lb watch=lights & box		6	
	It: To Cash pd bottle Renish & porter		8	
	It: To Cash pd horse hire to Rickmanseworth		2	2
	It: To Cash pd porter to walthamstow		2	
2	It: To Cash pd 2 ounce Creame tarter			6
	It: To Cash pd letts			9
	It: To Cash pd the watch at Algate			4
	It: To Cash pd lettr			4
	It: To Cash pd Geo: Balls Order	20		
4	It: To Cash pd porter to Sr D G			4
	It: To Cash pd lettr			3
	It: To Cash pd lettr			6
	It: To Cash pd lettr to Sr D:G			8
5	It: To Cash pd porter to Coach			4
	It: To Cash pd the petition writing		2	
	It: To Cash pd the Kings Orders in Signitt Office	1	6	8
7	It: To Cash pd boatig			6
	It: To Cash pd boatig to severall places			9
	It: To Cash pd postig letts		1	
	It: To Cash pd boat			9
9	It: To Cash pd postig letts		2	
	It: To Cash pd Boate			4
	It: To Cash pd Coppying Kings Ordrs & petition		5	
9	It: To Cash pd Boate			3
	It: To Cash pd Silke hds Scarves & 2lb Cumfits		14	
11	It: To Cash pd Rich Clipsham to the 23 7/mo 1674	5		
	It: To Cash pd porter to Carrier			5
12	It: To Cash pd porter to Sr D G			4
	It: To Cash pd Hicks Diolog			6
13	It: To Cash pd thy self at S H	2		
	It: To Cash pd a bottle Oyle		7	
	It: To Cash pd William Arion in full	1		
15	It: To Cash pd porter wth horse & books from Carr			4
	It: To Cash pd postig lettr			3
	It: To Cash pd My sallary to the ist 4/mo 1674	20		
16	It: To Cash pd for horse hay & Oates at London		1	8
	It: To Cash pd Rich Constable for Old books		10	
17	It: To Cash pd Expences at Chitingly			10

		£	s	d
	It: To Cash pd John Bennett postig lett^{rs}			6
18	It: To Cash pd Expences at Phimwell		2	6
	It: To Cash pd horse shooing			4
19	It: To Cash pd the horse at London one night		1	
	It: To Cash pd Nicholas Chandler 6/mo Kings tax	1	4	8
	It: To Cash pd Katherine Martins Kings tax	1	3	9
	It: To Cash pd John Venns Kings tax	5	16	3
	It: To Cash pd the poore tax: to Ditto	1	3	4
	It: To Cash pd tax for high wayes to John Venn		7	9
	It: To Cash pd Messuring 40 Acers wood		6	8
	It: To Cash pd Making 44 Rodd hedg to John V		7	4
	It: To Cash pd Making 3 gaites		5	
	It: To Cash pd the widdow Buss Kings tax		3	9
	It: To Cash pd Tho Archer the Kings tax		10	
19	It: To Cash pd in taxes to Mark Guyes	1	18	4
		616	5	½

[4/m]o	Debt^{r} *1674* as Follows	£	s	d
	It: To Cash pd as on the other side	616	5	½
[1]9	It: To Cash pd postig lett^{rs}			6
	It: To Cash pd for a lett^{r}			2
	It: To Cash pd porter to S^{r} D G			4
	It: To Cash pd postig lett^{s}		1	3
	It: To Cash pd Coppys the Kings Refferance to petition		1	
19	It: To Cash pd porter to Carrer wth horse			4
21	It: To Cash pd w w postig lett^{r}			8
	It: To Cash pd lett^{r}			4
23	It: To Cash pd lett^{r}			1
24	It: To Cash pd postig lett^{r} H S			2
25	It: To Cash pd lett^{r} & porter			4
	It: To Cash pd S Hersants bill in full	15	14	4
26	It: To Cash pd postig lett^{r}			2
	It: To Cash pd porter to tower			4
27	It: To Cash pd postig lett^{r}			8
29	It: To Cash pd T Robrts for S Mathews lent thee		11	
29	It: To Cash pd thy self sent in J C baskit beef	10		
29	It: To Cash pd porter to Carrer			3
	It: To Cash pd for a lett^{r}			3
30	It: To Cash pd Rich Mew in full for Biskitt	1	7	6
[5/mo]				
1	It: To Cash pd postig lett^{r}		4	9
	It: To Cash pd R^{t} Bridges 6/mo interst 50^{l} to the 2^{d} 4/mo per R P	1	10	
	It: To Cash pd lett^{r} to May feild			2
2	It: To Cash pd 4 petitions ingrosing		7	
3	It: To Cash pd postig lett^{s}		1	
	It: To Cash pd Expences at Hampton Coart		16	

		£	s	d
	It: To Cash pd porter to walthamstow		2	
	It: To Cash pd porter to Capt Poole			4
	It: To Cash pd porter to Capt Rooths wife			8
	It: To Cash pd porter to Sr D G			4
4	It: To Cash pd Boate to Fox hall			4
4	It: To Cash pd postig letts			6
6	It: To Cash pd lettr			[ ]
6	It: To Cash pd boatig to wt Hall			[ ]
7	It: To Cash pd John Bradsha per Edw Pyatt in full his Legacy	5		
	It: To Cash pd William Bartlett for Nicholas Cooke in full to the 12th Instant	30		
	It: To Cash pd the Lady Penn as per Acct given her to the 3d Instant	74	19	8
		757	7	11[½]
	Rests Due to Ballance at the stating Accts the 7th Day 5/mo 1674 the summe of	18		4
		775	7	3[½]

Errors Excepted in London
the 7th Day 5/mo 1674
per me Philip Ford

	Per Contra 1673 Criditr	£	s	d
10/mo	It: By Cash Remaineing in My hands at our last Accting the 9th 10/mo 1673	53	9	
20	It: By Cash of John Browne per the Articles		7	
26	It: By Cash Recd of Sr D G in pte Interest	80		
30	It: By Cash Recd of James Claypooll per Value given the Councell for Merry land	1	1	6
31	It: By Cash Recd of John Fuller in full one years quit Rent due the 29th 7/mo last past	8		
11/mo 12	It: By Cash Recd of the Lady Penn the ⅓ pte of 10l pd John Hamns Mother in full the plowland of Clogheane	3	6	8
	It: By Cash Recd of Ditto in full the ⅓ pte post fine 18l in Ireland	6		
	It: By Cash Recd Exchange 71l from Ireland Ditto	7	2	
	It: By Cash Recd of Andrew Robinson in pte woosteed Consigned H: Bowden	20		
	It: By Cash Recd of H Bawden the Ballance of his Acct of woosted Consigned	11	12	6
12/mo 2	It: By Cash Recd of John Browne per bill Exch on John Baning in pte wood sold in the Fright	100		
4	It: By Cash Recd of Richard Vickridg per pr geldings for Charrott	29	10	
5	It: By Cash Received of Simon Clement in full woosteed Consigned him	54	3	3
1/mo 20	It: By Cash Recd of Andrew Robinson in full woosteed Consigned H Bawden	25	18	

		£	s	d
25	It: By Cash for a years Rent Due for walthamstow the 24th 1/mo 1673/4 from Lady Penn	19		
	It: By Cash for Exch from Ireld 71:10^{s}:-	7	3	
	It: By Interest 85^{l} 3/mo before Received	1	5	
25	It: By half the Kings taxes for Walthamstow to the 16th 12/mo 1673/4	2		6
25	It: 11 yrd Friz at		13	9
	It: By Cash Recd of Isaac Hennis per a Chese Chad in F Roges Acct	1	7	
3/mo 8	It: By Cash Recd of John Full^{r} in full ½ y^{rs} Rent for How due the 25th 1/mo 1674	35		
	It: By Cash Recd of William Morris per bill Exchange on Math Crowther of Bristell in pte Rent due the ist 3/mo 1673	100		
	It: By Cash Recd of William Morris per Bill Exchange on M Bowdler in pte Rent Due the ist 3/mo 73	11		
4/mo 16	It: By Cash Recd of Nicholas Chandler in full half a years Rent for Bridges Due the 25th 1/mo 1674	20		
	It: By Cash Red of Ditto 2^{d} per shilling Kings tax		4	1
	It: By Cash Red of Ditto in full the widow Chandlers Arrears		9	7
17	It: By Cash Received of Kath Martin in full to the 25 1/mo	12		
	It: By Cash Received of Ditto 2^{d} per sh Kings tax		3	11
	It: By Cash Recd of John Venn in full to the 25 1/mo	11	10	
	It: By Cash Recd of Ditto 2^{d} per sh: Kings tax		4	
	It: By Cash Recd of the widdow Busse in full to the 25 1/mo	1	10	
18	It: By Cash Recd of Tho Archer in full to the 25 1/mo	5		
	It: By Cash Recd of Ditto 2^{d} per sh: Kings tax		1	8
	It: By Cash Recd of Mke Guyes in full to the 25 1/mo	6		
5/mo 2	It: By Cash Recd of John Hunt in full 5 bundles hollin whip stocks		3	
	It: By Cash Recd of w Morris per bill Exch on Christopher Devonshire in full ½ y^{rs} Rent Due the ist 3/mo 1673	40	2	10½
	It: By Cash per Bill Exch on Tho: Sherrden from William Morris payable the 13th Instant in pte half yers Rent Due the ist 9/mo 1673	100		
		775	8	3½

ADS. Philip Ford Accounts with William Penn, HSP. (*Micro.* 1:550). Docketed: P. F$^{s.}$ Acc^{t} 1673/74 10th/mo 11. 12 & 1.2.-4.5th/mo | No (6).

145
PHILIP FORD ACCOUNT NO. 12
28 APRIL 1677 – 17 NOVEMBER 1677

2/mo 1677	William Penn is Debter as Follows	£	s	d
	It: To Cash pd as on the other side	462	9	6
	It: To Cash pd porter for seeds			4
27	It: To Cash pd Rich Gunton the sadler in full	8	10	
	It: To Cash pd porter to S^r D G			6
	It: To Cash pd porter to Carrier			6
	It: To Cash pd porter to S^r D G			6
3/mo	It: To Cash pd Geo: Bowers for J Bradsha	1		
1	It: To Cash pd per 2^lb John Sheelds Balsome & portig		7	[ ]
	It: To Cash pd porter to S^r D G			[ ]
	It: To Cash pd postig lett^rs		1	[ ]
	It: To Cash pd portig box bottles & Barrells to Carrier			6
	It: To Cash pd porter to S^r D G			6
	It: To Cash pd for 12 y^rds Ribbin & 2 p^r shoose		5	[ ]
7	It: To Cash pd Sarah Mathew 9/mo inst 100^l due the 15 2/mo 77	6		
	It: To Cash pd postig letters			[ ]
	It: To Cash pd porter to William Russell			[ ]
	It: To Cash pd for Doggs Greace			[ ]
	It: To Cash pd porter to Carrier			6
	It: To Cash pd Carridge Oysters		1	[ ]
	It: To Cash pd Case the Vintn^r at Bow per R P	1	6	6
	It: To Cash pd postig lett^rs			[ ]
	It: To Cash pd for lett^r			[2]
	It: To Cash pd thy self in Geo: yard in Gould	2	6	4
	It: To Cash pd postig Edw Landys lett^r			6
	It: To Cash pd James Bradsha	2		[ ]
	It: To Cash pd for a lett^r			6
	It: To Cash pd lett^r Atturney & Bond per Ja Bradsha		2	[ ]
	It: To Cash pd for a lett^r			[ ]
18	It: To Cash pd the taylors bill	1	7	
	It: To Cash pd Elyas Marshall 6/mo inst 50^l Due the 3 3/mo 1677	1	10	
	It: To Cash pd Walter Redwood 6/mo interest 100^l due the 3 3/mo 77	3		
	It: To Cash pd for a lett^r			[ ]
	It: To Cash pd Coach to Victuling Office		1	[ ]
	It: To Cash pd Butcher per Livers		12	[ ]
19	It: To Cash pd thy self at Tho: Rudyards	1		
23	It: To Cash pd porter to S^r D G			[ ]
	It: To Cash pd postig lett^r			[ ]

26	It: To Cash pd thy self at my house	1		
28	It: To Cash pd George Thomlinson	3	7	[ ]
29	It: To Cash pd Ann Whitehead in pte	10		[ ]
	It: To Cash pd for a lett^{r} 4^{d}			[4]
30	It: To Cash pd porter			[ ]
31	It: To Cash pd thy self at My house	2		
	It: To Cash pd fright Sider		2	[ ]
4/mo	It: To Cash pd thy self sent per Ralph	2		
2	It: To Cash pd Geo Bowers in full per J B	1		[ ]
4	It: To Cash pd postig lett^{r}		1	[ ]
5	It: To Cash pd Sarah Hersant	3	1	[ ]
5	It: To Cash pd Pris Shippard	1	10	[ ]
5	It: To Cash pd thy wife	1		
	It: To Cash pd Boate & portig sid^{r} to w^{t} Chap		2	7
	It: To Cash pd postig lett^{r}			[ ]
7	It: To Cash pd thy self at William Russells		5	
7	It: To Cash pd Rich Snooke per a Caster	1		
	It: To Cash pd postig lett^{r}		2	6
	It: To Cash pd for p^{r} shooes per thy wife		2	[ ]
	It: To Cash pd Sarah Joanes	2		[ ]
9	It: To Cash pd the widow Gawthrop full	7	5	[ ]
13	It: To Cash pd Robert Scott in pte Books	3	16	[ ]
	It: To Cash pd for a Mare	17	5	[ ]
		549	11	[1]

[Four and a half month gap here, incomplete account]

William Penn is Debter as Follows

	1677	£	s	d
	It: To Cash pd as on the other side	961	11	
8/mo				
31	It: To Cash pd thy self at William Hagues	10		
9/mo				
1	It: To Cash pd Joshua Holland in full one yers interest 800^{l} due the 2^{d} 5/mo 77	48		
1	It: To Cash pd William Mead 6/mo inst 200^{l} due the 24 7/mo 77	6		
	It: To Cash pd John Chambers per a Release W M		1	6
2	It: To Cash pd the German that writes for thee		5	
5	It: To Cash pd postig lett^{r}		3	6
5	It: To Cash pd the Lady Penn as per Acct statd	178	7	4
	It: To Cash pd George Sevell in pt Ballance his Acct	13		
12	It: To Cash pd postig lett^{s}			6
13	It: To Cash pd Lydia Hersent	4	10	
15	It: To Cash pd Barnt Ossmans bill	1	3	6
16	It: To Cash pd William Hydes Note	3		

		£	s	d
16	It: To Cash pd thy self at Ellis Hookeses		6	
17	It: To Cash pd the Lady Penn more	9	16	6
		1236	4	1[0½]

Errors Excepted in London
the 17 9/mo 1677
per Philip Ford

ADS. Philip Ford Accounts with William Penn, Penn Papers, HSP. (*Micro.* 2:435). Docketed: P. Fs Acct *1676* 10mo 11.12 | & 1.2.3.4.5.6.7.8.9th/mo 77 | No (12).

146
PHILIP FORD ACCOUNT NO. 13
17 NOVEMBER 1677–9 JULY 1678

9/mo	An Acct of Disbursements since Acct stated the 17th 9/mo 1677	£	s	d
17	It: To Ballance at stating Acct	239		8½
19	It: To Cash pd Marke the German	1	10	
20	It: To Cash pd thy note to a woman Smith		10	
21	It: To Cash pd Elias Marshall 6/mo intst 50l Due the 3 9/mo 77	1	10	
21	It: To Cash pd Walter Redwood 6/mo interest 100l Due the 3 9/mo 77	3		
22	It: To Cash pd thy self per Marke	1		
24	It: To Cash pd Tho: Greene per M Brain	24	7	
24	It: To Cash pd William Hague	2		
	It: To Cash pd porter to Sr D G			4
	It: To Cash pd postig lettr			6
27	It: To Cash pd Sarah Mathew 6/mo interst 100l Due the 15 8/mo 77	4		
	It: To Cash pd for lettr			2
30	It: To Cash pd postig lettr		1	
30	It: To Cash pd Coach hire to & from Sr D G		2	
10/m				
3	It: To Cash pd postige lettr			6
3	It: To Cash pd Francis Bellos 1 yrs Intst 400l	24		
5	It: To Cash pd postig lettr			6
	It: To Cash pd postig lettr		1	6
6	It: To Cash pd Rebecka for Betty Cooke Made	1		
	It: To Cash pd Rich Colletts the Smiths bill		10	
7	It: To Cash pd Rebecka for thy self	2	10	
	It: To Cash pd postig lettrs		1	
	It: To Cash pd letts			6
17	It: To Cash pd lettr			3
	It: To Cash pd lettr & porter			6
10/mo	It: To Cash pd John Chambers 6/mo intrst 100l	3	10	
24	It: To Cash pd Sarah Joanes per my wife		5	
	It: To Cash pd per hoods for thy wife		9	4

31	It: To Cash pd postige lettrs		2	
11/mo				
4	It: To Cash pd postig letts			8
12	It: To Cash pd Nich: Cooks Order in full 6/mo intst 1000l Due the 12 11/mo 1677	30		
	It: To Cash pd intrst 167l for 6 wekes & 5 days	1	11	
	It: To Cash pd interst 239 for 3/mo to the 14 12/mo 77	2		
	It: To Cash pd for a lettr			3
	It: To Cash pd for letts		2	8
	It: To Cash pd Sarah Hersant per my wife	3		
	It: To Cash pd for letts		2	6
	It: To Cash pd thy self at Bristoll per P Lemon	2	5	
	It: To Cash pd Ballance Rich Vickridgs Acct	8	9	
	It: To Cash pd Robert Gibbins per thy horses	3	2	7
	It: To Cash pd Rich Sneed per 2 Mantles & Coate		16	6
	It: To Cash pd thy servt John Hays per thy wifes Order		10	
	It: To Cash pd Sarah Joanes	2		
12/mo				
19	It: To Cash sent thy wife in silver & gould	10	10	6
	It: To Cash pd postige lettr			9
	It: To Cash pd William Paddle 6/mo inst 100l due 15th Ditto	3		
	It: To Cash pd Stephen Crisp 6/mo intst 300l due 16	9		
27	It: To Cash pd Sarah Joanes	5		
	It: To Cash pd lettr & porter to John Fullr			6
	It: To Cash pd porter with suger loves			6
	It: To Cash pd portig box & Vines to Carrier			6
	It: To Cash pd postig lettr			6
1/mo				
4	It: To Cash pd postig lettr			6
	It: To Cash pd porter with Ale to w H			4
8	It: To Cash pd william Swann	5		
11	It: To Cash pd postig lettr			6
	It: To Cash pd pos{r}ter			2
	It: To Cash pd 4 pr shoose for thy son		4	
	It: To Cash pd porter to Carrier			6
	It: To Cash pd postige lettrs			6
		396	12	8½

William Penn is Debtr as Follows

1/mo	1678	£	s	d
	It: To Cash pd as on the other side	396	12	8½
27	It: To Cash pd Jane Woodcock in full 6/mo interst 300l Due the 8th Instant	9		
	It: To Cash pd postige lettr			6
	It: To Cash pd John Chambers per a Release		1	6

	It: To Cash pd postig lettr			6
	It: To Cash pd william Crooch per 2 & ½ doz tyle		3	9
2/mo	It: To Cash pd postige lettr			6
20	It: To Cash pd C Langhornes Mans note	3	5	1
27	It: To Cash pd Pris Shippard	2		
27	It: To Cash pd Jashua Holland Order 6/mo Interst 800l Due the 2d 11/mo 77	24		
27	It: To Cash pd per ½ firkin Sope		7	9
	It: To Cash pd portige the same			4
	It: To Cash pd postig lettr			9
30	It: To Cash pd postig lettr		1	
3/mo				
2	It: To Cash pd thy self	1		
4	It: To Cash pd Sarah Joanes	2	10	
4	It: To Cash pd William Meade 6/mo interst 200l Due the 24 1/mo last past	6		
	It: To Cash pd a white hood for thy daughtr		2	2
7	It: To Cash pd thy self at my house		10	
8	It: To Cash pd thy self 3 guines	3	4	6
11	It: To Cash pd Tho: Zachary per sperits		10	
11	It: To Cash pd postige lettr		1	
13	It: To Cash pd postige lettr			3
15	It: To Cash pd Betty the Cooke Maide	1	10	
17	It: To Cash pd Ann Hoggs bill	2	15	
17	It: To Cash pd a deale Box			10
17	It: To Cash pd porter to Carrier			6
17	It: To Cash pd Elias Marshall 6/mo interst 50l Due the 3 3/mo 78	1	10	
	~~It: To Cash pd Elias Marshall 6/mo intrest~~			
17	It: To Cash pd Walter Redwood 6/mo Interst 100l Due the 3 3/mo 1678	3		
17	It: To Cash pd Katherine Clarke thy note	2	9	
23	It: To Cash pd thy self at William Hagues		10	
	It: To Cash pd postig lettr			6
31	It: To Cash pd Barnet Osinn taylor	1	19	6
	It: To Cash pd postig lettrs		1	
4/mo				
6	It: To Cash pd Barrell Sope	3		
	It: To Cash pd portig Ditto to Carrier		1	
	It: To Cash pd Carridge parcell streniring			3
	It: To Cash pd Thy self per G Roberts 2 guines	2	3	
10	It: To Cash pd thy self at W Gagues		10	
	It: To Cash pd postige lettrs		1	
	It: To Cash pd postig lettr			3
18	It: To Cash pd porter at At Greenewich Parke gate 12d & 12d Aboard the Kings yate & thy self for Boateige 4s		6	
20	It: To Cash pd porter twise into wappin		1	6
21	It: To Cash pd porter to John Storkeys			4
25	It: To Cash pd postig lettrs		1	

		£	s	d
	It: To Cash pd Coach to Grayes Inn & 3[d] Expence		1	3
30	It: To Cash pd postig lettr			6
	It: To Cash pd John Senock per taxes for Coppice land Called Farmers Rocks		11	8
	It: To Cash pd 3 years Lords Rent for land by the Mannr of Frantfeild, Rox: V 1675 1676 1677 at 6:11d per Annum	1		9
5/mo 9	It: To Cash pd postig lettr			6
	It: To Cash pd the Lady Penn since the 17 9/mo 1677 as per Acct	113	6	10
		584	14	5

Errors Excepted
per Philip Ford

	Per Contra Criditr	£	s	d
	It: By Cash of William Morris per bill on Tho North	100		
	It: By Cash of William Morris per bill from Tho: Cooke on Sally Newton	50		
	It: By Cash of William Morris per bill from A Atkins	10		
10/mo 25	It: By Cash of William Hages servt	54		
	It: By Cash of William Morris per bill Francis Cornewell	100		
12/mo 14	It: By Cash of William Morris per bill on Z Shoote in full the 3/mo Gale 77	50	2	6
	It: By Cash from William Morris per bill on William Alloway per W End	80		
	It: By Cash of William Morris per bill on Z Shoote	100		
4/mo 7	It: By Cash of Gerrat Roberts on Acct of Mary=land Friend	9	7	
		553	9	6
	Rests Due to Ballance at stating Accts the 10th 5/mo 1678:	31	4	11
		584	14	5

Errors Excepted in London the 10th 5/mo 1678
per Philip Ford

ADS. Philip Ford Accounts with William Penn, Penn Papers, HSP. (*Micro.* 2:575). Docketed: P. F.s Acct *1677* 9/Mo to 12th | & 1.2.3.4.5th/mo78 | No (13).

147

PHILIP FORD ACCOUNT NO. 14
16 JULY 1678–18 JANUARY 1679

	An Acc^{t} of Disbursm^{ts} since Acc^{t} stated the 10th 5/mo 1678	£	s	d
12	It: To Ballance at stating Acc^{ts} the 10th 5/mo 1678	31	4	11
12	It: To Cash pd Mary Penington which she left at Warminghurst	15		
12	It: To Cash pd Carrege one pinte wine			9
13	It: To Cash pd postig lett^{r}		1	6
	It: To Cash pd Edmond Poore	1		
15	It: To Cash pd postig lett^{r}			9
6/mo				
6	It: To Cash pd per 4 p^{r} shoos per Child		4	
3	It: To Cash pd Richard Vickris 4^{l} widow Keene & 2^{l}:10:- John Bolton	6	10	
10	It: To Cash pd John Chambers 6/mo intrst 100^{l} due the 22 4/mo 78 wth Continuation	3	10	
	It: To Cash pd postig lett^{rs}		4	6
	It: To Cash pd fright Uskabah		1	2
	It: To Cash pd Carridge & portig to my house		2	6
	It: To Cash pd porter to Carrier			6
12	It: To Cash pd postig lett^{r}			3
13	It: To Cash pd postig lett^{r}			6
22	It: To Cash pd postig lett^{s}		10	
24	It: To Cash pd Benj Clarks note	5	4	6
31	It: To Cash pd Tho: Pade 6/mo intrst 100^{l} Due the 15th Instant	3		
7/mo				
4	It: To Cash pd postig lett^{r}			3
16	It: To Cash pd postig lett^{rs}		1	6
18	It: To Cash pd postig lett^{r}			6
	It: To Cash pd postig lett^{r}			6
26	It: To Cash pd postig lett^{r}			2
	It: To Cash pd postige lett^{r}		1	6
	It: To Cash pd Sarah Joanes	1		
	It: To Cash pd Recept in tally Office			6
	It: To Cash pd for the tally		2	
	It: To Cash pd postig lett^{r}			6
	It: To Cash pd thy self 5 Guins Merryland	5	7	6
8/mo 10	It: To Cash pd Costom warehouse Roome & portig 20^{lb} Flax		6	6
10	It: To Cash pd Tho Stratten in full	6	6	
	It: To Cash pd John Gawthrop in full	5	15	
11	It: To Cash pd Sarah Mathew one years intrst 100^{l} Due the 15th 8/mo 78	8		
	It: To Cash pd portig flax to Carrier			6

		£	s	d
12	It: To Cash pd postig lett^{r}			2
12	It: To Cash pd Alex: Parkes bill	4	4	6
14	It: To Cash pd Francis Borns note	2	8	
15	It: To Cash pd Barnet Osmans note	1	1	
15	It: To Cash pd postig lett^{r}			6
16	It: To Cash pd Edw Billing to Serg^{t} Raman	1	4	
18	It: To Cash pd John Pye	3	19	
18	It: To Cash pd Martha Sampson	5		
19	It: To Cash pd William Morris Release		1	6
25	It: To Cash pd Barnet Osmans bill	1	6	
26	It: To Cash pd entering lett^{r} Atturny in tally Office		4	
26	It: To Cash pd postig lett^{r}			2
26	It: To Cash pd postig lett^{r}		1	6
		113	9	1

	William Penn is Debt^{r}	£	s	d
8/mo	It: To Cash pd as on the other side	113	9	1
28	It: To Cash pd Ralph Cobbit	1	5	
	It: To Cash pd for play things per son		2	
9[/mo]				
8	It: To Cash pd postig lett^{r}			6
11	It: To Cash pd postig lett^{r}			4
13	It: To Cash pd Tho: Tanton in full	6	7	
14	It: To Cash pd postige lett^{r}			2
15	It: To Cash pd Elias Marshall 6/mo intrst 50^{l} Due the 3^{d} Instant	1	10	
16	It: To Cash pd Walter Scarffs bill	16		
16	It: To Cash pd Geo: Griffin in full	2	1	
	It: To Cash pd postig lett^{r}			2
	It: To Cash pd postig lett^{r}			4
22	It: To Cash pd postig lett^{r}			8
22	It: To Cash pd Coach hire to Westminster		2	6
22	It: To Cash pd per Orings Lemons glovs		5	
	It: To Cash pd the Lady Penn the 16th Instant in full one years Rent in Ireland due & ending the first 6/mo August 1678 & one years Interst 300^{l} Due & ending the 29th of September 1678 as per Acct given her	268	18	11
	It: To Cash pd lett^{rs}			8
	It: To Cash pd porter & lett^{r} to Coach			6
	It: To Cash pd for straw hatt for thy Sister Lowther Box Carridge & portig		15	10
10/mo				
3	It: To Cash pd per Cheny Oringes Cumfts & play=things		6	6
5	It: To Cash pd Harbert Springett for a booting Hutch per Tho Ellwood per thy wifes Order with portig & Caridge to Chalfont	3	16	
9	It: To Cash pd postig lett^{r}		4	

10	It: To Cash pd postig lett^{r}			4
11	It: To Cash pd for a p^{r} stockis from Martha Sampson		4	
11	It: To Cash pd porter & lett^{r}			3
13	It: To Cash pd lett^{r} & pap^{r} box to warminghurst			6
16	It: To Cash pd Richard Sneed lent at Bris	3		11½
16	It: To Cash pd postig lett^{r}			8
17	It: To Cash pd thy self at Ben Antrob	1		
17	It: To Cash pd Coach hire to Lest^{r} house & W		3	
17	It: To Cash pd Caleb Woods per thy Ord^{r}	26		
19	It: To Cash pd postig lett^{r}			2
20	It: To Cash pd Coach hire to Westm^{r}		1	6
	It: To Cash pd portig Venison		1	
	It: To Cash pd lett^{r}			3
	It: To Cash pd lett^{r}			2
21	It: To Cash pd Israll Branch	1		
	It: To Cash pd Coach hire to & from temple & torch		2	2
23	It: To Cash pd porter with hanch Venison			6
	It: To Cash pd Israll Branch	1		
24	It: To Cash pd postig lett^{r}			6
	It: To Cash pd Coach from Temple		1	
27	It: To Cash pd William Westcott in full	3	5	3
	It: To Cash pd Israll Branch	1		
	It: To Cash pd Coach hire to & from w^{t}		2	
	It: To Cash pd Francis Bourne	1	4	
28	It: To Cash pd postig lett^{r}			4
	It: To Cash pd postig lett^{r}			3
30	It: To Cash pd Coach hire to & from temple		2	
		453	16	11½

	D^{r} *1678* as Follows	£	s	d
10/mo	It: To Cash pd as on the other side	453	16	11½
31	It: To Cash pd John Chambers 6/mo intrest 100^{l} Due the 22 Instant wth Continuation	3	10	
11/m				
1	It: To Cash pd thy self at B Antribus		5	
1	It: To Cash Ralph Cobbit ¼ Anuity Due the 25 10/mo 78	1	5	
3	It: To Cash pd Barnett Ossmans	1	16	
	It: To Cash pd portige Box to Carrier			6
6	It: To Cash pd porter & lett^{s}			4
	It: To Cash pd postig lett^{rs}		1	6
8	It: To Cash pd John Martin, Stening	8	13	
	It: To Cash pd postig lett^{rs}			6
	It: To Cash pd porter & lett^{r} to Carrier			6
9	It: To Cash pd Sarah Joanes	2		
	It: To Cash pd portig lett^{r} Rebecca			4
	It: To Cash pd William Chandler bill in full	9	8	

		£	s	d
11/mo	It: To Cash pd William Browne in full 3^{l} pd Ellinor Keene	3		
9	It: To Cash pd Ann Whitehead in full	14		11
13	It: To Cash pd postig lett^{rs}			6
	It: To Cash pd lett^{r}			2
16	It: To Cash pd portig baskit			6
	It: To Cash pd the Lady Penn More to the 9th Instant	20		4
		518		0½

Errors Excepted in London the 18th 11/mo 1678
per Philip Ford

5/mo	Per Contra *1678* Criditr	£	s	d
5/mo				
12	It: By Cash of Tho: Lemon	46	5	
	It: By Cash of William Morris per bill on Zachary Shoote from Tho: Wight	50		
	It: By Cash of William Morris per bill on William Alloway per w End	50		
	It: By Cash of William Morris per bill on Zachary Shoote from Tho: Wight in full November Gale 1677	60		
	It: By Cash of William Morris per bill on John Swinton	100		
	It: By Cash of William Morris per bill on Edward Dymond from P Dymond	100		
	It: By one years Rent due the 29 7/mo 1678 for Walthomstow from Ldy Penn	19	10	
	It: By Exch 286^{l} from Ireland	28	12	
	It: By Intrest of Ditto for Money pd before Received	5		
9/mo 23	It: By a q^{rts} Interst Excq^{r} 93^{l}:6^{s}:6^{d} Due the 29th 7/mo last past	23	6	7½
28	It: By Cash Received of John Bennt in pte Fright Rent	6	17	4¾
29	It: By Cash of John Robins in pte timber	20		
10/mo 20	It: By Cash of Garrat Roberts in pte Ballance Acct to Make up 200^{l}	5	7	3
		514	18	3¼
	Rests Due to Ballance At stating Accts the 18th 11/mo 1678	3	1	9¼
		518		0¼

Errors Excepted in London the 18th 11/mo 1678
per Philip Ford
N^{o} (14)

ADS. Philip Ford Accounts with William Penn, Penn Papers, HSP. (*Micro.* 2:675).

PHILIP FORD ACCOUNT NO. 15
18 JANUARY 1679–28 MAY 1679

	William Penn is Debter 1678	£	s	d
18	It: To Ballance Acct then stated	3	1	9¼
18	It: To Cash pd porter to Marke			4
18	It: To Cash pd porter to G Roberts			3
18	It: To Cash pd William Ball for 2 trases		12	
19	It: To Cash pd thy self at my house	1		
	It: To Cash pd postig lett^{r}			2
	It: To Cash pd deale Box & port^{r} Carri^{r}		1	
	It: To Cash pd postig lett^{r}		1	3
	It: To Cash pd lett^{r}		1	
11/mo	It: To Cash pd Sarah Mathew 6/mo interest 100^{l}			
31	Due the 15th 2/mo 1679	4		
	It: To Cash pd Israll per my wife	10		
12/mo				
7	It: To Cash pd William Browne in full	3		
7	It: To Cash pd Tho: Zachary	1	12	8
7	It: To Cash pd Richard Vickridge on Ellinor Keenes Acct	4		
15	It: To Cash pd Tho: Padle 6/mo intrst 100^{l} Due the 15th 12/mo 1678	3		
	It: To Cash pd postig lett^{rs}		2	6
22	It: To Cash pd postig lett^{r}			6
	It: To Cash pd postig lett^{r} per Jemica		1	3
	It: To Cash pd postig lett^{s}			10
24	It: To Cash pd postig lett^{r}			3
	It: To Cash pd Exchq^{r} Acquittance			6
	It: To Cash pd for a tally per ¼ inst 25 10/mo		2	
	It: To Cash pd William Browne for quitt Rent & taxes for Coppis land at Withyham 13^{s}:1½^{d} & 4^{s} is		17	1½
	It: To Cash pd John Senocks taxes		11	2
25	It: To Cash pd Israll	1		
26	It: To Cash pd Francis Bourne in pte her 80^{l} bond 20^{l} & for intst to 2 2/mo 79	21	1	6
	It: To Cash pd thy self on the Exchange		5	
26	It: To Cash pd Edw: Brookes for his sister Massey in full 6/mo intrest 200^{l} due 25 10/mo last	6		
27	It: To Cash pd thy self per my wife	2		
28	It: To Cash pd Abell Wilkinsons note	1	13	9
28	It: To Cash pd Pris Shippards Order	5		
	It: To Cash pd portig Cheeses & box per Car: to Giles		2	
1/mo				
1	It: To Cash pd Marke		5	

	It: To Cash pd Peter Langley per John Furley		18	
6	It: To Cash pd for a lett^r			2
7	It: To Cash pd porter to Carrier			6
7	It: To Cash pd 3 q^rts Oyle & bottle		4	6
7	It: To Cash pd porter to Tho: Zacherys			4
7	It: To Cash pd porter to Lester house			6
10	It: To Cash pd Dolin in full Justus Boder bond	103	12	4
	It: To Cash pd Sarah Joanes		5	
	It: To Cash pd for a lett^r			4
12	It: To Cash pd porter from Carrer			8
	It: To Cash pd porter to T Z & S Herst			8
13	It: To Cash pd porter to Carrier			6
	It: To Cash pd goe Cart^r		3	6
14	It: To Cash pd postig lett^r			9
	It: To Cash pd Carridge truss dryd Solman		7	
	It: To Cash pd Sall: Hersant		12	
17	It: To Cash pd postig lett^r			2
18	It: To Cash pd Ralph the Oastler		18	4
19	It: To Cash pd thy self per thy note	1		
	It: To Cash pd Ann Hoggs bill	2	11	
	It: To Cash pd porter with truss sallmon to Car			6
20	It: To Cash pd for a lett^r			2
	It: To Cash pd porter to Carrier			4
21	It: To Cash pd William Wigan per Ch Mch^ll	5	2	
		185	13	0¾

	William Penn is Debt^r 1678	[£]	[s]	[d]
1/mo	It: To Cash pd as on the other side	185	13	0¾
22	It: To Cash pd for a lett^r			2
26	It: To Cash pd portig baskitt 1679			6
27	It: To Cash pd lett^rs			4
31	It: To Cash pd Marke the German		5	
31	It: To Cash pd for lett^s			2
31	It: To Cash pd porter to Andrew Soule			6
31	It: To Cash pd porter			3
	It: To Cash pd Geo: Griffin	1		
2/mo	It: To Cash pd Ralph Cobitt ¼ Annuety due the			
5	25 1/mo last	1	5	
5	It: To Cash pd portig letter			2
7	It: To Cash pd postig lett^r			2
	It: To Cash pd for two pound biskitt Caks		2	4
	It: To Cash pd Sarah Mathew in full	100		
	It: To Cash pd postig lett^r		1	
	It: To Cash pd Mary Sampson		10	
	It: To Cash pd for a lett^r			2
10	It: To Cash pd thy Man 12^s & 3^s:6^d per toyes		15	6
11	It: To Cash pd for a lett^r			2
	It: To Cash pd for a lett^r			3
12	It: To Cash pd portig potatoes to my house			4

		£	s	d
	It: To Cash pd Tho: Zachery per thy Ordr	3		
12	It: To Cash pd Dolins bond 200l in full	108		
	It: To Cash pd for a lettr			3
	It: To Cash pd for a Release per W Morris		1	6
	It: To Cash pd for a lettr			2
14	It: To Cash pd Coach hire from Westminster		2	
16	It: To Cash pd thy self at my house	1		
16	It: To Cash pd thy self 6 half Cro. Retrd in 95l		15	
17	It: To Cash pd porter with potatos to Car			4
19	It: To Cash pd postig lettrs		3	2
21	It: To Cash pd postig lettr			4
22	It: To Cash pd Coach hire from Temple		1	
	It: To Cash pd porter to Carrier			4
25	It: To Cash pd Israll	1	10	
	It: To Cash pd postig lettr			3
28	It: To Cash pd portig baskit plants			3
30	It: To Cash pd lettr			3
	It: To Cash pd postig bill Exch to & from Extr		1	
30	It: To Cash pd thy self at my house	1		
3/mo				
3	It: To Cash pd thy Man Israell per my wife	1	5	
	It: To Cash pd Abell Wilkinson per Ord	2		
5	It: To Cash pd for tally & Recept ¼ inst Ex		2	6
	It: To Cash pd botig			6
	It: To Cash pd postig 2 lettr from Exon			6
9	It: To Cash pd lettr			2
12	It: To Cash pd Sarah Joanes		5	
	It: To Cash pd postig lettrs		1	6
13	It: To Cash pd Charles Feltham S Joans	4	7	
14	It: To Cash pd Jane Woodcock & Martha Fisher 2 yrs intst 200l due the 4 2/mo 79	24		
16	It: To Cash pd postig lettr			3
19	It: To Cash pd postig lettrs		2	6
	It: To Cash pd Carridge & portig 2 barrells Scallops to my house		1	8
21	It: To Cash pd the Lady Penn since the 16 11/mo 1678 as per Acct given her	118	19	2
23	It: To Cash pd porter with 2 Bar Scallops Car			6
	It: To Cash pd for a lettr			2
28	It: To Cash pd Golins the German	10		
28	It: To Cash pd Barnett Osman		2	6
28	It: To Cash pd Tho: Baker per a Mastive	1	1	6
	It: To Cash pd Intrest 60l for 1/mo		6	
		568	7	3¾
3/mo				
28	Rests Due to Ballance the 28 3/mo 1679	48	3	2¾
		616	10	6½

	Per Contra	Criditr	£	s	d
	It: By Cash of William Morris per bill on Zachary Shute		50		
12/mo 22	It: By a ¼ interest due the 25 10/mo 78 Exchange		23	6	7½
1/mo 8	It: By Cash of Caleb Woods Ordr		130		
2/mo 2	It: By Cash of Caleb Woods Order		50		
	It: By Cash of William Morris per bill on James Burkin & Henry Wade in full the ½ years Rent due the ist 3/mo 1678		117	2	7
	It: By Cash of thy self from Warminghurst		95		
2/mo 15	It: By Cash of Samuell Heron the ⅙ pte 148l:6s:2d being the neat proceed of 12 hogsheads sugar 3 Caske Pementa & l Caske Indico		24	14	4
3/mo 23	It: By Cash of the Lady Penn for ⅓ pte Abatemt on John Southwells farme for 1 & ½ years ending the ist 3/mo 1678		2		
	It: By Cash of Ditto for her ⅓ pte loss on John Woods Farme		8	15	
	It: By Cash of Ditto for Intrest 120l 6/mo before Received		3	12	
	It: By Cash of Ditto for Exch 120l from Ireland		12		
	It: By Cash of William Morris per bill Exchange on Zachery Shute drawne per Tho: Wight		100		
		Sume totall:	616	10	6½

Errors Excepted in London the 28th 3/mo: 1679
per Philip Ford

ADS. Philip Ford Accounts with William Penn, Penn Papers, HSP. (*Micro.* 2:708). Docketed: P. F.s Acct *1678* per *bal* | 5, 6, 7, 8, 9, 10, 11, 12th: | & 1.2.3d *mo 79* | No (15) 14.

149
PHILIP FORD ACCOUNT NO. 16
29 MAY 1679–29 OCTOBER 1679

	William Penn is Debtr to Disbursmts since Acct stated the 28th 3/mo *1679*	£	s	d
3/mo 29	It: To Cash pd Pris Shipard	3	[ ]	[ ]
30	It: To Cash pd Rich Rogers		[ ]	[ ]
30	It: To Cash pd postig letts	[ ]	[ ]	[ ]
	It: To Cash pd John Hogg in pte his bill	[ ]	[ ]	[ ]
	It: To Cash pd John Moores bill	[ ]	[ ]	[ ]

	It: To Cash pd postig lettr	[ ]	[ ]	[ ]
	It: To Cash pd for a lettr	[ ]	[ ]	[ ]
4/mo				
2	It: To Cash pd John Pyes bill	[ ]	[ ]	[ ]
	It: To Cash pd Marke—on friends [torn]	[ ]	[ ]	[ ]
	It: To Cash pd Peter Langley per O[rder]	[ ]	[ ]	[ ]
	It: To Cash pd postig lettr	[ ]	[ ]	[ ]
5	It: To Cash pd postig bill from Exitr	[ ]	[ ]	[ ]
	It: To Cash pd protesting sd bill	[ ]	[ ]	[ ]
6	It: To Cash pd Elias Marshall 6/mo I[nterest] 50l Due the 3 3/mo 1679	[ ]	[ ]	[ ]
9	It: To Cash pd porter to Coach & Coachman	[ ]	[ ]	[ ]
	It: To Cash pd postig letts		3	[6]
	It: To Cash pd at Newgate		2	8
10	It: To Cash pd for Letts		1	2
12	It: To Cash pd thy Brothr Lowthers man	4	10	
13	It: To Cash pd Israll		10	
	It: To Cash pd Israll & Boatemen		2	6
14	It: To Cash pd thy wife		10	
	It: To Cash pd thy self at my house		5	
15	It: To Cash pd porter to William Russells			6
	It: To Cash pd thy self at my house per thy wife	1		
16	It: To Cash pd Tho: Tantons bill in full	3	17	
	It: To Cash pd postig letts		2	
17	It: To Cash pd porter to G Roberts			3
18	It: To Cash pd thy self at my house	1		
	It: To Cash pd Colines for 2 pr Knives		6	
	It: To Cash pd for Cherryes		1	
19	It: To Cash pd for 3lb Chereyes & bask		1	10
	It: To Cash pd Sarah Hersant per thy wife		5	
	It: To Cash pd Sarah Joanes		5	
	It: To Cash pd porter			3
	It: To Cash pd for a hood & Scarff for thy wife & a hood & Scarff for Rebecca Rowle & Looping	1	4	6
	It: To Cash pd wt Sessnet hood & Scarff & two boxes for thy wife		14	10
	It: To Cash pd Black Sessnet hood & Scarf & Rowle for thy wife		17	4
	It: To Cash pd Robt Gawthrop in pte	4	6	
	It: To Cash pd postig lettr			9
	It: To Cash pd lettr			2
23	It: To Cash pd Coach to Gileses		1	6
	It: To Cash pd 3 Lobsters		3	
	It: To Cash pd for Lickras			6
	It: To Cash pd Marke		1	
	It: To Cash pd boate			4
	It: To Cash pd letts		6	
23	It: To Cash pd the German for Boxes		17	
24	It: To Cash pd lettr			2
	It: To Cash pd our Maide per thy Ordr		2	6

	It: To Cash pd porter			3
	It: To Cash pd postig lett^{r}			4
26	It: To Cash pd News papers			5
	56^{l}:12:9	55	12	9
		1		

	William Penn is Debter as Follows	£	s	d
[4/mo]	[I]t: To Cash pd as on the other side	55	12	9
[ ]	It: To Cash pd sent with Hartechoks Colluts	5		
	[It:] To Cash pd for Hartechokes & Coluorts [&] Baskitt		3	6
[ ]	[It: To] Cash pd Tho: Zachary per Lilly vallu		6	
[5/mo]	[It: To] Cash pd Francis Burne 20^{l} in pt [torn] bond & 18^{s} in full Interst to 2 5/mo 79	20	18	
[ ]	[It: To] Cash pd porter to Carrier			6
[ ]	[It: To] Cash pd two bookes			2
[ ]	[It: To C]ash pd Capt Risby in full the 300^{l} [torn] payable to Rich Butler, Mathew [torn]sh & Allen Gaule	300		
[ ]	[It: To C]ash pd 5 Jesuetts tryalls & a Vindicote		3	1
[ ]	[It: To C]ash pd Marke	1		
[ ]	[It: To] Cash pd box for Councll^{r} Pettit			6
[ ]	It: To Cash pd portig Box to Ditto			4
	It: To Cash pd lett^{r} to Coll Sidney			6
	It: To Cash pd postig lett^{r}			3
	It: To Cash pd postig lett^{s}		3	5
5	It: To Cash pd Edwards Bill	6		
	It: To Cash pd Tho Tanton for 2 turkey tammy Coates Making		11	
5	It: To Cash pd postig lett^{s}			4
	It: To Cash pd Ralph Cobbitt ¼ Rent due the 24 4/mo 79	1	5	
7	It: To Cash pd severall tryalls & pap^{rs}		3	8
	It: To Cash pd lett^{r} & portige			5
	It: To Cash pd botig Exchq^{r}			6
	It: To Cash pd lett^{r}			3
8	It: To Cash pd Josua Holland Order	24		
10	It: To Cash pd postig lett^{r}			6
	It: To Cash pd news papers			4
	It: To Cash pd porter to Carrier			8
11	It: To Cash pd Nich Cooke in full	14		
	It: To Cash pd postige lett^{r}			6
14	It: To Cash pd postig lett^{r}			3
	It: To Cash pd pap^{r} bookes		3	6
17	It: To Cash pd John Chambers 6/mo Intrst 100^{l} Due the 22 4/mo 1679 with Continuation	3	10	
18	It: To Cash pd porter with lett^{r}			6
	It: To Cash pd porter to Carrier			8
	It: To Cash pd porter with Jenings		2	

	It: To Cash pd Edward Brookes for his sister 6/mo Interst 200l Due the 24 4/mo 79	6		
	It: To Cash pd porter to Carrier			8
1~~6~~9	It: To Cash pd protesting Ald Tutthills bill Exch		2	6
	It: To Cash pd news papers			3
	It: To Cash pd in full Elias Marshalls bond & Interst	50	15	
	It: To Cash pd Interst 80l for 1/mo		8	
12	It: To Cash pd Tho: Lemon in pt for Sr James Rushworths Interst	142		
	It: To Cash pd postig letts when at Bristol		4	8
	It: To Cash pd for shoose for thy wife		3	
	It: To Cash pd news papers			10
	It: To Cash pd Marke	1		
	It: To Cash pd the semen that brought the Salmon			6
	It: To Cash pd fright portig & other Charges the Cheeses		3	
15	It: To Cash pd Tho: Padle 6/mo Interst 100l due the 15th Instant	3		
	It: To Cash pd porter to Carrier			6
		637	8	

	William Penn is Debtr	[£]	[s]	[d]
6/mo	It: To Cash pd as on the other side	637	8	
19	It: To Cash pd news papers			4
19	It: To Cash pd postig letts		1	
	It: To Cash pd Mary Penington Value thou hadst of her at Warminghurst	10		
20	It: To Cash pd John Gawthrop in pte his bill	1	10	
	It: To Cash pd Exchqr Recpt & tally		2	6
	It: To Cash pd Botig to Westminstr			8
21	It: To Cash pd Brothr Howards bill for wine Oyle & Bottles	3		
23	It: To Cash pd papers			5
25	It: To Cash pd Interst 150l for 6/mo	1	2	6
26	It: To Cash pd news papers			2
28	It: To Cash pd Benj Furleys bill Exch	30		
	It: To Cash pd postig lettrs		1	2
29	It: To Cash pd lettr			2
	It: To Cash pd for Bookes		2	3
	It: To Cash pd postig lettr			2
7/mo				
3	It: To Cash pd postig lettr			6
	It: To Cash pd new sauce pann & tining the Old one		3	10
	It: To Cash pd for new Cullindr		4	
	It: To Cash pd porter & lettr			8
	It: To Cash pd porter with puter to Carrier			6

		£	s	d
	It: To Cash pd lettr			2
	It: To Cash pd news papers			4
	It: To Cash pd Deale Case for pewtr Dish		1	2
8	It: To Cash pd postig letts		2	
9	It: To Cash pd Rich Langhorne	2	3	2
9	It: To Cash pd news papers			1
10	It: To Cash pd postig lettrs		1	10
10	It: To Cash pd news papers			5
10	It: To Cash pd porter to Carrier			6
11	It: To Cash pd thy Cousen Markham	6		
15	It: To Cash pd 3 Doz: tinn plates		4	
	It: To Cash pd Coach hire & Expences with Tho: Rudyard at Temple		3	1
17	It: To Cash pd news papers			2
17	It: To Cash pd porter to Collenll Sidney			8
18	It: To Cash pd Coach hire to Southwarke		1	
19	It: To Cash pd Coach hire with T Rudy to Lester house		1	6
	It: To Cash pd bookes		2	6
20	It: To Cash pd Deale Box			8
	It: To Cash pd Marke	1		
	It: To Cash pd Fra: Burne in pte her bond & Intrest to the 2 8/mo 79	20	12	
	It: To Cash pd porter to Carrier			6
	It: To Cash pd Ciseraiy & botige		15	6
	It: To Cash pd postige lettr		1	
25	It: To Cash pd news papers			2
26	It: To Cash pd letts			8
	It: To Cash pd lettr			2
	It: To Cash pd letters & news papers & to porter			8
	It: To Cash pd porter the Cullinder			3
	It: To Cash pd St Adams for sope		14	6
	It: To Cash pd news papers			2
27	It: To Cash pd sider Engine	6	2	
29	It: To Cash pd postig lettrs		1	4
30	It: To Cash pd for papr bookes		3	10
30	It: To Cash pd porter to N Jenings		1	3
8/mo				
1	It: To Cash pd porter to Carrier			6
1	It: To Cash pd for lettr			4
4	It: To Cash pd Exchange the Cullinder		3	
	It: To Cash pd news papers & to Carrier		3	6
		723	3	2

	W P is Debtr	£	s	d
8/mo	It: To Cash pd as on the other side	723	3	2
4	It: To Cash pd News papers & forehead Rowles for Children			8
5	It: To Cash pd postige lettr			4
	It: To Cash pd Nicholas Jenings to Repay	3		

7	It: To Cash pd postige lett^{r}			6
	It: To Cash pd Ralph Cobbitt ¼ Annuity due the 29th 7/mo 1679	1	5	
9	It: To Cash pd news papers			10
11	It: To Cash pd Israll	1		
	It: To Cash pd Marke	1		
	It: To Cash pd Edmond thy serv^{t}	2	10	
13	It: To Cash pd lett^{s}			3
	It: To Cash pd Barnett Osman		11	6
16	It: To Cash pd thy wife	1		
	It: To Cash pd porter to John Peacock			6
17	It: To Cash pd Letters			4
	It: To Cash pd letters			2
	It: To Cash pd Israll		10	
18	It: To Cash pd lining washing			4
	It: To Cash pd the Bodyes Man		1	6
	It: To Cash pd postig lett^{s}			5
18	It: To Cash pd John Rance in full	2		
20	It: To Cash pd postige lett^{s}			4
21	It: To Cash pd Alex: Parker in full	2	7	
22	It: To Cash pd Israll		10	
	It: To Cash pd John Chambers per 2 Reless		3	
23	It: To Cash pd thy wife	1		
23	It: To Cash pd postig lett^{r}			2
27	It: To Cash pd postig lett^{s}			4
27	It: To Cash pd thy self at My house	2		
	It: To Cash pd the 1/5 pte Expences into Kent of 38^{s} is		7	7
	It: To Cash pd the serv^{ts} at Goodstone Coart		13	6
	It: To Cash pd Expences back the ¼ pte 32		8	
8/mo				
29	It: To Cash pd Mathew Bowmans bill	3		4
	It: To Cash pd the Lady Penn since the 29 3/mo 1679	82	12	
		829	7	9

P Ford

	Per Contra 1679 Cridit^{r}	£	s	d
	It: By Ballance Due at stating Accts the 28th 3/mo 1679	48	3	2¾
4/mo				
7	It: By Cash per bill Exchange from William Morris Drawne per William Honn^{d}	24		
	It: By Cash of Samuel Heron the ⅙ pte 75:11:2^{d} the proceed of goods per Swan	12	11	10
	It: By Cash of Ditto in full all Accts being due on Acct of Logwood in 1671 from Cary Heliard 44^{l} the ⅙ pt 7:6:8	5	15	2
	It: By Cash ¼ Intrest Exchq^{r} due 25 1/mo	23	6	7½

It: By Cash of G Roberts	300		
It: By Cash of William Morris per bill on Zachary Shute per T w	100		
It: By Cash of Ditto per bill Exchange on Geo: Tuttle	100		
It: By Cash of Ditto per bill Exchange on Alderman Tuthill	100		
It: By Cash ¼ Intrest Exchqr due 24 4/mo	23	6	7
It: By Ballance Due this 29 8/mo 1679	92	4	3¾
	829	7	9

At Stating Accts this 29 October 1679 there Remaines Due to me the Ballance being Ninety two pounds foure shillings & three pence three Farthings	92	4	3¾

Errors Excepted in London this 29
8/mo 1679
per Philip Ford

ADS. Philip Ford Accounts with William Penn, Penn Papers, HSP. (*Micro.* 2:724). Docketed: P. Fs. accountt | 3.4.5.6.7.8.9.10.11.12 1679 | & 1 | 80 | No (16) | The Acctt from the 1st mo 1679/80 is wanting.

150
PHILIP FORD ACCOUNT NO. 17
29 OCTOBER 1679–9 MARCH 1680

8/mo	William Penn is Debter since Acct Stated the 29th 8/mo 1679 as Followeth	£	s	d
29	It: To Ballance dew at stating Accts	92	4	3¾
9/mo 1	It: To Cash pd Rowly Titchburn for 2 pr shouse & 1 pr golosies		10	6
	It: To Cash pd postig lettrs			8
7	It: To Cash pd porter to Carrer & per letts			10
7	It: To Cash pd postig lettrs			6
8	It: To Cash pd lettr			2
	It: To Cash pd news paper			1
9	It: To Cash pd lettr			8
10	It: To Cash pd letts		1	
10	It: To Cash pd Ez: Woolly in full	1	19	4
12	It: To Cash pd lettr			2
13	It: To Cash pd porter to Carrier			6
	It: To Cash pd news papr			1
	It: To Cash pd portig hampr from Carrier			8
	It: To Cash pd porter to T Z & Ann Whitehead			6
14	It: To Cash pd news papers			2
	It: To Cash pd one doz: Lemons & Doz Orings		3	6
	It: To Cash pd porter to Allgate wth Baskt			6
	It: To Cash pd porter to Carrier			6

	It: To Cash pd lett^{r} S H			2
	It: To Cash pd 2 wt Sesst hoods one per thy wife & one for R Crisp the 23 8/mo 79		9	
	It: To Cash pd the Lady Penn the 15 1/mo 1676/7 as per Acc^{t} given her which is not before past to thy Acc^{t}	157	11	1½
	It: To Cash pd 2 & ¾ years Interst 98^{l}:1^{s}:8½^{d}	16	3	5
20	It: To Cash pd postig lett^{s}			6
22	It: To Cash pd news papers			1
	It: To Cash pd porter			2
24	It: To Cash pd postig lett^{rs}			7
26	It: To Cash pd lett^{s} for T Gent			2
27	It: To Cash pd tally Exchq^{r} & Recept		2	6
	It: To Cash pd lett^{r} & baskitt			6
	It: To Cash pd porter to M Willitts			4
	It: To Cash pd lining washing			8
	It: To Cash pd lett^{r}			2
10/mo				
2	It: To Cash pd postig lett^{r}		2	
	It: To Cash pd porter			3
3	It: To Cash pd lett^{r} S H			2
5	It: To Cash pd porter to J C			3
	It: To Cash pd postig lett^{r}			8
6	It: To Cash pd Francis Bourne in full	20	4	
	It: To Cash pd lining washing		1	
	It: To Cash pd lett^{r}			2
9	It: To Cash pd postig lett^{s}		2	6
11	It: To Cash pd porter & Lett^{r} to Rocks			6
	It: To Cash pd lett^{rs}			5
12	It: To Cash pd portig baskitt			6
	It: To Cash pd 2 news papers			2
	It: To Cash pd porter to Carrier			4
	It: To Cash pd lett^{r}			3
	It: To Cash pd 2 Doz: Larks		3	4
13	It: To Cash pd porter			3
15	It: To Cash pd postig lett^{s}			4
16	It: To Cash pd postig lett^{s}		1	4
	It: To Cash pd postig lett^{r}			4
	It: To Cash pd postig lett^{r}			3
22	It: To Cash pd postig lett^{r}			6
23	It: To Cash pd porter & lett^{r}			6
24	It: To Cash pd news pap^{r}			1
25	It: To Cash pd postig lett^{rs}			10
	It: To Cash pd porter & lett^{r} from Carrier			6
26	It: To Cash pd porter wth baskitt to Ld Penn			6
	It: To Cash pd news papers			2
	It: To Cash pd porter to Carrier gloves			4
27	It: To Cash pd lett^{r}			3
	It: To Cash pd postig lett^{r}			2
29	It: To Cash pd Ralph Cobbitt ¼ Annuity due the 25 Instant	1	5	
		292	1	10¼

10/mo	William Penn is Debt^r as Follows	£	s	d
	It: To Cash pd as on the other side	292	1	10¼
30	It: To Cash pd postig lett^r			6
	It: To Cash pd postig lett^s			8
	It: To Cash pd lett^r per S H			2
	It: To Cash pd news papers			1
	It: To Cash pd lining washing		1	
11/mo				
1	It: To Cash pd porter from Carrer			6
	It: To Cash pd porter to w^t Chappell			6
	It: To Cash pd porter to w^t Fryers			4
	It: To Cash pd news papers			1
	It: To Cash pd Nicholas Jenings	1	10	
*	It: To Cash pd Interst 261^l for 2/mo to the ist 11/mo 1679	2	12	
2	It: To Cash pd news papers			1
3	It: To Cash pd postig lett^s			6
5	It: To Cash pd postig lett^s			2
6	It: To Cash pd news pap^s			1
	It: To Cash pd lett^r			2
7	It: To Cash pd Fright 18 Load & 42 Foot timber one hogshead sid^r lights Cockits wharfidge Craneidge & porter	11	17	3
	It: To Cash pd lett^r			2
8	It: To Cash pd port^r 3 potts Venison			6
	It: To Cash pd porter with 2 potts to S^r A D & D Whisler			7
	It: To Cash pd porter to T T			6
9	It: To Cash pd boxes & news pap^rs		1	8
	It: To Cash pd porter to Carrier			6
13	It: To Cash pd postige lett^r			2
	It: To Cash pd news pap^r			1
14	It: To Cash pd for lett^r			2
15	It: To Cash pd postig lett^r			8
16	It: To Cash pd news pap^rs			4
	It: To Cash pd 400 Chesnutts & baskitt		3	
	It: To Cash pd porter to Carrier			6
	It: To Cash pd postig lett^r			6
	It: To Cash pd postig lett^r S H			2
17	It: To Cash pd news papers			2
17	It: To Cash pd the Lady Penn since the 29 8/mo 1679 as per Acct	62	17	3
	It: To Cash pd for lett^rs		3	2
	It: To Cash pd for lett^s			8
	It: To Cash pd lett^r from R C			4
	It: To Cash pd lett^r			6
	It: To Cash pd Jonathan Jenings	1		
	It: To Cash pd lett^r			4
	It: To Cash pd lett^r			6

		£	s	d
12/mo				
1	It: To Cash pd Richard Vickeridge for Widow Keene	8		
5	It: To Cash pd porter with box & hamp^{r} from Carrier		1	
	It: To Cash pd porter to Tho Z			4
	It: To Cash pd postig lett^{r}		1	
7	It: To Cash pd porter to Hen: Whisler			3
9	It: To Cash pd lett^{r}			2
	It: To Cash pd lett^{s}			6
10	It: To Cash pd James Gibsons bill of 6^{l}:15^{s}	5	2	
11	It: To Cash pd Benj Antrobus two bills in full	10		
11	It: To Cash pd Edw Brookes 6/mo Interst 200^{l} due the 25th 10/mo 79	6		
11	It: To Cash pd postig lett^{s}			8
14	It: To Cash pd portig & Carridge the Sparr Ribb to O Roberts			7
15	It: To Cash pd postige lett^{r}		1	
	It: To Cash pd postige lett^{r}			2
17	It: To Cash pd news pap^{r}			1
19	It: To Cash pd John Chambers 6/mo intst 100^{l} with Continuation due the 22 10/mo 79	3	10	
20	It: To Cash pd porter to Carrier			6
21	It: To Cash pd lett^{s}			2
23	It: To Cash pd lett^{s}		1	4
		405	18	1½

	William Penn is Debt^{r} 1679	£	s	d
12/mo	It: To Cash pd as on the other side	405	18	1½
23	It: To Cash pd Searching Prerogitive Office for S^{r} W P Inventory		2	4
24	It: To Cash pd John Chambers for a Release for William Morris to the ist 3/mo 1679		1	6
25	It: To Cash pd Tho: Padle 6/mo Interst 100^{l} due the 15th Instant	3		
26	It: To Cash pd lett^{r}			2
27	It: To Cash pd Cristopher Tucker for entering an Inventory of S^{r} W:P Estate & Engrosing to send for Dublin with Law tax	2	3	8
28	It: To Cash pd John Martins bill to William Beck	10		
28	It: To Cash pd John Martins bill to my self	8	13	
1/mo				
1	It: To Cash pd two letters			4
	It: To Cash pd 2 & ½ yrds Black sesnet scarff for thy wife & 1 peice Mixt woostd Crape for Martha Sampson	2	6	6
	It: To Cash pd Tho: Pratt for potts & glasses had in 1677		12	1
4	It: To Cash pd porter from Carrier			8
5	It: To Cash pd porter to Garrowayes & to			

		£	s	d
	Carrier			6
5	It: To Cash pd papr Box			2
6	It: To Cash pd postige lettrs			4
8	It: To Cash pd porter to T Z			3
	It: To Cash pd postig letters			8
9	It: To Cash pd John Martins bill to W Myers	10		
	It: To Cash pd Samuell Bolton in full paymt	17	1	8
9	It: To Cash pd the Lady Penn since the 17th 11/mo 1679 & is in full for Rent in Ireland to the first 12/mo last & for Intrest 300l to the 16 1/mo 1679	68	9	8
	It: To Cash pd Intrest 100l to the last 12/mo 79	1		
* 9	It: To Cash pd procklimation			1
	Summe is	529	11	8½

~~Ballance Due~~

529:11:8½d

Errors Excepted in London the 9th 1/mo
March 1679 per Philip Ford

	Per Contra 1679 Criditr	£	s	d
	It: By Cash past to Acct the 10th 10/mo 76 being pte of that Acct of 157:11:1½ paid the Lady Penn the 15: 1/mo 1676/7	36	15	1
	It: By Exchange 71:10s:- of the Lady Penn due the ist 9/mo 1676	5	16	
	It: By Interst 71:10s:- 6/mo before Recd	4	6	
	It: By Abatemt John Southwells farm the ⅓ pte for the ¼ due the ist 9/mo 76		6	8
	It: By Exch 71l:10s: due the ist 12/mo 76	7	4	
	It: By Interst 71:10s 6/mo before Recd	4	6	
	It: By Abatement John Southwells farm for the ¼ Due the ist 12/mo 76		6	8
9/mo	It: By ¼ Intrst Exchqr due the 29 7/mo 79	23	6	7½
24	It: By Cash of William Morris per bill on Z Shute per Tho: wight	100		
10/mo 30	It: By Cash of William Morris per bill on John Pemble per C Rye	100		
12/mo 24	It: By Cash of William Morris per bill on Ja: Claypoole per F R	100		
	It: By Cash of the Lady Penn for one years Rent at Walthomstow due the 29th 7/mo last past	19	10	
	It: By Cash of Ditto for Exchange from Ireland 181:7:9	14	10	
	It: By Cash of Ditto for Intrest 181l:7s:9d 6/mo before Received	5	8	
		421	15	0½
	Ballance Due to me this 9th 1/mo Mch 1679	107	16	8
		529	11	8½

Errors Excepted in London the 9th 1/mo
Mch 1679 per Philip Ford

151
WILLIAM PENN'S PROPERTY TRANSACTIONS IN ENGLAND, 1672-1678

WP and Gulielma sold large amounts of land in Kent and in Sussex in 1672, 1676, and 1678. All of this land had been inherited by Gulielma from her father, Sir William Springett (c. 1620-1644). In 1676 WP bought a sizable new property at Warminghurst, in Sussex. The indentures abstracted below document these transactions.

The first two sales (indentures *A* and *B*, below), and the mortgage of the manor of Hooe (included as part of indenture *C*, below) were controlled by a prenuptial trusteeship indenture, dated 10 January 1672, whereby five men—Richard Langhorne, Thomas Ellwood, Sir Henry Oxenden, James Master, and Demamine Worseley — could approve the sale of Gulielma's lands whenever the couple was in critical need of funds. In both indentures *A* and *B*, WP's difficulty in collecting debts in England and rents in Ireland is given as one reason for the sales, but his financial needs went deeper. He probably used some of the £1000 he received in July 1672 (indenture *A*) to cover the initial expenses incurred in setting up his house in Rickmansworth in April, upon his marriage. He probably used some of the £3000 he received in June 1676 (indenture *B*) to pay for his move, in September, to Warminghurst. Here he had a larger house, with a park, gardens, orchards, plowland, meadows, pasture, and woods, totaling about 300 acres of land. This estate cost WP £4450; to obtain it, he borrowed £4700 from Sir James Rushout and William Jarrett, who had just purchased the property, presumably as WP's agents. To secure this loan, WP had to mortgage the manor of Hooe, as well as other tracts of land in Sussex, to Rushout (indenture *C*). In June 1678, WP sold Hooe to a tenant for £2800 (indenture *D*). After 1678, Gulielma appears to have owned parts of three Sussex manors, Wickham, Kingston Bowsey, and Havertine, and probably had other Sussex lands as well.

In just six years, WP had sold well over 1250 acres of productive land for a total of £6800. As discussed in the headnote to doc. 139, WP contracted other sizable loans during these years; by June 1678 WP's outstanding loans, according to the Ford accounts, totaled £3256. Perhaps it was to free himself from some of these debts that WP, on 25 July 1678, one month after the sale of Hooe, borrowed from Rushout the sale price of £2800 for that property, which had been paid directly to Rushout as mortgagee, and £800 more. This increased the principal of his debt from £4700 to £5500; with the interest, he now owed Rushout £6231. In 1692, this loan was still unpaid, and Rushout and his relatives negotiated a new mortgage indenture with WP that increased his debt and kept Warminghurst and other WP Sussex land completely tied up.

Many of WP's deeds and other legal papers have apparently been lost (see doc. 137, above), but his Kent and Sussex transactions can be traced in some detail through three chancery indentures in the Public Record Office, London: C. 54/4342, case no. 4 (indenture *A*), C. 54/4459, case no. 9 (indenture *B*), and C. 54/4506, case no. 17 (indenture *D*); and in the extensive abstracts, made by Albert Cook Myers in 1915, of indentures in the possession of the duke of Norfolk, whose family acquired Warminghurst in 1805 (indenture *C*). These last indentures are now stored at Arundel Castle, Sussex, uncatalogued and not easily accessible. Myers' abstracts are in ACM, vol. 55, pp. 177-90 (typescripts), and vol. 56, pp. 53-94 (MSS). On the Springett family, see John Comber, *Sussex Genealogies, Lewes Centre* (Cambridge, England, 1933), pp. 279-82; on the Springetts' purchase of Sussex lands in the 1620s, see ACM, vol. 54B.

A
An Indenture between WP, Gulielma Penn, and Nicholas Cooke

Source: D. C. 54/4342, case no. 4, PRO. (Not filmed).
Date: 10 July 1672.
Grantors: (1) WP; (2) Gulielma Maria Springett Penn; (3) Richard Langhorne and Thomas Ellwood (trustees); (4) Sir Henry Oxenden, of Wingham, Kent, James Master, of Greys Inn, Middlesex, and Demamine Worseley, of Westin, Middlesex (trustees). Oxenden (d. 1686), knighted in 1660 and created a baronet in 1678, had been named an overseer of Sir William Springett's will in 1643. *DNB;* ACM, vol. 54B.
Grantee: Nicholas Cooke, of East Greenwich, Kent. In August 1672, Cooke would loan WP another £1000 (see doc. 140, above).
Purchase price: £1000.
Location of lands: (1) Fryth Okeley and Hernden, in Cranbrooke, Hawkehurst, and Sandhurst, Kent; (2) Duker's Hill and Lamplands, in Hawkehurst, Kent. Hawkehurst was an ancestral home of the Springett family; Gulielma's great-grandfather, Herbert Springett, had moved from Kent to Lewes and Ringmer, in Sussex, by 1590. See William Berry, *Pedigrees of the Families in the County of Kent*... (London, 1830), pp. 242-43; Comber, *Sussex Genealogies*, pp. 279-82.
Acreage: Not given.

B

An Indenture between WP, Gulielma Penn, William Pettyt, and Thomas Langhorne

Source: D. C. 54/4459, case no. 9, PRO. (*Micro.* 2:347).
Date: 3 June 1676.
Grantors: (1) WP; (2) Gulielma Maria Springett Penn; (3) Richard Langhorne and Thomas Ellwood (trustees); (4) Sir Henry Oxenden, James Master, and Demamine Worseley (trustees).
Grantees: William Pettyt, of the Inner Temple, London, and Thomas Langhorne, of London. Among WP's lost deeds (see doc. 137) is a land sale by Pettyt and Langhorne in 1679. WP paid attorney's fees to Pettyt in docs. 139 and 143. A Thomas Langhorne witnessed the quintipartite deed that divided New Jersey on 1 July 1676 (doc. 152).
Purchase Price: £3000.
Location of lands: (1) The manor of Wickham, Ickelsham, Sussex; (2) fifteen parcels of land in Ickelsham, Sussex; (3) one half of the manor of Kingston Dowry, including fourteen parcels of land, in Kingston-by-the-Sea, Sussex; and (4) three tenements in Withyham and Rotherfield, Sussex. It is not clear from the indenture whether the fifteen parcels in Ickelsham (2) were separate from the manor of Wickham (1), or are an itemization of those parts of the manor that were being sold, but the second case seems likely, because the manor of Wickham was still owned by Springett Penn (1738-1766), WP's great-grandson, in 1760. Wickham had been a manor from 1320, and was bought by Herbert Springett, Gulielma's grandfather, early in the seventeenth century. Kingston Dowry, or Kingston Bowsey, was bought by the overseers of the estate of Herbert Springett (c. 1591-1622) for his minor son, William, in 1623. The purchase price was £2400. *VCH: Sussex,* 9:187; ACM, vol. 54B.
Acreage: The land in (2) contained 201 acres; that in (3) contained about 700 acres. The acreage of (1), if it was distinct from (2), and that of (4) is not stated.

C

An Indenture between WP, Sir James Rushout, and William Jarrett

Source: ACM, vol. 55:186-89 (typescript summary); and see ACM, 55:179-80, 183-84 (typescript summaries), and 56:75-94 (MSS. summaries and engrossed indentures, 1678-1692). (Not filmed).
Date: 7 June 1676.
Grantors: Sir James Rushout, of Maylard Green, Essex, and William Jarrett, of London. Rushout (c. 1644-1698), the principal mortgagee and WP's principal creditor in the 1670s, was the son of a wealthy London merchant who had emigrated from Flanders in the reign of Charles I. Sir James became first baronet of Milnst-Maylards, Essex, in 1661, and was M.P. for Evesham, Worcs. (1670-1681, 1690-1698),

and for Worcestershire (1689-1690). *DNB;* Burke's *Peerage.*
Grantees: WP, and Gulielma Maria Springett Penn.
Amount of loan: £4700.
Purchase price for Warminghurst: £4450.
Security for the loan: (1) The manor of Hooe, Sussex (see indenture *D*, below); (2) parcels of land called Bridges, Cokeswith, and Youngs, in Laughton Ripe and Chaunton, Sussex.
Description of property purchased (from ACM, 55:183): a park, three messuages (dwelling houses), two cottages, two barns, two lofts, one water mill, one dove house, four gardens, four orchards, 20 acres of plowland, 80 acres of meadow, 200 acres of pasture, 40 acres of woods, 20 acres covered with water (including a mill pond), rights of pasture on a commons, and the advowson of the rectory of Warminghurst (the right to appoint the local vicar).
Acreage of property purchased: 360 or more. (Another document, summarized in ACM, 55:179-80, gives the acreage of Warminghurst as about 290).

D
An Indenture between WP, Sir James Rushout, William Jarrett, and John Fuller

Source: D. C. 54/4506, case no. 17, PRO. (Not filmed).
Date: 20 June 1678.
Grantors: (1) WP; (2) Sir James Rushout; (3) William Jarrett.
Grantee: John Fuller, of Sutton Hooe, Sussex, who had been Gulielma's tenant since before 1669; in July of that year he paid £180 in rent to Gulielma and agreed to pay £80 in rent for the ensuing year.
Purchase price: £2800.
Location of lands: The manor of Hooe and several adjacent plots in the parishes of Hooe, Ninfield, Wartling, Catsfield, and Bexhill, Sussex. The overseers of Herbert Springett's estate purchased Hooe for William Springett for £2500 in 1628. The five parishes in which the lands were located are adjacent, and lie just west of Hastings. *VCH: Sussex* 9:244-45; ACM, vol. 54B.
Acreage: 356 acres, with the several plots carefully located, and labeled according to agricultural use.

152
WEST NEW JERSEY PROPERTY TRANSACTIONS AND AGREEMENTS, 1675-1676

WP's role in the colonization of West New Jersey has been presented in docs. 112-18, above. But these documents do not describe the complex agreements among proprietors, trustees, and purchasers that determined the rights to the soil in that colony. The six property transactions summarized below do this.

Indenture *A*, dated 10 February 1675, was WP's attempt to resolve the John Fenwick-Edward Byllynge dispute over the control of their half interest in New Jersey (see docs. 112-14) by granting Fenwick ten shares of the disputed lands and £400. This was more land, but less cash, than WP, as arbitrator, had at first awarded Fenwick (see doc. 112, n. 3). Indenture *A* transferred the other ninety shares to Byllynge's trustees, WP, Gawen Lawrie, and Nicholas Lucas. The memorandum *B*, of 7 May 1675, recorded the numbers of the plots, in any grid of one hundred plots of land to be surveyed in New Jersey, that Fenwick had drawn by lot as his share. The trustees were here attempting to create a unified colony by mixing Fenwick's purchasers with Byllynge's. In the agreement *C*, of 28 June 1675, however, Fenwick and thirty-three of his purchasers effectively ignored the trustees' plan. They undertook to set up an independent community on thirty or forty thousand acres of land which Fenwick was to buy from the Indians upon his arrival in New Jersey.

To get to America, Fenwick had to raise more money and settle his debts. On 17 July 1675, immediately before his departure, he signed a mortgage arrangement *D* whereby he transferred all of his New Jersey lands that he had not already sold to the Quakers John Edridge and Edmond Warner for two years, in return for their forgiving a debt that he owed them. Edridge and Warner thereby acquired the right to sell land from Fenwick's shares.

Mortgage *D* gained particular importance when Edward Byllynge and his trustees came to negotiate the partition of New Jersey with Sir George Carteret in 1676 and had to secure title to all of Sir John Berkeley's original interest in New Jersey. This they did on 19 June 1676, through an indenture *E* with Edridge and Warner that allied these two men with Byllynge and his trustees, and against John Fenwick. Byllynge and his trustees then signed the partition indenture *F*, or quintipartite deed, of 1 July 1676 with Carteret. This agreement formally divided the colony into East and West New Jersey.

A

An Indenture between John Fenwick, Edward Byllynge, WP, Gawen Lawrie, and Nicholas Lucas

Source: Copy. Bureau of Archives and History, New Jersey State Library, Trenton, N. J. (Not filmed).
Date: 10 February 1675.
Parties: (1) John Fenwick; (2) Edward Byllynge; (3) WP, Gawen Lawrie, Nicholas Lucas.

Summary of the agreement: The text first recapitulates the instruments that determined English title to New Jersey lands: Charles II's grant of New Jersey and other lands in North America to James, Duke of York (12 March 1664); James' grant of New Jersey to Sir John Berkeley and Sir George Carteret (24 June 1664); and Berkeley's sale of his half interest in New Jersey to John Fenwick (18 March 1674). The indenture then transfers the half interest from Fenwick to WP, Lawrie, and Lucas, as trustees for Byllynge. In return for this tranfer, Fenwick is awarded ten out of the one hundred shares into which Byllynge's interest is, in this document, divided, and £400. The trustees paid Byllynge five shillings to seal the agreement.
Signatories: John Fenwick, Edward Byllynge, WP, Gawen Lawrie, Nicholas Lucas.
Witnesses: Thomas Langhorne, Henry West, James Bowers, John Richardson, and James Ball. All of the witnesses except Ball would sign the quintipartite deed (item *F*, below). Langhorne was a London merchant, a purchaser of WP Sussex land in 1676 (doc. 151, above), and probably of Pennsylvania land in the 1680s. West was an attorney who later did legal work for WP. Richardson was Richard Langhorne's servant.

B
A Memorandum of an Agreement between John Fenwick and Byllynge's Trustees

Source: Copy. Bureau of Archives and History, New Jersey State Library, Trenton, N. J. (Not filmed).
Date: 7 May 1675.
Substance of the agreement: "John Fenwick drew the Following numbers vizt 20. 21. 26. 27. 36. 47. 50. 57. 63. 72 as his proportion of the one Moyetie of New Cesaria or Jersey being divided into one hundred lotts. and that he hath accepted of the same and the Trustees [do accept] for the other lotts, well satisfied therein in testimony of which they have Interchangeably set their hands."
Signatories: WP, Gawen Lawrie, John Fenwick.
Witnesses: Robert Squibb, Jr., William Boydon.

C
An Agreement between John Fenwick and the Purchasers of New Jersey Lands

Source: Copy, dated 1 August 1676. T.S. 12/56, PRO, London. (Not filmed).
Date: 28 June 1675.
Parties: (1) John Fenwick; (2) thirty-three persons who purchased New Jersey lands from John Fenwick between February and July 1675. The names are given below, under "signatories."

Summary of the agreement: The parties agree to several provisions as the foundation of the Salem colony in New Jersey, which Fenwick would establish in November 1675; a summary of the major provisions follows. (1) John Fenwick stands possessed of ten parts of the one hundred parts into which Berkeley's half interest in New Jersey was divided on 10 February 1675 (see *A*, above). (2) Fenwick engages to purchase thirty or forty thousand acres from New Jersey's natives on which to plot out his purchasers' lands. (3) Fenwick and his purchasers agree on a system of marking and registering lands. (4) The colony is to be governed as follows: a governor and magistrates are to be chosen "by the advise and consent of the said proprietors & freeholders every yeare And tenn or twelve persons to bee elected as aforesaid to bee A Councell to remaine one yeare & then the one halfe of them to bee putt out & so many more chosen In their places and . . . after a yeares service to make A new Election of A Governor & halfe the Councell or the continuance of him or them as shall be most convenient who shall have full power to make . . . laws and Cus[t]omes." (5) Fenwick and his purchasers adopt a double register system of recording land sales, with one register to be kept in London, the other in New Jersey, a system similar to that which would be incorporated in the West New Jersey Concessions (doc. 115, chap. 24, above) the following year. (6) The lands that John Fenwick purchases from the natives are "to be devided amongst the said severall proprietors purchasers Freeholders & planters according to the equivolent share and proportion of his her or their severall . . . purchases. . . . And that every such person . . . herein concerned shall be satisfyed . . . with the remainder of his her and their severall parts and lotts as the said John Fenwick shall . . . purchase of the Indians to be within Fenwick's colony." (7) All who refuse to abide by the provisions of the agreement are to be excluded from all rights and benefits in Fenwick's Salem colony.

Signatories: Jn[o] Barkstead, Robert Wade, Richard Noble, John Maddocks[a], Thomas Mainwaring, Richard Guy[a], Thomas Duke, Edward Bradway[a], William Hughes[a], Edward Champnes, John Smyth[a], John Adams, Peter Huff, Edward Harding, John Test, John Conn [Cann], Edmond Warner, William Hancock, John Edridge, Roger Podrick[a], Thomas Anderson, J[oshua] Barkstead, Edward Duke, Henry Salter, Vicesimus Nettleship, Edward Wade, Roger Huckings, Samuell Nicolson, John Harding, William Molster, Samuell Land, Richard Hancock, Richard Morgan[a]. Twenty-nine of these signers purchased land from Fenwick between 25 February and 9 July 1675 and are listed in his "Salem Register No. 1," fols. 32-133, in the Bureau of Archives and History, New Jersey State Library, Trenton, N. J., reprinted in *New Jersey Archives,* 1st ser., 21:559-65. This list gives the occupation and place of residence in England of each purchaser, with the date and acreage of the purchase. Six or seven of these signers would sign the West New Jersey Concessions (doc. 115, above) sometime after November 1676. These signatures are marked with a superscript *a*; John Smyth is the doubtful case.

D
An Indenture between John Fenwick, John Edridge, and Edmond Warner

Source: Frank H. Stuart, *Major John Fenwick* (Woodbury, N.J., 1939), pp. 12-18; drawn from the chancery records in the PRO, London. (Not filmed).
Date: 17 July 1675.
Parties: (1) John Fenwick; (2) John Edridge, of Shadwell, Middlesex, a tanner, and Edmond Warner, of London, a poulterer.
Summary of the agreement: Fenwick consigns to Edridge and Warner his ten shares in the Berkeley half interest in New Jersey for 1000 years, from which they may sell land in order to recover Fenwick's debt of £110.15s.0d. owed to them. Fenwick also owes other debts to several persons (amounting to about £160, listed in a schedule attached to the end of the indenture), and he urges Edridge and Warner to pay off these debts from the proceeds of the sale of his lands. Fenwick has the option to recover control of his ten shares at the end of two years' time if Edridge and Warner have not, by then, received full payment of their debt, and Fenwick will make up the difference to them. The indenture does not appear, however, to require Edridge and Warner to return the shares to Fenwick.
Signatories: John Fenwick, John Edridge, Edmond Warner.

E
An Indenture between John Edridge, Edmond Warner, WP, Gawen Lawrie, and Nicholas Lucas

Source: D. C. 54/4459, case no. 19, PRO, London. (*Micro.* 2:354).
Date: 19 June 1676.
Parties: (1) John Edridge and Edmond Warner; (2) WP, Gawen Lawrie, Nicholas Lucas.
Substance of the Agreement: WP, Lawrie, and Lucas purchase John Fenwick's ten shares in the Berkeley half interest in New Jersey from Edridge and Warner for £205. It is evident from this brief indenture that the parties to it were acting upon the conviction that Fenwick had sold his ten shares to Edridge and Warner, although in indenture *D*, above, Fenwick had clearly mortgaged his shares, rather than sold them.

F

An Indenture between Sir George Carteret, WP, Gawen Lawrie, Nicholas Lucas, and Edward Byllynge.

Source: D. C. 54/4459, case no. 18, PRO, London. (*Micro.* 2:354; another version is *Micro.* 2:349). Bureau of Archives and History, New Jersey State Library, Trenton, N. J., also has a copy.
Date: 1 July 1676.
Parties: (1) Sir George Carteret; (2) WP; (3) Gawen Lawrie; (4) Nicholas Lucas; (5) Edward Byllynge.
Summary of the indenture: The indenture first recapitulates the titles to New Jersey lands as in indenture *A* above, but without any mention of John Fenwick or his ten shares. Byllynge and the trustees here treat the half interest in New Jersey acquired from Sir John Berkeley as an undivided whole. The substance of this indenture is the agreement between Carteret, on one side, and Byllynge, WP, Lawrie, and Lucas on the other, to divide New Jersey into two parts and to define the partition line between them. To seal the division, Byllynge's trustees pay Carteret five shillings for all of New Jersey west of the line, and Carteret pays the same amount to the trustees for all of New Jersey east of the line. The line itself is set as running from the northernmost point in New Jersey (which was defined in the duke of York's 1664 grant to Berkeley and Carteret as the intersection of the forty-first degree of latitude with the east bank of the Delaware River) to the eastern shore of Little Egg Harbor, in southern New Jersey on the Atlantic coast. A full description of this line, the attempts to survey it in the seventeenth and eighteenth centuries, and the impact of those surveys upon New Jersey's civil boundaries to the twentieth century, is in John P. Snyder, *The Story of New Jersey's Civil Boundaries, 1606-1968* (Trenton, 1969), pp. 8-14, and maps on pp. 5, 10-11, 20-21, 31, 33, 35.
Signatories: Sir George Carteret, WP, Gawen Lawrie, Nicholas Lucas, Edward Byllynge.
Witnesses: Henry West, James Bowers, Thomas Langhorne, Richard Langhorne, John Richardson.

CALENDAR OF MICROFILMED WP DOCUMENTS, 1644–1679

In the following list, figures in the first column give the reel and frame numbers of documents in the microfilm edition of The Papers of William Penn. Numbers in bold type identify documents printed in this volume.

1:003 Baptism, 23 October 1644, **1**
1:004 Verses on the Death of Henry, Duke of Gloucester, November 1660, **2**
1:006 WP's Matriculation at Christ Church, Oxford, 26 October 1660
1:007 List of Missing Business Records, 1649-1699, **137**
1:009 Ah, Tyrant Lust, 1664, **4**
1:012 Unknown Author to Sir William Penn, 24 April 1664, **3**
1:014 To Sir William Penn, 23 April 1665, **5**
1:015 To Sir William Penn, 6 May 1665, **6**
1:021 Sir William Penn to Sir George Lane, 8 February 1666, **7**
1:022 From Sir William Penn, 5 May 1666, **8**
1:023 From Sir William Penn, June 1666
1:024 From Sir William Penn, June 1666
1:025 From Sir William Penn, [1666]
1:026 To Sir William Penn, 4 July 1666, **9**
1:027 From Sir William Penn, 17 July 1666, **10**
1:028 From Sir William Penn, 17 July 1666
1:029 From Sir William Penn, 2 October 1666
1:030 From Sir William Penn, 8 January 1667
1:032 From Sir William Penn, 2 February 1667, **11**
1:033 From Sir William Penn, 6 April 1667, **12**
1:035 From Sir William Penn, 9 April 1667, **13**
1:039 From Lord O'Brien, 18 May 1670, **40**
1:041 From Lord O'Brien, 18 May [1670], **39**
1:042 From Sir William Penn, 21 May 1667, **14**
1:044 From Sir William Penn, 29 June 1667
1:045 From Lord Shannon, 20 August 1667, **15**
1:050 From Sir William Penn, 12 October 1667, **16**
1:052 From Lord Shannon, 14 October 1667
1:055 From Sir William Penn, 22 October 1667, **17**
1:057 To the Earl of Orrery, c. 4 November 1667, **18**
1:060 From the Earl of Orrery, 5 November 1667, **19**

1:064 A Catalogue of WP's Writings, 1668-1681
1:065 To Thomas Danson, [November 1668?], **25**
1:068 The Two Kingdoms of Darkness and Light, [c. 1668], **21**
1:092 An Answer to a Vain Flash, [c. 1668]
1:094 To London Friends, December 1668, **28**
1:097 To a Friend, 10 July 1668
1:098 Thomas Loe's Dying Words in Earnest, [October] 1668
1:100 To Gulielma Springett, 7 October 1668, **22**
1:102 To Isaac Penington, 17 October 1668, **23**
1:106 WP and George Whitehead to Thomas Vincent and Thomas Danson, 31 October 1668
1:108 To Gulielma Springett, December 1668, **29**
1:110 Warrants to John Warburton to take WP into custody and to Sir John Robinson to receive him, 12 December 1668
1:112 Liberty from Lord Arlington for Francis Cooke to see WP, 24 December 1668
1:114 Reply to Thomas Danson, [1668 or 1669], **25**
1:128 Ode on the death of Josiah Coale, [1669]
1:132 Lord Arlington to the Lieutenant of the Tower, 4 January 1669, **30**
1:134 To Lodowick Muggleton, 11 February 1669, **31**
1:137 Sir William Penn's petition to Charles II about WP, 31 March 1669
1:138 To Lord Arlington, 19 June 1669, **33**
1:142 To Lord Arlington, 19 June 1669, **32**
1:144 My Irish Journal, 15 September 1669–1 July 1670, **35**
1:180 From Sir William Penn, 6 October 1669
1:181 To Mayor Lewis Desmynieres [?], [5 November 1669?], **36**
1:183 From Sir William Penn, December 1669
1:184 A Prefatory Observation upon the Quakers Spiritual Court Proclaimed, [1670?]
1:193 God's Controversy Proclaimed, 1670, **55**
1:208 WP, George Whitehead, and others to the House of Commons, [1670?]
1:212 Petition to the King, [1673?]
1:215 From Sir William Penn, [c. 1670]
1:216 Will of Sir William Penn, 20 January 1670, **37**
1:225 From Sir William Penn, 29 April 1670, **38**
1:227 Ann Gay to WP and Philip Ford, 3 July 1670
1:230 From Gulielma Springett and Mary Penington, 16 July 1670, **41**
1:235 From Elizabeth Bowman, 16 July 1670, **42**
1:239 From John Gay, 23 July 1670, **43**
1:246 From Richard Bent, 1 August 1670
1:249 Jonathan Kealy to Philip Ford, 5 August 1670, **44**
1:253 From Philip Ford, 9 August 1670, **45**
1:261 Sir Samuel Starling to the Keeper of Newgate, 14 August 1670, **46**
1:262 To Sir William Penn, 15 August 1670, **47**
1:263 Exceptions Against the Procedure of the Court, 5? September 1670, **48**
1:267 To Sir William Penn, 5 September 1670, **49**
1:269 To Sir William Penn, 7 September 1670, **51**
1:270 From Dame Margaret Penn, 9 October 1670

1:271 To Peter Mews, November 1670, **53**
1:274 To Samuel Pepys, 4 November 1670, **52**
1:277 From Lord Massareene, 9 November 1670
1:279 To the Commissioners of the Navy, 2 December 1670, **54**
1:283 To the Commissioners of the Navy, 31 December 1670
1:286 Memorial tablet to Sir William Penn, [after 16 September 1670]
1:287 WP on the death of his father, [after 16 September 1670]
1:288 WP on his father's career, [after 16 September 1670]
1:289 To Richard Langhorne, 1671, **61**
1:293 An Holy Tryumph, 1671, **58**
1:294 Narrative of the Sufferings of Quakers in the Isle of Ely, November? 1671, **65**
1:312 To Isaac and G. Jacobs and Pieter and Elizabeth Hendricks, [1671?]
1:319 Sir John Robinson and Josiah Ricraft to the Keeper of Newgate, 5 February 1671, **56**
1:319a From Lord Broghill, 18 May 1670, **39**
1:320 Injustice Detected, February 1671, **57**
1:342 Petition to Parliament, April 1671, **59**
1:346 To the Sheriffs of London, 3 June 1671, **62**
1:348 From George Fox, 24 May 1671, **60**
1:349 To Samuel Pepys, 4 June 1671
1:351 A Trumpet Sounded, 9 September 1671
1:360 To John de Labadie's Company, October 1671, **63**
1:366 On Litigation Against Oaths, 15 November 1671, **64**
1:372 To E. Wadle, [c. 1672]
1:373 Declaration of Intention to Marriage, 7 February 1672, **67**
1:375 Approval of Intention to Marry, 6 March 1672, **68**
1:376 Marriage Certificate, 4 April 1672, **69**
1:379 Philip Ford Account No. 1, 23 April 1672–24 June 1672, **139**
1:385 WP and Upperside Friends to Friends at Missenden and elsewhere, 4 June 1672
1:389 To Dutch Friends, 14 June 1672
1:392 Philip Ford Account No. 2, 25 June 1672–14 August 1672, **140**
1:398 Philip Ford Account No. 3, 14 August 1672–29 October 1672, **141**
1:403 Certificate for Philip Ford from Upperside Meeting, 4 September 1672
1:405 On Truth's Account: Journey through Kent, Sussex, and Surrey, 11 September–4 October 1672, **70**
1:414 To William Mucklow, 11 October 1672, **71**
1:434 Philip Ford Account No. 4, 29 October 1672 – 14 February 1673, **142**
1:439 To Jan Willem Haasbaart, 22 November 1672
1:446 To John de Labadie, 24 November 1672
1:466 To J. L., 28 November 1672
1:469 To Lodowick Muggleton, 15 December 1672
1:471 To John Morse, 25 December 1672
1:472 To Daniel Fleming, 1673, **75**
1:476 Description of a True Quaker, [1673?]
1:483 Lawrence Steel's Anagram on WP, [1673?]
1:484 To George Fox, [1673?]

1:486 From John Morse, 4 January 1673
1:487 To John Morse, 9 January 1673
1:501 To Edward Terry, 29 January 1673
1:503 To John Morse, 2 February 1673
1:507 Philip Ford Account No. 5, 14 February 1673–9 December 1673, **143**
1:521 London Yearly Meeting Epistle, 26 May 1673
1:530 A Marriage Discipline, 4 June 1673, **73**
1:532 To Friends in Holland or Germany, 1 September 1673
1:535 To a Noble Friend, 23 September [1673?]
1:536 To Mary Pennyman, 22 November 1673, **74**
1:545 To The Little Flock & Family of God, 4 December 1673
1:550 Philip Ford Account No. 6, 9 December 1673–7 July 1674, **144**
1:559 Two Toleration Bills, [c.1678], **126**
1:567 To W. B[urroughs?], [1674?]
1:571 To W. B[urroughs?], [1674?]
1:575 To J. Keetch, [1674?]
1:578 To J. Keetch, [1674?]
1:583 To John Faldo, c. September 1674, **83**
1:585 To Neighbours, [1674?]
1:588 To Charles II, 1674, **80**
1:591 To Squire Bowles, 1674, **78**
1:594 To J. L., S. D., etc., 17 January 1674
1:596 To John Collinges, 22 January 1674, **76**
1:605 From Robert Barclay, 6 March 1674, **77**
1:608 To J[ohn]. H[awtrey?]. and Companion, 31 March 1674, **79**
1:619 To Henry Clark, 4 April, 8 June 1674
1:630 Crist. Kammerer to Nicolaus Bodeck, 11 May 1674
1:631 Latin Inscription to Dantzig Quakers, 22 June 1674
1:632 From George Fox and Thomas Lower, 28 August 1674, **81**
1:638 WP and others, Charges against Thomas Hicks, c. September 1674
1:639 To George Fox, 5 September 1674, **82**
1:643 William Kiffin and others to WP and others, 2 October 1674
1:644 WP and others to William Kiffin and others, 2 October 1674
1:645 William Kiffin and others to WP and others, 3 October 1674
1:646 WP and others to William Kiffin and others, 3 October 1674
1:647 To John Faldo, c. September 1674, **83**
1:648 From George Fox and Thomas Lower, 10 October 1674, **84**
1:651 William Kiffin and others to WP and others, 12 October 1674
1:652 WP and others to William Kiffin and others, 13 October 1674
1:653 Jeremy Ives and others to WP and others, 14 October 1674
1:654 WP and others to Jeremy Ives, 15 October 1674
1:655 WP and others to William Kiffin and others, 17 October 1674
1:656 WP and others to William Kiffin and others, 17 October 1674
1:657 William Kiffin and others to WP and others, 19 October 1674
1:658 Thomas Paul and others to WP and others, 22 October 1674
1:659 Answer to Jeremy Ives, 27 October 1674
1:660 To George Fox, 20, 21 November 1674
1:665 From George and Margaret Fox, 25 November 1674

1:668 To George Fox, 1 December 1674, **85**

1:673 To Friends in the Netherlands and Germany, c. 11 December 1674

2:007 To C. Pooley, [1675?]

2:012 Concerning Tythes, [1675?]

2:022 William Lodington, Poem to WP, c. 1675

2:025 George Fox to Friends, [c. 1674-75]

2:026 To Friends and Brethren, 10 March 1675

2:030 From George Fox, 11 January 1675, **86**

2:034 To John Fenwick, 20 January 1675, **112**

2:036 To John Faldo, 26 January 1675

2:037 To John Fenwick, 30 January 1675, **113**

2:039 To John Fenwick, 13 February 1675, **114**

2:041 To Margaret Fox, 16 March 1675

2:042 From Lord Broghill, 27 April 1675, **88**

2:044 From Henry More, 22 May 1675, **90**

2:094 Epistle from the London Yearly Meeting, 27 May 1675, **91**

2:107 Postscript to London Yearly Meeting Epistle, 27 May 1675

2:110 From Margaret Fox, 26 June 1675

2:114 To Sir William Petty, 30 July 1675, **92**

2:115 To George Fox, 9 September 1675

2:117 To George Fox, 9 September 1675 [another fragment of 2:115]

2:119 From Margaret Fox, 13 September 1675

2:121 From George Fox, 30 September 1675

2:128 To Richard Baxter, 6 October 1675 [LS], **94**

2:131 To Richard Baxter, 6 October 1675 [LBC]

2:134 From Richard Baxter, 6 October 1675, **95**

2:141 To Richard Baxter, c. 8 October 1675 [LS], **96**

2:150 To Richard Baxter, c. 8 October 1675 [LBC]

2:155 To a Roman Catholic, 9 October 1675

2:158 From Richard Baxter, 10 October 1675

2:160 To Richard Baxter, 11 October 1675 [LS], **97**

2:164 To Richard Baxter, 11 October 1675 [LBC]

2:167 To Richard Baxter, 11 October 1675

2:170 To Richard Baxter, c. January-March 1675 [LS]

2:175 To Richard Baxter, c. January-March 1675 [LBC]

2:177 From Richard Baxter, [post 11 October 1675], **98**

2:182 Richard Baxter's short account of a debate with WP, [after 14 October 1675]

2:197 Richard Baxter's long account of a debate with WP, [post 14 October 1675]

2:270 Advice to the Sussex Quarterly Meeting, 18 October 1675, **99**

2:274 From Anthony Lowther, 18 October 1675, **100**

2:278 To Lady Ann Conway, 20 October 1675, **101**

2:294 To the Princess and Countess at Hertford, 1676

2:325 To William Gibson, 1676?

2:326 WP and Upperside Friends to Friends at Uxbridge, etc., 2 February 1676

2:329 Submission of John Story and John Wilkinson, 7 April 1676

2:331 WP and others to Friends and Brethren, 8 May 1676

2:341 WP and London Yearly Meeting to English Friends, 18 May 1676
2:347 Indenture with William Pettyt and Thomas Langhorne, 3 June 1676, abstracted in **151**
2:349 Quinquipartite deed, Sir George Carteret, WP, Gawin Lawrie, Nicholas Lucas, and Edward Byllynge, 1 July 1676, variant version in 2:354
2:354 Indenture with John Edridge and Edmund Warner, 19 June 1676, and Quinquipartite deed, Sir George Carteret, WP, Gawin Lawrie, Nicholas Lucas, and Edward Byllynge, 1 July 1676, both abstracted in **152**
2:355 To Robert Clayton and Alderman Morris, 7 July 1676
2:356 From Robert Barclay, 20 July 1676, **105**
2:358 To the West New Jersey Commissioners, 18 August 1676,**116**
2:364 To Richard Hartshorne, 26 August 1676, **117**
2:367 To Prospective Settlers in West Jersey, September 1676, **118**
2:369 To John Raunce and Charles Harris, 11 September 1676, **107**
2:376 Sussex Quarterly Meeting Minute, corrected by WP, 25 September 1676
2:382 From Lord Baltimore, 11 December 1676, **108**
2:385 WP at Sussex Quarterly Meeting, 25 December 1676
2:390 Account of a meeting between WP and William Rogers, [February 1678]
2:396 To George Keith and Other Scottish Friends, c. 1677, **109**
2:401 On Keeping Quaker Prison Registers, 1677, **111**
2:405 The West Jersey Concessions, c. August 1677, **115**
2:421 To George Fox, 4 March 1676, **102**
2:429 To Robert Southwell, 11 March 1677
2:431 WP at Sussex Quarterly Meeting, 19 March 1677
2:435 Philip Ford Account No. 12, 28 April 1677 – 17 November 1677, **145**
2:438 From Princess Elizabeth, 2 May 1677
2:441 George Fox to Henry Sidon, 25 May 1677, **110**
2:444 To Robert Southwell, 19 June 1677
2:446 An Account of My Journey into Holland & Germany, 22 July – 23 October 1677, **119**
2:510 To the King of Poland, 4 August 1677, in **119**
2:512 To Princess Elizabeth and Countess Anna Maria van Hoorn, c. 24 August 1677, in **119**
2:513 To the Prince Elector of Heidelberg, 25 August 1677, in **119**
2:514 To Princess Elizabeth, c. September 1677
2:537 To Anna Maria van Hoorn, 10 October 1677, in **119**
2:539 To the Graef of Broich and Falkenstein, 3 September 1677, in **119**
2:540 From Princess Elizabeth, 4/14 September 1677
2:543 To Johanna Eleanora Merlan, 11 September 1677, in **119**
2:544 To the Countess of Falkenstein and Broich, 13 September 1677 [N. S.], in **119**
2:545 WP's address at the Somerdykes, 13 September 1677, variant copy in **119**
2:546 From Anna Maria van Hoorn, 14 September 1677
2:550 To Friends and Brethren, 16 September 1677, in **119**

2:558 From Margaret Fox, October 1677, **120**
2:563 To Anna Maria van Hoorn, 10 October 1677, in part in **119**
2:564 To Princess Elizabeth, 20 October 1677
2:565 To Anna Maria van Hoorn, 20/30 October 1677
2:566 To Friends in Holland and Germany, 24 October 1677
2:567 From Princess Elizabeth, 29 October 1677
2:572 WP, Ambrose Rigge, and Thomas Robinson to Friends in Sussex and Hampshire, 5 November 1677
2:575 Philip Ford Account No. 13, 17 November 1677–9 July 1678, **146**
2:580 From Princess Elizabeth, 17 November 1677
2:582 To the Earl of Middlesex and Dorset, 17 November 1677, **121**
2:588 To John Pennyman, 18 November 1677
2:589 To Pieter Hendricks, 19 November 1677, **122**
2:595 To Pieter and Elizabeth Hendricks and others, 10 December 1677
2:598 From Margaret Fox, 11 December 1677
2:601 Petition to the House of Commons, c. March 1673, variant of 14:765, **72**
2:602 To Margaret Fox, 8 January 1678, **123**
2:608 The Dissatisfactions of William Rogers and Others, 1 February 1678, **124**
2:648 Result of a meeting between John Story and WP, c. 12 February 1678
2:651 Two Speeches to a Committee of Parliament, 22 March 1678, **125**
2:654 Minute of a Meeting for Sufferings, 28 February 1678
2:662 To Friends in Lancashire, 11 March [1679], **130**
2:666 William Clark to WP, Gawen Lawrie, and Edward Byllynge, 20 April 1678
2:667 John Lindsay's Release and Quit Claim, 3 June 1678
2:669 From George Hutchinson, 7 June 1678, **127**
2:673 To Sir Robert Clayton and Alderman Morris, 8 July 1678
2:671 From Lord Broghill, 7 July 1678
2:675 Philip Ford Account No. 14, 10 July 1678–18 January 1679, **147**
2:680 From J. Fotherley, 19 July 1678
2:684 To Anthony Sharp, 14 August 1678
2:682 To Friends in Holland and Germany, 2 August 1678
2:686 To the Children of Light, 4 November 1678
2:697 To Algernon Sidney, 1 March 1679 (duplicate of 2:713)
2:698 From John Gratton, 19 December 1678, **128**
2:702 From George Fox, 13 January 1679
2:708 Philip Ford Account No. 15, 18 January 1679–28 May 1679, **148**
2:713 To Algernon Sidney, 1 March 1679, **129**
2:714 Testimony concerning Samuel Fisher, 27 March 1679
2:716 Release of Papers from Richard Langhorne's Custody, 16 April 1679, **131**
2:718 To Friends in Kent, 29 April 1679
2:724 Philip Ford Account No. 16, 29 May 1679–29 October 1679, **149**
2:731 From Sir John Pelham, 25 July 1679, **133**
2:734 To Algernon Sidney, 29 July 1679, **134**
2:735 Richard Creed to WP, George Whitehead, and Alexander Parker, 8 August 1679

2:737 John Story's Apology, 20 October 1679, **135**
2:739 Philip Ford Account No. 17, 29 October 1679–9 March 1680, **150**
2:744 To Pieter Hendricks and Jan Claus, 27 November 1679, **136**
2:749 To Charles Sackville, c. 1679-1680
14:669 From Lady Ranelagh, n. d.
14:670 From Lady Ranelagh, 12 February [n. y.]
14:672 From Lady Ranelagh, n. d.
14:673 From Robert Barrow, [c. 1678]
14:680 From Anthony Lowther, [1676?] **104**
14:684 To Charles Sackville, c. 1679-1680 (duplicate of 2:749)
14:701 From Lord Broghill, July [1678?]
14:703 To Margaret Fox, [before 1682]
14:713 WP and others to Dearly Beloved Friends and Brethren, c. 1675
14:715 From Lord Arran, n. d.
14:721 Petition of Quakers to the House of Lords, n. d.
14:765 Petition to the House of Commons, c. March 1673, **72**
14:766 Nathaniel Coleman's testimony concerning George Fox, [1673]
14:767 To Dearly Respected Friends, c. 1677?
14:795 From George Fox, 28 May c. 1674

CALENDAR OF DOCUMENTS NOT FILMED, 1644–1679

In the following list of documents accessioned since the publication of the microfilm edition of The Papers of William Penn, numbers in bold type identify documents printed in this volume.

1. Secretary Williamson to Sir William Penn, 20 December 1662
2. Memorandum of Charles II's decision about Sir William Penn's Irish Lands, 10 March 1664
3. To Sir William Penn, 18 December 1666
4. List of Sir William Penn's Lands in County Cork, 22 April 1667, printed as part of **138**
5. George Bishop to Sir William Penn, 30 November 1667, **20**
6. Incomplete draft of *No Cross, No Crown*, c. 1668
7. Order of the Privy Council, 16 December 1668, **27**
8. Warrant to the Lieutenant of the Tower to keep WP prisoner, 18 December 1668
9. Release from the Tower, 28 July 1669, **34**
10. Testimonies concerning George Fox's proposals of marriage, 18 and 22 October 1669
11. Fragment from the Penn-Mead trial, c. 1670
12. William Poole to Sir William Penn, 2 June 1670
13. To Sir William Penn, 6 September 1670, **50**
14. Right Marriage, c. 1671, **66**
15. Indenture between WP and Nicholas Cooke, 10 July 1672, abstracted in **151**
16. To Friends in Maryland, 1673
17. From George Fox, 8 October 1673
18. From John Faldo, 21 January 1675
19. From John Faldo, 1 February 1675
20. To John Faldo, 2 February 1675
21. Indenture between John Fenwick, Edward Byllynge, WP, Gawen Lawrie, and Nicholas Lucas, 10 February 1675, abstracted in **152**
22. From Lord Broghill, c. April 1675, **87**
23. Memorandum between John Fenwick and Byllynge's Trustees, 7 May 1675, abstracted in **152**
24. Agreement between John Fenwick and the purchasers of New Jersey land, 28 June 1675, abstracted in **152**
25. Indenture between John Fenwick, John Edridge, and Edmund Warner, 17 July 1675, abstracted in **152**

26. On Creating Quaker History, May 1676, **103**
27. From William Penn of Bucks., 1 May 1676
28. Indenture between WP, Sir James Rushout, and William Jarret, 7 June 1676, abstracted in **151**
29. From Robert Barclay, 6 September 1676, **106**
30. Indenture between WP, Gawen Lawry, Nicholas Lucas, Edward Byllynge, and Thomas Hooten, 8 November 1676
31. Indenture between WP and others and John Fuller, 20 June 1678, abstracted in **151**
32. From Algernon Sidney, 10 July [1678]
33. From Algernon Sidney, 29 August [1678]
34. Draft of a Bill for Preserving Property, c. 1678, printed as part of **126**
35. Incomplete draft of an Act for Preserving Property and for the Repeal of Penal Laws, c. 1678, printed as part of **126**
36. To Friends in Kent, 29 April 1679, variant version of 2:718, **132**

INDEX

Page references to identifications are set in **bold face type.**